1990 Jays Day By Day

MW01706781

CONTENTS

Detailed Index 3

Special Feature: 1991 All-Star Game 4
Toronto hosts baseball's 62nd dream game

Year-by-Year Review 8
Each season, 1990 to 1977

SkyDome 37

Blue Jays Personnel 40
Photos and year-by-year stats for every Jay

Career Fielding 123
Career fielding stats for current Jays

1990 Statistics 127
Game synopses and stats from last season

Team History and Awards 158
All-time roster and year-by-year leaders

Championship Series 1989 and 1985 161

Jays Record Book 174
Top season and single-game performances

Opponents' Statistics 214
1990 and lifetime individual stats vs. the Jays

Important Dates 230
Trading, waiver and arbitration deadlines in 1991

Items of Interest 232
Special rules, free-agency, the disabled list, etc.

Radio and Television 236

Spring Training 238
Preseason schedule and all-time spring results

1991 Spring Roster 242

ISBN 0-7710-1547-X

McClelland & Stewart Inc.
The Canadian Publishers
481 University Avenue
Toronto, Ontario
M5G 2E9

Printed and bound in Canada by Thorn Press

TORONTO BLUE JAYS 1991

Detailed Index

AL Stats 1990 . . . 127-130
All-Star Break . . . 194
All-Star Selections . . . 161
Attendance Data . . . 196; 188; 154-157
Awards . . . 164
Back-To-Back-To-Back . . . 186
Batting:
- All-Time Blue Jays Leaders . . . 178
- Big "RBI" Games . . . 198
- Career, as Blue Jays . . . 167
- Detailed, Blue Jays 1990 . . . 141
- 1990 Blue Jays . . . 138
- .300 Hitters . . . 182
- DH Hitting . . . 140
- Pinch Hitting . . . 65; 140; 182
- Road . . . 140
- Single Season Highs . . . 178
- Streaks . . . 196
- Top Ten . . . 178
- Year-By-Year . . . 175

BBWAA, Toronto Chapter . . . 131
Beeston, Paul . . . 43
Biographies:
- Front Office . . . 43-45
- Manager & Coaches . . . 46-54
- Players . . . 55-118

Behind the Scenes . . . 118-119
Biggest Innings . . . 189
Birthdays, 1991 . . . 54
Broadcasting . . . 236-237
Canadian Baseball Hall of Fame . . . 166
Canadian Players . . . 196-197
Championship Series, 1985, 1989
Climate, Toronto . . . 83
Coaches, BIOS . . . 47-54
Craig, Tommy . . . 118
Dates to Remember, 1991 . . . 23
Day-By-Day, 1990 . . . 146-147
Directly to the Majors . . . 92
Directory . . . 40
Doubleheader Shutouts . . . 69
Dunedin Stadium . . . 239
Exhibition Stadium, First & Lasts . . . 39
Extra-Innings . . . 196
Farm System . . . 42
Fielding:
- By Position, 1990 . . . 139
- Career by Position . . . 123; 169
- League Leaders . . . 196
- Season . . . 139; 175
- Triple Plays . . . 193
- Year-By-Year . . . 175
- Gold Glove Award . . . 198

First Major League Appearance . . . 169
First Place, Blue Jays . . . 130
Forfeit Game . . . 213
Games by Position . . . 169
Gaston, Cito . . . 46
Gillick, Pat . . . 44
Grant Field . . . 239
Highest Scoring Games . . . 191
Highs & Lows, 1990 . . . 143
History . . . 158
Hitting For The Cycle . . . 140
Home Runs:
- Grand Slams . . . 229
- In Consecutive Games . . . 187
- Inside the Park . . . 186
- Lifetime AL Parks . . . 193
- Pinch-Hit . . . 185
- 20 Home Runs . . . 182
- Opponents . . . 227
- Ten Home Run Game . . . 117
- Two (Three) in a Game . . . 198; 184; 186
- Yearly Leaders . . . 183

Homestands/Best-Worst . . . 126
Hotels, Out of Town . . . 51
How They Were Acquired . . . 70
Innings, Biggest . . . 189
Iron Man Streak . . . 194
Items of Interest . . . 232
Labatt's "Blue" Award . . . 164
Last Time . . . 153
Latest Ending Games . . . 197
Leaders, Year-by-Year . . . 176
Logo, Blue Jays . . . 197
Low Hit Games . . . 229
Major League Draft . . . 177
Major League Leaders, 1990 . . . 131
Manager, Gaston . . . 46
Marathons . . . 192
Mileage . . . 86
Milestones, Upcoming . . . 145
Milestones, Victories . . . 183
Minor League Review, 1990 . . . 148-152
Monthly Records . . . 190
Multiple Hit Games . . . 188
Name the Team . . . 197
No-Hitters . . . 98
Non-Pitchers . . . 185
1-0 Games . . . 198
Opening Day Lineups . . . 172
Openers, Home . . . 173
Opponents Records:
- vs AL Clubs . . . 214
- Batters . . . 220
- Pitchers . . . 224
- Leading (Season) . . . 231

Original Blue Jays . . . 159
Ownership . . . 42
Pitchers at the Plate . . . 122
Pitchers - Batting . . . 122
Pitching:
- All-Time Blue Jays Leaders . . . 181
- Career, as Blue Jays . . . 168
- Detailed, Blue Jays, 1990
- 15-Game Winners . . . 182
- Low-Hit Games . . . 199
- 1990, Blue Jays . . . 128
- More Than Nine Innings . . . 183
- Relief . . . 138
- Single Season Highs . . . 179
- Starting . . . 138
- 10 or More Strikeouts . . . 199
- Top Ten . . . 179
- Year-By-Year . . . 177

Player Transactions, 1990 . . . 142
Player Development . . . 41; 120-122
Postponements . . . 193
Radio . . . 237
Rain Delays . . . 197
Rainouts . . . 193
Records:
- Club & Individual . . . 200
- Miscellaneous . . . 204
- Fielding . . . 205
- Game . . . 207
- Month . . . 210
- Rookies . . . 212
- Held or Tied . . . 195

Review, 1990 . . . 132
Rookies . . . 213
Rosters:
- All-Time . . . 160
- 1991, Spring . . . 214-216
- Rules of Interest . . . 232

Schedules:
- Season . . . Inside Front Cover
- Spring . . . 241

Scouts . . . 41
Season, 1990 in Review . . . 132
Seasons, Most With Blue Jays . . . 74
Shares, WS/LCS . . . 190
Short-Term Blue Jays . . . 56
SkyDome . . . 36-38
Spring Training . . . 238
Stolen Bases . . . 182
Streaks:
- Hitting . . . 196
- Winning and Losing . . . 183

Switch-Hitters . . . 187
Suspend Games . . . 197
Tied Games . . . 122
Time . . . 187
Trades . . . 170
Transactions, 1990 . . . 142
Triple Plays . . . 193
TV . . . 236
Uniform . . . 197
Webster, R. Howard (Awards) . . . 165
Won-Lost Breakdown . . . 149; 189
Won-Lost, Best . . . 192
Year-By-Year . . . 174; 228
Youngest Blue Jays . . . 181

BLUE JAYS PUBLIC RELATIONS DEPARTMENT

Howard Starkman,
Director, Public Relations

Mark Leno,
Assistant Director, Public Relations

Administrative Assistant,
Bonnie Way

Public Relations Coordinator,
Monique Walsh

Baseball's 62nd Dream Game Comes to Toronto

Dave Stieb equals an A.L. pitchers' record with his seventh All-Star appearance in the 1990 All-Star Game at Wrigley Field in Chicago.

TORONTO '91 ALL-STAR GAME

WHEN THE ALL-STAR GAME comes to Toronto on July 9, 1991, it will mark the 62nd staging of what started out as a one-time event. The architect of the first All-Star Game was Arch Ward, former sports editor for the Chicago Tribune. In 1933, Ward convinced his publisher and baseball's leadership that a "Dream Game" matching the best players from the American and National Leagues would be a fitting attraction for the 1933 World's Fair in Chicago. "The Game of the Century" was set for July 6, with Comiskey Park chosen over Wrigley Field by the flip of a coin. When the first game was played, media coverage was very limited. Some Major League teams didn't even have one newspaper reporter from their home city in attendance. The 1991 game in SkyDome will be very different. More than 700 writers, photographers and broadcasters will cover the action with more than 80 million baseball fans in North America and millions more around the world watching or listening to the game.

Twenty-four future Hall of Famers were on the first All-Star Game's rosters. But few, if anyone, grasped the magnitude of the event. Joe Cronin, a Hall of Famer and the A.L.'s starting shortstop, said fifty years later, "Although much is being made today of the fact that we played in the 1933 All-Star Game, we also considered it a great honor because we thought it would be the one and only All-Star Game."

But even before the end of the A.L.'s 4-2 victory, sentiment was strong to continue the game on at least a year-to-year basis. Since 1933, the All-Star Game has been an annual event with two exceptions: wartime travel restrictions forced cancellation in 1945 and for a four-year period beginning in 1959, two games were played each summer. Through 1990, The National League holds the lead in the series 37 games to 23 with one game tied.

SELECTING THE PLAYERS

Ballots were inserted in newspapers for the first two all-star games in 1933 and 1934. From 1935 to 1946, the managers of the eight teams in each league selected the participants with the All-Star Game managers choosing the starters. Balloting for the starting lineups, with tabulation by the Associated Press, was returned to the fans from 1947 to 1957, but a case of ballot stuffing by Cincinnati fans prompted Commissioner Ford Frick to to leave player selection to managers, players and coaches from 1958 to 1969. In the Cincinnati incident in 1957, seven Reds were selected to the National League starting lineup. Commissioner Frick arbitrarily replaced two of those selections – outfielders Gus Bell and Wally Post – with Willie Mays and Hank Aaron.

Fan balloting was restored in 1970 and since then more than 140,000,000 ballots have been cast. The single-season record for ballots cast was set in 1977 when 12,562,746 fans voted.

When the first All-Star Game was played in 1933, each team had 18 players. Thirty players got into the game, which was won 4-2 by the American League, though the A.L. stayed with its starting lineup – except for pitching changes – until Sam West replaced Babe Ruth defensively in the ninth inning.

Since 1969, the standard roster limit for the All-Star Game has been 28 per team, though exceptions have been made. It is not uncommon for about 50 players to see action during the game.

In 1987, George Bell, at left, became the only Blue Jay elected to an All-Star starting lineup by fan balloting. Bell was in the midst of a 47HR, 134RBI season and went on to be named A.L. MVP. Kelly Gruber, below, played in the 1990 All-Star Game in Chicago.

ALL-STAR JAYS

Eighteen members of the Toronto Blue Jays have represented the club in All-Star Games. Dave Stieb and former Jays' broadcaster Early Wynn are co-holders of the A.L. record for All-Star Game appearances by a pitcher with seven. Jays with more than one All-Star selection include Tony Fernandez in 1986, 1987 and 1989; Damaso Garcia in 1984 and 1985; George Bell in 1987 and 1990; and Kelly Gruber in 1989 and 1990.

The Blue Jays sent their largest contingent to the All-Star Game in in 1985 when Stieb, Garcia, Jimmy Key, Ernie Whitt and coach Bobby Cox were named to the team. Other non-playing Jays' All-Stars include coach Roy Hartsfield in 1978 and trainer Ken Carson in 1980. Other Jays' players selected to the A.L. All-Star Team include Ron Fairly (1977), Roy Howell (1978), Dave Lemanczyk (1979), Jim Clancy (1982), Alfredo Griffin (1984), Jesse Barfield and Lloyd Moseby (1986) and Tom Henke (1987). Though Dave Stieb started on the mound in 1983 and 1984, George Bell's 1987 All-Star selection was the only occasion a Blue Jay was voted to the starting lineup by fan balloting.

Arch Ward's 1933 World's Fair exhibition was the forerunner to Major League baseball's modern All-Star Game which, in 1991, will be watched by more than 100 million fans worldwide. At the 1991 All-Star Game, Ward's name can be found engraved on the trophy awarded to the MVP in what has become the greatest single-game event in baseball.

1990 September rally can't undo August slide

Manager	W	L	Pct.	Pos.	GB	Attendance
Cito Gaston	**86**	**76**	**.531**	**2nd**	**2**	**3,885,284**

David Wells joined the rotation in 1990, making 25 starts. He pitched a career-high 189 innings and finished at 11-6.

COMING OFF A HOT SECOND HALF and a Division Championship in 1989, the Blue Jays began their fourteenth season winning six of their first ten games against the Rangers, Royals and Orioles. They spent eight days in first place and ended the month with a record of 12 and 9.

But as the season progressed, the Jays found themselves playing a bit better than .500 baseball; always in contention but unable to combine pitching, hitting and defense in a way that would produce a prolonged winning streak. The club spent time in first place in every month of the season except August when eight losses in 10 games against New York, Boston and Milwaukee dropped the Jays further back – 6½ games – than they had been at any other point in the season. But this late-season deficit was overcome as the Jays won 14 of September's first 18 games and moved back into first place.

The Jays held or shared the lead until two three-game series – one with the Red Sox and one with the Orioles – remained to be played. In Boston, the Sox got wins from reliever Jeff Reardon and Roger Clemens before Jimmy Key won his 13th of the season in a 10-5 Jays' victory. In 1990, the Jays won only three of 13 games against the Red Sox.

Trailing Boston by two games with three to play, the Jays split a pair with Baltimore before Greg Olson won a 2-1 game in relief for the Orioles, denying the Jays their last opportunity to earn a share of first place.

1990 saw several rookie ballplayers make their marks with the Jays. John Olerud had 14 HRs and 48 RBIs in 358 at-bats. Glenallen Hill had 12 HRs in 84 games. Greg Myers, who was classified as a rookie, worked with Pat Borders to form the club's catching tandem despite spending time on the disabled list.

Borders, who was selected as the Jays' most improved ballplayer in 1990, was behind the plate when Dave Stieb pitched the first no-hitter in franchise history against Cleveland on September 2. Stieb also pitched the 100th complete game of his career in 1990, shutting out Oakland 1-0 on May 28. Todd Stottlemyre emerged as a workhorse pitcher this season, starting 33 games with 203 IP.

1990 Blue Jays Statistics

BATTER	Pos.	Avg.	G	AB	R	H	HR	RBI
BELL, George	OF	.265	142	562	67	149	21	86
BORDERS, Pat	C	.286	125	346	36	99	15	49
DIAZ, Carlos	C	.333	9	3	1	1	0	0
DUCEY, Rob	OF	.302	19	53	7	16	0	7
EPPARD, Jim	PH	.200	6	5	0	1	0	0
FELIX, Junior	OF	.263	127	463	73	122	15	65
FERNANDEZ, Tony	SS	.276	161	635	84	175	4	66
GRUBER, Kelly	3B	.274	150	592	92	162	31	118
HILL, Glenallen	OF	.231	84	260	47	60	12	32
LAWLESS, Tom	IF-OF	.083	15	12	1	1	0	1
LEE, Manny	2B	.243	117	391	45	95	6	41
LIRIANO, Nelson	2B	.212	50	170	16	36	1	15
McGRIFF, Fred	1B	.300	153	557	91	167	35	88
MULLINIKS, Rance	3B-DH	.289	57	97	11	28	2	16
MYERS, Greg	C	.236	87	250	33	59	5	22
OLERUD, John	DH-1B	.265	111	358	43	95	14	48
QUINLAN, Tom	3B	.500	1	2	0	1	0	0
SOJO, Luis	IF	.225	33	80	14	18	1	9
VIRGIL, Ozzie	DH	.000	3	5	0	0	0	0
WHITEN, Mark	OF	.273	33	88	12	24	2	7
WILLIAMS, Kenny	OF	.194	49	72	13	14	0	8
WILSON, Mookie	OF	.265	147	588	81	156	3	51
Designated Hitters		.220	162	604	68	133	14	68
Pinch-Hitters		.216	71	97	4	21	0	14
1990 Totals		**.260**	**162**	**5589**	**767**	**1479**	**167**	**729**

Labatt's Most Valuable Player
KELLY GRUBER

Labatt's Most Valuable Pitcher
DAVE STIEB

BBWAA
Player of the Year
KELLY GRUBER

BBWAA
Pitcher of the Year
DAVE STIEB

BBWAA
Rookie of the Year
JOHN OLERUD

Most Improved Player
PAT BORDERS

PITCHER	ERA	W-L	SV	G	IP	H	ER	BB	SO
ACKER, Jim	3.83	4-4	1	59	91.2	103	39	30	54
BLACK, Bud	4.02	2-1	0	3	15.2	10	7	3	3
BLAIR, Willie	4.06	3-5	0	27	68.2	66	31	28	43
CANDELARIA, John	5.48	0-3	1	13	21.1	32	13	11	19
CERUTTI, John	4.76	9-9	0	30	140.0	162	74	49	49
CUMMINGS, Steve	5.40	0-0	0	3	12.1	22	7	5	4
FLANAGAN, Mike	5.31	2-2	0	5	20.1	28	12	8	5
GILLES, Tom	6.75	2-0	0	5	1.1	2	1	0	1
HENKE, Tom	2.17	2-4	32	61	74.2	58	18	19	75
KEY, Jimmy	4.25	13-7	0	27	154.2	169	73	22	88
KILGUS, Paul	7.71	0-0	0	7	16.1	19	11	7	7
LEITER, Al	0.00	0-0	0	4	6.1	1	0	2	5
LUECKEN, Rick	9.00	0-0	0	1	1.0	2	1	1	0
MacDONALD, Bob	0.00	0-0	0	4	2.1	0	0	2	0
STIEB, Dave	2.93	18-6	0	33	208.2	179	68	64	125
STOTTLEMYRE, Todd	4.34	13-17	0	33	203.0	214	98	69	115
WARD, Duane	3.45	2-8	11	73	127.2	101	49	42	112
WELLS, David	3.14	11-6	3	43	189.0	165	66	45	115
WILLS, Frank	4.73	6-4	0	44	99.0	101	52	38	72
1990 Totals	**3.84**	**86-76**	**48**	**162**	**1454.0**	**1434**	**620**	**445**	**892**

John Olerud became the 16th player since the start of the amateur draft in 1965 to make his pro debut at the M.L. level.

Pat Borders set career highs in games, AB, HRs and RBIs. He ranked third in the A.L. in throwing out runners with a .426 success rate.

The Jays' 86 wins in 1990 equalled the club's output in 1986 and were the fewest recorded by the franchise since breaking .500 for the first time in 1983.

The Blue Jays and their fans set a Major League attendance record in 1990. The club averaged 47,966 fans per game, sold out 66 of 81 dates and drew a total attendance of 3,885,284. Overall home and road, the club drew 5,925,056, breaking the previous record held by the 1982 Los Angeles Dodgers by 65,984.

1989 Hot when it counts, Jays win A.L. East by 2 games

Manager	W	L	Pct.	Pos.	GA/GB	Attendance
Jimy Williams	**12**	**24**	**.333**			
Cito Gaston	**77**	**49**	**.611**			
Total	**89**	**73**	**.549**	**1st**	**+2**	**3,375,883**

Switch-hitting rookie Junior Felix hit .283 batting right-handed.

THE TORONTO BLUE JAYS won their second A.L. East Division Championship in 1989, enduring a slow start and a managerial change before putting together a strong second half.

The season began with the Jays losing four of five one-run ballgames. Tony Fernandez suffered a broken right cheekbone when hit in the face by a pitch on April 7. Nine days later, Kelly Gruber became the first Jay to hit for the cycle as the Jays scored 15 runs against Kansas City.

But by mid-May the Jays were 12-24 and had lost 12 one-run games. Manager Jimy Williams was replaced by batting instructor Cito Gaston on May 15. The club went 8-7 for the balance of May and then exploded for 30 runs in three games against the Red Sox in Fenway Park, getting 11 RBIs from rookie Junior Felix.

The Jays played their SkyDome opener on June 5 and went on to record their first plus-.500 month at 17-10. A three-game sweep of the Tigers in Detroit just before the All-Star Break hoisted the Jays into a tie for fourth and heralded a revitalized Toronto bullpen. Tom Henke, who had just three saves in the first half of the season, reasserted himself as the club's top stopper and finished the season with 20 saves.

The Jays closed out the month of July one game under .500 at 52-53, four games back and tied for second. Early August saw the acquisition of Lee Mazzilli and Mookie Wilson, two players who would play vital roles down the stretch for the Blue Jays.

August 1989 proved to be the most successful month in franchise history with 20 wins against just nine defeats. The club finally broke the .500 barrier on August 15 and, on August 31, pulled into a first-place tie with Baltimore.

The Jays continued to play well through September, but needed back-to-back wins over the Orioles on the last weekend of the season to clinch the A.L. East.

The American League Championship series pitted the Jays against the Oakland Athletics. Although the Jays got their share of hits against Oakland pitching, the A's superb attack was too much for Toronto to handle. The A's won in five games with the Jays winning game three in front of a record SkyDome crowd of 50,268.

The Jays' comeback from a 12-24 start and a 10-game deficit to win the A.L. East was witnessed by the largest paid attendance – 3,375,883 – in American League history.

1989 Blue Jays Statistics

BATTER	Pos.	Avg.	G	AB	R	H	HR	RBI
BARFIELD, Jesse	OF	.200	21	80	8	16	5	11
BATISTE, Kevin	OF	.250	6	8	1	2	0	0
BELL, George	OF	.297	153	613	88	182	18	104
BORDERS, Pat	C	.257	94	241	22	62	3	29
BRENLY, Bob	C	.170	48	88	9	15	1	6
CABRERA, Francisco	C	.167	3	12	1	2	0	0
DUCEY, Rob	OF	.211	41	76	5	16	0	7
FELIX, Junior	OF	.258	110	415	62	107	9	46
FERNANDEZ, Tony	SS	.257	140	573	64	147	11	64
GRUBER, Kelly	3B	.290	135	545	83	158	18	73
HILL, Glenallen	OF	.288	19	52	4	15	1	7
INFANTE, Alexis	IF	.167	20	12	1	2	0	0
LAWLESS, Tom	IF-OF	.229	59	70	20	16	0	3
LEE, Manny	2B	.260	99	300	27	78	3	34
LIRIANO, Nelson	2B	.263	132	418	51	110	5	53
MAZZILLI, Lee	1B-DH	.227	28	66	12	15	4	11
McGRIFF, Fred	1B	.269	161	551	98	148	36	92
MOSEBY, Lloyd	OF	.221	135	502	72	111	11	43
MULLINIKS, Rance	DH	.238	103	273	25	65	3	29
MYERS, Greg	C	.114	17	44	0	5	0	1
OLERUD, John	1B	.375	6	8	2	3	0	0
VIRGIL, Ozzie	DH/C	.182	9	11	2	2	1	2
WHITT, Ernie	C	.262	129	385	42	101	11	53
WILSON, Mookie	OF	.298	54	238	32	71	2	17
Designated Hitters		.216	162	589	66	127	8	55
Pinch-Hitters		.264	88	121	14	32	3	13
1989 Totals		**.260**	**162**	**5581**	**731**	**1449**	**142**	**685**

PITCHER	ERA	W-L	SV	G	IP	H	ER	BB	SO
ACKER, Jim	1.59	2-1	0	14	28.1	24	5	12	24
BUICE, DeWayne	5.82	1-0	0	7	17.0	13	11	13	10
CASTILLO, Tony	6.11	1-1	1	17	17.2	23	12	10	10
CERUTTI, John	3.07	11-11	0	33	205.1	214	70	53	69
CUMMINGS, Steve	3.00	2-0	0	5	21.0	18	7	11	8
FLANAGAN, Mike	3.93	8-10	0	30	171.2	186	75	47	47
GOZZO, Mauro	4.83	4-1	0	9	31.2	35	17	9	10
HENKE, Tom	1.92	8-3	20	64	89.0	66	19	25	116
HERNANDEZ, Xavier	4.76	1-0	0	7	22.2	25	12	8	7
KEY, Jimmy	3.88	13-14	0	33	216.0	226	93	27	118
LEITER, Al	4.05	0-0	0	2	6.2	9	3	2	4
MUSSELMAN, Jeff	10.64	0-1	0	5	11.0	19	13	9	3
NUNEZ, Jose	2.53	0-0	0	6	10.2	8	3	2	14
SANCHEZ, Alex	10.03	0-1	0	4	11.2	16	13	14	4
STIEB, Dave	3.35	17-8	0	33	206.2	164	77	76	101
STOTTLEMYRE, Todd	3.88	7-7	0	27	127.2	137	55	44	63
WARD, Duane	3.77	4-10	15	66	114.2	94	48	58	122
WELLS, David	2.40	7-4	2	54	86.1	66	23	28	78
WILLS, Frank	3.66	3-1	0	24	71.1	65	29	30	41
1989 Totals	**3.58**	**89-73**	**38**	**162**	**1467.0**	**651**	**584**	**478**	**849**

Labatt's Most Valuable Player
GEORGE BELL

Labatt's Most Valuable Pitcher
DAVE STIEB

BBWAA
Player of the Year
GEORGE BELL

BBWAA
Pitcher of the Year
TOM HENKE

BBWAA
Rookie of the Year
JUNIOR FELIX

Most Improved Player
TODD STOTTLEMYRE

George Bell reached 100 RBIS for the third time in four seasons.

John Cerutti led the Jays' starters with an ERA of 3.07.

1988 Late-season streak sees Jays finish 2 games back

Manager	W	L	Pct.	Pos.	GB	Attendance
Jimy Williams	**87**	**75**	**.537**	**T-3rd**	**2**	**2,595,175**

Jays' MVP Fred McGriff led the club with 34 HRs and 100 runs scored in 1988.

HAVING SO NARROWLY MISSED winning the A.L. East title in 1987, the 1988 Blue Jays entered the season as an acknowledged contender. But the club started slowly, winning only 9 of 22 games in April and 13 of 26 games in May. By the end of May the Jays were in sixth place – 12 games back and 7 games under .500. At the All-Star Break the club was 42-46 and 11½ games back.

After the All-Star Break, and with the return of pitchers Jimmy Key and Jeff Musselman from the disabled list, the Jays played their most consistent baseball of the season. The team registered the Division's best post-All-Star record with 45 wins and 29 losses for a 22-7 record in September and October. But this late-season drive wasn't enough to catch the Red Sox, who had also surged in the standings. The Jays ended 1988 tied for third place, two games behind Boston.

The Blue Jays did well at the plate in 1988, leading the A.L. in home runs (158), triples (47), total bases (2330), and slugging percentage (.419). On the mound, the Jays' staff led the League and tied a club mark with 17 shutouts. Fred McGriff led all first basemen with a .997 fielding percentage, while three-time Gold Glove winner Tony Fernandez finished third among shortstops with a .981 fielding percentage despite being hampered by off-season surgery. Fred McGriff led the club with 34 home runs and hit .282. Kelly Gruber enjoyed his finest season as a Jay, and his first as the club's regular third baseman, hitting .278 with 81 RBI. George Bell, who had a major-league record three home runs on opening day, was the club's RBI leader with 97. Tony Fernandez hit .287 with 70 RBI and Rance Mulliniks, employed largely as a DH, hit .300. Rookie catcher Pat Borders hit .273 in 56 games while first-year outfielder Rob Ducey hit .315 in 27 games. The DH spot hit a League-leading .288 with 25 HRs and 95 RBI.

Dave Stieb had his best season since 1985, finishing with an ERA of 3.04 and a record of 16-8. He recorded three one-hitters in 1988 and had no-hit bids spoiled with two out in the ninth inning in each of his last two starts of the season. Jimmy Key, who started three games in April before requiring elbow surgery that placed him on the disabled list for 75 days, finished at 12-5 with an ERA of 3.29. Tom Henke led the relief corps with 25 saves and a 2.91 ERA while Duane Ward earned 15 saves and a 9-3 record.

1988 Blue Jays Statistics

BATTER	Pos.	Avg.	G	AB	R	H	HR	RBI
BARFIELD, Jesse	OF	.244	136	468	62	114	18	56
BELL, George	OF	.269	156	614	78	165	24	97
BENIQUEZ, Juan	DH	.293	30	58	9	17	1	8
BORDERS, Pat	C	.273	56	154	15	42	5	21
BUTERA, Sal	C	.233	23	60	3	14	1	6
CAMPUSANO, Sylvestre	OF	.218	73	142	14	31	2	12
DUCEY, Rob	OF	.315	27	54	15	17	0	6
FERNANDEZ, Tony	SS	.287	154	648	76	186	5	70
FIELDER, Cecil	DH-1B	.230	74	174	24	40	9	23
GRUBER, Kelly	3B	.278	158	569	75	158	16	81
INFANTE, Alexis	IF	.200	19	15	7	3	0	0
LEACH, Rick	OF	.276	87	199	21	55	0	23
LEE, Manny	2B-SS	.291	117	381	38	111	2	38
LIRIANO, Nelson	2B	.264	103	276	36	73	3	23
McGRIFF, Fred	1B	.282	154	536	100	151	34	82
MOSEBY, Lloyd	OF	.239	128	472	77	113	10	42
MULLINIKS, Rance	DH-3B	.300	119	337	49	101	12	48
WHITT, Ernie	C	.251	127	398	63	100	16	70
Designated Hitters		.288	162	612	90	176	25	95
Pinch-Hitters		.202	81	129	14	26	2	18
1988 Totals		**.268**	**162**	**5557**	**763**	**1491**	**158**	**706**

Labatt's Most Valuable Player
FRED McGRIFF

Labatt's Most Valuable Pitcher
DAVE STIEB

BBWAA
Player of the Year
FRED MCGRIFF

BBWAA
Pitcher of the Year
DAVE STIEB

BBWAA
Rookie of the Year
PAT BORDERS

Most Improved Player
KELLY GRUBER

PITCHER	ERA	W-L	SV	G	IP	H	ER	BB	SO
BAIR, Doug	4.05	0-0	0	10	13	14	6	3	8
CASTILLO, Tony	3.00	1-0	0	14	15	10	5	2	14
CERUTTI, John	3.13	6-7	1	46	124	120	43	42	65
CLANCY, Jim	4.49	11-13	1	36	196	207	98	47	118
EICHHORN, Mark	4.19	0-3	1	37	67	79	31	27	28
FLANAGAN, Mike	4.18	13-13	0	34	211	220	98	80	99
HENKE, Tom	2.91	4-4	25	52	68	60	22	24	66
KEY, Jimmy	3.29	12-5	0	21	131	127	48	30	65
MUSSELMAN, Jeff	3.18	8-5	0	15	85	80	30	30	39
NUNEZ, Jose	3.07	0-1	0	13	29	28	10	17	18
STIEB, Dave	3.04	16-8	0	32	207	157	70	79	147
STOTTLEMYRE, Todd	5.69	4-8	0	28	98	109	62	46	67
WARD, Duane	3.30	9-3	15	64	112	101	41	60	91
WELLS, David	4.62	3-5	4	41	64	65	33	31	56
WILLS, Frank	5.23	0-0	0	10	26	22	12	6	19
1988 Totals	**3.80**	**87-75**	**47**	**162**	**1449**	**1404**	**611**	**528**	**904**

Above: Dave Stieb was 16-8 with three one-hitters.
Below: Kelly Gruber's 81 RBI set a club record for third basemen.

1987 Duel with Detroit sees Jays a close second

Manager	W	L	Pct.	Pos.	GB	Attendance
Jimy Williams	**96**	**66**	**.593**	**2nd**	**2**	**2,778,459**

Lloyd Moseby's 26 HRs, 96 RBIs and 106 runs were career highs for the Jays' centerfielder.

IF YOU WROTE a story about a baseball pennant race, you wouldn't and couldn't pack in as many thrills as were contained in the last ten games of the Toronto Blue Jays' 1987 season. Leading the Tigers by a half game with ten left, the Jays played home and home series against Detroit on the last two weekends of the year. These seven games – with the division championship on the line – were all one-run contests.

The Jays won the first three against Detroit to stretch their lead to 3½. They led the fourth game going into the ninth before a Kirk Gibson home run paved the way for an eventual Tiger victory in extra innings. Three losses to Milwaukee sent the Jays into Tiger Stadium with a one game lead and three to play. The Tigers swept the series, despite marvelous pitching performances from Mike Flanagan and Jimmy Key in the final two games of the season. The Jays finished two games behind Detroit at 96-66/.593 – the second best-record in the majors and three games short of the franchise record of 99 wins in 1985.

Despite the disappointment of the last week of the season, 1987 was a year of superlatives for the Jays. The club led the A.L. in attendance, drawing almost 2.8 million, and registered the sixth-highest home run total in league history with 215 including an incredible 10 HR single-game barrage against Baltimore on September 14th.

George Bell (47 HRs and 134 RBIs) had a career year, earning A.L. MVP honours. Jimmy Key allowed no more than three earned runs in 30 of 36 starts, finished at 17-6 with an ERA of 2.76 and was runner-up in balloting for the Cy Young Award. Tony Fernandez, despite a sore knee, was one of baseball's top defensive shortstops, while hitting .322 with 32 stolen bases. Tom Henke led the A.L. in saves with 34.

Rookie Fred McGriff hit 20 HRs while first-year lefthander Jeff Musselman finished at 12-5 with 68 appearances. Nelson Liriano played in the final 37 games of the season, starting at second base and hitting out of the leadoff spot. Mike Flanagan yielded two runs or less in five of seven starts for the Jays after being acquired from Baltimore on August 30. Hard-throwing relievers David Wells and Duane Ward combined for 25 appearances from the bullpen after being called up for the stretch run.

The Jays' starting lineup and pitching rotation changed considerably during the course of 1987. The 1988 squad combined veterans at the peak of their abilities with talented younger players ready to play and improve at the major-league level.

1987 Blue Jays Statistics

BATTER	Pos.	Avg.	G	AB	R	H	HR	RBI
BARFIELD, Jesse	OF	.263	159	590	89	155	28	84
BELL, George	OF	.308	156	610	111	188	47	134
BENIQUEZ, Juan	OF-DH	.284	39	81	6	23	5	21
DEWILLIS, Jeff	C	.120	13	25	2	3	1	2
DUCEY, Rob	OF	.188	34	48	12	9	1	6
FERNANDEZ, Tony	SS	.322	146	578	90	186	5	67
FIELDER, Cecil	DH-1B	.269	82	175	30	47	14	32
GRUBER, Kelly	3B	.235	138	341	50	80	12	36
INFANTE, Alexis	IF	.000	1	0	0	0	0	0
IORG, Garth	IF	.210	122	310	35	65	4	30
LEACH, Rick	1B-OF-DH	.282	98	195	26	55	3	25
LEE, Manny	SS	.256	56	121	14	31	1	11
LIRIANO, Nelson	2B	.241	37	158	29	38	2	10
McGRIFF, Fred	DH-1B	.247	107	295	58	73	20	43
MOORE, Charlie	C	.215	51	107	15	23	1	7
MOSEBY, Lloyd	OF	.282	155	592	106	167	26	96
MULLINIKS, Rance	3B-DH	.310	124	332	37	103	11	44
MYERS, Greg	C	.111	7	9	1	1	0	0
SHARPERSON, Mike	2B	.208	32	96	4	20	0	9
STARK, Matt	C	.083	5	12	0	1	0	0
THORNTON, Lou	OF	.500	12	2	5	1	0	0
UPSHAW, Willie	1B	.244	150	512	68	125	15	58
WHITT, Ernie	C	.269	135	446	57	120	19	75
Designated Hitters		.258	162	592	101	153	38	97
Pinch-Hitters		.234	108	167	0	39	3	28
1987 Totals		**.269**	**162**	**5,635**	**845**	**1,514**	**215**	**790**

PITCHER	ERA	W-L	SV	G	IP	H	ER	BB	SO
CERUTTI, John	4.40	11-4	0	44	151	144	74	59	92
CLANCY, Jim	3.54	15-11	0	37	241	234	95	80	180
EICHHORN, Mark	3.17	10-6	4	89	128	110	45	52	96
FLANAGAN, Mike	2.37	3-2	0	7	49	46	13	15	43
GORDON, Don	4.09	0-0	0	5	11	8	5	3	3
HENKE, Tom	2.49	0-6	34	72	94	62	26	25	128
JOHNSON, Joey	5.13	3-5	0	14	67	77	38	18	27
KEY, Jimmy	2.76	17-8	0	36	261	210	80	66	161
LAVELLE, Gary	5.53	2-3	1	23	27	36	17	19	17
MUSSELMAN, Jeff	4.15	12-5	3	68	90	75	41	54	54
NIEKRO, Phil	8.25	0-2	0	3	12	15	11	7	7
NUNEZ, Jose	5.01	5-2	0	37	97	91	54	58	99
STIEB, Dave	4.09	13-9	0	33	185	164	84	87	115
WARD, Duane	6.94	1-0	0	12	12	14	9	12	10
WELLS, David	3.99	4-3	1	18	29	37	13	12	32
1987 Totals	**3.74**	**96-66**	**43**	**162**	**1454**	**1323**	**605**	**567**	**1064**

Labatt's Most Valuable Player
GEORGE BELL
Labatt's Most Valuable Pitcher
JIMMY KEY
BBWAA
Player of the Year
GEORGE BELL
BBWAA
Pitcher of the Year
JIMMY KEY
BBWAA
Rookie of the Year
JEFF MUSSELMAN
Most Improved Player
LLOYD MOSEBY

Above: Fred McGriff's 20 HRs set a new Jays' rookie mark. *Below*: Lefthander Jeff Musselman earned 10 of 12 wins at home.

1986 All-Star Performances but a slow start hurts

Manager	W	L	Pct.	Pos.	GB	Attendance
Jimy Williams	**86**	**76**	**.531**	**4th**	**9½**	**2,455,477**

All-star Jesse Barfield hit 40 home runs.

THE BLUE JAYS' tenth anniversary season proved the baseball adage that it's easier to win a title than to defend one. The American League pennant and World Series Championship would have to wait at least another season as the club, under new manager Jimy Williams, finished the season in fourth, 9½ games behind the Boston Red Sox.

George Bell and Jesse Barfield had the finest seasons of their careers. Bell had 31 home runs and 38 doubles along with a club record 108 RBIs – tied with Barfield, who established club records with 40 homers, 107 runs, a .559 slugging percentage, and 108 RBIs. Tony Fernandez, again playing in every game, led the club with a .310 average and showed himself to be one of the top shortstops in the game. Barfield, Bell, and Fernandez were selected to post-season all-star teams and Barfield and Fernandez became the first Blue Jays to win Gold Glove awards. Rick Leach finished at .309, appearing in 104 games at first base, in the outfield, and as a designated hitter. He had ten pinch-hits.

Jim Clancy and Dave Stieb became the club's first 100-game winners. Clancy was the most consistent of the Jays' starters for most of the season, though he lost his final seven decisions. Dave Stieb lost his first six decisions; he was 2-9 at the All-Star break but improved to finish at 7-12. Jimmy Key was also winless in his first six starts, but found his groove to finish the season at 11-11. He did not allow a run in his last 19.1 innings of work. Mark Eichhorn, who earned a spot on the roster in spring training, won fourteen games in relief in 1986, and set the club record for lowest ERA at 1.72. Eichhorn, who had adopted a submarine-style delivery, held opposing teams scoreless in 42 of his 69 appearances and was selected rookie relief pitcher of the year by *The Sporting News*. Tom Henke continued as the team's top stopper, finishing with a club record of 27 saves.

In their first ten seasons, the Blue Jays grew from a raw expansion franchise to a multi-talented team. The club's second decade began with a nucleus of players among the best in baseball.

1986 Blue Jays Statistics

BATTER	Pos.	Avg.	G	AB	R	H	HR	RBI
BARFIELD, Jesse	OF	.289	158	589	107	170	40	108
BELL, George	OF	.309	159	641	101	198	31	108
FERNANDEZ, Tony	SS	.310	163	689	91	213	10	65
FIELDER, Cecil	1B-DH	.157	34	83	7	13	4	13
GARCIA, Damaso	2B	.281	122	424	57	119	6	46
GRUBER, Kelly	IF	.196	87	143	20	28	5	15
HEARRON, Jeff	C	.217	12	23	2	5	0	4
IORG, Garth	IF	.260	137	327	30	85	3	44
JOHNSON, Cliff	DH	.250	107	336	48	84	15	55
LEACH, Rick	1B-OF-DH	.309	110	246	35	76	5	39
LEE, Manny	T	.205	35	78	8	16	1	7
MARTINEZ, Buck	C	.181	81	160	13	29	2	12
McGRIFF, Fred	IF	.200	3	5	1	1	0	0
MOSEBY, Lloyd	OF	.253	152	589	89	149	21	86
MULLINIKS, Rance	3B	.259	117	348	50	90	11	45
SHEPHERD, Ron	OF	.203	65	69	16	14	2	4
UPSHAW, Willie	1B	.251	155	573	85	144	9	60
WHITT, Ernie	C	.268	131	395	48	106	16	56
Designated Hitters		.242		616	86	149	20	83
Pinch-Hitters		.277		155	19	43	4	32
1986 Totals		**.269**	**163**	**5716**	**809**	**1540**	**81**	**767**

PITCHER	ERA	W-L	SV	G	IP	H	ER	BB	SO
ACKER, Jim	4.35	2-4	0	23	60	63	29	22	32
ALEXANDER, Doyle	4.46	5-4	0	17	111	120	55	20	65
AQUINO, Luis	6.35	1-1	0	7	11	14	8	3	5
CAUDILL, Bill	6.19	2-4	2	40	36	36	25	17	32
CERUTTI, John	4.15	9-4	1	34	145	150	67	47	89
CLANCY, Jim	3.94	14-14	0	34	219	202	96	63	126
CLARKE, Stan	9.24	0-1	0	10	13	18	13	10	9
DAVIS, Steve	17.18	0-0	0	3	4	8	7	5	5
EICHHORN, Mark	1.72	14-6	10	69	157	105	30	45	166
GORDON, Don	7.06	0-1	1	14	22	28	17	8	13
HENKE, Tom	3.25	9-5	27	63	91	63	34	38	118
JOHNSON, Joe	3.89	7-2	0	16	88	94	38	22	39
KEY, Jimmy	3.57	14-11	0	36	232	222	92	74	141
LAMP, Dennis	5.05	2-6	2	40	73	93	41	23	30
MAHLER, Mickey	0.00	0-0	0	2	1	1	0	0	0
MUSSELMAN, Jeff	10.13	0-0	0	6	5	8	6	5	4
STIEB, Dave	4.74	7-12	1	37	205	239	108	87	127
WARD, Duane	13.50	0-1	0	2	2	3	3	4	1
1986 Totals	**4.08**	**86-76**	**44**	**163**	**1476**	**1467**	**669**	**487**	**1002**

Labatt's Most Valuable Player
GEORGE BELL
Labatt's Most Valuable Pitcher
JIMMY KEY
BBWAA Player of the Year
JESSE BARFIELD
BBWAA Pitcher of the Year
MARK EICHHORN
Most Improved Player
RICK LEACH

Above: Mark Eichhorn had ten saves and a 1.72 ERA in 157 IP. *Below:* Tony Fernandez hit .310 with 213 base hits.

1985 A Dream Season: 99 wins and a championship

Manager	W	L	Pct.	Pos.	GA	Attendance
Bobby Cox	**99**	**62**	**.615**	**1st**	**2**	**2,468,925**

Lefthander Jimmy Key won 14 games with 213 IP.

A FIRST-PLACE FINISH and the American League East Division Championship came to the Blue Jays on October 5, 1985 when Doyle Alexander pitched a complete game to beat the New York Yankees 5-1. The Jays finished with 99 wins and went on to take a 3-1 lead in games against the Kansas City Royals in the American League Championship Series, before the Royals battled back to win in seven games.

The Jays had made changes. In December of 1984, Griffin and Collins had gone to Oakland for relief ace Bill Caudill. Jim Gott and two minor leaguers had gone to San Francisco for lefthander Gary Lavelle in January of 1985. Dennis Lamp had been moved to middle relief and Jimmy Key had become part of the starting rotation. Bell, Barfield, and Fernandez were now everyday players. Cliff Johnson, who was later reacquired in mid-season, signed with Texas as a free agent, and as compensation, the Jays received little-known pitcher Tom Henke, who began the year in "AAA".

The team moved into first place on May 13. The Jays' bullpen had its best record ever, with 47 saves and a 35-20 won-lost record. After a fast start, Caudill's production tailed off and Jim Acker got the call in short-relief situations. Acker registered ten saves, seven wins, and a 3.23 ERA. Dennis Lamp, pitching long or middle relief, had a remarkable 11-0 season and was the Jays' most consistent pitcher. But the big bullpen story was Tom Henke. Called up in late July, the hard-throwing righthander became the club's top reliever, saving thirteen of fifteen games. Jimmy Key had a fine season in his first year as a starter, going 14-6 and giving the Jays their first wins by a lefthanded starter since Paul Mirabella defeated Boston on October 4, 1980.

Barfield and Bell were friendly rivals for Player of the Year; both hit and fielded their positions strongly. Tony Fernandez appeared in all 161 games, batting .289. Garth Iorg had his best season, hitting .313. Ernie Whitt had nineteen homers.

The Jays had come within one win of the American League pennant. Nine seasons of player development and roster moves had established the club as one of baseball's best.

1985 Blue Jays Statistics

BATTER	Pos.	Avg.	G	AB	R	H	HR	RBI
AIKENS, Willie	DH	.200	12	20	2	4	1	5
ALLENSON, Gary	C	.118	14	34	2	4	0	3
BARFIELD, Jesse	OF	.289	155	539	94	156	27	84
BELL, George	OF	.275	157	607	87	167	28	95
BURROUGHS, Jeff	DH	.257	86	191	19	49	6	28
FERNANDEZ, Tony	SS	.289	161	564	71	163	2	51
FIELDER, Cecil	1B-DH	.311	30	74	6	23	4	16
GARCIA, Damaso	2B	.282	146	600	70	169	8	65
GRUBER, Kelly	IF	.231	5	13	0	13	0	1
HEARRON, Jeff	C	.143	4	7	0	1	0	0
IORG, Garth	IF	.313	131	288	33	90	7	37
JOHNSON, Cliff	DH-1B	.260	106	369	35	96	13	66
LEACH, Rick	1B-OF	.200	16	35	2	7	0	1
LEE, Manny	IF	.200	64	40	9	8	0	0
MARTINEZ, Buck	C	.162	42	99	11	16	4	14
MATUSZEK, Len	DH-1B	.212	62	151	23	32	2	15
MOSEBY, Lloyd	OF	.259	152	584	92	151	18	71
MULLINIKS, Rance	3B	.295	129	366	55	108	10	56
NICOSIA, Steve	C	.267	6	15	0	4	0	1
OLIVER, Al	DH	.251	61	187	20	47	5	23
SHEPHERD, Ron	OF	.114	38	35	7	4	0	1
THORNTON, Lou	OF	.236	56	72	18	17	1	8
UPSHAW, Willie	1B	.275	148	501	79	138	15	65
WEBSTER, Mitch	OF	.000	4	1	0	0	0	0
WHITT, Ernie	C	.245	139	412	55	101	19	64
Designated Hitters		.247	161	600	77	148	13	78
Pinch-Hitters		.222	–	167	18	37	4	29
1985 Totals		**.269**	**161**	**5,508**	**759**	**1,482**	**158**	**714**

PITCHER	ERA	W-L	SV	G	IP	H	ER	BB	SO
ACKER, Jim	3.23	7-2	10	61	86	86	31	43	42
ALEXANDER, Doyle	3.45	17-10	0	36	261	268	100	67	142
CAUDILL, Bill	2.99	4-6	14	67	69	53	23	35	46
CERUTTI, John	5.40	0-2	4	4	7	10	4	4	5
CLANCY, Jim	3.78	9-6	0	23	129	117	54	37	66
CLARKE, Stan	4.50	0-0	0	4	4	3	2	2	2
DAVIS, Steve	3.54	2-1	0	10	28	23	11	13	22
FILER, Tom	3.88	7-0	0	11	49	38	21	18	24
HENKE, Tom	2.03	3-3	13	28	40	29	9	8	42
KEY, Jimmy	3.00	14-6	0	35	213	188	71	50	85
LAMP, Dennis	3.32	11-0	2	53	106	96	39	27	68
LAVELLE, Gary	3.10	5-7	8	69	73	54	25	36	50
LEAL, Luis	5.75	3-6	0	15	67	82	43	24	33
MUSSELMAN, Ron	4.47	3-0	0	25	52	59	26	24	29
STIEB, Dave	2.48	14-13	0	36	265	206	73	96	167
1985 Totals	**3.29**	**99-62**	**47**	**161**	**1,448**	**1,312**	**529**	**484**	**823**

Labatt's Most Valuable Player
JESSE BARFIELD
Labatt's Most Valuable Pitcher
DAVE STIEB
BBWAA Player of the Year
JESSE BARFIELD
BBWAA Pitcher of the Year
DENNIS LAMP
Most Improved Player
DENNIS LAMP

Above: Tom Henke was 3-3 with 13 saves and a 2.03 ERA in 40 IP. *Below:* George Bell had 28 home runs and 95 RBIS.

1984 Unstoppable Tigers hide Jays' strong season

Manager	W	L	Pct.	Pos.	GB	Attendance
Bobby Cox	**89**	**73**	**.549**	**2nd**	**15**	**2,110,009**

Doyle Alexander was 17-6 with an ERA of 3.13.

THE JAYS MADE MOVES to improve their bullpen, as late or extra-inning losses had hurt the club in 1983. Dennis Lamp became Toronto's first significant free agent signing, and a trade that sent Barry Bonnell to Seattle brought lefthander Bryan Clark to the Jays' relief corps.

Despite these efforts, the year was marked by the inability of the Jays' bullpen to close games. After a seemingly charmed streak of nineteen one-run victories in the first half of the season, the Jays dropped 25 of 40 one-run games over the rest of the schedule. They finished with 89 wins, matching their 1983 total and winding up in second place. This was the year of the "flying Tigers", as the Detroit club's fast start (35 wins in their first 40 games) allowed them to lead from wire to wire.

Player of the Year for the Jays was Dave Collins, whose .308 batting average with 41 extra base hits and 60 stolen bases made him the team's rally-starter. Moseby had his second fine season, hitting .280 with eighteen homers and 39 stolen bases. Rance Mulliniks, part of the Jays' third-base platoon, hit .349 with runners in scoring position. His .326 average was the best on the club. Tony Fernandez played in 88 games with the Jays, hitting .270 and staking claim to the starting shortstop's job for 1985.

Doyle Alexander had a great year on the mound, going 17-6 with 262 innings pitched and eleven complete games. Stieb had another fine year at 16-8 with an ERA of 2.83. Jim Clancy and Luis Leal each won thirteen games.

For the first time in franchise history more than two million fans made their way to Exhibition Stadium to be part of a pennant race. But the Tigers never faltered; the Blue Jays were a good team, but a piece or two was still missing from the championship puzzle.

1984 Blue Jays Statistics

BATTER	Pos.	Avg.	G	AB	R	H	HR	RBI
AIKENS, Willie	DH	.205	93	234	21	48	11	26
BARFIELD, Jesse	OF	.284	110	320	51	91	14	49
BELL, George	OF	.292	159	606	85	177	26	87
COLLINS, Dave	OF	.308	128	441	59	136	2	44
FERNANDEZ, Tony	SS	.270	88	233	29	63	3	19
GARCIA, Damaso	2B	.284	152	633	79	180	5	46
GRIFFIN, Alfredo	SS-2B	.241	140	419	53	101	4	30
GRUBER, Kelly	IF	.063	15	16	1	1	1	2
HERNANDEZ, Toby	C	.500	3	2	1	1	0	0
IORG, Garth	IF	.227	121	247	24	56	1	25
JOHNSON, Cliff	DH	.304	127	359	51	109	16	61
LEACH, Rick	1B-OF	.261	65	88	11	23	0	7
MANRIQUE, Fred	IF	.333	10	9	0	3	0	1
MARTINEZ, Buck	C	.220	102	232	24	51	5	37
MOSEBY, Lloyd	OF	.280	158	592	97	166	18	92
MULLINIKS, Rance	IF	.324	125	343	41	111	3	42
PETRALLI, Geno	C	.000	3	3	0	0	0	0
SHEPHERD, Ron	OF	.000	12	4	0	0	0	0
UPSHAW, Willie	IB	.278	152	569	79	158	19	84
WEBSTER, Mitch	OF	.227	26	22	9	5	0	4
WHITT, Ernie	C	.238	124	315	35	72	15	46
Designated Hitters		.270	162	612	91	165	27	93
Pinch-Hitters		.284	–	215	29	61	6	39
1984 Totals		**.273**	**162**	**5,678**	**750**	**1,555**	**143**	**702**

PITCHER	ERA	W-L	SV	G	IP	H	ER	BB	SO
ACKER, Jim	4.38	3-5	1	32	72	79	35	25	33
ALEXANDER, Doyle	3.13	17-6	0	36	262	238	91	59	139
CLANCY, Jim	5.12	13-15	0	36	220	249	125	88	118
CLARK, Bryan	5.91	1-2	0	20	46	66	30	22	21
GOTT, Jim	4.02	7-6	2	35	110	93	49	49	73
JACKSON, Roy Lee	3.56	7-8	10	54	86	73	34	31	58
KEY, Jimmy	4.65	4-5	10	63	62	70	32	32	44
LAMP, Dennis	4.55	8-8	9	56	85	97	38	38	45
LEACH, Rick	2.70	0-0	0	1	1	2	3	2	0
LEAL, Luis	3.89	13-8	0	35	222	221	96	77	134
MUSSELMAN, Ron	2.11	0-2	1	11	21	18	5	10	9
McLAUGHLIN, Joey	2.53	0-0	0	6	11	12	3	7	3
STIEB, Dave	2.83	16-8	0	35	267	215	84	88	198
1984 Totals	**3.86**	**89-73**	**33**	**162**	**1,464**	**1,433**	**628**	**528**	**875**

Labatt's Most Valuable Player
GEORGE BELL

Labatt's Most Valuable Pitcher
DAVE STIEB

BBWAA
Player of the Year
DAVE COLLINS

BBWAA
Pitcher of the Year
DOYLE ALEXANDER

BBWAA
Rookie of the Year
TONY FERNANDEZ

Most Improved Player
DAVE COLLINS

Above: Cliff Johnson hit .304 as DH. *Below:* Willie Upshaw had 19 home runs.

1983 Maturing Jays leave the cellar behind

Manager	W	L	Pct.	Pos.	GB	Attendance
Bobby Cox	**89**	**73**	**.549**	**4th**	**9**	**1,930,415**

Leftfielder Dave Collins

THE BLUE JAYS had at last become serious contenders. This season saw the ballclub only 1½ games out of first place in late August when, in one disastrous week, the Jays lost six times either in extra innings or in the ninth.

The team strengthened its designated hitting, acquiring veteran sluggers Cliff Johnson and Jorge Orta through trades. The two combined for 34 home runs and 113 RBIs, the top totals in the league. The Jays increased their total run production to 795, up almost a full run per game on 1982, and their .277 team batting average and .436 slugging average led the American League.

Lloyd Moseby had his finest season, becoming the first Jay to score more than 100 runs. He hit .315 with eighteen home runs, 81 RBIs, and 27 stolen bases. Power came from Willie Upshaw who became the first Jay to record 100 RBIs. He had 27 homers and 99 runs scored, sharing Player of the Year honours with Moseby. Damaso Garcia had another strong year, finishing at .307 with 31 stolen bases despite being hampered by knee problems.

The outfield had a different look due to the acquisition of Dave Collins from the New York Yankees. Collins platooned in left with Bonnell and, later in the season, George Bell. Bonnell did spot duty in all outfield positions, hitting .318. Barfield had 27 homers in right.

The pitching staff depended on Stieb, Clancy, Leal, and Jim Gott as starters, but when Gott was sidelined with recurring blister problems, the Jays acquired veteran righthander Doyle Alexander who had been released by the Yankees in June. Alexander won seven and lost six for the Jays.

It was quite a year in baseball. George Brett had a home run disallowed because he had too much pine tar on his bat and Dave Winfield accidently hit one of Exhibition Stadium's ever-present outfield seagulls with a baseball. More important, it was the year of Toronto's first exposure to pennant fever. Fans were ready for more.

1983 Blue Jays Statistics

BATTER	Pos.	Avg.	G	AB	R	H	HR	RBI
BARFIELD, Jesse	OF	.253	128	388	58	98	27	68
BELL, George	OF	.268	39	112	5	30	2	17
BONNELL, Barry	OF	.318	121	377	49	120	10	54
COLLINS, Dave	OF	.271	118	402	55	109	1	34
FERNANDEZ, Tony	SS	.265	15	34	5	9	0	2
GARCIA, Damaso	2B	.307	131	525	84	161	3	38
GRIFFIN, Alfredo	SS	.250	162	528	62	132	4	47
IORG, Garth	IF	.275	122	375	40	103	2	39
JOHNSON, Cliff	DH-1B	.265	142	407	59	108	22	76
KLUTTS, Mickey	3B	.256	22	43	3	11	3	5
MARTINEZ, Buck	C	.253	88	221	27	56	10	33
MOSEBY, Lloyd	OF	.315	151	539	104	170	18	81
MULLINIKS, Rance	IF	.275	129	364	54	100	10	49
ORTA, Jorge	DH-OF	.237	103	245	30	58	10	38
PETRALLI, Geno	C	.000	6	4	0	0	0	0
POWELL, Hosken	OF	.169	40	83	6	14	1	7
UPSHAW, Willie	1B	.306	160	579	99	177	27	104
WEBSTER, Mitch	OF	.182	11	11	2	2	0	0
WHITT, Ernie	C	.256	123	344	53	88	17	56
Designated Hitters		.250	162	604	86	151	34	113
Pinch-Hitters		.290	—	200	26	58	5	42
1983 Totals		**.277**	**162**	**5,581**	**795**	**1,546**	**167**	**748**

PITCHER	ERA	W-L	SV	G	IP	H	ER	BB	SO
ACKER, Jim	4.33	5-1	1	38	98	103	47	38	44
ALEXANDER, Doyle	3.93	7-6	0	17	117	126	51	26	46
CLANCY, Jim	3.91	15-11	0	34	223	238	97	61	99
CLARKE, Stan	3.27	1-1	0	10	11	10	4	5	7
COOPER, Don	6.75	0-0	0	4	5	8	4	0	5
GEISEL, Dave	4.64	0-3	5	47	52	47	27	31	50
GOTT, Jim	4.74	9-14	0	34	177	195	93	68	121
JACKSON, Roy Lee	4.50	8-3	7	49	92	92	46	41	48
LEAL, Luis	4.31	13-12	0	35	217	216	104	65	116
MOFFITT, Randy	3.77	6-2	10	45	57	52	24	24	38
MORGAN, Mike	5.16	0-3	0	16	45	48	26	21	22
McLAUGHLIN, Joey	4.45	7-4	9	50	65	63	32	37	47
STIEB, Dave	3.04	17-12	0	36	278	223	94	93	187
WILLIAMS, Matt	14.63	1-1	0	4	8	13	13	7	5
1983 Totals	**4.12**	**89-73**	**32**	**162**	**1,445**	**1,434**	**662**	**517**	**835**

Labatt's
Player of the Year
LLOYD MOSEBY & WILLIE UPSHAW

Labatt's
Pitcher of the Year
DAVE STIEB

BBWAA
Player of the Year
LLOYD MOSEBY

BBWAA
Pitcher of the Year
DAVE STIEB

BBWAA
Rookie of the Year
JIM ACKER

Most Improved Player
LLOYD MOSEBY

Above: Manager Bobby Cox. *Below:* Luis Leal was 13-12.

1982 Cox's platooning Jays on verge of contention

Manager	W	L	Pct.	Pos.	GB	Attendance
Bobby Cox	**78**	**84**	**.481**	**T6**	**17**	**1,275,978**

Damaso Garcia hit .310 in 1982.

THIS WAS THE YEAR that the Jays finally escaped seventh place in the American League East Division standings. A late-season surge saw them win ten of their last twelve games and finish in a tie with Cleveland for sixth. The club's winning percentage showed its greatest improvement, as the Jays finished at .481 with 78 wins.

Bobby Cox's first season as manager saw some of the club's promising young players take increasingly large roles. Willie Upshaw took over at first base after John Mayberry was traded to Kansas City in May. In 580 at-bats, Upshaw had 75 RBIs and 21 home runs. Damaso Garcia had his best season yet, hitting .310 with 185 hits and 58 stolen bases. He was the toughest Blue Jay to strike out in 1982, and could have posted even greater numbers had he not suffered a hand injury when he was again hit by a pitch in late August. Garcia was the Jays' Player of the Year. Jesse Barfield, playing rightfield almost exclusively against lefthanded pitching, had eighteen home runs and 97 hits, including a pinch-hit grand slam. Despite being a platoon player, Barfield was second in the American League in outfield assists, with fifteen, and was selected as the club's Rookie of the Year.

Platooning was an important part of Cox's strategy. Barfield shared rightfield with Hosken Powell. Garth Iorg and newly acquired Rance Mulliniks shared third and Ernie Whitt and Buck Martinez handled the catching responsibilities.

Meanwhile Dave Stieb was blossoming into one of the American League's top pitchers. He led the league with 288.1 innings pitched, nineteen complete games, and five shutouts. He won a club-record seventeen games for the Jays, despite being unable to register a win until his fifth start of the season. Jim Clancy rebounded from his injuries of the previous season to post a 16-14 record and Luis Leal gave the Jays their first effective third starter, going 12-15 with 250 innings pitched. In relief, Dale Murray became the Jays' ace, with eleven saves and eight wins in 111 innings pitched.

The club appeared ready to move up the standings in the American League East.

1982 Blue Jays Statistics

BATTER	Pos.	Avg.	G	AB	R	H	HR	RBI
ADAMS, Glenn	DH	.258	30	66	2	17	1	11
BAKER, Dave	3B	.250	9	20	3	5	0	2
BARFIELD, Jesse	OF	.246	139	394	54	97	18	58
BONNELL, Barry	OF	.293	140	437	59	128	6	49
DAVIS, Dick	OF	.286	3	7	0	2	0	2
GARCIA, Damaso	2B	.310	147	597	89	185	5	42
GRIFFIN, Alfredo	SS	.241	162	539	57	130	1	48
HERNANDEZ, Pedro	3B	.000	8	9	1	0	0	0
IORG, Garth	3B-2B	.285	129	417	45	119	1	36
JOHNSON, Anthony	OF	.235	70	98	17	23	3	14
MARTINEZ, Buck	C	.242	96	260	26	63	10	37
MAYBERRY, John	1B	.273	17	33	7	9	2	3
MOSEBY, Lloyd	OF	.236	147	487	51	115	9	52
MULLINIKS, Rance	3B-SS	.244	112	311	32	76	4	35
NORDHAGEN, Wayne	DH-OF	.270	72	185	12	50	1	20
PETRALLI, Geno	C-3B	.364	16	44	3	16	0	1
POWELL, Hosken	OF	.275	112	265	43	73	3	26
REVERING, Dave	1B	.215	55	135	15	29	5	18
ROBERTS, Leon	OF	.229	40	105	6	24	1	5
UPSHAW, Willie	1B	.267	160	580	77	155	21	75
VELEZ, Otto	DH	.192	28	52	4	10	1	5
WHITT, Ernie	C	.261	105	284	28	74	11	42
WOODS, Al	OF	.234	85	201	20	47	3	24
Designated Hitters		.238	162	596	52	142	8	56
Pinch-Hitters		.271	—	262	24	71	4	53
1982 Totals		**.262**	**162**	**5,526**	**651**	**1,447**	**106**	**605**

PITCHER	ERA	W-L	SV	G	IP	H	ER	BB	SO
BOMBACK, Mark	6.03	1-5	0	16	60	87	40	25	22
CLANCY, Jim	3.71	16-14	0	40	267	251	110	77	139
EICHHORN, Mark	5.45	0-3	0	7	38	40	23	14	16
GARVIN, Jerry	7.25	1-1	0	32	58	81	47	26	35
GEISEL, Dave	3.98	1-1	0	16	32	32	14	17	22
GOTT, Jim	4.43	5-10	0	30	136	134	67	66	82
JACKSON, Roy Lee	3.06	8-8	6	48	97	77	33	31	71
LEAL, Luis	3.93	12-15	0	38	250	250	109	79	111
McLAUGHLIN, Joey	3.21	8-6	8	44	70	54	25	30	49
MURRAY, Dale	3.16	8-7	11	56	111	115	39	32	60
SCHROM, Ken	5.87	1-0	0	6	15	13	10	15	8
SENTENEY, Steve	4.91	0-0	0	11	22	23	12	6	20
STIEB, Dave	3.25	17-14	0	38	288	271	104	75	141
1982 Totals	**3.95**	**78-84**	**25**	**162**	**1,444**	**1,428**	**633**	**493**	**776**

Labatt's
Player of the Year
DAMASO GARCIA

Labatt's
Pitcher of the Year
DAVE STIEB

BBWAA
Player of the Year
DAMASO GARCIA

BBWAA
Pitcher of the Year
DAVE STIEB

BBWAA
Rookie of the Year
JESSE BARFIELD

Most Improved Player
JIM CLANCY

Above: Outfielder Barry Bonnell hit .293. *Below:* Ernie Whitt split the catcher's job with Buck Martinez.

1981

A split season sees the Jays turn around

Manager	W	L	Pct.	Pos.	GB	Attendance
Bob Mattick	**16**	**42**	**.276**	**7th**	**19**	
(split season)	**21**	**27**	**.438**	**7th**	**$7^1/_2$**	**755,083**

Dave Stieb was 11-10 with 184 IP.

IN A SEASON SPLIT in half by a 59-day players' strike, the Blue Jays' performance combined the worst start and the strongest finish in the franchise's five-year history. When the strike began, the Jays' record was a mediocre 16-42 for a .276 winning percentage. After the strike was over, the Jays played .500 baseball for all but the last two weeks of the season.

Dave Stieb became the first Jays regular starter to win more decisions than he lost, finishing the year at 11-10 with an ERA of 3.19. Jim Clancy, troubled by nagging injuries, finished at 6-12. Luis Leal, a righthander in his second year with the club, was 7-13 with a 3.68 ERA in 130 innings pitched. In the bullpen, Joey McLaughlin recorded ten saves and a 2.85 ERA and Roy Lee Jackson, acquired from the Mets for Bob Bailor, had seven saves and an ERA of 2.61.

Damaso Garcia had an excellent second half for the Jays, hitting .375 before being struck by a pitch that broke his wrist in late August. Jesse Barfield and George Bell, who had been acquired from the Phillies in the major-league draft, began to play in the outfield after the strike. Barfield and Bell started in the outfield with Lloyd Moseby for the first time on September 3, 1981. Moseby, in his first full season with the Jays, tied with first baseman John Mayberry for the club lead in RBIs.

Tony Fernandez, a gifted eighteen-year-old Dominican shortstop, began his rapid climb through the minors. He finished the year in "AAA", hitting .278 in Syracuse. At the close of the season, the Jays – almost without realizing it – had become a promising, capable team loaded with young talent and ready to move forward. Manager Bobby Mattick was replaced by Bobby Cox at the end of the season as the Jays continued to improve.

1981 Blue Jays Statistics

BATTER	Pos.	Avg.	G	AB	R	H	HR	RBI
AINGE, Danny	IF-OF	.187	86	246	20	46	0	14
BARFIELD, Jesse	OF	.232	25	95	7	22	2	9
BEAMON, Charlie	1B	.200	8	15	1	3	0	0
BELL, George	OF	.233	60	163	19	38	5	12
BONNELL, Barry	OF	.220	66	227	21	50	4	28
BOSETTI, Rick	OF	.234	25	47	5	11	0	4
COX, Ted	IF	.300	16	50	6	15	2	9
GARCIA, Damaso	2B	.252	64	250	24	63	1	13
GRIFFIN, Alfredo	SS	.209	101	388	30	81	0	21
IORG, Garth	IF	.242	70	215	17	52	0	10
MACHA, Ken	IF-C	.200	37	85	4	17	0	6
MANRIQUE, Fred	IF	.143	14	28	1	4	0	1
MARTINEZ, Buck	C	.227	45	128	13	29	4	21
MAYBERRY, John	1B	.248	94	290	34	72	17	43
MOSEBY, Lloyd	OF	.233	100	378	36	88	9	43
STIEB, Dave	PR	.000	1	0	1	0	0	0
UPSHAW, Willie	1B	.171	61	111	15	19	4	10
VELEZ, Otto	1B	.213	80	240	32	51	11	28
WELLS, Greg	1B-DH	.247	32	73	7	18	0	5
WHITMER, Dan	C	.111	7	9	0	1	0	0
WHITT, Ernie	C	.236	74	195	16	46	1	16
WOODS, Al	OF	.247	85	288	20	71	1	21
Designated Hitters		.212	106	363	45	77	13	36
Pinch-Hitters		.234	–	77	4	18	1	15
1981 Totals		**.226**	**106**	**3,521**	**329**	**797**	**61**	**314**

PITCHER	ERA	W-L	SV	G	IP	H	ER	BB	SO
BARLOW, Mike	4.20	0-0	0	12	15	22	7	6	5
BERENGUER, Juan	4.31	2-9	0	12	71	62	34	35	29
BOMBACK, Mark	3.89	5-5	0	20	90	84	39	35	33
CLANCY, Jim	4.90	6-12	0	22	125	126	68	64	56
ESPINOSA, Nino	9.00	0-0	0	1	1	4	1	0	0
GARVIN, Jerry	3.40	1-2	0	35	53	46	20	23	25
JACKSON, Roy Lee	2.61	1-2	7	39	62	65	18	25	27
LEAL, Luis	3.68	7-13	1	29	130	127	53	44	71
McLAUGHLIN, Joey	2.85	1-5	10	40	60	55	19	21	38
MIRABELLA, Paul	7.36	0-0	0	8	15	20	12	7	9
MURRAY, Dale	1.17	1-0	0	11	15	12	2	5	12
STIEB, Dave	3.19	11-10	0	25	184	148	65	61	89
TODD, Jackson	3.96	2-7	0	21	98	94	43	31	41
WILLIS, Mike	5.91	0-4	0	20	35	43	23	20	16
1981 Totals	**3.81**	**37-69**	**18**	**106**	**953**	**908**	**404**	**377**	**451**

Labatt's
Player of the Year
DAVE STIEB

Labatt's
Pitcher of the Year
DAVE STIEB

BBWAA
Player of the Year
DAVE STIEB

BBWAA
Pitcher of the Year
DAVE STIEB

Most Improved Player
JOEY McLAUGHLIN

Above: Roy Lee Jackson had an ERA of 2.61. *Below:* Lloyd Moseby had 43 RBIs in 100 games.

1980 A new manager and the best season yet

Manager	W	L	Pct.	Pos.	GB	Attendance
Bob Mattick	**67**	**95**	**.414**	**7th**	**36**	**1,400,327**

John Mayberry hit a club-record 30 home runs.

BOBBY MATTICK was made the club's new manager. As the Jays' scouting supervisor, Mattick had been responsible for recruiting and developing the talented young ballplayers in the Blue Jays' system. Though he was a managerial rookie, his forty years in baseball, and his familiarity with the Jays' personnel, made Mattick a natural for the job. The Jays responded with their best season to date, 67-95, for a winning percentage of .414. It was the club's first season with fewer than 100 losses.

An important trade sent Tom Underwood and Rick Cerone to the New York Yankees for first baseman Chris Chambliss, lefthander Paul Mirabella, and minor-league infielder Damaso Garcia. Chambliss was then traded to Atlanta for outfielder Barry Bonnell and relief pitcher Joey McLaughlin.

John Mayberry had 30 home runs, establishing a club record that would stand for six seasons. Alvis Woods hit .300 with fifteen home runs and Barry Bonnell had 56 RBIs. Injuries eventually subdued the Jays' offence as Bonnell, Bob Bailor, Rick Bosetti, and Otto Velez were forced out of the lineup.

Jim Clancy and Dave Stieb had become the club's top two starters, with 13 and 12 wins. Stieb was American League Pitcher of the Month for April and represented the Jays at the All-Star Game. Jerry Garvin moved to the bullpen and recorded a 2.28 ERA in 61 appearances. Joey McLaughlin, Paul Mirabella, and Jesse Jefferson all pitched more than 120 innings.

Garth Iorg, who had seen spot duty with the Jays in earlier seasons, had 222 at-bats. Damaso Garcia played regularly at second, hit .278, and combined with shortstop Alfredo Griffin to give the club excellent middle-infield defence. Danny Ainge, a professional prospect in both basketball and baseball, had 111 at-bats as a utility infielder. Ernie Whitt became the team's number-one catcher and Lloyd Moseby and Willie Upshaw made the Blue Jays to stay.

More pieces of the puzzle were beginning to fall into place.

1980 Blue Jays Statistics

BATTER	Pos.	Avg.	G	AB	R	H	HR	RBI
AINGE, Dan	IF	.243	38	111	11	27	0	4
AULT, Doug	1B	.194	64	144	12	28	3	15
BAILOR, Bob	IF-OF	.236	117	347	44	82	1	16
BONNELL, Barry	OF	.268	130	463	55	124	13	56
BOSETTI, Rick	OF	.213	53	188	24	40	4	18
BRAUN, Steve	PH-1B	.273	37	55	4	15	1	9
CANNON, J.J.	OF	.080	7C	50	16	4	0	4
DAVIS, Bob	C	.216	91	218	18	47	4	19
GARCIA, Damaso	2B	.278	140	543	50	151	4	46
GRIFFIN, Alfredo	SS	.254	155	653	63	166	2	41
HODGSON, Paul	OF	.220	20	41	5	9	1	5
HOWELL, Roy	3B	.269	142	528	51	142	10	57
IORG, Garth	IF	.248	80	222	24	55	2	14
KELLY, Pat	C	.286	3	7	0	2	0	0
MACHA, Mike	3B-C	.000	5	8	0	0	0	0
MAYBERRY, John	1B	.248	149	501	62	124	30	82
MOSEBY, Lloyd	OF	.229	114	389	44	89	9	46
RAMOS, Domingo	IF	.125	5	16	0	2	0	0
STIEB, Dave	P-OF	.000	1	1	0	0	0	0
UPSHAW, Willie	1B	.213	34	61	10	13	1	5
VELEZ, Otto	DH-1B	.269	104	357	54	96	20	62
WHITT, Ernie	C	.237	106	295	23	70	6	34
WOODS, Al	OF	.300	109	373	54	112	15	47
Designated Hitters		.229	162	599	73	137	22	84
Pinch-Hitters		.280	–	100	10	28	3	15
1980 Totals		**.251**	**162**	**5,571**	**624**	**1,398**	**126**	**580**

PITCHER	ERA	W-L	SV	G	IP	H	ER	BB	SO
BAILOR, Bob	7.71	0-0	0	3	2	4	2	1	0
BARLOW, Mike	4.09	3-1	5	40	55	57	25	21	19
BUSKEY, Tom	4.46	3-1	0	33	67	68	33	26	34
CLANCY, Jim	3.30	13-16	0	34	251	217	92	128	152
GARVIN, Jerry	2.29	4-7	8	61	83	70	21	27	52
JEFFERSON, Jesse	5.47	4-13	0	29	122	130	74	52	53
KUCEK, Jack	6.75	3-8	1	23	68	83	51	41	35
LEAL, Luis	4.53	3-4	0	13	60	72	30	31	26
LEMANCZYK, Dave	5.40	2-5	0	10	43	57	26	15	10
McLAUGHLIN, Joey	4.51	6-9	4	55	136	159	68	53	70
MIRABELLA, Paul	4.34	5-12	0	33	131	151	63	66	53
MOORE, Balor	5.29	1-1	1	31	65	76	38	21	22
SCHROM, Ken	5.23	1-0	1	17	31	32	18	19	13
STIEB, Dave	3.71	12-15	0	34	242	232	100	83	108
TODD, Jackson	4.02	5-2	0	12	85	90	38	30	34
WILLIS, Mike	1.71	2-1	3	20	26	25	5	11	14
1980 Totals	**4.19**	**67-95**	**23**	**162**	**1,466**	**1,523**	**683**	**635**	**705**

Labatt's
Player of the Year
JOHN MAYBERRY

Labatt's
Pitcher of the Year
JIM CLANCY

BBWAA
Player of the Year
JOHN MAYBERRY

BBWAA
Pitcher of the Year
JIM CLANCY

BBWAA
Rookie of the Year
DAMASO GARCIA

Above: Manager Bobby Mattick. *Below:* Otto Velez had 20 home runs and 62 RBIS.

1979

Youthful Jays: talent in the wings

Manager	W	L	Pct.	Pos.	GB	Attendance
Roy Hartsfield	**53**	**109**	**.327**	**7th**	**$50^1/_2$**	**1,431,651**

Alfredo Griffin was Player of the Year in 1979.

WINS WERE SCARCER than ever for the Jays. Though some of the club's young players began to show their talents, the Jays won only 53 times in 1979.

The youth movement continued with the trade of veteran catcher Alan Ashby to Houston for righthander Mark Lemongello, outfielder J.J. Cannon, and infielder Pedro Hernandez. With Ashby gone, Rick Cerone became the club's number-one catcher and delivered 61 RBIs hitting from the number-nine spot in the batting order. Another deal sent Victor Cruz, Rookie of the Year on last year's club, to Cleveland for Phil Lansford and a young shortstop from the Dominican Republic, Alfredo Griffin. Griffin started slowly in Toronto, but went on to become a co-winner of the American League Rookie of the Year award, along with John Castino of Minnesota. Griffin hit .287 with 179 hits, 81 runs scored, ten triples, and 21 stolen bases – club records, all of them.

Jim Clancy worked only 64 innings as a serious ankle injury put him on the disabled list. Tom Underwood lost his first nine decisions before going 9-7 for the rest of the season; he was the only Jays pitcher to go 200 innings.

On June 26 a talented rookie pitcher completed the almost unheard-of leap from "A" ball to the majors in one season. Dave Stieb, who had been converted from the outfield the previous year, was 5-0 with Dunedin in "A", 5-2 with Syracuse in "AAA", and 8-8 with Toronto, for a combined record of 18-10. Most of the Jays' other prospects were still honing their skills in Dunedin, Florida. Lloyd Moseby hit .332 and Jesse Barfield had 71 RBIs in the Florida State League.

Roy Hartsfield, who had managed the Jays for their first three seasons, was fired after the campaign. The second phase of building the Blue Jays was about to begin.

1979 Blue Jays Statistics

BATTER	Pos.	Avg.	G	AB	R	H	HR	RBI
AINGE, Dan	2B	.237	87	308	26	73	2	19
BAILOR, Bob	3B-OF	.229	130	414	50	95	1	38
BOSETTI, Rick	OF	.260	162	619	59	161	8	65
BROWN, Bobby	OF	.000	4	10	1	0	0	0
CANNON, J.J.	OF	.211	61	142	14	30	1	5
CARTY, Rico	DH	.256	132	461	48	118	12	55
CERONE, Rick	C	.239	136	469	47	112	7	61
DAVIS, Bob	C	.124	32	89	6	11	1	8
GOMEZ, Luis	IF	.239	59	163	11	39	0	11
GRIFFIN, Alfredo	SS	.287	153	624	81	179	2	31
HERNANDEZ, Pedro	IF	.000	3	0	1	0	0	0
HOWELL, Roy	3B	.247	138	511	60	126	15	72
JOHNSON, Tim	IF	.186	43	86	6	16	0	6
KUSICK, Craig	1B	.222	48	108	11	24	5	13
MAYBERRY, John	1B	.274	137	464	61	127	21	74
McKAY, Dave	IF	.218	47	156	19	34	0	12
ROBERTSON, Bob	1B	.103	15	29	1	3	1	1
SOLAITA, Tony	1B	.265	36	102	14	27	2	13
VELEZ, Otto	OF	.288	99	274	45	79	15	48
WILBORN, Ted	OF	.000	22	12	3	0	0	0
WOODS, Al	OF	.278	132	436	57	121	5	36
Designated Hitters		.260	162	599	70	156	18	82
Pinch-Hitters		.231	–	52	5	12	4	14
1979 Totals		**.251**	**162**	**5,423**	**613**	**1,362**	**95**	**562**

PITCHER	ERA	W-L	SV	G	IP	H	ER	BB	SO
BUSKEY, Tom	3.43	6-10	7	44	79	74	30	25	44
CLANCY, Jim	5.51	2-7	0	12	64	65	39	31	33
EDGE, Butch	5.23	3-4	0	9	52	60	30	24	19
FREISLEBEN, Dave	4.95	2-3	3	42	91	101	50	54	33
GARVIN, Jerry	2.78	0-1	0	8	23	15	7	10	14
GRILLI, Steve	0.00	0-0	0	1	2	1	0	0	1
HUFFMAN, Phil	5.77	6-18	0	31	173	220	111	68	56
JEFFERSON, Jesse	5.51	2-10	1	34	116	150	71	45	43
KUSICK, Craig	4.91	0-0	0	1	4	3	2	0	0
LEMANCZYK, Dave	3.71	8-10	0	22	143	137	59	45	63
LEMONGELLO, Mark	6.29	1-9	0	18	83	97	58	34	40
LUEBBER, Steve	INF	0-0	0	1	0	2	1	1	0
MILLER, Dyar	10.57	0-0	0	10	15	27	18	5	7
MOORE, Balor	4.84	5-7	0	34	139	135	75	79	51
MURPHY, Tom	5.40	1-2	0	10	18	23	11	8	6
STIEB, Dave	4.31	8-8	0	18	129	139	62	48	52
TODD, Jackson	5.85	0-1	0	12	32	40	21	7	14
UNDERWOOD, Tom	3.69	9-16	0	32	227	213	93	95	127
WILLIS, Mike	8.44	0-3	0	17	27	35	25	15	8
1979 Totals	**4.81**	**53-109**	**11**	**162**	**1,417**	**1,537**	**758**	**594**	**611**

Labatt's
Player of the Year
ALFREDO GRIFFIN

Labatt's
Pitcher of the Year
TOM UNDERWOOD

BBWAA
Player of the Year
ALFREDO GRIFFIN

BBWAA
Pitcher of the Year
TOM UNDERWOOD

Top: Tom Underwood.
Above: Rick Cerone.
Below: Rick Bosetti.

1978

Player changes help but wins still scarce

Manager	W	L	Pct.	Pos.	GB	Attendance
Roy Hartsfield	**59**	**102**	**.366**	**7th**	**40**	**1,562,585**

Victor Cruz had 9 saves and an ERA of 1.71.

TWO EXPERIENCED HITTERS joined the Jays for their second season. Righthanded-hitting designated hitter Rico Carty and lefthanded-hitting first baseman John Mayberry joined the club to add to the offensive punch expected to come from Ault, Velez, Bailor, and third baseman Roy Howell.

The club's first free agent, Luis Gomez, played shortstop, and Canadian infielder Dave McKay was shifted to second. In the bullpen, Pete Vuckovich was traded for two pitchers, lefthanded starter Tom Underwood and twenty-year-old reliever Victor Cruz.

Despite the changes and the improvement in many of the Jays' young players, this was a tough year on the field, as the club lost 102 games. Consistent offence and pitching proved elusive, as the Jays were outscored by their opponents 775-590 over the course of the season. Carty and Mayberry each hit 20 home runs and combined to drive in 138, but it wasn't enough.

A bright spot was rookie centrefielder Rick Bosetti who had seventeen assists and established a Blue Jays tradition of fast, young outfielders. Roy Howell, 1978's Player of the Year, played strongly at third base, while contributing eight homers and 61 RBIs.

Jim Clancy, in his first full season in the big leagues, was the club's only pitcher to win ten games. Tom Underwood led the staff in strikeouts with 140 while Victor Cruz topped all Toronto relievers with nine saves and a minuscule ERA of 1.71. Underwood got the win in the highest-scoring game in Jays history, a 24-10 win over Baltimore on June 26. Mike Willis, a lefthanded reliever, had his first start of the season on September 20 when he faced Ron Guidry of the Yankees. Guidry was enjoying a sensational season and was 22 and 2 coming into Toronto. Willis responded with his only complete major-league game, beating Guidry and the Yankees 8-1.

In the June free-agent draft, the Jays, picking second, selected a young outfielder named Lloyd Moseby. Down in "A" ball, eighteen-year-old Jesse Barfield hit just .206, and another struggling slugger, Dave Stieb, was switched from the outfield to the pitcher's mound.

1978 Blue Jays Statistics

BATTER	Pos.	Avg.	G	AB	R	H	HR	RBI
ALBERTS, Butch	DH	.278	6	18	1	5	0	0
ASHBY, Alan	C	.261	81	264	27	69	9	29
AULT, Doug	1B	.240	54	104	10	25	3	7
BAILOR, Bob	IF-OF	.264	154	621	74	164	1	52
BOSETTI, Rick	OF	.259	136	568	61	147	5	42
CARTY, Rico	DH	.284	104	387	51	110	20	68
CERONE, Rick	C	.223	88	282	25	63	3	20
EWING, Sam	OF	.179	40	56	3	10	2	9
GOMEZ, Luis	SS-2B	.223	153	413	39	92	0	31
HORTON, Willie	DH	.252	115	393	38	99	11	60
HOWELL, Roy	3B	.270	140	551	67	149	8	61
HUTTON, Tommy	IF-OF	.270	64	173	19	44	2	9
IORG, Garth	2B	.163	19	49	3	8	0	3
JOHNSON, Tim	SS	.232	70	82	10	19	0	3
MAYBERRY, John	1B	.250	152	515	51	129	22	70
McKAY, Dave	1F	.238	145	504	59	120	7	45
MILNER, Brian	C	.444	2	9	3	4	0	2
NORDBROOK, Tim	SS	.000	7	0	1	0	0	0
UPSHAW, Willie	1B-OF	.237	95	224	26	53	1	17
VELEZ, Otto	OF	.266	91	248	29	66	9	38
WHITT, Ernie	C	.000	2	4	0	0	0	0
WOODS, Al	OF	.241	62	220	19	53	3	25
WOODS, Gary	OF	.158	8	19	1	3	0	0
Designated Hitters		.250	161	621	75	155	25	96
Pinch-Hitters		.236	–	123	11	29	2	18
1978 Totals		**.250**	**161**	**5,430**	**590**	**1,358**	**98**	**550**

PITCHER	ERA	W-L	SV	G	IP	H	ER	BB	SO
BUSKEY, Tom	3.37	0-1	0	8	13	14	5	4	7
CLANCY, Jim	4.09	10-12	0	31	194	199	88	91	106
COLEMAN, Joe	3.81	5-0	0	41	80	79	34	35	32
CRUZ, Victor	1.71	7-3	9	32	47	28	9	36	51
GARVIN, Jerry	5.66	4-12	0	26	145	189	91	48	67
JEFFERSON, Jesse	4.38	7-16	0	31	212	214	103	86	97
KIRKWOOD, Don	4.24	4-5	0	16	68	76	32	25	29
LEMANCZYK, Dave	6.26	4-14	0	29	137	170	95	65	62
MOORE, Balor	4.93	6-9	0	37	144	165	79	54	75
MURPHY, Tom	3.93	6-9	7	50	94	87	41	37	35
UNDERWOOD, Tom	4.10	6-14	0	31	198	201	90	87	140
WALLACE, Dave	3.86	0-0	0	6	14	12	6	11	7
WILEY, Mark	6.75	0-0	0	2	3	3	2	1	2
WILLIS, Mike	4.56	3-7	7	44	100	104	51	39	52
1978 Totals	**4.55**	**59-102**	**23**	**161**	**1,429**	**1,529**	**723**	**614**	**758**

Labatt's
Player of the Year
ROY HOWELL

Labatt's
Pitcher of the Year
JIM CLANCY & TOM UNDERWOOD

BBWAA
Player of the Year
BOB BAILOR

BBWAA
Pitcher of the Year
JIM CLANCY & VICTOR CRUZ

BBWAA
Rookie of the Year
VICTOR CRUZ

Most Improved Player
ALAN ASHBY

Above: Manager Roy Hartsfield. *Below:* Third baseman Roy Howell hit .270 with 61 RBIS.

1977 Major League Baseball comes to Toronto

Manager	W	L	Pct.	Pos.	GB	Attendance
Roy Hartsfield	**54**	**107**	**.335**	**7th**	**45½**	**1,701,052**

Dave Lemanczyk had 13 wins and 278 IP.

APRIL 7, 1977: Big-league baseball came to Toronto, to a snow-covered field. The 1977 Blue Jays – a team of rookies, career minor-leaguers, and players other clubs didn't want – played the Chicago White Sox, a team then in its seventy-sixth year of existence. And, just as in the story books, the unknown Blue Jays won – and Torontonians were won over. That season, 1,701,052 fans turned out to share the city's first taste of major-league baseball.

The first-year Jays never threatened to win the pennant – they finished with 54 wins and 107 losses – but the team was entertaining and surprisingly competitive, with 77 of its 161 games decided by only one or two runs. And the club had character; players began emerging as fans' favourites right from that first game on April 7.

Doug Ault, a 27-year-old rookie first baseman, homered twice in the Jays' first game. Outfielder Otto Velez, acquired from the New York Yankees, started the season with a bang, hitting .442 for the month of April and winning the American League Player of the Month award. Bob Bailor, the Jays' first pick in the 1976 expansion draft, turned in a gritty first-season performance which saw him hit .310, the highest-ever mark for a player on a first-year expansion club. Ron Fairly, a twenty-year veteran, led the club with nineteen home runs and became the first player since Stan Musial to play more than 1,000 games in both the infield and the outfield.

On the mound, Dave Lemanczyk led the staff, working 252 innings and recording thirteen wins, another first-year expansion club record. Second in wins and innings pitched was lefthanded forkballer Jerry Garvin, who led the A.L. in pickoffs with 22. The club's first relief specialist was Pete Vuckovich who finished with eight saves, a 7-7 record, and an ERA of 3.47. Vuckovich, who went on to win the Cy Young Award with Milwaukee in 1982, pitched the Jays' first shutout, a 2-0 win over Baltimore on June 26.

The Blue Jays were in the big leagues, and the slow process of building a ballclub had begun.

1977 Blue Jays Statistics

BATTER	Pos.	Avg.	G	AB	R	H	HR	RBI
ASHBY, Alan	C	.210	124	396	25	83	2	29
AULT, Doug	1B	.245	129	445	44	109	11	64
BAILOR, Bob	IF-OF	.310	122	496	62	154	5	32
BOWLING, Steve	OF	.206	89	194	19	40	1	13
CERONE, Rick	C	.200	31	100	7	20	1	10
EWING, Sam	OF	.287	97	244	24	70	4	34
FAIRLY, Ron	1B-OF	.279	132	458	60	128	19	64
GARCIA, Pedro	2B	.208	41	130	10	27	0	9
HOWELL, Roy	3B	.302	103	381	41	115	10	44
MASON, Jim	SS	.165	22	79	10	13	0	2
McKAY, Dave	IF	.197	95	274	18	54	3	22
NORDBROOK, Tim	SS	.193	39	83	11	16	0	2
ROOF, Phil	C	.000	3	5	0	0	0	0
RADER, Doug	IF	.240	96	313	47	75	13	40
STAGGS, Steve	2B	.258	72	291	37	75	2	28
SCOTT, John	OF	.240	79	233	26	56	2	15
TORRES, Hector	OF	.241	91	266	33	64	5	26
VELEZ, Otto	OF	.256	120	360	50	92	16	62
WHITT, Ernie	C	.171	23	41	4	7	0	6
WOODS, Al	OF	.284	122	440	58	125	6	35
WOODS, Gary	OF	.216	60	227	21	49	0	17
Designated Hitters		.269	161	583	75	22	22	87
Pinch-Hitters		.280	—	93	—	5	5	23
1977 Totals		**.252**	**161**	**5,419**	**605**	**1,367**	**100**	**553**

PITCHER	ERA	W-L	SV	G	IP	H	ER	BB	SO
BRUNO, Tom	8.00	0-1	0	12	18	30	16	13	8
BYRD, Jeff	6.21	2-13	0	17	87	98	60	68	40
CLANCY, Jim	5.03	4-9	0	13	77	80	43	47	44
DARR, Mike	4.50	0-1	0	1	1	3	5	4	1
DeBARR, Dennis	6.00	0-1	0	14	21	29	14	8	10
GARVIN, Jerry	4.19	10-18	0	34	245	247	114	85	27
HARTENSTEIN, Chuck	6.67	0-2	0	13	27	40	20	6	15
HARGAN, Steve	5.28	1-3	0	6	29	26	17	14	11
JEFFERSON, Jesse	4.31	9-17	0	33	217	224	104	83	114
JOHNSON, Jerry	4.60	2-4	5	43	86	91	44	54	54
LEMANCZYK, Dave	4.25	13-16	0	34	252	278	119	87	105
MURPHY, Tom	4.77	2-2	2	35	83	107	44	30	39
SINGER, Bill	6.75	2-8	0	13	60	71	45	39	33
VUCKOVICH, Pete	3.47	7-7	8	53	148	143	57	59	123
WILLIS, Mike	3.95	2-6	5	43	107	105	47	38	59
1977 Totals	**4.57**	**54-107**	**20**	**161**	**1,428**	**1,538**	**726**	**623**	**771**

Labatt's MVP
BOB BAILOR

BBWAA
Player of the Year
BOB BAILOR

BBWAA
Pitcher of the Year
DAVE LEMANCZYK

BBWAA
Rookie of the Year
BOB BAILOR

Above: Bob Bailor hit .310 and was Player of the Year.
Below: Doug Ault hit two homers on Opening Day in Toronto.

SKYDOME

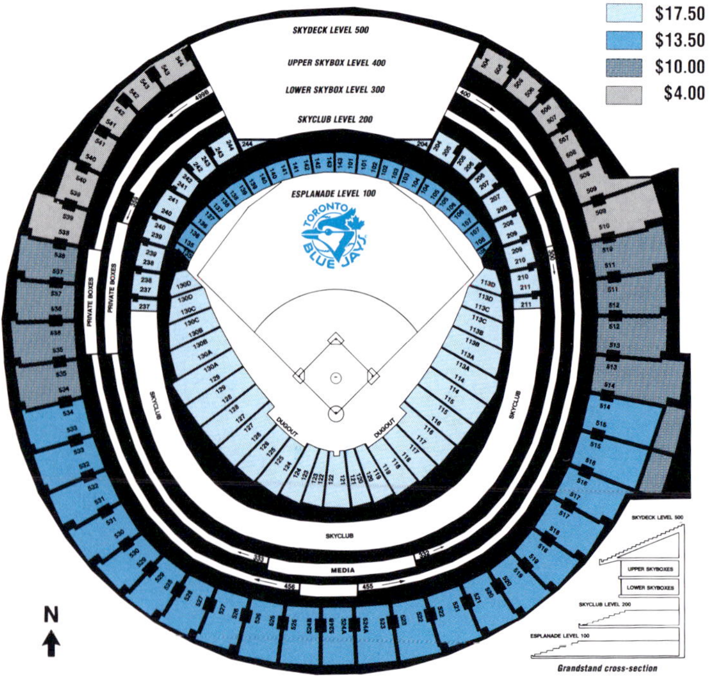

Seating Chart

SKYDOME

Toronto's superb new stadium with a retractable roof became the official home park of the Blue Jays on Monday, June 5, 1989.

In moving to SkyDome, the Jays find themselves playing in the world's most advanced and luxurious ballpark. From bottom to top, everything from the artificial turf to the seating, video scoreboard, and roof employs the finest and newest technology available. Located to the west and south of the CN Tower and north of the Esplanade between John and Peter Streets, the very scale of the project is astonishing. When closed, the retractable roof covers an area of eight acres and rises to an inside height equivalent to that of a 31-storey building — almost twice as high as Minnesota's Metrodome.

From its conception, SkyDome took an innovative approach to financing, construction and design. The stadium is owned by Stadium Corporation of Ontario Ltd., a partnership that incorporates both government and private investors. The Province of Ontario and the Municipality of Metropolitan Toronto contributed $30 million each. Joining these two levels of government are 25 Canadian corporations — including the Toronto Blue Jays Baseball Club — each of which has contributed $5 million in exchange for preferred-supplier status and a SkyBox. Canada's three major breweries have also joined the partnership with $5 million contributions. This blending of public- and private-sector investment stands as a unique model in the financing of a showpiece project. The final cost of SkyDome construction is more than $500 million.

Architects Rod Robbie and Michael Allen designed SkyDome and have patented its retractable-roof system. Site preparation began in April of 1986, with groundbreaking taking place in October of that same year. The last exterior concrete was poured in November of 1988 and the first test of the moveable roof panels took place in January of 1989. More than 10,000 person-years of employment were created by the construction of the new stadium.

SKYDOME FIRSTS

GAME — Monday June 5, 1989 (Blue Jays-3, Milwaukee Brewers-5)
ATTENDANCE — 48,378
TIME/TEMP — 2:43/18°C
PITCHER — Jimmy Key, Toronto
BATTER — Paul Molitor, Milwaukee (doubled)
PLATE UMPIRE — Rocky Roe
PITCH — Fastball, called strike
HIT — Double by Molitor in 1st inning
RUN — Molitor in 1st inning
SINGLE — Kelly Gruber, Toronto, 1st inning
DOUBLE — Paul Molitor, 1st inning
HOME RUN — Fred McGriff, Toronto, 2nd inning
RBI — Gary Sheffield, Milwaukee, 1st inning
WINNING PITCHER — Don August, Milwaukee
LOSING PITCHER — Jimmy Key, Toronto
SAVE — Dan Plesac
PUTOUT — Nelson Liriano, Toronto
ASSIST — Kelly Gruber, Toronto
STOLEN BASE — Fred McGriff, 6th inning
WALK — George Bell, Toronto, 2nd inning

ADMISSION PRICES FOR 1991

$17.50
$13.50
$10.00
$ 4.00

SkyDome Data
The Blue Jays were 44-37 at home in '90...12-18 when the roof was open, 29-17 when closed, and 5-2 when closed during the game.

SkyDome Home Runs
Toronto hit a total of 93 HR's at home in 1990 while opponents hit 82...30 of the home games saw the roof open...The Blue Jays hit 26 HR's with the roof open and hit 67 when it was closed...
Sky Dome Home Runs: Bell 11, Borders 10, Felix 7, Fernandez 2, Gruber 23, Hill 7, Lee 2, McGriff 14, Mulliniks 1, Myers 3, Olerud 11, Whiten 1.

SOME FACTS ABOUT SKYDOME

ROOF

- roof area — 339,343 square feet (31,525 sq. metres)
- weight — 11,000 tons
- span at widest point — 674 feet (206 metres)
- height — 282 feet (from field level) at highest point
- type of covering (skin) — single PVC membrane on insulated acoustic steel deck.
- percentage of openess — 91%
- time to open/close — 20 minutes (moves at a rate of 71 feet (21 metres) per minute)
- concept of opening system — panels 2 and 3 which slide on parallel rails and panel 1 which rotates on a circular rail
- major mechanical components — multi-wheel bogie assemblies, electric DC motors, direct drive

JUMBOTRON SCOREBOARD

- largest video display board in the world
- the Sony system uses 420,000 light bulbs
- 33 feet (10.3 metres) by 115 (35 metres)
- cost — $17 million

SEATING

- five levels: Esplanade level, Club level, 161 Skyboxes on two levels, SkyDeck
- approximately 51,000 for baseball
- approximately 53,000 for football
- up to 62,000 for concerts
- half mode for concerts between 10,000 and 25,000
- 41,000 are located within the foul lines
- SkyBoxes range in price from $150,000 to $225,000 per year

HOTEL

- 348 distinctively designed guest rooms
- 70 rooms with stadium view

FOOD SERVICES

- concessionaire-McDonald's of Canada
- four counter service restaurants
- 20 SkySnack locations
- 48 beverage stations
- nine vending kitchens
- fine dining-Bitove Corporation
- Windows on SkyDome — 650 seat restaurant
- Sightlines — 300 foot long bar overlooking the field
- Hard Rock Cafe

FIELD

- artificial-turf system — Astro-Turf 8, $1\frac{1}{4}$ in thickness
- dimensions-symmetrical; 328 feet down the lines, 375 to power alleys and 400 feet to centre field
- diamond is centred exactly two degress off perfect north
- outfield wall — 10 feet in height
- bullpens — located just beyond the left and right field fences
- pitcher's mound is on a hydraulic system
- conversion — takes approximately 10-12 hours to convert from baseball-football (and vice-versa)

FIRST GAME PLAYED AT EXHIBITION STADIUM

The Blue Jays slugged their way to a 9—5 triumph over the Chicago White Sox in their April 7, 1977, debut.

Despite snow flurries before the game and near-freezing temperatures, 44,649 fans witnessed the exciting contest, which featured 16 hits by the Blue Jays and 15 by Chicago.

Doug Ault smacked two homers and a single and rookie Al Woods hit a pinch-homer in his first big-league at bat for Toronto. Richie Zisk had four hits for the visitors.

The Blue Jays played 968-games from April 7, 1977-May 28, 1989 at Exhibition Stadium posting a record of 491-475 with 23,213,557 fans passing through the turnstiles.

EXHIBITION STADIUM FIRSTS

GAME — Thurs. April 7, 1977 (Blue Jays 9, Chicago White Sox 5)
ATTENDANCE — 44,649 **TIME/TEMP.** — 3:22/0°C. (32°F)
PITCHER — Bill Singer, Toronto
BATTER — Ralph Garr, Chicago (walked)
PLATE UMPIRE — Nestor Chylak
PITCH — Called strike
HIT — Home run by Richie Zisk, first inning, none on
RUN — Ralph Garr (scored on sacrifice fly by Jorge Orta)
SINGLE — Jim Spencer, Chicago, April 7, 1977, first inning
DOUBLE — Richie Zisk, Chicago, April 7, 1977, second inning
TRIPLE — Ron LeFlore, Detroit, April 12, 1977, fifth inning
HOME RUN — Richie Zisk, April 7, 1977, first inning
FIRST RBI — Jorge Orta, Chicago, April 7, 1977, 1st inning
INSIDE-THE-PARK HOME RUN — Cecil Cooper, Milwaukee, May 5, 1977 (fifth inning)
GRAND SLAM HOME RUN — Hector Torres vs. New York, June 27, 1977 (fifth inning, off Ron Guidry)
TWO HOME-RUN GAME — Doug Ault, Toronto, April 7, 1977
THREE HOME-RUN GAME — John Mayberry, K.C., June 1, 1977
PINCH-HIT HOME RUN — Al Woods, Toronto, April 7, 1977 (fifth inning)
WINNING PITCHER — Jerry Johnson, Toronto (in relief), April 7, 1977
LOSING PITCHER — Ken Brett, Chicago (starter), April 7, 1977
SAVE — Pete Vuckovich, Toronto, April 7, 1977
PUTOUT — Steve Bowling, Toronto (fly ball to right field) April 7, 1977
ASSIST — Hector Torres, Toronto (ground ball to shortstop) April 7, 1977
ERROR — Rick Cerone, Toronto, April 7, 1977
SHUTOUT — Ferguson Jenkins, Boston, Sun. April 24, 1977 (9—0)
COMPLETE GAME — Dave Lemanczyk, Toronto vs. Chicago, April 9, 1977
WALK — Ralph Garr by Bill Singer, April 7, 1977 (first inning)
STRIKEOUT — John Scott by Ken Brett, April 7, 1977 (first inning)
FORFEIT — Baltimore, Thurs. September 15, 1977 (Blue Jays 9, Baltimore 0)
NIGHT GAME — Mon., May 2, 1977 vs. Milwaukee (Brewers 3, Blue Jays 1)
STOLEN BASE — Ralph Garr, Chicago, April 7, 1977 (first inning)
TRIPLE PLAY — Clancy to Mayberry to Gomez, April 22, 1978 (sixth inning)
BALK — Balor Moore, Toronto vs. Seattle, May 13, 1978
ONE-HITTER — Chris Knapp, California, September 3, 1978 (Angels 3, Blue Jays 1)
NO-HITTER — Never happened

EXHIBITION STADIUM LASTS

GAME — May 28, 1989 (Blue Jays 7, Chicago White Sox 5), 10 innings
ATTENDANCE — 46,120 **TIME/TEMP.** — 3:19/20°C. (68°F)
PITCHER — Bobby Thigpen, Chicago
BATTER — George Bell, Toronto, home run
PLATE UMPIRE — Dan Morrison
PITCH — fastball, home run
HIT — Home Run by George Bell, 10th inning
RUN — George Bell on home run
SINGLE — Steve Lyons, Chicago, 10th inning
DOUBLE — Kelly Gruber, Toronto 10th inning
HOME RUN — George Bell, 10th inning
RBI — George Bell, 10th inning
WINNING PITCHER — Tom Henke
LOSING PITCHER — Bobby Thigpen
PUT OUT — Fred McGriff, Toronto, 10th inning
ASSIST — Nelson Liriano, Toronto, 10th inning
ERROR — Matt Merullo, Chicago, 4th inning
STOLEN BASE — Steve Lyons, Chicago, 10th inning

TORONTO BLUE JAYS—CLUB DIRECTORY

BOARD OF DIRECTORS

Honorary Chairman	N.E. Hardy
Chairman	William R. Ferguson

Directors . . . . . John Craig Eaton, N.E. Hardy, William Ferguson, G.W. Radford, P.N.T. Widdrington

OFFICERS

Vice-Chairman & Chief Executive Officer	P.N.T. Widdrington
President & Chief Operating Officer	Paul Beeston
Executive Vice-President, Baseball	Pat Gillick
Vice-President, Baseball	Bob Mattick
Vice-President, Baseball	Al LaMacchia
Vice-President, Business	Bob Nicholson

EXECUTIVE OFFICE

Executive Administrative Assistant	Sue Cannell

BASEBALL

Assistant General Manager	Gord Ash
Director, Development	Mel Queen
Director, Scouting	Bob Engle
Director, International Scouting	Wayne Morgan
Director, Canadian Scouting	Bob Prentice
Special Assistant to Executive Vice President, Baseball	Al Widmar
Administrator, Player Personnel	Bob Nelson
Trainer	Tommy Craig
Assistant Trainer	Brent Andrews
Clubhouse Manager, Blue Jays	Jeff Ross
Video Operations	Robert Baumander
Team Physician	Dr. Ron Taylor
Consulting Orthopaedic Surgeon	Dr. James Andrews
Consulting Orthopaedic Surgeon	Dr. Allan Gross
Consulting Orthopaedic Surgeon	Dr. Martin Kornreich
Consulting Physician	Dr. William Forder
Employee Assistance Program Director	Sam McDowell
Executive Administrative Assistant	Fran Brown
Administrative Assistant	Donna Kuzoff
Administrative Assistant	Heather Connolly
Administrative Assistant	Trina Hiscock

BUSINESS

Director, Minor League Business Operations:	Ken Carson
Executive Administrative Assistant	Anne Jarvis
Receptionist	Isabel Barnes
Switchboard	Mary Anne Sturley
Security/Information	Don Alden

PUBLIC RELATIONS

Director, Public Relations	Howard Starkman
Assistant Director, Public Relations	Mark Leno
Manager, Team Travel	John Brioux
Administrative Assistant	Bonnie Way
Public Relations Co-ordinator	Monique Walsh

MARKETING

Director, Marketing	Paul Markle
Manager, Promotions & Advertising	Rick Amos
Manager, Community Relations	Mark Edwards
Manager, Commerce Court Store	Helen Maunder
Administrative Assistant	Darla McKeen-Burnett
Customer Service Representative	Teresa Michalski

OPERATIONS

Director, Stadium & Ticket Operations	George Holm
Assistant Director & Manager, Field Operations	Len Frejlich
Manager, Security	Fred Wootton
Manager, Game Operations	Mario Coutinho
Clubhouse Manager, Visitors	Ian Duff
Supervisor, Grounds	Brad Bujold
Supervisor, Office Services	Mick Bazinet
Administrative Assistant	June Sym
Office Services Assistant	Sam Platsis
Operations Assistant	Marion Farrell

TICKETS

Director, Stadium & Ticket Operations	George Holm
Assistant Director, Tickets & Box Office Manager	Randy Low
Manager, Group Sales	Maureen Haffey
Manager, Ticket Vault Services	Paul Goodyear
Manager, Subscriber Services	Mike Maunder
Manager, Event Ticket Services	Allan Koyanagi
Manager, Mail Order Services	Doug Barr
Manager, Commerce Court Tickets	Barb Walker
Manager, Special Ticket Services	Sheila Cantarutti
Manager, Telephone Order Services	Jan Marshall
Co-ordinator, Group Sales	Steve Porter
Group Sales Assistant	Betty Ann Armstrong
Group Sales Assistant	Sue Mallabon
Customer Service Representative	Donna Calderone
Customer Service Representative	Sandra Coulson
Advance Ticket Seller	Peter Galbraith
Advance Ticket Seller	Paul Leech
Advance Ticket Seller	Al Ross

FINANCE

Director, Finance	Susan Quigley
Manager, Employee Compensation	Catherine Elwood
Manager, Information Systems	Hans Frauenlob
Systems Administrator	Mark Graham
Manager, Accounting	Cathy McNamara
Accounts Payable	Chris Wensley
Financial Analyst	Marion Bell
Administrative Assistant	Nancy Carmichael

BLUE JAYS PLAYER DEVELOPMENT & SCOUTING

Pat Gillick	Executive Vice-President, Baseball
Bob Mattick	Vice-President, Baseball
Al LaMacchia	Vice-President, Baseball
Al Widmar	Assistant to Executive Vice-President
Gord Ash	Assistant General Manager
Bob Nelson	Administrator, Player Personnel
Bob Engle	Director, Scouting
Wayne Morgan	Director, International Scouting
Bob Prentice	Director, Canadian Scouting
Mel Queen	Director, Development
Epy Guerrero	Co-ordinator Latin America
Moose Johnson	Special Assignment Scout
Gordon Lakey	Special Assignment Scout
Tim Wilken	Special Assignment Scout
Dave Yoakum	Advance Scout
Larry Hisle	Roving Hitting Instructor
Scott Breeden	Roving Pitching Instructor
Jim Hoff	Roving Instructor
Bob Didier	Roving Catcher Instructor
Mike Easler	Roving Hitting Instructor
Fran Brown	Executive Administrative Assistant
Heather Connolly	Administrative Assistant
Donna Kuzoff	Administrative Assistant
Trina Hiscock	Administrative Assistant
Tim Ringler	Minor League Equipment Co-ordinator

SCOUTING SUPERVISORS

David Blume	Elk Grove, CA
Chris Bourjos	Chicago, IL
Chris Buckley	Temple Terrace, FL
Ellis Clary	Valdosta, GA
John Cole	Irvine, CA
Ellis Dungan	Pensacola, FL
Joe Ford	Yukon, OK
Tim Hewes	Bakersfield, CA
Tom Hinkle	Atascadero, CA
Jim Hughes	McKinney, TX
Duane Larson	Harrisburg, NC
Ted Lekas	Worcester, MA
Ben McLure	Palmyra, PA
Andy Pienovi	Portland, OR
Jorge Rivera	Puerto Nuevo, PR
Mark Snipp	Fort Worth, TX
Jerry Sobeck	San Jose, CA
Ron Tostenson	Stanton, CA
Neil Summers	Merrick, NY
Don Welke	Louisville, KY

SCOUTS—ASSOCIATE

Jeff Allen	Bend, OR
Patrick Anderson	Pine Bluff, AR
Buddy Bear	Port Angeles, WA
John Blatnick	Fraser, MI
Leonard Boers III	Saginaw, MI
Jake Boss	Holt, MI
Ron Cabot	Mississauga, ON
Carlos Cambo	Miami, FL
Domingo Carrasquel	Lara, Venezuela
Richard Cerrone	Boulder City, NV
Dell Carter	Fresno, CA
Osvaldo Chavarria	Burnaby, BC
Wayne Davis	Huntington, MO
Dick Finn	Columbus, OH
John Galloway	Victoria, Australia
Kurt Geese	Tyler, TX
John Gill	Burlington, ON
Bob Goodin	Perth, Australia
Melvin Gomes	S. P. de Macoris, DR
James Graffam	Gorham, ME
Dave Gutierrez	Felton, CA
Don Hara	Long Beach, CA
Jim Headley	South Gate, CA
Paul Hodgson	Fredericton, NB
Jerry Howard	Kalispell, MT
Chuck Jacques	Boise, ID
Ignacio Javier	Santo Domingo, DR
Walter Jeffries	Dresden, ON
John Kemmerly	Dover, PA
Terry Kieffer	Beaver Dam, WI
Glen Kwiatkowski	Taylor, MI
Elton Lash	Buchanan, MI
Bill Lechner	Little Canada, MN
Jeff Long	Middleburg, FL
Duncan MacDonald	Nepean, ON
Mike McAlpin	Delran, NJ
John Mabry	Montgomery, AL
Ron Mace	Nelson, BC
Robert Masterson	Cincinnati, OH
Ron Mertus	Chatsworth, CA
Jim Mitchell	Bakersfield, CA
Ken Montgomery	Houston, TX
Rodger Morphew	Alexandria, IN
Pete Ness	Portland, OR
Steve Partington	Sidney, OH
Daryl Patterson	Clovis, CA
Frank Pottie	Dartmouth, NS
Jim Ridley	Milton, ON
Ron Roncetti	Toronto, ON
Joe Saunders	Canton, MI
Gladwyn Scott	Warren, MB
Glennis Scott	Minnedosa, MB
Tim Sever	Homasassa, FL
William Slack	Montreal, PQ
John Smillie	Corinth, MS
James Smith	Milton, FL
Scott Sutherland	Spokane, WA
Allan Thom	Monroe, MI
Ron Thompson	Detroit, MI
Jeff Trundy	Manchester, ME
Larry Tuttle	Blissfield, MI
Noel Vester	Dunedin, FL
Don Vernholm	Marquette, MI
Vic Vernholm	Wixom, MI
Greg Wade	Brisbane, Australia
Ramon Webster	Colon, Panama
Grant Weir	Melbourne, Australia
Doug Wilson	Vancouver, BC
Rod Wilson	St. Stephen, NB
Patrick Wolff	Agana, Guam
Peter Worboys	Sydney, Australia

BLUE JAYS FARM CLUBS

AAA—International
Syracuse Chiefs
MacArthur Stadium
Syracuse, NY 13208
(315) 474-7833
Fax: (315) 474-2658
General Manager & Executive Vice-President: Anthony "Tex Simone"
Assistant General Manager: John Simone
Field Manager: Bob Bailor
Coaches: Rocket Wheeler, Bob Shirley
Trainer: Randy Holland
Stadium: MacArthur Stadium
Capacity: 10,500
Outfield Distances: LF-320, CF-434, RF-320

A—Florida State
Dunedin Blue Jays
P.O. Box 957
Dunedin, Florida 34697
(813) 733-9302
Fax: (813) 734-7661
General Manager: Gary Rigley
Assistant General Manager: Benji Meleras
Administrative Assistant: Vicki Pruitt
Clubhouse Manager: Scott Donovan
Grounds Superintendent Eric Hansen
Grounds Staff: Mike Ryan, Ed Vonnes, Dick Swisher, Jeff Harrington
Concession Manager & Secretary: Pat Smith
Field Manager: Dennis Holmberg
Coaches: Bill Monbouquette, Peter Rowe
Trainer: Jon Woodworth
Stadium: Dunedin Stadium
Capacity: 6218
Outfield Distances: LF-335, CF-400, RF-315

A—New York—Penn
St. Catharines Blue Jays
P.O. Box 1088
St. Catharines, Ontario
L2R 3B0
(416) 641-5297
Fax: (416) 641-3007
General Manager: Ellen Harrigan-Charles
Assistant General Manager: Marilyn Finn
Administrative: Eleanor Bowman
Field Manager: Doug Ault
Coaches: Mike McAlpin, Darren Balsley
Trainer: Scott Shannon
Stadium: Community Park
Capacity: 2,000
Outfield Distances: LF-310, CF-400, RF-310

Rookie-Gulf Coast
Gulf Coast Blue Jays
P.O. Box 669
Murdock, Florida 33938 - 0669

AA—Southern
Knoxville Blue Jays
Bill Meyer Stadium
633 Jessamine St.
Knoxville, Tennessee 37917
(615) 637-9494
Fax: (615) 523-9913
Chairman of the Board: Pat Gillick
President: Paul Beeston
General Manager: Dan Rajkowski
Assistant General Manager: Bill Dyke
Director, Public Relations: Brian Cox
Administrative Assistant: Andrea Pruitt
Field Manager: John Stearns
Coaches: J.J. Cannon, John Poloni
Trainer: Doug Merrifield
Stadium: Bill Meyer Stadium
Capacity: 8000
Outfield Distances: LF-330, CF-405, RF-330

A—South Atlantic
Myrtle Beach Hurricanes
P.O. Box 1110
Myrtle Beach, South Carolina 29578-1110
(803) 626-1987
Fax: (803) 626-8335
President: Winston Blenckstone
General Manager: TBA
Assistant General Manager: Jim Roberts
Field Manager: Garth Iorg
Coaches: Leroy Stanton, Steve Mingori
Trainer: TBA
Stadium: Coastal Carolina College Stadium
Capacity: 3200
Outfield Distances: LF-315, CF-400, RF-315

Rookie Advanced—Pioneer
Medicine Hat Blue Jays
P.O. Box 465
Medicine Hat, Alberta T1A 7G2
(403) 526-0404
Fax: (403) 526-4000
President: Bill Yuill
Vice-President: Russ Williams
General Manager: Kevin Friesen
Field Manager: TBA
Coaches: Omar Malave, Reggie Cleveland
Trainer: TBA
Stadium: Athletic Park
Capacity: 3,200
Outfield Distances: LF-350, CF-380, RF-350

Dominican Summer League
Santo Domingo Blue Jays
Latin America Co-ordinator: Epy Guerrero
General Manager: Ignacio Javier
Administrator: Rosario Guerrero
Manager: Ramon Webster
Trainer: Jose DeLeon

TORONTO BLUE JAYS OWNERSHIP PARTNERS

On March 26, 1976, the American League granted an expansion franchise to a group consisting of Labatt's Breweries, Imperial Trust Limited and The Canadian Imperial Bank of Commerce. Both Labatt's Breweries and Imperial Trust each own 45% of the team. The C.I.B.C. owns the other 10% of the club. Imperial Trust is a holding company set up by the late R. Howard Webster, who was instrumental in the granting of the franchise in 1976. The Webster family still maintains their share of the ownership. The ownership of the club has remained unchanged since the team was formed.

TORONTO BLUE JAYS CLUB OFFICERS

NORMAN EDGAR (Peter) HARDY
HONORARY CHAIRMAN

Has been with the BLUE JAYS since the club's inception, serving through 1988 as Vice-Chairman on the club's Board of Directors...Appointed Chief Executive Officer of the club on July 22/82...Appointed Honorary Chairman on December 14, 1990...Resides in London, Ontario.

WILLIAM R. FERGUSON
CHAIRMAN OF THE BOARD

Was born in Saint John, New Brunswick and was educated in Saint John...Attended Clarkson College in Potsdam, New York...Is a Certified Management Accountant...Is the Executive Vice-President and Director of the Imperial Windsor Group Inc. of Montreal...He is also a Member/Trustee and Vice-President of the RHW Foundation...He has served on the Board of Directors of the Toronto Blue Jays since 1981...Is a Director for the Dalhousie Medical Research Foundation, the Quebec-Labrador Foundation; and the Confederation Centre of the Arts in Charlottetown, Prince Edward Island...He is married to the former Mary Ann Foley and has five children...He resides in Montreal, Quebec.

P.N.T. WIDDRINGTON
VICE-CHAIRMAN AND CHIEF EXECUTIVE OFFICER

Was born in Toronto, Ontario in 1930...Attended Queens University and graduated with an Honours Degree in Economics...He also attended Harvard Business School where he received his M.B.A...He is currently the Chairman of the Board of John Labatt Limited and Laidlaw Incorporated, has been a board member of the BLUE JAYS since 1980...He began his career at Labatt's in 1955 as a salesman and has held progressively senior positions within the company including: Regional Manager, Ontario (1957-58), General Manager, Manitoba (1958-61), General Manager, B.C. (1962-65), President of Lucky Breweries, San Francisco, California (then a subsidiary of LBC) (1968-71)...Joined the corporate head office of John Labatt Limited as Vice-President, Corporate Development in 1971...In 1973 he was appointed President and Chief Executive Officer, positions he held until 1989... In 1987 he was appointed chairman and presently holds that office...He is married and has two children.

PAUL BEESTON
PRESIDENT AND CHIEF OPERATING OFFICER

Born, June 20, 1945 at Welland, Ontario...Married the former Kaye Doherty (8/29/69)...Two children, Aimee (11/15/75) and David (4/10/78)...Graduated in 1964 from Welland Vocational and High School...Started at the University of Western Ontario in fall of 1964 and graduated in 1968 with a Bachelor of Arts degree, majoring in economics and political science...Began working with Coopers & Lybrand in London in summer on 1968...Received Chartered Accountant designation in 1971...Became a manager with Coopers & Lybrand in 1973...Left Coopers and Lybrand to become the first employee of the BLUE JAYS on May 10, 1976, only 1 1/2 months after the granting of the franchise...Became the BLUE JAYS Vice-President, Administration...Became Vice-President, Business Operations on November, 24, 1977 and assumed the title of Executive Vice-President, Business, September 24, 1984...Appointed President and Chief Operating Officer on January 10, 1989...Received designation- Fellow of the Institute of Chartered Accountants of Ontario, March 23, 1988...Resides in Toronto.

PAT GILLICK
VICE-PRESIDENT, BASEBALL

Born, August 22, 1937 at Chico, California...Father, the late Larry Gillick was a former star pitcher with Sacramento in the Pacific Coast League and former sheriff of Butte County, California...Married the former Doris Sander in November, 1968...One child, Kimberley (11/24/72)...Graduated in 1954 at the age of 16 from Notre Dame High School in Sherman Oaks, California where he played baseball and football...Enrolled in University of Southern California in the fall and graduated in 1958 at the age of 20 with a Bachelor of Science Degree in business...Played baseball at USC under coach Rod Dedeaux and was a member of USC's N.C.A.A College World Series championship team in 1958...Pitched semi-professional for Edmonton in the Western Canada League in summer of 1958...Batted and threw lefthanded...Was signed to his first professional contract by Mike Catron in the Orioles organization...Made professional debut in 1959 at Stockton (C) with a 9-5 record and 3.78 ERA...Advanced to Fox Cities (B) in 1960 where he was 11-2 with a 1.91 ERA and finished season at Vancouver (AAA)...Spent the next three seasons between Little Rock (AA), Elmira (A) and Rochester (AAA) including 10 wins at Little Rock in 1961...Compiled a 45-32 record and 3.42 ERA in five seasons in Baltimore chain...Played under former Baltimore manager Earl Weaver for three seasons at Fox Cities (1960) and Elmira (1962-63)...Retired in 1963 at age 26 due to arm trouble to accept position in Houston organization as Assistant Farm Director under Eddie Robinson...Spent 10 years with Houston working his way to Regional Scouting Co-ordinator and to Director of Scouting...Joined New York Yankees in September 1974 as Co-ordinator of Player Development and Scouting under Tal Smith...Accepted challenge of building the BLUE JAYS and joined Toronto on August 16, 1976 as Vice President of Player Personnel...Responsible for all Baseball-related activities including scouting, the farm system and the major league team...Became Vice-President, Baseball Operations on November 24, 1977...Voted Canada's 1983 Baseball Man of the Year by the Toronto and Montreal Chapters of the BBWAA...Appointed Executive Vice-President, Baseball, September 24, 1984...Named UPI's 1985 ML Baseball Executive of the Year...Resides in the Toronto suburb of Mississauga.

BOB MATTICK
VICE-PRESIDENT, BASEBALL

Born, December 5, 1915 at Sioux City, Iowa but grew up in St. Louis...Father, Wally (Chick) Mattick was a former major league player with the White Sox (1912-1913) and the Cardinals (1918)...Signed first professional contract as a shortstop with Chicago Cubs in 1933...Best season was 1937 when he hit .279 with 66 RBI and 39 doubles for Los Angeles of Pacific Coast League...After playing for both the Cubs and Cincinnati he retired in 1942 finishing with a career major league average of .233 with 64 RBI in 206 games...Suffered serious eye injury in 1936 (fractured skull above the right eye due to a foul ball) while with Los Angeles which seriously hampered career...Resulted in double vision...Managed in Southern League, 1944-1945...From 1946 through 1979 worked in administrative and scouting capacites working for 10 different organizations including a 20 year association with Gabe Paul...Left Montreal in 1976 to join the BLUE JAYS as scouting supervisor...In 1978 was appointed Director of Player Development overseeing all minor league field activities...Replaced Roy Hartsfield as BLUE JAYS field manager in 1980 becoming the oldest rookie manager to start a season (64 years)...Served that position for two seasons compiling a 104-164 record...Appointed Executive Co-ordinator, Baseball Operations with responsibilities including on-field, player personnel and field staff recruitment activities at all levels of the organization with emphasis at the major league level...Appointed Vice-President, Baseball, September 24, 1984...Oversaw the operation of the BLUE JAYS' entry in the Florida Instructional League, 1977-1988...Some of the top starters recruited, signed and developed by Mattick include: Curt Flood, Vada Pinson, Rusty Staub, Tommy Harper, Darrell Porter, Gorman Thomas, Bobby Grich, Don Baylor, Gary Carter, Ellis Valentine and Dave Stieb...Married, wife's name, Jacqueline on October 6, 1945...Resides in Bellevue, Washington.

AL LaMACCHIA
VICE-PRESIDENT, BASEBALL

Born, July 22, 1921 at St. Louis, Missouri...The former right handed pitcher spent three seasons in the Major Leagues with the St. Louis Browns from 1943-1946...He compiled a career record of 2-2 with a 6.46 ERA in 16 games...Making his Major League debut with the Browns, he finished his career in 1946 with the Washington Senators...Moved into baseball's front office scouting for four years for the Philadelphia Phillies and 16 years with the Atlanta Braves...Involved in the drafting and signing of such players as Cito Gaston, Larvell Blanks, Jamie Easterly, Joey McLaughlin, Adrian Devine, Bruce Benedict and Dale Murphy...Joined the BLUE JAYS in 1977...Aided in drafting and signing many of the players in the BLUE JAYS' system including Dave Stieb and George Bell...Was a scouting supervisor prior to being named Assistant to the President, Baseball Operations on January 12, 1984...Appointed Vice-President, Baseball on September 24, 1984...Married the former Ann Monaco (1/9/44)...Resides in San Antonio, Texas.

BOB NICHOLSON
VICE-PRESIDENT, BUSINESS

Born, April 20, 1955...Graduate of University of Toronto with a Bachelor of Commerce in 1978...Joined Coopers & Lybrand the same year and stayed with the company until November, 1982 at the time leaving as an audit supervisor...Attained chartered accountant status in 1980...Joined the BLUE JAYS on November 29, 1982 serving as Director of Finance...Elevated to Vice-President, Finance on September 24, 1984...Serves as corporate secretary...Responsibilities include, stadium & ticket operations, marketing, finance, broadcast rights, personnel and minor league business operations...Married...Wife's name Carolyn (12/27/86)...Daughter Kristy (7/9/89) and son Derek (10/3/90).

R. HOWARD WEBSTER

R. Howard Webster lives in the memory as a low-profile team owner, an accomplished financier who once owned the old Lord Simcoe Hotel in Toronto as well as the Globe and Mail newspaper. He was a keen sportsman who won intercollegiate golf titles in his youth. Back in the 1970s, Webster tried to buy the San Diego Padres to move the team to Toronto. When that didn't work out, he threw in his lot with Labatt's Breweries, which was equally intent on bringing major league baseball to the city.

They added a third partner, the Canadian Imperial Bank of Commerce, and in 1976, came within a whisker of purchasing the San Francisco Giants for Toronto. But that city found new owners for its team, and Webster and his partners set their sights elsewhere. The Blue Jays franchise was acquired from the American League for the sum of $7 million in 1977. Then as now, the Webster family and Labatt's owned 45 percent each of the Blue Jays and the bank 10 percent.

Because of failing health, Webster did not attend games in recent years, but his associates have said he watched the Jays faithfully on television and enjoyed seeing the young players mature.

Fitting enough, then, that the farm club MVP awards should honor his name.

43 CITO GASTON
MANAGER

Born: March 17, 1944 San Antonio, TX
Resides: Mississauga, ON
B-R T-R 6-4 210

APPOINTED: Joined the BLUE JAYS' coaching staff on November 4, 1981...Appointed interim manager on May 15, 1989...Named to the permanent post on May 29, 1989.

PERSONAL: Clarence Edwin Gaston..Married...Wife's name Denise...Two children, Adrian and Carly...1962 graduate of Holy Cross High School in Corpus Christi...Part owner of Studebakers', a local night spot...Is the 4th black manager in ML history (others are Frank Robinson, Larry Doby and Maury Wills).

PLAYING CAREER: **1964:** Originally signed by the Milwaukee Braves after an all-star career at Holy Cross High School (3 letters)...Collected hits in 43 of 60 games at Binghamton (NYP) and Greenville (WCL)...**1965:** Spent the season at the Class A level with West Palm Beach...Averaged 1 hit every 2 games...**1966:** Led the New York-Penn League in HR (28), RBI (104), TB (255) and was 4th in runs (84)...Named to the All-Star team and was the league MVP...**1967:** Made his ML debut, appearing in 9 games for the Atlanta Braves...Had started the season with Austin of the Texas League where he was named to the League's All-Star team...**1968:** Split the season between Richmond and Shreveport, batting .279 with the latter...**1969:** Was the Padres' 30th and final selection in the NL Expansion Draft...Hit .230 for the expansion Padres...**1970:** Set career best with 29 HR and 93 RBI while batting .318...Represented the Padres in the All-Star Game going 0-2...Was named the Padres' MVP...**1971:** Hit just .228 with 39 of 118 hits going for extra bases...**1972:** Hit .269 and averaged close to 1 hit per game (102/111)...On supplemental DL, 5/17-6/2...Hit a PH grand slam HR vs the Cubs' Ferguson Jenkins on 6/14, the 2nd in franchise history and the 1st time since 5/2/69...**1973:** 38 of 119 hits were extra base hits...Marked 3rd time in 4 years that he had reached double figures in HR...**1974:** Final season with the Padres and had average drop to .213, his lowest for a full ML season...**1975:** Returned to the Braves organization after being traded for Danny Frisella on 11/7/74...Roomed with Home Run great Hank Aaron...Saw limited duty appearing in only 64 games...**1976:** Had best season since 1970 hitting .291 while appearing in 69 games...**1977:** Played in just 56 games and hit .271...Had three sacrifice flies...**1978:** Final season at ML level...Started the season with the Braves and was sold to the Pirates on 9/22...combined to hit .233 in 62 games...**1979:** Was granted free agency on 11/2/78 and invited to the Braves' spring training camp...Subsequently released and played in the Inter-American League before the league folded on 6/30...Joined Leon (Mexican League) to finish season, batting .337 in 24 games...**1980:** Completed playing career with Leon while playing in 48 games and collecting 44 hits.

COACHING AND MANAGING CAREER: **1981: At the urging of Brave VP of Player Personnel, Hank Aaron, he joined the Braves as a minor league hitting instructor...1982-1989:** Hired by then-manager Bobby Cox as the club's first full-time batting instructor, replacing the part-time Bobby Doerr...Improved club's overall average in 1982 by 36 points...Club batting average while hitting instructor: 1982: (.262), 1983: (.277), 1984: (.273), 1985: (.269)...1986: (.269), 1987: (.269), 1988: (.268), 1989: (.260)...1989: Appointed interim manager on 5/15 upon the dismissal of Jimy Williams...Posted an 8-7 record before assuming the full-time title on 5/31...Club was 77-49 overall from 5/15 through season's end- the best record in the Major Leagues...Became the 24th rookie manager since 1900 to finish in first place...Named Baseball Man of the Year in Canada by Toronto-Montreal BBWAA...**1990:** Led the BLUE JAYS to a second place finish in the AL East, 2.0 games behind the Red Sox.

CITO GASTON—PLAYING RECORD

Year	Club & League	AVG	G	AB	R	H	2B	3B	HR	RBI
1964	Binghamton (NYP)	.238	11	21	1	5	2	0	1	4
1964	Greenville (Cal)	.230	49	165	15	38	6	3	0	16
1965	West Palm Beach (FSL)	.188	70	202	14	38	5	3	0	9
1966	Batavia (NYP)	.330	114	433	84	143	18	5	28	104
1966	Austin (Tex)	.300	4	10	2	3	1	1	0	4
1967	Austin (Tex)	.305	136	505	72	154	24	6	10	70
1967	ATLANTA (NL)	.120	9	25	1	3	0	1	0	1
1968	Richmond (Int).	239	21	71	9	17	4	0	2	8
1968	Shreveport (Tex)	.279	96	340	49	95	15	4	6	57
1969	SAN DIEGO (NL)	.230	129	391	20	90	11	7	2	28
1970	SAN DIEGO (NL)	.318	146	584	92	186	26	9	29	93
1971	SAN DIEGO (NL)	.228	141	518	57	118	13	9	17	61
1972	SAN DIEGO (NL)	.269	111	379	30	102	14	0	7	44
1973	SAN DIEGO (NL)	.250	133	476	51	119	18	4	16	57
1974	SAN DIEGO (NL)	.213	106	267	19	57	11	0	6	33
1975	ATLANTA (NL)	.241	64	141	17	34	4	0	6	15
1976	ATLANTA (NL)	.291	69	134	15	39	4	0	4	25
1977	ATLANTA (NL)	.271	56	85	6	23	4	0	3	21
1978	ATL. PITTS (NL)	.233	62	120	6	28	1	0	1	9
1979	Santo Dom. (Int-am)	.324	40	148	22	48	5	0	1	14
1979	Leon (Mex)	.337	24	83	5	28	2	0	1	8
1980	Leon (Mex)	.238	48	185	16	44	5	0	4	27
ML TOTALS		.256	1026	3120	314	799	106	30	91	387

ALL-STAR GAME RECORD

Year	Club & League	AVG	G	AB	R	H	2B	3B	HR	RBI
1970	NL, at Cinn	.000	1	2	0	0	0	0	0	0

GASTON - TRANSACTIONS

- Selected by San Diego Padres from Atlanta in expansion draft, October 14, 1968.
- On disabled list, May 17 to June 2, 1972.
- Traded to Atlanta Braves for Pitcher Danny Frisella, November 7, 1974.
- Sold to Pittsburgh Pirates, September 22, 1978.
- Granted free agency, November 2, 1978; signed by Santo Domingo of Mexican League, April 10, 1979.
- On suspended list, June 21 to July 21, 1979.
- Released, July 22, 1979; signed by Leon Of Mexican League, July 22, 1979.
- Minor League hitting instructor, Atlanta Braves, 1981.
- Coach, Toronto Blue Jays, 1982-1989.
- Appointed interim manager of Blue Jays, May 15, 1989.
- Named as manager of Blue Jays, May 29, 1989.

MANAGERIAL RECORD

Year	Club & League	W-L	Position
1989	TORONTO (AL)	77-49	1st, East Division *
1990	TORONTO (AL)	86-76	2nd East Division

* Club finished overall at 89-73 and were 12-24 when the managerial change was made.

BLUE JAYS MANAGERS

	G *	W	L	PCT	YEARS
Cox, Bobby	648	355	292	.549	1982-85
Williams, Jimy	523	281	241	.537	1986-89
Hartsfield, Roy	484	166	318	.343	1977-79
Gaston, Cito	288	163	125	.566	1989-90
Mattick, Bobby	268	104	164	.388	1980-81

* Includes Tie Games

COACHES

42 GALEN CISCO
PITCHING COACH

Born: March 7, 1937 St. Mary's, OH
Resides: St. Mary's, OH
B-R T-R 5-11 205

APPOINTED: October 23, 1989.

PERSONAL: Galen Bernard Cisco...Married...Wife's name, Martha...Two sons, Chip (9/5/58) and Jeff (12/13/62)...Both played professional ball...Attended Ohio State University earning a Bachelor of Science in Education...Was an outstanding football player at O.S.U. under Woody Hayes (FB/LB)...Captain of the O.S.U. team that defeated Oregon 10-7 in the 1958 Rose Bowl...Baseball roomate was Frank Howard...Hobbies include golf and flying model airplanes.

PLAYING CAREER: **1958:** Turned professional with Raleigh of the Carolina League and was promoted to Corning where he joined the starting rotation, finishing the year with a combined 6-12 mark...1959: Made three stops combining for a 17-10 record...With Waterloo of the Midwest League he led the league in ERA with 2.23 and struck out a career high 165...**1960:** Spent the season with Minneapolis surrendering less than 1H/IP...**1961:** Started the season with Seattle (AAA) of the Pacific Coast League, posting a 6-1 record in 9 GS, 5 of which were complete games...Subsequently made debut with Red Sox...**1962:** Started the season with the Red Sox and was then dealt to the expansion Mets...**1963:** Won 7 games for the Mets posting a career high 51 appearances...**1964:** Won 6 games for the Mets, 1 short of ML high and lost a career high 19 games...**1965:** Final season with the NL Mets...Finished with a combined 18-42 record with the Mets...**1966:** Split the season between Jacksonville and Toronto as he returned to the Red Sox organization...Finished with a combined 11-6 record; his first winning record since 1961 with Seattle...**1967:** Started the season as a member of the Boston Red Sox...Optioned to Pittsfield (AA) of the Eastern League and then returned to Toronto...Allowed only 16 ER in 76 IP that season in the minors...**1968:** Reached double figures in wins for 3rd time of professional career (11-12)...Led the IL in ERA (2.21) and ShO (6)...**1969:** Again joined the ranks of expansion, joining the new Royals in Kansas City...Started the season with Omaha and was then promoted to the parent club...**1970:** Finished professional career with Omaha and was used primarily in relief.

Cisco (cont...)

MANAGING AND COACHING CAREER: 1971-79: Served as pitching coach of the Royals under Bob Lemon, Jack McKeon and Whitey Herzog...Member of West Division Champs three times (1976-1978)...**1980-1984:** Served as pitching coach under Dick Williams (whom he had played for in 1967) and Jim Fanning in Montreal...A member of the 1981 NL East Championship team...**1985-1987:** Served as pitching coach under Dick Williams, Steve Boros and Larry Bowa...Was the 7th pitching coach in Padres' history...**1988-1989:** Served as pitching coach under Bob Bailor at Syracuse (AAA) of the International League...Spent part of 1988 as interim pitching coach for the BLUE JAYS when Al Widmar underwent back and neck surgery...**1990:** Was appointed as the full-time pitching coach for TORONTO, marking the first time in 10 seasons that he had spent a full season with an AL club.

GALEN CISCO—PLAYING RECORD

Year	Club & League	W-L	ERA	G	GS	CG	ShO	SV	IP	H	R	ER	HR	HB	BB	SO	WP
1958	Raleigh (Caro)	2-2	4.34	14	0	0	0	0	29.0	33	16	14	0	0	20	27	0
1958	Corning (NYP)	4-10	3.91	18	16	8	0	0	122.0	124	71	53	5	3	64	100	7
1959	Allentown (East)	0-1	18.00	2	0	0	0	0	1.0	3	2	2	0	0	1	0	0
1959	Waterloo (Mid)	16-7	2.23	23	23	20	5	0	182.0	142	63	45	0	0	62	165	0
1960	Minneapolis(AmAs)	3-7	2.93	33	17	2	1	0	138.0	122	54	45	8	6	45	70	3
1961	Seattle (PCL)	6-1	1.54	9	9	5	3	0	70.0	55	20	12	3	1	20	37	3
1961	BOSTON (AL)	2-4	6.75	17	8	0	0	0	52.0	67	40	39	5	0	26	39	1
1962	BOSTON (AL)	4-7	6.72	23	9	1	0	0	83.0	95	66	62	11	3	50	43	2
1962	NEW YORK (NL)	1-1	3.32	4	2	1	0	0	19.0	15	7	7	0	3	11	13	1
1963	NEW YORK (NL)	7-15	4.33	51	17	1	0	0	156.0	165	88	75	15	7	64	81	10
1964	NEW YORK (NL)	6-19	3.61	36	25	5	2	0	192.0	182	85	77	17	6	54	78	5
1965	NEW YORK (NL)	4-8	4.50	35	17	1	1	0	110.0	119	63	56	12	1	51	58	3
1966	Jack'ville/Tor (Int)	11-6	4.11	30	14	8	2	0	140.0	157	71	64	16	4	40	98	5
1967	BOSTON (AL)	0-1	3.68	11	0	0	0	0	22.0	21	10	9	4	0	8	8	0
1967	Pittsfield (East)	0-0	0.82	4	1	0	0	0	11.0	5	3	1	0	1	1	7	0
1967	Toronto (Int)	3-5	2.08	10	9	3	1	0	65.0	63	20	15	2	1	13	46	1
1968	Louisville (Int)	11-12	2.21	29	29	13	6	0	204.0	157	58	50	16	4	60	157	3
1969	Omaha (A.A.)	3-4	5.00	10	9	5	0	0	63.0	77	40	35	4	2	15	42	1
1969	KANSAS CITY (AL)	1-1	3.68	15	0	0	0	1	22.0	17	11	9	4	0	15	18	2
1970	Omaha (AmAs)	6-3	2.49	24	4	1	0	2	76.0	63	25	21	6	3	17	49	0
AL TOTALS		7-13	5.98	51	19	1	0	1	179.0	200	127	119	24	3	99	108	5
NL TOTALS		18-43	4.04	126	61	8	3	0	479.0	481	243	215	44	17	180	230	19
ML TOTALS		25-56	4.62	187	80	9	3	1	650.0	681	370	334	68	20	279	338	24

MANAGERIAL/COACHING CAREER

(Joined Blue Jays Organization in 1988)

1971-79 Pitching Coach, Kansas City Royals (AL)

1980-84 Pitching Coach, Montreal Expos (NL)

1985-87 Pitching Coach, San Diego Padres (NL)

1988-89 Pitching Coach, Syracuse, International League (Blue Jays)

1990- Pitching Coach, Toronto (AL)

7 RICH HACKER

THIRDBASE COACH

Born: April 4, 1947 Belleville, IL

Resides: Belleville, IL

B-S T-R 6-0 185

APPOINTED: Richard Hacker...Joined the BLUE JAYS' coaching staff on October 24, 1990.

PERSONAL: Married...Wife's name Kathryn...Has two sons, Roger Paul (9/16/77) and Scott Alexander (6/8/81) and a daughter, Katie Ann (9/16/83)...Nephew of former Major League pitcher Warren Hacker...Graduated from Southern Illinois University-Carbondale in 1967...Enjoys hunting, fishing and skiing.

PLAYING CAREER: **1967:** Was drafted by the Mets and played at Mankato of the Northern League...**1968:** Played in the California League (A) at Visiala for the season where he collected a then career high 26 RBI and 9 doubles...**1969:** Began the season at Visiala and was promoted to Memphis (AA) of the Texas League after having played just 27 games...**1970:** Spent the entire year at Memphis (AA) and hit .326 in 13 games...**1971:** Started the season at Winnipeg (AAA) of the International League, playing in 98 games...He was called up to the Expos where he played in just 16 games...**1972:** Played at Peninsula (AAA) of the International League where he scored a career high 35 runs...**1973:** Again spent the season at Peninsula (AAA) where he played in a career high 107 games...Struck out only 28 times in 248 at-bats.

MANAGING AND COACHING CAREER: **1979-1980:** Served as a minor league manager and scout for the San Diego Padres...**1981:** Midwest area scout for the TORONTO BLUE JAYS...**1982:** Had been hired in November '81 by the Cardinal Organization as manager at Johnson City where his team placed 4th in the Appalacian League...**1983:** Again managed at Johnson City (Rookie) and finished 6th with a record of 30 and 42...**1984:** Moved to the New York-Penn League where he managed the Erie (A) club to a 43 and 31 record (2nd place)...**1985:** Returned to the Johnson City club of the Appalachian League and finished in 2nd with 39 wins and 29 losses...**1986:** Was promoted to the Major League team after the '85 season succeeding Hal Lanier...Coached first base...**1987:** Served as first base coach for Whitey Herzog...**1988:** Again coached at first base for the Cardinals under Herzog...**1989:** Was moved across the diamond to coach third base for the Cardinals...**1990:** Remained at third base under Herzog, Schoendienst and Joe Torre.

RICH HACKER—PLAYING RECORD

Year	Club & League	AVG	G	AB	R	H	2B	3B	HR	RBI	BB	SO	SB
1967	Mankato (Nor)	.221	49	163	21	36	4	2	0	9	18	29	6
1968	Visalia (Cal)	.224	76	250	27	56	9	1	2	26	18	56	3
1969	Visalia (Cal)	.244	27	90	9	22	1	0	0	11	3	16	2
1969	Memphis (Tex)	.190	34	100	7	19	5	1	0	11	7	18	0
1970	Memphis (Tex)	.326	13	43	7	14	2	0	1	3	6	6	0
1971	Winnipeg (Int)	.235	98	327	29	77	95	2	2	8	31	59	4
1971	MONTREAL (NL)	.121	16	33	2	4	1	0	0	2	3	12	0
1972	Peninsula (Int)	.223	102	323	35	72	4	0	0	8	34	52	0
1973	Peninsula (Int)	.222	107	248	18	55	2	3	0	16	23	28	2
ML TOTALS		.121	16	33	2	4	1	0	0	2	3	12	0

MANAGERIAL/COACHING CAREER

1982-83, Johnson City Manager

1984- , Erie Manager

1985- , Johnson City Manager

1986-90, St. Louis (NL) Coach

RECORD AS MANAGER

Year	Club & League	W-L	Finished
1982	Johnson City (Appy)	30-42	6th
1983	Johnson City (Appy)	30-42	6th
1984	Erie (NYP)	43-31	2nd
1985	Johnson City (Appy)	39-29	2nd

25 MIKE SQUIRES

FIRSTBASE COACH

Born: March 5, 1951 Kalamazoo, MI

Resides: Kalamazoo, MI

B-L T-L 5-10 191

APPOINTED: November 22, 1988.

PERSONAL: Michael Lynn Squires...Married the former Maureen Mentor (9/22/72)...Three children; Lisa (11/9/76), Connie (3/2/78) and Steven (6/17/83)...Nicknamed Spanky...Played baseball for 4 years at Kalamazoo Valley Community College and Western Michigan...Captained Kalamazoo High School in football and baseball...Father, Lynn, served in the White Sox scouting department.

PLAYING CAREER: **1973:** Was Chicago's 18th round selection in the June 1973 Free Agent Draft...Averaged a hit per game (68 games) with Appleton of the Midwest League...**1974:** Played for Knoxville (AA) of the Southern League and was named to All-Star team...Set a Southern League fielding record with a .996 fielding percentage...**1975:** Named Southern League's MVP and to All-Star team while batting .308...ML debut, 9/1 vs Kansas City and appeared in 20 games...**1976:** Promoted to Iowa (AAA) of the American Association where he went 76 games without an error and led AmAs first basemen in fielding (.995)...**1977:** Hit for highest average of career...Tied for AmAs league lead in CS (13)...**1978:** Set a club record at Iowa by hitting safely in 33 consecutive games...**1979:** Was first full season at the ML level...Played in 122 games...**1980:** Committed only 5 errors in 997 total chances for a .995 fielding percentage, 3rd in the AL...Did not commit an error until 8/12, his 83rd game...Caught in games of 5/4 and 5/7 to become the first LH catcher in the ML since Dale Long (Cubs-1958)...**1981:** AL Gold Glove Award winner, committing only 6 errors in 793 TC for a .995 fielding average...Named to the Sporting News AL All-Star fielding team...**1982:** Started 42 of 116 games...Suffered a strained left hamstring in mid- September...HR vs California's Mike Witt on 9/13 was first since 8/19/80...**1983:** Saw action in 143 games for the Western Division Champions, including 4 ALCS games...As an 11 year veteran of the organization, he was chosen to hoist the division championship flag above Comiskey Park on that clinching day (9/18...Led AL first basemen in fielding (.996), committing only 2 errors in 557 TC...1st career appearance at 3B, 8/23 at Kansas City...**1984:** Made 77 appearances at 1B, 13 at 3B, 3 in OF and 1 on the mound...Errorless at all positions...Made history on 5/2 when he started the game at 3B- first start by a LH at 3B since at least 1936...In total, 4 GS at 3B...Pitching appearance, 4/22

Squires (cont...)

at Detroit...Started the game at 1B, moved to 3B in the 8th and pitched after 8.2 IP...Did not bat in September...**1985**...Released by White Sox in spring.

MANAGING AND COACHING CAREER: **1985:** Served as an advance ML scout for the White Sox after being released as a player in spring training...**1986-1988:** Advance scout for Oakland...**1989-1990:** Has served last two seasons as first base coach for the BLUE JAYS.

MIKE SQUIRES—PLAYING RECORD

Year	Club & League	AVG	G	AB	R	H	2B	3B	HR	RBI	SH-SF	HP	BB	SO	SB-CS
1973	Appleton (Mid)	.298	68	228	42	68	7	3	3	29	3-2	0	52	19	7-1
1974	Knoxville (Sou)	.287	136	481	74	138	23	5	6	69	2-5	0	74	39	16-14
1975	Knoxville (Sou)	.304	129	448	68	136	23	5	3	50	6-3	1	67	31	24-13
1975	Chicago (AL)	.231	20	65	5	15	0	0	0	4	0-1	0	8	5	3-0
1976	Iowa (AmAs)	.253	124	336	37	851	18	1	2	40	3-4	1	50	32	10-7
1977	Iowa (AmAs)	.323	126	415	67	134	29	4	1	45	2-3	3	84	37	24-13
1977	Chicago (AL)	.000	3	3	0	0	0	0	0	0	0-0	0	0	1	0-0
1978	Iowa (AmAs)	.312	115	449	70	140	24	3	5	48	3-2	0	63	39	30-12
1978	CHICAGO (AL)	.280	46	150	25	42	9	2	0	19	2-3	0	16	21	4-4
1979	CHICAGO (AL)	.264	122	295	44	78	10	1	2	22	5-2	2	22	9	15-5
1980	CHICAGO (AL)	.283	131	343	38	97	11	3	2	33	11-0	1	33	24	8-9
1981	CHICAGO (AL)	.265	92	294	35	78	9	0	0	25	13-5	0	22	17	7-2
1982	CHICAGO (AL)	.267	116	195	33	52	9	3	1	21	4-0	0	14	13	3-3
1983	CHICAGO (AL)	.222	143	153	21	34	4	1	1	11	2-1	2	22	11	3-3
1984	CHICAGO (AL)	.183	104	82	9	15	1	0	0	6	1-0	0	6	7	3-0
ML TOTALS		.260	777	1580	210	411	53	10	6	141	38-12	5	143	108	46-25

MANAGERIAL/COACHING CAREER

1985, Chicago White Sox, Advance Scout

1986-88, Oakland Athletics, Advance Scout

1989-90, Toronto Blue Jays, Coach

8 JOHN SULLIVAN
BULLPEN COACH

Born: Jan. 3, 1941 Somerville, NJ

Resides: Dansville, NY

B-L T-R 6-0 210

APPOINTED: November 4, 1981.

PERSONAL: John Peter Sullivan...Married, wife's name Elizabeth (Betsy)...Four children: Carrie Ann (8/4/62), James (9/15/63), Margaret (10/9/64) and Jeffrey (7/7/68)...Graduated from Bernards High School, Bernardsville, N.J. in 1958- was inducted into school's Hall of Fame in 1990...Enjoys hunting and golf.

PLAYING CAREER: **1959:** Signed by the Tigers and assigned to Erie (Summer A) of the New York-Penn League...43 of 112 hits were extra base hits...**1960:** Played for Durham (A) of the Carolina League, where he set a personal high for RBI (71)...**1961:** Set a career high for games played (126) while at Birmingham (AA) of the Southern League...**1962:** Spent the season with Knoxville (A) of the South Atlantic League where he once again averaged almost 1 hit per game (104H/117games)...**1963:** Started the season with Syracuse (AAA) of the International League where 21 of 85 hits went for extra bases...**1964:** Started the season with Syracuse hitting a career low .220 (min. 90 games)...Called up to the Tigers, making 2 appearances...**1965:** 1st ML HR vs Kansas City's Wes Stock...Played 34 games for the Tigers prior to being optioned to Syracuse...**1966:** Hit a then career high .328 for Vancouver...Drafted by the Mets from Syracuse on 11/28...**1967:** Played 65 games in NL with the Mets...**1968:** Sold to the Phillies organization and spent the season at San Diego (AAA) of the Pacific Coast League...**1969:** Appeared in 12 games for the Phillies prior to being sold to the Orioles on 4/8...Finished the season with Rochester, hitting .253- his highest average in 3 seasons...**1970:** Sold to the Royals on 4/13 and was assigned to Omaha (AAA) of the American Association...**1971:** Set a personal high with a .330 batting average...**1972:** Served as a player/coach for Jacksonville (AA) of the Southern League.

MANAGING AND COACHING CAREER: **1972:** Served as a player/coach with Jacksonville...**1973:** Managerial debut with Kingsport (A) of the Appalachian League, leading them to a first place finish...Was named Manager-of-the-Year...**1974:** 1st season with Waterloo (A) of the Midwest League finishing at 68-56, 2nd in the 1st half and 3rd in the second half...**1975:** Managed Waterloo to a .727 overall winning percentage and a league championship...Named Midwest Manager of the Year and the Ewing M. Kaufmann Award for outstanding contributions to the Royals' organization...**1976:** Won the Midwest championship, going 38-24 in the first half and 40-28 in the second half...**1977:** Moved to Omaha (AAA) of the American Association where he managed a first place club only to lose the championship in 6 games to Denver...**1978:** Final season with Omaha, finishing first and winning the championship...Club won 21 of final 30 games...**1979:** Joined the Royals' ML coaching staff as bullpen coach...**1980-81:** Joined Atlanta and Bobby Cox as bullpen coach...**1982-83:** Served as first base coach for the BLUE JAYS...**1984-1990:** Served as bullpen coach for the BLUE JAYS.

JOHN SULLIVAN—PLAYING RECORD

Year	Club & League	AVG	G	AB	R	H	2B	3B	HR	RBI
1959	Erie (NYP)	.322	110	348	69	112	29	1	13	58
1960	Durham (Cal)	.279	125	419	59	117	18	4	11	71
1961	Birmingham (Sou)	.229	126	415	47	95	14	2	8	57
1962	Knoxville (SAL)	.267	116	389	50	104	18	2	6	36
1963	Syracuse (Int)	.263	106	323	35	85	14	1	6	35
1963	DETROIT (AL)	.000	3	5	0	0	0	0	0	0
1964	Syracuse (Int)	.220	93	264	29	58	9	4	6	27
1964	DETROIT (AL)	.000	2	3	0	0	0	0	0	0
1965	DETROIT (AL)	.267	34	86	5	23	0	0	2	11
1965	Syracuse (Int)	.169	29	77	10	13	2	0	2	8
1966	Vancouver (PCL)	.328	83	238	34	78	12	2	5	34
1967	NEW YORK (NL)	.218	65	147	4	32	5	0	0	6
1968	San Diego (PCL)	.246	83	256	18	63	11	0	1	23
1969	PHILADELPHIA (NL)	.222	12	18	0	4	0	0	0	1
1969	Rochester (Int)	.253	95	293	26	74	17	0	4	44
1970	Omaha (AmAs)	.256	64	160	10	41	12	0	1	20
1971	Omaha (AmAs)	.330	82	215	22	71	14	2	4	40
1972	Jacksonville (Sou)	.255	88	220	19	56	11	0	3	32
AL TOTALS		.245	39	94	5	23	0	0	2	11
NL TOTALS		.218	77	165	4	36	5	0	0	7
ML TOTALS		.228	116	259	9	59	5	0	2	18

SULLIVAN - TRANSACTIONS

- Drafted by New York Mets from Syracuse (Detroit Tigers' organization), November 28, 1966.
- Sold to Philadelphia Phillies' organization, February, 19, 1968.
- Sold to Baltimore Orioles' organization, April 8, 1969.
- Sold to Kansas City Royals' organization, April 13, 1970.
- Player-Coach for Jacksonville, 1972.

MANAGERIAL/COACHING CAREER

(Joined Blue Jays Organization in 1982)
1972, Player-Coach, Jacksonville, Southern League (Royals)
1973, Manager, Kingsport, Appalachian League (Royals)
1974-76, Manager, Waterloo, Midwest League (Royals)
1977-78, Manager, Omaha, American Association (Royals)
1979, Bullpen Coach, Kansas City Royals, American League
1980-81, Bullpen Coach, Atlanta Braves, National League
1982-90, Bullpen Coach, Toronto Blue Jays, American League

RECORD AS MANAGER

Year	Club & League	W-L	PCT	Finish
1973	Kingsport (Appy)	53-17	.757	(1st)
1974	Waterloo (Mid)	68-56	548	2nd in Div., 3rd in Div.
1975	Waterloo (Mid)	93-35	.727	(1st in Div., 1st in Div.)
1976	Waterloo (Mid)	78-52	.600	(1st in Div., 1st in Div.)
1977	Omaha (AmAs)	76-59	.608	(1st in Div.)
1978	Omaha (AmAs)	66-69	.489	(1st in Div.)
CAREER TOTALS (6 years)		434-288	.601	

BLUE JAYS OUT-OF-TOWN HOTELS

Baltimore	Stouffer Harborplace	(310) 547-1200
Boston	Sheraton Boston	(617) 236-2000
California	Doubletree	(714) 634-4500
Chicago	Westin Hotel	(312) 943-7200
Cleveland	Stouffer's	(216) 696-5600
Detroit	Ritz Carlton	(313) 441-2000
Kansas City	Adam's Mark	(816) 737-0200
Milwaukee	Hyatt Regency	(414) 276-1234
Minneapolis	Hyatt Regency	(612) 370-1234
New York	Grand Hyatt	(212) 883-1234
Oakland	Oakland Airport Hilton	(415) 635-5000
Seattle	Crowne Plaza	(206) 464-1980
Texas	Sheraton Centre Park	(817) 261-8200

18 GENE TENACE

BATTING COACH

Born: Oct. 10, 1946 Russellton, PA
Resides: Poway, CA
B-R T-R 6-0 195

APPOINTED: October 25, 1989.
PERSONAL: Gene Fury Tenace...Married...Wife's name Linda...Three children: Stacey, Merinda and Gina...Graduate of Valley Local High School in Lucasville, Ohio where he played football and baseball...Enjoys hunting.
PLAYING CAREER: **1965:** Was the Kansas City Athletics' 11th pick in the 6/65 Draft...Turned professional with Shelby of the West Carolina League appearing exclusively in the outfield...**1966:** Spent the season with Leesburg (A) of the Florida State League where he split duty between 1B and OF...**1967:** Split the season between Peninsula (A) and Leesburg striking out only 66 times in 361 AB...**1968:** Spent the season at Peninsula, splitting duty at catcher and outfield...Set then personal highs with 21 HR and 71 RBI...Was 4 RBI short of equalling his RBI total for the first 3 seasons combined...**1969:** Started the season with Birmingham (AA) of the Southern League and set personal high with .319 average...Earned a promotion to the Athletics appearing in 16 games for his ML debut...**1970:** 1st season that he was used exclusively as a catcher...Started season with Iowa (AAA) of the American Association and was promoted to the Athletics...20 RBI in 38 games for the A's...**1971:** 1st full season at the ML level...Also faced the Orioles in the ALCS going 0-3...**1972:** Hit 5 HR in 82 games during the regular season and then hit 3 HR in a 5 game ALCS vs the Tigers...Then tied Babe Ruth's record of 4 World Series HR vs the Reds in the World Series and became the first player to hit HR in his first 2 World Series AB (10/14)...Set a World Series record with a .913 slugging percentage...**1973:** 6th in the AL in HR (24) and 5th in games (160) among catchers...11 BB in 30 plate appearances vs the Mets in the World Series...**1974:** 3rd in AL HR (26) and 1st in BB (110)...**1975:** Set personal highs in HR (29) and RBI (87)...Led all AL first basemen in fielding percentage (.998)...**1976:** Final season with the A's...Hit 22 HR, marking the 4th consecutive season that he had reached the 20 HR plateau...**1977:** Signed by the Padres after going through the Re-entry Draft...Played 3B, 1B and OF...Set club mark with 125 BB...1 of 7 Padres with 100+ hits...**1978:** Played 80 games at 1B and caught 71 games...**1979:** Led NL in fielding percentage among catchers (.998)...18 of 20 HR came on the road...**1980:** 29 of 70 hits were for extra bases...Hit 15+ HR for the eighth consecutive season...Acquired by the Cardinals with pitchers Rollie Fingers and Bob Shirley and catcher Bob Geren for catchers Terry Kennedy and Steve Swisher, infielder Mike Phillips and pitchers Al Omstead, Kim Seaman, John Littlefield and John Urrea on 12/8...**1981:** Was used by Cardinals as a spot starter and pinch hitter...38 BB, fourth highest total on the club...**1982:**Used again as a spot starter and pinch hitter vs LHP...15-day DL with fractured right thumb, 5/22...Was batting .419 at the time...Obtained by the Pirates as a re-entry Free Agent, signed on 12/1...1983: Final season as an active player...Saw limited duty at Pittsburg (53 games).
MANAGING AND COACHING CAREER: **1984:** Minor league hitting instructor with the Milwaukee Brewers...**1986-87:** Bullpen coach for the Houston Astros...**1988:** Minor league hitting instructor for the New York Yankees and interim manager of Prince William of the Carolina League...**1989:** Minor league hitting instructor with the BLUE JAYS...**1990:-** Major League hitting instructor with the TORONTO BLUE JAYS.

GENE TENACE—PLAYING RECORD

Year	Club & League	AVG	G	AB	R	H	2B	3B	HR	RBI	SH-SF	HP	BB	SO	SB-CS
1965	Shelby (WCL)	.183	32	93	10	17	2	1	2	6	1-1	2	13	36	0-0
1966	Leesburg (FSL)	.211	91	228	28	48	8	2	1	24	1-2	4	36	48	3-2
1967	Peninsula (Cal)	.000	3	7	0	0	0	0	0	1	0-0	0	2	1	0-0
1967	Leesburg (FSL)	.266	106	354	47	94	12	2	6	44	1-7	4	43	65	4-3
1968	Peninsula (Cal)	.283	132	435	78	123	20	3	21	71	5-3	5	66	87	18-2
1969	Birmingham (Sou)	.319	89	276	56	88	20	4	20	74	0-3	5	56	47	2-3
1969	OAKLAND (AL)	.158	16	38	1	6	0	0	1	2	0-0	1	1	15	0-0
1970	Iowa (AmAs)	.282	93	319	54	90	24	1	16	63	1-1	4	49	81	5-1
1970	OAKLAND (AL)	.305	38	105	19	32	6	0	7	20	0-0	2	23	30	0-2
1971	OAKLAND (AL)	.274	65	179	26	49	7	0	7	25	1-0	2	29	34	2-1
1972	OAKLAND (AL)	.225	82	227	22	51	5	3	5	32	2-0	3	24	42	0-0
1973	OAKLAND (AL)	.259	160	510	83	132	18	2	24	84	8-7	10	101	94	2-2
1974	OAKLAND (AL)	.211	158	484	71	102	17	1	26	73	2-4	12	110	105	2-9
1975	OAKLAND (AL)	.255	158	498	83	127	17	0	29	87	3-4	12	106	127	7-4
1976	OAKLAND (AL)	.249	128	417	64	104	19	1	22	66	1-5	4	81	91	5-4
1977	SAN DIEGO (NL)	.233	147	437	66	102	24	4	15	61	2-4	13	125	119	5-3
1978	SAN DIEGO (NL)	.224	142	401	60	90	18	4	16	61	0-2	11	101	98	6-5
1979	SAN DIEGO (NL)	.263	151	463	61	122	16	4	20	67	1-6	7	105	106	2-6
1980	SAN DIEGO (NL)	.222	133	316	46	70	11	1	17	50	0-4	4	92	63	4-4
1981	ST. LOUIS (NL)	.233	58	129	26	30	7	0	5	22	1-2	4	38	26	0-0
1982	ST. LOUIS (NL)	.258	66	124	18	32	9	0	7	18	0-1	4	36	31	1-1
1983	PITTSBURGH (NL)	.177	53	62	7	11	5	0	0	6	0-0	4	12	17	0-1
NL TOTALS		.237	750	1932	284	457	90	13	80	285	4-19	47	509	460	18-20
AL TOTALS		.245	805	2458	369	603	89	7	121	389	17-20	46	475	538	18-22
ML TOTALS		.241	1555	4390	653	1060	179	20	201	674	21-39	93	984	998	36-42

TENACE - TRANSACTIONS

- On disabled list, April 30-May 27, 1976.
- Granted free agency, November 1, 1976; signed by San Diego, December 14, 1976.
- Traded with pitchers Rollie Fingers and Bob Shirley and a player to be named later (catcher Bob Geren) to St. Louis for catchers Terry Kennedy and Steve Swisher, pitchers John Littlefield, Al Olmsted, Kim Seaman and John Urrea and Infielder Mike Phillips, December 8, 1980.
- On disabled list, March 22-April 12; May 20-June 14, 1982.
- Granted free agency, November 10, 1982; signed by Pittsburgh, December 1, 1982.
- On supplemental disabled list, August 8-September 1, 1983.

MANAGERIAL/COACHING CAREER

(Joined Blue Jays Organization in 1989)
1984, Minor League Hitting Instructor, Milwaukee Brewers
1986-87, Bullpen Coach, Houston Astros
1988, Minor League Instructor, New York Yankees
Manager, Prince William, Carolina League (Yankees)
1989, Minor League Hitting Instructor, Toronto Blue Jays
1990, Major League Hitting Instructor, Toronto Blue Jays

RECORD AS MANAGER

Year	Club & League	W-L	PCT	Finish
1988	Prince William (Caro)	22-39	.361	7th

56 HECTOR TORRES
COACH

Born: Sept. 16, 1945 Monterrey, MX
Resides: Liverpool, NY
B-R T-R 6-0 180

PERSONAL: Hector Epitacio Torres...Married the former Glenda Draper, October 5, 1968...Three children: twins (Karissa and Tiffany) and Ginger...Father Epitacio played professional ball in Mexico from 1938-1957.

PLAYING CAREER: **1962: Signed as a free agent by the San Francisco Giants in 1962: Played at Decatur (A) in the Midwest League where he played in 96 games and struck out 84 times...1963:** Spent the season at Fresno (A) of the California League where he hit 11 doubles and had 38 RBI...**1964:** Again spent the season at Fresno where he hit 42 points higher than the previous year (.223)...Set career high in AB (511)...**1965:** Moved to Springfield (AA) of the Eastern League and played in only 44 games before being sent back to Decatur where he hit .257 in 64 games...Struck out only 55 times in 391 (combined) at bats...**1966:** Was traded to the Angels for Dave Marshall on April 6/1966...Spent the season at Seattle (AAA) of the Pacific Coast League where he had 86 hits in 102 games...**1967:** Played the entire season at Seattle (AAA) and tied career high for games (139) and hit 14 doubles...Was traded to the Astros on November 21 to complete the deal on August 7th, which sent Jim Weaver to the Angels...**1968:** Played the entire season with Houston and set a career high for ML hits in a season (104)...**1969:** Split time between Oklahoma City (AAA) of the American Association and Houston...**1970:** Began the season at Oklahoma City hitting .305 in 38 games and was then promoted to Houston where he played in just 31 games...Was traded to the Cubs on October 12 for Roger Metzger...**1971:** Spent the season at Chicago playing SS and 2B...**1972:** Traded to Montreal with Hal Breeden on April 7, for Dan McGinn...Played 83 games at Montreal...**1973:** Sold to the Houston Astros on April 4th...Six base hits in 38 games...Traded to the White Sox on October 23 for player to be named later (Dan Neumeier)...**1974:** Played at Hawaii (AAA) of the Pacific Coast League where he played in 123 games- the most since he played 128 in 1968...**1975:** Was sold to the Padres on April 3, 1975...Hit .259 in 112 games for San Diego...**1976:** Again spent the season at San Diego splitting duty at SS and 3B...Traded to Cleveland with John Grubb and Fred Kendall on December 8, 1976...**1977:** Traded to the BLUE JAYS on March 29 for John Lowenstein...Played in 91 games for TORONTO and scored the most runs while with a ML team (33) since 1968 when he scored 44...**1978:** Played at Syracuse (AAA) of the International League until he was released by the BLUE JAYS on March 27th...Picked up by the Yankees and was assigned to Columbus (AAA) of the IL.

MANAGING AND COACHING CAREER: **1979-1984:** Minor League Instructor for the TORONTO BLUE JAYS...**1985-1986:** Manager of Florence (A) of the South Atlantic League...**1987-1989:** Coach at (AAA) Syracuse of the International League...**1990:**-Coach at the BLUE JAYS' Florida State League affiliate, Dunedin (A)...Also spent some time in TORONTO, as a coach during the last five weeks of the season.

HECTOR TORRES—PLAYING RECORD

Year	Club & League	AVG	G	AB	R	H	2B	3B	HR	RBI	BB	SO	SB
1962	Decatur (Mid)	.191	96	304	44	58	6	3	3	33	36	84	1
1963	Fresno (Cal)	.181	104	343	38	62	11	2	4	38	46	111	2
1964	Fresno (Cal)	.223	139	511	69	114	16	4	18	60	47	140	4
1965	Springfield (East)	.187	44	150	6	28	4	1	2	10	11	26	0
1965	Decatur (Mid)	.257	64	241	25	62	6	0	5	35	13	29	3
1966	Seattle (PCL)	.249	102	346	34	86	9	3	3	24	15	54	1
1967	Seattle (PCL)	.214	139	472	29	101	14	7	2	39	15	76	4
1968	HOUSTON (NL)	.223	128	466	44	104	11	1	1	24	18	64	2
1969	Okla City (AmAs)	.238	29	105	13	25	3	0	0	5	6	9	2
1969	HOUSTON (NL)	.159	34	69	5	11	1	0	1	8	2	12	0
1970	Okla City (AmAs)	.305	38	151	15	46	7	3	2	20	6	19	1
1970	HOUSTON (NL)	.246	31	65	6	16	1	2	0	5	6	8	0
1971	CHICAGO (NL)	.224	31	58	4	13	3	0	0	2	4	10	0
1972	MONTREAL (NL)	.155	83	181	14	28	4	1	2	7	13	26	0
1973	HOUSTON (NL)	.091	38	66	3	6	1	0	0	2	7	13	0
1974	Hawaii (PCL)	.259	123	425	41	110	14	1	7	47	23	42	2
1975	SAN DIEGO (NL)	.259	112	352	31	91	12	0	5	26	22	32	2
1976	SAN DIEGO (NL)	.195	74	215	8	42	6	0	4	15	16	31	2
1977	TORONTO (AL)	.241	91	266	33	64	7	3	5	26	16	33	1
1978	Syra/Colum (Int)	.206	111	344	37	71	10	2	7	41	16	54	1
ML TOTALS		.216	622	1738	148	375	46	7	18	115	104	229	7

MANAGERIAL/COACHING CAREER (All in Blue Jays Organization)

1979-84, Minor League Instructor, Toronto Blue Jays
1985-86, Manager, Florence, South Atlantic League
1987-89, Coach, Syracuse, International League
1990, Coach, Infield Instructor/Bullpen Employee, Toronto Blue Jays

RECORD AS MANAGER

Year	Club & League	W-L	PCT	Finish
1985	Florence (SAL)	82-55	.599	2nd in Div., 1st in Div.)
1986	Florence (SAL)	65-76	.424	5th in Div., 3rd in Div.)
CAREER TOTALS (2 years)		138-131	.513	

TORONTO BLUE JAYS BIRTHDAYS IN 1991

JANUARY
3—John Sullivan (51)
15—Rance Mulliniks (35)
FEBRUARY
2—Pat Tabler (33)
5—Roberto Alomar (23)
9—Mookie Wilson (35)
10—Eddie Zosky (23)
25—Ken Dayley (32)
26—Kelly Gruber (29)
MARCH
5—Mike Squires (40)
7—Denis Boucher (23)
7—Joe Carter (31)
10—Mike Timlin (25)
17—Cito Gaston (47)
22—Glenallen Hill (26)
24—Steve Karsay (19)
27—Tom Quinlan (23)
APRIL
6—Kenny Williams (27)
8—Alex Sanchez (25)
14—Greg Myers (25)
22—Jimmy Key (30)
26—Ricky Trlicek (22)
27—Bob MacDonald (26)
27—Jim Eppard (31)
MAY
14—Pat Borders (28)
20—David Wells (28)
20—Todd Stottlemyre (26)
24—Rob Ducey (26)
26—Willie Fraser (27)
28—Ricky Rhodes (23)
28—Duane Ward (27)
JUNE
17—Manny Lee (26)
20—Paul Beeston (46)
25—Carlos Delgado (19)
JULY
22—Dave Stieb (34)
25—Ed Sprague (24)
31—Chris Weinke (19)
AUGUST
5—John Olerud (23)
22—Pat Gillick (54)
23—Nate Cromwell (23)
SEPTEMBER
3—Rene Gonzales (30)
16—Hector Torres (46)
24—Jim Acker (22)
25—David Weathers (22)
OCTOBER
4—Rich Hacker (44)
5—Jerry Schunk (26)
10—Gene Tenace (45)
17—Ravello Manzanillo (28)
23—Al Leiter (26)
26—Frank Wills (33)
NOVEMBER
7—William Suero (24)
12—Randy Knorr (23)
25—Mark Whiten (25)
DECEMBER
11—Derek Bell (23)
13—Pat Hentgen (23)
21—Tom Henke (34)
24—Carlos Diaz (27)

34 JIM ACKER

PITCHER

Born: Sept. 24, 1958 Freer, TX
Resides: Freer, TX
B-R T-R 6-2 215
M.L. Service: 8.000

PERSONAL: James Justin Acker . . . Married, wife's name Jamye...Attended Freer High School, graduating in 1977...Attended University of Texas...Was considered one of the Braves' top minor league prospects before suffering arm trouble...Brother Bill was an NFL defensive lineman for the Chiefs, Bills and Cardinals...Is an avid hunter and fisherman...During the off-season works his ranch in Freer, Texas.

LAST SEASON: Was used exclusively in relief during 1990...His longest outing of the year was 4.0IP (three times); vs SEA 5/15, NYY 6/24 and vs MILW 8/27...His ERA was at its lowest point at the end of May- 1.77...Had an ERA of less than 2.00 vs Baltimore (1.42), Boston (0.00), California (0.00) and Detroit (1.86)...Had a 0.45 ERA for the month of May (11G, 20.0IP, 14H, 1R/ER, 5BB, 9K)...Retired the first batter faced, 56% of the time...Had his first save since leaving the Atlanta Braves, on 6/24 vs the New York Yankees...His prior save had come on 8/12/89 vs San Diego Padres...Third on the BLUE JAYS in Appearances with 59...Opponents Hit .281 and .320 in his first inning of work...At the SkyDome, had an ERA of 3.76 in 52.2IP.

PROFESSIONAL CAREER: **1980**: Began career in Gulf Coast League, pitching 5.0 innings of shutout ball in his only game with Bradenton...Promoted to Savannah (AA) and was used exclusively in starting rotation...**1981**: Began season with Savannah, ERA 2.69...Earned promotion to Richmond (AAA) of the International League, pitching 7 complete games...**1982**: Endured first losing season while pitching at Savannah...Underwent arthroscopic surgery at season's end to repair the labrium muscle and remove bone chips in right shoulder...**1983**: After being acquired by the BLUE JAYS he was the only rookie to start the season with the club...Major League debut came on 4/7 at Fenway Park, pitching 2.0 shutout innings...First Major League game start and win, 6/21 vs the Twins...First Major League save came on 9/6 vs California...Only rookie to spend the entire season with the club...**1984**: Was used sporadically and spent time on the DL (8/16-9/1)...Suffered from tendinitis of the right shoulder...**1985**: Two saves in first 6 appearances, to tie career total prior to the season...Set personal highs in wins (7) and then season high in SV (10)...Was first professional season that he did not start a game...Used in a stopper role for the early season, collecting 4 of 10 saves through the end of May...**1986**: Traded to Braves on 7/6 and made 7 consecutive relief appearances...Finished the season with 14 consecutive game starts...Won first GS with the Braves, defeating the Mets 8-5 on 7/26...Was first win as a game starter since 9/18/83...**1987**: First full season with the Braves...Workhorse of the staff, appearing in a career high 68 games...Recorded career high 14 SV...Was 4-4-7 with a 1.96 ERA over his last 23 games after 8/8...Was successful in 14 of 21 save situations...**1988**: Appeared in 10 games in April and then tore muscle fibers in the in the right elbow and missed the next three months...Started the season finale, 10/2 at Cincinnati, losing a 1-0 decision...Was first GS since 10/3/86 at the Astrodome...**1989**: Started the season with the Braves posting an 0-6 record with a 2.67 ERA and 2 SV in 59 games...Pitched exclusively in relief...Prior to joining the BLUE JAYS, had not won since 9/24/87 (13 decisions)...Acquired by TORONTO from Atlanta for LHP Tony Castillo and catcher Francisco Cabrera on 8/24...Posted 1.59 ERA in 28 innings for the BLUE JAYS...Held opponents to .237 combined batting average-lowest of his career...Snapped his losing streak (14 decisions) with a 5-4 win at Cleveland on 9/10...Only pitcher to appear in all 5 ALCS games vs Oakland.

CAREER NOTES: With the BLUE JAYS as a starter; (3-3, 5.29ERA, 68.0IP, 40ER, 13GS)...In the bullpen with Toronto; (20-14-13, 3.57ERA, 214G, 367.2IP, 146ER)...Is 11-3-1, 3.87 ERA lifetime for the BLUE JAYS post ASG...With Cliff Johnson, only player to be a BLUE JAY twice...His 227 appearances is 5th on the BLUE JAYS All-Time list.

JIM ACKER

Year	Club & League	W-L	ERA	G	GS	CG	ShO	SV	IP	H	R	ER	HR	HB	BB	SO	WP
1980	Bradenton (Gulf)	1-0	0.00	1	1	0	0	0	5.0	1	0	0	0	0	0	5	0
1980	Savannah (Sou)	5-5	2.65	13	13	3	0	0	95.0	33	33	28	6	5	29	47	4
1981	Savannah (Sou)	5-5	2.69	10	10	6	0	0	77.0	57	34	23	9	3	34	37	3
1981	Richmond (Int)	8-7	4.19	21	21	7	0	0	118.0	112	63	55	6	1	74	72	5
1982	Savannah (Sou)	9-14	4.44	26	24	7	1	1	142.0	120	96	70	12	6	86	96	7
1983	TORONTO (AL)	5-1	4.33	38	5	0	0	1	97.2	103	52	47	7	8	38	44	1
1984	TORONTO (AL)	3-5	4.38	32	3	0	0	1	72.0	79	39	35	3	6	25	33	5
1985	TORONTO (AL)	7-2	3.23	61	0	0	0	10	86.1	86	35	31	7	3	43	42	2
1986	TORONTO (AL)	2-4	4.35	23	5	0	0	0	60.0	63	34	29	6	2	22	32	3
1986	ATLANTA (NL)	3-8	3.79	21	14	0	0	0	95.0	100	47	40	7	1	26	37	2
1987	ATLANTA (NL)	4-9	4.16	68	0	0	0	14	114.2	109	57	53	11	4	51	68	1
1988	ATLANTA (NL)	0-4	4.71	21	1	0	0	0	42.0	43	26	22	6	1	14	23	2
1988	Greenville (Sou)	0-0	1.72	8	4	0	0	0	15.2	7	3	3	1	0	3	5	2
1989	ATLANTA (NL)	0-6	2.67	59	0	0	0	2	97.2	84	29	29	5	1	20	68	2
1989	TORONTO (AL)	2-1	1.59	14	0	0	0	0	28.1	24	7	5	1	1	12	24	1
1990	TORONTO (AL)	4-4	3.83	59	0	0	0	1	91.2	103	49	39	9	3	30	54	4
AL Totals		23-17	3.84	227	13	0	0	13	436.0	458	216	186	33	23	170	229	16
NL Totals		7-27	3.71	169	15	0	0	16	349.1	338	159	144	29	7	111	198	7
ML Totals		30-44	3.78	396	28	0	0	29	785.1	796	375	330	62	30	281	427	22

CHAMPIONSHIP SERIES RECORD

Year Club & League	W-L	ERA	G	GS	CG	ShO	SV	IP	H	R	ER	HR	HB	BB	SO	WP
1985 TORONTO (AL)	0-0	0.00	2	0	0	0	0	6.0	2	0	0	0	0	0	5	0
1989 TORONTO (AL)	0-0	1.42	5	0	0	0	0	6.1	4	2	1	0	1	1	4	0

ACKER—TRANSACTIONS

- Selected by Atlanta Braves in 1st round (21st player selected) of free-agent draft, June 3, 1980.
- On disabled list. April 9 to April 20, 1982.
- Drafted by Toronto Blue Jays, December 6, 1982, in Major League Draft.
- On disabled list, August 16 to September 1, 1984.
- Traded to Atlanta Braves for Pitcher Joe Johnson, July 6, 1986.
- On disabled list, May 9 to August 19, 1988; included rehabilitation disability assignment to Greenville, July 30 to August 18, 1988.
- Granted free agency, November 4, 1988; re-signed by Richmond (Atlanta Braves' organization), January 6, 1989.
- Traded to Toronto Blue Jays for Pitcher Tony Castillo and a player to be named later, August 24, 1989; Atlanta Braves' organization acquired Catch Francisco Cabrera to complete deal, August 24, 1989.

JIM ACKER vs AMERICAN LEAGUE

	1990						CAREER					
	W-L-S	ERA	IP	H	ER	SO	W-L-S	ERA	IP	H	ER	SO
SEASON	4-4-1	3.83	91.2	103	39	54	23-17-13	3.84	436.0	458	186	229
TORONTO	2-3-1	3.76	52.2	63	22	27	10-7-7	3.92	225.0	226	98	122
AWAY	2-1-0	3.92	39.0	40	17	27	13-10-6	3.75	211.0	232	88	107
vs BALTIMORE	0-0-0	1.42	6.1	7	1	4	0-0-1	4.15	21.2	25	7	10
BOSTON	0-0-0	0.00	3.1	3	0	2	2-3-0	3.16	37.0	27	13	16
CLEVELAND	2-0-0	6.52	9.2	10	7	6	5-3-3	4.20	4.91	47	23	32
DETROIT	0-0-0	1.86	9.2	6	2	7	3-0-0	3.65	37.0	30	15	19
MILWAUKEE	0-1-0	5.14	7.0	8	4	5	1-2-1	4.17	36.2	41	17	24
NEW YORK	0-2-1	4.00	9.0	11	4	2	3-2-1	5.58	30.2	41	19	13
TORONTO	-	-	-	-	-	-	-	-	-	-	-	-
A.L. EAST	2-3-1	3.68	45.0	45	18	26	14-11-6	3.98	211.1	211	94	114
vs CALIFORNIA	0-0-0	0.00	6.0	6	0	3	0-2-2	4.91	33.0	44	18	21
CHICAGO	0-0-0	7.94	5.2	9	5	6	1-1-0	3.62	27.1	29	11	12
KANSAS CITY	0-0-0	3.00	3.0	7	1	2	0-1-1	1.56	34.2	36	6	17
MINNESOTA	0-0-0	6.75	4.0	5	3	1	1-0-2	7.11	25.1	30	20	11
OAKLAND	0-0-0	3.86	9.1	8	4	4	2-0-1	3.31	38.2	23	8	18
SEATTLE	1-1-0	3.00	12.0	14	4	5	3-2-1	4.50	44.0	45	22	26
TEXAS	1-0-0	5.40	6.2	9	4	7	2-0-0	2.37	20.2	25	7	10
A.L. WEST	2-1-0	4.05	46.2	58	21	28	9-6-7	3.70	223.2	247	92	115
Pre-ASG	1-2-1	3.00	54.0	51	18	30	12-13-12	3.82	273.0	280	116	136
Post-ASG	3-2-0	5.02	37.2	52	21	24	11-4-1	3.87	163.0	178	70	93
STARTER	-	-	-	-	-	-	3-3-0	5.29	68.0	66	40	46
RELIEVER	4-4-1	3.83	91.2	103	39	54	20-14-13	3.57	368.0	392	146	192
in APRIL	0-0-0	3.45	15.2	16	6	13	1-2-3	2.42	67.0	66	18	38
MAY	1-1-0	0.45	20.0	14	1	9	2-4-5	3.73	82.0	78	34	38
JUNE	0-1-1	7.62	13.0	16	11	4	7-6-3	5.04	84.0	93	47	42
JULY	1-0-0	3.38	16.0	21	6	11	4-2-1	3.98	63.1	77	28	32
AUGUST	1-2-0	5.19	17.1	21	10	10	3-2-0	3.27	63.1	63	23	30
SEPT/OCT	1-0-0	4.66	9.2	15	5	7	6-1-1	4.24	76.1	81	36	49

CAREER HIGHS

SEASON **Wins** 7-1985 **ERA** 2.43-198 **Saves** 14-1987
IP 126.0-1989 **SO** 92-1989

GAME **Low Hit CG** Never **SO** 7, vs KC, April 12, 1986
BB 5, vs CHI (NL), August 20, 1987

Last ML Win: vs CLEV, Sept. 23, 1990
Last Save: vs NY (AL), June 24, 1990
Last CG: Never
Last SHO: Never
Last Relief Appearance: at BOST, Sept, 30, 1990
Last GS: at CINN. Oct. 2, 1988
Winning Streak: 3

SHORT-TERM BLUE JAYS

The Blue Jays have had five players whose BLUE JAY career consisted of one and only one regular season game:

Mike Darr-RHP (1977) Nino Espinosa-RHP (1981)
Steve Grilli-RHP (1979) Steve Luebber-RHP (1979)
Rick Luecken-RHP (1990)

12 ROBERTO ALOMAR

INFIELDER

Born: February 5, 1968 Ponce, PR

Resides: Salinas, PR

B-S T-R 6-0 175

M.L. Service: 3.000

PERSONAL: Roberto Velazquez Alomar...Single...Comes from a baseball family- his father Sandy, coached for the Padres for five seasons and played in the Major Leagues for 15 seasons with 7 different clubs...His brother Sandy Jr. is a catcher for the Cleveland Indians and was awarded Rookie of the Year in the American League for 1990.

LAST SEASON: Was his 3rd season in the Major Leagues...Had a career high 60 RBI-most by a Padre second baseman...From April 27 - May 15 he hit 30-67/.448 with 8 doubles raising his average to .367...Had two four hit games in May- May 6th at Chicago and May 10th at St. Louis...Was selected to the All-Star team for the first time in his career...Committed just 6 errors after the All-Star break (13 before)...Missed 14 of the last 24 games due to an elbow injury...Was second in the National League in putouts with 311.

PROFESSIONAL CAREER: **1985:** Spent the season at Charleston (A) of the South Atlantic League, splitting time between second base and shortstop...Played in a league leading 137 games as well as leading the league in AB (546)...Tied for 5th in runs scored with 89...Averaged better than a hit per game (160H/137G)**...1986:** Played at Reno (A) in the California League and led the league in batting average (.346)...Played exclusively at second base...Cut his errors in half from the previous season (18)...Named to Baseball America's League All-Star Team as the second baseman...**1987:** Moved up to AA with Wichita in the Texas League...Led the league in putouts with 167...Played mainly at second base, seeing some action at shortstop also...57 of 171 hits went for extra bases...Had a career high 41 doubles, second in the league...Batted .366 in June...Second consecutive season with a plus .300 batting average- (.319)- 8th in the league...Hit a career high 12 HR...**1988:** Began the season at Las Vegas (AAA) of the Pacific Coast League, playing in just 9 games before being recalled to San Diego...Received his first ML hit off of Nolan Ryan in his first ML game on 4/20...Hit .316 in the final 55 games of the season...Had 3 hitting streaks of at least 10 games during the months of August and September...Had the most sacrifices in the NL of any non-pitcher (16)...Led the club in runs, doubles and sacrifices...Voted the Padres' Rookie of the Year...Made just 4 errors in the last 64 contests...Tied for 2nd in the NL in double plays turned with 88...**1989:** Was his first full season at the Major League level...Was the youngest player on any NL opening-day roster...Played exclusively at second base and led the league in errors at that position with 28- 11 by the end of April...Had a career high 184 hits to go along with a career high for AB (623)...Had a career best 17 game hitting streak...Hit .365 for the month of September...Had a pair of 4 hit contests, 6/21 vs the Dodgers and 8/17 vs the New York Mets...Led the NL in sacrifice hits with 17...Hit safely in 31 of the last 33 games...Tied for 2nd in the NL in stolen bases (42) and was 3rd in hits (184)...Hit .313 vs right hand pitching.

CAREER NOTES: Hit .295 in 1989 for his highest seasonal average...Has 22 ML home runs (9 in 1988)...Drove in 60 runs in 1990...Longest hit streak- 17 games in 1989...Last ML HR- September 17, 1990.

ROBERTO ALOMAR

Year	Club and League	AVG	G	AB	R	H	2B	3B	HR	RBI	SH-SF	HP	BB	SO	SB-CS
1985	Charleston (SAL)	.293	137	546	89	160	14	3	0	54	12-4	0	61	73	36-19
1986	Reno (Cal)	.346	90	356	53	123	16	4	4	49	6-7	3	32	38	14-8
1987	Wichita (Tex)	.319	130	536	88	171	41	4	12	68	1-7	2	49	74	43-15
1988	Las Vegas (PCL)	.270	9	37	5	10	1	0	2	14	2-1	0	1	4	3-0
1988	SAN DIEGO (NL)	.266	143	545	84	145	24	6	9	41	16-0	3	47	83	24-6
1989	SAN DIEGO (NL)	.295	158	623	82	184	27	1	7	56	17-8	1	53	76	42-17
1990	SAN DIEGO (NL)	.287	'47	586	80	168	27	5	6	60	5-5	2	48	72	24-7
ML TOTALS		.283	448	1754	246	497	78	12	22	157	38-13	5	148	231	90-30

ALOMAR - TRANSACTIONS

- Signed as a free agent by San Diego Padres, February 16, 1985
- Traded to Toronto Blue Jays December 1990, along with outfielder Joe Carter for shortstop Tony Fernandez and firstbaseman Fred McGriff.

CAREER HIGHS

SEASON: **AVG** .295-1989 **H** 184-1989 **HR** 9-1988 **RBI** 60-1990

GAME: **H** 4 (4 times, last May 10 at ST. LOUIS) **HR** 1 (22 times)
RBI 5, Aug. 27, 1989 vs NY METS
SB 3, Aug. 23, 1989 at PHILADELPHIA

Longest Hit Streak 17-1989

Last ML HR Sept. 17, 1990 at HOUSTON

14 DEREK BELL

OUTFIELDER

Born: Dec. 11, 1968 Tampa, FL
Resides: Tampa, FL
B-R T-R 6-2 200
M.L. Service: 0.000

PERSONAL: Derek Nathaniel Bell...Graduate of King High School in 1987 where he played baseball...Named club MVP two years in a row and was recipient of Leading Hitter Award three years...Played for Belmont Heights Little League team which advanced to the World Series three times in a row.

LAST SEASON: Spent the season at Syracuse (AAA) of the International League and hit .261 with 7 HR and 56 RBI...Led the Chiefs in stolen bases with 21...Was his first season at the AAA level...Hit his first (AAA) HR on 4/23 vs Toledo...Injured his hamstring twice during the season and spent 17 days on the DL...Had nine consecutive stolen bases until 6/10...Tied for second on the club in triples with 5...Played in 109 games at Syracuse...Was second on the club in sacrifice hits with 6...In 104 games in the outfield he made just 5 errors.

PROFESSIONAL CAREER: **1987**: Tied for second in the New York-Penn League in game winning RBI (8)...Led St. Catharines in HR (10), RBI (42), runs (46) and HP (6)...Hit .305 in August, including a 12 game hit streak; 8/4 - 8/16...Named as R. Howard Webster Award winner as St. Catharines' MVP...**1988**: Named as South Atlantic League MVP...Named as Baseball America's Most Outstanding Prospect...Led league in batting (.344) by 30 points, despite being promoted to Knoxville on 7/16...At Knoxville was second in slugging percentage (.557) and tied for third in 2B (29)...Had 40 multiple hit games...On the DL at Knoxville 7/30-9/1 with a broken left hand as the result of being hit by a pitch...**1989**: Spent the season with Knoxville (AA) of the Southern League...Fifth in the league in AB (513)...Made 9 errors in 237 total chances...Sixth in OF assists with 12...Led the team in H (124), TB (205), 2B (22) and RBI (75)...Second on the club in runs (72) and tied for second in HR with 16...Winner of R. Howard Webster Award as M.V.P...Baseball America's pick as second-best prospect in BLUE JAYS organization.

DEREK BELL

Year	Club and League	AVG	G	AB	R	H	2B	3B	HR	RBI	SH-SF	HP	BB	SO	SB-CS
1987	St. Catharines (NYP)	.264	74	273	46	72	11	3	10	42	2-3	6	18	60	12-4
1988	Myrtle Beach (SAL)	.344	91	352	55	121	29	5	12	60	0-4	6	15	67	18-6
1988	Knoxville (Sou)	.250	14	52	5	13	3	1	0	4	0-0	0	1	14	2-1
1989	Knoxville (Sou)	.242	136	513	72	124	22	6	16	75	0-4	6	26	92	15-7
1990	Syracuse (Int)	.261	109	402	57	105	13	5	7	56	0-6	3	23	75	21-7

DEREK BELL—TRANSACTIONS

- Selected by Toronto Blue Jays in 2nd round (49th overall) of free-agent draft, June 2, 1987.
- On disabled list, July 30-September 1, 1988.
- On disabled list June 13-June 21; July 2-July 12, 1990.

10 PAT BORDERS

CATCHER

Born: May 14, 1963 Columbus, OH
Resides: Lake Wales, FL
B-R T-R 6-2 200
M.L. Service: 3.000

PERSONAL: Patrick Lance Borders...Married...Wife's name, Kathy...Daughter, Lindsay Rae...Graduate of Lake Wales High School in 1982...Played baseball and football where he set a school mark in HR...Was ranked 2nd in the state in baseball...Baseball hero is Pete Rose...Hit .440 in 1981 when his school finished runner-up in the state finals...Hit .513 with 10 HR and 36 RBI in 25 games in his senior year...Offered baseball and football scholarships from Mississippi State University...Originally signed as a third baseman.

LAST SEASON: Third year in Major Leagues and only his fifth season as a catcher...Career highs in Games(125), AB(346), Doubles(24), HRS(15) and RBI(49)...vs LHP hit .285, 10HR, 27RBI-186AB...Ranked first in Slugging Pct off LHP among catchers(.554)...vs RHP hit .288, 5HR, 32RBI-160AB...Hit .355, 11-31 for April- (14G, 3HR, .710% SLG)...Had a four hit game on 4/30 vs Indians...Had a season high seven game hit streak from 7/28- 8/3...hit 5 HR in May...15 HRS, 10 vs LHP/5 vs RHP/10 at SkyDome/5 on Road...at the All-Star Break as a game starter was hitting .307, 47-153, 9HR, 23RBI...Was third on the BLUE JAYS in Slugging % with .497...Ranked third in % CS off catchers(34 for 88/38.6%...As PH was 5-25, 3RBI...At SkyDome, hit .274 vs .297 on the Road.

PROFESSIONAL CAREER: **1982: Spent the season with Medicine Hat (A) of the Pioneer League where he was used exclusively at 3B...Averaged over 1H per game (66H/61G)...1983:** Led SAL third basemen in games (125) and T/2nd in 2B (31)...**1984:** T/1st in South Atlantic league RBI (85), T/2nd in TB (205), 3rd in 2B (32) and slugging % (.443), T/3rd in GW RBI (11), 4th in runs produced (142)...Named to SAL All-Star team and earned league's Star of Stars honours as MVP of All-Star game...Winner of R. Howard Webster Award as club's MVP...**1985:** T/1st in league for games by a first baseman (110)...Was used exclusively at 1B...**1986:** Was 1st season as a catcher...Started the season with Florence (A) of SAL...Contract purchased by Knoxville (AA) of the Southern League on 5/13...Sent to Kinston (A) of the Carolina League on 6/22...Batted a combined .339 with three teams...**1987**: Started the season with Dunedin (A) of FSL prior to being promoted to Knoxville (AA) of the Southern League on 4/17...Tied for league lead in PB (16)...Played 1 game at 1B...Led team with 13 GIDP...**1988:** 1 of 9 Major Leaguers to open the season without Triple A experience...ML debut, 3-4, 1 triple, 5RBI, 4/6 at Kansas City...Only ML game start at 2B, 5/3 at Seattle in an emergency situation due to Manny Lee injury...Injured left rib cage during batting practice prior to an exhibition game at Syracuse on 7/7...15-Day DL, 7/15 retro to 7/5...Assigned to Syracuse for medical rehabilitation on 7/30...Activated from DL and optioned to Syracuse on 8/18...Recalled to Toronto for 9/1...1989: Career high 7 game hit streak (10-28/.357, 3RBI, 4/7-16)...1st career grand slam HR, 7/7 at Tiger Stadium vs Guillermo Hernandez...Started 59 games- 45 at catcher and 14 as DH...26 appearances as the DH- most on the club...Threw out 17 of 48 runners (35.4%)...Hit .387 in June and .361 in July...Hit .389 vs Texas, .368 vs Detroit and .350 vs Milwaukee.

CAREER NOTES: Is a career .333 hitter in June and .306 in July...23 career home runs, 16 vs LHP/7 vs RHP.

PAT BORDERS

Year	Club and League	AVG	G	AB	R	H	2B	3B	HR	RBI	SH-SF	HP	BB	SO	SB-CS
1982	Medicine Hat (Pio)	.304	61	217	30	66	12	2	5	33	1-1	2	24	52	1-2
1983	Florence (SAL)	.274	131	457	62	125	31	4	5	54	1-1	1	46	116	4-1
1984	Florence (SAL)	.276	131	467	69	129	32	5	12	85	0-3	1	56	109	3-4
1985	Kinston (Caro)	.261	127	460	43	120	16	1	10	60	0-2	1	45	116	6-5
1986	Florence (SAL)	.375	16	40	8	15	7	0	3	9	0-0	0	2	9	0-0
1986	Kinston (Caro)	.328	49	174	24	57	10	0	6	26	0-1	1	10	42	0-0
1986	Knoxville (Sou)	.353	12	34	3	12	1	0	2	5	2-0	0	1	6	0-3
1987	Dunedin (FSL)	.364	3	11	0	4	0	0	0	1	0-0	0	0	3	0-0
1987	Knoxville (Sou)	.292	94	349	44	102	14	1	11	51	0-3	2	20	56	2-5
1988	TORONTO (AL)	.273	56	154	15	42	6	3	5	21	2-1	0	3	24	0-0
1988	Syracuse (Int)	.242	35	120	11	29	8	0	3	14	0-2	0	16	22	0-0
1989	TORONTO (AL)	.257	94	241	22	62	11	1	3	29	1-2	1	11	45	2-1
1990	TORONTO (AL)	.286	125	346	36	99	24	2	15	49	1-3	0	18	57	0-1
ML TOTALS		.274	275	741	73	203	41	6	23	99	4-6	1	32	126	2-2

CHAMPIONSHIP SERIES RECORD

Year	Club and League	AVG	G	AB	R	H	2B	3B	HR	RBI	SH-SF	HP	BB	SO	SB-CS
1989	TORONTO (AL)	1.000	1	1	0	1	0	0	0	1	0-0	0	0	0	0-0

BORDERS-TRANSACTIONS

- Selected by Toronto Blue Jays' organization in sixth round of free-agent draft, June 7, 1982.
- On disabled list, July 5 to August 19, 1988; included rehabilitation disability assignment to Syracuse, July 30 to August 19, 1988.

PAT BORDERS vs AMERICAN LEAGUE

	1990					CAREER				
	AB	H	HR	RBI	AVG	AB	H	HR	RBI	AVG
SEASON	346	99	15	49	.286	741	203	23	99	.274
TORONTO	164	45	10	28	.274	341	92	13	46	.270
ROAD	182	54	5	21	.297	400	111	10	53	.278
vs BALTIMORE	26	11	2	7	.423	56	18	2	7	.321
BOSTON	18	2	0	2	.111	39	8	1	5	.205
CLEVELAND	31	10	1	3	.323	66	20	1	4	.303
DETROIT	34	12	3	8	.353	64	23	4	19	.359
MILWAUKEE	22	4	1	4	.182	51	13	3	10	.255
NEW YORK	34	11	0	3	.324	77	22	1	6	.286
TORONTO	-	-	-	-	-	-	-	-	-	-
AL. EAST	165	50	7	27	.303	353	104	12	51	.295
vs CALIFORNIA	31	8	1	4	.258	61	13	1	5	.213
CHICAGO	24	5	0	0	.208	49	11	2	5	.224
KANSAS CITY	16	4	1	2	.250	39	11	1	9	.282
MINNESOTA	28	7	2	5	.250	64	13	2	8	.203
OAKLAND	31	12	2	7	.387	60	21	2	11	.350
SEATTLE	30	6	1	2	.200	60	12	2	3	.200
TEXAS	21	7	1	2	.333	55	18	1	7	.327
A.L.WEST	181	49	8	22	.271	388	99	11	48	.255
Pre-ASG	184	52	10	28	.283	454	126	17	67	.278
Pos-ASG	162	47	5	21	.290	287	77	6	32	.268
vs RHP	160	46	5	22	.288	252	65	7	30	.258
LHP	186	53	10	27	.285	489	138	16	69	.282
PINCH HITTING	25	5	0	3	.200	60	15	0	7	.250
DESIGNATED HITTING	1	0	0	0	.000	60	14	1	10	233
in APRIL	31	11	3	4	.355	133	40	5	15	.301
MAY	84	23	4	10	.274	175	40	7	24	.229
JUNE	54	16	3	13	.296	114	38	4	21	.333
JULY	56	17	2	9	.304	98	30	3	17	.306
AUGUST	65	18	2	8	.277	90	24	3	12	.267
SEPT/OCT	56	14	1	5	.250	131	31	1	10	.237

Borders (cont...)

CAREER HIGHS

SEASON:	**Avg.** .286-1990	**H** 99-1990	**HR** 15-1990	**SB** 2-1989
GAME:	**H** 4-April 30/90 at CLEV	**HR** 1-23 times		
	RBI 5-April 6/88 at K.C.	**SB** 1-2 times		
Last ML HR	Sept. 11/90 at K.C.			

Longest Hitting Streak: 8 - July 28-August 8, 1990

35 DENIS BOUCHER
PITCHER

Born: March 7, 1968 Montreal, PQ
Resides: Lachine, PQ
B-R T-L 6-1 195
M.L. Service: 0.000

PERSONAL: Denis Boucher...Single...Was a member of Canada's entry in the 1987 Pan-Am Games, completing the tournament with a 1-1 record, his only loss was to the U.S.A. in the playoff round...Attended the National Baseball Institute in 1986 and '87 and was a member of Canada's Youth Team at the 1986 World Youth Tournament...Attended the BLUE JAYS' Florida Instructional League entry at the end of the 1987 season....Name is pronounced Den-EE Boo-SHAY.

LAST SEASON: Began the season at Dunedin (A) of the Florida State League where he had a perfect 7-0 record with a 0.75 ERA in 9 game starts...Struck out 62 while walking only 8 batters...Was promoted to Syracuse (AAA) of the International League on June 5th...Appeared in 17 games (all game starts)...Was 8-5 with 2 complete games after the promotion...Tied for 2nd on the club in winning pct. with .615...Had better than a 2-1 strikeout to walk ratio (80-37)...Had arthroscopic surgery at the end of the season by Dr. James Andrews to remove bone chips from his left elbow.

PROFESSIONAL CAREER: **1987:** Sent to the BLUE JAYS' entry in the Florida Instructional League at Dunedin...**1988:** Tied for the lead in the South Atlantic League in games started (32), 2nd in strikeouts (169) and innings pitched (197)...Won six games in as many starts May 3-23 (0.96 ERA)...Had 10 or more strikeouts in a game twice...**1989:** Spent the season at Dunedin (A) of the Florida State League where he was second in the league in GS (28)...Pitched a 2-hitter on August 17 vs West Palm Beach...Second on the team with 10 wins...Won 8 of 10 decisions from July 12 to August 25 with a 1.88 ERA during that span.

DENIS BOUCHER

Year	Club & League	W-L	ERA	G	GS	CG	ShO	SV	IP	H	R	ER	HR	HB	BB	SO	WP
1988	Myrtle Beach (SAL)	13-12	2.84	33	32	1	0	0	196.2	161	81	62	11	8	63	169	15
1989	Dunedin (FSL)	10-10	3.06	33	28	1	1	0	164.2	142	80	56	6	6	58	117	13
1990	Dunedin (FSL)	7-0	0.75	9	9	2	2	0	60.0	45	8	5	1	2	8	62	4
1990	Syracuse (Int.)	8-5	3.85	17	17	2	1	0	107.2	100	51	46	7	2	37	80	6

BOUCHER—TRANSACTIONS

- Signed as a free agent by the Toronto Blue Jays on August 18, 1987

29 JOE CARTER
OUTFIELDER

Born: March 7, 1960 Oklahoma City, OK
Resides: Leawood, KS
B-R T-R 6-3 215
M.L. Service: 6.143

PERSONAL: Joseph Chris Carter...Married, wife's name is Diana...Has two daughters, Kia Kionne (9/16/82) and Ebony Shante (10/9/84) as well as a son Jordan Alexander (12/25/89)...Attended Wichita State University where he was an All Missouri Valley Conference and NCAA All-District Five first teamer...Was All-America second team in 1979 and '80...Was the Sporting News' College Player-of-the-Year in 1981...As a member of the 1980 Boulder, Colorado summer league team, Joe teamed with Tony Gwynn and Mark Langston during collegiate days...Graduated from Millwood High School in Oklahoma City, OK where he played baseball, basketball, football and ran track.

LAST SEASON: Played his first and only season with the Padres, leading the club and 3rd in the National League in RBI (115)...Has had 100+ RBI seasons four out of the last five...Posted an RBI once every 5.5 at bats (8th in the NL)...Had 10 RBI more than previous season, yet had 11 fewer HR (24)...Had career high 7 runs batted in on April 23rd vs San Francisco...Appeared in all 162 games- the only National Leaguer to do so...His consecutive games played streak now stands at 341- the second highest active streak in baseball behind the Orioles' Cal Ripken...Recorded a .988 fielding percentage- his highest since the 1984 season (.987).

PROFESSIONAL CAREER: **1981:** Was the first round pick of the Chicago Cubs in the June 1981 Free Agent Draft (second overall)...Began at AA Midland of the Texas League hitting .269 while driving in 35 runs in 67 games...**1982:** Was assigned to Midland (AA) for the second season in a row...Played exclusively in the outfield and managed better than a hit per game (136H/110G)...More than a third of his hits went for extra bases...Chosen as a Texas League All-Star...Missed having a 100 RBI season by two (98 RBI)...**1983:** Was promoted to AAA Iowa of the American Association leading the league in AB with 522...Was named the American Association Rookie of the Year batting .307 with 27 doubles and 22 HR...Called up to the parent club and collected his first Major League hit on August 1st vs Philadelphia...**1984:** Began the season at Iowa (AAA) seeing action in 61 games before being dealt to the Indians along with Mel Hall, Don Schulze and Darryl Banks for Ron Hassey, Rick Sutcliffe and George Frazier on June 13th...Hit his first Major League HR off of Texas' Frank Tanana on June 28...Had his first 6 RBI game of his career on August 12 vs the Yankees...Had bone chips removed from his left knee during the off-season...**1985:** First full season at the Major League level...Played the outfield as well as all three bases...Season was hampered by a series of groin pulls and a sprained left wrist...Hit his first career inside-the-park HR on September 10 at Seattle...Played at both second and third base in the same inning at Oakland on September 23rd...**1986:** Had a club All-Time high for at-bats with 663...Led the Major Leagues in both RBI (121) and runs produced (200)...Had a 21 game hitting streak, the 2nd longest in the American League that season...Never went more than 2 games without collecting at least one hit...First 3 HR game came on August 29 in Boston...More than doubled his previous seasons RBI total of 59...Posted highest batting average of Major League career (.302)...**1987:** Became the first ever 30-30 man in Indians history, hitting 32 HR and stealing 31 bases...Was also the 3rd American League player to ever have a 30-30 season with 100 RBI...Hit 3 HR at Fenway on May 28th, becoming the first player ever to have two 3 HR games at Fenway Park- other on August 29, 1986...Missed 5 games due to a broken nose from a Keith Atherton pitch at Minnesota on June 23rd...Second consecutive season with 100+ RBI (106)...**1988:** Finished in the AL's top 10 in HR (27), RBI (98), total bases (297), game winning RBI (13), extra base hits (69) and triples (6)...Became the first Indian ever to record 100 HR and 100 stolen bases in his career as an Indian...Had 36 doubles for the second time in his career...Hit his fourth career grand slam HR in Minnesota on April 22...The next day he had the second 6 RBI game of his career at the Metrodome...Lined into a triple play in Minnesota on August 8- the first by an Indian since Toby Harrah in 1980...Suffered a bruised left shoulder while making a diving catch on 9/11 at Boston, contributing to a season ending 8 for 52 at the plate...**1989:** Hit a career high 35 HR (the most since Rocky Colavito hit 42 in 1959) and drove in 105 runs for the Tribe...Was second in the AL in HR behind Fred McGriff (36)...Finished fourth in the league in RBI, third in total bases (303), second in extra base hits (71) and ninth in slugging percentage (.465)...Had 6 multiple HR games...Hit three HR on June 24th at Texas and repeated the feat on July 19th at Minnesota and was named AL Player-of-the-Week...Of his 35 HR, 20 of them either tied the game or put the Indians ahead...A two homer game at the Metrodome on July 18th gave him 5 HR in back-to-back games, tying a major league record (15th time)- one of his 5 HR was his second career inside-the-park HR...One of only three AL players to start every game (Cal Ripken Jr. and Rueben Sierra)...Was tied for first in the league in AB with Steve Sax (651)...Hit .301 during the month of May (29 games)...Hit into just 6 double plays (6th best in the AL).

CAREER NOTES: Has never been selected to an All-Star team...Over 100 RBI in four of past five seasons.

JOE CARTER

Year	Club & League	AVG.	G	AB	R	H	2B	3B	HR	RBI	SH-SF	HP	BB	SO	SB-CS
1981	Midland (Tex)	.269	67	249	42	67	15	3	5	35	1-1	2	8	30	12-2
1982	Midland (Tex)	.319	110	427	84	136	22	8	25	98	3-7	4	26	51	15-4
1983	Iowa (AmAs)	.307	124	522	82	160	27	6	22	83	6-1	0	17	103	40-12
1983	CHICAGO (NL)	.176	23	51	6	9	1	1	0	1	1-0	0	0	21	1-0
1984	Iowa (AmAs)	.310	61	248	45	77	12	7	14	67	0-2	3	20	31	11-6
1984	CLEVELAND (AL)	.275	66	244	32	67	6	1	13	41	0-1	1	11	48	2-4
1985	CLEVELAND (AL)	.262	143	489	64	128	27	0	15	59	3-4	2	25	74	24-6
1986	CLEVELAND (AL)	.302	162	663	108	200	36	9	29	121	1-8	5	32	95	29-7
1987	CLEVELAND (AL)	.264	149	588	83	155	27	2	32	106	1-4	9	27	105	31-6
1988	CLEVELAND (AL)	.271	157	621	85	168	36	6	27	98	1-6	7	27	98	27-5
1989	CLEVELAND (AL)	.243	162	651	84	158	32	4	35	105	2-5	8	39	112	13-5
1990	SAN DIEGO (NL)	.232	162	634	79	147	27	12	24	115	0-8	7	48	93	22-6
AL TOTALS		.269	839	3256	456	876	164	22	151	530	8-28	32	169	516	126-33
NL TOTALS		.228	185	685	85	156	28	2	24	116	0-8	7	48	114	23-6
ML TOTALS		.262	1024	3941	541	1032	192	24	175	648	8-36	39	217	630	149-39

CARTER—TRANSACTIONS

- Selected by Chicago Cubs' organization in 1st round (second player selected) of free-agent draft, June 8, 1981.
- On disabled list, April 9 to April 19, 1982.
- Traded with Outfielder Mel Hall and Pitchers Don Schulze and Darryl Banks to Cleveland Indians for Catcher Ron Hassey and Pitchers Rick Sutcliffe and George Frazier, June 13, 1984.
- On disabled list, July 2 to July 17, 1984.
- Traded to San Diego Padres for Catcher Sandy Alomar, Outfielder Chris James and Third Baseman Carlos Baerga, December 6, 1989.
- Traded to Toronto Blue Jays with Second baseman Roberto Alomar for Shortstop Tony Fernandez and First baseman Fred McGriff, December 5, 1990.

JOE CARTER vs AMERICAN LEAGUE

	1990					Career				
	AB	H	HR	RBI	AVG	AB	H	HR	RBI	AVG
AL Total	-	-	-	-	-	3256	876	151	530	.269
HOME	-	-	-	-	-	1603	440	69	254	.274
AWAY	-	-	-	-	-	1653	436	82	276	.264
vs BALTIMORE	-	-	-	-	-	259	61	12	34	.235
BOSTON	-	-	-	-	-	256	69	18	40	.269
CLEVELAND	-	-	-	-	-	-	-	-	-	-
DETROIT	-	-	-	-	-	246	55	6	31	.224
MILWAUKEE	-	-	-	-	-	284	85	21	50	.299
NEW YORK	-	-	-	-	-	239	61	14	46	.255
TORONTO	-	-	-	-	-	251	63	9	37	.251
AL EAST	-	-	-	-	-	1535	394	80	238	.257
vs CALIFORNIA	-	-	-	-	-	261	67	7	37	.257
CHICAGO	-	-	-	-	-	228	56	6	29	.246
KANSAS CITY	-	-	-	-	-	241	67	7	33	.278
MINNESOTA	-	-	-	-	-	267	82	19	54	.307
OAKLAND	-	-	-	-	-	250	72	10	50	.288
SEATTLE	-	-	-	-	-	261	80	12	50	.288
TEXAS	-	-	-	-	-	213	58	10	39	.272
AL WEST	-	-	-	-	-	1721	482	71	292	.280
PRE-ASG	-	-	-	-	-	1613	427	71	271	.265
POST-ASG	-	-	-	-	-	1643	449	80	259	.273
vs RHP	-	-	-	-	-	2363	633	109	390	..268
LHP	-	-	-	-	-	893	243	42	140	.272
PINCH HITTING	-	-	-	-	-	16	6	0	3	.375
DESIGNATED HITTING	-	-	-	-	-	17	3	0	1	.176
in APRIL	-	-	-	-	-	387	100	20	62	.258
MAY	-	-	-	-	-	515	139	17	88	270
JUNE	-	-	-	-	-	483	125	25	76	.259
JULY	-	-	-	-	-	571	152	25	94	.266
AUGUST	-	-	-	-	-	599	158	32	90	.264
SEPT/OCT	-	-	-	-	-	701	202	32	120	.288

CAREER HIGHS

SEASON: **AVG.** .302-1986 **H** 200-1986 **HR** 35-1989
RBI 121 - 1986 **SB** 31-1987

GAME: **H** 5 (3 times, last Sept. 6/86 at MILW)
HR 3 (4 times, last July 19/89 at MINN)
RBI 7, April 23, 1990 vs SAN FRAN
SB 3, Sept.1, 1985 at MILW

Last ML HR: SEPT. 9, 1990 vs ATL
Longest Hitting Streak: 21 - 1986

38 NATE CROMWELL

PITCHER

Born: Aug. 23, 1968 Las Vegas, NV
Resides: Las Vegas, NV
B-L T-L 6-1 185
M.L. Service: 0.000

PERSONAL: Nathaniel Cromwell. . .Married - Roshon...Graduate of Chaparral High School in Las Vegas in 1987 where he lettered for three years in baseball and also played basketball.

LAST SEASON: Spent the season at Knoxville (AA) of the Southern League where he was 3rd on the club in GS (23)...Walked 91 batters in 121.1 IP while striking out only 79...Tied for 2nd on the squad with 2 complete games...Allowed 119 hits in 121.1 IP...Was picked up on waivers by the Braves on September 24 after having been designated for assignment on September 17...Was re-acquired by TORONTO from Atlanta on November 6th in exchange for RHP Earl Sanders.

PROFESSIONAL CAREER: **1987:** Turned professional with Medicine Hat (Rookie) of the Pioneer League...Used primarily as a game starter, winning 4 of 10 decisions...**1988:** Held South Atlantic League opponents to a .207 batting average...Did not allow a run in 21 innings at one point...**1989:** Spent the season with Dunedin (A) of the Florida State League...Used almost exclusively in the starting rotation...Club's top winner (12) and also led the club in GS (30) and K (161) while finishing 2nd in IP (151.2)...Winner of the R. Howard Webster Award as Dunedin MVP...Among the league leaders in wins (T/5th-12), GS (1st-30), K (1st-161) and WP (25)...had league's highest K/9IP ratio (9.48).

NATE CROMWELL

Year	Club & League	W-L	ERA	G	GS	CG	ShO	SV	IP	H	R	ER	HR	HB	BB	SO	WP
1987	Med. Hat (Pio)	4-6	4.31	15	11	1	0	0	54.1	54	36	26	1	1	37	47	10
1988	Myrtle Beach (SAL)	8-8	2.90	21	20	1	1	0	124.1	88	47	40	6	8	67	86	8
1989	Dunedin (FSL)	12-6	3.62	31	30	0	0	0	151.2	136	70	61	5	4	84	161	25
1990	Knoxville (Sou)	5-14	5.56	27	23	2	0	0	121.1	119	85	75	11	4	91	79	8

CROMWELL—TRANSACTIONS

- Blue Jays 11th round selection (283rd overall) in June 1987 Free Agent Draft
- On disabled list, June 17-28, 1987

46 KEN DAYLEY
PITCHER

Born: Feb. 25, 1959 Jerome, ID
Resides: Chesterfield, Missouri
B-L T-L 6-0 180
M.L. Service: 7.094

PERSONAL: Kenneth Grant Dayley II...Married the former Jill Pilakowski 11/22/80...Has four children: Sara Jill, Ashley Nichole, Kenneth Grant and Brooke...Graduated from the Dalles (Oregon) High School in 1977...Attended the University of Portland, majoring in marketing...While there he played both baseball and basketball...Enjoys listening to music and fishing.

LAST SEASON: Spent the entire season at St. Louis where he appeared in 58 games...Didn't allow an ER until 5/18 vs the Reds (11.1 innings)...Picked up his first save on 4/18 vs the Pirates...Struck out five in 2.2 innings vs the Dodgers on 5/27...Received 2 of his 4 wins vs the Expos...Had 10 fewer saves than in 1989...Allowed just 5 HR during the entire season...Achieved his 40th career save on 9/8 vs the Cubs...Second on the club in appearances with 58 (Di Pino-62)...Longest outing was vs Pittsburg when he pitched 3.1 innings on 8/10...Did not hit a batter all season (last time was '88)...Opposing batters hit .233...Has appeared in at least 50 games or more in each of the last 4 seasons.

PROFESSIONAL CAREER: **1980:** Selected in the first round by Atlanta (3rd overall) in the June Free Agent Draft...Went directly to Savannah (AA) of the Southern League where he compiled an 8-3 record with a 2.57 ERA and 104 strikeouts in 105 innings...**1981:** Led the International League in games started (31), innings (200.0), strikeouts (162) and tied for first in league wins (13) while at Richmond (AAA)...**1982:** Opened the season at Richmond (AAA) of the International League and was promoted to Atlanta in early May...First ML appearance came in a start vs St. Louis on 5/13...Gave up 5 hits and 4 runs in 1.1 innings...Gained first ML win 5/19 vs Montreal going 6.2 innings and allowing only 3 hits and 1 run...With a 4-6 mark was returned to AAA in early August...Recalled on 9/1, working 5 games in relief for the remainder of the season...**1983:** Opened season at Richmond (AAA) of the International League, winning first five decisions to give him nine straight at Richmond, dating back to 1982...Promoted to Atlanta, where he spent the remainder of the year...**1984:** Started the year at Atlanta and was 0-3 after four starts...Was sent to Richmond (AAA) where he accumulated a 5-1 record in 9 appearances and an ERA of 4.04...Traded to the Cardinals on June 15th along with first baseman Mike Jorgensen for third baseman Ken Oberkfell...After 3 appearances (2 starts) he had added two more defeats...Optioned to Louisville (AAA) of the American Association where he had a 4-6 record and 3.27 ERA in 13 starts, with 3 complete games...Walked only 22 and struck out 79 in 96.1 innings with the American Association champions...Did not join the Cardinals in September after Louisville season ended because rest was prescribed for an abdominal muscle spasm...**1985:** Allowed only 1 run, 15 hits and struck out 15 in his first 13 appearances, covering 18.2 innings...Over 8 appearances from 4/26-5/22, working 12.2 scoreless innings...Recorded first ML save on 5/9 at Los Angeles in a 5-4 win...Struck out 5 of 10 batters at New York on 6/7...From 6/21-7/26, he pitched 11 shutout innings (11 games) allowing only 4 hits and 13 strikeouts...Went six appearances (5.2IP) without allowing a run from 8/10-18 and picked up saves 8 and 9...Notched save #10 on 8/22 at Houston to the the Cardinals two pitchers with double figures in saves for the first time since 1975...Led the club in appearances and strikeouts per innings pitched (.9)...His 11 saves were second on the club to Jeff Lahti's 19...In post-season play, he allowed only 3 hits and walked 4 in 12 innings...Struck out 8 while appearing in 9 of 13 post-season games...Had two saves vs the Dodgers during the NL Championship Series...Was the only pitcher in the World Series who appeared in two or more games that was not scored on...**1986:** Allowed a run of more in 8 of first 11 appearances (13 ER in 17.0IP, 6.88ERA)...Went on the disabled list on 7/13...Came back and didn't allow an earned run in 18.2 IP...Recorded seven strikeouts in four innings of relief 4/19 at Montreal- a high for a Cardinals relief pitcher in '86...Allowed only one HR over the season (5/1 vs the Dodgers' Marshall)...Averaged 7.68 strikeouts per 9 IP...Was placed on disabled list on 7/16 retroactive to 7/13 with continuing elbow stiffness...Missed the remainder of the season and underwent surgery in October by Dr. Frank Jobe to repair damaged ligament on the inside of his left elbow and to transfer nerves nearby...**1987:** Made recovery from the injury and became the Cardinals #1 short man out of the bullpen from the left side...Started the rehabilitation at Louisville (AAA) of the American Association where he pitched 2 innings...Activated from the DL on 5/21 and pitched two perfect innings vs the Braves...Picked up his first victory of the season on 6/28 at Montreal in extra innings...First save of the season came the next day vs New York...Won three games in four days (7/19-23)...Tied for the NL high with five wins in July...Surpassed career high for wins (5) on 7/31 with his sixth...Averaged 9.3 strikeouts per nine innings...Won 4 more games than his previous career high...Tied Todd Worrell for 6th best ERA (2.66) among NL relievers..Did not allow a run until his 11th appearance of the season...Earned saves in NLCS games #1 and #6...Added another save in the World Series (game 6)...Posted a team best 1.04 ERA in 7 post-season games...**1988:** Suffered a torn muscle in his lower back while pitching on opening day at Cincinnati...Placed on the 15-day DL on 4/5 and was sidelined until 5/11...After returning from the DL, he allowed just one run in his first nine appearances and had an ERA of 0.87...Struck out a season high 4 batters 9/19 vs Pittsburg...Held opponents to a .239 batting average...Was second on club in games (54), saves (5) and games finished (21)...Was unscored upon in 37 of 54 (69%) relief appearances...Allowed just two HR in 55.1 IP...Was successful in 5 of 8 save opportunities...Posted 4 saves and

(Dayley (cont...)

a 1.71 ERA at Busch Stadium (32 games)...**1989:** Was used in more save opportunities due to injury to Todd Worrell...Appeared in a club high 71 games (4th in NL)...Recorded his first save of the season vs San Francisco on 4/26...Won 3 straight decisions 5/9-20...Tied for the NL lead with 13 appearances in April...Allowed just 2 ER in 24 IP (0.75ERA) from July 1 - September 1...Pitched 14.1 consecutive scoreless innings 7/21-8/26...Was 3-1 with a 2.06 ERA in 30 games vs NL West teams...Held opponents to a .228 batting average...Was involved in 9 of the 10 Cardinals' combined shutouts...Was 2nd among Cardinal relievers in saves (12), 3rd in IP (75.1) and 3rd in games finished (28)...His 75.1 IP were the most since 1983...Made the first error of his big-league career, 7/18 vs the Giants.

CAREER HIGHS

Most Strikeouts: 9, June 24, 1983
Most Strikeouts in Relief 7, April 19, 1986 at MTL
Longest Scoreless Streak: 14.1 IP, twice, last time July 21-August 26, 1989
Longest Relief Appearance: 4 IP, twice, last time April 19, 1986 at MTL
Longest Win Streak: 4 games, July 19-31, 1987
Longest Losing Streak: 5 games, 1984

KEN DAYLEY

Year	Club & League	W-L	ERA	G	GS	CG	ShO	SV	IP	H	R	ER	HR	HB	BB	SO	WP
1980	Savannah (Sou)	8-3	2.57	16	16	3	0	0	105	86	38	30	8	6	54	104	4
1981	Richmond (Int)	13-8	3.33	31	31	4	1	0	200	180	82	74	14	3	117	162	6
1982	Richmond (Int)	8-3	3.11	13	13	6	0	0	98.1	89	43	34	6	1	47	79	4
1982	ATLANTA (NL)	5-6	4.54	20	11	0	0	0	71.1	79	39	36	9	0	25	34	2
1983	Richmond (Int)	9-3	3.28	14	14	4	1	0	90.2	79	39	33	7	0	49	74	4
1983	ATLANTA (NL)	5-8	4.30	24	16	0	0	0	104.2	100	59	50	12	2	39	70	3
1984	Richmond (Int)	5-1	4.04	9	9	2	1	0	62.1	66	31	28	6	0	24	45	4
1984	Louisville (AmAs)	4-6	3.27	13	13	3	0	0	96.1	86	42	35	6	2	22	79	3
1984	ATLANTA (NL)	0-3	5.30	4	4	0	0	0	18.2	28	18	11	5	1	6	10	0
1984	ST. LOUIS (NL)	0-2	18.00	3	2	0	0	0	5.0	16	10	10	1	0	5	0	0
1985	ST. LOUIS (NL)	4-4	2.76	57	0	0	0	11	65.1	65	24	20	2	0	18	62	4
1986	ST. LOUIS (NL)	0-3	3.26	31	0	0	0	5	38.2	42	19	14	1	1	11	33	0
1987	Louisville (AmAs)	0-0	4.50	1	1	0	0	0	2.0	1	1	1	0	0	1	1	1
1987	ST. LOUIS (NL)	9.5	2.66	53	3	0	0	4	61.0	52	21	18	2	2	33	63	5
1988	ST. LOUIS (NL)	2-7	2.77	54	0	0	0	5	55.1	48	20	17	2	1	19	38	2
1989	ST. LOUIS (NL)	4-3	2.87	71	0	0	0	12	75.1	63	26	24	3	0	30	40	2
1990	ST. LOUIS (NL)	4-4	3.56	58	0	0	0	4	73.1	63	32	29	5	0	31	51	6
ML TOTALS		33-45	3.62	375	33	0	0	41	568.2	556	268	229	85	19	217	401	60

DAYLEY—TRANSACTIONS

- Selected by Atlanta Braves' organization in 1st round (third player selected) of free-agent draft, June 3, 1980.
- Traded with First Baseman Mike Jorgensen to St. Louis Cardinals for Third Baseman Ken Oberkfell, June 15, 1984.
- On disabled list, July 13, 1986 through remainder of season.
- Released, December 20, 1986; re-signed by Cardinals, January 19, 1987.
- On St. Louis disabled list, April 5 to May 21, 1987; included rehabilitation disability assignment to Louisville, May 12 to May 21, 1987.
- On disabled list, April 5 to May 9, 1988.
- Granted Free Agency.
- Signed with the Blue Jays, November 26th, 1990.

58 CARLOS DELGADO

CATCHER

Born: June 25, 1972 Aquadilla, PR
Resides: Aquadilla, PR
B-L T-R 6-3 206
M.L. Service: 0.000

PERSONAL: Carlos Juan Delgado...Attended Jose de Diego High School in Puerto Rico and participated in Baseball, Volleyball and Track and Field...His baseball hero is Roberto Clemente...Enjoys water and beach sports.

LAST SEASON: Was named the R. Howard Webster Award winner for the St. Catharines Blue Jays (A) of the New York-Penn League as the club's most outstanding player...Was second on the team in batting with a .283 average...Tied for second on the club in HR (6), while leading St. Catharines with 19 extra base hits...Had team highs in slugging percentage (.420), RBI (39) and sacrifice flies (4)...Played 60 games at the catcher position, committing 7 errors.

PROFESSIONAL CAREER: **1989:** Spent the season at St. Catharines (A) appearing in just 31 games sporting a .180 batting average...Five of 16 hits were doubles.

CARLOS DELGADO

Year	Club & League	AVG.	G	AB	R	H	2B	3B	HR	RBI	SH-SF	HP	BB	SO	SB-CS
1989	St. Catharines (NYP)	.180	31	89	9	16	5	0	0	11	0-1	0	23	39	0-0
1990	St. Catharines (NYP)	.283	67	226	29	64	13	0	6	39	1-4	5	35	65	2-7

DELGADO-TRANSACTIONS

- Signed as a Free Agent by Blue Jays on October 9, 1988.

39 CARLOS DIAZ

CATCHER

Born: Dec. 24, 1964 Elizabeth, NJ

Resides: Palm Harbor, FL

B-R T-R 6-3 190

M.L. Service: 0.053

PERSONAL: Carlos Franciso Diaz...Married...Wife's name, Natalie...One son, Anthony Francisco (Dec. 19/90)...Attended and was drafted from Oklahoma State University.

LAST SEASON: Spent most of the season at Syracuse (AAA) of the International League where he played in 77 games and hit .203, 51-251, 1 HR, 19 RBI, 17 BB, 51 K...Led the Syracuse Chiefs in games played at the catcher position...Was called up to Toronto on May 5th to replace the injured Greg Myers and hit .333 in 4 games...Had first ML hit on 5/17th vs Seattle...Optioned back on May 27th...Was recalled to Toronto in September where he played in 5 games but did not have an at bat but had a key sacrifice hit in 9/23 win over Cleveland...Was used in primarily a defensive role.

PROFESSIONAL CAREER: **1986:** Started professional career with Ventura (A) of the California League and was moved to Medicine Hat (Rookie) of the Pioneer League on 6/26...Finished season with St. Catharines (A) of the New York-Penn League, helping them to a league championship...Hit a combined 41-162/.253...**1987:** Spent the season with Dunedin (A) of the Florida State League...Placed on DL with shoulder separation, 4/19-5/14...71 games as a catcher, 2-games at 1B...7 errors in 73 games...**1988:** Started the season with Knoxville of the Southern League, appearing in only 7 games...Assigned to Dunedin (A) of the FSL on 4/19...Promoted to Syracuse (AAA) of the International League on 7/7 where he remained for the duration of the season...**1989:** Spent the season with Knoxville (AA) of the Southern League...96 games behind the plate...Club's 1st string catcher...Threw out 45 of 141 runners (31.9%)...11 errors (2nd highest among catchers) in 694 TC...2nd in league with 15 PB.

CARLOS DIAZ

Year	Club & League	AVG.	G	AB	R	H	2B	3B	HR	RBI	SH-SF	HP	BB	SO	SB-CS
1986	Ventura (Cal)	.400	2	5	1	2	1	0	0	0	0-0	0	1	2	0-0
1986	Medicine Hat (Pio)	.313	20	83	11	26	5	2	0	16	0-1	0	6	17	1-0
1986	St. Catharines (NYP)	.176	24	74	9	13	3	1	1	5	0-1	2	7	18	1-0
1987	Dunedin (FSL)	.230	73	230	24	53	6	0	0	27	1-1	1	22	41	3-2
1988	Knoxville (Sou)	.217	7	23	2	5	1	0	0	0	0-0	0	2	4	0-1
1988	Dunedin (FSL)	.196	68	235	20	46	11	0	6	23	2-1	2	20	56	2-2
1988	Syracuse (Int)	.169	27	83	4	14	5	0	1	8	2-1	0	1	23	0-0
1989	Knoxville (Sou)	.250	100	320	28	80	12	1	6	36	4-3	3	17	55	3-1
1990	Syracuse (Int)	.203	77	251	18	51	10	0	1	19	5-2	0	17	51	2-2
1991	TORONTO (AL)	.333	9	3	1	1	0	0	0	0	1-0	0	0	2	0-0
ML TOTALS		.333	9	3	1	1	0	0	0	0	1-0	0	0	2	0-0

DIAZ - TRANSACTIONS

- Blue Jays 14th selection (367the overall) in June 1986.
- Free Agent Draft.
- On disabled list, April 19-May 14, 1987.

PINCH HIT POTENTIAL: The Blue Jays set a club mark with three pinch hit HR's in three consecutive at bats, August 1, 3, 5, 1984...After going126 at bats in 1984 without a round-tripper Ernie Whitt lit up Kansas City's Bret Saberhagen, for two runs on August 1st...Then at Baltimore on August 3rd Orioles reliever Bill Swaggerty fell victim to a three-run shot by Willie Aikens...The final HR was a solo blast by Cliff Johnson vs Orioles Tippy Martinez on August 5th...It was Johnson's 19th career PH HR which set a new major league record...The Blue Jays also set a club mark with 6 pinch hits in as many at bats, June 28-29, 1987 at Milwaukee and vs New York...On June 28th the club registered pinch hits from Fred McGriff (HR), Rance Mulliniks and Rick Leach in the 8th inning...The next night the Blue Jays got pinch hits from Manny Lee, Ernie Whitt and Rance Mulliniks.

CARLOS DIAZ vs AMERICAN LEAGUE

	1990					CAREER				
	AB	H	HR	RBI	AVG	AB	H	HR	RBI	AVG
SEASON	3	1	0	0	.333	3	1	0	0	.333
TORONTO	2	1	0	0	.500	2	1	0	0	.500
AWAY	1	0	0	0	.000	1	0	0	0	.000
vs BALTIMORE	0	0	0	0	.000	0	0	0	0	.000
BOSTON	0	0	0	0	.000	0	0	0	0	.000
CLEVELAND	0	0	0	0	.000	0	0	0	0	.000
DETROIT	1	0	0	0	.000	1	0	0	0	.000
MILWAUKEE	-	-	-	-	-	-	-	-	-	-
NEW YORK	-	-	-	-	-	-	-	-	-	-
TORONTO	-	-	-	-	-	-	-	-	-	-
A.L. EAST	1	0	0	0	.000	1	0	0	0	.000
vs CALIFORNIA	-	-	-	-	-	-	-	-	-	-
KANSAS CITY	0	0	0	0	.000	0	0	0	0	.000
MINNESOTA	-	-	-	-	-	-	-	-	-	-
OAKLAND	-	-	-	-	-	-	-	-	-	-
SEATTLE	2	1	0	0	.500	2	1	0	0	.500
TEXAS	-	-	-	-	-	-	-	-	-	-
A.L. WEST	2	1	0	0	.500	2	1	0	0	.500
Pre- ASG	3	1	0	0	.333	3	1	0	0	.333
Post- ASG	0	0	0	0	.000	0	0	0	0	.000
vs RHP	1	1	0	0	1.000	1	1	0	0	.000
LHP	2	0	0	0	.000	0	0	0	0	.000
PINCH HITTING	-	-	-	-	-	-	-	-	-	-
DESIGNATED HITTING	0	0	0	0	.000	0	0	0	0	.000
in APRIL	-	-	-	-	-	-	-	-	-	-
MAY	3	1	0	0	.333	3	1	0	0	.333
JUNE	-	-	-	-	-	-	-	-	-	-
JULY	-	-	-	-	-	-	-	-	-	-
AUGUST	-	-	-	-	-	-	-	-	-	-
SEPT/OCT	0	0	0	0	.000	0	0	0	0	.000

20 ROB DUCEY

OUTFIELDER

Born: May 24, 1965 Toronto, ON

Resides: Palm Harbor, FL

B-L T-R 6-2 180

M.L. Service: 1.158

PERSONAL: Robert Thomas Ducey...Married...Wife's name, Yanitza, a former Miss Venezuela...One son, Thomas Gregory (April 23, 1990)...Played for the Cambridge Jr's and Sr's in the 1983 Intercounty League...Also played for and attended Seminole Community College in Sanford, Florida...Graduate of Glenview Park High School in 1983, where he was a competitive wrestler...Earned Athlete-of-the-Year honours in his senior year...Fourth Canadian to be on the BLUE JAYS 40 man roster...Others were Dave McKay, Paul Hodgson and Dave Shipanoff...Did not play baseball until age 15...Previously had played softball exclusively and at age 15 was a member of the Canadian National Midget Softball Team...Youngest of five children and only boy.

LAST SEASON: Spent the season at Syracuse where he hit .267, 7 HR, 47 RBI in 127 games...After coming off knee injury suffered in 1989, got off to a slow start...Batted .241 in first 64-games, .296 in final 63-games...Led Chiefs with 32-doubles, 60-walks..Appeared in 127-games, 52-CF, 35-RF, 28-LF....Was among International League leaders in triples (7) and doubles (32)...Led Syracuse in games played in the outfield with 119...Was called up to TORONTO in September and hit .302 16/53, with 7 RBI, 7 BB, 15 K, 1 SB...Made 18 starts all in left-field...Had a three hit game vs Detroit in his first start on 9/5...Hit .500, 6-12 with runners in scoring position....Had a .396 slugging % while with TORONTO...Only Canadian player to play on the ML club this season.

PROFESSIONAL CAREER: **1984:** Was 3rd in the Pioneer League in HR (12 while hitting .302...Was the winner of the R. Howard Webster Award as Medicine Hat's MVP...**1985:** Tied for 3rd in South Atlantic League AB (529) and enjoyed a 12 game hit streak, 8/8-18, going 21-51/.412 in the process...**1986:** Started the season with Ventura (A) of the California League...Averaged over 1 hit per game and was promoted to Knoxville (AA) of Southern League on 5/31...Batted a combined .318 for season...Named winner of the James (Tip) O'Neill Award given annually on behalf of the Canadian Baseball Hall of Fame to the Canadian baseball player excelling in individual achievement and team contribution...**1987:** Started the season with Syracuse (AAA) of the International League, batting .318 in 12 games...Promoted to the BLUE JAYS on 4/29...ML debut, 1-2, 1 RBI vs Texas on 5/1...3rd Canadian to play for TORONTO...Optioned to Syracuse on 5/31 where he remained until 9/1...Tied lead in IL in triples (10) and finished fifth in on base percentage (.388)...IL Player of the Week 8/24-31...Organization's Minor League Player of the Month for August...1st ML HR, 3R vs Baltimore's Mike Kinnunen 9/14...**1988:** Started the season with Syracuse (AAA) of the IL after vying for the starting BLUE JAYS CF job during spring training...With Syracuse batted .256 in 90 games, with 7 HR and 42 RBI...Club's top producer in July...Contract purchased by BLUE JAYS on 8/2 and was held hitless in each of his 1st 6 appearances (0-13)...Tied then personal high with 2 H vs New York on 8/9...Hit safely in 9 of next 10 GS through season's end...1st career 4H game, 9/26 vs Boston...Set personal high with 4 game hit streak, 9/24-27...Was 13-32/.406 in September/October and 15-48/.313, 6 RBI in 15 GS...Was 10-28/.357, 2 RBI vs LHP...**1989:** Made the club after leading the BLUE JAYS during spring training with a .448 average and 18 RBI...Appeared in 12 games (9GS) in April...1st multiple hit appearance of the season on 5/2 going 2-4 vs Oakland...Placed on the 15-day DL with a sprained right knee on June 9th after running into a dislodged outfield fence during batting practice at SkyDome...Assigned to Syracuse (AAA) on medical rehabilitation on July 5th...Returned July 14th after reinjuring his knee...Moved to 21-day DL on August 7th and then continued his rehabilitation in Syracuse on August 24th...Overall at Syracuse, hit .103 in 10 games...Rejoined BLUE JAYS on September 2nd...Appeared defensively in LF on September 3rd vs the Twins for his first ML appearance since June 7th...Was activated for ALCS.

ROB DUCEY

Year	Club & League	AVG	G	AB	R	H	2B	3B	HR	RBI	SH-SF	HP	BB	SO	SB-CS
1984	Medicine Hat (Pio)	.302	63	235	49	71	10	3	12	49	1-1	1	41	61	13-6
1985	Florence (SAL)	.251	134	529	78	133	22	2	13	86	3-7	1	49	103	12-4
1986	Ventura (Cal)	.337	47	178	36	60	11	3	12	38	1-2	1	21	24	17-5
1986	Knoxville (Sou)	.308	88	344	49	106	22	3	11	58	0-4	0	29	59	7-7
1987	Syracuse (Int)	.284	100	359	62	102	14	10	10	60	0-5	3	61	89	8-7
1987	TORONTO (AL)	.188	34	48	12	9	1	0	1	6	0-1	0	8	10	2-0
1988	Syracuse (Int)	.256	90	317	40	81	14	4	7	42	2-4	3	43	81	7-6
1988	TORONTO (AL)	.315	27	54	15	17	4	1	0	6	2-2	0	5	7	1-0
1989	Syracuse (Int)	.103	10	29	0	3	0	1	0	3	0-1	0	10	13	0-0
1989	TORONTO (AL)	.211	41	76	5	16	4	0	0	7	1-0	0	9	25	
1990	Syracuse (Int)	.267	127	438	53	117	32	7	7	47	1-1	4	60	87	13-9
1990	TORONTO (AL)	.302	19	53	7	16	5	0	0	7	0-1	1	7	15	1-1
ML TOTALS		.251	121	231	39	58	14	1	1	26	3-4	1	29	57	6-2

CHAMPIONSHIP SERIES RECORD

Year	Club & League	AVG	G	AB	R	H	2B	3B	HR	RBI	SH-SF	HP	BB	SO	SB-CS
1989	TORONTO (AL)	.000	0	0	0	0	0	0	0	0	0-0	0	0	0	0-0

DUCEY - TRANSACTIONS

- Signed as a free agent by Blue Jays, May 16, 1984.
- On disabled list, June 9 to September 2, 1989; included rehabilitation disability assignment to Syracuse, July 5-July 14 and August 24 - September 2, 1989.

ROB DUCEY vs AMERICAN LEAGUE

	1990					CAREER				
	AB	H	HR	RBI	AVG	AB	H	HR	RBI	AVG
SEASON	53	16	0	7	.302	231	58	1	26	.251
HOME	29	7	0	2	.241	118	27	1	14	.229
AWAY	24	9	0	5	.375	113	31	0	12	.274
vs BALTIMORE	9	2	0	1	.222	27	9	1	8	.333
BOSTON	0	0	0	0	.000	12	6	0	1	.500
CLEVELAND	7	2	0	0	.286	23	5	0	3	.217
DETROIT	5	3	0	2	.600	7	3	0	2	.428
MILWAUKEE	8	2	0	2	.250	17	3	0	3	.176
NEW YORK	5	2	0	1	.400	25	8	0	2	.320
TORONTO	-	-	-	-	-	-	-	-	-	-
A.L. EAST	34	11	0	6	.314	111	34	1	19	.304
vs CALIFORNIA	-	-	-	-	-	26	5	0	1	.192
CHICAGO	8	1	0	0	.125	10	2	0	0	.200
KANSAS CITY	11	4	0	1	.364	27	5	0	1	.185
MINNESOTA	-	-	-	-	-	14	2	0	1	.143
OAKLAND	-	-	-	-	-	12	3	0	0	.200
SEATTLE	-	-	-	-	-	15	3	0	2	.200
TEXAS	-	-	-	-	-	16	4	0	2	.250
A.L. WEST	19	5	0	1	.263	120	24	0	7	.200
Pre- ASG	-	-	-	-	-	97	19	0	8	.196
Post- ASG	53	16	0	7	.302	134	39	1	18	.291
vs RHP	47	14	0	5	.298	162	39	0	17	.241
LHP	6	2	0	2	.333	69	19	1	9	.275
PINCH HITTING	-	-	-	-	-	9	1	0	0	.111
DESIGNATED HITTING	-	-	-	-	-	1	0	0	0	.000
in APRIL	-	-	-	-	-	27	5	0	1	.185
MAY	-	-	-	-	-	65	13	0	6	.200
JUNE	-	-	-	-	-	5	1	0	1	.200
JULY	-	-	-	-	-	-	-	-	-	-
AUGUST	-	-	-	-	-	22	4	0	1	.182
SEPT/OCT	53	16	0	7	.302	112	35	1	17	.313

CAREER HIGHS

SEASON: **AVG.** .315-1988 **H** 17-1988 **HR** 1-1987 **SB** 2-1987, 1990

GAME: **H** 4-at BOST., Sept. 26, 1988 **HR** 1-vs BALT., Sept. 14, 1987
RBI 3-vs BALT., Sept. 14, 1987 **SB** 1-6 times

Last ML HR: - vs BALT., Sept. 14, 1987
Longest Hitting Streak: 4 - 1989

26 JIM EPPARD

FIRST BASEMAN/OUTFIELDER

Born: April 27, 1960 South Bend, ID
Resides: Huntington Beach, CA
B-L T-L 6-2 181
M.L. Service: 1.079

PERSONAL: James Gerhard Eppard...Married the former Lou Ann Sherman, October 17, 1987...Graduated from Azusa High School (CA) in 1978...Played baseball and basketball during prep career...Attended Citrus Junior College and U.C. Berkeley...Began career as first baseman.

LAST SEASON: Was puchased by the BLUE JAYS in the off season as a six-year free agent...Spent the year at Syracuse (AAA) of the International League where he became the first Syracuse player ever to lead the IL in hitting (.310)...Also led the league in hits with 143...Played exclusively at first base with the Chiefs (131 games)...Was second on the club in AB with 461...Scored a team high 72 runs...Struck out only two times more than he walked (49K/47BB)...Contract was purchased by the BLUE JAYS in September...He appeared in 6 games and had 5 at-bats (all pinch hitting) with 1 hit and 2 strikeouts.

PROFESSIONAL CAREER: **1982:** Played at Medford (A) of the Northwest League where he led the league in hitting with a .376 batting average while splitting time between first base and the outfield...Also led the league in assists (38) and hits (91)...**1983:** Moved the the California League (A) at Modesto, leading the loop in fielding percentage (.991) while playing first base...Averaged better than a hit per game (138H/134G)...**1984:** Promoted to Albany (AA) of the Eastern League and finished sixth in the league in hitting with a .312 batting average...Went 5-5 on April 20 vs Waterbury...Split time between the outfield and first base...**1985:** Returned to Modesto of the California League (A) where he led the league in batting average (.345) and hits (183)...Set a California League record for assists by a first baseman with 125...Had then career high 88 RBI...**1986:** Made the jump to AAA with Tacoma of the Pacific Coast League...Played in just 95 games- fewest since his first professional season...Played mainly in the outfield...**1987:** Was sold in the off-season to the Angels organization and played at Edmonton (AAA) of the Pacific Coast League...Played exclusively at first base and led the loop in batting average (.341) and doubles (33)...Led Edmonton in RBI with 94...Was called up to the parent club in September...Made debut on September 8th with a pinch-hit single off of the Royals' Mark Gubicza...**1988:** Started the season at Edmonton (AAA) and appeared in 41 games at first base before being called up to California on May 27th...Struck out 15 times in 126 plate appearances...Had five multiple hit games...Hit .308 as a pinch-hitter with the Angels and tied for the AL lead in that category with 8 pinch-hits...Fourth on the team in on-base percentage (.347)...**1989:** Started the season at Edmonton (AAA) where he played at first base as well as the outfield...Had 16 doubles in 90 games...Was called up to the parent club in May and again in September...Hit .250 in 12 AB with California...Saw action defensively at first base only.

JIM EPPARD

Year	Club & League	AVG	G	AB	T	H	2B	3B	HR	RBI	SH-SF	HP	BB	SO	SB-CS
1982	Medford ((Nwst)	.376	64	242	58	91	13	2	1	41	0-2	1	50	15	6-3
1983	Modesto (Cal)	.283	134	488	68	138	18	4	4	45	7-2	0	42	40	14-4
1984	Albany (East)	.312	118	417	58	130	14	6	0	51	5-4	2	71	40	7-7
1985	Modesto (Cal)	.345	141	531	97	183	23	4	3	88	5-11	2	69	49	14-6
1986	Tacoma (PCL)	.274	95	321	39	88	15	1	0	34	5-4	0	32	31	2-3
1987	Edmonton (PCL)	.341	132	446	68	152	33	3	3	94	1-7	2	74	30	1-5
1987	CALIFORNIA (AL)	.333	8	9	2	3	0	0	0	0	0-0	0	2	0	0-0
1988	Edmonton (PCL)	.262	41	141	18	37	6	1	0	16	0-0	0	16	9	0-1
1988	CALIFORNIA (AL)	.283	56	113	7	32	3	1	0	14	2-0	0	11	15	0-0
1989	Edmonton (PCL)	.274	90	292	40	80	16	1	2	34	2-4	1	45	37	5-5
1989	CALIFORNIA (AL)	.250	12	12	0	3	0	0	0	2	0-0	0	1	4	0-0
1990	Syracuse (Int)	.310	133	461	72	143	18	3	4	48	6-4	2	47	49	5-7
1990	TORONTO (AL)	.200	6	5	0	1	0	0	0	0	0-0	1	0	2	0-0
M L TOTALS		.281	82	139	9	39	3	1	0	16	2-0	1	14	21	0-0

EPPARD - TRANSACTIONS

- Selected by Chicago Cubs' organization in 11th round of free-agent draft, January 8, 1980.
- Selected by Oakland A's organization in 13th round of free-agent draft, June 7, 1982.
- On disabled list, April 11 to April 21, 1986.
- Sold to California Angels' organization, January 12, 1987.
- Released, October 5, 1989.
- Released by Blue Jays Oct. 30, 1990
- Signed to Blue Jays organization (AAA contract) Nov. 30, 1990

CAREER HIGHS

SEASON: **AVG.** 283 - 1988 **H** 32 - 1988 **RBI** 14 - 1988

GAME: **H** 2 (last time, at BALT., AUG. 21, 1988)
RBI 2 (last time, vs BALT., AUG. 31, 1988)

Longest Hitting Streak: 4 - 1988

27 WILLIE FRASER

PITCHER

Born: May 26, 1964 New York, NY
Resides: Irvine, CA
B-R T-R 6-1 206
M.L. Service: 4.031

PERSONAL: William Patrick Fraser...Married the former Annie Gutowski (November 12, 1988)...Graduated from Newburgh High (NY) in 1982...Lettered in baseball and football (four overall)...Attended Concordia College (Bronxville, New York), gaining All-State selection two years.

LAST SEASON: Spent the majority of the season (45 games) with California going 5-4 with a 3.08 ERA...Was sent to Edmonton (AAA) of the Pacific Coast League on April 30th and was recalled on May 14th...While at Edmonton, he was 1-0 in 3 games (all game starts) with a 3.14 ERA...While with California, he allowed just 69 hits in 76 innings of work...From August 5th-September 12, was 3-0 in 14 appearances with 2 SV and 0.40 ERA...Yielded just one HR to a left handed batter (Raphael Palmeiro)...Retired 32 of the 45 first batters he faced...Opposing batters hit .241 off of the RHP.

PROFESSIONAL CAREER: **1985:** Was the Angels' first round pick of the June 1985 Free Agent Draft...Played at Quad Cities (A) of the Midwest League where he appeared in 13 G/GS, posting a 2-6 won-loss record in 81.2 innings...Had a better than 2-1 strikeout to walk ratio (72/32)...Pitched one complete game...**1986:** Began the season at Palm Springs (A) of the California League, pitching in 19 games...Was 9-2 with a 3.55 ERA in 19 GS...Earned selection to California League All-Star team...Was promoted to Edmonton (AAA) of the Pacific Coast League on August 1st...Went 4-1, 3.15 ERA with the Trappers in 6 games (all game starts)...Earned promotion to the ML squad where he started one game (4.1IP, 6H, 4ER, 1BB, 2K) giving him an 8.31 ERA...Was the co-winner of the Kenny Myers Award given annually to the player judged best in minor league system...**1987:** First full Major League season...Spent the entire season with California, appearing in 36 games and starting 23...First ML win vs the Athletics on April 11 (in relief)...First win as a starter came vs the Red Sox in Boston on May 9th...Of 26 HR allowed, 25 were hit when he was the starting pitcher...Collected first ML save on April 21st vs Oakland...**1988:** Set personal bests with 12 wins, 32 games started and 194.2 innings pitched...Second straight season in which he had recorded double figures in wins...Pitched a complete game one-hitter vs the Mariners on August 10th at Anaheim...2nd on the Angels in wins (12)...Struck out only six batters more than he walked (86K/80BB)...Was his first sub-.500 (12-13) year since 1985 when he was 2-6...**1989:** Was first season without at least one game start...Achieved a then career-best 3.24 ERA, while appearing in 44 games (91.2IP)...Posted first save since April 21, 1987 on August 4th vs the Brewers...Had a 2-1 strikeout to walk ratio (46K/23BB)...Used primarily in middle relief...Was ranked 11th among AL relief pitchers in innings pitched...Right handed batters hit just .227 and left handed hitters managed a .248 clip...Was 3-2 at home with one save and a 1.98 ERA (50.0IP, 11ER).

WILLIE FRASER

Year	Club & League	W-L	ERA	G	GS	CG	ShO	SV	IP	H	R	ER	HR	HB	BB	SO	WP
1985	Quad Cities (Mid)	2-6	5.40	13	13	1	0	0	81.2	95	53	49	8	8	32	72	12
1986	Palm Springs (Cal)	9-2	3.55	19	19	2	0	0	124.1	115	60	49	8	7	29	99	4
1986	Edmonton (PCL)	4-1	3.15	6	6	2	2	0	40.0	25	15	14	5	0	8	24	0
1986	CALIFORNIA (AL)	0-0	8.31	1	1	0	0	0	4.1	6	4	4	0	0	1	2	0
1987	CALIFORNIA (AL)	10-10	3.92	36	23	5	1	1	176.2	160	85	77	26	6	63	106	12
1988	CALIFORNIA (AL)	12-13	5.41	34	32	2	0	0	194.2	203	129	117	33	9	80	86	12
1989	CALIFORNIA (AL)	4-7	3.24	44	0	0	0	2	91.2	80	33	33	6	5	23	46	5
1990	CALIFORNIA (AL)	5-4	3.08	45	0	0	0	2	76.0	69	29	26	4	0	24	32	1
1990	Edmonton (PCL)	1-0	3.14	3	3	0	0	0	14.1	11	8	5	1	0	6	12	2
ML TOTALS		31-34	4.24	160	56	7	1	5	543.1	518	280	256	69	20	191	272	30

FRASER - TRANSACTIONS

- Selected by California Angel's organization in 1st round (15th player selected) of free-agent draft, June 3, 1985.
- Traded with Outfielder DEVON WHITE to the Toronto Blue Jays for Outfielder Junior Felix and Infielder Luis Sojo on December 2, 1990.

DOUBLEHEADER SHUTOUTS: Did you know that the Blue Jays have never shut out opponents in both ends of a doubleheader?...Conversely, the Blue Jays have been shut out in both ends of a doubleheader twice, losing 8-0 and 6-0 to Boston at Toronto on September 5, 1977 and losing 15-0 and 2-0 to New York at Toronto on September 25, 1977...The Blue Jays have been shut out in one end of a doubleheader on 13 occasions (nine DH losses and four splits)...The Blue Jays have also shut out the opposition in one end of a doubleheader on three occasions (two wins, one split).

WILLIE FRASER vs AMERICAN LEAGUE

	1990						CAREER					
	W-L-S	ERA	IP	H	ER	SO	W-L-W	ERA	IP	H	ER	SO
SEASON	5-4-2	3.08	76.0	69	26	32	31-34-5	4.26	543.1	518	257	272
HOME	4-1-1	2.62	44.2	40	13	22	14-15-3	4.02	255.1	-	114	141
ROAD	1-3-1	3.73	31.1	29	13	10	17-19-2	4.47	288.0	-	143	131
vs BALTIMORE	1-0-0	0.00	4.0	2	0	1	3-3-0	3.42	47.1	-	18	22
BOSTON	1-0-0	0.00	2.1	4	0	0	4-2-0	4.71	36.1	-	19	15
CLEVELAND	0-0-0	3.38	5.1	7	2	3	1-3-0	6.19	36.1	-	25	21
DETROIT	0-0-0	7.20	5.0	4	4	5	1-4-0	5.49	39.1	-	24	18
MILWAUKEE	1-1-0	2.03	13.1	12	3	4	2-4-2	3.74	43.1	-	18	19
NEW YORK	0-1-2	1.00	9.0	5	1	1	3-4-2	4.97	50.2	-	28	22
TORONTO	1-0-0	3.24	8.1	6	3	2	2-1-0	4.28	33.2	-	16	19
AL EAST	4-2-2	2.47	47.1	40	13	16	16-21-4	4.64	287.0	-	148	136
vs CALIFORNIA	-	-	-	-	-		-	-	-	-	-	-
CHICAGO	0-0-0	2.08	4.1	1	1	2	2-3-0	3.33	46.0	-	17	18
KANSAS CITY	0-0-0	0.00	2.0	2	0	1	3-4-0	3.83	56.1	-	24	34
MINNESOTA	0-0-0	7.20	5.0	7	4	2	0-2-0	5.76	29.2	-	19	19
OAKLAND	0-2-0	4.15	8.2	7	4	6	3-2-1	3.27	33.0	-	12	20
SEATTLE	0-0-0	18.00	1.0	3	2	0	3-1-0	4.46	36.1	-	18	17
TEXAS	1-0-0	2.35	7.2	9	2	5	4-1-0	3.11	55.0	-	19	28
AL WEST	1-2-0	4.08	28.2	29	13	16	15-13-1	3.83	256.1	-	109	136
1st HALF	2-2-0	5.47	26.1	37	16	10	14-20-1	4.64	252.1	-	130	118
2nd HALF	3-2-2	1.81	49.2	32	10	22	17-14-4	3.93	291.0	-	127	154
STARTER	-	-	-	-	-	-	18-22-0	6.95	238.1	338	184	162
RELIEVER	5-4-2	3.08	76.0	69	26	32	13-12-5	2.15	305.0	180	73	11i0
in APRIL	0-0-0	11.81	5.1	10	7	2	4-2-1	4.57	63.0	-	32	30
MAY	2-1-0	3.86	9.1	14	4	2	5-8-0	4.96	74.1	-	41	31
JUNE	0-0-0	4.82	9.1	11	5	7	4-7-0	4.32	98.0	-	47	49
JULY	0-0-0	1.47	18.1	9	3	7	5-6-0	4.18	97.0	-	45	51
AUGUST	3-1-1	1.27	21.1	15	3	8	9-3-2	4.17	95.0	-	44	39
SEPT/OCT	0-1-1	2.92	12.1	10	4	7	4-7-2	3.72	116.0	-	48	73

CAREER HIGHS

SEASON: **W** 12 - 1988 **ERA** 3.08 - 1990 **SV** 2 - 1989, 1990
IP 194.2 - 1988 **SO** 106 - 1987

GAME: **Low Hit CG** 1 vs SEA, Aug. 10, 1988
SO 6 Last time at K.C. June 13, 1987 **BB** 6 vs N.Y., May 23, 1987

Last Win vs TEX, Aug. 27, 1990
Last Save at N.Y., Sept. 3, 1990
Last CG at MINN, Oct. 2, 1988
Last ShO at K.C., June 13, 1987
Last GS at MINN, Oct. 2, 1988
Last Relief at OAK, Oct. 2, 1990
Longest Winning Streak 6 - 1988

HOW THEY WERE ACQUIRED
(40-MAN ROSTER)

***FARM SYSTEM* (21)**

BELL	BORDERS	BOUCHER	CROMWELL
DIAZ	DUCEY	HENTGEN	HILL
KEY	KNORR	MacDONALD	MYERS
OLERUD	QUINLAN	SANCHEZ	STIEB
STOTTLEMYRE	SUERO	TIMLIN	WELLS
WHITEN			

***FREE AGENTS* (3)**

DAYLEY TABLER WILLS

***WAIVERS* (1)**

WILLIAMS

***TRADES* (11)**

ACKER	ALOMAR	CARTER	FRASER
GONZALES	LEITER	MULLINIKS	TRLICEK
WARD	WHITE	WILSON	

***ML DRAFT* (3)**

GRUBER LEE RHODES

***COMPENSATION DRAFT* (1)**

HENKE

88 RENE GONZALES

INFIELDER

Born: Sept. 3, 1961 Austin, TX

Resides: Covina, CA

B-R T-R 6-3 195

M.L. Service: 4.024

PERSONAL: Rene Adrian Gonzales...Single...Wears the highest number in BLUE JAYS history-88...Attended California State-Los Angeles where he led his team in doubles and RBI during his junior year...Also played at Glendale Junior College...Graduated from Rosemead High School (California)...Worked as an usher at Dodger Stadium for 2 seasons while in college...His father Ben, played minor league ball between 1956 and 1960.

LAST SEASON: Played at second base, third base, shortstop, rightfield, pinch running and pinch hitting...Saw action in 67 games but batted in only 48 of them...Had 3 hits in a game twice during 1990- May 30th at Minnesota and August 12 at California (at California he had a double, triple and a career high 4 RBI)...Started in the outfield on June 12 vs Milwaukee for his first start there since June 4th, 1988 vs the Yankees...He hit .375 (3-8) with runners on third base...Played 9 games at shortstop in 1990 compared to 4 in his first 3 years with the Orioles.

PROFESSIONAL CAREER: **1982: Was selected by the Expos in the 5th round of the 1982 Free Agent Draft...Hit .213 at Memphis (AA) of the Southern League while playing at shortstop...Played in just 56 games...1983:** Spent the entire season at Memphis where he batted .269 with 16 extra base hits and 44 RBI...Played in 144 games- all at shortstop...Led the Southern League in putouts (258) and fielding average for shortstops (.972)...He also led the league in double plays with 102...**1984:** Began the season with Indianapolis (AAA) of the American Association...Was called up to Montreal and made his debut on July 27th at home vs the Phillies...Returned to Indianapolis until the conclusion of the American Association playoffs...Hit .234 with 32 RBI in 114 games for the AAA club...Closed out the season with Montreal, beginning September 10th...Started 7 consecutive games at shortstop between September 15th and 22nd...Got his first ML hit off of Jerry Koosman at Philadelphia on September 15th...Won a "Silver Glove" with Indianapolis...**1985:** Spent the entire season at AAA Indianapolis where he led American Association shortstops with 345 assists and 79 double plays...Was second in games for shortstops with 127...**1986:** Began the season at Indianapolis of the American Association where he played third base, shortstop and second base...Was recalled by Montreal on July 20th and made three starts at shortstop...Was sent back on July 24th when the Expos obtained Tom Foley...Was recalled again on September 19th and played in 8 of Expos' final 16 games...Established a career high for extra base hits with 19...Was traded to the Orioles on December 16th...**1987:** Began the season with Baltimore, playing at third base, shortstop and second base...Hit .207 (6-29) in 24 games with the Orioles...Was optioned to Rochester (AAA) of the American Association on July 10th where he hit .300 in 42 games...Had a career high 3 triples at Rochester...Returned to Baltimore on September 10th and hit .323 (10-31) in the final 13 games...Hit safely in his first six games after his return to Baltimore...**1988:** Spent the entire season at Baltimore...Started a career high 72 games, including 63 at third base...Played five positions-shortstop, third base, second base, first base and outfield...Batted a club high .361 (13-36) vs the Yankees...Hit .326 in 14 games after moving into the the starting lineup on May 15th...Started 28 of 34 games, May 15 - June 21 and committed just one error during that span...Made 28 straight starts from August 10 - September 9...**1989:** Again spent the full season at Baltimore, playing second base, shortstop and third base...Started the first 12 games of the season and was the Orioles' fifth different starting second baseman in as many years...Made 40 starts at second base and nine at third base...Hit in a personal high six consecutive games, May 3 - June 2 .476 (10-21)...Hit his only home run of the season at Detroit off of rookie pitcher Randy Nosek...Batted .462 during the month of May (6-13).

RENE GONZALES

Year	Club and League	AVG	G	AB	R	H	2B	3B	HR	RBI	SH-SF	HP	BB	SO	SB-CS
1982	Memphis (Sou)	.213	56	183	10	39	3	1	1	11	5-0	3	9	44	2-3
1983	Memphis (Sou)	.269	144	476	67	128	12	2	2	44	16-2	3	40	53	5-2
1984	Indianapolis (AmAs)	.234	114	359	41	84	12	2	2	32	10-4	2	20	33	10-4
1984	MONTREAL (NL)	.233	29	30	5	7	1	0	0	2	0-0	1	2	5	0-3
1985	Indianapolis (AmAs)	.226	130	340	21	77	11	1	0	25	4-1	0	22	49	3-5
1986	Indianapolis (AmAs)	.273	116	395	57	108	14	2	3	43	7-4	2	41	47	8-6
1986	MONTREAL (NL)	.115	11	26	1	3	0	0	0	0	0-0	0	2	7	0-2
1987	BALTIMORE (AL)	.267	37	60	14	16	2	1	1	7	2-0	0	3	11	1-0
1987	Rochester (Int)	.300	42	170	20	51	9	3	0	24	4-4	1	13	17	4-2
1988	BALTIMORE (AL)	.215	92	237	13	51	6	0	2	15	5-2	3	13	32	2-0
1989	BALTOMORE (AL)	.217	71	166	16	36	4	0	1	11	6-1	-	12	30	5-3
1990	BALTIMORE (AL)	.214	67	103	13	22	3	1	1	12	6-0	0	12	14	1-2
NL TOTALS		.179	40	56	6	10	1	0	0	2	0-0	1	4	12	0-5
AL TOTALS		.221	267	566	56	125	15	2	5	45	19-3	3	40	87	9-5
ML TOTALS		.217	307	622	62	135	16	2	5	47	19-3	4	44	99	9-10

GONZALES - TRANSACTIONS

- Selected by Montreal Expos' organization in 5th round of free-agent draft, June 7, 1982.
- Traded to Baltimore Orioles, December 16, 1986, completing deals in which Baltimore traded Pitcher Dennis Martinez to Montreal Expos on June 16, 1986 and Catcher John Stefero to Montreal on December 8, 1986, both for a player to be named later.
- Traded to Toronto Blue Jays, January 15, 1991 in exchange for Pitcher Robert Blumberg.

RENE GONZALES vs AMERICAN LEAGUE

	1990					CAREER				
	AB	H	HR	RBI	AVG	AB	H	HR	RBI	AVG
SEASON	103	22	1	12	.214	566	125	5	47	.221
HOME	47	9	1	3	.191	282	64	3	19	.227
AWAY	56	13	0	9	.232	284	61	2	26	.284
vs BALTIMORE	-	-	-	-	-	-	-	-	-	-
BOSTON	2	0	0	0	.000	48	10	0	3	.208
CLEVELAND	0	0	0	0	.000	14	4	0	1	.286
DETROIT	5	1	0	0	.200	60	9	1	3	.150
MILWAUKEE	1	0	0	0	.000	35	7	0	4	.200
NEW YORK	8	1	0	0	.125	78	23	0	6	.295
TORONTO	6	0	0	0	.000	37	4	0	3	.108
A.L. EAST	22	2	0	0	.091	272	57	1	20	.210
vs CALIFORNIA	19	7	0	5	.368	65	20	0	7	.308
CHICAGO	7	1	0	1	.143	30	7	1	2	.233
KANSAS CITY	5	0	0	0	.000	45	7	0	4	.156
MINNESOTA	19	5	0	1	.263	40	9	0	2	.225
OAKLAND	7	0	0	0	.000	35	6	1	2	.171
SEATTLE	15	4	1	2	.267	60	15	2	5	.250
TEXAS	9	3	0	3	.333	19	4	0	3	.211
A.L. WEST	81	20	1	12	.247	294	68	4	25	.231
Pre-ASG	57	12	1	7	.211	324	75	5	31	.232
Post-ASG	46	10	0	5	.217	242	50	0	14	.207
vs RHP	76	16	1	7	.211	192	49	1	19	.255
LHP	27	6	0	5	.222	374	76	4	26	.203
PINCH HITTING	0	0	0	0	.000	000	2	0	0	.000
DESIGNATED HITTING	-	-	-	-	-	-	-	-	-	-
in APRIL	19	4	1	2	.211	-	-	-	-	-
MAY	32	8	0	5	.250	-	-	-	-	-
JUNE	6	0	0	0	.000	-	-	-	-	-
JULY	8	1	0	0	.125	-	-	-	-	-
AUGUST	33	8	0	5	.242	-	-	-	-	-
SEPT/OCT	5	1	0	0	.200	-	-	-	-	-

CAREER HIGHS

SEASON: **AVG.** .267 - 1987 **H** 51 - 1988 **HR** 2 - 1988
RBI 15-1988 **SB** 5 - 1989

GAME: **H** 4, at PHIL, Sept. 16, 1984 **HR** 1, 5 times
RBI 4, at CALF, Aug. 12, 1990

Last ML HR: vs SEA April 29, 1990
Longest Hitting Streak: 5 - 1988

17 KELLY GRUBER
THIRD BASEMAN

Born: Feb. 26, 1962 Bellaire, TX
Resides: Austin, TX
B-R T-R 6-0 185
M.L. Service: 5.108

PERSONAL: Kelly Wayne Gruber...Married, Lynn Seguin (10/18/86), a former Toronto resident...One son, Kody Robert- (July 4, 1990)...Was four sport standout at Westlake (Texas) High School and named to All-State and All-American teams in senior year, 1980...Was All-District quarterback in football and district qualifier in track...Attended University of Texas for one semester...Was Cleveland's first round selection (10th overall) in June, 1980 Free Agent Draft...Name is pronounced GREW-ber.

LAST SEASON: Labatt's "BLUE" Player of Year...Hit seven Home Runs in his first 17 Games...Was the American League Player of the Week for the week of 4/23-29 (first time)...Was the Labatt's "Blue" Player of the Month for April (.325, 7 HR, 20 RBI), May (.300, 6 HR, 20 RBI) and Sept/Oct(...AL Player of the Month for Sept(.352)...Selected to his second All-Star game- (the first he has played in) ...Tied Willie Mays record of most stolen bases in an All Star game with 2...Ranked third in the AL in fielding for 3rd basemen with a .955 fielding percentage-was first in putouts(123)...Led the BLUE JAYS in hit by pitch category with 8-3rd in AL...Started five games in RF, between 8/4-8...Named AL Player of the Week for the week ending 9/16; (.464 13/28, 2HR, 14RBI, 5R)...Hit .434 vs Cleveland.., Hit .313 with Runners in Scoring Position...Led the BLUE JAYS with 13 Sacrifice Flies- 2nd in AL...Only the 4th BLUE JAY individual to attain 100 or more RBI in a season...Led the BLUE JAYS in RBI with 118, placing him 2nd in the AL in RBI...In September, hit .424, 28-66, 5 HR and 22 RBI...Had a 15 game hit streak from September 10-25 (tying his career high)...Only BLUE JAY regular to bat in the same spot (# 3) in the batting order all season...Had 4, 2HR games in 1990...Only eight of his 31 Home Runs were solo shots...Of his 31 HR, 8 vs LHP/23 vs RHP/23 @ SkyDome/8 on Road...Had career high 48 walks...Winner of the 1990 Rawlings Gold Glove Award for fielding excellence for thirdbasemen...Named to the

Sporting News All-Star Team and UPI team for the American League...Was part of the Major Legaue All-Star team that toured Japan after the 1990 season...In the AL ranked 2nd in RBI(118), 5th in the in HR (31), 2nd in Total Bases (303), 2nd in Extra Base Hits (73), 6th in Slugging Percentage (.512), T7th in Runs (92), 8th in HR frequency, 31HR/592AB, 9th in doubles(36)...Broke Jessie Barfield's record for Home Runs hit at home (22) by hitting (23) at SkyDome this year...

PROFESSIONAL CAREER: **1980: Debuted with Batavia after signing with the Indians...1981: Rebounded well after a dismal year in 1980, setting a career high .290 average...Also hit career high in 2B (25)- 2nd in Carolina League...8th in batting (.290) while leading all Midwest SS in games (125), putouts (180), assists (389) and total chances (569)...1982**: Received first taste of AA ball with Chattanooga and was productive despite a slide in average...**1983**: Was last season in Cleveland chain 4 HR for 3rd straight season...Was also on the Indians' ML roster...Switched to 3B...**1984**: Started the season with the BLUE JAYS, making ML debut, 4/20 at California as a 3B defensive replacement...Youngest player on opening day roster...Optioned to Syracuse on 5/16...Led IL in slugging pct. (.500) and 2nd in HR (21)...Club's Minor League Player of the Month for June (.390, 5HR, 17RBI)...Recalled to parent club on 9/2...After 11 ML AB, 1st ML hit- a PH HR vs Boston's Al Nipper on 9/25...**1985**: Spent the season at Syracuse and was T/3rd in HR (21) while leading his club in HR, K (92) and HBP (7)...Led IL third basemen in games (121), total chances (309) and assists (217)...Named to post season All-Star team...Recalled to TORONTO on 9/1...Appeared in 5 games, primarily as a defensive replacement...**1986**: First full season at ML level...Hit .204, 2 HR, 8 RBI as a game starter in 34 games...1st career inside-the-park HR, 6/12 vs Detroit's Scherrer- was also 1st career 3H game...**1987**: Nagged with a variety of injuries during the season...Then career high 7 game hit streak 5/9-15...Set personal highs with 4H, 2HR, 5/22 at Seattle...Set then personal high with 4 RBI, 8/3 at Chicago...**1988**: Went 4-6, 2 HR, 5 RBI subbing for Mulliniks in the Home Opener on 4/11 vs New York and became the club's regular third baseman...Labatt's "Blue" Player of the Month for April (.288, 3HR, 11RBI)...Then career high 12 game hit streak- 6/22-7/4...Had club's only inside-the-park HR, 5/16 vs Chicago's Jeff Bittiger...Hit on the little finger of the left hand by New York's Dave Eilnad on 8/11 and hit only .258 from that point...Labatt's "Blue" Player of the Month for June (.318, 6HR, 19RBI)...**1989**: Missed starting the season opener due to a sprained middle finger of the left hand sustained on 3/30...Became the fist BLUE JAY to hit for the cycle, 4/16 vs the Royals (1st-solo HR vs Bannister/ 2nd-2R-2B vs Saberhagen/ 7th-2R-3B vs Gordon/ 8th-RBI 1B vs Gleaton)...Tied then career high 4H game and set personal high with 6 RBI...Set personal high with 15 game hit streak- 27-62/.435, 1 HR, 12 RBI), 6/9-23...Set personal high and became the 5th franchise player fo have 5H in a game- 6/12 vs the Tigers...9 consecutive outfield GS, 6/16-24...Returned to 3B on 6/27 at Baltimore, tying club mark with 3 errors...Labatt's "Blue" Player of the Month for June (.351, 4HR, 17RBI)...Injured right hand on 8/9 vs Texas in a collision with 3B umpire Don Denkinger...On DL on 8/19, retroactive to 8/10...Activated on 8/25...18 HR were career high...Picked for All-Star Game but did not play...Hit .471 vs the Royals and .381 vs the Tigers...Hit .308 before All-Star Game and .263 after.

KELLY GRUBER

Year	Club & League	AVG	G	AB	R	H	2B	3B	HR	RBI	SH-SF	HP	BB	SO	SB-CS
1980	Batavia (NYP)	.217	61	212	27	46	3	2	2	19	3-2	3	15	46	6-3
1981	Waterloo (Mid)	.290	127	458	64	133	25	4	14	59	10-2	6	24	85	15-7
1982	Chattanooga (Sou)	.243	128	441	53	107	18	4	13	54	4-7	3	21	89	11-6
1983	Buffalo (East)	.263	111	403	60	106	20	4	15	54	3-2	5	23	44	15-7
1984	Syracuse (Int)	.269	97	342	53	92	12	2	21	55	0-1	7	23	67	12-2
1984	TORONTO (AL)	.063	15	16	1	1	0	0	1	2	0-0	0	0	5	0-0
1985	Syracuse (Int)	.249	121	473	71	118	16	5	21	69	1-5	7	28	92	20-8
1985	TORONTO (AL)	.231	5	13	0	3	0	0	0	1	0-0	0	0	3	0-0
1986	TORONTO (AL)	.196	87	143	20	28	4	1	5	15	2-2	0	5	27	2-5
1987	TORONTO (AL)	.235	138	341	50	80	14	3	12	36	1-2	7	17	70	12-2
1988	TORONTO (AL)	.278	158	569	75	158	33	5	16	81	5-4	7	38	92	23-5
1989	TORONTO (AL)	.290	135	545	83	158	24	4	18	73	0-5	3	30	60	10-5
1990	TORONTO (AL)	.274	150	592	92	162	36	6	31	118	1-13	8	48	94	14-2
ML TOTALS		.266	688	2219	321	590	111	19	83	326	9-26	25	138	351	61-19

CHAMPIONSHIP SERIES RECORD

Year	Club & League	AVG	G	AB	R	H	2B	3B	HR	RBI	SH-SF	HP	BB	SO	SB-CS
1989	TORONTO (AL)	.294	5	17	2	5	1	0	0	1	0-1	0	3	2	1-0

ALL-STAR GAME RECORD

Year	Club & League	AVG	G	AB	R	H	2B	3B	HR	RBI	SH-SF	HP	BB	SO	SB-CS
1989	AL at Calf.						DID NOT PLAY								
1990	AL at Chi (NL)	.000	1	1	0	0	0	0	0	0	0-0	0	1	0	0- 0

GRUBER - TRANSACTIONS

- Selected by Cleveland Indians in 1st round (10th player selected) of free-agent draft, June 3, 1980.
- Drafted by Toronto Blue Jays, December 5, 1983, in Major League Draft.
- On disabled list, August 10 to August 25, 1989.

KELLY GRUBER vs AMERICAN LEAGUE

	1990					CAREER				
	AB	H	HR	RBI	AVG	AB	H	HR	RBI	AVG
SEASON	592	162	31	118	.274	2219	640	83	326	.288
TORONTO	305	89	23	62	.292	1107	297	45	165	.268
ROAD	287	73	8	56	.254	1112	293	38	161	.263
vs BALTIMORE	54	19	4	16	.352	174	57	10	34	.328
BOSTON	55	9	4	13	.164	188	41	10	33	.218
CLEVELAND	53	23	7	17	.434	186	54	9	32	.290
DETROIT	35	9	2	10	.257	159	45	7	30	.283
MILWAUKEE	48	12	2	7	.250	195	56	4	22	.287
NEW YORK	49	14	0	6	.286	191	46	6	27	.241
TORONTO	-	-	-	-	-	-	-	-	-	-
A.L. EAST	294	86	19	69	.293	1093	299	46	178	.274
vs CALIFORNIA	34	7	0	3	.206	166	42	1	12	.253
CHICAGO	47	15	3	9	.319	153	43	7	24	.281
KANSAS CITY	50	11	1	9	.220	155	45	3	21	.290
MINNESOTA	41	14	3	9	.341	157	40	6	21	.255
OAKLAND	45	10	3	6	.222	156	39	8	23	.250
SEATTLE	36	7	1	5	.194	166	38	6	20	.229
TEXAS	45	12	1	8	.267	173	44	6	27	.254
A.L. WEST	298	76	12	49	.255	1126	291	37	148	.258
Pre-ASG	321	95	20	66	.296	1251	360	49	190	.288
Post-ASG	271	67	11	52	.247	968	230	34	136	.238
vs RHP	426	113	23	84	.265	1472	391	61	224	.266
LHP	166	49	8	34	.295	747	199	22	102	.266
PINCH HITTING	2	1	0	3	.500	36	8	2	8	.222
DESIGNATED HITTING	1	1	0	3	1.000	12	2	1	4	.167
in APRIL	83	27	7	20	.325	263	82	15	51	.312
MAY	100	30	6	20	.300	415	114	13	55	.275
JUNE	116	35	7	24	.302	434	133	21	73	.306
JULY	89	15	2	11	.169	376	82	11	38	.218
AUGUST	102	21	1	12	.206	341	75	6	38	.220
SEPT/OCT	102	34	8	31	.333	390	104	17	71	.267

CAREER HIGHS

SEASON: **AVG.** .290-1989 **H** 162-1990 **HR** 31-1990
RBI 118-1990 **SB** 23-1988

GAME: **H** 5-at DET. June 12, 1989; vs NY April 11, 1988
HR 2-6 times; last Sept. 8, 1990 vs CHI (AL) **RBI** 6-vs K.C. Sept. 8, 1990
SB 1-61 times [2 in 1990 ALL-STAR GAME]

Last ML HR: Sept. 29, 1990 at BOST
Longest Hitting Streak: 15 - 1989

PLAYERS WITH MOST SEASONS WITH BLUE JAYS

SEASONS	PLAYER	YEARS
12	Jim Clancy	1977-88
12	Ernie Whitt	1977-78; 1980-89
12	Dave Stieb	1979-1990
10	Lloyd Moseby	1980-90
9	Rance Mulliniks	1982-90
9	Jesse Barfield	1981-89
9	George Bell	1981; 1983-90
8	Tony Fernandez	1983-90
7	Damaso Garcia	1980-86
7	Kelly Gruber	1984-90
7	Jimmy Key	1984-90

50 TOM HENKE
PITCHER

Born: Dec. 21, 1957 Kansas City, MO
Resides: Jefferson City, MO
B-R T-R 6-5 225
M.L. Service: 6.059

PERSONAL: Tom Anthony Henke...Married the former Kathleen (Kathy) Swoboda on 9/13/80...Four children, Ryan (1/13/81), Kimberly (11/10/83), Amanda (7/18/86), and Lindsay (10/7/89)...Graduated from Blair Oaks High School in Wardsville, Missouri in 1976...Attended East Central Junior College in Union, MO., with a degree in building construction...Hobbies include fishing, hunting and trapping...Is a bricklayer by trade.

LAST SEASON: Is the TORONTO BLUE JAYS All-Time leader in saves with 151(186 opportun-ites)...His 32 saves(6th in AL), was the second highest season save total of his career (34 in '87)...Had 32 saves in 38 opportunities...Finished 7th in the AL in the Rolaids Relief Man standings with 80 points...Averaged better than a strikeout per inning; has accomplished this feat 5 out of the 6 seasons he has been with the BLUE JAYS...Allowed only 18 earned runs in '90...ERA for the month of June was 0.73 (8G, 12.1IP, 6SV, 1R/ER, 1BB, 13K)...Labatt's "Blue" Pitcher of the Month for the month of June (0-0-6, .73ERA, 8G, 13K, 1BB)...Was his 5th season in a row with at least 20 saves or more...Blew just 6 save opportunities ...Had a 0.75ERA for the month of August (12.0IP, 1R/ER, 1BB, 12K, 9G)...Opposing Batting Average was .213 and with Runners in scoring position was .130

PROFESSIONAL CAREER: **1980**: Turned professional after being selected by the Rangers in the 4th round (secondary phase) of the 6/80 Free Agent Draft after being previously selected by the Cubs and Mariners...Split the season between Sarasota (Rookie) and Asheville (A) posting a combined 3-5 record in 13 games, 9GS...**1981**: Split the season between Asheville and Tulsa (AAA) of the American Association...Combined for a 12-9 record...Used primarily in relief...**1982**: Enjoyed his finest season leading the Texas League in games (52), 2nd in GF (42) and T/3rd in SV (14)...Major League debut- September 10/82...Won his 1st ML game 9/29 vs the Athletics pitching 3 shutout innings...**1983**: Posted a 9-6 record at Oklahoma City prior to being promoted to the Rangers on 8/11...Recorded first ML save, 8/20 vs White Sox...Allowed one run in his first eight innings covering four appearances after being recalled on August 11/83...**1984**: Split the season between Oklahoma City (AAA) and Texas...Broke camp with Texas before being optioned on 4/24...Recalled on 6/27 but returned on 7/1...Returned to Texas on 8/9 for remainder of season...Used primarily in short relief...At Oklahoma City, was one of four American Association pitchers to have more strikeouts than IP (64.2IP/65K)...Gave up one HR in 65 innings with Oklahoma City and none in his 28 innings with Texas...**1985**: Started the season with Syracuse (AAA) where he posted an amazing 2-1-18 record and an 0.88ERA allowing only 5 ER and 13 hits in 58.1 innings...Tied for International League lead in saves (18) and led all pitchers in batting average against (.081)...Did not allow a run 4/19-7/1 (38.0IP)...Named to IL All-Star Team and was named Most Valuable Pitcher...BLUE JAYS Minor League Pitcher of the Month for May...Contract purchased by TORONTO on 7/28...Recorded wins at Baltimore in 1st 2 appearances, 7/31 and 8/1...Led AL in SV (8) during August and set new club mark for 1 month...13 SV in 15 SV situations...Labatt's "Blue" Pitcher of the Month for August...**1986**: Career high 7 K, 5/10 vs Seattle...Allowed a HR to Seattle's Dave Henderson on 5/10: his first HR to a righ-handed batter in 244 faced at ML level...Won 6 in a row 5/31-9/1...Became club's first pitcher to save both ends of a double-header, 8/27 at Cleveland...8 SV in September/October to tie then club mark...3rd on AL SV (27), 9th in appearances (63) while averaging 11.63K/9.0IP...**1987**: 3rd overall in AL Rolaids Relief Award standings behind Dave Righetti and Jeff Reardon...18 consecutive ShO appearances (21.2IP) to start season...Rolaids AL Reliever for July setting club mark with 10 SV...Named to AL All-Star team- pitched 2.2 innings...Only 2nd time that a pitcher without a win has been named to a mid-summer classic team...Struck out seven consecutive batters over two games 8/20-22...Set club mark with 28th save, 8/20 at Oakland...Rolaids AL Reliever of the Month for August (0-1-7, 2.00ERA, 13 games)...Averaged 12.26K/9IP- highest in ML...Set club marks and career highs inSV (34) as well as career highs in games (92), IP (94.0) and strikeouts (128)...Most appearances in a winless season by any pitcher on baseball history (72)...Among league leaders in saves (1st) and appearances (3rd)...Named as Relief Pitcher on UPI AL All-Star team and Baseball America All-Star team...**1988**: Won 7-6 at California on 7/19 for 1st win in 120 games, dating back to 9/1/86...Also snapped 9 game losing streak...Lost consecutive outings 7/22 and 7/25 for first time in ML...Among league leaders in SV (T/7th-25)...Successful in 25 of 29 save situations (86.2%)- best in AL...**1989**: 100th save for the BLUE JAYS, opening day 4/3 at Kansas City...did not have consecutive scoreless outings from 4/9-5/13...Won last 7 decisions of the season and did not lose a game after 4/30...Allowed a 3R PH HR to Boston's Heep on 7/2 for only ER (1) in 19 games 6/13-7/31...Saved a 10-8 win at Oakland on 6/23 for 1st SV since 4/7...Labatt's "Blue" Pitcher of the Month for July (0-0-6, 0.55ERA, 12 games)...Held opposition scoreless in 13 consecutive appearances 8/7-9/9...Blew his first save since 5/2 at Detroit on 9/26...3 saves in last week of season as well as the AL East clincher vs the Orioles on 9/30...Among league leaders in GF (T/4th-56)...15 of 20 SV after the All-Star game and 11 of 20 from August through season's end with 0.91 ERA- (5ER, 49.0IP)...Rolaids AL Reliever for the Month of July (0-0-6, 0.55ERA, 12 games)...Named BLUE JAYS Pitcher of the Year by BBWAA.

TOM HENKE

Year	Club & League	W-L	ERA	G	GS	CG	ShO	SV	IP	H	R	ER	HR	HB	BB	SO	WP
1980	Sarasota (Gulf)	3-3	0.95	8	4	1	1	0	38	33	11	4	0	4	12	34	2
1980	Asheville (SAL)	0-2	7.83	5	5	0	0	0	23	25	21	20	5	3	20	19	11
1981	Asheville (SAL)	8-6	2.93	28	8	0	0	3	92	77	36	30	5	3	35	67	6
1981	Tulsa (Tex)	4-3	3.94	15	0	0	0	1	32	31	16	14	2	2	14	37	1
1982	Tulsa (Tex)	3-6	2.67	52	1	0	0	14	87.2	69	35	26	8	3	40	100	5
1982	TEXAS (AL)	1-0	1.15	8	0	0	0	0	15.2	14	2	2	0	1	8	9	0
1983	Okla. City (AmAs)	9-6	3.01	47	0	0	0	2	77.2	71	33	26	2	2	33	90	1
1983	TEXAS (AL)	1-0	3.38	8	0	0	0	1	16.0	16	6	6	1	0	4	17	0
1984	TEXAS (AL)	1-1	6.35	25	0	0	0	2	28.1	36	21	20	0	1	20	25	2
1984	Okla. City (AmAs)	6-2	2.64	39	0	0	0	7	64.2	59	21	19	1	1	25	65	5
1985	Syracuse (Int)	2-1	0.88	39	0	0	0	18	51.1	13	5	5	2	1	18	60	1
1985	TORONTO (AL)	3-3	2.03	28	0	0	0	13	40.0	29	12	9	4	0	8	42	0
1986	TORONTO (AL)	9-5	3.35	63	0	0	0	27	91.1	63	39	34	6	1	32	118	3
1987	TORONTO (AL)	0-6	2.49	72	0	0	0	34	94.0	62	27	26	10	0	25	128	5
1988	TORONTO (AL)	4-4	2.91	52	0	0	0	25	68.0	60	23	22	6	2	24	66	0
1989	TORONTO (AL)	8-3	1.92	64	0	0	0	20	89.0	66	20	19	5	2	25	116	2
1990	TORONTO (AL)	2-4	2.17	61	0	0	0	32	74.2	58	18	18	8	1	19	75	6
ML TOTALS		29-26	2.72	381	0	0	0	154	517.0	404	168	156	40	27	165	596	18

CHAMPIONSHIP SERIES RECORD

Year	Club & League	W-L	ERA	G	GS	CG	ShO	SV	IP	H	R	ER	HR	HB	BB	SO	WP
1985	TORONTO (AL)	2-0	4.26	3	0	0	0	0	6.1	5	3	3	1	0	4	4	0
1989	TORONTO (AL)	0-0	0.00	3	0	0	0	0	2.2	0	0	0	0	0	0	3	0
LCS Totals		2-0	3.00	6	0	0	0	0	9.0	5	3	3	1	0	4	4	0

ALL-STAR GAME RECORD

Year	Club & League	W-L	ERA	G	GS	CG	ShO	SV	IP	H	R	ER	HR	HB	BB	SO	WP
1987	AL at Oak.	0-0	.00	0	0	0	0	0	2.2	2	0	0	0	0	0	1	0

HENKE - TRANSACTIONS

- Selected by Seattle Mariners in 20th round of free-agent draft, June 5, 1979.
- Selected by Chicago Cubs in secondary phase of free-agent draft, January 8, 1980.
- Selected by Texas Rangers in secondary phase of free-agent draft, June 3, 1980.
- Selected by Toronto Blue Jays' organization in player compensation pool draft, January 24, 1985. (Toronto received compensation for Texas Rangers' signing of free agent Designated Hitter Cliff Johnson, a Type A player, December 5, 1984.

TOM HENKE vs AMERICAN LEAGUE

	1990						CAREER					
	W-L-S	ERA	IP	H	ER	SO	W-L-S	ERA	IP	H	ER	SO
SEASON	2-4-32	2.17	74.2	58	18	75	29-26-154	2.72	516.1	404	156	596
TORONTO	2-0-16	2.39	37.2	31	10	40	15-7-70	2.42	219.1	157	59	263
ROAD	0-4-16	1.95	37.0	27	8	35	14-19-84	2.94	297.0	247	97	333
vs BALTIMORE	1-1-3	4.15	8.2	4	4	4	5-2-10	3.12	40.1	27	14	48
BOSTON	1-1-1	5.79	4.2	6	3	7	2-1-12	2.78	32.1	31	10	40
CLEVELAND	0-0-1	5.40	5.0	7	3	4	3-1-9	2.61	41.1	27	12	45
DETROIT	0-0-1	1.42	6.1	5	1	6	2-1-17	1.67	43.0	27	8	48
MILWAUKEE	0-0-3	0.00	7.2	6	0	5	1-2-9	3.66	39.1	38	16	43
NEW YORK	0-0-4	3.86	4.2	3	2	8	1-4-13	5.08	44.1	45	25	54
TORONTO	-	-	-	-	-	-	-	-	-	-	-	-
A.L. EAST	2-2-13	3.16	37.0	31	13	34	14-11-70	3.18	240.2	195	85	278
vs CALIFORNIA	0-2-3	2.00	9.0	7	2	9	4--5-11	2.23	48.1	36	12	54
CHICAGO	0-0-3	0.00	5.0	1	0	6	3-0-16	1.43	44.0	33	7	47
KANSAS CITY	0-0-1	6.75	4.0	7	3	6	1-1-12	2.78	32.1	31	10	39
MINNESOTA	0-0--3	0.00	6.1	4	0	5	1-3-13	3.12	43.1	36	15	48
OAKLAND	0-0-4	1.93	4.2	3	1	8	1-2-10	3.67	34.1	30	14	51
SEATTLE	0-0-3	0.00	4.0	1	0	2	2-2-8	2.50	36.0	21	10	38
TEXAS	0-0-2	0.00	4.2	4	0	5	3-2-4	1.19	30.1	22	4	41
A.L. WEST	0-2-19	1.43	37.2	27	6	41	15-15-84	2.41	268.2	209	72	318
Pre-ASG	0-1-16	1.54	41.0	25	7	40	12-12-68	3.00	228.1	175	76	259
Post-ASG	2-3-16	2.94	33.2	33	11	35	17-14-86	2.49	288.2	239	80	337
STARTER	-	-	-	-	-	-	-	-	-	-	-	-
RELIEVER	2-4-32	2.17	74.2	58	18	75	29-26-154	2.72	516.3	404	156	596
in APRIL	0-0-1	2.89	9.1	11	3	8	3-4-15	4.17	49.2	45	23	53
MAY	0-1-5	1.76	15.1	9	3	19						
JUNE	0-0-6	0.73	12.1	4	1	13	5-2-25	2.66	70.3	56	21	80
JULY	0-1-9	3.38	13.1	12	5	12	4-4-32	2.36	83.3	50	22	96
AUGUST	1-0-5	0.75	12.0	12	1	12	5-2-35	1.97	118.2	97	26	141
SEPT/OCT	1-2-6	3.65	12.1	10	5	11	8-9-33	2.98	120.3	107	40	136

CAREER HIGHS

SEASON: **WINS** 9-1986 **ERA** 1.15-1982 **SV** 34-1987
IP 94.0-1987 **SO** 128 - 1987

GAME: **LOW HIT CG** Never **SO** 7-at SEA May 10, 1986; vs NY April 11, 1988
BB 4-at MILW June 26, 1987; vs DET Sept 12, 1986.

Last Win: vs BALT Sept. 16, 1990
Last Save: at BALT Oct. 2, 1990
Last CG: Never
Last ShO: Never
Last Relief: at BALT Oct. 3, 1990
Longest Winning Streak: 7 - 1989

WINNING PITCHERS VIA HENKE SAVES

(BLUE JAYS ONLY)

PITCHER	1990	1989	1988	1987	1986	1985	TOTAL
Jim Acker	1	–	–	–	1	–	2
Doyle Alexander	–	–	–	–	2	2	4
Bud Black	1	-	-	-	-	-	1
Willie Blair	1	-	-	-	-	-	1
Dewayne Buice	–	1	–	–	–	–	1
Tony Castillo	–	1	–	–	–	–	1
Bill Caudill	–	–	–	–	1	–	1
John Cerutti	7	1	3	4	1	1	17
Jim Clancy	–	–	1	3	5	0	9
Steve Cummings	–	1	–	–	–	–	1
Mark Eichhorn	–	–	–	5	9	0	14
Tom Filer	–	–	–	–	–	3	3
Mike Flanagan	–	1	2	2	–	–	5
Mauro Gozzo	-	1	–	–	–	–	1
Tom Gilles	1	-	-	-	-	-	1
Joe Johnson	–	–	–	2	1	–	3
Jimmy Key	5	5	4	7	3	3	27
Dennis Lamp	–	–	–	–	1	1	2
Gary Lavelle	–	–	–	1	–	1	2
Jeff Musselman	–	–	2	5	–	–	7
Jose Nunez	–	–	–	1	–	–	1
Dave Stieb	8	2	7	3	3	2	25
Todd Stottlemyre	3	2	2	–	–	–	7
Duane Ward	1	–	3	1	–	–	5
David Wells	3	4	1	–	–	–	8
Frank Wills	1	1	–	–	–	–	2
Totals	32	20	25	34	27	13	151

41 PAT HENTGEN

PITCHER

Born: Nov. 13, 1968 Detroit, MI

Resides: Fraser, MI

B-R T-R 6-2 200

M.L. Service: 0.000

PERSONAL: Patrick George Hentgen...Single...1986 graduate of Fraser High School...Played varsity baseball for 3 years and varsity football for 2 years...Was captain of the baseball team...Baseball hero is Dwight Gooden...Original baseball position was SS...Hobbies include: fishing and waterskiing...Had been offered a baseball scholarship at Western Michigan University.

LAST SEASON: Spent the season at Knoxville (AA) of the Southern League...Led the Knoxville starters in ERA with 3.05 (28G, 26GS, 153.1IP, 57R, 52ER, 10HR, 68BB, 142K)...Was second in the Southern League in K (142)...Opponents hit just .218 against him...Finished 6th in the League in ERA in'90.

PROFESSIONAL CAREER: **1986:** Turned professional with St. Catharines (Summer A) of the New York-Penn League and helped them to a league title...Used primarily as a game starter and had trouble with control (30BB/40IP)...**1987:** Led the South Atlantic League in GS (31) and in IP (188)...4th in batting average allowed (.214), fewest baserunners allowed per 9 innings (10.16) and caught stealing against (.600)...**1988:** Led the FSL in GS (30) while with Dunedin...4th in K (125)...Was the game starter in a combined no-hitter (Willie Blair and Entique Burgos) at Osceola on 5/10...10 K in 5.0 IP, 8/13 vs Tampa...**1989:** Finished second in the FSL in GS (28) and strikeouts (148)...Placed 8th in ERA (2.68)...Struck out 8.73 batters per nine innings as a starter-3rd in FSL...Opponents batted only .219 against him...Went 8-4 with a 2.14 ERA after 5/15.

PAT HENTGEN

Year	Club & League	W-L	ERA	G	GS	CG	ShO	SV	IP	H	R	ER	HR	HB	BB	SO	WP
1986	St. Catharines (NYP)	0-4	4.50	13	11	0	0	1	40.0	38	27	20	3	2	30	30	3
1987	Myrtle Beach (SAL)	11-5	2.35	32	31	2	2	0	188.0	145	62	49	5	8	60	131	14
1988	Dunedin (FSL)	3-12	3.45	31	30	0	0	0	151.1	139	80	58	10	4	65	125	14
1989	Dunedin (FSL)	9-8	2.68	29	28	0	0	0	151.1	123	53	45	5	6	71	148	16
1990	Knoxville (Sou)	9-5	3.05	28	26	0	0	0	153.1	121	57	52	10	3	68	142	8

HENGTEN - TRANSACTIONS

- Selected by Blue Jays in 5th round (133rd overall) in June, 1986, Free Agent Draft.

24 GLENALLEN HILL

OUTFIELDER

Born: March 22, 1965 Santa Cruz, CA

Resides: Santa Cruz, CA

B-R T-R 6-2 210

M.L. Service: 1.034

PERSONAL: Glenallen Hill...Married...Wife's name, Mika...Graduated from Santa Cruz High School in 1983 where he was named All-County in basketball and named Player-of-the-Year in football...Also played varsity basketball...Nicknamed "Thrill".

LAST SEASON: Had a season high hit streak of six games from 4/25-5/1...Batted .310 (27/83) during the month of April...Had his first career 2 HR game vs Seattle on 5/17...Was Hill's first full season at the Major League level...Placed on the D.L. (15 day) retroactive to July 6th due to cuts and scrapes on both feet, knees and right elbow due to a nightmare- arachnophobia...Had two 4 RBI games this season, setting a career high...Started 68 games in 1990, 32 in RF/22 in LF/14 as DH...Hit his second career Grand Slam home run on August 14th at Chicago...Had an emergency appendectomy in Boston on 10/1...Hit .236, (33-140) at home as opposed to hitting .225 (27-120) on the road...Hit .250 with runners in scoring position (14-56)...Struck out once every 4.2 at bats.

PROFESSIONAL CAREER: **1983**: Debuted with Medicine Hat and batted .256...**1984**: Tied for 4th in the league with 16 HR and named to Baseball America's South Atlantic All-Star team...**1985**: Spent the season with Kinston (A) where he was 2nd in the league with 20 HR and 4th with 42 SB...Led the club in HR, RBI, SB and K (211)...**1986**: Spent the season with Knoxville (AA) of the Southern League and led the league in TB (286), HR (31) and AB (570)...BLUE JAYS' 1st player in minor league system to hit 30+ HR in a season...Named to National Association Class AA and Southern League All-Star team...Won R. Howard Webster Award as club's MVP...Still led league in K (153) but figure was decreased significantly...**1987**: Contract assigned outright to Syracuse (AAA) of International League on 3/28 after being on the major league roster since 11/13/85...Led the IL in games, (137) and 2nd in AB (536)...47 of 126 hits went for extra bases...**1988**: Started the season with Syracuse (AAA) of the IL appearing in 51 games wtih 40 hits and 59 K...Optioned to Knoxville (AA) of the Southern League on 6/6...2 HR and 7 RBI, 7/16 vs Jacksonville...Combined for 134 K in 130 games, his lowest total since rookie year of 1983...**1989**: Played entire season at Syracuse (AAA) of IL...HIt .316 for April (24-76)...Hit 312 for June (34-109)...Batted .309 on the road with 6 HR and 26 RBI in 53 games, compared to .280 at home with 2 HR and 19 RBI, 53 games...10 of 45 RBI vs Columbus...Purchased by the BLUE JAYS on 7/31...ML debut 7/31 vs the Yankees, going 2-3, 1 RBI...Optioned to Syracuse on 8/2 after 2 appearances...Recalled to TORONTO for 9/1...Hit only career grand slam HR, 9/1 vs the Twins' Mark Guthrie...Was 1st ML extra base hit and set personal high for RBI with 4...Appeared in 17 games in September/October, hitting safely in 12 of them...Among IL leaders in runs (1st-86), TB (1st-279), 3B (1st 15), RBI (T/4th-72), Slugging Pct. (1st-.578), AB (T/4th-483), Hits (1st-155) and HR (1st-21)...Named to IL All-Star team...Seven OF errors was most in the league...Winner of the R. Howard Webster Award as Syracuse's MVP.

GLENALLEN HILL

Year	Club & League	AVG	G	AB	T	H	2B	3B	HR	RBI	SH-SF	HP	BB	SO	SB-CS
1983	Medicine Hat (Pio)	.256	46	133	26	34	3	4	6	27	2-0	1	17	49	4-4
1984	Florence (SAL)	.239	129	440	75	105	19	5	16	64	0-6	3	63	150	30-15
1985	Kinston (Caro)	.210	131	466	57	98	13	0	20	56	2-4	1	57	211	42-15
1986	Knoxville (Sou)	.277	141	570	87	158	23	6	31	97	0-13	1	39	153	18-19
1987	Syracuse (Int)	.235	137	536	65	126	25	6	16	77	1-5	1	25	151	22-9
1988	Syracuse (Int)	.233	51	172	21	40	7	0	4	19	0-3	2	15	59	7-2
1988	Knoxville (Sou)	.264	79	269	37	71	13	2	12	38	0-3	2	28	75	10-4
1989	Syracuse (Int)	.321	125	483	86	155	31	15	21	72	3-4	5	34	107	21-7
1989	TORONTO (AL)	.288	19	52	4	15	0	0	1	7	0-0	0	3	12	2-1
1990	TORONTO (AL)	.231	84	260	47	60	11	3	12	32	0-0	0	18	62	8-3
ML TOTALS		.240	103	312	51	75	11	3	13	39	0-0	0	21	74	10-4

HILL - TRANSACTIONS

- Selected by Toronto Blue Jays in 9th round (219th overall), June, 1983 Free Agent Draft.
- On disabled list July 6-23, 1990.

DÉJA VU: Tom Henke became the first Blue Jays pitcher to record saves in both ends of a doubleheader, August 27, 1988 at Cleveland...Henke pitched one shutout inning to secure a 3-2, 12 inning win in the opener and then 1.2 shutout innings (3 strikeouts) to preserve a 6-3 win in the nightcap...Henke duplicated the feat, saving both ends of a July 17, 1989 doubleheader against the Angels (6-4; 5-4)...David Wells was the winning pitcher in both games.

GLENALLEN HILL vs AMERICAN LEAGUE

	1990					CAREER				
	AB	H	HR	RBI	AVG	AB	H	HR	RBI	AVG
SEASON	260	60	12	32	.231	312	75	13	39	.240
TORONTO	140	33	7	17	.236	160	38	8	21	.238
AWAY	120	27	5	15	.225	152	37	5	18	.243
vs BALTIMORE	17	5	1	2	.294	23	7	1	2	.304
BOSTON	6	1	0	0	.167	6	1	0	0	.167
CLEVELAND	31	8	3	5	.258	43	12	3	7	.279
DETROIT	32	5	1	4	.156	38	5	1	4	.132
MILWAUKEE	18	3	0	2	.167	24	6	0	2	.250
NEW YORK	32	7	0	3	.219	35	9	0	4	.257
TORONTO	-	-	-	-	-	-	-	-	-	-
A.L. EAST	136	29	5	16	.213	169	40	5	19	.237
vs CALIFORNIA	17	5	1	3	.294	17	5	1	3	.294
CHICAGO	19	8	1	5	.421	23	9	1	5	.391
KANSAS CITY	20	4	1	1	.200	23	4	1	1	.174
MINNESOTA	29	6	1	2	.207	41	9	2	6	.220
OAKLAND	9	1	0	0	.111	9	1	0	0	.111
SEATTLE	7	3	2	4	.429	7	3	2	4	.429
TEXAS	23	4	1	1	.174	23	4	1	1	.174
A.L. WEST	124	31	7	16	.250	143	35	8	20	.245
Pre-ASG	142	34	7	20	.239	142	34	7	20	.239
Post-ASG	118	26	5	12	.220	170	41	6	19	.241
vs RHP	117	28	7	20	.239	138	35	7	22	.254
LHP	143	32	5	12	.224	174	40	6	17	.230
PINCH HITTING	7	2	0	0	.286	7	2	0	0	.286
DESIGNATED HITTING	56	17	0	3	.196	63	13	0	3	.
in APRIL	42	13	2	4	.310	42	13	2	4	.310
MAY	56	9	3	8	.161	56	9	3	8	.161
JUNE	36	8	1	6	.222	36	8	1	6	.222
JULY	34	9	3	5	.265	37	11	3	6	.297
AUGUST	71	17	3	9	.239	74	17	3	9	.230
SEPT/OCT	21	4	0	0	.190	67	17	1	6	.254

CAREER HIGHS

SEASON: **AVG**. .288-1989 **H** 60-1990 **HR** 12-1990
RBI 32 - 1990 **SB** 8 - 1990

GAMES: **H** 3-vs SEA May 17, 1990; vs NY June 22, 1990: vs CAL July 5, 1990
HR 2-vs SEA May 17, 1990
RBI 4-vs MINN Sept. 1, 1989; vs SEA May 17, 1990; at CHI Aug. 14, 1990
SB: 1 - 10 times

Last ML HR: at CHI Aug. 14, 1990
Longest Hitting Streak: 7 - 1989

47 STEVE KARSAY

PITCHER

Born: March 24, 1972 Flushing, NY
Resides: College Point, NY
B-R T-R 6-3 185
M.L. Service: 0.000

PERSONAL: Steven Andrew Karsay...Single...Graduate of Christ the King High School in Queens, New York, 1990...Was named Player of the Year in his senior year of high school baseball...Favourite baseball player is Don Mattingly...Enjoys watching college basketball.

LAST SEASON: Played at St. Catharines (A) of the New York-Penn League where he compiled a 1-1 record with a 0.79 ERA while pitching 22.2 innings and appearing in 5 games (all game starts)...Struck out 25 while walking just 12 batters...Was sent to the Florida Instructional League in the off-season at Dunedin.

STEVE KARSAY

Year	Club & League	W-L	ERA	G	GS	CG	ShO	SV	IP	H	R	ER	HR	HB	BB	SO	WP
1990	St. Catharines (NYP)	1-1	0.79	5	5	0	0	0	22.2	11	4	2	0	0	12	25	0

KARSAY - TRANSACTIONS

- Selected in 1st round (22nd overall) of June 1990, Free Agent Draft.

22 JIMMY KEY
PITCHER

Born: April 22, 1961 Huntsville, AL
Resides: Tarpon Springs, FL
B-R T-L 6-1 190
M.L. Service: 7.000

PERSONAL: James Edward Key...Married (9/24/83)...Wife's name, Cynthia (Cindy) who doubles as his agent...Daughter, Jordan...Met at Clemson University where both were attending on athletic scholarships (baseball and swimming respectively)...Graduated from Butler High School in 1979...Attended Clemson University majoring in Recreation and Park Administration...Was All-Conference in 1982 as DH-LHP...In 1982, led club with 116 innings and a 2.79 ERA while compiling a 9-3 record...Set club mark with 21-2B and enjoyed a career .300 average...Named as Clemson's MVP first team ACC Pitcher and DH as well as the All-Regional team...Participated in the College World Series once while attending Clemson (freshman year) and the Regionals twice...Hobbies include hunting and fishing...Drafted by Chicago White Sox in 10th round (6/79) but did not sign...Club's co-player representative.

LAST SEASON: Began the 1990 campaign with a 4-1 record in his first five decisions...Experienced a pulled right hamstring in late May, causing him to be placed on the 15-day D.L. on 6/1, retroactive to 5/23...Spent time rehabilitating his hamstring in Dunedin- going 2-0, 2.50 ERA...Had a 2.12 ERA for the month of July; (5G/GS, 34.0IP, 27J, 8R/ER, 7BB, 14K)...All Time franchise leader in LHP wins (83)...Was named Labatt's "BLUE" Pitcher of the Month for the month of August-(3-1, 3.38ERA, 6G/GS, 37.1IP, 14ER, 24K, 1BB) and Sept/Oct...Longest outing of the seaon was 8.1IP vs Detroit on 8/7...Had a 4-1 strikeout to walk ratio- (best among starters)...Had a NO-HITTER through 5 innings vs Baltimore on 9/14 before leaving after feeling a slight twinge in his right hamstring...After being activated from the D.L. on 6/22 he was (7-5, 17GS, 106.2IP, 2.95ERA...K high was 7 vs Minnesota on 8/18...Gave up just 22 BB in 154.2IP- best on the BLUE JAYS...Won four of his last five starts...LH batters hit only .182...Opposition Batters hit .352 in 1st inning of work.

PROFESSIONAL CAREER: **1982: Debuted with Medicine Hat prior to being promoted to Florence on 7/15...Combined that year for a 7-3 record with a 3.24 ERA...1983**: Started the season with Knoxville (AA) and was named organization's Pitcher of the Month for April (2-1, 0.70ERA)...Threw a two-hitter vs Savannah, 4/14...Subsequently promoted to Syracuse (AAA) where he was 5-8 and made 1st professional relief appearance...**1984**: Was 1st ML season and was the only rookie to spend the entire season with the club...ML debut, 4/6 at California, winning 11-5...1st ML SV, 3-2 at Texas on 4/13...Retired first 16 batters faced...Set club rookie mark in SV (10) and then club marks for games (63) and appearances (63)...Had been invited to camp as a non-roster player...Ninth in AL in appearances (63)...**1985**: Lost 1st ML GS, 7-2 at Baltimore, 4/12...Became the first BLUE JAYS' starting LHP to win a game since Paul Mirabella when he defeated California 6-3 on 5/1...1st ML CG, 6-1 vs Chicago on 5/20...Won 6 in a row, 5/1-6/27...Carried a no-hitter into the ninth on 6/6 vs Detroit leaving the game after 10 IP having allowed 2H, 0R...18 consecutive scoreless IP, 6/1-16 without registering a decision...Appeared in All-Star game, retiring only batter faced...Led club with 2.12 BB/9IP (10th in AL) and was 2nd on club (4th in AL) in ERA (3.00), winning percentage (.700-5th in AL) and wins (14)...Did not lose two consecutive starts...**1986**: 1st ShO and one-hitter, 5-0 vs Chicago on 5/22 allowing a 2-out 5th inning single to Ozzie Guillen...Labatt's "Blue" Pitcher of the Month for June (3-2, 2.09ERA)...Set career K high with 10, 7/7 vs Seattle...Twice tied career high of 10IP, 6/7 vs Milwaukee and 7/27 at Oakland...Labatt's "Blue" Pitcher of the Year...11th in AL in ERA (3.57) and T/5th in GS (35)...Season totals of 14-8, 2.70ERA after first seven games (0-3, 13.05ERA)...9-4 vs teams above .500...Allowed only one HR to a left handed batter (Rich Gedman)...**1987**: Second to Roger Clemens in Cy Young balloting...Named to The Sporting News AL All-Star team and was publications AL Pitcher of the Year...Named to Baseball America AL All-Star team...Labatt's "Blue" Pitcher of the Year, after capturing Labatt's honours for April (4-1, 3.03ERA)), June (2-2, 1.55ERA) and July (4-1, 2.87ERA)...Career high 8 games win streak, 7/16-9/25...3ER or less in 30 of 36GS...Career highs in wins (17 [tying then a club mark]), IP (261.0), ERA (2.76 [led AL]) and K (161)...Led BLUE JAYS' staff with an average of 7.25 innings per start...Named Alabama's Pro Athlete of the Year...**1988**: Won season opener 5-3 at Kansas City on 4/4 becoming 1st pitcher in franchise history to win consecutive home openers...Experienced swelling in left elbow on 4/14 after losing to New York on 4/13...Placed on 15-day DL on 4/15 and underwent arthroscopic surgery on 5/4 for the removal of 2 bone chips (Dr. James Andrews)...Moved to 21-day DL on 5/16...Medical rehabilitation assignment at Dunedin (A) on 6/10-29...Activated from DL on 6/29 and won first 4 GS and five of 1st six...Labatt's "Blue" Pitcher of the Month for July (3-1, 2.25ERA)...Among league leaders in winning percentage (4th-.706), ShO (T/8th-2)...Named to ML team which toured Japan at season's end...**1989**: Club's Opening Day pitcher, winning 4-3 at Kansas City on 4/3...Also won Home Opener 3-0 vs Kansas City on 4/14...Back-to-back CG's, 3-2 vs Seattle on 5/10 and 5-3 vs Cleveland on 5/15...Won a season high 4 in a row 5/10-26 vs (Seattle, Cleveland, Chicago)...Set personal high with 10 K vs Oakland 4/24...Through 5/26, had held opposition to 3 ER or less in 9 of 1st 12 GS...3 BB in 8 GS, 4/24-5/31...Was losing pitcher in SkyDome Opener, 6/5 (5-3 vs Milwaukee)...Was 1-11, 5.74 ERA in 13 GS, 5/31-8/3...Included 6 losses in as many GS, 7/5-8/3 and a career high 7 games losing streak,6/25-8/3...On 15-day DL, 8/4-19 with a mild inflamation of the left shoulder...Returned from DL and won his first 4 GS and first 5 decisions...After returning from DL was 6-1, 9 GS, 53.0 IP, 20 ER, 3.40 ERA...Among the league leaders in GS (T/10th-33), BB/9IP (1st-1.10), ER (10th-93)...Won club's only ALCS game vs Oakland, 7-3 (Game #4 10/6)...Underwent arthroscopic surgery on his left shoulder (Dr. James Andrews) on 10/24 to repair a partial tear of the left rotator cuff.

JIMMY KEY

Year	Club & League	W-L	ERA	G	GS	CG	ShO	SV	IP	H	R	ER	HR	HB	BB	SO	WP
1982	Med. Hat (Pio)	2-1	2.30	5	5	1	0	0	31.1	27	12	8	0	0	10	25	1
1982	Florence (SAL)	5-2	3.72	9	9	0	0	0	58.0	59	33	24	10	4	18	49	2
1983	Knoxville (Sou)	6-5	2.85	14	14	2	0	0	101.0	86	35	32	4	5	40	57	6
1983	Syracuse (Int)	4-8	4.13	16	15	2	0	0	89.1	87	58	41	14	3	33	71	6
1984	TORONTO (AL)	4-5	4.65	63	0	0	0	10	62.0	70	37	32	8	1	32	44	3
1985	TORONTO (AL)	14-6	3.00	35	32	3	0	0	212.2	188	77	71	22	2	50	85	6
1986	TORONTO (AL)	14-11	3.57	36	35	4	2	0	232.0	222	98	92	24	3	74	141	3
1987	TORONTO (AL)	17-8	2.76	36	36	8	1	0	261.0	210	93	80	24	2	66	161	8
1988	TORONTO (AL)	12-5	3.29	21	21	0	0	0	131.1	127	55	48	13	5	30	65	1
1988	Dunedin (FSL)	2-0	0.00	4	4	0	0	0	21.1	15	2	0	1	0	1	11	0
1989	TORONTO (AL)	13-14	3.88	33	33	5	1	0	216.0	226	99	93	18	3	27	118	4
1990	TORONTO (AL)	13-7	4.25	27	27	0	0	0	154.2	169	79	73	20	1	22	88	0
ML TOTALS		87-56	3.47	251	184	20	4	10	1269.2	1212	538	489	129	17	301	702	25

+ Appeared in one game as a pinch-runner, 1985.

ALL-STAR GAME RECORD

Year	Club & League	W-L	ERA	G	GS	CG	ShO	SV	IP	H	R	ER	HR	HB	BB	SO	WP
1985	AL at Minn.	0-0	0.00	1	0	0	0	0	.1	0	0	0	0	0	0	0	0

CHAMPIONSHIP SERIES RECORD

Year	Club & League	W-L	ERA	G	GS	CG	ShO	SV	IP	H	R	ER	HR	HB	BB	SO	WP
1985	TORONTO (AL)	0-1	5.19	2	2	0	0	0	8.2	15	5	5	1	0	2	5	0
1989	TORONTO (AL)	1-0	4.50	1	1	0	0	0	6.0	7	3	3	1	0	2	2	0
LCS Totals		1-1	4.91	3	3	0	0	0	14.2	22	8	8	2	0	4	7	0

KEY - TRANSACTIONS

- Selected by Chicago White Sox in 10th round of free-agent draft, June 5, 1979.
- Selected by Toronto Blue Jays in 3rd round of free-agent draft, June 7, 1982.
- On disabled list, Apriln 15 to June 29, 1988; included rehabilitation disability assignment to Dunedin, June 10 to June 27, 1988.
- On disabled list, August 4 to August 19, 1989.
- On disabled list, May 23 to June 22, 1990: included rehabilitation assignment to Dunedin June 7 to June 18, 1990.

JIMMY KEY vs AMERICAN LEAGUE

	1990						CAREER					
	W-L-S	ERA	IP	H	ER	SO	W-L-S	ERA	IP	H	ER	SO
SEASON	13-7-0	4.25	154.2	169	73	88	87-56-10	3.47	1268.1	1212	489	702
TORONTO	7-3-0	4.47	88.2	97	44	52	46-32-3	3.57	688.1	658	273	378
ROAD	6-4-0	3.95	66.0	72	29	36	41-24-7	3.35	580.0	554	216	324
vs BALTIMORE	0-0-0	3.60	10.0	7	4	5	6-7-0	4.31	94.0	99	45	51
BOSTON	1-1-0	5.00	18.0	24	10	12	7-3-0	3.00	102.0	97	34	49
CLEVELAND	1-0-0	1.80	5.0	5	1	3	9-4-1	4.50	116.0	119	58	63
DETROIT	3-1-0	4.62	25.1	31	13	13	8-6-1	2.84	120.1	114	38	84
MILWAUKEE	2-0-0	3.46	13.0	11	5	11	6-5-1	3.23	92.0	78	33	49
NEW YORK	1-0-0	6.17	11.2	15	8	8	8-6-1	3.17	133.1	142	47	62
TORONTO	-	-	-	-	-	-	-	-	-	-	-	-
A.L. EAST	8-2-0	4.45	83.0	93	41	52	44-31-4	3.49	657.2	649	255	358
vs CALF	-	-	-	-	-	-	5-4-0	3.73	99.0	91	41	54
CHICAGO	1-1-0	5.40	10.0	15	6	5	12-5-3	2.82	121.1	103	38	68
KANSAS CITY	1-0-0	1.50	6.0	5	1	4	6-4-0	2.89	81.0	67	26	48
MINNESOTA	1-1-0	4.50	10.0	13	5	10	4-1-2	3.14	43.0	42	15	29
OAKLAND	0-2-0	3.94	16.0	17	7	7	4-7-0	3.77	93.0	93	39	48
SEATTLE	2-1-0	5.94	16.2	13	11	6	9-2-0	4.33	89.1	87	43	52
TEXAS	0-0-0	1.38	13.0	13	2	4	3-2-0	3.51	82.0	80	32	44
A.L. WEST	5-5-0	4.02	71.2	76	32	36	43-25-5	3.46	608.2	563	234	343
Pre-ASG	5-4-0	6.10	59.0	78	40	28	43-33-4	3.63	645.1	609	260	363
Post-ASG	8-3-0	3.10	95.2	91	33	60	44-23-5	3.30	623.4	603	229	329
STARTER	13-7-0	4.25	154.2	169	73	88	82-51-0	3.30	1200.3	1140	457	654
RELIEVER	-	-	-	-	-	-	5-5-10	5.50	68.2	72	42	48
in APRIL	2-1-0	5.21	19.0	25	11	10	12-9-1	4.19	156.2	154	73	89
MAY	2-1-0	8.10	16.2	21	15	7	14-7-3	4.14	186.3	176	86	98
JUNE	0-1-0	7.84	10.1	19	9	5	10-11-0	2.80	195.3	174	61	116
JULY	2-2-0	2.12	34.0	27	8	14	15-12-0	3.46	252.0	248	97	129
AUGUST	3-1-0	3.38	37.1	41	14	24	17-10-3	3.47	207.1	206	80	109
SEPT/OCT	4-1-0	3.86	37.1	36	16	28	17-10-3	2.93	270.2	254	92	161

CAREER HIGHS

SEASON: **W** 17-1987 **ERA** 2.76-1987 **SV** 10-1984
IP 261.0-1987 **SO** 161-1987

GAME: **Low Hit CG** 1-at CHI Aug. 22, 1986
SO 10-vs OAK April 24, 1989; July 7, 1986 vs SEA **BB** 6-at CALF July 17, 1986

Last Win: at BOST Sept. 30, 1990 **Last Save:** vs MILW Sept. 20, 1984
Last CG: vs CALF July 18, 1989 **Last ShO:** vs K.C. April 14, 1989
Last Relief: at CALF May 8, 1986 **Longest Winning Streak:** 8 - 1987

49 RANDY KNORR

CATCHER

Born: Nov. 12, 1968 San Gabriel, CA

Resides: Baldwin Park, CA

B-R T-R 6-2 205

M.L. Service: 0.000

PERSONAL: Randy Duane Knorr...Single...A 1986 graduate of Baldwin Park High School...Earned All-League and All-Valley honours in baseball...Baseball hero is Dale Murphy...Enjoys reading.

LAST SEASON: Played at Knoxville (AA) in the Southern League and hit .276 with 51 R, 13 HR, 64 RBI, 31 BB, 83K...He led the team in starts at the catcher position with 96...He was second in RBI with 64...Overall, appeared in 116 games...Was second on the team in sacrifice flies with 6...Had a .327 on base percentage.

PROFESSIONAL CAREER: **1986: Played 55 games at first base for Medicine Hat (Rookie) of the Pioneer League...Averaged more than a hit per game (58H/55 games)...On DL with dislocated left shoulder, 6/24-7/4...Underwent surgery on 12/4...1987:** Started the season with Myrtle Beach (A) of the South Atlantic League prior to being sent to Medicine Hat on 6/5...8 HR, 16 RBI in first 14 games...Recalled to Myrtle Beach on 7/19 and hit .342 for the remainder of the season...Led SAL catchers in games (117), TC (960) and putouts (870)...Was 2nd consecutive season that he had split time as DH-C...**1988:** Spent the entire season with Myrtle Beach appearing in 117 games, setting a personal high in RBI (42) and tying personal high with 13 doubles...**1989:** Spent the season with Dunedin (A) of the Florida State League...Appeared in only 33 games, driving in 23 runs and averaging close to 1 H per game (32H/33 games)...Didn't play after 5/10 due to a sprain of the medial collateral ligament of the left knee...Attended the Florida Instructional League, batting .307 and proceeded to play winter baseball in the Australian Baseball League for Melbourne...ABL Player of the Week for period ending 11/29...Had 5 HR in 1st 6 games.

RANDY KNORR

Year	Club & League	AVG	G	AB	T	H	2B	3B	HR	RBI	SH-SF	HP	BB	SO	SB-CS
1986	Medicine Hat (Pio)	.270	55	215	21	58	13	0	4	32	3-3	0	17	53	0-0
1987	Myrtle Beach (SAL)	.264	46	129	17	34	4	0	6	21	0-2	0	6	46	0-0
1987	Medicine Hat (Pio)	.292	26	106	21	31	7	0	10	24	0-3	1	5	26	0-0
1988	Myrtle Beach (SAL)	.234	117	364	43	85	13	0	9	42	9-2	0	41	91	0-1
1989	Dunedin (FSL)	.262	33	122	13	32	6	0	6	23	0-2	0	6	21	0-2
1990	Knoxville (Sou)	.276	116	392	51	108	12	1	13	64	4-6	2	31	83	0-3

KNORR - TRANSACTIONS

- Selected by Toronto Blue Jays in 10th round. (263rd overall) in June 1986, Free Agent Draft.
- On disabled list June 24—July 4, 1986.
- On disabled list May 10—September 1, 1989.

4 MANNY LEE

SHORTSTOP

Born: June 17, 1965 San Pedro de Macoris, DR

Resides: San Pedro de Macoris, DR

B-S T-R 5-9 161

M.L. Service: 4.149

PERSONAL: Manuel Lora Lee...Completed one year of college in the Dominican Republic prior to singing with the Mets on May 10, 1982 as a free agent...Was signed by Mets' scout Eddy Toledo...Single...Grew up on same street as Pedro Guerrero.

LAST SEASON: Played in 117 games most in his career...His 6 HR were a career high for a season (career total prior to '90 was 7)...Ranked 1st among American League second basemen in fielding with a .993 fielding percentage- Only 4 errors...Hit .306 (11/36) in April...Had a career high hit streak of 9 games- 5/17-30...At the All-Star Break was hitting .271 (45-166)...Had 95 hits; the second highest season total of his career (111 in '88)...Batted .248 with runners in scoring position...All of his 6 HR came vs LHP...Did not hit a home run after the ALL-STAR Break...After becoming the everyday second baseman after the Liriano trade on 7/27, hit .240 (46-192), 0HR, 21RBI...Is first All-Time, among BLUE JAY second basemen in fielding percentage for a season (.993), surpassing Damaso Garcia (.985) in 1986.

PROFESSIONAL CAREER: **1982**: Turned professional after signing as a free agent on 5/10...Spent season both at 2B and SS appearing in only 16 games and setting a career high in SH (2)...**1983**: Spent season with Little Falls (NY-PENN) and Sarasota (Gulf Coast) batting a combined .261 with 17 RBI...**1984**: Spent season with Columbia (A) of SAL where he led the league in batting (.329) finished third in on-base-percentage (.424) and was named as the league's ALL-STAR SS...**1985**: Was youngest and only teenager in ML on Opening Day...ML debut, as a PR, 4/10 at Kansas City...1st ML hit vs Cleveland's Rick Behenna, 6/2 (2nd game)...Started 4 games, 1st one being 6/23 vs Boston (2B)...Used primarily as a defensive replacement and PR...**1986**: Started the season with Syracuse (AAA) of the IL prior to being sent to Knoxville (AA) of the Southern League on 5/6...Recalled to Syracuse on 6/18...Promoted to TORONTO on 8/11 appearing for 1st time on 8/19 vs Chicago...1st ML RBI, 8/27 vs Cleveland...1st ML HR, 8/29 vs Minnesota's Smithson...**1987**: Started the season with Syracuse (AAA) of the IL before contract was purchased by the BLUE JAYS on 5/27...Went 1-3 vs California for 1st ML hit since 9/22/86...Tied personal high with 3 H, 6/9 at New York...Assigned outright to Syracuse on 7/23...Contract purchased by BLUE JAYS on 8/30 and became the regular SS on 9/25 with Fernandez undergoing elbow surgery...2nd career HR, 3R vs Detroit's Alexander on 9/2...**1988**: Started the season on DL with tendinitis in his right shoulder...Activated on 4/12...On DL 5/12-6/1 with contusion of right shoulder...8 game hit streak 9/6-25...Didn't play after 9/25 due to pulled right hamstring...**1989**: Started the season at 2B and moved to SS on 4/7-5/1 when Fernandez was disabled...Hit .225 in the 20 GS at SS...Set personal high with 4 H, 4/11 at New York...Sprained left ankle in 1B slide at Anaheim on 4/29...21-day DL 4/30-6/2...Hit .349 in 1st 16 games after returning from DL...Hit .352 in June...RBI on 7/17 vs Angels, snapped 17 game drought...Started the first game of a double header on 7/17 at SS for his first GS at SS since 4/29...Filled in defensively at RF on 7/5 vs the Orioles for only ML outfield appearance...1st HR of season, 2R shot vs Cecilio Guante, 7/24 at Texas...Tied personal highs with 3 RBI games 8/6 vs the Yankees and 9/22 at Milwaukee...Started 2 of 5 ALCS games vs Oakland...Hit .429 vs Chicago, .367 vs Texas and .345 vs Detroit...Hit .295 vs LHP...Hit .279 before the All-Star break and .239 afterward.

MANNY LEE

Year	Club & League	AVG	G	AB	T	H	2B	3B	HR	RBI	SH-SF	HP	BB	SO	SB-CS
1982	Kingsport (Appy)	.222	16	54	2	12	1	0	0	3	2-0	0	3	12	0-1
1983	Little Falls (NYP)	.289	17	45	10	13	0	0	0	5	2-0	0	9	11	2-1
1983	Sarasota (Gulf)	.247	32	97	8	24	2	1	0	12	1-0	1	13	14	2-3
1984	Columbia (SAL)	.329	102	346	84	114	12	5	2	33	1-4	0	60	42	24-6
1985	TORONTO (AL)	.200	64	40	9	8	0	0	0	0	1-0	0	2	9	1-4
1986	Knoxville (Sou)	.272	41	158	21	43	1	2	0	11	0-1	0	20	29	8-4
1986	Syracuse (Int)	.246	76	236	34	58	6	1	1	19	3-0	0	21	39	7-9
1986	TORONTO (AL)	.205	35	78	8	16	0	1	1	7	2-1	0	4	10	0-1
1987	Syracuse (Int)	.283	74	251	25	71	9	5	3	26	3-2	0	18	50	2-2
1987	TORONTO (AL)	.256	56	121	14	31	2	3	1	11	1-1	0	6	13	2-0
1988	TORONTO (AL)	.291	116	381	38	111	16	3	2	38	4-4	0	26	64	3-3
1989	TORONTO (AL)	.260	99	300	27	78	9	2	3	34	1-1	0	22	60	4-1
1990	TORONTO (AL)	.243	117	391	45	95	12	4	6	41	1-3	0	26	90	3-1
ML TOTALS		.259	487	1311	141	339	39	13	13	131	10-10	0	86	246	13-11

LEE - TRANSACTIONS

- Signed as free agent by New York Mets' organization, May 10, 1982.
- On disabled list, April 9 to April 22, 1984.
- Traded with Outfielder Gerald Young to Houston Astros, August 31, 1984, as partial completion of deal in which New York Mets acquired Infielder Ray Knight for three players to be named later, August 28, 1984; Houston acquired Pitcher Mitch Cook to complete deal, September 10, 1984.
- Drafted by Toronto Blue Jays, December 3, 1984.
- On disabled list, March 28 to April 12 and May 12 to June 1, 1988.
- On disabled list, April 30 to June 6, 1989.

CHAMPIONSHIP SERIES

Year	Club & League	AVG	G	AB	R	H	2B	3B	HR	RBI	SH-SF	HP	BB	SO	SB-CS
1985	TORONTO (AL)	.000	1	0	0	0	0	0	0	0	0-0	0	0	0	0-0
1989	TORONTO (AL)	.250	2	8	2	2	0	0	0	0	0-0	0	0	1	0-0

TORONTO CLIMATE

	High	Low	Rain	Rain days/ MO		High	Low	Rain	Rain days/ MO
Jan. . . .	30°F	16°F	2.7"	16	July . . .	79°F	59°F	2.9"	10
Feb. . . .	30°F	15°F	2.4"	12	Aug. . .	77°F	58°F	2.7"	9
Mar. . . .	37°F	23°F	2.6	13	Sept. . .	69°F	51°F	2.9"	12
Apr. . . .	50°F	34°F	2.5"	12	Oct. . . .	56°F	40F°	2.4"	11
May . . .	63°F	44°F	2.9"	13	Nov. . .	43°F	31°F	2.8"	13
June . . .	73°F	54°F	2.7"	11	Dec. . .	33°F	21°F	2.6"	13

Temperatures shown above are daily highs and lows for the month indicated, based on weather bureau statistics from previous years. Rain days per month indicates the number of days (on average) that measurable precipitation is recorded.

MANNY LEE vs AMERICAN LEAGUE

	1990					CAREER				
	AB	H	HR	RBI	AVG	AB	H	HR	RBI	AVG
SEASON	391	95	6	41	.243	1311	339	13	131	.259
TORONTO	190	50	2	19	.263	639	164	6	62	.257
AWAY	201	45	4	22	.224	672	175	7	69	.260
vs BALTIMORE	24	4	0	2	.167	99	25	0	5	.253
BOSTON	29	6	0	0	.207	67	14	2	2	.209
CLEVELAND	36	7	0	2	.194	96	23	0	7	.240
DETROIT	31	5	2	4	.161	149	37	3	17	.248
MILWAUKEE	33	11	0	8	.333	108	35	0	16	.324
NEW YORK	36	11	1	7	.306	132	40	2	22	.303
TORONTO	-	-	-	-	-	-	-	-	-	-
A.L. EAST	189	44	3	23	.233	651	174	7	69	.267
vs CALIFORNIA	33	9	0	1	.273	110	29	0	12	.264
CHICAGO	23	4	0	1	.174	64	17	0	6	.266
KANSAS CITY	29	10	0	1	.345	112	29	1	7	.259
MINNESOTA	34	8	0	2	.235	101	23	1	8	.228
OAKLAND	34	6	2	6	.176	114	24	2	12	.211
SEATTLE	18	4	1	1	.222	73	17	1	4	.233
TEXAS	31	10	0	6	.323	86	26	1	13	.302
A.L. WEST	202	51	3	18	.252	660	165	6	62	.250
Pre-ASG	166	45	6	19	.271	579	156	7	55	.269
Post-ASG	225	50	0	22	.222	732	183	6	76	.250
vs RHP	213	52	0	21	.244	781	189	4	66	.242
LHP	178	43	6	20	.242	530	150	9	65	.283
PINCH HITTING	0	0	0	0	.000	21	4	0	1	.190
DESIGNATED HITTING	-	-	-	-	-	24	3	0	4	.125
in APRIL	36	11	0	3	.306	160	40	0	15	.250
MAY	48	13	5	8	.271	78	17	5	9	.218
JUNE	62	17	1	6	.274	251	78	2	26	.311
JULY	69	11	0	6	.159	244	58	1	23	.238
AUGUST	95	21	0	11	.221	284	73	4	33	.257
SEPT/OCT	81	22	0	7	.272	294	73	1	25	.248

CAREER HIGHS

SEASON: **AVG.** .291-1988 **H** 111-1988 **HR** 6 -1990
RBI 41 - 1990 **SB** 4-1989

GAME: **H** 4 - April 11, 1989 at NY **HR** 1-13 times
RBI 3- 7 times (last Aug. 29, 1990 vs MILW) **SB** 1-13 times

Last ML HR: June 17, 1990 at NY
Longest Hitting Streak: 9 - 1990

28 AL LEITER

PITCHER

Born: Oct. 23, 1965 Toms River, NJ

Resides: North Caldwell, NJ

B-L T-L 6-3 215

M.L. Service 2.033

PERSONAL: Alois Terry Leiter...Married the former Lorene Salsburg (01/26/91)...Graduate of Central Regional High School in Bayville, NJ. (1984) where he played baseball, football and track, leading the baseball team to the state championship...An All-American selection for baseball and All-county in football for 1984...Older brother Kurt was a pither in Baltimore chain from 1982-1984 while other brother Mark, is currently in the Yankees' organization...Hobbies include: water sports, college basketball...Favourite city- Chicago, favourite stadium- Anaheim Stadium...A fan of Bruce Springsteen...Most memorable moment- 1st 6 ML outs were strikeouts.

LAST SEASON: Started the season with Dunedin(A) of the Florida State League...Was sent to Syracuse on May 20th and placed on DL...Activated from DL on June 13th....At Syracuse (AAA) he was 3-8 with a 4.62ERA in 15G, 14GS, 78.0IP, 43R, 40ER, 4HR, 68BB, 69K...Made first GS on June 16th vs Richmond...Did not allow a home run in his final 42.0 IP...Was 2-2, 1.151ERA in his last 7GS...Was called up on September 4th to TORONTO...Was used in relief and went 0-0, 4G, 6.1IP, 1H, 0R/ER for a 0.00ERA...Longest outing was 3.0 innings vs Baltimore on 9/13.

PROFESSIONAL CAREER: **1984**: Selected by the Yankees in 2nd round (regular phase) of 6/84 Free Agent Draft and began professional career with Oneonta (A) of the New York- Penn League...48 K in 57.0 IP...**1985**: Started season with Ft. Lauderdale (A) or FSL losing 6 of 7 decisions in 17 GS...Finished season at Oneonta and was 2.37 ERA with 34 K in 38 IP...**1986**: Started the season with Ft. Lauderdale of the FSL winning 4 of 12 decisions with one CG being a 2H 6-0 ShO of West Palm Beach on 5/24...Sidelined with bruised left elbow from 7/26-8/8...In 21 GS, allowed 6 or more BB six times...**1987**: Started the season with Columbus (AAA) of the IL but disabled on 5/1 with a broken nose sustained while running sprints in the OF...Reinstated on 5/23

Leiter (cont...)

re-optioned to Albany on 5/24...Placed on DL again on 6/14 with tender left shoulder...Activated on 7/3 and remained at Albany until being re-optioned to Columbus on8/27...Recalled by the Yankees on 9/10...2 GS in IL playoffs winning both decisions...Pitched for Yankees vs Atlanta in Hall of Fame game on 7/27 with 2 scoreless innings...ML debut, a GS vs the Brewers on 9/15...Became the youngest player to play for Yankees (21+ years) since Jose Rijo appeared on 7/6/84 at Minnesota...Was the 48th man to play for the Yankees that season, breaking the club mark...Became youngest game starter to win a game since Gene Nelson (6/4/81- 20 yrs)...1st ML loss, 9/20, 6-2 at New York to the BLUE JAYS allowing HR to BELL and LIRIANO...**1988**: Opponents batted .213 against him, 2nd lowest on team...Only Yankees pitcher to record more K (60) than IP (57.1)...Won 1st three GS striking out 23 in 20 IP... Forced to leave 5/6 game at Texas with flu-like symptoms...No-hitter through 5.2 IP vs Angels on 5/24 before allowing a Joyner single...**1989**: Lost his 1st GS of the season, 11-1 to the Indians at New York despite 9 strikeouts in 5.1 IP...1st win of the season, 8-5 at New York vs the Twins on 4/14...Fell 1 K short of personal high with 10...Marked 3rd time in career that he had reached double figures in strikeouts...Also set personal high with 9 BB and was the most by a Yankees' pitcher since Bob Shirley walked 9...Lost last appearance with Yankees, a 5-3 verdict at Kansas City on 4/26...Traded to TORONTO for outfielder Jessie Barfield on April 30...Was placed on the DL shortly after the trade due to a sore left shoulder...Pitched on rehabilitation at Dunedin before undergoing arthroscopic surgery on September 6.

AL LEITER

Year	Club & League	W-L	ERA	G	GS	CG	ShO	SV	IP	H	R	ER	HR	HB	BB	SO	WP
1984	Oneonta (NYP)	3-2	3.63	10	10	0	0	0	57.0	52	32	23	1	2	26	48	5
1985	Ft. Laud'dale (FSL)	1-6	6.48	17	17	1	0	0	82.0	87	70	59	3	2	57	44	3
1985	Oneonta (NYP)	3-2	2.37	6	6	2	0	0	38.0	27	14	10	5	1	6	12	0
1986	Ft. Laud'dale (FSL)	4-8	4.05	22	21	1	1	0	117.2	96	64	53	2	5	90	101	7
1987	Columbus (Int)	1-4	6.17	5	5	0	0	0	23.1	21	18	16	1	0	15	23	3
1987	Albany (East)	3-3	3.35	15	14	2	0	0	78.0	64	34	29	4	2	37	71	3
1987	NEW YORK (AL)	2-2	6.35	4	4	0	0	0	22.2	24	16	16	2	0	15	28	4
1988	Columbus (Int)	0-2	3.46	4	4	0	0	0	13.0	5	7	5	0	3	14	12	1
1988	NEW YORK (AL)	4-4	3.92	14	14	0	0	0	57.1	49	27	25	1	0	14	33	2
1989	NEW YORK (AL)	1-2	6.08	4	4	0	0	0	26.2	23	20	18	1	2	21	22	1
1989	TORONTO (AL)	0-0	4.05	1	1	0	0	0	6.2	9	3	3	1	0	2	4	1
1989	Dunedin (FSL)	0-2	5.63	3	3	0	0	0	8.0	11	5	5	0	0	5	4	0
1990	Dunedin (FSL)	0-0	2.63	6	6	0	0	0	24.0	18	8	7	1	0	12	14	2
1990	Syracuse (Int)	3-8	4.62	15	14	1	1	0	78.0	59	43	40	4	5	68	69	5
1990	TORONTO (AL)	0-0	0.00	4	0	0	0	0	6.1	1	0	0	0	0	2	5	0
ML TOTALS		7-8	4.66	27	23	0	0	0	119.2	106	66	62	5	2	73	119	8

LEITER - TRANSACTIONS

- Selected by New York Yankees' organization in 2nd round of free-agent draft, June 4, 1984.
- On disabled list, June 22 to July 26, 1988; included rehabilitation disability assignment to Columbus, July 17 to July 25, 1988.
- Traded to Toronto Blue Jays for Outfielder Jesse Barfield, April 30, 1989.
- On disabled list, May 11, 1989 through remainder of season; included rehabilitation disability assignment to Dunedin, August 12 to August 29, 1989.

AL LEITER vs AMERICAN LEAGUE

	1990						CAREER					
	W-L-S	ERA	IP	H	ER	SO	W-L-S	ERA	IP	H	ER	SO
SEASON	0-0-0	0.00	6.1	1	0	5	7-8-0	4.66	119.2	106	62	119
TORONTO	0-0-0	0.00	5.0	1	0	5	1-0-0	2.75	19.2	14	6	11
ROAD	0-0-0	0.00	1.1	0	0	0	6-8-0	5.04	100.0	92	56	108
vs BALTIMORE	0-0-0	0.00	3.0	0	0	2	1-0-0	3.72	9.2	8	4	12
BOSTON	0-0-0	0.00	1.0	0	0	0	0-2-0	15.26	7.2	11	13	3
CLEVELAND	0-0-0	0.00	2.0	1	0	3	0-2-0	5.79	18.2	17	12	19
DETROIT	-	-	-	-	-	-	0-0-0	1.23	7.1	6	1	6
MILWAUKEE	0-0-0	0.00	0.1	0	0	0	2-0-0	1.35	13.1	8	2	15
NEW YORK	-	-	-	-	-	-	-	-	-	-	-	-
TORONTO	-	-	-	-	-	-	1-1-0	5.02	14.1	11	8	18
A.L. EAST	0-0-0	0.00	6.1	1	0	5	4-5-0	5.68	63.1	60	40	69
vs CALIFORNIA	-	-	-	-	-	-	1-0-0	2.93	15.1	15	5	14
CHICAGO	-	-	-	-	-	-	-	-	-	-	-	-
KANSAS CITY	-	-	-	-	-	-	0-1-0	5.54	13.0	9	8	7
MINNESOTA	-	-	-	-	-	-	2-0-0	3.46	13.0	13	5	15
OAKLAND	-	-	-	-	-	-	0-0-0	0.00	0.0	1	0	0
SEATTLE	-	-	-	-	-	-	-	-	-	-	-	-
TEXAS	-	-	-	-	-	-	0-2-0	5.14	7.0	7	4	10
A.L. WEST	-	-	-	-	-	-	3-3-0	2.41	82.0	74	42	79
Pre-ASG	-	-	-	-	-	-	5-5-0	4.69	80.2	74	42	79
Post-ASG	0-0-0	0.00	6.1	0	0	0	2-3-0	4.62	39.0	31	20	35
STARTER	-	-	-	-	-	-	7-8-0	4.92	113.1	105	62	114
RELIEVER	0-0-0	0.00	6.1	1	0	5	0-0-0	0.00	6.1	1	0	5
in APRIL	-	-	-	-	-	-	4-2-0	4.78	52.2	43	28	51
MAY	-	-	-	-	-	-	1-2-0	3.63	22.1	23	9	24
JUNE	-	-	-	-	-	-	0-1-0	7.94	6.2	8	5	4
JULY	-	-	-	-	-	-	-	-	-	-	-	-
AUGUST	-	-	-	-	-	-	-	-	-	-	-	-
SEPT/OCT	0-0-0	0.00	6.1	1	0	6	2-3-0	4.62	39.0	32	20	40

Leiter (cont...)

CAREER HIGHS

SEASON:	**W** 4-1988 **IP** 57.1-1988	**ERA** 3.92-1988 **SO** 60 - 1985	**SV** NONE
GAME:	**SO** 11 vs TOR April 14, 1988		**BB** 6 vs CALF May 3, 1988

Last Win vs MINN April 14, 1989
Last Relief at BOST Sept. 29, 1990

45 BOB MacDONALD

PITCHER

Born: April 27, 1965 East Orange, NJ

Resides: Toms River, NJ

B-L T-L 6-2 180

M.L. Service: 0.046

PERSONAL: Robert Joseph MacDonald...Single...1983 graduate of Point Pleasant Beach High School...Named to All-Ocean County team in baseball and member of the championship team in his senior year...Also played football and basketball...Attended Rutgers University where he played baseball...Played in the New Jersey League against former BLUE JAY pitcher, Jeff Musselman.

LAST SEASON: Began the season with Syracuse(AAA)...Assigned to Knoxville Blue Jays (AA) in the Southern League on May 4th where he went 1-2, 1.89ERA, 36G, 29GF, 57.0IP, 17R, 12ER, 15SV, 29BB, 54K...Led the Knoxville Blue Jays in saves with 15...Was called up to TORONTO on Aug. 13th and made three appearances in relief...Optioned to Syracuse on Aug. 29 and returned to the BLUE JAYS on Sept. 4th...Made one appearance in Sept., a one batter relief outing on the 23rd vs Cleveland...With TORONTO, was 0-0, 0.00ERA, 4G, 2.1IP, 2BB, 0K.

PROFESSIONAL CAREER: 1987: Turned professional with St. Catharines (A) of the New York-Penn League...Made only one GS prior to being assigned to Medicine Hat (Rookie) of the Pioneer League on 6/23...Was used exclusively in relief...Promoted to Myrtle Beach (A) of the South Atlantic League on 7/25...**1988:** Spent the season with Myrtle Beach...Led SAL in GF (48), 2nd in appearances (52), 4th in SV (15) and relief points (43)...**1989:** Started the season with Knoxville (AA) of the Southern League, striking out close to 1 batter per inning (58K/63IP)...Led club in games (43) and SV (9)...Promoted to Syracuse (AAA) of the International League on 7/31...Made 12 relief appearances for the Chiefs.

Bob MacDONALD

Year	Club & League	W-L	ERA	G	GS	CG	ShO	SV	IP	H	R	ER	HR	HB	BB	SO	WP
1987	St. Catharines (NYP)	0-0	4.50	1	1	0	0	0	4.0	8	4	2	0	0	0	4	0
1987	Myrtle Beach (SAL)	2-1	5.66	10	0	0	0	0	20.2	24	18	13	1	0	7	12	2
1988	Myrtle Beach (SAL)	3-4	1.69	52	0	0	0	15	53.1	42	13	10	2	0	18	43	2
1989	Knoxville (Sou)	3-5	3.29	43	0	0	0	9	63.0	52	27	23	0	2	23	58	0
1989	Syracuse (Int)	2-0	5.63	12	0	0	0	0	16.0	10	1	0	0	1	6	12	0
1990	Knoxville (Sou)	1-2	1.89	36	0	0	0	15	57.0	37	17	12	2	0	29	54	3
1990	Syracuse (Int)	0-2	5.40	9	0	0	0	2	8.1	4	5	5	1	0	9	6	0
1990	TORONTO (AL)	0-0	0.00	4	0	0	0	0	2.1	0	0	0	0	0	0	2	0

MacDONALD - TRANSACTIONS

- Selected by Toronto Blue Jays in 19th round (491st overall) in June 1987, Free Agent Draft.

OFFICIAL MILEAGES BETWEEN CITIES
AMERICAN LEAGUE

	BAL	BOS	CAL	CHI	CLE	DET	KC	MIL	MIN	NY	OAK	SEA	TEX	TOR
BAL		370	2329	622	314	404	961	641	936	184	2456	2334	1209	384
BOS	370		2611	867	563	632	1257	860	1124	187	2704	2496	1561	446
CAL	2329	2611		1744	2053	1979	1363	1756	1536	2475	337	954	1235	2176
CHI	622	867	1744		316	238	403	66	334	740	1835	1720	802	436
CLE	314	563	2053	316		94	695	328	622	425	2151	2021	1021	193
DET	404	632	1979	238	94		630	237	528	504	2068	1927	987	214
KC	961	1257	1363	403	695	630		436	394	1113	1498	1489	460	8224
MIL	641	860	1756	67	328	237	436		297	746	1845	1694	853	420
MIN	936	1124	1536	334	624	528	394	297		1028	1578	1399	852	679
NY	184	187	2475	740	425	504	1113	746	1028		2576	2421	1391	366
OAK	2456	2693	337	1835	2151	2068	1489	1845	1578	2576		671	1465	2260
SEA	2334	2495	954	720	2021	1927	1498	1694	1399	2421	671		1660	2060
TEX	1209	1555	1235	802	1021	987	460	853	852	1391	1465	1660		1199
TOR	384	446	2176	437	193	214	822	420	679	366	2260	2060	1199	

	1990						CAREER					
	W-L-S	ERA	IP	H	ER	SO	W-L-S	ERA	IP	H	ER	SO
SEASON	0-0-0	0.00	2.1	0	0	0	0-0-0	0.00	2.1	0	0	0
TORONTO	0-0-0	0.00	0.1	0	0	0	0-0-0	0.00	0.1	0	0	0
ROAD	0-0-0	0.00	2.0	0	0	0	0-0-0	0.00	2.0	0	0	0
vs BALTIMORE	-	-	-	-	-	-	-	-	-	-	-	-
BOSTON	-	-	-	-	-	-	-	-	-	-	-	-
CLEVELAND	0-0-0	0.00	0.1	0	0	0	0-0-0	0.00	0.1	0	0	0
DETROIT	-	-	-	-	-	-	-	-	-	-	-	-
MILWAUKEE	-	-	-	-	-	-	-	-	-	-	-	-
NEW YORK	0-0-0	-	0.0	0	0	0	0-0-0	-	0.0	0	0	0
TORONTO	-	-	-	-	-	-	-	-	-	-	-	-
A.L. EAST	0-0-0	0.00	0.1	0	0	0	0-0-0	0.00	0.1	0	0	0
vs CALIFORNIA	-	-	-	-	-	-	-	-	-	-	-	-
CHICAGO	0-0-0	0.00	1.0	0	0	0	0-0-0	0.00	1.0	0	0	0
KANSAS CITY	-	-	-	-	-	-	-	-	-	-	-	-
MINNESOTA	0-0-0	0.00	1.0	0	0	0	0-0-0	0.00	1.0	0	0	0
OAKLAND	-	-	-	-	-	-	-	-	-	-	-	-
SEATTLE	-	-	-	-	-	-	-	-	-	-	-	-
TEXAS	-	-	-	-	-	-	-	-	-	-	-	-
A.L. WEST	0-0-0	0.00	2.0	0	0	0	0-0-0	0.00	2.0	0	0	0
PRE-ASG	-	-	-	-	-	-	-	-	-	-	-	-
POST-ASG	0-0-0	0.00	2.1	0	0	0	0-0-0	0.00	2.1	0	0	0
STARTER	-	-	-	-	-	-	-	-	-	-	-	-
RELIEVER	0-0-0	0.00	2.1	0	0	0	0-0-0	0.00	2.1	0	0	0
in APRIL	-	-	-	-	-	-	-	-	-	-	-	-
MAY	-	-	-	-	-	-	-	-	-	-	-	-
JUNE	-	-	-	-	-	-	-	-	-	-	-	-
JULY	-	-	-	-	-	-	-	-	-	-	-	-
AUGUST	0-0-0	0.00	2.0	0	0	0	0-0-0	0.00	2.0	0	0	0
SEPT/OCT	0-0-0	0.00	0.1	0	0	0	0-0-0	0.00	0.1	0	0	0

57 RAVELO MANZANILLO
PITCHER

Born: October 17, 1963 San Pedro de Macoris, DR

Resides: San Pedro de Macoris, DR

B-L T-L 5-10 190

M.L. Service: 0.010

PERSONAL: Ravello Manzanillo...Brother, Josias, is a pitcher in the Red Sox organization.

LAST SEASON: Pitched at Vancouver (AAA) of the Pacific Coast League, going 7-3 with 3.61 ERA...Appeared in 38 games (6 GS) giving up just 2 HR in 92.1 IP...Allowed less than a hit per inning (74H/92.1IP)...Tied for third on the squad in wins (7) and was second in appearances (38)...Was fewest GS since he was with Veracruz of the Mexican League in 1986 (5 GS)...Achieved first save since 1985 when he was with Nashua.

PROFESSIONAL CAREER: **1981:** Fell five innings short of the ERA title with 1.13 while pitching for Bradenton (A) of the Gulf Coast League...Had better than a 3-1 strikeout to walk ratio (34K/10BB)...**1982:** Moved to Greenwood (A) of the South Atlantic League where he appeared in 27 games (25 GS) and logged 157.2 IP...Earned first save of professional career...Had seven complete games and 2 shutouts (the first of his career)...**1983:** Pitched at Alexandria (A) of the Carolina League...Had 2 more appearances than GS for the third season in a row (22G/20GS)...Allowed more hits than IP for first time in career (107H/105.1IP)...**1984:** Promoted to AA Nashua of of the Eastern League where he had a .500 record (4-4) for the third consecutive season...Was on the disabled list July 30th through the remainder of the season...**1985:** Was assigned to Nashua (AA) for the second consecutive season...Appeared in a career high 33 games, 17 of which were GS...Allowed just 99 hits in 123.1 innings of work...Was his first sub-.500 season of his professional career...**1986:** Played at Veracruz of the Mexican League and recorded one win in 5 GS...Pitched just 21 innings and posted highest ERA of his minor league career (5.57)...Was released on May 1/86...**1987:** DID NOT PLAY...**1988:** Returned to professional baseball with the White Sox organization...Pitched at Tampa (A) of the Florida State League...Delivered lowest ERA since 1981 season (3.04)...Made 20 game starts which included a one-hit shutout vs Dunedin in August 15th...Close to a 3-1 strikeout to walk ratio (140K/49BB)...Averaged 9.47 strikeouts per 9.0IP...10 wins were the most in his career...Finished second in the FSL in strikeouts (140)...Hitters managed just .194 vs the LHP (fourth in the FSL)...Was called up to Chicago in September and made debut vs the Royals on September 25th, striking out eight in 4 IP but didn't record a decision...**1989:** Reported to spring training with his leg in a cast due to an off-season car accident in the Dominican Republic...Returned to AA ball with Birmingham of the Southern League where he had 22G/GS and sported a 3.90 ERA...Best month was June (3-1, 2.16ERA, 6GS)...Had third plus .500 season of his career (8-7).

RAVELO MANZANILLO

Year	Club & League	W-L	ERA	G	GS	CG	ShO	SV	IP	H	R	ER	HR	HB	BB	SO	WP
1981	Bradenton (Gulf)	3-1	1.13	9	7	0	0	0	48	35	11	6	0	2	10	34	4
1982	Greenwood (SAL)	9-9	4.97	27	25	7	2	1	158	156	108	87	15	1	109	93	6
1983	Alexandria (Caro)	7-7	4.44	22	20	1	0	0	105	107	68	52	9	2	79	66	6
1984	Nashua (East)	4-4	4.24	14	13	2	1	0	74	56	40	35	6	1	62	50	6
1985	Nashua (East)	6-10	4.67	33	17	2	0	5	123	99	70	64	4	3	96	62	11
1986	Veracruz (Mex)	1-3	5.57	5	5	1	0	0	21	19	16	13	2	0	20	16	0
1987					DID NOT PLAY												
1988	Tampa (FSL)	10-6	3.04	24	10	2	2	0	130	93	53	44	2	4	49	140	10
1988	CHICAGO (AL)	0-1	5.79	2	2	0	0	0	9.1	7	6	6	1	1	12	10	1
1989	Birmingham (Sou)	8-7	3.90	22	22	2	0	0	129.1	105	66	56	11	6	72	89	2
1990	Vancouver (PCL)	7-3	3.61	38	6	0	0	4	92.1	74	41	37	2	3	60	64	3
ML TOTALS		0-1	5.79	2	2	0	0	0	9.1	7	6	6	1	1	12	10	1

MANZANILLO - TRANSACTIONS

- Signed as free agent by Pittsburgh Pirates' organization, August 21, 1980.
- On disabled list, July 30, 1984 through remainder of season.
- Released, May 1, 1986; signed by Tampa (Chicago White Sox' organization), March, 1988.
- Signed as a six-year free agent by Toronto (Syracuse roster) Dec. 4, 1990.

5 RANCE MULLINIKS

INFIELDER

Born: Jan.15, 1956 Tulare, CA

Resides: El Paso, TX

B-L T-R 6-0 175

M.L. Service: 12.115

PERSONAL: Steven Rance Mulliniks...Married Jeannette (Jeannie) Geck...Three children, Rance Ryan (7/11/78), Merissa Erin (11/23/86) and Whitney (1/28/90)...Enjoys all sports...Graduated from Monache H.S. in Porterville, California in 1974...Son of Harvey Mulliniks, pitcher in Yankees organization, 1956-57.

LAST SEASON: Appeared in only 57 games, lowest total since 1981 when he played in 24 games...Made his first career appearance at first base on 5/26 vs Seattle...Started 20 games, 14 at third and six at DH...Was used primarily as a Pinch Hitter-was 8-22/.364, 7RBI, 4BB...His eight pinch-hits led the BLUE JAYS...Hit .364(12-33), 12 BB with Runners in Scoring Position...Had .417 average(5-12) on 3-2 count...Hit .429(3-7) vs LHP ...As a GS'er was .288(15-52), 2 HR, 7 RBI, 19 GS...At SkyDome hit .318(14-44) and .264(14-53) on the road.

PROFESSIONAL CAREER: **1974: Originally signed by California following selection in the 3rd round of the 1974 June Free Agent Draft...Was sent to the Pioneer League at Idaho Falls...On DL 5/4-6/9 with fractured thumb...1975:** Moved to A ball at Quad Cities where he stroked his 1st professional HR...Subsequently moved to Salinas of the California League...**1976:** Finished 8th in the Texas League in batting average (.315) despite missing the final six weeks of the season with a fractured left thumb...Was named as Texas League All-Star SS...**1977:** Started the season at Triple A where he batted .307 prior to joining the Angels on 6/14...Was leading Salt Lake City in HR (11) and RBI (51) at the time of recall...Became the club's regular SS on 6/23...**1978:** Started the season with California but hit only .185 prior to being sent to Salt Lake City...Batted .343 at Salt Lake City...**1979:** Split season between the Angels and Salt Lake City for the third straight season, batting .147 with the Angels...Named to the league and National Association class AAA All-Star teams...**1980:** Was traded during the off-season, along with Willie Aikens, to the Royals...Was used primarily as a utility infielder, seeing action primarily at SS and 2B...**1981:** Spent the season with Kansas City as a utility infielder at 3B, 2B and SS...**1982:** Was traded to the BLUE JAYS in March and hit his first HR as a BLUE JAY during Grapefruit League play, 3/29 off of Jeff Reardon...Was his first full ML season as a regular at 3B...Achieved then personal highs in AB (311), R (32), hits (76), 2B (25), HR (4) and RBI (35)...**1983:** Set then personal highs in average (.275), 3B (3), and career highs in games (129), HR (10) and RBI (49)...Led club in 2B (34)- one short of then club mark...Was 2nd among AL 3B in fielding pct. (.971)...Led club in PH (10) and led AL pinch hitters in slugging pct., (.652) and on base pct. (.519)...**1984:** Led AL third basemen in fielding pct. (.968)...Led club when batting with runners in scoring position (.349, 35RBI)...Set club mark and personal high with 8 consecutive hits and 10 times reaching base safely, 8/24-27 vs Minnesota...Playing vs Minnesota on 8/31, registered 9th consecutive hit prior to being retired...Labatt's "Blue" Player of the Month for July (.426, 1HR, 9RBI)...**1985:** 1st career 4 hit game, 4/14 vs Baltimore...1st career PH HR vs New York's Bordi, 6/12 in 11th inning to win game...Winner of the Good Guy Award by Toronto's BBWAA...Average did not slump below .300 after 5/24...Set then career high with a 9 game hit streak...500th ML hit, 8/19 vs Cleveland's Tom Waddell...Set personal highs in R (55), games (129) and RBI (56)...Led AL third basemen in fielding pct. (.971) for second straigh season...Was 4 for 11 in ALCS vs Kansas City, including a HR off of Bret Saberhadgen in game 3...**1986:** Set a personal high in HR (11) but filed to reach the 3 figure mark in hits for the 1st time since 1982...Tied a personal high with a 9 game hit streak (12-34/.353, 2HR, 3RBI), 6/9-20...4 HR in 7 games, 6/15-25 capping a successful June (.315, 4HR, 11RBI)...1st career 2 HR game, 7/3 at Boston vs Boyd and Brown...Placed on 15-day DL with compressed nerve in lower back on 8/10 retroactive to 8/6 after going 3-26...Reinstated on 9/1 and collected 7 hits in his next 41 AB before closing the season with a 4 game hit streak...Led AL 3B in fielding pct. (.975) for the third straigt season...**1987:** Started the season as the DH vs RHP but moved to 3B when Gruber faltered...RBI on May 23 at Seattle, snapped drought of 22 games...2nd career 2HR game, 6/24 at Detroit...Tied then personal high with 11 HR...Finished season batting .352 (51-145) for the last two months...Started 92 games, all but two of them vs RHP...Was 1st season that he wore glasses...**1988:** On 15-day DL, 4/12-5/1 with mild capsular strain of the left knee...3 appearances at 3B from 4/12, used exclusively as a PH/DH...Set personal high with 11 games hit streak 7/3-20...Led all AL DH (minimun 300 AB) with a .300 average...**1989:** Club's Opening Day 3B due to a Spring Training injury to Kelly Gruber...Game started 7 of 8 games at 3B, 4/25-5/3...1st career grand slam HR, 5/2 vs Oakland's Bob Welch...Tied personal high in that game with 4 RBI...2 hits in the next 14 games...Season high 4 games hit streak, 6/3-6...Game started at 3B on 7/31 vs Baltimore for 1st GS there since 5/3...5 RBI in 4 games, 7/26-8/2...11 of 13 games at 3B to close out August...HR in consecutive games, 8/14-15 at Boston...Best month was July (7-23/.304)...11 of 29 RBI recorded in 1st two months...Hit .417 vs Baltimore, .389 vs Detroit and .316 vs Texas.

RANCE MULLINIKS

Year	Club & League	AVG	G	AB	T	H	2B	3B	HR	RBI	SH-SF	HP	BB	SO	SB-CS
1974	Idaho Falls (Pio)	.218	66	202	28	44	8	3	0	24	7-1	3	31	41	14-7
1975	Quad Cities (Mid)	.269	52	186	34	50	6	2	1	21	2-4	1	30	25	7-0
1975	Salinas (Cal)	.258	59	209	38	54	8	0	0	10	3-2	1	32	30	13-6
1976	El Paso (Tex)	.315	90	333	81	105	22	4	7	51	5-4	0	68	61	20-4
1977	Salt Lake City (PCL)	.309	58	220	48	68	17	3	11	51	1-4	0	34	27	11-9
1977	CALIFORNIA (AL)	.269	78	271	36	73	13	2	3	21	0-1	1	23	36	1-1
1978	Salt Lake City (PCL)	.307	34	127	34	39	6	2	3	21	0-0	1	29	11	0-2
1978	CALIFORNIA (AL)	.185	50	119	6	22	3	1	1	6	0-2	1	8	23	2-0
1979	Salt Lake City (PCL)	.343	116	402	94	138	21	7	3	59	0-5	4	98	45	21-11
1979	CALIFORNIA (AL)	.147	22	68	7	10	0	0	1	8	0-5	1	4	14	0-0
1980	KANSAS CITY (AL)	.259	36	54	8	14	3	0	0	6	1-1	0	7	10	0-0
1981	KANSAS CITY (AL)	.227	24	44	6	10	3	0	0	5	0-0	2	0	7	0-1
1982	TORONTO (AL)	.244	112	311	32	76	25	0	4	35	3-1	1	37	49	3-2
1983	TORONTO (AL)	.275	129	364	54	100	34	3	10	49	3-2	1	57	43	0-2
1984	TORONTO (AL)	.324	125	343	41	111	21	5	3	42	0-2	1	33	43	2-3
1985	TORONTO (AL)	.295	129	366	55	108	26	1	10	56	1-5	0	55	54	2-0
1986	TORONTO (AL)	.259	117	348	50	90	22	0	11	45	1-2	1	43	60	1-1
1987	TORONTO (AL)	.310	124	332	37	103	28	1	11	44	3-3	0	34	55	1-1
1988	TORONTO (AL)	.300	119	337	49	101	21	1	12	48	2-4	0	56	57	1-0
1989	TORONTO (AL)	.238	103	273	25	65	11	2	3	29	0-2	0	34	40	0-0
1990	TORONTO (AL)	.289	57	97	11	28	4	0	2	16	0-1	0	22	19	2-1
ML TOTALS		.274	1225	3327	417	911	214	16	71	410	12-31	9	413	510	15-12

CHAMPIONSHIP SERIES RECORD

Year	Club & League	AVG	G	AB	T	H	2B	3B	HR	RBI	SH-SF	HP	BB	SO	SB-CS
1985	TORONTO (AL)	.364	5	11	1	4	1	0	1	3	0-0	0	2	2	0-0
1989	TORONTO (AL)	.000	1	1	0	0	0	0	0	0	0-0	0	0	1	0-0

MULINIKS - TRANSACTIONS

- Selected by California Angels' organization in 3rd round of free-agent draft, June 5, 1974.
- On disabled list, May 4 to June 9 and September 2 to September 24, 1976.
- Traded with First Baseman Willie Aikens to Kansas City Royals for Outfielder Al Cowens, Shortstop Todd Cruz and a player to be named later, December 6, 1979; California Angels acquired Pitcher Craig Eaton to complete deal, April 1, 1980.
- Traded to toronto Blue Jays for Pitcher Phil Huffman, March 25, 1982.
- On disabled list, August 6 to September 1, 1986.
- On disabled list, April 12 to May 2, 1988.

RANCE MULLINIKS vs AMERICAN LEAGUE

	1990					CAREER				
	AB	H	HR	RBI	AVG	AB	H	HR	RBI	AVG
SEASON	97	28	2	16	.289	3327	911	71	411	.274
TORONTO	44	14	1	11	.318	1385	406	31	202	.293
AWAY	53	14	1	5	.264	1942	505	40	209	.260
vs BALTIMORE	3	2	0	3	.667	263	65	5	27	.247
BOSTON	3	1	0	1	.333	293	84	9	61	.287
CLEVELAND	10	0	0	0	.000	286	75	4	34	.262
DETROIT	22	9	1	5	.409	307	87	9	35	.283
MILWAUKEE	4	0	0	0	.000	225	60	5	20	.267
NEW YORK	8	1	0	1	.125	202	59	4	22	.292
TORONTO	-	-	-	-	-	55	14	0	7	.255
A.L. EAST	50	13	1	10	.260	1631	444	36	206	.272
vs CALIFORNIA	14	2	1	1	.143	251	78	7	34	.311
CHICAGO	3	0	0	0	.000	226	58	4	20	.257
KANAS CITY	2	2	0	1	1.000	191	46	0	16	.241
MINNESOTA	6	1	0	1	.167	236	67	6	30	.284
OAKLAND	1	0	0	0	.000	281	68	8	35	.242
SEATTLE	11	5	0	2	.455	279	90	6	38	.323
TEXAS	10	5	0	1	.500	232	60	4	32	.259
A.L. WEST	47	15	1	6	.319	1696	467	35	205	.275
Pre-ASG	45	10	1	5	.222	1818	486	38	218	.267
Post-ASG	52	18	1	11	.346	1509	425	33	193	.282
vs RHP	90	25	2	15	.278	3059	850	66	385	.278
LHP	7	3	0	1	.429	268	61	5	26	.228
PINCH HITTING	22	8	0	7	.364	182	55	2	32	.302
DESIGNATED HITTING	26	1	0	1	.038	601	162	14	71	.270
in APRIL	2	2	0	1	1.000	495	114	6	54	.230
MAY	27	8	1	4	.296	511	146	13	72	.286
JUNE	12	0	0	0	.000	597	155	10	60	.260
JULY	11	2	0	1	.182	553	75	18	81	.316
AUGUST	24	9	0	3	.375	627	167	13	81	.266
SEPT/OCT	21	7	1	7	.333	544	154	11	63	.283

Mulliniks (cont...)

CAREER HIGHS

SEASON: **AVG.** .324 - 1984 **H** 111 - 1984 **HR** 12 - 1988
RBI 57 - 1985 **SB** - 3 - 1983

GAME: **H** 4 at BALT April 14, 1985 **HR** 2 - 3 times
RBI 4 at NY [2] Aug. 2, 1983 at BOST July 3, 1986
SB 1 - 15 times

Longest Hitting Streak: 11 - 1988

21 GREG MYERS

CATCHER

Born: April 14, 1966 Riverside, CA

Resides: Riverside, CA

B-L T-R 6-2 206

M.L. Service: 1.155

PERSONAL: Gregory Richard Myers...Married...Wife's name, Paula...Two daughters, Megan Lee (8/18/84) and Amanda (5/31/88)...Attended Riverside (California) Polytechnical High School...Participated in baseball and was All-League on 3 occasions...Helped club to a baseball championship in 1982...Baseball hero is Lance Parrish.

LAST SEASON: Was classified as a rookie year...Hit first M.L. home run vs the Royals' Luis Aquino on April 20...Had a career high hit streak (7 games) , April 17-26...Injured his left shoulder in a collision at home plate with Lou Whitaker on May 4 and place on disabled list May 5...Went to Syracuse for medical rehabilitation for three games May 22-25th...Activated from DL on May 25th...Had back to back career high hit games, 3 hits on June 9 and 4 hits on June 10 vs the Brewers...Recorded only three extra base hits after the All-Star Break...Started 79 games as catcher...Overall played in 87 games (.236, 59-250, 5HR, 22RBI)...Threw out 29.8 % 17-57 baserunners...Hit .169 (12-71) with runners in scoring position...Hit .242 vs RHP , 55-227...Hit .326 (14-43) for the month of August in 14 games...At SkyDome, hit .238 (29-122), 3HR, 13RBI while hitting .234, 30-128, 2HR, 9RBI on the road...As PH'er was 2-7...Hit .387 when hitting the 0-0 pitch.

PROFESSIONAL CAREER: **1984:** Professional debut with Medicine Hat of the Pioneer League...Batted .316 with only 6 K in 133 AB (38 games)...**1985:** Spent the season with Florence (A) of the South Atlantic League, catching 77 games...Tied Rob Ducey for the club lead in games (134)...Led all catchers in SAL in fielding pct. (.989)...Had five hits vs Macon on May 5...**1986:** Spent the season with Ventura County (A) of the California League...Set career highs in HR (20), RBI (79) and hits (133)...Baseball America's All-Star catcher for the league...Was 4th in same publication's Top 10 ML prospects from California League...Recipient of the R. Howard Webster Award as MVP on Ventura club...**1987:** Spent the season with Syracuse (AAA) of the International League...Led all catchers in games (106), TC (698) and PO (637)...15 game hit streak 4/29-5/15...Hit 7 of 10 HR in the second half...Contract purchased by TORONTO on 9/1...ML debut, 9/12, defensively vs the Yankees...1st ML GS, 10/2 at Detroit, collecting 1st ML hit vs Doyle Alexander...**1988:** Spent season with Syracuse (AAA) of the IL...Caught only 10 games and none after 4/20...Organization's Player of the Month for April and IL Player of the Week for 1st week of the season...Used primarily as the DH due to sore shoulder...Didn't play after 6/10 after jamming right shoulder in 2B slide... On DL 6/19-9/1 due to right rotator cuff surgery on 7/1...**1989:** Started the season with Knoxville (AA) of the Southern League after recovering from shoulder surgery...Collected 30 hits in 29 games, starting 24 games as catcher...Contract by the BLUE JAYS on 7/2...Went 0-2 as the DH on 7/3 vs Boston for 1st ML appearance since 10/3/87...Went 0-15 (0-23 dating back to 1987) from 7/3-7/14...1st ML RBI, 7/30 at New York...1st ML multiple hit game, 2-4 (2-2B), 7/31 at New York...Optioned to Syracuse (AAA) on 8/2...Appeared in 24 games, 24 hits, playing 12 games as catcher...Recalled to the BLUE JAYS on 9/3 and appeared in 3 games (1-6)...Game started 14 times for TORONTO, 7 as DH and 7 as catcher.

GREG MYERS

Year	Club & League	AVG	G	AB	T	H	2B	3B	HR	RBI	SH-SF	HP	BB	SO	SB-CS
1984	Medicine Hat (Pio)	.316	38	133	20	42	9	0	2	20	3-1	0	16	6	0-0
1985	Florence (SAL)	.223	134	489	52	109	19	2	5	62	2-7	2	39	54	0-0
1986	Ventura (Cal)	.295	124	451	65	133	23	4	20	79	1-5	2	43	46	9-4
1987	Syracuse (Int)	.246	107	342	35	84	19	1	10	47	3-2	1	22	46	3-3
1987	TORONTO (AL)	.111	7	9	1	1	0	0	0	0	0-0	0	0	3	0-0
1988	Syracuse (Int)	.283	34	120	18	34	7	1	7	21	0-0	0	8	24	1-0
1989	Syracuse (Int)	.270	24	89	8	24	6	0	1	11	1-0	0	4	9	0-0
1989	TORONTO (AL)	.114	17	44	0	5	2	0	0	1	0-0	0	2	9	0-1
1990	TORONTO (AL)	.236	87	250	33	59	7	1	5	22	1-4	0	22	33	0-1
ML TOTALS		.215	111	303	34	65	9	1	5	23	1-4	0	24	45	0-2

MYERS - TRANSACTIONS

- Selected by Toronto Blue Jays' organization in 3rd round of free-agent draft, June 4, 1984.
- On disabled list, June 17, 1988 through remainder of season.
- On Toronto disabled list, March 26 to June 5, 1989; included rehabilitation disability assignment to Knoxville, May 17 to June 5, 1989.
- On disabled list, May 5 to May 25, 1990, including rehabilitation disability assignment to Syracuse, May 22-25, 1990.

GREG MYERS vs AMERICAN LEAGUE

	1990					CAREER				
	AB	H	HR	RBI	AVG	AB	H	HR	RBI	AVG
SEASON	250	59	5	22	.236	303	65	5	23	.215
TORONTO	122	29	3	13	.238	146	31	3	13	.212
AWAY	128	30	2	9	.234	157	34	2	10	.217
vs BALTIMORE	18	3	0	3	.167	27	3	0	3	.111
BOSTON	27	6	0	0	.222	30	7	0	0	.233
CLEVELAND	18	4	1	3	.222	19	4	1	3	.211
DETROIT	11	2	0	0	.182	23	3	0	0	.131
MILWAUKEE	29	8	1	2	.276	29	8	1	2	.276
NEW YORK	19	4	1	2	.211	25	6	1	3	.240
TORONTO	-	-	-	-	-	-	-	-	-	-
A.L. EAST	122	27	3	10	221	153	31	3	11	.203
vs CALIFORNIA	15	3	0	3	.200	16	3	0	3	.188
CHICAGO	16	5	1	1	.313	16	5	1	1	.313
KANSAS CITY	28	9	1	6	.321	28	9	1	6	.321
MINNESOTA	22	7	0	1	.318	22	7	0	1	.318
OAKLAND	11	1	0	0	.091	22	2	0	0	.091
SEATTLE	14	0	0	1	.000	22	1	0	1	.045
TEXAS	22	7	0	0	.318	24	7	0	0	.292
A.L. WEST	128	32	2	12	.250	150	34	2	12	.227
Pre-ASG	129	31	4	11	.240	139	31	4	11	.223
Post-ASG	121	28	1	11	.231	164	34	1	12	.207
vs RHP	227	55	5	20	.242	277	60	5	21	.217
LHP	23	4	0	2	.174	26	5	0	2	.192
PINCH HITTING	7	2	0	0	.286	8	2	0	0	.250
DESIGNATED HITTING	-	-	-	-	-	-	-	-	-	-
in APRIL	43	13	2	8	.302	43	13	2	8	.302
MAY	14	0	0	0	.000	14	0	0	0	.000
JUNE	59	15	2	3	.254	59	15	2	3	.254
JULY	41	9	0	8	.220	79	13	0	9	.165
AUGUST	43	14	0	1	.326	43	14	0	1	.160
SEPT/OCT	50	8	1	2	.160	65	10	1	2	.154

CAREER HIGHS

SEASON: **AVG.** .236-1990 **H** 59-1990 **HR** 5-1990 **RBI** 22-1990 **SB** 0

GAME: **H** 4-at MILW June 10, 1990 **HR** 1-5 times
RBI 3-vs K.C. April 20, 1990: vs CLEV, April 26, 1990 **SB** 0

Last ML HR vs CHI, Sept. 9, 1990
Longest Hitting Streak: 7 - 1990

9 JOHN OLERUD

FIRST BASEMAN

Born: Aug. 5, 1968 Seattle, WA
Resides: Bellevue, WA
B-L T-L 6-5 218
M.L. Service 1.031

PERSONAL: John Garrett Olerud...Single...Father (John) and Mother (Lynda) both attended Washington State...Father was twice WSU MVP and an All-American catcher in 1965...Father is also a member of the WSU Hall of Fame...John was a general studies major at WSU...Member of the US National Team which competed in the Intercontinental Cup Baseball Tournament at Havana in October 1988...Lettered in 3 sports during High School and was All-State and team MVP in baseball...Was Baseball America's NCAA Player of the Year for 1987-1988...Set Washington State records in average (.464), H (108), HR (23), TB (204), Slugging Pct (.876), hit streak (22 games), wins (15), consecutive wins (16), IP (122.2) and K (113) for the same season.

LAST SEASON: Was the youngest player on the club...His first Professional and Major League HR and RBI came on 4/18 vs the Baltimore Orioles...Had only two HR game on 6/20 vs the Yankees...At the ALL-STAR Break he led all Major League rookies in HR (10), RBI (33), BB (35), SLG % (.465) and OBA (.375)...Started 15 games at first base and 86 games at designated hitter...Batted .333(25-75) for the month of June, 4 HR, 15 RBI, 10 R...Had nine game hitting streak between 7/24 and 8/2(.412, 13-34, 4 RBI, 2 HR) also had two, eight game streaks...Was .294 hitter with Runners in Scoring Position...Hit .342, 25-73 vs LHP...Batted .273 at SkyDome with 11 HR and 26 RBI...On the Road hit .257, 2HR, 22RBI...Was named National Baseball Graduate of the Year...Went to Florida Instructional League to work out in left field.

PROFESSIONAL CAREER: **1989:** Became only the 16th player since the start of the amateur draft in 1965 to make his professional debut in the Major Leagues...Was hospitalized on 1/11/89 after collapsing in Washington State's Fieldhouse following an early morning workout...Diagnosis was subarachnoid hemorrage which caused bleeding into the spinal column...Underwent surgery

Olerud (cont...)

on 2/27 for the removal of a brain aneurism at the base of the brain...Finished the season batting .359 with 5 HR and 30 RBI in 27 games and was 3-2, 6.68 ERA in 6 game starts at WSU...ML debut, 9/3 vs the Twins, defensive replacement at 1B...Collected 1st ML hit in that game, a single vs German Gonzales...1st ML game start, 2-4 outing at 1B vs the Orioles on 10/1...Played for the BLUE JAYS' entry in the Florida Instructional League.

JOHN OLERUD

Year	Club & League	AVG	G	AB	R	H	2B	3B	HR	RBI	SH-SF	HP	BB	SO	SB-CS
1989	TORONTO (AL)	.375	6	8	2	3	0	0	0	0	0-0	0	0	1	0-0
1990	TORONTO (AL)	.265	111	358	43	95	15	1	14	48	1-4	1	57	75	0-2
ML TOTALS		.268	117	366	45	98	15	1	14	48	1-4	1	57	76	0-2

OLERUD - TRANSACTIONS

- Selected by New York Mets' organization in 27th round of free-agent draft, June 2, 1986.
- Selected by Toronto Blue Jays' organization in 3rd round of free-agent draft, June 5, 1989.

JOHN OLERUD vs AMERICAN LEAGUE

	1990					CAREER				
	AB	H	HR	RBI	AVG	AB	H	HR	RBI	AVG
SEASON	358	95	14	48	.265	366	98	14	48	.268
TORONTO	187	51	11	26	.273	194	54	11	26	.278
ROAD	171	44	3	22	.257	172	44	3	22	.256
vs BALTIMORE	30	11	3	7	.367	35	13	3	7	.371
BOSTON	43	11	1	6	.256	44	11	1	6	.250
CLEVELAND	18	8	1	3	.444	19	8	1	3	.421
DETROIT	35	9	2	7	.257	0	0	0	0	.257
MILWAUKEE	30	11	0	3	.367	0	0	0	0	.367
NEW YORK	22	10	3	7	.455	0	0	0	0	.455
TORONTO	-	-	-	-	-	-	-	-	-	-
A.L. EAST	178	60	10	33	.337	185	62	10	33	.335
Vs CALIFORNIA	25	7	1	4	.280	25	7	1	4	.280
CHICAGO	17	4	1	4	.235	17	4	1	4	.235
KANSAS CITY	31	6	1	1	.194	0	0	0	0	.194
MINNESOTA	13	1	0	0	.077	14	2	0	0	.143
OAKLAND	32	2	0	0	.063	0	0	0	0	.063
SEATTLE	31	7	1	4	.226	31	7	1	4	.226
TEXAS	31	8	0	2	.258	31	8	0	2	.258
A.L. WEST	180	35	4	15	.194	181	36	4	15	.199
Pre-ASG	215	59	10	33	.274	215	59	10	33	.274
Post-ASG	143	36	4	15	.252	151	39	4	15	.258
vs RHP	285	70	11	33	.246	292	73	11	33	.250
LHP	73	25	3	15	.342	74	25	3	15	.338
PINCH HITTING	7	1	0	1	.143	8	1	0	1	.125
DESIGNATED HITTING	302	78	10	38	.258	303	78	10	38	.257
in APRIL	48	12	2	5	.250	48	12	2	5	.250
MAY	71	17	2	10	.239	71	17	2	10	.239
JUNE	75	25	4	15	.333	75	25	4	15	.333
JULY	67	19	3	7	.284	67	19	3	7	.284
AUGUST	66	14	2	7	.212	66	14	2	7	.212
SEPT/OCT	31	8	1	4	.258	39	11	1	4	.282

CAREER HIGHS

SEASON: **AVG** .265 - 1990 **H** 95 - 1990 **HR** 14 - 1990
RBI 48 - 1990 **SO** 0

GAME: **H** 3 - at CLEV April 30, 1990; at MILW June 10, 1990; vs NY June 21, 1990
HR 2 vs NY June 21, 1990
RBI 3 vs NY June 22, 1990; at BOST June 25, 1990; vs DET Aug. 7, 1990
SB 0

DIRECTLY TO THE MAJORS

Since the start of the amateur free-agent draft in 1965, 16 players have made their professional baseball debuts in the major leagues. The complete list:
N—Has never played in the minor leagues

DRAFT, YEAR	PLAYER	TEAM
June '67 (secondary)	Mike Adamson, rhp	Baltimore
June '69 (regular)	Steve Dunning, rhp	Cleveland
June '71 (secondary)	Pete Broberg, rhp	Washington
	Burt Hooton, rhp	Chicago Cubs
June '72 (regular)	Dave Roberts, 3b	San Diego
January '73 (secondary)	Dick Ruthven, rhp	Philadelphia
June '73 (regular)	David Clyde, lph	Texas
	N–Dave Winfield, of	San Diego
	Eddie Bane, lhp	Minnesota
June '78 (regular)	N–Bob Horner, 3b	Atlanta
	Brian Milner, c	Toronto
	Mike Morgan, rhp	Oakland
	Tim Conroy, lhp	Oakland
June '85 (regular)	N–Pete Incaviglia, of	Texas
June '88 (regular	N–Jim Abbott, lhp	California
June '89 (regular)	N–John Olerud, dh/1b	Toronto

16

TOM QUINLAN

THIRD BASEMAN

Born: March 27, 1968 St. Paul, MN

Resides: Maplewood, MN

B-R T-R 6-3 214

M.L. Service: 0.031

PERSONAL: Tom Raymond Quinlan...Single...Attended Hill-Murray High School in St. Paul, graduating in 1986...Participated in both hockey and baseball at the high school level, reaching All-State status in each sport...Selected by the NHL Calgary Flames in the 4th round of the June, 1986 Entry Draft (their 3rd selection)...Had been offered a baseball and hockey scholarship at the University of Minnesota.

LAST SEASON: Chosen the R. Howard Webster Award winner(MVP) for Knoxville...Spent the full season at Knoxville (AA) of the Southern League where he hit .258 in 141 games with 15 HR and 51 RBI...Was fourth in the league in games with 141...Was second on the club in SLG pct. with .426...played 139 games at third base and committed 31 errors...Led the team in strikeouts with 159...Was called up to TORONTO on 9/2...Started his first and only Major League game of his career vs the Tigers at Detroit on 9/4 and went 1 for 2.

PROFESSIONAL CAREER: **1987:** Started his professional career with Myrtle Beach (A) of South Atlantic League...Led all SAL third basemen in games (130), DP (29), putouts (96) and TC (368)...**1988:** 4 HR in 1st week, 4/17-23...Hit .300 in August...On DL, 6/10-7/14 with fractured right foot...**1989:** Spent the season with Knoxville (AA) of the Southern League...Was the club's regular third baseman...Led the club in strikeouts (118) but 3rd in BB (34)...Also 3rd on club in runs (62)...Tied among league third basemen in turning DP (21)...Recorded a .909 fielding pct., committing 34 errors, highest among Southern League third basemen...Also led 3B in TC (374), assists (259 and T/3rd in putouts [81]).

TOM QUINLAN

Year	Club & League	AVG	G	AB	R	H	2B	3B	HR	RBI	SH-SF	HP	BB	SO	SB-CS
1987	Myrtle Beach (SAL)	.223	132	435	42	97	20	3	5	51	3-6	6	34	130	0-2
1988	Knoxville (Sou)	.218	98	326	33	71	18	1	8	47	3-2	5	35	99	4-9
1989	Knoxville (Sou)	.210	139	452	62	95	21	3	16	57	3-4	9	41	118	6-4
1990	Knoxville (Sou)	.258	141	481	70	124	24	6	15	51	7-1	14	49	157	8-9
1990	TORONTO (AL)	.500	1	2	0	1	0	0	0	0	0-0	1	0	1	0-0
ML TOTALS		.500	1	2	0	1	0	0	0	0	0-0	1	0	1	0-0

QUINLAN - TRANSACTIONS

- Selected by Toronto Blue Jays' organization in 27th round (605th overall) of free-agent draft, June 2, 1986.
- On disabled list, June 10 to July 14, 1989.

TOM QUINLAN vs AMERICAN LEAGUE

	1990					CAREER				
	AB	H	HR	RBI	AVG	AB	H	HR	RBI	AVG
SEASON	2	1	0	0	.500	2	1	0	0	.500
TORONTO	-	-	-	-	-	-	-	-	-	-
AWAY	2	1	0	0	.500	2	1	0	0	.500
vs BALTIMORE	-	-	-	-	-	-	-	-	-	-
BOSTON	-	-	-	-	-	-	-	-	-	--
CLEVELAND	-	-	-	-	-	-	-	-	-	--
DETROIT	2	1	0	0	.500	2	1	0	0	.500
MILWAUKEE	-	-	-	-	-	-	-	-	-	-
NEW YORK	-	-	-	-	-	-	-	-	-	-
TORONTO	-	-	-	-	-	-	-	-	-	-
A.L. EAST	2	1	0	0	.500	2	1	0	0	.500
vs CALIFORNIA	-	-	-	-	-	-	-	-	-	-
CHICAGO	-	-	-	-	-	-	-	-	-	-
KANSAS CITY	-	-	-	-	-	-	-	-	-	-
MINNESOTA	-	-	-	-	-	-	-	-	-	-
OAKLAND	-	-	-	-	-	-	-	-	-	-
SEATTLE	-	-	-	-	-	-	-	-	-	-
TEXAS	-	-	-	-	-	-	-	-	-	-
A.L. WEST	-	-	-	-	-	-	-	-	-	-
Pre- ASG	-	-	-	-	-	-	-	-	-	-
Post- ASG	2	1	0	0	.500	2	1	0	0	.500
vs RHP	-	-	-	-	-	-	-	-	-	-
LHP	2	1	0	0	.500	2	1	0	0	.500
PINCH HITTING	-	-	-	-	-	-	-	-	-	-
DESIGNATED HITTING	-	-	-	-	-	-	-	-	-	-
in APRIL	-	-	-	-	-	-	-	-	-	-
MAY	-	-	-	-	-	-	-	-	-	-
JUNE	-	-	-	-	-	-	-	-	-	-
JULY	-	-	-	-	-	-	-	-	-	-
AUGUST	-	-	-	-	-	-	-	-	-	-
SEPT/OCT	2	1	0	0	.500	2	1	0	0	.500

54 RICKY RHODES

PITCHER

Born: May 28, 1968 Waco, Texas

Resides: Waco, Texas

B-R T-R 6-4 T-R

M.L. Service: 0.000

PERSONAL: Ricky Lee Rhodes...Single...Graduated from Richfield High School in Waco, Texas (1986) where he played baseball, basketball and football...Attended Navarro Junior College (TX) from 1986-1988 majoring in social studies...Played baseball at Navarro also...Brother, Arthur, is a LHP in the Baltimore organization...Enjoys fishing, bowling and billiards.

LAST SEASON: Spent the 1990 season at Greensboro (A) of the South Atlantic League, where he appeared in 27 games (all game starts)...Posted a 3.73 ERA along with a 7-10 record...Allowed fewer than a hit per inning (121H/154.1IP)...Was tied for 1st on the squad in GS and wild pitches (17)...Was second on the club in innings pitched (154.1) and strikeouts (147).

PROFESSIONAL CAREER: **1988:** Was assigned to Sarasota (Summer A) of the Gulf Coast League...Appeared in 12 games (all game starts) with one complete game shutout...Had close to a 3-1 strikeout to walk ratio (76K/27BB)...Allowed just 43 hits in 69.2 IP...**1989:** Moved to the New York-Penn League affiliate Oneonta (A) where he appeared in and started 12 games for the second year in a row...Posted a 2-3 record in 53.2 IP...Averaged almost a strikeout per inning (52K/53.2IP)...

RICKY RHODES

Year	Club & League	W-L	ERA	G	GS	CG	ShO	SV	IP	H	R	ER	HR	HB	BB	SO	WP
1988	Sarasota (Gulf)	6-3	2.33	12	12	1	1	0	69.2	43	26	18	4	4	27	76	1
1989	Oneonta (NYP)	2-3	4.70	12	12	0	0	0	53.2	46	35	28	3	1	35	52	3
1990	Greensboro (SAL)	7-10	3.73	27	27	0	0	0	154.1	121	75	64	8	5	95	147	17

RHODES - TRANSACTIONS

- Selected by New York Yankees' organization in 35th round of free-agent draft, June 1988.
- Drafted by Toronto Blue Jays December, 1990.

32 ALEX SANCHEZ

PITCHER

Born: April 8, 1966 Antioch, CA

Resides: Antioch, CA

B-R T-R 6-2 201

M.L. Service: 0.025

PERSONAL: Alex Anthony Sanchez...Was an All-American in 1986 at UCLA (16-3) and majored in economics...1 of 5 pitchers to make All-American team with Major Leaguers, Greg Swindell and Mike Loynd on that team...Disappointing junior year (4-5, 5.92 ERA) but 101 K in 106 IP...Was Cubs' 20th pick in June 1984 Free Agent Draft being drafted as an outfielder...Holds UCLA record for wins in a season, 16 in 1986 and strikeouts in a season, 142 in 1986.

LAST SEASON: Started 22 games at Syracuse (AAA) of the International League...Was second on the club in GS and had one CG...Allowed almost one hit per inning (111H in 112.0IP)...Walked 14 batters more than he struck out...Was picked up on waivers by Cleveland on September 24th in conjunction with the Bud Black acquisition...He was then re-acquired by TORONTO in a trade with the Indians on November 6 which sent RHP Willie Blair to Cleveland.

PROFESSIONAL CAREER: **1987:** Spent the season with St. Catharines of the New York-Penn League...Had a very successful professional debut, leading the league in games started (17) and strikeouts (116), winning the Robert Stedler Award as the top prospect in the NY-Penn League; also named to the All-Star team as a right handed pitcher; led St. Catharines hurlers in games started, strikeouts, wins (8) and innings pitched (95)...Went 4-0 with an ERA of 2.13 during six appearances in August...Was involved in four combination shutouts...Promoted to Myrtle Beach at end of season and recorded a save in only appearance...**1988:** Started season with Knoxville (AA) of Southern League and named to All-Star team...Among Southern League leaders in wins (T/4th-12), K (1st-166) and had the 3rd highest strikeout per nine innings ratio (10) and 2nd lowest batting average allowed (.185)...Promoted to Syracuse (AAA) of the International League on 7/18...**1989:** Spent much of the season with Syracuse (AAA) of the IL...Named as the IL Most Valuable Pitcher...Among IL leaders in wins (T/1st-13), GS (T/1st-27), K (2nd-144) and IP (4th-169.2)...Contract purchased by TORONTO on 5/15...ML debut, 5/23 GS vs Minnesota...Not involved in a 2-1 BLUE JAYS win (6.0IP, 5H, 1R-ER, 5BB, 1K)...Only ML decision, next GS, 6-2 loss at Cleveland on 5/30...Last ML game start, 0.1 IP in BLUE JAYS' 13-11, 12 inning win over the Red Sox on 6/4...Walked 14 in only 11.2 IP including 5 in his last 1.0 IP (2 games, 1GS).

ALEX SANCHEZ

Year	Club & League	W-L	ERA	G	GS	CG	ShO	SV	IP	H	R	ER	HR	HB	BB	SO	WP
1987	St.Catharines (NYP)	8-3	2.64	17	17	0	0	0	95.1	72	33	28	3	0	38	116	6
1987	Myrtle Beach (SAL)	0-0	3.00	1	0	0	0	1	3.0	2	1	1	1	0	0	4	0
1988	Knoxville (Sou)	12-5	2.53	24	24	2	0	0	149.1	100	56	42	8	3	74	166	5
1988	Syracuse (Int)	4-3	3.59	10	10	1	0	0	57.2	47	26	23	8	0	43	57	4
1989	Syracuse (Int)	13-7	3.13	28	27	1	1	0	169.2	125	68	59	14	1	74	141	11
1989	TORONTO (AL)	0-1	10.03	4	3	0	0	0	11.2	16	13	13	1	0	14	4	1
1990	Syracuse (Int)	5-9	5.71	22	22	1	0	0	112.0	111	77	71	15	4	79	65	5
ML TOTALS		0-1	10.03	4	3	0	0	0	11.2	16	13	13	1	0	14	4	1

SANCHEZ - TRANSACTIONS

- Selected by Chicago Cubs in 20th round of free-agent draft, June, 1984.
- Selected by Toronto in 1st round (17th overall) in free-agent draft, June 2, 1987.
- On disabled list July 19-Aug. 16, 1990.
- Claimed on waivers by Cleveland, Sept. 24, 1990.
- Traded to Toronto by Cleveland in exchange for pitcher Willie Blair, Nov. 6, 1990.

ALEX SANCHEZ vs AMERICAN LEAGUE

	1990						CAREER					
	W-L-S	ERA	IP	H	ER	SO	W-L-S	ERA	IP	H	ER	SO
SEASON	-	-	-	-	-	-	0-1-0	10.03	11.2	16	13	4
TORONTO	-	-	-	-	-	-	0-0-0	6.75	6.2	9	5	1
ROAD	-	-	-	-	-	-	0-1-0	14.40	5.0	7	8	3
vs BALTIMORE	-	-	-	-	-	-	-	-	-	-	-	-
BOSTON	-	-	-	-	-	-	0-0-0	135.00	0.1	3	5	0
CLEVELAND	-	-	-	-	-	-	0-1-0	5.79	4.2	4	3	3
DETROIT	-	-	-	-	-	-	0-0-0	54.00	0.2	4	4	0
MILWAUKEE	-	-	-	-	-	-	-	-	-	-	-	-
NEW YORK	-	-	-	-	-	-	-	-	-	-	-	-
TORONTO	-	-	-	-	-	-	-	-	-	-	-	-
A.L. EAST	-	-	-	-	-	-	0-1-0	19.06	5.2	11	12	3
vs CALIFORNIA	-	-	-	-	-	-	-	-	-	-	-	-
CHICAGO	-	-	-	-	-	-	-	-	-	-	-	-
KANSAS CITY	-	-	-	-	-	-	-	-	-	-	-	-
MINNESOTA	-	-	-	-	-	-	0-0-0	1.50	6.0	5	1	1
OAKLAND	-	-	-	-	-	-	-	-	-	-	-	-
SEATTLE	-	-	-	-	-	-	-	-	-	-	-	-
TEXAS	-	-	-	-	-	-	-	-	-	-	-	-
A.L. WEST	-	-	-	-	-	-	0-0-0	1.50	6.0	5	1	1
PRE-ASG	-	-	-	-	-	-	0-1-0	10.03	11.2	16	13	4
POST-ASG	-	-	-	-	-	-	-	-	-	-	-	-
STARTER	-	-	-	-	-	-	0-1-0	7.36	11.0	12	9	4
RELIEVER	-	-	-	-	-	-	0-0-0	54.00	0.2	4	4	0
in APRIL	-	-	-	-	-	-	-	-	-	-	-	-
MAY	-	-	-	-	-	-	0-1-0	3.38	10.2	9	4	4
JUNE	-	-	-	-	-	-	0-0-0	81.00	1.0	7	9	0
JULY	-	-	-	-	-	-	-	-	-	-	-	-
AUGUST	-	-	-	-	-	-	-	-	-	-	-	-
SEPT/OCT	-	-	-	-	-	-	-	-	-	-	-	-

CAREER HIGHS

GAME: **SO** 3 - at CLEV May 30, 1989 **BB** 5 - at MINN May 23, 1989

Last Relief: vs DET June 10, 1989

59 JERRY SCHUNK

INFIELDER

Born: October 5, 1965 Hamilton, OH

Resides: Cincinnati, OH

B-R T-R 5-11 180

M.L. Service: 0.000

PERSONAL: Jerry Alan Schunk...1983 Graduate of Colerain High School where he played baseball, football and basketball...Was All-City selection in baseball and basketball and named to 3rd team All-Ohio in football...Attended the University of Toledo where he was named to the All-Mid American Conference baseball team...Played on the national champion Midland in semi-pro ball in 1984.

LAST SEASON: Began the season at Knoxville (AA) of the Southern League...Played at SS and in the outfield and hit .288 in 85 games...Struck out just 25 times in 274 at-bats...Was promoted

Schunk (cont...)

to Syracuse (AAA) of the International League and averaged close to one hit per game (24 H in 26 G).

PROFESSIONAL CAREER: **1986:** Started his first professional season at St. Catharines (Summer A) of the New York-Penn League, playing third base and hitting .276 in 71 games...Led all NY-Penn League third basemen in fielding percentage (.955), games (71), assists (127) and double plays (16)...Averaged better than a hit per game (71 G/ 75 H)...Had a career high 18 stolen bases...**1987:** Spent the entire year at Dunedin (A) of the Florida State League, splitting time between second base and shortstop...Played in a then career high, 98 games...21 of 88 hits were extra base hits...**1988:** Had a 10 game hitting streak July 1-11 during which he hit .372...Was third season with double digit figures in steals (11)...Had a stretch of 20 games without an error...**1989:** Was moved to Knoxville (AA) of the Southern League for the season...First taste of Double A ball...Played all four infield positions and also played outfield on occasion...Stuck out just 19 times in 270 at-bats...Batted .299 with 1 HR and 10 RBI in August.

JERRY SCHUNK

Year	Club & League	AVG	G	AB	R	H	2B	3B	HR	RBI	SH-SF	HP	BB	SO	SB-CS
1986	St. Catharines (NYP)	.276	71	272	39	75	12	0	7	33	6-3	2	21	25	18-6
1987	Dunedin (FSL)	.246	98	358	40	88	15	2	4	39	0-2	2	17	38	11-4
1988	Dunedin (FSL)	.257	87	343	36	88	17	2	5	28	8-1	2	19	30	11-7
1989	Knoxville (Sou)	.241	95	270	32	65	13	4	4	31	8-5	3	17	19	6-3
1990	Knoxville (Sou)	.288	85	274	32	79	13	1	3	31	14-3	3	9	25	8-7
1990	Syracuse (Int)	.240	26	100	8	24	4	0	0	7	1-0	0	3	10	1-2

SCHUNK - TRANSACTIONS

- Selected by Toronto in 6th round of free-agent draft, June 1986.
- Disabled April 18-June 5, 1988.

33 ED SPRAGUE

THIRD BASEMAN/CATCHER

Born: July 25, 1967 Castro Valley, CA

Resides: Stockton, California

B-R T-R 6-2 215

M.L. Service: 0.000

PERSONAL: Edward Nelson Sprague...Graduated from St. Mary's High School in Stockton, California in 1985...Attended Stanford University where he played baseball and led the PAC-10 Conference in HR (19) and RBI (71) during his senior year and helped club to a 2nd straight NCAA World Series Championship in 1988...Is second on the Cardinals all-time HR list (41) and 4th in RBI (178)...Played on the 1988 Gold Medal winning U.S. Olympic Baseball team, hitting .290...Graduated from Stanford in 1988...Was an economics major...Father Ed was a Major League pitcher (1968-76)...Originally drafted by the Red Sox in in 1986 in the 26th round.

LAST SEASON: Played in a league leading 142 games for the Syracuse Chiefs (AAA) of the International League...Led the Chiefs and was fourth in the IL in total bases (217)...Led the club in HR (20) and RBI (75)...Was third on the team in runs scored (60)...Tied for fourth on the squad with a .418 slugging percentage...Played 132 games at third base, nine games at first base and caught six games...Was his first full year at the AAA level.

PROFESSIONAL CAREER: **1989:** Started the season at Dunedin (A) of the Florida State League where he hit .219 in 52 games...18 of his 42 hits went for extra bases...Was promoted to the Syracuse Chiefs (AAA) of the International League on May 30th where he played in 86 games and hit .208 in 288 at bats...Had 20 extra base hits at Syracuse.

ED SPRAGUE

Year	Club & League	AVG	G	AB	R	H	2B	3B	HR	RBI	SH-SF	HP	BB	SO	SB-CS
1989	Dunedin (FSL)	.219	52	192	21	42	9	2	7	23	0-2	2	16	40	1-1
1989	Syracuse (Int)	.208	86	288	23	60	14	1	5	33	1-3	5	18	73	0-0
1990	Syracuse (Int)	.239	142	519	60	124	23	5	20	75	3-4	10	31	100	4-2

SPRAGUE - TRANSACTIONS

- Selected by Toronto in 1st round (25th overall) in June, 1988 Free-Agent Draft.

37 DAVE STIEB
PITCHER

Born: July 22, 1957 Santa Ana, CA
Resides: Gilroy, CA
B-R T-R 6-1 195
M.L. Service: 11.96

PERSONAL: David Andrew Stieb...Married the former Pattie Faso, 8/14/81...Two children, Andrew David (5/14/82), Ashley Danielle (11/4/85)...Graduated from Oak Grove High School in San Jose...Attended Southern Illinois University where he played the outfield as well as pitched...Named to The Sporting News All-American team as an outfielder...Played semi-pro ball in Alaska before signing with TORONTO...Name pronounced, STEEB...Hobbies include music with an extensive guitar collection...Actively involved in the Cystic Fibrosis Foundation.

LAST SEASON: Has the most ML service of any player on the BLUE JAYS Roster- (11 yrs, 96 Days)...Set club marks with his 18 wins and Winning PCt, .750(18-6)...Pitched the first NO-HITTER in Blue Jays history on Sept 2 at Cleveland...Is first on the clubs' All-Time list for wins (166)...Was selected as the Labatt's "BLUE" Pitcher of the Year for 1990- the seventh time he has captured the honour...Also was voted Pitcher of the Year by Toronto Chapter of BBWAA- was 4th in Cy Young Award voting...Pitched a complete game 1-0 shutout at Oakland on 5/28 for his 100th complete game and his 29th shutout...He won 5 straight games from May 28 through June 20th...Selected for the All-Star Game and appeared for the 7th time in his career, tying him with Early Wynn for most appearances by an AL pitcher...Was the first year that he had won 11 games by the All-Star Break...Won first game of his career at Memorial Stadium in Baltimore on 8/1...Had the shortest outing of his career on 6/25 at Boston(0.0IP, 3H, 6R/ER, 4BB) facing only 7 batters, 6 of which scored...Was the Labatt's "BLUE" Pitcher of The Month for May and July...Strikeout high was 9 vs the Angels on 7/5...On the Road was 9-1, 2.73ERA, 16GS, 2CG, 2Sho, 105.2IP, 77H, 35R, 32ER, 29BB, 61K...Right handed batters hit .205, 77-375...In the AL, ranked 5th in ERA(2.93), T4th in Wins(18), T3rd in Winning Pct(.750, 18-6), 4th in Opposing Batters Average(.230), 2nd in Hit Batters(10), 7th in fewest Base Runners per 9 IP(10.91).

PROFESSIONAL CAREER: **1978:** Debuted in 8/78 with Dunedin (A) as a pitcher, DH and OF...**1979:** After working in Instructional League as a pitcher, quickly advancing to AAA, posting a combined 10-2 mark prior to promotion to parent club...ML debut, 6/26/79 starting and losing at Baltimore, 6-1...1st ML win came at home in his 1st home GS, 7/9/79, 7-1 CG over Milwaukee...Finished 2nd on the club in wins (8) despite playing only a half season...**1980:** AL Pitcher of the Month for April (3-0, 1.09ERA) and was the youngest pitcher chosen to play in the All-Star Game...Became the 1st BLUE JAYS pitcher to bat and play a fielding position when he played LF on 8/29/80 in completion of a suspended game vs Minnesota...Set a club mark for consecutive CG (7), 6/18-7/21...**1981:** Led the BLUE JAYS pitchers in wins (11), ERA (3.18), GS (25, IP (184) and K (89 while becoming the 1st BLUE JAY pitcher to have a plus .500 winning pct. (.524)...Named as Labatt's "Blue" and Toronto BBWAA MVP while finishing among league leaders in several categories including GS (2nd-25), CG (6th-11), innings (5th-184), K (10th-89) and wins (10th-11)...Pitched 1.2 IP in All-Star game, making 2nd straight appearance...**1982:** Finished 2nd in Labatt's MVP voting to Damaso Garcia...The Sporting News AL Pitcher of the Year...Set club marks in wins (17) and decisions (31) while finishing fifth in the AL with a 3.25 ERA...Led AL in IP (288.1), CG (19) and ShO (5)...Led AL pitchers defensively in total chances (82) and assists (53)...Sporting News AL Pitcher of the Year...**1983:** AL Player of the Week, 5/16-22...AL and Labatt's "Blue" Pitcher of the Month for May (5-1, 1.73ERA) while pitching club record 57.1IP...Labatt's "Blue" Pitcher of the Month for August (2-2, 2.19ERA)...2nd in AL in IP (278), tied for 2nd in ShO (4), 3rd in K (187), ERA (3.04) and CG (14), tied for 3rd in GS (36), tied for 7th in wins (17)...Opponents hit .219...Named Pitcher of the Year by Toronto's BBWAA for 3rd consecutive season...**1984:** Led the AL in IP (267), 2nd in K (198) and ERA (2.83), T/4th in GS (35), T/5th in winning pct. (.667), T/9th in CG (10) and ShO (2), T/10th in wins (16)...Labatt's "Blue" Pitcher of the Month for April (4-0, 1.88ERA), June (1-2, 3.02ERA), July (4-1, 2.25ERA) and co-winner for August (2-1, 2.25ERA)...Struck out 11 at Minnesota, 8/26 and followed with 10 in his next GS against the same club...Labatt's "Blue" Pitcher of the Year...Starting and losing pitcher of All-Star game...**1985:** Signed richest contract in ML history through '95 on 3/8...Had streak of 26 consecutive IP without an ER, 5/17-6/2...AL Pitcher of the Month for May (4-1, 5CG, 1.69ERA)...Labatt's "Blue" Pitcher of Month for May and June (3-2, 1.51ERA; 2-1, 2.03ERA)..Pitched 3rd consecutive and 5th All-Star game...Held opposition to 2R or less in 15 of 1st 17 GS...No-hitter through 8 IP, 8/24 prior to surrendering consecutive HR to Law and Little...Led AL in ERA (2.48), third in innings pitched (265) and T/4th in GS (36) and T/9th in ShO (2)...Tied for lead in assists by pitcher (53) and led in TC (92)...Won 1 of last 6 decisions...Labatt's "Blue" Pitcher of the Year...**1986:** Lost 1st 5 decisions...Recorded 1000th ML strikeout, June 23 when he fanned Brewers' Bill Schroeder...Only CG, 6-0 vs Chicago, 5/30...Appeared in relief 7/12 vs Oakland for 1st ML relief appearance since 10/4/80, snapping string of 189 consecutive GS...1st professional save, 6-2 for Clancy, at Seattle, 7/23...Allowed 29 first inning runs (4th highest in AL) in 34 GS...Led AL in Hit batters (15) for fourth time in past six seasons...Tied for AL lead with 15 no-decision starts...Compiled highest ERA in majors (7.43) over first four weeks (minimum 5GS) and didn't win after August 18...But in between was 13-3 with a 3.07 ERA...**1987:** Defeated California, 3-1 (5/29), Seattle, 7-2 (6/3) and New York 11-0 (6/8) marking the 1st time since 7/4-19/85 that he had won 3 consecutive GS...7-0 4-hitter vs Kansas City on 7/10 was 1st complete game- ShO in 40 GS dating back to 5/30/86...Then personal high 7 game win streak, 7/10-8/18...4 wins in 4 consecutive GS, 8/2-18 for the first time since 4/18-5/4/84...Winless in last 9 games, 7 GS...In 14 wins, BLUE JAYS outscored opponents 116-37...**1988:** Won a career 9 games in a row, 5/1-6/20...Tossed first career one hitter vs Milwaukee on 5/31...10 wins at the All-Star game to tie personal high...Club's lone representative at the mid-summer classic...Then shortest career GS, 1.0IP, 9/2 vs Texas...1 relief outing, 5.0 IP at Chicago on 8/16...Finished season with back-to-back 1-hitters, each lost with 2 out in the ninth (1-0 at Cleveland on 9/24 and 4-0 vs Baltimore on 9/30)...Both no hit bids were spoiled with the count at 2-2...Finished season with 3 consecutive CG ShO...Labatt's "Blue" Pitcher of the Month for May (6-0 [club mark], 1.99ERA) and September/October (4-0, 1.50ERA)...Tied club mark and set personal high with 12 K, 8/22 vs Chicago...Among league leaders in ShO (T/2nd-4), ERA (7th-3.04), winning pct. (T/7th-.667) and wins (T/8th-16)...**1989:** Allowed 1 R in 8 IP on 4/5 at KC to snap consecutive scoreless streak at 34IP...Tossed a one-hitter in 8-0 win over New York on 4/10 for 3rd one-hitter in 4 GS dating back to '88...Won 1st 3 decisions through 5/8...Won 4 consecutive GS, 6/3-19, defeating Boston, Detroit, Milwaukee and Seattle...Allowed a 3R HR to Seattle's Briley on 7/20- it was the first HR with someone on base since 5/17...2nd CG of the season 2-1 two hitter vs Yankees on 8/4...3rd CG of season 7-0, one-hitter vs Milwaukee on 8/26 (infield hit to Yount- 6th)...3rd one-hitter in 29 GS...Lost perfect game with a 9th inning, two out double to Roberto Kelly on 8/4...26 consecutive ER-less innings streak snapped on 9/10 vs Indians...Tied personal high and club mark with 17 wins...Opponents batted .219 against him- (.188 vs right)...10-3 vs the AL East...Labatt's "Blue" Pitcher of the Month for September/October (3-0, 2.04ERA, 5GS)...Lost 3 of 12 decisions post All-Star break...Was 2-0 vs Detroit and Milwaukee...Lost 2 times to Baltimore- the only team to beat him twice...Among league leaders in wins (T/6th-17), GS (T/10th-33), winning pct. (9th-.680), ShO (T/7th-2), opponents average (4th-.219), HB (1st-13)...Labatt's "Blue" Pitcher of the Year.

DAVE STIEB

Year	Club & League	W-L	ERA	G	GS	CG	ShO	SV	IP	H	R	ER	HR	HB	BB	SO	WP
1978	Dunedin (FSL)	2-0	2.08	4	4	1	0	0	26.1	23	10	6	1	0	1	8	0
1979	Dunedin (FSL)	5-0	4.24	8	8	2	1	0	51.1	54	30	24	0	4	28	38	3
1979	Syracuse (Int)	5-2	2.13	7	7	4	0	0	51.1	39	15	12	0	2	14	20	1
1979	TORONTO (AL)	8-8	4.31	18	18	7	1	0	129.1	139	70	62	11	4	48	52	3
1980	TORONTO (AL)†	12-15	3.70	34	32	14	4	0	242.0	232	108	100	12	6	83	108	6
1981	TORONTO (AL)	11-10	3.19	25	25	11	2	0	183.2	148	70	65	10	11	61	89	1
1982	TORONTO (AL)	17-14	3.25	38	38	19	5	0	288.1	271	116	104	27	5	75	141	3
1983	TORONTO (AL)	17-12	3.04	36	36	14	4	0	278.0	223	105	94	21	14	93	187	5
1984	TORONTO (AL)	16-8	2.83	35	35	11	2	0	267.0	215	87	84	19	11	88	198	2
1985	TORONTO (AL)	14-13	2.48	36	36	8	2	0	265.0	206	89	73	22	9	96	167	4
1986	TORONTO (AL) ‡	7-12	4.74	37	34	1	1	1	205.0	239	128	108	29	15	87	127	7
1987	TORONTO (AL)	13-9	4.09	33	31	3	1	0	185.0	164	92	84	16	7	87	115	4
1988	TORONTO (AL) ‡	16-8	3.04	32	31	8	4	0	207.1	157	76	70	15	13	79	147	4
1989	TORONTO (AL)	17-8	3.35	33	33	3	2	0	206.2	164	83	77	12	13	76	101	3
1990	TORONTO (AL)	18-6	2.93	33	33	2	2	0	208.2	179	73	68	11	10	64	125	5
ML TOTALS		166-123	3.37	390	382	101	30	1	2666.2	2337	1097	989	205	118	937	1557	47

CHAMPIONSHIP SERIES RECORD

Year	Club & League	W-L	ERA	G	GS	CG	ShO	SV	IP	H	R	ER	HR	HB	BB	SO	WP
1985	TORONTO (AL)	1-1	3.10	3	3	0	0	0	20.1	11	7	7	1	1	10	18	0
1989	TORONTO (AL)	0-2	6.35	2	2	0	0	0	11.1	12	8	8	2	0	6	10	0
LCS Total		1-3	4.26	5	5	0	0	0	31.2	23	15	15	3	1	16	28	0

ALL-STAR GAME RECORD

Year	Club & League	W-L	ERA	G	GS	CG	ShO	SV	IP	H	R	ER	HR	HB	BB	SO	WP
1980	AL., at L.A.	0-0	0.00	1	0	0	0	0	1.0	1	1	0	0	2	0	0	1
1981	AL., at Clev.	0-0	0.00	1	0	0	0	0	1.2	1	0	0	0	1	1	1	0
1983	AL., at Chi. (AL)	1-0	0.00	1	1	0	0	0	3.0	0	1	0	0	0	1	4	0
1984	AL., at S.F.	0-1	4.50	1	1	0	0	0	2.0	3	2	1	1	0	0	2	0
1985	AL., at Minn.	0-0	0.00	1	0	0	0	0	1.0	0	0	0	0	0	1	2	0
1988	AL., at Cinn.	0-0	0.00	1	0	0	0	0	1.0	1	0	0	0	0	0	0	0
1990	AL., at Chi (NL)	0-0	0.00	1	0	0	0	0	2.0	0	0	0	0	0	1	1	0

† - Appeared in one game as an outfielder with no chances.

‡ - Appeared in one game as a pinch-runner.

STIEB - TRANSACTIONS

- Selected by Toronto Blue Jays in 5th round (106th overall) of free-agent draft, June 6, 1978.

STIEB'S NO-HITTER

SEPTEMBER 2, 1990 at CLEVELAND — TORONTO 3, CLEVELAND 0

DAVE STIEB chalked up his first no-hitter and the first in BLUE JAYS history as he stopped the Cleveland Indians on a sunny Sunday afternoon at Cleveland Stadium before a crowd of 23,640.

The game ended as Cleveland's Jerry Browne whacked a fly to right field where JUNIOR FELIX put the squeeze on it.

Stieb had a season high nine strikeouts and walked four over his 122-pitch afternoon.

There were no tough plays and only a couple of well hit balls. Closest the Tribe came to a hit was KEN PHELPS pulling a liner about three feet foul to open the eighth inning.

The BLUE JAYS and STIEB got their offensive support from FRED McGRIFF who hit two solo home runs and from MANNY LEE who doubled home KENNY WILLIAMS in the fifth inning.

Stieb had previously gone 8.2 innings, three times, protecting no-hitters. He had back-to-back attempts in September 1988; on September 24, 1988 at Cleveland Stadium, JULIO FRANCO's had a bad hop single over second baseman MANNY LEE's head. In his next start, against Baltimore at Exhibition Stadium, JIM TRABER looped a single over first baseman FRED McGRIFF's outstretch glove hand. Both no-hit bids were lost on 2-2 pitches. STIEB also had a perfect game for 8.2 innings on August 4, 1989 vs the Yankees at SkyDome. ROBERTO KELLY doubled to left to break it up.

TORONTO	000	110	001 — 3	8	0
CLEVELAND	000	000	000 — 0	0	1

STIEB and BORDERS
BLACK, OROSCO (8), OLIN (9) and SKINNER
WP—STIEB (17-5) LP-BLACK (10-9)
STIEB PITCHING LINE: 9 IP 0 H 0 R 0 ER 4 BB 9 SO

DAVE STIEB vs AMERICAN LEAGUE

	1990						CAREER					
	W-L-S	ERA	IP	H	ER	SO	W-L-S	ERA	IP	H	ER	SO
SEASON	18-6-0	2.93	208.2	179	68	125	166-123-1	3.34	2665.2	2337	989	1557
TORONTO	9-5-0	3.15	103.0	102	36	64	87-64-0	3.45	1315.1	1192	504	765
ROAD	9-1-0	2.73	105.2	77	32	61	79-59-1	3.23	1350.1	1145	485	792
vs BALTIMORE	1-1-0	5.30	18.2	21	11	12	6-10-0	3.76	177.1	152	74	94
BOSTON	1-0-0	4.15	21.2	27	10	17	12-8-0	4.07	181.1	186	82	121
CLEVELAND	2-1-0	2.81	25.2	16	8	17	15-9-0	3.32	225.1	200	83	126
DETROIT	0-0-0	4.50	6.0	5	3	4	12-9-0	3.56	184.1	161	73	117
MILWAUKEE	2-1-0	2.81	25.2	16	8	17	17-12-0	2.96	240.1	209	79	133
NEW YORK	0-0-0	1.29	7.0	5	1	6	8-10-0	3.00	219.0	180	73	135
TORONTO	-	-	-	-	-	-	-	-	-	-	-	-
A.L. EAST	6-3-0	3.53	104.2	90	41	73	70-58-0	3.40	1227.2	1088	464	726
vs CALIFORNIA	1-1-0	2.63	24.0	16	7	16	13-8-0	3.09	210.0	182	72	135
CHICAGO	2-0-0	0.57	15.2	13	1	8	20-4-0	1.76	214.1	149	42	132
KANSAS CITY	2-0-0	2.45	11.0	15	3	7	13-10-0	3.21	199.0	177	71	123
MINNESOTA	3-0-0	1.74	20.2	12	4	11	12-13-0	3.32	230.1	199	85	148
OAKLAND	2-1-0	3.44	18.1	12	7	7	11-13-0	3.73	205.1	182	85	97
SEATTLE	-	-	-	-	-	-	14-8-1	3.88	181.0	169	78	103
TEXAS	2-1-0	1.89	19.0	14	4	11	13-9-0	4.14	198.0	184	91	101
A.L. WEST	12-3-0	2.15	108.2	82	26	60	96-65-1	3.28	1438.0	1242	524	839
Pre-ASG	11-3-0	3.15	100.0	90	35	60	86-66-0	3.31	1358.1	1183	499	785
PosT-ASG	7-3-0	2.73	108.2	89	33	65	80-57-1	3.37	1307.4	1154	490	772
STARTER	18-6-0	2.93	208.2	179	68	125	166-123-0	3.34	2647.3	2322	982	1546
RELIEVER	-	-	-	-	-	-	0-0-1	3.38	18.2	15	7	11
In APRIL	3-1-0	2.35	23.0	22	6	13	19-18-0	3.32	328.1	306	121	194
MAY	3-1-0	2.48	40.0	30	11	20	34-18-0	3.08	482.2	392	165	285
JUNE	4-1-0	5.40	30.0	36	18	18	25-24-0	3.92	397.1	377	173	216
JULY	3-0-0	0.94	28.2	16	3	17	27-17-1	3.03	414.4	357	140	212
AUGUST	3-2-0	3.86	39.2	34	17	22	29-22-0	3.42	507.4	429	193	312
SEPT/OCT	2-1-0	2.47	47.1	41	13	35	32-24-0	3.32	534.2	476	197	338

CAREER HIGHS

SEASON: **W** 18-1990 **ERA** 2.48-1985 **SV** 1-1986
IP 288.1-1985 **SO** 198-1984

GAME: **LOW HIT CG** NO HITTER at CLEV Sept. 2, 1990 **SO** 12-vs CHI May 22, 1988
BB 8 at MILW May 16, 1983

Last Win: vs CHI Sept. 8, 1990 **Last Save:** at SEA July 23, 1986
Last CG: at CLEV Sept. 2, 1990 **Last ShO:** at CLEV Sept. 2, 1990
Last Relief: at CHI Aug. 16, 1988 **Longest Winning Streak:** 9 - 1988
Longest Losing Streak: 6 - 1986

30 TODD STOTTLEMYRE
PITCHER

Born: May 20, 1965 Yakima, WA
Resides: Yakima, WA
B-L T-R 6-3 195
M.L. Service: 2.111

PERSONAL: Todd Vernon Stottlemyre...Married, wife's name is Sherri...Had previously been drafted by the Yankees (6/84) and the Cardinals (1/85)...Son of former Yankee RHP and current Mets Pitching coach Mel and brother of Mel Jr. who is currently in the Royals chain...Had a perfect 10-0 record with a 0.72 ERA in his senior year at Davis High School in Yakima...Then attended University of Nevada-Las Vegas, posting a 10-4 record with a team leading 4.20 ERA...Withdrew from the program to be eligible for January, 1985 Free Agent Draft...Sat out all of 1984 due to sore right elbow but attended Yakima Valley Community College.

LAST SEASON: In his first full season in the Majors was in the rotation all year...Was the youngest Blue Jay pitcher to ever start a season opener- 4/9...Brother Mel Stottlemyre Jr. pitched for the Kansas City Royals...Father Mel Stottlemyre was pitching coach for the Mets...Lost the season opener to Texas 4-2...Tied with Dave Stieb for the club lead in games started with 33...Had a 4 game win streak in 4GS from 6/7 - 6/23...Led the BLUE JAYS in complete games with 4...Was second on the club in innings pitched with 203.0...Tied David Wells for second in team strikeouts-(115)...Allowed only 4H in 8.0IP on 7/13 vs the Angels...Went at least 6.0IP in 20 of his 33 starts this season...6-9, 4.41 ERA on the road...Strikeout high was 8 on 7/3 vs California...Longest outing was 9.0IP vs the Detroit Tigers on 5/5 and 6/17 vs the Yankees...Career W-L record is 24-31...Shortest outing was 2.0IP vs Detroit on 5/10...Opposing Batters, .300 vs LH, .247 vs RH...Was 2nd in AL in run support per 9.0 IP, 5.808, 131 runs for 203.0 inning...17 losses were 5th in AL.

PROFESSIONAL CAREER: **1986:** Started the season with Ventura County (A) of California League prior to promotion to Knoxville (AA) on 6/21...Was 2nd on club in wins (9), 4th in GS (17)

Stottlemyre (cont...)

3rd in K (104)...Named by Baseball America as league's best prospect...Named California League's TOPPS player of the Month for May and BLUE JAYS' minor league pitcher of the Month for June...3rd on Knoxville in wins (8), GS (18) and K (81)...**1987:** Spent the season with Syracuse (AAA) of the International League...Reported to the BLUE JAYS on 9/1 as a non-roster player...Led the IL in GS (34), losses (13), runs (103), ER (92), BB (87), 2nd in K (143) and IP (186.2) and K/9IP for a starter (6.89)...Named as one of the league's top prospects by Baseball America...9 of 11 wins by 7/2...Set club mark for GS...Was recipient of R. Howard Webster Award as MVP for Syracuse...**1988:** Made the club as a non-roster invitee with contract purchased on 4/3...ML debut 4/6 at Kansas City with 1.2 ShO IP...1st ML GS, 4-2 loss at Minnesota, 4/10...Was 1st of 8 consecutive losses through 5/23...1st ML win 9-2 at Seattle on 5/3...Perfect game through 6.1 IP before hitting Alvin Davis...Lost next 6 decisions, 5/8-28...Assigned outright to Syracuse (AAA) of IL on 7/27...Organization's Minor League Pitcher of the Month for August (5-0, 2.05ERA, 7GS)...Contract purchased by BLUE JAYS on 9/2 and appeared in 5-games in September...**1989:** Started the season with 7 consecutive relief appearances...Went 6.0 IP vs New York on 4/18 which was the longest outing by a club reliever in 1989...Lost 1st GS of season, 4-1 vs Texas on 4.23...Subsequently lost next GS, 9-0 at California (2.1IP) on 4/28 and was relegated to the bullpen...2 appearances in bullpen (5.0IP, 7H, 5R/ER) and then assigned outright to Syracuse (AAA) of the IL on 5/15...Was 3-2, 3.23 ERA with Chiefs...Contract purchased on 6/30...Proceeded to win 7 of 8 decisions, 7/6-9/6...Included career high 5-games win streak over New York (6-5, 8/6), Kansas City (2-0, 8/12), Milwaukee (5-4, 8/27), Minnesota (7-3, 9/1) and Chicago (4-2, 9/6)...Winless in last 4 GS (0-2) to finish season...Lost only ALCS game start, (game 2) by a score of 10-4...Father, Mel, had pitched in post season 25 years earlier in the 1964 World Series...With ALCS appearance, the Stottlemyres are only the 2nd father/son combination to have post season experience...The others were Jim Bagby and Jim Junior...3-2, 2.97 ERA vs the East Division and 4-5, 7.11 ERA vs AL West clubs...6-3, 3.43 ERA post All-Star Game...Had ERA under 2.00 vs Baltimore (1.64), Cleveland (1.29) and New York (1.23).

TODD STOTTLEMYRE

Year	Club & League	W-L	ERA	G	GS	CG	ShO	SV	IP	H	R	ER	HR	HB	BB	SO	WP
1986	Ventura (Cal)	9-4	2.43	17	17	2	0	0	103.2	76	39	28	4	2	36	104	7
1986	Knoxville (Sou)	8-7	4.18	18	18	1	0	0	99.0	93	56	46	5	1	49	81	4
1987	Syracuse (Int)	11-13	4.44	34	34	1	0	0	186.2	189	103	92	14	6	87	143	10
1988	TORONTO (AL)	4-8	5.69	28	16	0	0	0	98.0	109	70	62	15	4	46	67	2
1988	Syracuse (Int)	5-0	2.05	7	7	1	0	0	48.1	36	12	11	1	0	8	51	2
1989	Syracuse (Int)	3-2	3.23	10	9	2	0	0	55.2	46	23	20	4	2	15	45	0
1989	TORONTO (AL)	7-7	3.88	27	18	0	0	0	127.2	137	56	55	11	5	44	63	4
1990	TORONTO (AL)	13-17	4.34	33	33	4	0	0	203.0	214	101	98	18	8	69	115	6
ML TOTALS		24-32	4.51	88	67	4	0	0	428.2	460	227	215	44	17	159	245	12

LEAGUE CHAMPIONSHIP SERIES

Year	Club & League	W-L	ERA	G	GS	CG	ShO	SV	IP	H	R	ER	HR	HB	BB	SO	WP
1989	TORONTO (AL)	0-1	7.20	1	1	0	0	0	5.0	7	4	4	1	0	2	3	0

STOTTLEMYRE - TRANSACTIONS

- Selected by New York Yankees' organization in 5th round of free-agent draft, June 6, 1983.
- Selected by St. Louis Cardinals' organization in secondary phase of free-agent draft, January 9, 1985.
- Selected by Toronto Blue Jays' organization in secondary phase of free-agent draft, June 3, 1985.

TODD STOTTLEMYRE vs AMERICAN LEAGUE

	1990						CAREER					
	W-L-S	ERA	IP	H	ER	SO	W-L-S	ERA	IP	H	ER	SO
SEASON	13-17-0	4.34	203.0	214	98	115	24-32-0	4.52	428.2	460	215	245
TORONTO	7-8-0	4.28	103.0	112	49	62	12-15-0	4.52	220.2	250	111	129
AWAY	6-9-0	4.41	100.0	102	49	53	12-17-0	4.50	208.0	210	104	116
vs BALTIMORE	1-0-0	1.50	6.0	6	1	2	2-0-0	1.42	19.0	16	3	10
BOSTON	0-3-0	3.74	21.2	17	9	15	1-4-0	4.23	38.1	35	18	22
CLEVELAND	3-1-0	3.65	24.2	24	10	9	3-1-0	3.69	46.1	48	19	17
DETROIT	1-2-0	5.40	16.2	21	10	11	3-2-0	3.66	39.1	42	16	23
MILWAUKEE	0-1-0	3.38	8.0	9	3	3	1-3-0	5.85	20.0	27	13	13
NEW YORK	2-0-0	3.94	29.2	32	13	14	3-0-0	3.12	43.1	47	15	20
TORONTO	-	-	-	-	-	-	-	-	-	-	-	-
A.L. EAST	7-7-0	3.88	106.2	109	46	54	13-10-0	3.66	206.1	215	84	105
vs CALIFORNIA	1-1-0	2.77	13.0	14	4	14	1-3-0	4.82	28.0	37	15	21
CHICAGO	2-0-0	0.60	15.0	6	1	11	3-2-0	2.45	29.1	23	8	18
KANSAS CITY	1-3-0	7.58	19.0	29	16	10	2-5-0	5.45	38.0	49	23	22
MINNESOTA	2-0-0	3.21	14.0	15	5	4	3-2-0	5.21	38.0	41	22	17
OAKLAND	0-1-0	4.50	8.0	7	4	6	0-2-0	8.14	21.0	28	19	18
SEATTLE	0-3-0	8.47	17.0	22	16	7	1-4-0	7.80	30.0	35	26	15
TEXAS	0-2-0	5.06	10.2	12	6	9	1-4-0	5.01	32.1	32	18	29
A.L. WEST	6-10-0	4.84	96.2	105	52	61	11-22-0	5.44	216.2	245	131	140
Pre-ASG	9-8-0	4.45	111.1	121	55	54	13-20-0	4.65	235.3	261	122	137
Post-ASG	4-9-0	4.22	91.2	93	43	61	11-12-0	4.34	192.2	199	93	108
STARTER	13-17-0	4.34	203.0	214	98	115	22-30-0	4.48	391.2	420	195	231
RELIEVER	-	-	-	-	-	-	2-2-0	3.16	57.0	40	20	14
in APRIL	3-2-0	4.67	27.0	25	14	13	3-7-0	5.37	60.1	66	36	37
MAY	1-3-0	5.04	30.1	31	17	17	2-8-0	5.45	65.3	71	40	44
JUNE	4-2-0	3.13	46.0	47	16	15	6-2-0	2.76	81.2	78	25	32
JULY	2-4-0	5.86	27.2	39	18	20	4-5-0	4.78	52.2	64	28	34
AUGUST	1-3-0	3.31	35.1	29	13	26	4-5-0	4.42	89.2	97	44	55
SEPT/OCT	2-3-0	4.91	36.2	43	20	24	5-5-0	4.75	77.4	89	42	43

11 WILLIAM SUERO

INFIELDER

Born: Nov. 7, 1966 Santo Domingo, DR

Resides: Santo Domingo, DR

B-R T-R 5-9 175

M.L. Service: 0.000

PERSONAL: William Urban Suero...Graduate of Francisco Rasario Sanchez High School in Santo Domingo, Dominican Republic in 1984.

LAST SEASON: Played the entire season at Knoxville (AA) of the Southern League...Led the club in slugging pct. (.451) and at-bats (483)...Was second on the team in HR (16) and SB (40), third in games played (133) and RBI (60)...Selected to the Topps Double A All-Star Team...Played 130 games at second base...Was named to the AA All-Star Team.

PROFESSIONAL CAREER: **1985:** DID NOT PLAY...Was on the DL for the entire season at Bradenton...**1986:** Spent the season at Medicine Hat of the Pioneer League where he led all second basemen in games (63), fielding percentage (.947), total chances (701), putouts (159), assists (182) and double plays (34)...Was second in the league in at bats (273)...**1987:** Spent the year with St. Catharines of the New York-Penn League...Was named to the post season All-Star team and selected to Topps' Class A All-Star team...Led all second basemen in games (77), total chances (362), and putouts (149)...Finished third in batting (.316), second in at bats (297) and second in hits (94)...**1988:** Played at Myrtle Beach of the South Atlantic League...Named to the South Atlantic All-Star team after finishing second in the league in runs scored (88) and tenth in batting (.284)...Had a 16 game hitting streak, June 17-July 5...Had 36 multiple hit games including two 4 hit games...**1989:** Started the season at Dunedin (A) of the Florida State League where he hit .333 (39-117) in May; with 5 doubles, 5 triples, 2 HR and 12 RBI...Posted a slugging percentage of .513 for the month...Batted .310 (31-100) in May and June after being promoted to Knoxville-(10 extra base hits and 10 RBI)...Set a new career high for games played in a season with (138) and walks (50).

WILLIAM SUERO

Year	Club & League	AVG	G	AB	R	H	2B	3B	HR	RBI	SH-SF	HP	BB	SO	SB-CS
1985	Bradenton (Gulf)						DID NOT PLAY								
1986	Medicine Hat (Pio)	.278	64	273	39	76	7	5	2	28	4-2	3	15	36	13-4
1987	St. Catharines (NYP)	.316	77	297	43	94	12	4	4	24	2-1	1	35	35	23-11
1988	Myrtle Beach (SAL)	.284	125	493	88	140	21	6	6	52	3-6	4	49	72	21-7
1989	Dunedin (FSL)	.291	51	206	35	60	10	5	2	17	1-0	3	16	32	9-3
1990	Knoxville (Sou)	.263	133	483	80	127	29	7	16	60	6-2	7	78	78	40-21

SUERO - TRANSACTIONS

- Signed as a free-agent by the Toronto Blue Jays, May 1, 1985.
- On disabled list June 21-Sept. 9, 1985.
- On disabled list August 17-Sept.3, 1988.

15 PAT TABLER

INFIELDER

Born: Feb. 2, 1958 Hamilton, OH

Resides: Cincinnati, OH

B-R T-R 6-2 200

M.L. SERVICE: 8.078

PERSONAL: Patrick Sean Tabler...Married, wife's name Susan...Three children: Tyler (12/1/82), Kathryn (6/30/84) and Troy (10/7/88)...Graduated from McNicholas High in Cincinnati in 1976 where he participated in baseball, basketball, track and football...Was All-City and All-State in baseball and basketball...Named Cincinnati's MVP and Player-of-the-Year and All-American in baseball...Played Little League and American Legion ball as a youth.

LAST SEASON: Spent most of the 1990 season with the Kansas City Royals...Posted fewest at-bats with one Major League club (195) since 1982 when he had 85 with the Cubs...18 of his 65 hits went for extra-bases...Struck out just one time more than he walked (21K/20BB)...Played in his 1000th Major League game on May 4th vs the White Sox...Collected his 1000th ML hit (a double) off of the Orioles' Ben McDonald on July 27th at Kansas City...Was dealt to the Mets on August 30th for pitcher Archie Corbin...Made nine starts for the Mets and appeared in 17 games for them...Hit in 6 of his last 8 games of the season while with the Mets.

PROFESSIONAL CAREER: **1976:** Played third base and outfield at Oneonta (A) of the New York-Penn League...Was the Yankees' first round selection in the June 1976 Free Agent Draft

(16th overall)...Batted .231 in 65 games...**1977:** Assigned to Ft. Lauderdale (A) of the Florida State League where he almost doubled his hit total from the previous season...Led FSL first basemen in errors with 35...Played exclusively at first base...**1978:** Spent the season at Ft. Lauderdale (A) and managed to boost his average by 35 points from the previous season to .273...Cut his errors in half, making just 15 while spending time at first base, outfield and third base...Drove in 70 runs in a then career high 138 games...**1979:** Began the season at Ft. Lauderdale for the third consecutive year...Hit .316- (43 points higher than the previous season) in 75 games with 12 doubles before being promoted to West Haven (AA) of the Eastern League...Played 56 games at second base and the outfield and had 24 extra-base hits...Averaged better than a hit per contest (57H/56G)...**1980:** Spent the entire season at Nashville (AA) of the Southen League, playing solely at second base...Had then career high AB (479) and continued to hit close to .300 (.296)...Had 62 extra-base hits (38 doubles, 8 triples and 16 HR) which accounted for almost half of his total hits (142)...Led all Southern League second basemen in errors with 27...**1981:** Made the jump to AAA ball with the Columbus Clippers of the International League...Split duty between second and third base...Played in 52 games and was hitting at a .296 clip before being sent to Iowa AAA-(Cubs) of the American Association on June 12th...While with Iowa, he participated in 63 games and added 10 points to his .296 average...Made just 4 errors while with Iowa...Traded to the Chicago Cubs on August 19th...Promoted to the big league club and saw action in 35 games with the Cubs...**1982:** Started the season with Iowa (AAA) where he was chosen as the league's All-Star third baseman while hitting .342...Led the league in triples (11), putouts (112) and assists (215)...Drove in a career high 105 RBI as well as delivering 60 extra-base hits...Promoted to the Senior Loop club and hit .235 in 25 games...**1983:** Traded to the White Sox on January 25th and was later sent to Cleveland on April 1...Went to Charleston (AAA) of the International League and played in just 4 games before being called up to the parent club on April 18th...Led the team with a .291 batting average...Played at three positions (outfield, third base and second base)...Averaged better than a hit per game (125H/124G)...**1984:** Enjoyed his second straight .290 ML season...Hit his first ML Grand Slam HR off of Seattle's Dave Beard on September 25th on his way to a 6 RBI game...Reached double figures in HR (10) for the first time in his ML career...Played at all three bases and the outfield...**1985:** Enjoyed a 6 RBI game vs Seattle on June 8th which included his second career grand slam HR in the 1st inning off of Jim Beattie...Put together a career high 15 game hitting streak, April 13-28...Spent considerably more time at first base than the previous two seasons...Underwent arthroscopic surgery on his left knee on September 5th, keeping him sidelined for the rest of the season...**1986:** Hit a career high .326, which was good for 4th place overall in the AL batting department...Posted the highest batting average gain of any AL player from 1985 to 1986 (51 points)...Placed on the 15-day DL on June 11 with a deep henmatoma of the right thigh...Reported to Maine (AAA) of the International League for medical rehabilitation on June 26...Rejoined the ML club on June 29...Named the AL Player of the Week for the week ending August 31...Collected his 500th hit on August 12 at New York...Led AL players with a .374 batting average during the second half...**1987:** Achieved career highs in 7 offensive categories: HR (11), RBI (86), Hits (170), Doubles (34), Stolen Bases (5), Games (151) and at-bats (553)...Tied a career best with 66 runs scored...Was the AL Player of the Week for the week ending May 31- (14-29/.483, 2HR, 10RBI)...Named to the AL All-Star Team for the first time in his career...Was hitting .308 with 7 HR and 48 RBI at the All-Star Break...Reached base in 8 straight plate appearances August 21 (game 2) and August 22 (7 hits, 1BB)...Was 5-9 with 11 RBI with the bases loaded...**1988:** Began the season with the Indians but was traded to the Royals on June 3 in exchange for LHP Buddy Black...Prior to the trade he was hitting .224 in 41 games...After his arrival at Kansas City, he batted .309 in 89 games, raising his overall average to .282 for the season...Was 8-9 with the bases loaded (20 RBI) including going 5-5 (12 RBI) while with the Royals...Royals Player of the Month for August (.312, 29H, 17 RBI)...**1989:** Opened the season as the designated hitter but also saw action at first base, second base and the outfield...Hit his 1st HR of the season and 1st career at Royals Stadium vs the Indians on July 23...Had a 10 game hitting streak, June 21-July 2 (14-38/.368)...Played first base at Texas on September 1 for his first appearance there since June 23, 1985...His 2nd HR of the season was a PH-HR in the bottom of the ninth vs the Rangers on September 12...Hit .350 vs LHP- 6th in the American League.

PAT TABLER'S HITTING WITH THE BASES LOADED

Tabler is a career .500 hitter (40-80) with 98 RBI in bases loaded situations. Here is a year by year breakdown of how he's produced in those situations.

YEAR	CLUB	H	AB	HR	RBI	AVG.
1982	CHICAGO	0	1	0	0	.000
1983	CLEVELAND	11	19	0	25	.579
1984	CLEVELAND	5	9	1	14	.556
1985	CLEVELAND	6	7	1	15	.857
1986	CLEVELAND	2	10	0	3	.200
1987	CLEVELAND	5	9	0	11	.556
1988	CLEVELAND	3	4	0	8	.750
	KANSAS CITY	5	5	0	12	1.000
1989	KANSAS CITY	1	11	0	5	.091
1990	KANSAS CITY	0	0	0	0	.000
	NEW YORK (NL)	2	5	0	5	.400
TOTAL		40	80	2	98	.500

PAT TABLER

Year	Club & League	AVG	G	AB	R	H	2B	3B	HR	RBI	SH-SF	HP	BB	SO	SB-CS
1976	Oneonta (NYP)	.231	65	238	27	55	3	0	1	20	2-3	2	27	35	6-2
1977	Ft. Lauderdale (FSL)	.238	110	391	35	93	7	1	1	36	3-3	0	43	62	4-8
1978	Ft. Lauderdale (FSL)	.273	138	455	56	124	9	5	5	70	6-7	1	76	69	5-1
1979	Ft. Lauderdale (FSL)	.316	75	247	39	78	12	4	2	33	1-1	5	51	46	4-3
1979	West Haven (East)	.300	56	190	33	57	15	3	6	36	1-3	2	36	44	9-4
1980	Nashville (Sou)	.296	136	479	82	142	38	8	16	83	4-2	7	66	74	9-6
1981	Columbus (Int)	.296	52	179	41	53	14	3	11	33	1-3	4	27	43	0-1
1981	Iowa (AmAs)	.206	63	222	41	68	13	3	6	37	1-3	3	25	40	2-3
1981	CHICAGO (NL)	.188	35	101	11	19	3	1	1	5	3-0	0	13	26	0-1
1982	Iowa (AmAs)	.342	129	441	89	151	32	11	17	105	3-9	3	85	74	15-7
1982	CHICAGO (NL)	.235	25	85	9	20	4	2	1	7	0-2	1	6	20	0-0
1983	Charleston (Int)	.214	4	14	2	3	0	1	0	2	0-0	0	4	2	0-0
1983	CLEVELAND (AL)	.291	124	430	56	125	23	5	6	65	0-5	1	56	63	2-4
1984	CLEVELAND (AL)	.290	144	473	66	137	21	3	10	68	0-2	3	47	62	3-1
1985	CLEVELAND (AL)	.275	117	404	47	111	18	3	5	59	2-3	2	27	55	0-6
1986	Maine (Int)	.250	3	12	5	3	1	0	0	1	0-1	0	2	1	0-0
1986	CLEVELAND (AL)	.326	130	473	61	154	29	2	6	48	2-1	3	29	75	3-1
1987	CLEVELAND (AL)	.307	151	553	66	170	34	3	11	86	3-5	6	51	84	5-2
1988	CLEVELAND (AL)	.224	41	143	16	32	5	1	1	17	0-1	1	23	27	1-0
1988	KANSAS CITY (AL)	.309	89	301	37	93	17	2	1	49	0-4	2	23	41	2-3
1989	KANSAS CITY (AL)	.259	123	390	36	101	11	1	2	42	3-2	2	37	42	0-0
1990	KANSAS CITY (AL)	.272	75	195	12	53	14	0	1	19	0-3	1	20	21	0-2
1990	NEW YORK (NL)	.279	17	43	6	12	1	1	1	10	0-0	1	3	8	0-0
AL TOTALS		.290	994	3362	397	976	172	20	43	453	10-29	21	313	470	15-19
NL TOTALS		.222	77	229	26	51	8	4	3	22	3-2	2	22	54	0-1
ML TOTALS		.286	1071	3591	423	1027	180	24	46	475	13-31	23	335	524	16-20

ALL-STAR GAME RECORD

Year	Club & League	AVG	G	AB	R	H	2B	3B	HR	RBI	SH-SF	HP	BB	SO	SB-CS
1987	AL at Oak	.000	1	1	0	0	0	0	0	0	0-0	0	0	1	0-0

TABLER - TRANSACTIONS

- Selected by New York Yankees' organization in 1st round (16th player selected) of free-agent draft, June 8, 1976.
- Loaned to Iowa (Chicago Cubs' organization), June 12, 1981; returned, August 19, 1981.
- Acquired on waivers by Chicago Cubs for two players to be named later, August 19, 1981; New York Yankees acquired Pitcher Bill Caudill, April 1, 1982, and New York organization acquired Pitcher Jay Howell, August 2, 1982, to complete deal.
- Traded with Pitchers Dick Tidrow and Randy Martz and Infielder Scott Fletcher to Chicago white Sox for Pitchers Steve Trout and Warren Brusstar, January 25, 1983.
- Traded to Cleveland Indians for Shortstop Jerry Dybzinski, April 1, 1983.
- On disabled list, June 11 to June 30, 1986; included rehabilitation disability disability assignment to Maine, June 26 to June 30, 1986.
- Traded to Kansas City Royals for Pitcher Bud Black, June 3, 1988.
- Traded to New York Mets for Pitcher Archie Corbin, August 30, 1990.
- Sign as a free-agent with Toronto Blue Jays, December 5, 1990.

TABLER vs AMERICAN LEAGUE

	1990					CAREER				
	AB	H	HR	RBI	AVG.	AB	H	HR	RBI	AVG.
SEASON	195	53	1	19	.272	3362	976	43	453	.290
HOME	98	24	0	6	.245	1666	514	25	245	.309
ROAD	97	29	1	13	.299	1696	462	18	205	.272
vs BALTIMORE	15	1	0	1	.067	304	100	3	41	.329
BOSTON	24	9	1	8	.375	256	78	6	36	.305
CLEVELAND	13	6	0	3	.462	69	21	1	11	.304
DETROIT	5	1	0	0	.200	218	67	6	32	.307
MILWAUKEE	20	7	0	3	.350	290	81	1	41	.279
NEW YORK	21	7	0	2	.333	283	93	1	44	.328
TORONTO	16	3	0	1	.188	284	78	4	35	.275
AL EAST	114	34	1	18	.298	1704	518	22	240	.204
vs CALIFORNIA	4	0	0	0	.000	224	65	3	31	.290
CHICAGO	24	6	0	0	.250	292	76	2	26	.260
KANSAS CITY	-	-	-	-	-	200	51	3	24	.255
MINNESOTA	16	6	0	1	.375	234	62	1	30	.265
OAKLAND	5	0	0	0	.000	208	61	2	35	.293
SEATTLE	19	4	0	0	.211	234	61	4	31	.261
TEXAS	13	3	0	0	.231	266	82	6	36	.308
AL WEST	77	19	0	1	.247	1658	458	21	213	.276
Pre-ASG	98	24	0	5	.245	1729	411	19	226	.238
Post-ASG	97	29	1	14	.299	1633	565	24	227	.346
vs RHP	114	26	0	10	.228	2208	603	22	269	.273
LHP	81	27	1	9	.333	1154	373	21	184	.323
PINCH HITTING	12	3	0	3	.250	68	17	1	16	.250
DES HITTING	49	13	0	4	.265	862	244	4	112	.283
in APRIL	30	7	0	1	.233	487	149	6	64	.306
MAY	26	6	0	3	.231	594	162	7	77	.273
JUNE	35	8	0	1	.229	499	132	3	65	.265
JULY	67	21	1	13	.313	602	181	11	77	.301
AUGUST	37	11	0	1	.297	718	223	8	97	.311
SEPT/OCT	-	-	-	-	-	462	129	8	73	.279

Tabler (cont...)

CAREER HIGHS

SEASON: **AVG.** .326-1986 **H** 170-1987 **HR** 11-1987 **RBI** 86-1987 **SB** 5-1987

GAME: **H** 4-5 times, last time vs DET Aug. 22, 1987 **HR** 1- 46 times
RBI 6 vs SEA June 8, 1985: vs SEA Sept. 25, 1984 **SB** 1-15 times

Last ML HR: vs CHI (NL) 9/28/90 **Longest Hitting Streak:** 15 - 1985

40 MIKE TIMLIN
PITCHER

Born: March 10, 1966 Midland, TX
Resides: Midland, TX
B-R T-R 6-4 205
M.L. Service: 0.000

PERSONAL: Michael August Timlin...Graduated from Midland High School (Texas) where he captained the baseball team...Attended Southwestern University in Georgetown, Texas where he played baseball.

LAST SEASON: Began the season at Dunedin (A) of the Florida State League where he appeared in 42 games and saved 22 (4th in FSL)...Had nearly a 3-1 strikeout to walk ratio (46-16)...Was promoted to Knoxville (AA) of the Southern League on July 23rd and managed 8 saves (second on the club) while appearing in 17 games...Had a 3-1 K to BB ratio at Knoxville and had an ERA of 1.73 at Knoxville.

PROFESSIONAL CAREER: **1987:** Was 4-8 at Medicine Hat (Rookie) of the Pioneer League and had close to a 3-1 strikeout to walk ratio (66K/26BB)...**1988:** Spent the entire season at Myrtle Beach (A) of the South Atlantic League where he was 7-3 with a 2.16 ERA in the final two months of the season...Pitched a career high 155 innings...**1989:** Played at Dunedin (A) of the Florida State League...Struck out 40 batters and allowed only 43 hits in 49 innings of relief work...Achieved first save of his professional career.

Year	Club & League	W-L	ERA	G	GS	CG	ShO	SV	IP	H	R	ER	HR	HB	BB	SO	WP
1987	Medicine Hat (Pio)	4-8	5.14	13	12	2	0	0	75.1	79	50	43	4	5	26	66	9
1988	Myrtle Beach (SAL)	10-6	2.86	35	22	0	0	0	151.0	119	68	48	4	19	77	106	8
1989	Dunedin (FSL)	5-8	3.25	33	7	1	0	7	88.2	90	44	32	2	5	36	64	10
1990	Dunedin (FSL)	7-2	1.43	42	0	0	0	22	50.1	36	11	8	0	1	16	46	3
1990	Knoxville (Sou)	1-2	1.73	17	0	0	0	8	26.0	20	6	5	0	1	7	21	0

TIMLIN - TRANSACTIONS

- Selected by Toronto Blue Jays' organization in 5th round (127th overall) of free-agent draft June, 1987.
- On disabled list April 4 - May 2, 1989.

52 RICKY TRLICEK
PITCHER

Born: April 26, 1969 Houston, TX
Resides: Houston, TX
B-R T-R 6-2 200
M.L. Service: 0.000

PERSONAL: Richard Alan Trlicek...Graduate of LaGrange High School...Pronounced TRiLL-i-SeCK.

LAST SEASON: Spent the season at Dunedin (A) in the Florida State League where he was 5-8, 3.75ERA, 26G/GS, 154.1IP, 64ER, 2HR, 72BB, 125K...Was 3rd on the Dunedin club in strikeouts and 5th overall in the FSL...Led the club with 22 wild pitches.

PROFESSIONAL CAREER: **1987:** Was Phillies' fourth pick in the June 1987 Free Agent Draft...Signed by Don Williams, Tony Roig and Bob Reasonover...Spent the season with Utica (Summer A) of the New York-Penn League where he was used primarily as a game starter...Encountered control problems with 31 BB in 37.1 IP...**1988:** Second consecutive season in the New York-Penn League...Tied then personal high with 2 wins...Used exclusively as a game starter...Control problems persisted with 31 BB in 31.2 IP...**1989:** Spent most of the season with Sumter (A) of the South Atlantic League where he was 2nd on the club in GS (15) and K (72) while finishing 3rd in IP (93.2)...Made 1 GS for Durham (A) of the Carolina League, pitching 8 innings.

Year	Club & League	W-L	ERA	G	GS	CG	ShO	SV	IP	H	R	ER	HR	HB	BB	SO	WP
1987	Utica (NYP)	2-5	4.10	10	8	1	1	0	37.1	43	28	17	2	1	31	22	5
1988	Batavia (NYP)	2-3	7.39	8	8	0	0	0	31.2	27	32	26	2	4	31	26	7
1989	Sumter (Sal)	6-5	2.59	15	15	0	0	0	93.2	73	40	27	7	4	40	72	3
1989	Durham (Cal)	0-0	1.13	1	1	0	0	0	8.0	3	2	1	0	1	1	4	2
1990	Dunedin (FSL)	5-8	3.73	26	26	0	0	0	154.1	128	74	64	2	6	72	125	22

TRLICEK - TRANSACTIONS

- Selected by Philadelphia Phillies' organization in 4th round of free-agent draft, June 2, 1987.
- Released, March 23, 1989; signed by Atlanta Braves' organization, april 2, 1989.
- Traded to Toronto Blue Jays for Catcher Ernie Whitt and Outfielder Kevin Batiste, December 17, 1989.

31 DUANE WARD

PITCHER

Born: May 28, 1964 Parkview, NM

Resides: Las Vegas, NV

B-R T-R 6-4 215

M.L. Service 3.154

PERSONAL: Roy Duane Ward...Single...While at Farmington (NM) High School, he was All-State, All-State Tournament and All-District Player for 2 years...All-American his senior year.

LAST SEASON: Was the Labatt's "BLUE" Pitcher of The Month for the month of April- 3SV, 0.54ERA, 10GMS...Set a new career high for strikeouts with 7 on 8/2 at Texas...Longest outing was on 8/1 at Texas, going 4.0IP... First Batter Efficiency was 83.6%(61-73)...Had career high 73 appearances-all in relief...At Home was 0-4, 5 saves, 3.02...On the Road was 2-4, 6 Saves, 3.92.. Finished 39 games - second to Henke-(58)...Opposing batters hit .221 (.259[L], .194[R])...Led the AL in innings pitched by a reliever with 127.2...T2nd in the AL in games with 73-...Had a 1.52 ERA for August 13G, 23.2IP, 4R/ER, 2BB, 22K...Second on the Blue Jays in saves with 11...Set a new career high for IP with 127.2- previous high was 114.2 in 1989...Had a better than 2-1 strikeout to walk ratio...Issued lowest number of walks (42) since joining the BLUE JAYS in 1988...Had seven Holds...11 saves came in 18 opportunites.

PROFESSIONAL CAREER: **1982:** Was Braves' 1st round selection (9th overall) in the June Free Agent Draft...Began professional career with Bradenton...Started 8 games while pitching a total of 45.2 IP...**1983:** Remained at the Class A level but with Durham...Set personal high with 11 wins...**1984:** Spent the season with Greenville (AA) of the Southern League, finishing 4th on the club in K (54)...Proceeded to lead the Florida Instructional League in ERA (1.45)...**1985:** Started the season with Greenville (AA) where he dropped each of his 1st 5 decisions but rebounded to go 10-2 in his next 18 games...Finished season at Richmond going 0-1 in 5 games...Was named by Baseball America as 1 of the top 3 Major League Prospects in Southern League behing Jose Canseco and Eric Plunk...**1986:** Started season with Atlanta making ML debut, 4/12 vs Houston...1st ML decision, 3-2 loss to Houston on 4/22...Optioned to Richmond (AAA) of International League on 6/6 due to inactivity...Acquired by TORONTO for Doyle Alexander on 7/5 and assigned to Syracuse (AAA) of the IL...Recalled to TORONTO on 9/1...BLUE JAYS debut, 1 ShO IP, 9/17 vs Detroit...1st ML GS, 12-3 loss on 9/28 at Fenway which eliminated BLUE JAYS from post season play...**1987:** Began the season with the BLUE JAYS prior to being optioned to Syracuse (AAA) of the IL on 4/29...Played most of the season at Syracuse...Recalled on 9/1...Went 14 consecutive outings (16.1IP) at Syracuse without allowing a run, 6/5-7/31 (2-0-10, 0.96 ERA...Led the Chiefs in SV (14), ERA (2.74) and appearances (46)...1st ML win, 5-3 at Milwaukee, 9/7 in relief...**1988:** Underwent surgery on 10/15/87 to repair a slight ligament tear in left knee sustained with Syracuse on 8/87...1st ML SV, 10-0 vs Twins on 4/9...8 consecutive scoreless outings, 4/19-5/5...Solo HR to Cleveland's Kittle- 1st HR in 40 AL appearances and 1st since 4/27/86 (Dodgers' Landreaux)...Lost 6-3 at Minnesota on 7/26 for 1st ML loss since 9/28/86...Career high 6 K, 9/3 vs Texas...15-18 in save situations...T/5th in AL in appearances (64)...1989: Shared the stopper role with Tom Henke...Endured control problems, walking 58 batters in 114.2 IP...Walked at least on batter (9) in his first 7 appearances...Lost 3 of 4 decisions in April...In May was 0-3-2 despite 1.77 ERA...5R/ER in 7.1 IP 6/13-20...Season high consecutive ShO appearances, 6/29-7/14 (12.2IP)...Saves in 4 consecutive appearances, 7/3-14 and 7 saves in 9 appearances 7/3-25...Only 4 BB in 12 appearances...Left 9/29 game vs the Orioles after being hit on the throwing hand by the batted ball...Ineffective in post season play, allowing 3R/ER, 6H in 3.2 IP...Led ML in blown saves (12)...Among League leader in games (8th-66), WP (T/3rd-13)...Was 42-65 in First Batter Efficiency...All 4 wins recorded before All-Star Game...3 of 10 losses came vs California...6 of 15 saves in June.

Year	Club & League	W-L	ERA	G	GS	CG	ShO	SV	IP	H	R	ER	HR	HB	BB	SO	WP
1982	Bradenton (Gulf)	2-3	4.53	8	8	1	0	0	45.2	45	25	23	0	3	24	31	2
1982	Anderson (SAL)	1-2	5.32	5	4	0	0	0	23.2	24	16	14	0	1	15	18	4
1983	Durham (Cal)	11-13	4.29	28	28	6	2	0	178.1	165	103	85	20	6	75	115	6
1984	Greenville (Sou)	4-9	4.99	21	20	4	0	0	104.2	108	71	58	9	2	57	54	8
1985	Greenville (Sou)	11-10	4.20	28	24	3	0	0	150.0	141	83	70	4	4	105	100	9
1985	Richmond (Int)	0-1	11.81	5	1	0	0	0	5.1	8	9	7	1	1	8	3	0
1986	ATLANTA (NL)	0-1	7.31	10	0	0	0	0	16.0	22	13	13	2	0	8	8	0
1986	Richmond (Int)	1-1	3.38	6	6	0	0	0	34.2	34	13	13	0	1	23	17	0
1986	Syracuse (Int)	6-4	4.23	14	14	3	0	0	83.0	91	43	39	9	2	29	50	4
1986	TORONTO (AL)	0-1	3.50	2	1	0	0	0	2.0	3	4	3	0	0	4	1	0
1987	TORONTO (AL)	1-0	6.94	12	1	0	0	0	11.2	14	9	9	0	0	12	10	0
1987	Syracuse (Int)	2-2	3.89	46	3	0	0	14	76.1	59	35	33	7	2	42	67	7
1988	TORONTO (AL)	9-3	3.30	64	0	0	0	15	111.2	101	46	41	5	5	60	91	10
1989	TORONTO (AL)	4-10	3.77	66	0	0	0	15	114.2	94	55	48	4	5	58	122	13
1990	TORONTO (AL)	2-8	3.45	73	0	0	0	11	127.2	101	51	49	9	1	42	112	5
AL TOTALS		16-22	3.67	217	2	0	0	41	367.2	313	165	150	18	11	176	336	28
NL TOTALS		0-1	7.31	10	0	0	0	0	16.0	22	13	13	2	0	8	8	0
ML TOTALS		16-23	3.82	227	2	0	0	41	383.2	335	178	163	20	11	184	344	28

WARD - TRANSACTIONS

- Selected by Atlanta Braves' organization in 1st round (ninth player selected) of free-agent draft, June 7, 1982.
- On disabled list, May 7 to May 29 and July 14 to August 7, 1984.
- Traded to Toronto Blue Jays for Pitcher Doyle Alexander, July 6, 1986.

DUANE WARD vs AMERICAN LEAGUE

	1990						CAREER					
	W-L-S	ERA	IP	H	ER	SO	W-L-S	ERA	IP	H	ER	SO
SEASON	2-8-11	3.45	127.2	101	49 1	12	16-22-41	3.68	366.2	313	150	336
TORONTO	0-4-5	3.02	65.2	48	22	53	7-11-21	3.27	187.1	153	68	171
ROAD	2-4-6	3.92	62.0	53	27	59	9-11-20	4.12	179.1	160	82	165
vs BALTIMORE	0-0-1	0.76	71.0	6	6	8	0-0-3	1.55	87.0	28	15	25
BOSTON	0-2-0	6.55	11.0	10	8	6	3-3-6	3.83	40.0	31	17	25
CLEVELAND	0-0-2	0.00	13.0	6	0	13	1-1-3	1.09	33.0	20	4	37
DETROIT	1-1-0	4.50	10.0	6	5	12	3-2-4	4.50	26.0	15	13	31
MILWAUKEE	0-0-1	9.72	8.1	12	9	3	2-2-3	8.10	30.0	46	27	20
NEW YORK	0-0-1	1.86	9.2	11	2	8	1-2-2	3.34	32.1	33	12	32
TORONTO	-	-	-	-	-	-	-	-	-	-	-	-
A.L. EAST	1-3-5	2.20	123.0	51	30	50	10-10-21	3.19	248.1	173	88	170
vs CALIFORNIA	0-3-0	11.25	8.0	11	10	8	0-6-1	7.00	18.0	25	14	14
CHICAGO	1-0-1	2.57	7.0	6	2	8	2-0-5	1.73	26.0	19	5	23
KANSAS CITY	0-1-2	1.17	15.1	9	2	12	1-3-3	2.78	32.1	21	10	26
MINNESOTA	0-0-2	0.90	10.0	6	1	7	0-1-3	3.54	20.1	17	8	14
OAKLAND	0-0-0	0.96	9.1	5	1	7	1-1-1	3.45	31.1	21	12	31
SEATTLE	0-1-1	3.00	9.0	9	3	9	1-1-4	2.57	28.0	25	8	26
TEXAS	0-0-0	0.00	9.2	4	0	11	1-0-3	1.93	23.1	12	5	32
A.L. WEST	1-5-6	2.50	68.1	50	19	62	6-12-20	3.11	179.1	140	62	166
Pre-ASG	1-3-7	3.48	67.1	59	26	58	10-10-22	3.20	196.3	168	70	180
Post-ASG	1-5-4	3.43	60.1	42	23	54	6-79-19	4.22	170.2	145	80	156
STARTER	0-0-0	0.0	0	0	0	0	1-0 3	6.00	2.0	7	8	1
RELIEVER	2-8-11	3.45	127.2	101	49	112	16-21-26	3.49	365.2	306	142	335
in APRIL	0-0-3	1.08	16.2	10	2	18	1-3- 5	3.33	45.3	41	17	44
MAY	1-2-1	4.64	21.1	21	11	22	2-4-4	3.12	57.2	50	20	55
JUNE	0-1-2	5.09	23.0	27	13	15	7-2-7	4.04	71.1	65	32	59
JULY	0-3-2	3.15	20.0	15	7	16	1-5-10	3.58	60.1	59	24	51
AUGUST	1-1-2	1.52	23.2	14	4	22	3-2- 8	3.43	59.4	49	23	53
SEPT/OCT	0-1-1	4.76	22.2	14	12	19	2-4-7	4.27	71.2	49	34	74

CAREER HIGHS

SEASON: **W** 9-1988 **ERA** 3.30-1988 **SV** 15-1988; 1989
IP 127.2-1990 **SO** 122-1989

GAME: **LOW HIT CG** - Never **SO** 7- at TEX Aug. 12, 1990
BB 4-at OAK June 25, 1989; at DET May 11,1990

Last Win: at CHI Aug. 2, 1990 **Last Save:** at KC Sept. 11, 1990
Last CG: Never **Last ShO:** - Never
Last Relief: at BALT Oct. 1, 1990 **Last GS:** vs BOST April 17, 1989
Longest Winning Streak: 6-1988

53 DAVE WEATHERS

PITCHER

Born: Sept. 25, 1969 Lawrenceburg, TN

Resides: Leoma, TN

B-R T-R 6-3 205

M.L. Service: 0.000

PERSONAL: John David Weathers...Single...Attended Loretto High School, graduating in 1987...Was All-State and All-District in his Sophomore, Junior and Senior years...Attended Motlow State Community College in Tullahoma, Tennessee...Set school mark for strikeouts in a season (67)...Childhood hero was Dwight Gooden and Todd Worrell...Hobbies include fishing and skiing...Greatest baseball thrill was a high school game where he pitched a no-hitter and hit three HR.

LAST SEASON: Spent the entire season at Dunedin (A) of the Florida State League where he went 10-7 while starting 27 games...Pitched two complete games to tie for the team lead...Allowed two home runs in 158.0 IP...Was third on the club in BB with (59)...Led the team in GS (27) and balks (9)...Hit 9 batters- second on the squad.

PROFESSIONAL CAREER: **1988: Turned professional with St. Catharines (Summer A) of the New York-Penn League...Won 4 consecutive game starts, 6/22-7/4...Was used primarily as a game starter...1989:** Spent the season with Myrtle Beach (A) of the South Atlantic League...Led the staff in wins (11) and losses (13)...Also led club in GS (31), IP (172.2) and was third in strikeouts (111)...Led the league in GS (31)...Pitched two complete games...Led the league in TBF (759)...Third in SAL in IP (172.2)...Base stealers were successful 15 of 47 times while he was on the mound (.319)...Tossed a two hitter, losing 2-1 to Spartanburg on 5/16...Tossed a three hitter, losing 3-2 to Charleston on 6/21...6 errors in 42 total chances (.857).

DAVID WEATHERS

Year	Club & League	W-L	ERA	G	GS	CG	ShO	SV	IP	H	R	ER	HR	HB	BB	SO	WP
1988	St. Catharines (NYP)	4-4	3.02	15	12	0	0	0	62.2	58	30	21	3	2	26	36	5
1989	Myrtle Beach (SAL)	11-13	3.86	31	31	2	0	0	172.2	163	99	74	3	7	86	111	12
1990	Dunedin (FSL)	10-7	3.70	27	27	2	0	0	158.0	158	82	65	2	9	59	96	10

WEATHERS - TRANSACTIONS

- Selected by Toronto Blue Jays in 3rd round (82nd overall) in June 1988 free-agent draft.

48 CHRIS WEINKE

THIRD BASEMAN

Born: July 31, 1972 St. Paul, MN

Resides: St. Paul, MN

B-L T-R 6-4 205

M.L. Service: 0.000

PERSONAL: Christopher Jon Weinke...Single...Attended Cretin-Derham High School in St. Paul, Minnesota where he played first base and third base...Also played football at Cretin-Derham...Offered a football scholarship from Florida State University.

LAST SEASON: Was drafted by the BLUE JAYS in the second round of the June Free Agent Draft (62nd overall)...Spent the rest of the season working out with the club...Attended the BLUE JAYS' entry in the Florida Instructional League at Dunedin.

PROFESSIONAL CAREER: Did not play during 1990.

WEINKE - TRANSACTIONS

- Selected by Toronto Blue Jays in 2nd round (62nd overall) in June 1990 free-agent draft.

36 DAVID WELLS

PITCHER

Born: May 20, 1963 Torrance, CA

Resides: San Diego, CA

B-L T-L 6-4 225

M.L. Service: 3.020

PERSONAL: David Lee Wells...Married, wife's name, Wendy...A graduate of Point Loma High School in San Diego...Graduated in 1982 where he played baseball and basketball...Was named Conference Player of the Year...Baseball heros were Willie Mays and Rod Carew...Hobbies include basketball and surfing.

LAST SEASON: Began the season in the bullpen...Had made 126 consecutive relief appearances between starts...Moved into the starting rotation after starting the season with 16 consecutive relief appearances...His first win of the season came in relief with a 6-3 win at Detroit on 5/13...Had a 0.93ERA in April 9.2IP, 0-0, 1ER, 1BB, 8K...For the month of July, had 1.82ERA in 6G/GS, 39.2IP, 8ER, 7BB, 20K...Pitched the most innings of his career (189.0)...Had the 2nd best ERA on the BLUE JAYS (among starters) - 3.14...In 20 of his 25 starts, lasted at least 6.0IP ...On the road was 8-4, 3.55ERA, 22G, 15GS, 106.1IP, 42ER, 25BB, 67K..K high was 9 vs the the Twins on 6/5...At SkyDome was 3-2, 2.61ERA, 21G, 10GS, 82.2IP, 71H, 25R, 24ER, 20BB, 48K...As a GS'er, Wells was 10-5, 3.11ERA, 167.2IP, 152H, 58ER, 11HR, 42BB, 97K...In Relief was 1-1-1, 3.38ERA, 18G, 21.1IP, 13H, 9R, 8ER, 3HR, 3BB, 18K...Ranked 7th in ERA(3.14), 8th in Lowest BA Allowed RHB, .230(136-591) & Lowest BA Allowed(.235).

PROFESSIONAL CAREER: **1982:** Started the season with Medicine Hat (Rookie) of the Pioneer League and was used exclusively as a game starter...1 of 6 LHP to pitch for the Pioneer League champs...**1983:** Spent the entire season with Kinston (A) losing 6 of 7 GS...Promoted to Knoxville (AA) on 5/14...Pitched a 2H ShO vs Memphis on 6/5...Placed on the disabled list with an injured left elbow...**1985:** Did not play due to left elbow surgery to the ulnar collateral ligament...Was placed on the disabled list on 4/10 when the operation was conducted...**1986:** Started the season with Florence (A) of the South Atlantic League prior to being promoted to Ventura (A) of the California League on 4/26...Was 2-1 with a 1.89 ERA in 5 games for Ventura...Promoted to Knoxville (AA) on 5/14 and was placed on the DL from 7/7-8/20 with tendinitis in his left shoulder...Promoted to Syracuse on 8/25...Posted a combined 3-5 record during the season...**1987:** Started the season with Syracuse (AAA) of the International League...Was organization's top pitcher for month of May (2-0, 0.87ERA)...Contract purchased by TORONTO on 6/22...ML debut, starting and losing 4-0 to New York on 6/30 (4.0IP, 9H, 4R/ER, 2BB, 4K)...Optioned to Syracuse on 7/12 and remained there through their season end...1st ML win, 7-6 vs California on 9/2 after recall...1st ML save, 9/18 at New York...Was workhorse down the stretch posting a 4-1-1 record with a 1.50 ERA in 16 games (26K in 24.0IP)...**1988:** Winning pitcher in Home Opener, vs New York, 4/11...After allowing 15R in 23.2 IP, was optioned to Syracuse (AAA) on 7/10...Subsequently went 28 days without pitching due to tenderness of the left arm...Recalled by BLUE JAYS on 8/26...Went 21 days without an appearance in August/September...4-5 in SV situations...**1989:** Only left hand reliever to spend the entire season with the club...Won 15-8 vs New York on 4/16 for first win since 6/2/88...Tied personal high with 6 K, 5/16 vs Cleveland (5.1IP)...Lost consecutive outings 3-1 to Boston on 6/30 and 4-1 on 7/2...3 wins in 4 appearances, 7/17-29...Winner in both ends of a Double Header vs the Angels...Won 3-2 (11 innings) vs Cleveland on 9/16 for 7th win of season after entering season with 7 lifetime wins...3R in last 23 appearances (31.0IP), holding opposition scoreless in 20 of those...2 of 4 losses to Boston...3-1-2, 2.51 ERA in July and 1-0-0, 0.79 ERA in September/October...Monthly ERA decreased each month from June onward...5 of 7 wins at home.

DAVID WELLS

Year	Club & League	W-L	ERA	G	GS	CG	ShO	SV	IP	H	R	ER	HR	HB	BB	SO	WP
1982	Med. Hat (Pio)	4-3	5.18	12	12	1	0	0	64.1	71	42	37	5	0	32	53	5
1983	Kingston (Caro)	6-5	3.73	25	25	5	0	0	157.0	141	81	65	13	1	71	115	7
1984	Kingston (Caro)	1-6	4.71	7	7	0	0	0	42.0	51	29	22	1	1	19	44	4
1984	Knoxville (Sou)	3-2	2.59	8	8	3	1	0	59.0	58	22	17	3	0	17	34	1
1985	Syracuse (Int)				DID NOT PLAY												
1986	Florence (SAL)	0-0	3.55	4	1	0	0	0	12.2	7	6	5	1	0	9	14	0
1986	Ventura (Cal)	2-1	1.89	5	2	0	0	0	19.0	13	5	4	0	0	4	26	0
1986	Knoxville (Sou)	1-3	4.05	10	7	1	0	0	40.0	42	24	18	1	1	18	32	4
1986	Syracuse (Int)	0-1	9.82	3	0	0	0	0	3.2	6	4	4	0	0	1	2	0
1987	Syracuse (Int)	4-6	3.87	43	12	0	0	6	109.1	102	49	47	9	0	32	106	9
1987	TORONTO (AL)	4-3	3.99	18	2	0	0	1	29.1	37	14	13	0	0	12	32	4
1988	TORONTO (AL)	3-5	4.62	41	0	0	0	4	64.1	65	36	33	12	2	31	56	6
1988	Syracuse (Int)	0-0	0.00	6	0	0	0	3	5.2	7	1	0	0	0	2	8	2
1989	TORONTO (AL)	7-4	2.40	54	0	0	0	2	86.1	66	25	23	5	0	28	78	6
1990	TORONTO (AL)	11-6	3.14	43	25	0	0	3	189.0	165	72	66	14	2	45	115	7
ML TOTALS		25-18	3.29	156	27	0	0	10	369.0	333	147	135	31	4	116	281	23

WELLS - TRANSACTIONS

- Selected by Toronto Blue Jays' organization in 2nd round (30th overall) of free-agent draft, June 7, 1982.
- On disabled list, June 28, 1984, through remainder of season.
- On disabled list, April 10, 1985, through entire season.
- On disabled list, July 7 to August 20, 1986.

DAVID WELLS vs AMERICAN LEAGUE

	1990						CAREER					
	W-L-S	ERA	IP	H	ER	SO	W-L-S	ERA	IP	H	ER	SO
SEASON	11-6-3	3.14	189.0	165	66	115	25-18-10	3.29	369.0	333	135	281
TORONTO	3-2-2	2.61	82.2	71	24	48	11-8-5	2.81	176.1	154	55	126
ROAD	8-4-1	3.55	106.1	94	42	67	14-10-5	3.74	192.1	179	80	155
vs BALTIMORE	0-1-0	3.78	16.2	18	7	8	1-1-1	4.15	30.1	31	14	24
BOSTON	0-2-0	2.40	15.0	11	4	3	2-4-0	3.16	37.0	31	13	20
CLEVELAND	0-0-1	3.14	14.1	13	5	6	1-1-1	2.49	25.1	20	7	17
DETROIT	3-0-0	5.82	17.0	20	11	13	3-1-1	3.92	41.1	48	18	33
MILKAUKEE	1-2-0	4.61	13.2	16	7	10	1-3-1	4.57	21.2	23	11	15
NEW YORK	1-0-0	3.86	14.0	15	6	12	6-1-1	2.48	40.0	36	11	40
TORONTO	-	-	-	-	-	-	-	-	-	-	-	-
A.L. EAST	5-5-1	3.97	90.2	83	40	52	14-11-5	3.40	195.2	189	74	149
vs CALIFORNIA	1-0-0	1.84	14.2	11	3	11	4-2-1	4.10	37.1	35	17	35
CHICAGO	0-0-0	3.24	8.1	6	3	5	0-0-1	1.84	14.2	10	3	8
KANSAS CITY	1-0-1	0.50	18.0	7	1	2	2-1-1	3.51	25.2	24	10	9
MIINNESOTA	2-0-0	2.40	15.0	9	4	11	3-2-0	2.45	25.2	15	7	23
OAKLAND	1-0-0	2.03	13.1	11	3	9	1-0-1	2.89	18.2	17	6	14
SEATTLE	1-0-0	0.53	17.0	12	1	13	1-0-0	1.04	26.0	15	3	20
TEXAS	0-1-1	8.25	12.0	16	11	9	0-1-1	5.33	25.1	28	15	23
A.L. WEST	6-1-2	2.38	98.1	72	26	63	11-7-5	3.16	173.2	144	61	132
Pre-ASG	6-2-3	3.35	80.2	68	30	64	11-13-9	3.94	201.2	188	88	172
Post-ASG	5-4-0	2.99	108.1	97	36	51	14-5-1	2.53	167.1	145	47	106
STARTER	10-5-0	3.11	167.2	152	58	97	10-7-0	3.49	173.0	167	67	103
RELIEVER	1-1-3	3.38	21.1	13	8	18	15-11-10	3.12	196.0	166	68	178
in APRIL	0-0-3	0.93	9.2	3	1	8	3-3-3	3.97	45.1	35	20	43
MAY	2-0-0	4.57	21.0	16	9	19	3-1-3	2.39	52.2	36	14	50
JUNE	3-2-0	4.41	34.2	33	17	27	4-6-3	4.58	76.2	83	39	65
JULY	2-0-0	1.82	39.2	34	8	20	5-3-0	2.95	61.0	56	20	38
AUGUST	2-2-0	3.89	39.1	41	17	16	3-2-0	3.60	50.0	51	20	24
SEPT/OCT	2-2-0	2.28	44.2	38	14	25	7-3-0	2.39	83.0	72	22	61

CAREER HIGHS

SEASON: **W** 11-1990 **ERA** 2.40-1989 **SV** 4-1988 **IP** 189.0-1990, **SO** 115-1990

GAME: **LOW HIT CG** Never **SO** 9-vs MINN.June 5, 1990

BB 5-vs MINN June 5, 1990 at TEX Aug. 3, 1990

Last Win: at KC, Sept. 11, 1990 **Last Save:** vs CLEV, April 24, 1990

Last CG: Never **Last ShO:** Never

Last Relief: vs MILW, June 2, 1990 **Last GS:** at BALT, Oct 1, 1990

19

DEVON WHITE

OUTFIELDER

Born: Dec. 29, 1962 Kingston, JA

Resides: Mesa, AZ

B-S T-R 6-2 172

M.L. Service: 4.061

PERSONAL: Devon Markes White...Married, wife's name, Colleen (November 1, 1986)...One child Thaddeus...Attended Park West High School (New York)...Was four year varsity letterman in baseball and also played basketball.

LAST SEASON: Finished the season with 11 HR, the fourth season in a row with double digits in HR...Appeared in just 125 games after totalling 156 in 1986...Was second on the club in sacrifice hits (10), trailing Dick Schofield's 13...Registered career hit number 500 vs Detroit's Jack Morris on June 16th (a solo HR)...Tied Luis Polonia for the club lead in steals with 21...Was one of only 11 AL outfielders to register double digits in outfield assists (11)...Was optioned to Edmonton (AAA) of the Pacific Coast League on July 6...Hit .364 with 4 doubles and 4 triples while with the Trappers...Was recalled to California on July 27...Hit .198 with runners in scoring position and .200 in bases loaded situations.

PROFESSIONAL CAREER: **1981:** Began professional career in the Pioneer League (Rookie) with Idaho Falls where he played outfield, third base and first base...Batted just .179 in 30 games and had 2 extra base hits...**1982:** Moved up to Danville (A) of the Midwest League where he played exclusively in the outfield and improved his previous season's average by .36 points...Had 11 stolen bases, seven more than in '81...**1983:** Began the season at Peoria (A) of the Midwest League and improved in almost every offensive and defensive category...Batted .253, an increase of .38 points over 1982...Led Midwest League outfielders in TC with 286...Had 36 extra base hits, including 17 doubles and 13 HR...Promoted to Nashua (AA) of the Eastern League and played in 17 games, posting a .257 average...**1984:** Led the California League (A) in outfield putouts (322) and total chances (351) while playing for Redwood...Continued to raise batting average to .283 while averaging better than a hit per contest (147H/138G)...His 25 doubles marked his second straight season with 20+ doubles...Was named California League's "Best Defensive Outfielder" in Baseball America's "Best Tools Survey"...**1985:** Started the season with Midland (AA) of the Texas League hitting .296 in 70 games...Had 38 stolen bases and scored 52 runs before being promoted to AAA Edmonton of the Pacific Coast League...Boosted season extra base hit total to 43 with his 16 doubles, 5 triples and 4 HR while with the Trappers...Was called up to the parent club in September and made his debut on September 2nd in Detroit...Stole 3 bases during call-up...Overall, made just 6 errors on the season- his fewest since 1981 (3)...Had 61 stolen bases on the year...**1986:** Opened the season with the AAA Edmonton club in the P.C.L. and tied for the league lead in outfield assists with 16...Was fourth consecutive season with 55+ RBI (63)...Led the Trappers in runs (84), triples (10) and stolen bases (42)...Was recalled by California on August 31 and saw action in 29 games...Hit his first career M.L. HR off of Texas' Jeff Russell on October 2nd...1987: Selected to the TOPPS Rookie All-Star Team for his efforts with the Angels...Led the AL in putouts for outfielders with 424...Recorded switch hit HR in one game on June 23 vs the Yankees...Tallied 16 OF assists which tied him for third in the AL along with Cory Snyder...Established club rookie records in at-bats (639), runs (103), total bases (283), extra base hits (62) and strikeouts (135)...Career best hitting streak, May 8-22 (18-52/.346)...Led the club in games played with 159...First Angel rookie to record 20+ HR and 20+ steals in the same season...1988: Recorded 100th career RBI at Toronto on April 29...Missed 1/4 of the season due to various injuries, including ailing right rib cage and surgery on his right knee- placed on the D.L. on May 21 and underwent surgery on the same day...Reactivated on June 10th...Had just 17 stolen bases- his lowest total since 1982...Awarded Rawlings Gold Glove for fielding excellence in the outfield...1989: First Angel ever to reach double figures in doubles, triples, home runs and stolen bases...Stole home on September 9 vs Boston for 22nd time in Angels history and completed stealing for the cycle...The stealing of home was the first since Gary Pettis in 1985...Named to the American League All-Star Team for the first time in his career...636 AB ranked sixth all-time on the Angels' single season list...His 44 stolen bases was the 4th highest total in Angels history...Won a his second consecutive Rawlings Gold Glove Award- only the 4th Angel to do so.

DEVON WHITE

Year	Club & League	AVG	G	AB	R	H	2B	3B	HR	RBI	SH-SF	HP	BB	SO	SB-CS
1981	Idaho Falls (Pio)	.179	30	106	10	19	2	0	0	10	0-0	0	12	34	4-3
1982	Danville (Mid)	.215	57	186	21	40	6	1	1	11	1-0	0	11	41	11-0
1983	Nashua (East)	.257	17	70	11	18	7	2	0	2	0-1	1	7	22	5-1
1983	Peoria (Mid)	.253	117	430	69	109	17	6	13	66	6-3	12	36	124	32-15
1984	Redwood (Cal)	.283	138	520	101	147	25	5	7	55	17-5	11	56	118	36-12
1985	Midland (Tex)	.296	70	260	52	77	10	4	4	35	3-6	6	35	46	38-8
1985	Edmonton (PCL)	.253	66	277	53	70	16	5	4	39	1-3	4	24	77	21-9
1985	CALIFORNIA (AL)	.143	21	7	7	1	0	0	0	0	0-0	0	1	3	3-1
1986	Edmonton (PCL)	.291	112	461	84	134	25	10	14	60	1-1	3	31	90	42-12
1986	CALIFORNIA (AL)	.235	29	51	8	12	1	1	1	3	0-4	0	6	8	13-8
1987	CALIFORNIA (AL)	.263	159	639	103	168	33	5	24	87	14-2	2	39	135	32-11
1988	CALIFORNIA (AL)	.259	122	455	76	118	22	2	11	51	5-1	2	23	84	17-8
1989	CALIFORNIA (AL)	.245	156	636	86	156	18	13	12	56	7-2	2	31	129	44-16
1990	CALIFORNIA (AL)	.217	125	443	57	96	17	3	11	44	10-3	3	44	116	21-6
1990	Edmonton (PCL)	.364	14	55	9	20	4	4	0	6	0-0	0	7	12	4-2
AL TOTALS		.247	612	2231	337	551	91	24	59	241	36-8	10	144	475	123-42

White (cont...)

CHAMPIONSHIP SERIES RECORD

Year	Club & League	AVG	G	AB	R	H	2B	3B	HR	RBI	SH-SF	HP	BB	SO	SB-CS
1986	CALIFORNIA (AL)	.500	4	2	2	1	0	0	0	0	0-0	0	0	1	0-1

ALL-STAR GAME RECORD

Year	Club & League	AVG	G	AB	R	H	2B	3B	HR	RBI	SH-SF	HP	BB	SO	SB-CS
1989	American	.000	1	1	0	0	0	0	0	0	0-0	0	0	0	0-0

WHITE - TRANSACTIONS

- Selected by California Angels' organization in 6th round of free-agent draft, June 8, 1981.
- On suspended list, June 11 to June 12 and July 19, 1982 through remainder of season.
- On disabled list, May 12 to May 22, 1986.
- On disabled list, May 7 to June 10, 1988.
- Traded along with pitchers Willie Fraser and Marcus Moore to Toronto in exchange for Outfielder Junior Felix, Infielder Luis Sojo and Catcher Ken Rivers on December 2, 1990.

DEVON WHITE vs AMERICAN LEAGUE

	1990					CAREER				
	AB	H	HR	RBI	AVG	AB	H	HR	RBI	AVG
SEASON	443	96	11	44	.217	2231	241	59	241	.247
HOME	219	47	5	20	.215	1084	256	28	113	.236
AWAY	224	49	6	24	.219	1147	295	31	128	.257
vs BALTIMORE	39	4	1	3	.103	159	35	3	12	.220
BOSTON	35	3	1	1	.086	143	30	3	12	.210
CLEVELAND	38	11	2	5	.289	166	48	9	20	.289
DETROIT	23	6	1	2	.261	159	43	2	13	.270
MILWAUKEE	21	9	0	3	.429	141	38	4	14	.270
NEW YORK	49	15	2	8	.306	178	49	4	25	.275
TORONTO	30	3	1	2	.100	1687	35	5	19	.208
A.L. EAST	235	51	8	24	.217	1114	278	30	115	.250
vs CALIFORNIA	-	-	-	-	-	-	-	-	-	-
CHICAGO	30	5	0	3	.167	205	58	7	31	.283
KANSAS CITY	38	7	0	3	.184	189	39	0	14	.206
MINNESOTA	43	13	1	5	.302	174	45	6	24	.259
OAKLAND	28	6	1	4	.214	187	47	4	25	.251
SEATTLE	39	8	0	2	.205	195	48	6	20	.246
TEXAS	30	6	1	3	.200	167	36	6	12	.216
A.L. WEST	208	45	3	20	.216	1117	273	29	126	.244
Pre-ASG	263	56	7	22	.213	1102	279	36	127	.253
Post-ASG	180	40	4	22	.222	1129	272	23	114	.241
vs RHP	313	64	18	34	.204	1521	373	37	172	.247
LHP	130	32	3	10	.246	710	176	22	69	.248
PINCH HITTING	3	0	0	0	.000	9	2	0	1	.222
DESIGNATED HITTING	-	-	-	-	-	1	0	0	0	.000
in APRIL	66	12	1	2	.182	337	87	13	41	.149
MAY	108	25	3	10	.231	340	88	8	34	.259
JUNE	69	15	3	9	.217	353	90	13	43	.255
JULY	37	9	0	2	.243	379	101	9	45	.266
AUGUST	91	18	3	12	.198	430	94	10	46	.219
SEPT/OCT	72	17	1	9	.236	392	91	6	32	.232

CAREER HIGHS

SEASON: AVG. .263 - 1987 **H** 168 - 1987 **HR** 24 - 1987
RBI 87 - 1987 **SB** 44 - 1989

GAME: **H** 4 - Last time: at CHI July 30, 1988 **HR** 2 - at TEX June 23, 1987
RBI 5 - vs CHI April 12, 1988
SB 4 vs BOST Sept. 9, 1989

Last ML HR: vs MINN Sept. 12, 1990 **Longest Hitting Streak:** 13-1987

23 MARK WHITEN

OUTFIELDER

Born: Nov. 25, 1966 Pensacola, FL
Resides: Pensacola, FL
B-S T-R 6-3 215
M.L. Service: 0.067

PERSONAL: Mark Anthony Whiten...Single...1984 graduate of Pensacola High School where he played baseball...Attended Pensacola Jr. College where he also played baseball earning MVP honours...From the same home town as Pittsburg Pirates product, Jay Bell and BLUE JAYS broadcaster, Tom Cheek...Pronounced WHITT-EN.

LAST SEASON: Started the season at Syracuse (AAA) of the International League...Had 13 game hit streak, June 13-24...Had five hit game June 30 vs Oklahoma City...Named to AAA-All-Star Game in Las Vegas...Named to season ending International League All-Star team and was named

Baseball America's Top Prospect for the International League...Hit .290, 113-390, 14 HR, 48 RBI, 14 SB with the Chiefs...Was called up to TORONTO for the first time on 7/12 and hit his first M.L. HR off of Kevin Appier of the Kansas City Royals on 7/26...Was optioned back to Syracuse on 8/13...Was recalled on 8/30...Hit .273, 24-88, 2 HR, 7 RBI...A switch-hitter, hit .76 pts higher from the right side (.316)...Started 20 games all in right field.

PROFESSIONAL CAREER: **1986:** First professional season with Medicine Hat (Rookie) of the Pioneer League...Played in all 70 games...3rd in the league in AB (270), T/3rd in H (81), 5th in TB (133), T/5th in HR (10) and T/5th in SB (22)...Winner of R. Howard Webster Award as the club's MVP...**1987:** Spent the season with Myrtle Beach (A) of the South Atlantic League...Named as the outfielder with the best arm in the SAL by Baseball America...Named to the SAL All-Star team and was named by Howe News Bureau as the SAL's Star of Stars Award winner for statistical excellence...Led SAL in games (135), TC (322), assists (18) and DP by an outfielder (4)...Also led the SAL in HBP (16) and 4th in BB (76)...Led club in runs (90) and GW RBI (11)...6 RBI, 4/27 vs Sumter...Grand slam HR vs Greensboro on 5/9...**1988:** Started season with Dunedin (A) of the Florida State League and led FSL outfielders in assists with (21)...Was promoted to Knoxville (AA) of the Southern League on 8/3...125 hits combined in 127 games...**1989:** Spent the season with Knoxville (AA) of the Southern League where he led the team in Runs (75) and BB (60)...Struck out 114 times in 129 games...Led the league in HB (11)...Had 17 OF assists (2nd in the league) and made 8 errors in 248 total chances.

MARK WHITEN

Year	Club & League	AVG.	G	AB	R	H	2B	3B	HR	RBI	SH-SF	HP	BB	SO	SB-CS
1986	Medicine Hat (Pio)	.300	70	270	53	81	16	3	10	44	1-2	6	29	56	22-3
1987	Myrtle Beach (SAL)	.253	139	494	90	125	22	5	15	64	0-1	16	76	149	49-14
1988	Dunedin (FSL)	.252	99	385	61	97	8	5	7	37	2-3	3	41	69	17-14
1988	Knoxville (Sou)	.259	28	108	20	28	3	1	2	9	0-0	1	12	20	6-0
1989	Knoxville (Sou)	.258	129	423	75	109	13	6	12	47	0-2	11	60	114	11-10
1990	Syracuse (Int)	.290	104	390	65	113	19	4	14	48	0-4	3	37	72	14-5
1990	TORONTO (AL)	.273	33	88	12	24	1	1	2	7	0-1	0	7	14	2-0
ML TOTALS		.273	33	88	12	24	1	1	2	7	0-1	0	7	14	2-0

WHITEN - TRANSACTIONS

- Selected by Toronto Blue Jays' reorganization in 5th round of free-agent draft, January 14, 1986.

MARK WHITEN vs AMERICAN LEAGUE

	1990					CAREER				
	AB	H	HR	RBI	AVG	AB	H	HR	RBI	AVG
SEASON	88	24	2	7	.273	88	24	2	7	.273
TORONTO	29	7	1	3	.241	29	7	1	3	.241
AWAY	59	17	1	4	.288	59	17	1	4	.288
vs BALTIMORE	2	1	0	0	.500	2	1	0	0	.500
BOSTON	-	-	-	-	-	-	-	-	-	-
CLEVELAND	7	3	0	1	.429	7	3	0	1	.429
DETROIT	6	2	0	1	.333	6	2	0	1	.333
MILWAUKEE	10	5	1	3	.500	10	5	1	3	.500
NEW YORK	0	0	0	0	.000	0	0	0	0	.000
TORONTO	-	-	-	-	-	-	-	-	-	-
A.L. EAST	25	11	1	5	.440	25	11	1	5	.440
vs CALIFORNIA	15	5	0	0	.333	15	5	0	0	.333
CHICAGO	0	0	0	0	.000	0	0	0	0	.000
KANSAS CITY	10	4	1	2	.400	10	4	1	2	.400
MINNESOTA	3	0	0	0	.000	3	0	0	0	.000
OAKLAND	9	0	0	0	.000	9	0	0	0	.000
SEATTLE	12	3	0	0	.250	12	3	0	0	.250
TEXAS	14	1	0	0	.071	14	1	0	0	.071
A.L. WEST	63	13	1	2	.206	63	13	1	2	.206
Pre-ASG	-	-	-	-	-	-	-	-	-	-
Post-ASG	88	24	2	7	.273	88	24	2	7	.273
vs RHP	50	12	1	3	.240	50	12	1	3	.240
LHP38	12	1	4	.316	38	12	1	4	.316	
PINCH HITTING	3	0	0	0	.000	3	0	0	0	.000
DESIGNATED HITTING	2	0	0	0	.000	2	0	0	0	.000
in APRIL	-	-	-	-	-	-	-	-	-	-
MAY	-	-	-	-	-	-	-	-	-	-
JUNE	-	-	-	-	-	-	-	-	-	-
JULY	59	14	1	2	.237	59	14	1	2	.237
AUGUST	10	3	0	2	.300	10	3	0	2	.300
SEPT/OCT	19	7	1	3	.368	19	7	1	3	.368

CAREER HIGHS

SEASON: **AVG.** .273 - 1990 **H** 24 - 1990 **HR** 2 - 1990
RBI 7 - 1990 **SB** 2 - 1990

GAME: **H** 3 - at CAL July 14, 1990 **HR** 1 - twice
RBI 2 - vs KC July 26, 1990; at MILW Sept. 24, 1990 **SB** 1 - twice

Last ML HR: at MILW Sept. 24, 1990 **Longest Hitting Streak:** 4 - 1990

13 KENNY WILLIAMS

OUTFIELDER

Born: April 6, 1964 Berkeley, CA

Resides: Puyallup, WA

B-R T-R 6-1 195

M.L. Service: 4.065

PERSONAL: Kenneth Royal Williams...Married the former Jessica Estrada...Has two chidren, Kenneth Jr. (5/23/86) and Kyle (6/18/87...Attended Stanford University and played football during his freshman year...One of the most highly recruited 2 sport athletes in the nation as a high school senior.

LAST SEASON: Began the season with the Tigers...Claimed on waivers by the BLUE JAYS on 6/18...Hit .194 after coming to the BLUE JAYS...Had a .272 on base percentage and a .306 slugging percentage...Was used primarily in pinch hitting and pinch running situations while in Toronto...Started 16 games(6-RF/2-CF/5-LF/3-DH)...With runners in scoring position he batted .176, 3-17...Hit .308, 4-13 for the month of August with 1 RBI and 4 Runs in 15 games...As a PH'er he was .125, 1-8 with TORONTO and .111, 2-18 on the season...Hit .071(1-14) on 3-2 count.

PROFESSIONAL CAREER: **1982:** Selected in the third round of the June Free Agent Draft in 1982...First professional season with Sarasota (Rookie) of the Gulf Coast League where he played in 31 games and had 31 hits...**1983:** Spent the entire year at Appleton (A) in the Midwest League where he had 12 HR and 53 RBI in 124 games and helped Appleton win the Midwest League title...**1984:** Started the season at Appleton (A) where he played in 38 games and hit .286 but was promoted to Glens Falls (AA) where he hit .246 in 97 games and hit 8 HR, 47 RBI and stole 16 bases...**1985:** Spent the entire 1985 season at Glens Falls (AA) of the Eastern League where he batted .250 with 16 HR (second on the club) and had 66 RBI...Was his first full year at the AA level...**1986:** Spent the season splitting time between Birmingham (AA) of the Southern League and Buffalo (AAA) of the American Association before being called up when the ML rosters expanded in September...Hit .129 in 15 games and 31 AB...Collected his first ML HR on 9/27 off of Minnesota's Neal Heaton at Comiskey Park...**1987:** Began the season with Hawaii (AAA) of the Pacific Coast League before he was promoted to the parent club on May 18 and became the regular CF...Batted .281 in 116 games for the White Sox with 18 2B, 11 HR and 50 RBI...Had an 8 game hitting streak from 9/14-21, (11-30/.367)...**1988:** Was switched to 3B and was the White Sox regular 3B until a bothersome left ankle injury forced him out of the lineup...Placed on the DL and remained there until June 30...Moved back to OF...Assigned outright to Vancouver (AAA) of the Pacific Coast League on July 28 and returned to the parent club on August 19...Hit 8 HR with Chicago...**1989:** Was traded to the Tigers in a 2-man trade on March 23, 1989...Played 94 games for Detroit in the OF (started 71)...Hit .204 with 6 HR and 23 RBI...Placed on the 15 day DL on June 23 with a pulled side muscle...Reactivated on July 28...Also spent time at Toledo (AAA) of the International League where he appeared in 14 games and hit .255 with 3 HR and 2 SB.

KENNY WILLIAMS

Year	Club & League	AVG	G	AB	R	H	2B	3B	HR	RBI	SH-SF	HP	BB	SO	SB-CS
1982	Sarasota (Gulf)	.298	31	104	19	31	2	1	1	11	1-2	1	10	27	9-4
1983	Appleton (Mid)	.231	124	415	60	96	18	2	12	53	5-3	4	26	148	27-8
1984	Appleton (Mid)	.286	38	147	23	42	11	2	5	26	1-2	2	15	48	13-5
1984	Glens Falls (East)	.246	97	309	35	76	7	5	8	47	1-4	4	21	70	16-7
1985	Glens Falls (East)	.250	133	520	87	130	16	6	16	66	7-5	6	47	83	27-14
1986	Buffalo (AmAs)	.212	50	189	21	40	4	2	4	15	1-0	5	6	53	5-4
1986	Birmingham (Sou)	.331	68	272	41	90	16	5	6	40	1-0	5	18	48	26-9
1986	CHICAGO (AL)	.129	15	31	2	4	0	0	1	1	0-0	1	1	11	1-1
1987	Hawaii (PCL)	.269	35	134	19	36	4	4	3	14	1-2	0	9	27	5-4
1987	CHICAGO (AL)	.281	116	391	48	110	18	2	11	50	3-1	9	10	83	21-10
1988	CHICAGO (AL)	.159	73	220	18	35	4	2	8	28	3-2	8	10	64	5-2
1988	Vancouver (PCL)	.250	16	60	8	15	2	1	1	7	1-1	2	2	14	2-1
1989	DETROIT (AL)	.205	94	258	29	53	5	1	6	23	2-2	5	18	63	9-4
1989	Toledo (Int)	.255	14	51	8	13	2	0	3	8	0-0	1	5	9	2-0
1990	DETROIT (AL)	.133	57	83	10	11	2	0	0	5	0-1	1	3	24	2-2
1990	TORONTO (AL)	.194	49	72	13	14	6	1	0	8	0-1	1	7	18	7-2
ML TOTALS		.215	404	1055	120	227	35	6	26	115	8-7	25	49	268	46-24

WILLIAMS - TRANSACTIONS

- Selected by Chicago White Sox' organization in 3rd round of free-agent draft, June 7, 1982.
- On disabled list, May 25 to June 30, 1988.
- Traded to Detroit Tigers for Pitcher Eric King, March 23, 1989.
- On disabled list, June 23 to July 29, 1989; included rehabilitation disability assignment to Toledo, July 14 to July 29, 1989.
- Claimed on waivers by Toronto Blue Jays June 18, 1990.

	1990					CAREER				
	AB	H	HR	RBI	AVG	AB	H	HR	RBI	AVG
SEASON	155	25	0	13	.161	1055	227	26	115	.215
TORONTO	46	7	0	5	.152	103	21	2	9	.204
AWAY	109	18	0	8	.165	952	206	24	106	.216
vs BALTIMORE	11	2	0	0	.182	67	10	2	8	.149
BOSTON	7	0	0	1	.000	84	15	2	10	.179
CLEVELAND	14	2	0	0	.143	98	17	3	9	.173
DETROIT	3	1	0	0	.333	48	15	1	5	.313
MILWAUKEE	15	3	0	2	.200	74	16	1	10	.216
NEW YORK	18	2	0	4	.071	87	15	1	10	.172
TORONTO	6	1	0	0	.167	63	15	2	4	.238
A.L. EAST	74	11	0	7	.149	521	103	12	56	.198
vs CALIFORNIA	22	5	0	2	.227	88	14	3	9	.159
CHICAGO	9	2	0	1	.222	25	11	0	3	.440
KANSAS CITY	5	1	0	0	.200	60	12	1	5	.200
MINNESOTA	15	5	0	1	.333	107	31	2	7	.290
OAKLAND	-	-	-	-	-	91	24	2	13	.264
SEATTLE	20	3	0	11	.150	82	15	3	10	.183
TEXAS	10	0	0	1	.000	81	17	3	12	.210
A.L. WEST	811	1	0	6		534	124	14	59	.232
Pre-ASG	105	14	0	7	.133	546	110	13	63	.201
Post-ASG	50	11	0	6	.220	509	117	13	52	.230
vs RHP	42	4	0	1	.095	-	-	-	-	-
LHP	113	21	0	12	.186	-	-	-	-	-
PINCH HITTING	18	2	0	0	.111	31	4	0	1	.129
DESIGNATED HITTING	13	1	0	2	.077	21	1	0	2	.048
in APRIL	20	4	0	3	.200	155	29	6	24	.187
MAY	46	5	0	2	.109	203	37	3	16	.182
JUNE	27	2	0	1	.074	125	31	3	14	.248
JULY	27	5	0	3	.185	147	29	2	18	.197
AUGUST	13	4	0	1	.308	203	56	6	23	.276
SEPT/OCT	22	5	0	3	.227	222	45	6	20	.203

CAREER HIGHS

SEASON: **AVG.** .281 - 1987 **H** 110 - 1987 **HR** 11 - 1987 **SB** 21 - 1987

GAME: **H** 4 vs BOST Aug. 18, 1987 **HR** 1, 26 times **RBI** 4 at CLEV July 4, 1987
Last ML HR: at TOR Aug. 24, 1989 **Longest Hitting Streak:** 8 - 1987

44 FRANK WILLS
PITCHER

Born: Oct. 26, 1958 New Orleans, LA
Resides: Destrehan, LA
B-R T-R 6-2 220
M.L. Service: 4.035

PERSONAL: Frank Lee Wills...Married the former Kimberly Mumphrey (2/13/82)...Two children, Dorian Dee (9/3/83) and Olivia Lea (11/25/90)...Attended Tulane University where he compiled a 3 year collegiate record of 14-13 with 221 K in 213 IP...Also was a 3 year football letterman (punter)...Played baseball, football and basketball at De La Salle (La.) High School, graduating in 1977...Played Little League, Babe Ruth and American Legion ball as a youth...Was named RHP on The Sporting News College Baseball All-America team, 1980.

LAST SEASON: Slimmed down for the season...His 99.0 innings were the most since he threw 123.0 innings in 1985 for Seattle...Spent most of year in the bullpen...His first 36 appearances were in relief...In relief, was 5-4, 5.01ERA, 40G, 79.0IP, 84H, 45R, 44ER, 12HR, 28BB, 61K...Made his first start of the season on 8/27 vs Milwaukee...As a starter, 1-0, 3.60ERA, 4GS, 20.0IP, 17H, 9R, 8ER, 10BB, 11K...Made 4 consecutive game starts between 8/27 and 9/16...In his first GS, went 5.0IP when the game was halted due to bugs (gnats)...At SkyDome Wills was 3-4, 4.50ERA...On the road, 3-0, 5.11ERA...Allowed only 1HR as a starter(20.0IP)...ERA for August was 2.37 in 6G (1GS), 19.0IP, 5R/ER, 6BB, 11K...Opposition hit .390 on the 0-0 pitch.

PROFESSIONAL CAREER: **1980:** Was Kansas City's 1st round draft pick (16th overall) in the June 1980 Free Agent draft...Split season between Sarasota (Rookie-Gulf Coast) and Charleston (A-South Atlantic)...Collectively was 4-5...**1981:** Played for Jacksonville (AA) of the Southern League...Was 2nd in league in K (174), 3rd in CG (11) and 4th in IP (192)...Joined the parent club during the final week of the season but did not appear in a game...**1982:** Spent the season with Omaha (AAA) of the American Association and was used in relidf for 1st time in career (also made 12 GS)...**1983:** Made ML debut on July 31 at Detroit...First ML win came on September 23 vs Minnesota...Spent time at Jacksonville (AA) in the Southern League where he was 5-2 with a 2.48 ERA...Eventually moved to Omaha (AAA) of the American Association where he gave up 96 hits in 95 innings ...**1984:** Was on the Royals' Opening Day roster but was optioned to Omaha (AAA) on 4/12...Recalled by the royals on 7/17...Voted as the Pitcher with the best fastball in the American Association by league's managers and scouts...**1985:** Traded to the Mariners in a multi-team deal that sent Jim Sundberg to Kansas City and Don Slaught to Texas on 1/18...Started the season with the Mariner's Triple A Calgary club...Tossed a 7 IP no-hitter at Tacoma on 5/31...Joined the

Wills (cont...)

Mariners on 6/5...Game started 18 of 24 games, winning 4 of first 5 GS before losing his next 8...1st ML save, 7/31 vs Minnesota...Set ML bests in wins (5), GS (18), IP (123) and K (67)...**1986:** Signed as a Free Agent by the Indians on 3/27...Began the season with Maine (AAA) of the IL...Contract purchased by Indians on 7/22 and made 26 relief appearances...8/5-26 was 1-1, 1.23 ERA...3 SV and 1 win in span of 5 games, 9/2-20...**1987:** Started the season with Buffalo (AAA) of the American Association prior to joining the Indians on 4/24...Save in 1st appearance, 4/25 vs New York...Assinged outright to Buffalo on 5/13...Allowed 53 H in 56.2 IP while posting a 3-2-6 mark with a 3.34 ERA...**1988:** Started the season with Syracuse (AAA) of the IL...Contract purchased by BLUE JAYS on 7/13...BLUE JAYS' debut, 7/20 at California with 0.2 ShO IP...Stranded 7 of 11 inherited runners and retired 8 of 10 1st batters faced...**1989:** Started the season with Syracuse (AAA) of IL...Contract purchased by the BLUE JAYS on 5/15...Made 4 consecutive relief appearances allowing 2R/ER in 12.2 IP...1st game start for BLUE JAYS, 6/6 vs Brewers...No decision in BLUE JAYS 6-4 loss...1st decision, 8-2 loss to Seattle on 6/18...1st decision since 5/5/87 for Indians...4 consecutive GS, 6/6-23...On 15 day DL, 7/2-18 with a strained hamstring...Returned making 5 relief appearances (6R/ER, 13.2IP)...Won 11-4 vs Detroit on 8/23 for 1st ML win since 10/3/86 while with the Indians...Contract assigned outright to Syracuse on 8/25...Contract purchased by BLUE JAYS on 9/4...Appeared in 6 games going 2-0 woth 0.63 ERA (1ER/14.1IP).

FRANK WILLS

Year	Club & League	W-L	ERA	G	GS	CG	ShO	SV	IP	H	R	ER	HR	HB	BB	SO	WP
1980	Sarasota (Gulf)	2-0	1.96	4	4	0	0	0	23.0	18	7	5	0	3	8	20	3
1980	Charleston (SAL)	2-5	3.63	9	9	3	0	0	57.0	59	33	23	1	5	32	48	6
1981	Jacksonville (Sou)	9-14	3.98	27	27	11	1	0	192.0	199	104	85	16	9	91	174	15
1982	Omaha (AmAs)	7-10	5.20	41	12	2	0	3	107.1	110	71	62	8	4	81	77	7
1983	Jacksonville (Sou)	5-2	2.48	8	8	2	0	0	54.1	44	19	15	3	1	23	40	4
1983	Omaha (AmAs)	4-11	4.74	16	16	4	1	0	95.0	96	56	50	8	1	45	65	6
1983	KANSAS CITY (AL)	2-1	4.15	6	4	0	0	0	34.2	35	17	16	2	0	15	23	3
1984	Omaha (AmAs)	7-4	2.81	15	15	2	1	0	89.2	75	32	28	9	0	49	69	2
1984	KANSAS CITY (AL)	2-3	5.11	10	5	0	0	0	37.0	39	21	21	3	0	13	21	2
1985	Calgary (PCL)	4-3	4.86	9	9	3	2	0	46.1	44	27	25	5	0	25	31	3
1985	SEATTLE (AL)	5-11	6.00	24	18	1	0	1	1 23.0	122	85	82	18	3	68	67	9
1986	Maine Int)	4-3	2.87	22	1	0	0	6	3 1.1	37	10	10	4	0	1	2	0
1986	CLEVELAND (AL)	4-4	4.91	26	0	0	0	4	40.1	43	23	22	6	6	16	32	6
1987	Buffalo (AmAs)	3-2	3.34	36	0	0	0	6	56.2	53	28	21	5	0	22	45	1
1987	CLEVELAND (AL)	0-1	5.06	6	0	0	0	1	5.1	3	3	3	0	0	7	4	0
1988	Syracuse (Int)	6-4	3.24	25	10	0	0	3	80.2	70	40	29	4	4	25	53	7
1988	TORONTO AL)	0-0	5.23	10	0	0	0	0	20.2	22	12	12	2	0	6	19	1
1989	Syracuse (Int)	1-0	1.59	14	0	0	0	5	17.0	8	7	3	1	0	8	13	1
1989	TORONTO (AL)	3-1	3.66	24	4	0	0	0	71.1	65	31	29	4	1	30	41	4
1990	TORONTO (AL)	6-4	4.73	44	4	0	0	0	99.0	101	54	52	13	1	38	72	1
ML TOTALS		22-25	4.95	150	35	1	0	6	431.1	430	246	237	48	11	193	279	26

WILLS - TRANSACTIONS

- Selected by Kansas City Royals' organization in 1st round (16th playerselected) of free-agent draft, June 3, 1980.
- On disabled list, August 1 to August 16, 1984.
- Traded to New York Mets' organization as part of a six-player, four-team deal in which Kansas City Roaysl acquired Catcher Jim Sundberg from Milwaukee Brewers, Texas Rangers acquired Catcher Don Slaught from Kansas City, Milwaukee acquired Pitcher Danny Darwin and a player to be named later from Texas and Pitcher Tim Leary from New York, January 18, 1985; Milwaukee organization acquired Catcher Bill Hance from Texas to complete deal, January 30, 1985.
- Traded to Seattle Mariners' organization for Pitcher Wray Bergendahl, March 29, 1985
- Released March 20, 1986; signed by Maine (Cleveland Indians' organization), March 27, 1986.
- On disabled list, May 4 to May 31, 1986.
- Released, March 29, 1988; signed by Knoxville (Toronto Blue Jays' organization) April 7, 1988.
- Released, October 28, 1988; re-signed by Blue Jays' organization, January 12, 1989.

EIGHT STRAIGHT WINNING SEASONS

The **BLUE JAYS** have a string of eight consecutive winning seasons (1983 thru 1990) the current longest of any MAJOR LEAGUE team.

The New York Yankees' 39 year string (1926 thru 1964) represents the Major League record.

The Baltimore Orioles have the 2nd longest in baseball history with 18 consecutive winning seasons (1968 thru 1985).

FRANK WILLS vs AMERICAN LEAGUE

	1990						CAREER					
	W-L-S	ERA	IP	H	ER	SO	W-L-S	ERA	IP	H	ER	SO
SEASON	6-4-0	4.73	99.0	101	52	72	22-25-6	4.95	431.1	430	237	279
TORONTO	3-4-0	4.50	62.0	60	31	40	3-4-0	4.50	62.0	60	31	40
ROAD	3-0-0	5.11	37.0	41	21	32	3-0-0	5.11	37.0	41	21	32
vs BALTIMORE	0-1-0	5.40	11.2	15	7	11	2-1-0	6.04	28.1	33	19	20
BOSTON	0-0-0	0.00	0.0	3	3	0	0-2-1	5.03	34.0	36	19	21
CLEVELAND	1-1-0	3.86	7.0	6	3	5	3-4-0	5.05	41.0	38	23	30
DETROIT	0-0-0	1.35	6.2	1	1	7	1-1-0	2.73	26.1	16	8	22
MILWAUKEE	0-0-0	6.75	6.2	7	5	2	0-1-0	3.67	34.1	30	14	13
NEW YORK	1-0-0	0.87	10.1	6	1	11	1-2-1	5.75	20.1	24	13	17
TORONTO	-	-	-	-	-	-	1-3-1	9.87	17.1	26	19	10
A.L. EAST	2-2-0	4.25	42.1	38	20	36	8-14-3	5.13	201.2	203	115	133
vs CALIFORNIA	1-0-0	2.16	8.1	10	2	3	1-1-0	6.46	15.1	23	11	9
CHICAGO	1-0-0	4.91	7.1	6	4	5	2-1-0	4.44	24.1	24	12	17
KANSAS CITY	1-0-0	7.20	10.0	14	8	6	2-0-0	7.33	27.0	33	22	21
MINNESOTA	0-0-0	5.14	7.0	9	4	4	1-1-2	3.07	44.0	43	15	26
OAKLAND	0-1-0	6.75	6.2	6	5	5	2-2-1	5.29	32.1	28	19	20
SEATTLE	1-0-0	7.56	8.1	12	7	4	4-1-0	5.08	28.1	32	16	18
TEXAS	0-1-0	2.00	9.0	6	2	9	2-5-0	4.58	53.0	44	27	35
A.L. WEST	4-2-0	5.08	56.2	63	32	36	14-11-3	4.89	224.1	227	122	146
Pre-ASG	5-2-0	5.36	48.2	54	29	36	9-7-1	5.05	140.2	138	79	90
Post-ASG	1-2-0	4.11	50.1	47	23	36	13-18-0	4.89	290.2	292	158	189
STARTER	1-0-0	3.60	20.0	17	8	11	9-16-0	5.64	188.1	191	118	98
RELIEVER	5-4-0	5.01	79.0	84	44	61	13-9-6	4.41	243.0	239	119	181
in APRIL	1-1-0	8.74	11.1	17	11	11	1-1-1	8.10	13.1	18	12	14
MAY	3-1-0	5.59	19.1	20	12	10	3-2-0	3.96	36.1	35	16	23
JUNE	1-0-0	3.86	14.0	12	6	12	4-2-0	5.63	62.1	57	39	36
JULY	0-1-0	3.00	15.0	13	5	11	2-6-1	4.28	88.1	78	42	58
AUGUST	0-0-0	2.37	19.0	14	5	11	2-6-1	5.40	103.1	117	62	67
SEPT/OCT	1-1-0	5.75	20.1	25	13	17	10-8-3	4.65	127.2	125	66	87

CAREER HIGHS

SEASON: **W** 6 - 1990 **ERA** 3.66 - 1989
SV 4 - 1986 **IP** 123.0 - 1985 **SO** 72 - 1990

GAME: **Low Hit CG** 6 vs MINN Aug. 17, 1985 **SO** 7 vs TOR July 23, 1984

Last Win: at KC Sept. 11, 1990
Last CG vs MINN Aug. 17, 1985
Last GS: vs BALT Sept. 16, 1990
Last Save: vs NY April 25, 1987
Last Relief: at BALT Oct. 1, 1990

3 MOOKIE WILSON
OUTFIELDER

Born: Feb. 9, 1956 Bamberg, SC
Resides: Bamberg, SC
B-S T-R 5-10 174
M.L. Service: 10.034

PERSONAL: William Hayward Wilson...Married, 6/22/78 at home plate before a game at Jackson, Mississippi...Wife's name, Rosa...Helped lead Bamberg-Ehrhardt in High School to South Carolina AA Championship as a senior...Graduate of Spartanburg Junior College (South Carolina) with A.A. degree in liberal arts...Attended University of South Carolina for 2 years and majored in Business Administration...Member of the Gamecocks 1977 NCAA Atlantic Region Championship and 2nd place on the College World Series...Drafted by the Dodgers in 1976 but did not sign...With wife Rosa has established the "Mookie's Roses" Foundation, an educational center for high school girls in New Jersey (11/86)...Named to many 1977 All-American teams.

LAST SEASON: Ranked 9th in AL in 2B(36)-a career high and 5th SB Success % with .852(23 for 27)...Surpassed the 1300 career hit mark(1339)...Tied his career high, with 4 RBI on 8/19 vs Minnesota...Tied for the Blue Jays team lead in doubles with 36 and was 2nd in Stolen base(23)...Hit streak of 12 games (.358, 19-53, 6 RBI), 9/4-17...Batted in the second spot in the order until June 2nd (.225, 1 HR, 10 RBI, 9 SB)...Started 132 games in centerfield...Had most at-bats (588) since 1983 when he had 638 while with the Mets...Had 51 RBI, his most since 1984...Made only 3 errors all season and was ranked 6th in American League for outfielders...Hit 30 points higher from the left side.

PROFESSIONAL CAREER: **1977: Turned professional with Wausau, collecting 71 hits in 68 games...1978:** Led the Texas League in 3B (15) and 5th in SB (38)...**1979:** Was the International League's All-Star CF while with Tidewater and was club's MVP...**1980:** A natural right-handed hitter, he started to switch-hit in spring training to take advantage of his speed...Won IL and TOPPS All-Class AAA All-Star honours...6th in IL batting (.295) and led league in runs (92), hits (152) and 3B (14)...Extended his Tidewater streak (started in 1979) for not hitting into a double play to 655 AB before hitting into one on 5/18...Called up to Mets in September...Named to 1st team of National Association Class AAA All-Star team...Joined the Mets on 9/2 vs the Dodgers and was hitless in 1st 8 AB before delivering his first ML hit, 9/4 vs San Diego's John Curtis...**1981:** Was selected to numerous All-Rookie teams and was 7th in Rookie of the Year Voting...Led Mets in runs (49), 3B (8) and SB (24) despite appearing in only 92 games...Became the 9th Mets' player to hit 8 triples in one season...Became the everyday CF on 5/22...1st ML HR, 6/2 vs Phillies Nino Espinosa...Set personal high with 4H on 9/20 vs Cardinals...**1982:** Hit safely in 115 of 159 games...Set Mets' mark with 58 SB...9 3B tied a club mark...Led club in games (159), AB (639), runs (90), hits (178), TB (236), 2B (25) and SB (58)...Then career high 13 game hit streak...Went 4-4 vs Dodgers' Valenzuela on 5/4 marking the 1st time anyone had collected 4 H vs the LHP...**1983:** Set career high in runs (91) and stole 54 bases (4th in the NL) to take over Lee Mazilli as the club leader in that category...Only Met to steal 50 or more in consecutive years...Led NL in AB (638) and was 8th in hits (176) and runs...**1984:** One of six ML players to reach double figures in 2B, 3B, HR and SB- others (Ryne Sandberg, Jose Cruz, Juan Samuel, Kirk Gibson and LLOYD MOSEBY)...Led the Mets in SB (46) for 4th consecutive season...Tied for club lead in games (154) and led club in AB (587), runs (88) and set club mark with 10 3B...Tied personal high with 4 H and set personal high with 4 RBI, 7/7 vs Reds...**1985:** Experienced right shoulder problems during spring and forced him to sidelines in April...Did not GS from 4/24-5/8...Appeared in oly 5 games during that span...Placed on 21 day DL on 7/1 and underwi=ent arthroscopic surgery on 7/3 by DR's. James Parkes and Fiske Warren...Repaired fraying and tears of the labrum...Underwent further medical procedure on right shoulder on 10/19 by Dr. Parkes to repair minor impingement of right shoulder...1st Met to reach 200 SB, 5/15 vs Houston...Activated from DL on 9/1...Hit .301 after being activated...**1986:** Hit in the right eye by Rafael Santana on a rundown drill on 3/5 and was cut for 21 stitches...15 DL on 3/30...Assigned to Tidewater on medical rehabilitation on 4/25...Activated on 5/9...Hit .330 from 5/18-6/20...Set career high with 5 hits on 5/23 at San Diego...4th career lead-off HR, 5/31 vs San Francisco...Started each of the 6 NL LCS games (4 in LF, 2 in CF)...Started six of the seven World Series games (5 in LF and 1 in CF)...2 hits and 2 SB in game 4...In game 6, hit an infield dribbler that went between Bill Buckner's legs at 1B allowing the winning run to score...**1987:** Was batting .436 in 1st 12 games...Longest hit streak was 7 games...Scored 1250th career run, 9/5 at Los Angeles...Ranked sixth in the NL in pinch hitting (.313)...**1988:** Was senior member in terms of continuous service with club...Scored 61 runs to surpass Leon Jones as Mets' All-Time leader...1,000th ML hit, 7/22 vs the Braves...11 game hit streak, 4/10-5/2...10 game hit streak 8/22-9/2...Tied career high with 4 RBI , 9/5 vs the Pirates...1,000th ML game, 8/14 vs Expos...hit .385 from 8/3 through season's end...Started 3 games vs the Dodgers during NLCS...Hit game winning single in game 3 on 10/8...**1989:** While with the Mets, longest hit streak, 5 games, 4/21-30 and 7/9-18...Had gone 36 games prior to trade without a HR...Last HR, 6/9 at Pittsburg...Named as the player to be named later from the Mets for LHP, Jeff Musselman and minor league RHP Mike Brady...BLUE JAYS debut, 0-4 vs Kansas City in LF on 8/2...14 game hit streak, (30-65/.462, 1HR, 10RBI), 8/13-27...1st 4 hit game of the season, 8/15 at Boston...1st BLUE JAYS HR, solo vs Baltimore's Johnson on 8/18...Hit safely in 38 of 54 games for BLUE JAYS...20 game starts in RF and CF and 14 starts in LF...Hit .351 with 1 HR and 9 RBI on the road...13-13 in SB attempts...Hit safely in 4 of 5 ALCS games vs Oakland...Of the 38 games hit safely in, 21 were multiple hit outings...Hit .346 vs LHP.

MOOKIE WILSON

Year	Club & League	AVG	G	AB	R	H	2B	3B	HR	RBI	SH-SF	HP	BB	SO	SB-CS
1977	Wausau (Mid)	.290	68	245	50	71	10	2	6	32	1-4	3	33	57	23-7
1978	Jackson (Tex.)	.292	132	497	72	145	13	15	7	72	6-6	6	39	70	38-9
1979	Tidewater (Int)	.267	141	529	84	141	22	10	5	36	6-2	8	45	91	49-12
1980	Tidewater (Int)	.295	132	515	92	152	11	14	4	44	9-4	4	44	86	50-14
1980	NEW YORK (NL)	.248	27	105	16	26	5	3	0	4	2-0	0	12	19	7-7
1981	NEW YORK (NL)	.271	92	328	49	89	8	8	3	14	0-0	2	20	59	24 12
1982	NEW YORK (NL)	.279	159	639	90	178	25	9	5	55	1-3	2	32	102	58-16
1983	NEW YORK (NL)	.276	152	638	91	176	25	6	7	51	2-1	4	18	103	54-16
1984	NEW YORK (NL)	.276	154	587	88	162	28	10	10	54	2-2	2	26	90	46-9
1985	NEW YORK (NL)	.276	93	337	56	93	16	8	6	26	1-1	0	28	52	24-9
1986	Tidewater (IL)	.258	9	31	4	8	1	0	0	4	0-0	0	3	7	4-2
1986	NEW YORK (NL)	.289	123	381	61	110	17	5	9	45	0-1	1	5	72	25-7
1987	NEW YORK (NL)	.299	124	385	58	115	19	7	9	34	2-1	2	35	85	21-6
1988	NEW YORK (NL)	.296	112	378	61	112	17	5	8	41	1-2	2	27	63	15-4
1989	NEW YORK (NL)	.205	80	249	22	51	10	1	3	18	0-1	0	10	47	7-4
1989	TORONTO (AL)	.298	54	238	32	71	9	1	2	17	3-1	0	3	37	12-1
1990	TORONTO (AL)	.265	147	588	81	156	36	4	3	51	6-4	0	31	102	23-4
AL TOTALS		.275	201	826	113	227	45	5	5	68	9-5	0	34	139	35-5
NL TOTALS		.276	1116	4027	592	1112	170	62	60	342	11-11	15	240	692	281-86
ML TOTALS		.276	1317	4853	705	1339	215	67	65	410	20-16	15	274	831	316-91

WILSON - TRANSACTIONS

- Selected by Los Angeles Dodgers' organization in 4th round of free-agent draft, January 7, 1976.
- Selected by New York Mets' organization in 2nd round of free-agent draft, June 7, 1977.
- On disabled list, July 2 to September 1, 1985.
- On New York disabled list, March 30 to May 9, 1986; included rehabilitation disability assignment to Tidewater, April 26 to May 9, 1986.
- Traded to Toronto Blue Jays, August 1, 1989, completing deal in which Toronto traded Pitcher Jeff Musselman and Pitcher Mike Brady to New York Mets for a player to be named later, July 31, 1989.
- Granted free-agency, November 13, 1989; re-signed by Blue Jays, November 27, 1989.

LEAGUE CHAMPIONSHIP SERIES

Year	Club & League	AVG	G	AB	R	H	2B	3B	HR	RBI	SH-SF	HP	BB	SO	SB-CS
1986	NEW YORK (NL)	.115	6	26	2	3	0	0	0	1	0-0	0	1	7	1-0
1988	NEW YORK (NL)	.154	4	13	2	2	0	0	0	1	0-0	0	2	2	1-0
1989	TORONTO (AL)	.263	5	19	2	5	0	0	0	2	0-0	0	2	2	1-0

WORLD SERIES RECORD

Year	Club & League	AVG	G	AB	R	H	2B	3B	HR	RBI	SH-SF	HP	BB	SO	SB-CS
1986	Mets vs Red Sox	.269	7	26	3	7	1	0	0	0	0-0	1	1	6	3-0

MOOKIE WILSON vs AMERICAN LEAGUE

	1990					CAREER				
	AB	H	HR	RBI	AVG	AB	H	HR	RBI	AVG
SEASON	588	156	3	51	.265	826	227	5	68	.275
TORONTO	271	67	0	20	.247	398	99	1	28	.249
ROAD	317	89	3	31	.281	428	128	4	40	.299
vs BALTIMORE	59	21	0	1	.356	86	31	1	7	.360
BOSTON	51	14	0	5	.275	80	24	0	6	.300
CLEVELAND	54	13	0	4	.241	84	22	0	6	.262
DETROIT	37	10	2	5	.270	65	17	2	7	.262
MILWAUKEE	49	10	0	6	.204	80	23	0	9	.288
NEW YORK	43	8	0	6	.186	54	9	0	7	.167
TORONTO	-	-	-	-	-	-	-	-	-	-
A.L. EAST	293	76	2	27	.259	449	126	3	42	.281
vs CALIFORNIA	43	12	0	3	.279	43	12	0	3	.279
CHICAGO	43	10	0	4	.233	67	16	1	5	.239
KANSAS CITY	46	10	0	3	.217	67	13	0	3	.194
MINNESOTA	34	16	0	7	.471	59	25	0	8	.424
OAKLAND	34	5	0	1	.147	34	5	0	1	.147
SEATTLE	44	11	0	3	.250	44	0	0	0	.314
TEXAS	51	16	1	3	.314	63	19	1	3	.302
A.L. WEST	295	80	1	24	.271	377	101	2	26	.268
Pre-ASG	288	70	1	22	.243	288	70	1	22	.243
Post-ASG	300	86	2	29	.287	538	157	4	46	.292
vs RHP	400	110	1	30	.275	560	154	3	42	.275
LHP	188	46	2	21	.245	266	73	2	26	.274
PINCH HITTING	-	-	-	-	-	-	-	-	-	-
DESIGNATED HITTING	25	4	0	1	.160	25	4	0	1	.160
in APRIL	78	16	0	2	.205	78	16	0	2	.205
MAY	91	23	1	8	.253	91	23	1	8	.253
JUNE	96	24	0	11	.250	96	24	0	11	.250
JULY	93	25	0	3	.269	93	25	0	3	.269
AUGUST	99	33	1	16	.333	217	72	3	28	.332
SEPT/OCT	131	35	1	11	.267	251	67	1	16	.267

CAREER HIGHS

SEASON: **AVG.** .299-1987 **H** 178-1982 **HR** 10-1984
RBI 55-1982 SB 58-1982

GAME: **H** 5 at SAN DIEGO, May 23, 1986
HR 2 at PHIL, April 10, 1988
RBI 4-5 times (last time at MINN, Aug. 19, 1990)
SB 3 at MILW, Sept. 23, 1989

Last ML HR: at DET, Sept. 4, 1990

TEN HOME RUN GAME: The BLUE JAYS etched a page in the record book with a 10 HR performance against the Baltimore Orioles on September 14th, 1987. Following is a list of highlights from that game: In the 18-3 victory the BLUE JAYS received HR's from ERNIE WHITT (3), GEORGE BELL (2), RANCE MULLINIKS (2), FRED McGRIFF (1), ROB DUCEY (1) and LLOYD MOSEBY (1)...WHITT became the second BLUE JAYS player since Otto Velez on May 10, 1980 to hit three HR's in one game...The clubs combined to hit 11 HR's in the game, to tie the Mmajor League mark...RANCE MULLINIKS hit his 10th and 11th of the season, enabling the BLUE JAYS to become the 12th team in major league history to have at least nine players with at least 10 HR's...A club mark with 53 total bases in the game was set...The club hit three HR's in the second inning, marking the third time in 1987 and seventh time in franchise history that the club had a three HR inning... ROB DUCEY hit his first Major League HR...Most players with two or more home runs, club, game was tied as three BLUE JAYS, Bell, Mulliniks and Whitt had multiple home run games. The 10 home runs surpassed the previosu record of eight.

1 EDDIE ZOSKY

SHORTSTOP

Born: Feb. 10, 1968 Whittier, CA
Resides: Whittier, CA
B-R T-R 6-0 175
M.L. Service: 0.000

PERSONAL: Edward James Zosky...Single...Part of signing bonus was donated to Toronto's Hospital for Sick Children as well as the baseball programs at Fresno State and St. Paul's High School of Santa Fe Springs, California...Graduated from the latter in 1986...Named to the 1989 All-American team by The Sporting News and Baseball America...Favourite players include Ozzie Smith and Cal Ripken, Jr.

LAST SEASON: Hit .271 in 115 games at Knoxville (AA) of the Southern League...Fourth on the team in hits with 122...Tied for the club lead in triples with 7...All 115 games were at the shortstop position...Had a .316 on base percentage...Tied for fifth on Knoxville in doubles (20).

PROFESSIONAL CAREER: **1989:** Started the season with Fresno State batting .370 (101-273) with 3 HR and 51 RBI...Joined Dunedin (A) of the Florida State League on 6/30 after being drafted in the first round of the June Free Agent Draft (19th overall)...Didn't play before promotion to Knoxville (AA) of the Southern League...Hit .221 with 10 of 56 hits going for extra bases.

EDDIE ZOSKY

Year	Club & League	AVG	G	AB	R	H	2B	3B	HR	RBI	SH-SF	HP	BB	SO	SB-CS
1989	Knoxville (Sou)	.221	56	208	21	46	5	3	2	14	2-1	0	10	32	1-1
1990	Knoxville (Sou)	.271	115	450	53	122	20	7	3	45	6-3	5	26	72	3-13

ZOSKY - TRANSACTIONS

- Selected by Toronto in 1st round (19th overall) in June 1989 free-agent draft.

BLUE JAYS BEHIND THE SCENES

DR. RON TAYLOR

Team Physician

A Toronto native, became the first former Major League player to return to the game in the capacity of team physician-February 1979...Spent 11 years in the Major Leagues with five teams before retiring from the game in 1972...Began his Major League career with the Cleveland Indians in 1962...Played the next 10 seasons with National League teams including 2 plus seasons with St. Louis and five with the New York Mets...Other teams were Houston and San Diego...Finished career with a 45-43 record, 72 saves and a 3.93 ERA...Pitched on two World Series teams - 1964 Cardinals and 1969 Mets...Obtained degree in electrical engineering from University of Toronto while playing baseball...Began medical studies in 1972 and graduated from University of Toronto in 1977...Served internship at Mount Sinai Hospital in Toronto and returned for a second year in 1978, specializing in sports medicine...Currently runs a sports medicine clinic at Mount Sinai Hospital...Elected to the Canadian Baseball Hall of Fame in 1985.

DR. ALLAN GROSS

Consulting Orthopaedic Surgeon

Has been involved with the BLUE JAYS since 1979...Graduated from the University of Toronto in 1962 with his Doctor of Medicine Degree...Began working at Mt. Sinai Hospital in June of 1971...Interested in bone and cartilage transplantation, he established the Mount Sinai Hospital Bone Bank in 1972...Has pioneered many transplant surgery techniques...From 1975-1982 he was the Surgeon-In-Chief of Mt. Sinai Hospital...From 1982-1986 was the Head, Combined Division of Orthopaedic Surgery, Toronto General Hospital/Mt. Sinai Hospital...Is the Head of Orthopaedic Surgery at Mt. Sinai Hospital and the A.J. Latner Professor and Chairman, Division of Orthopaedic Surgery at The University of Toronto...He is also a Fellow of The Royal College of Surgeons of Canada in Orthopaedic Surgery (1969)...Married, wife's name Penny Gross PhD...Wife is a Senior Research and Program Evaluation Analyst with the Ontario Government...Has four children: Lowell, Tony, Robyn and Jeremy...Resides in Toronto.

TOMMY CRAIG
Trainer

This will be his 6th full season with the BLUE JAYS and fifth as Head Trainer...Attained a BSc in Health and Physical Education with emphasis in sports medicine from East Carolina University...Graduated in December 1979...Started training career with Cincinnati's Shelby, NC affiliate in 1978...Joined the BLUE JAYS organization in 1980 as head trainer for Kinston, NC...Moved to Knoxville (AA) in 1981 before spending the 1982-84 seasons at Syracuse...Joined the BLUE JAYS in September 1984...Certified athletic trainer with the National Athletic Trainers Association and member of the Professional Baseball Athletic Trainers Society...Spent winter '84 working at the Hughston Sports Medicine Hospital in Columbus, GA focusing on arthroscopic surgery cases...Married the former Theresa Rosick, 9/12/81...Three children, Sarah (4/26/83), Geoffrey (12/20/85) and Natalie (12/18/89)...Resides in Palm Harbor, Florida.

BRENT ANDREWS
Assistant Trainer

This is his 3rd season with the BLUE JAYS...Has a Bachelor of Physical Education from the University of Calgary and a physical education diploma from Calgary's Mt. Royal College...Worked with the BLUE JAYS Medicine Hat team in 1987 and 1988...Has served as a ski instructor at Canada Olympic Park and for the Canadian Association of Disabled Skiing...Is a certified YMCA fitness instructor and is a member of the National Athletic Trainers Association, Canadian Association of Sports Sciences and Canadian Therapists Association...Served three years in an Athletic Therapy position with the University of Calgary football program as well as the university's athletic therapy clinic...Single and is a resident of Toronto.

JEFF ROSS
Equipment Manager

Is starting his 11th season as Equipment Manager after succeeding John Silverman prior to the start of the 1981 season...Is a 37 year old Montreal native who now lives in Palm Harbor, Florida...Ran the visiting clubhouse at Exhibition Stadium during the BLUE JAYS first four seasons of operation...Responsibilities include maintenance of all uniforms and equipment as well as overseeing the transport of such items during the regular season...Graduated from Darcy McGee High School in Montreal...Attended Dawson College and worked part-time for the Montreal Expos as a member of their grounds crew and in the clubhouses...Enjoys golf and fishing...Married, wife's name Christine...Has three children, Matthew (16), Christian (10) and Leah (4).

IAN DUFF
Visiting Clubhouse Manager

Single...31 yrs old...Born in Lachine, Quebec and moved to Toronto 13 years later...Graduate of Silverthorn Collegiate Institute...Started with the BLUE JAYS in 1977 as a home clubhouse attendant, a position he held through 1979...Spent the 1980 season as the visiting clubhouse attendant...Appointed Visiting Clubhouse Manager in November 1981, succeeding Jeff Ross...Acts as Home Clubhouse Manager during spring training...Occasionally travels with the team duing the season in the position of acting BLUE JAYS Equipment Manager...Primary responsibility is to handle any and all requests of the visiting team while at SkyDome...Resides in Mississauga, Ontario.

MINOR LEAGUE PLAYER DEVELOPMENT

MEL QUEEN

Director of Player Development...Has been with the BLUE JAYS organization since 1986 when he was a roving pitching instructor...Was promoted to his present position in 1990...Began his playing career in the Reds' organization in 1960 as a third baseman...Moved to the outfield in 1963 before becoming a pitcher in 1966...Had his best season in 1967 when he finished 10th in the NL in ERA (2.76)...Finished his career with the Angels (AL) in 1972 where he was used in a relief role...Started coaching in 1979 with Waterloo (A) of the Midwest League, a Cleveland affiliate...Became the Cleveland Indians' pitching coach in 1982...Was out of organized baseball from 1983-1986.

SCOTT BREEDEN

Minor League Pitching Instructor...Pitched in the Reds' chain for 12 seasons beginning in 1956 with Kokoma of the Midwest League...Played seven seasons at the triple A level...Began his coaching career as the manager of Wytheville (A) of the Appalachian League in 1967...Stayed in the Reds' organization as a minor league instructor and as Cincinnati's pitching coach (NL) from 1986-1989...Moved to the BLUE JAYS in 1990, serving as a minor league instructor.

BOB DIDIER

Minor League Catching Instructor...Played for three Major League clubs during his career: Atlanta, Detroit and Boston- from 1969-1974...Caught Hoyt Wilhelm's 1000th game...Once threw out Lou Brock twice in a game...Retired from professional baseball in 1976...Was a player/coach during his last season in 1976...Began his professional coaching career as a manager with Kingsport (Rookie) of the Appalachian League in 1977...Spent three seasons on the Oakland A's coaching staff (1984-1986)...Joined the Mariners' coaching staff prior to the 1989 season...1991 will be his first season in the BLUE JAYS organization.

LARRY HISLE

Minor League Hitting Instructor...Last season was his first in the BLUE JAYS chain, serving in the same capacity...Was an outfield instructor for the Milwaukee Brewers from 1983-1984...Was not involved in professional baseball for four years (1985-1988)...Returned with the Houston Astros organization in 1989 as a minor league hitting instructor...Played in the Majors for Philadelphia, Minnesota and Milwaukee during his playing career...Had his best ML season in 1977 when he hit .302 with 28 HR and 119 RBI during his last season with the Twins.

JIM HOFF

Minor League Instructor...Was the Cincinnati Reds' minor league Field Coordinator from September 30th, 1983 to the end of the 1990 minor league season...Supervised and directed all spring training activities for the Reds' farm system...Also directed the Reds' Florida Instructional League operation...Was a former infielder in the Reds' system from 1967 to 1972...Managed in the Cincinnati farm system for 11 years...Graduated from Xavier University (Cincinnati) and later attended Notre Dame Law School.

MIKE EASLER

Minor League Hitting Instructor...1991 will be his first season as an instructor in the BLUE JAYS organization...Began his professional career as an outfielder in 1969 with the Houston Astros organization...Made his major league debut in 1973 with the Astros...Played for the Pirates from 1979-1983 hitting .338 in 1980...Finished his major league career with the Yankees in 1987...Was a career .293 hitter and drove in 522 runs during his ML career...Played professional baseball in Japan for two years (1988-89) with the Nippon Ham Fighters...Last season managed the Miami (Independent) entry in the Florida State League.

SYRACUSE CHIEFS

BOB BAILOR

Begins his fifth season as a minor league manager; his fourth at Syracuse (AAA) of the International League...Was a former BLUE JAY shortstop from 1977-1980...In 1977, posted the highest batting average (.310) ever, for a player on a first year expansion team...Voted BLUE JAYS player of the year in 1977...Finished his professional career in 1985 with the Los Angeles Dodgers hitting .246 in 74 games...Started managerial career in 1987 as manager of the Dunedin BLUE JAYS (A) of the Florida State League...Led the 1989 Chiefs to the divisional crown, only to lose to Richmond 3 games to 1 in post season play...Was named IL Manager-of-the-Year for 1989...Last season, he managed Syracuse to a 62-83 record (6th overall).

BOB SHIRLEY

Starts his fourth season as a member of the BLUE JAYS minor league coaching staff...Played 11 seasons at the Major League level and recorded a career best 2.64 ERA in 48 games with the Yankees in 1985...Began coaching career as a player/coach in 1988 with Syracuse (AAA) of the International League...Managed the St. Catharines BLUE JAYS of the New York-Penn League in 1989...Will serve as the Chiefs' pitching coach for the second consecutive season in 1991.

ROCKET WHEELER

Began coaching career in the BLUE JAYS organization as a player/coach in 1981 with Florence (A) of the South Atlantic League...Became a full-time coach in 1983 with Florence...Has previously managed at Medicine Hat (Rookie) of the Pioneer League in 1984, 1988 and 1989, as well as at Bradenton (Summer A) of the Gulf Coast League in 1985...Will be returning for his third season as a coach at Syracuse.

KNOXVILLE BLUE JAYS

JOHN STEARNS

This season will be his second as Manager of the Knoxville BLUE JAYS (AA) of the Southern League...Last season was his first in the BLUE JAYS organization after having scouted for the Brewers and coached for both the Astros and the Yankees organizations...Played as a catcher and first baseman for the Mets for most of his Major League career (1975-1984), hitting a career high .297 in 98 games during the 1982 season...Last season, claimed a 67-77 record in his rookie year as a manager.

JOHN POLONI

1991 will see his return to Knoxville (AA) as the pitching coach...Also spent last season at Knoxville serving in the same capacity with the club...Broke into professional ball with the Texas Rangers organization in 1975...Saw just 2 games of Major League action during his playing career (1977)...Played briefly in the BLUE JAYS organization with Knoxville in 1979 and 1980...Began coaching career in 1983 with the Mariners organization...Joined the BLUE JAYS coaching staff in 1987 with the Myrtle Beach club (A).

J.J. CANNON

1991 will be his seventh consecutive season as a coach with Knoxville (AA) and eighth as a full-time coach...Served as a player-coach in 1983 with Kinston (A) of the Carolina League...Began his professional playing career in 1974 in the Astros chain as an outfielder...Played in the BLUE JAYS system from 1979-1983, including 131 games with TORONTO during 1979 and 1980.

DUNEDIN BLUE JAYS

DENNIS HOLMBERG

Begins his second season as Manager of the Dunedin BLUE JAYS (A) of the Florida State League...This will be his fifth season with Dunedin and his fourteenth season as a manager/coach in the BLUE JAYS organization...Best professional season came in 1976 when he hit .299 with Burlington (A) of the Midwest League and had 12 HR with 62 RBI...His last season came in 1977 while playing and coaching for Holyoke (AA) of the Eastern League.

BILL MONBOUQUETTE

Returns for his second season as the Dunedin pitching coach...Began coaching career in 1969 with the Yankees organization...Came to the BLUE JAYS in 1988 and was appointed to the pitching coach position at Myrtle Beach (South Atlantic League)...Pitched for over 10 seasons at the Major League level (1958-1965)...Most of his playing career was spent with the Red Sox...His best season came in 1963 when he won 20 games and posted a 3.81 ERA in 258 innings...Closed out his playing days in 1968 with the Yankees and the Giants.

PETER ROWE

Will be returning to Dunedin as a coach...Last season was his first season coaching in the BLUE JAYS organization...Began his professional career with the BLUE JAYS in 1978 when he played at Dunedin (A) of the Florida State League...In 1980 while with the Knoxville club he hit .277 with 11 HR and 40 RBI in 99 games...His last season as a player came in 1980 with Knoxville.

MYRTLE BEACH HURRICANES

GARTH IORG

This will be his first season as manager of the Myrtle Beach HURRICANES (A) of the South Atlantic League...Last season, he managed the Medicine Hat BLUE JAYS (Rookie) of the Pioneer League...1990 was his first season as a minor league manager...At Medicine Hat he posted a 20-46 record (7th overall)...Platooned at third base, along with current BLUE JAY DH, Rance Mulliniks from 1982 until 1987...Hit a career high .313 with 7 HR and 37 RBI in 1985.

STEVE MINGORI

1991 will mark his sixth season of pitching coach duties in the BLUE JAYS organization...Began in 1986 with Syracuse (AAA) of the International League...Spent the next three seasons with Dunedin (A) in the FSL...Last season was moved to Myrtle Beach and assisted the club in displaying a 3.12 ERA and a .550 winning percentage...Played in the Major Leagues with Cleveland and Kansas City from 1970-1979...Compiled a 5-5 record with 10 saves and a 2.33 ERA in 1976 while with the Royals.

LEROY STANTON

Has spent his entire coaching career with the BLUE JAYS organization...Began coaching with Medicine Hat in 1981, after retiring as a player in 1980...Has been assigned to Myrtle Beach since 1987...Began his Major League career in 1970 when he debuted with the Mets...Was traded to the Angels along with Nolan Ryan, Francisco Estrada and Don Rose in 1971...Moved on to Seattle in 1977 where he finished his ML career...Hit 27 HR and had 90 RBI in 1977 with the Mariners...Retired from playing in 1980.

ST. CATHARINES BLUE JAYS

DOUG AULT
Returns for his second season as Manager of the St. Catharines Blue Jays...Last season, compiled a 29-47 record in the New York-Penn League circuit...Prior to coming to St. Catharines, he had managed at Dunedin, Syracuse and Kinston...His managerial career began with the BLUE JAYS in 1983 with Kinston in the Carolina League...Played for TORONTO from 1977-1980 and has been with the organization ever since.

DARREN BALSLEY
This will be his second season as a coach in the BLUE JAY organization...Pitched in the BLUE JAYS chain from 1987-1989...Worked as a pitching coach at St. Catharines in 1990...Started his professional career with the Athletics in 1984 and was picked up by TORONTO in December 1986 via the Minor League Draft...He will handle the pitching coach duties at St. Catharines during 1991.

MIKE McALPIN
A former outfielder at the University of Delaware returns for his fourth season as a coach at St. Catharines...Began in the BLUE JAYS organization in 1980 as a scout...Coached at Medicine Hat from 1982-1984...Moved to Bradenton of the Gulf Coast League for the 1985 season...Was assigned to St. Catharines in 1988.

MEDICINE HAT BLUE JAYS

REGGIE CLEVELAND
This will be his first season as a pitching coach in the BLUE JAYS organization...The Swift Current, Saskatchewan native played in the Major Leagues for twelve seasons...His career led him to play in various cities including St. Louis, Boston, Texas and Milwaukee...Was inducted into the Canadian Baseball Hall of Fame in 1986...He holds the distinction of being the only Canadian pitcher to ever start a World Series game.

OMAR MALAVE
Returns for his second season as a coach with the Medicine Hat Blue Jays...Played his entire career with the BLUE JAYS organization beginning with the Bradenton Blue Jays (Summer A) of the Gulf Coast League in 1981 and retiring after the 1989 season at Knoxville/Syracuse.

SANTO DOMINGO BLUE JAYS

RAMON WEBSTER
Santo Domingo Blue Jays Field Manager...Played professionally from 1963-79...Saw action in both the American and National Leagues...First full ML season was in 1967 with the Kansas City Royals where he hit .256 in 122 games...Ended his ML career in 1971 when he played in 26 games for the Chicago Cubs...Has had managerial experience in the Blue Jays organization with the Bradenton Blue Jays of the Gulf Coast League during the mid-80's...Will manage the Santo Domingo Blue Jays this coming season in the Dominican Republic...He also works closely with Epy Guerrero in the scouting of Latin American players.

PITCHERS AT THE PLATE

The Blue Jays have never had a pitcher bat in a regular season game in their first thirteen seasons.

DAVE STIEB batted against Minnesota Twins on August 29, 1980 at Exhibition Stadium but he was playing the outfield.

Stieb had gone in to play left field in the 15th inning of a suspended game started on August 28th.

In his only time at the plate he flied out to the center-fielder, Ken Landreaux in the bottom of the 15th....The pitcher was Al Williams.

He played one inning and had no fielding opportunities as the Jays lost 7-5 in 15 innings.

CALL IT A DRAW! The Blue Jays have played two tie games in their history. The first one was May 13, 1984 at Cleveland...with one out in the top of the 8th inning the rains came and play could not continue with the score 4-4...The game had to be completely replayed as part of a TWDH on August 15th...The second occurrence was at Cleveland on August 26, 1986...Play was halted after 9 innings due to rain...The game was completely replayed as part of an August 27th TWDH...Even though the games were rained out, the statistics from the games were entered into the books.

ACKER, Jim—P

Year	PCT	G	PO	A	E	TC	DP
1983	1.000	38	12	15	0	27	4
1984	.938	32	7	8	1	16	0
1985	1.000	61	10	16	0	26	1
1986 (AL)	1.000	23	9	11	0	20	2
1986 (NL)	1.000	21	7	17	0	24	2
1987 (NL)	1.000	68	6	23	0	29	2
1988 (NL)	1.000	21	3	7	0	10	0
1989 (NL)	1.000	59	12	14	0	26	0
1989 (AL)	,917	14	1	10	1	12	0
1990 (AL)	1.000	59	5	19	0	24	0
Total	.991	396	72	140	2	214	11

ALOMAR, Roberto—2B

Year	PCT	G	PO	A	E	TC	DP
1988 (NL)	.980	143	319	459	16	794	88
1989 (NL)	.967	157	341	472	28	841	91
1990 (NL)	.976	137	311	392	17	720	73
Total	.974	437	971	1233	61	2355	252

ALOMAR, Roberto—SS

Year	PCT	G	PO	A	E	TC	DP
1990	.895	5	5	12	2	19	4

BORDERS, Pat—C

Year	PCT	G	PO	A	E	TC	DP
1988	.973	43	205	14	6	225	0
1989	.980	68	261	27	6	294	1
1990 (AL)	.993	115	515	46	4	565	6
Total	.985	226	981	87	16	1084	7

BORDERS, Pat—2B

Year	PCT	G	PO	A	E	TC	DP
1988	1.000	1	0	3	0	3	0

BORDERS, Pat—3B

Year	PCT	G	PO	A	E	TCDP	
1988	.667	1	0	2	1	3	0
Total	.667	1	0	2	1	3	0

CARTER, Joe—1B

Year	PCT	G	PO	A	E	TC	DP
1984 (AL)	1.000	7	47	2	0	49	4
1985 (AL)	.974	11	33	5	1	39	2
1986 (AL)	.993	70	559	47	4	610	50
1987 (AL)	.983	84	644	45	12	701	61
1989 (AL)	.991	11	93	14	1	108	4
1990 (NL)	.948	14	107	3	6	116	15
Total	.985	197	1483	116	24	1623	136

CARTER, Joe—2B

Year	PCT	G	PO	A	E	TC	DP
1985	1.000	1	0	1	0	1	0

CARTER, Joe—3B

Year	PCT	G	PO	A	E	TC	DP
1985	.000	1	0	0	0	0	0

CARTER, Joe—OF

Year	PCT	G	PO	A	E	TC	DP
1983 (NL)	1.000	16	26	0	0	26	0
1984(AL)	.956	59	122	9	6	137	0
1985 (AL)	.983	135	278	11	5	294	2
1986 (AL)	.976	104	241	8	6	255	2
1988 (AL)	.985	156	444	8	7	459	3
1989 (AL)	.978	146	350	6	8	364	3
1990 (NL)	.988	150	385	13	5	403	4
Total	.980	828	1984	56	42	2082	14

DAYLEY, Ken—P

Year	PCT	G	PO	A	E	TC	DP
1982	1.000	20	3	5	0	8	0
1983	1.000	24	0	7	0	7	0
1984	1.000	7	1	4	0	5	0
1985	1.000	57	5	15	0	20	0
1986	1.000	31	1	7	0	8	0
1987	1.000	53	3	4	0	7	1
1988	1.000	54	2	7	0	9	0
1989	.875	71	2	5	1	8	0
1990	.929	58	5	8	1	14	1
Total	.975	375	22	62	2	79	2

DIAZ, Carlos—C

Year	PCT	G	PO	A	E	TC	DP
1990	1.000	9	13	3	0	16	0

DUCEY, Rob—OF

Year	PCT	G	PO	A	ET	C	DP
1987	1.000	28	31	0	0	31	0
1988	1.000	26	35	1	0	36	0
1989	1.000	35	56	3	0	59	2
1990	1.000	19	37	0	0	37	0
Total	1.000	108	159	4	0	163	2

EPPARD, Jim—1B

Year	PCT	G	PO	A	E	TC	DP
1988 (AL)	.971	6	29	4	1	34	2
1989 (AL)	1.000	4	12	0	0	12	2
Total	.978	10	41	4	1	46	4

EPPARD, Jim—OF

Year	PCT	G	PO	A	E	TC	DP
1987	1.000	1	1	0	0	1	0
1988	.971	17	34	0	1	35	0
Total	.972	18	35	0	1	36	0

FRASER, Willie—P

Year	PCT	G	PO	A	E	TC	DP
1986	.000	1	0	0	0	0	0
1987	.955	36	6	15	1	22	0
1988	.932	34	21	20	3	44	3
1989	1.000	44	6	14	0	20	1
1990	1.000	45	2	6	0	8	0
Total	.957	160	35	55	4	94	4

GONZALES, Rene—1B

Year	PCT	G	PO	A	E	TC	DP
1988 (AL)	1.000	1	2	0	0	2	0
Total	1.000	1	2	0	0	2	0

GONZALES, Rene—2B

Year	PCT	G	PO	A	E	TC	DP
1987 (AL)	1.000	6	0	4	0	4	1
1988 (AL)	.979	14	17	29	1	47	6
1989 (AL)	.978	54	93	125	5	223	35
1990 (AL)	.994	43	61	94	1	156	19
Total	.984	117	171	252	7	430	61

GONZALES, Rene—3B

Year	PCT	G	PO	A	E	TC	DP
1986 (NL)	1.000	5	5	8	0	13	1
1987 (AL)	.963	29	18	34	2	54	2
1988 (AL)	.966	80	45	153	7	205	19
1989 (AL)	.923	17	8	16	2	26	1
1990 (AL)	.929	16	3	10	1	14	1
Total	.968	147	79	221	12	312	24

GONZALES, Rene—SS

Year	PCT	G	PO	A	E	TC	DP
1984 (NL)	.957	27	17	28	2	47	5
1986 (NL)	1.000	6	2	11	0	13	2
1987 (AL)	1.000	1	4	5	0	9	2
1988 (AL)	1.000	2	1	3	0	4	1
1989 (AL)	1.000	1	2	5	0	7	1
1990 (AL)	1.000	9	4	10	0	14	3
Total	.979	46	30	62	2	94	14

GONAZLES, Rene—OF

Year	PCT	G	PO	A	E	TC	DP
1988 (AL)	1.000	1	1	0	0	1	0
1990 (AL)	.000	1	0	0	0	0	0
Total	1.000	2	1	0	0	1	0

GRUBER, Kelly—2B

Year	PCT	G	PO	A	E	TC	DP
1985	.000	1	0	0	0	0	0
1986	.969	14	15	16	1	32	5
1987	1.000	7	3	4	0	7	1
1988	.909	7	4	16	2	22	4
Total	.951	29	22	36	3	61	10

GRUBER, Kelly—SS

Year	PCT	G	PO	A	E	TC	DP
1984	.667	1	0	2	1	3	0
1986	1.000	5	3	2	0	5	0
1987	.980	21	20	28	1	49	7
1988	.000	1	0	0	0	0	0
1989	1.000	1	0	2	0	2	0
Total	.966	29	23	34	2	59	7

GRUBER, Kelly—3B

Year	PCT	G	PO	A	E	TC	DP
1984	.933	12	4	10	1	15	0
1985	1.000	5	2	6	0	8	0
1986	.940	42	19	59	5	83	3
1987	.948	119	52	168	12	232	11
1988	.971	156	114	349	14	477	31
1989	.945	119	86	291	22	399	15
1990	.955	145	123	280	19	422	21
Total	.955	598	400	1163	73	1636	81

GRUBER, Kelly—OF

Year	PCT	G	PO	A	E	TC	DP
1988	1.000	2	3	0	0	3	0
1989	1.000	16	35	2	0	37	1
1990	1.000	6	6	0	0	6	0
Total	1.000	24	44	2	0	46	1

HENKE, Tom—P

Year	PCT	G	PO	A	E	TC	DP
1982	1.000	8	2	2	0	4	0
1983	.750	8	0	3	1	4	0
1984	1.000	25	1	2	0	3	0
1985	1.000	28	3	3	0	6	0
1986	1.000	63	2	2	0	4	1
1987	1.000	72	9	12	0	21	1
1988	1.000	52	1	9	0	10	1
1989	.929	64	3	10	1	14	0
1990	1.000	61	6	5	0	11	0
Total	.974	381	27	48	2	77	3

HILL, Glenallen—OF

Year	PCT	G	PO	A	E	TC	DP
1989	.964	16	27	0	1	28	0
1990	.983	60	115	4	2	121	0
Total	.980	76	142	4	3	149	0

KEY, Jimmy—P

Year	PCT	G	PO	A	E	TC	DP
1984	.952	63	9	11	1	21	0
1985	.957	35	15	52	3	70	3
1986	1.000	36	18	42	0	60	4
1987	.953	36	17	44	3	64	5
1988	1.000	21	5	19	0	24	1
1989	.965	33	11	44	2	57	2
1990	.968	27	8	22	1	31	3
Total	.969	251	83	234	10	327	18

LEE, Manny—2B

Year	PCT	G	PO	A	E	TC	DP
1985	.971	38	27	40	2	69	8
1986	.990	29	32	72	1	105	10
1987	.966	27	51	61	4	116	16
1988	.988	98	221	261	6	488	64
1989	.985	40	103	96	3	202	29
1990	.993	112	259	286	4	549	65
Total	.989	344	693	816	21	1529	192

LEE, Manny—3B

Year	PCT	G	PO	A	E	TC	DP
1987	1.000	2	1	1	0	2	0
1988	.867	8	1	12	2	15	1
1989	.891	17	9	32	5	46	4
Total	.889	27	11	45	7	63	5

LEE, Manny—SS

Year	PCT	G	PO	A	E	TC	DP
1985	.952	8	7	13	1	21	3
1986	.857	5	3	3	1	7	1
1987	.987	26	26	49	1	76	10
1988	.940	23	28	35	4	67	6
1989	.974	28	40	73	3	116	18
1990	1.000	9	6	15	0	21	1
Total	.968	99	110	188	10	308	39

LEE, Manny—OF

Year	PCT	G	PO	A	E	TC	DP
1989	.000	1	0	0	0	0	0
Total	.000	1	0	0	0	0	0

LEITER, Al—P

Year	PCT	G	PO	A	E	TC	DP
1987	1.000	4	0	2	0	2	0
1988	.917	14	0	11	1	12	0
1989	1.000	5	1	2	0	3	0
1990	1.000	4	1	1	0	2	0
Total	.947	27	2	16	1	19	0

MacDONALD, Bob—P

Year	PCT	G	PO	A	E	TC	DP
1990	.000	4	0	0	0	0	0

MANZANILLO, Ravelo—P

Year	PCT	G	PO	A	E	TC	DP
1988	1.000	2	0	1	0	1	0

MULLINIKS, Rance—1B

Year	PCT	G	PO	A	E	TC	DP
1990	1.000	3	11	0	0	11	1

MULLINIKS, Rance—3B

Year	PCT	G	PO	A	E	TC	DP
1981	.900	5	4	5	1	10	1
1982	.928	102	60	137	13	210	13
1983	.971	116	70	161	7	220	13
1985	.971	119	75	162	7	244	16
1986	.975	110	60	176	6	242	13
1987	.927	96	29	137	13	179	14
1988	1.000	7	3	5	0	8	0
1989	.985	29	15	50	1	66	9
1990	.949	22	12	25	2	39	4
Total	.961	606	393	1006	57	1456	95

MULLINIKS, Rance—2B

Year	PCT	G	PO	A	E	TC	DP
1980	1.000	14	11	19	0	30	4
1981	.900	10	14	13	3	30	4
1983	1.000	2	0	1	0	1	0
1984	.000	1	0	0	0	0	0
1986	.000	1	0	0	0	0	0
Total	.967	28	25	33	3	60	8

MULLINIKS, Rance—SS

Year	PCT	G	PO	A	E	TC	DP
1977	..963	77	112	229	13	354	37
1978	.953	47	68	93	8	169	22
1979	.957	22	46	43	4	93	13
1980	.981	18	19	34	1	54	5
1981	.966	7	7	21	1	29	4
1982	.963	16	9	17	1	27	3
1983	1.000	15	7	23	0	30	7
1984	.857	3	2	4	1	7	2
1987	-	1	0	0	0	0	0
Total	.962	206	270	464	29	763	93

MYERS, Greg—C

Year	PCT	G	PO	A	E	TC	DP
1987	1.000	7	24	1	0	25	0
1989	1.000	11	46	6	0	52	1
1990	.993	87	411	30	3	444	4
Total	.994	105	481	37	3	521	5

OLERUD, John—1B

Year	PCT	G	PO	A	E	TC	DP
1989	1.000	5	19	2	0	21	0
1990	.986	18	133	10	2	145	10
Total	.988	23	152	12	2	166	10

SANCHEZ, Alex—P

Year	PCT	G	PO	A	E	TC	DP
1989	1.000	4	1	6	0	7	1
Total	1.000	4	1	6	0	7	1

STIEB, Dave—P

Year	PCT	G	PO	A	E	TC	DP
1979	.977	18	12	31	1	44	1
1980	.987	34	20	58	1	79	8
1981	.980	25	11	38	1	50	3
1982	.976	36	27	53	2	82	6
1983	.968	36	28	33	2	63	1
1984	.982	35	22	34	1	57	4
1985	.946	36	34	53	5	92	5
1986	.980	37	15	33	1	49	4
1987	.961	33	24	25	2	51	2
1988	1.000	32	19	26	0	45	3
1989	1.000	33	18	29	0	47	1
1990	.941	33	24	40	4	68	3
Total	.972	388	254	453	20	727	41

STOTTLEMYRE, Todd—P

Year	PCT	G	PO	A	E	TC	DP
1988	1.000	28	7	11	0	18	0
1989	.821	27	7	16	5	28	1
1990	.979	33	17	30	1	48	5
Total	.936	88	31	57	6	94	6

TABLER, Pat—1B

Year	PCT	G	PO	A	E	TC	DP
1984	.998	67	433	39	1	473	46
1985	.983	92	739	72	14	825	77
1986	.990	107	846	84	9	939	87
1987	.984	82	650	75	12	737	49
1988	.969	17	114	9	4	127	11
1989	.993	20	126	13	1	140	10
1990	1.000	5	31	1	0	32	6
Total	.987	390	2939	293	41	3273	286

TABLER, Pat—OF

Year	PCT	G	PO	A	E	TC	DP
1983	.948	88	180	4	10	194	0
1984	.973	43	72	1	2	75	1
1988	.986	37	68	1	1	70	0
1989	.970	55	89	8	3	100	1
1990 (NL)	1.000	10	20	1	0	21	1
1990 (AL)	.986	42	68	4	1	73	1
Total	.968	275	497	19	17	533	4

TABLER, Pat—2B

Year	PCT	G	PO	A	E	TC	DP
1981 (NL)	.982	35	70	93	3	166	17
1983 (AL)	.000	2	0	0	0	0	0
1984 (AL)	.000	1	0	0	0	0	0
1985	1.000	1	1	2	0	3	1
1989	1.000	3	2	4	0	6	0
1990	.875	6	2	5	1	8	0
Total	.978	48	75	104	4	183	18

TABLER, Pat—3B

Year	PCT	G	PO	A	E	TC	DP
1982(NL)	.949	25	23	33	3	59	3
1983(AL)	.986	25	17	51	1	69	6
1984 (AL)	.950	36	27	49	4	80	7
1985 (AL)	1.000	4	4	3	0	7	0
1988 (AL)	.000	1	0	0	0	0	0
1989 (AL)	.000	1	0	0	0	0	0
1990 (AL)	.875	6	2	5	1	8	0
Total	.960	98	73	141	9	223	16

WARD, Duane—P

Year	PCT	G	PO	A	E	TC	DP
1986 (NL)	1.000	10	0	6	0	6	0
1986 (AL)	1.000	2	1	0	0	1	0
1987	1.000	12	2	2	0	4	0
1988	.947	64	6	12	1	19	0
1989	.963	66	5	21	1	27	2
1990	.964	73	9	18	1	28	0
Total	.965	227	23	59	3	85	2

WELLS, David—P

Year	PCT	G	PO	A	E	TC	DP
1987	1.000	18	2	4	0	6	1
1988	1.000	41	5	5	0	10	1
1989	.952	54	9	11	1	21	0
1990	1.000	43	7	32	0	39	1
Total	.987	156	23	52	1	76	3

WHITE, Devon—OF

Year	PCT	G	PO	A	E	TC	DP
1985	1.000	16	10	1	0	11	0
1986	.961	28	49	0	2	51	0
1987	.980	159	424	16	9	449	3
1988	.976	116	364	7	9	380	2
1989	.989	154	430	10	5	445	3
1990	.972	122	302	11	9	322	4
Total	.979	595	1579	45	34	1658	12

WHITEN, Mark—OF

Year	PCT	G	PO	A	E	TC	DP
1990	1.000	30	60	3	0	63	0

WILLIAMS, Kenny—1B

Year	PCT	G	PO	A	E	TC	DP
1989	.000	1	0	0	0	0	0

WILLIAMS, Kenny—3B

Year	PCT	G	PO	A	E	TC	DP
1988	.860	32	19	67	14	100	3

WILLIAMS, Kenny—OF

Year	PCT	G	PO	A	E	TC	DP
1986	1.000	10	18	1	0	19	1
1987	.981	115	303	5	6	314	2
1988	.959	38	68	2	3	73	1
1989	.979	87	180	11	4	195	3
1990	1.000	77	103	5	0	108	2
Total	.982	327	672	24	13	709	9

WILLS, Frank—P

Year	PCT	G	PO	A	E	TC	DP
1983	.800	6	1	3	1	5	1
1984	.714	10	3	2	2	7	0
1986	.900	26	3	6	1	10	0
1987	1.000	6	0	2	0	2	0
1988	1.000	10	1	5	0	6	0
1989	1.000	24	5	10	0	15	0
1990	1.000	44	9	10	0	19	2
Total	.938	126	22	38	4	64	3

WILSON, Mookie—OF

Year	PCT	G	PO	A	E	TC	DP
1980 (NL)	.973	26	72	1	2	75	0
1981 (NL)	.983	80	226	3	4	233	2
1982 (NL)	.988	156	415	12	5	432	4
1983 (NL)	.984	148	422	5	7	434	1
1984 (NL)	.990	146	396	8	4	408	6
1985 (NL)	.964	83	216	0	8	224	0
1986 (NL)	.979	114	228	77	5	240	2
1987 (NL)	.963	109	205	3	8	216	2
1988 (NL)	.976	104	200	4	5	209	1
1989 (NL)	.975	71	152	2	4	158	0
1989 (AL)	.991	54	111	2	1	114	1
1990 (AL)	.992	141	370	5	3	378	2
Total	.982	1232	3013	52	56	3121	21

BEST/WORST HOMESTANDS AND ROADTRIPS (MINIMUM 6 GAMES)

PCT.	W-L	DATES	OPPONENTS
BEST HOMESTANDS			
.909	10-1	May 9-16, 1978	Oakland, Seattle, California
.857	6-1	August 7-13, 1978	Baltimore, Chicago, Kansas City
.857	6-1	Sept. 28- Oct. 3, 1982	Minnesota, Seattle
.857	6-1	July 6-12, 1987	Texas, Kansas City
.846	11-2	Aug. 22-Sept. 3, 1989	Detroit, Milwaukee, Chicago, Minnesota
.833	5-1	May 9-16, 1978	Oakland, Seattle, California
.818	9-2	July 18-28, 1985	Oakland, Seattle, California
BEST ROADTRIPS			
.900	9-1	June 8-17, 1990	Milwaukee, Minnesota, New York
.857	6-1	June 8-14, 1987	New York, Baltimore
.833	5-1	May 23-29, 1985	Cleveland, Chigago
.833	5-1	Sept. 23-28, 1988	Cleveland, Boston
.714	5-2	une 23-30, 1983	Seattle, Minnesota
.700	7-3	April 26- May 5, 1985	Texas, Oakland, California, Seattle
.700	7-3	July 3-12, 1987	Chicago, Cleveland, Boston
WORST HOMESTANDS			
.000	0-6	Sept. 26- Oct. 1, 1980	Boston, Detroit
.111	1-8	September 1-9, 1978	California, Cleveland, Milw., Baltimore
.125	1-7	September 2-8, 1977	Seattle, Boston
.125	1-7	May 15-22, 1990	Seattle, California, Oakland
.143	1-6	May 23- June 1, 1977	Oakland, California, Kansas City
.182	2-10	May 18-31, 1979	Baltimore, Cleveland, Boston, Detroit
WORST ROADTRIPS			
.000	0-6	September 3-9, 1979	Baltimore, Cleveland
.143	1-6	August 20-26, 1982	New York, Baltimore
.143	1-6	April 24-30, 1989	Oakland, Seattle, California
.200	2-8	July 4-14, 1977	Boston, Cleveland, Detroit, Chicago
.250	2-6	June 21-27, 1984	Boston, Milwaukee
.300	3-7	June 10-19, 1985	New York, Boston, Milwaukee

1990 AMERICAN LEAGUE STATISTICS

1990 AMERICAN LEAGUE STANDINGS

AMERICAN LEAGUE EAST

	WON	LOST	PCT.	GB	HOME	ROAD	vs EAST	vs WEST
BOSTON	88	74	.543	-	51-30	37-44	50-28	38-46
TORONTO	86	76	.531	2.0	44-37	42-39	42-36	44-40
DETROIT	79	83	.488	9.0	39-42	40-41	35-43	44-40
CLEVELAND	77	85	.475	11.0	41-40	36-45	34-44	43-41
BALTIMORE	76	85	.472	11.5	40-40	36-45	34-44	42-41
MILWAUKEE	74	88	.457	14.0	39-42	35-46	41-37	33-51
NEW YORK	67	95	.414	21.0	37-44	30-51	37-41	30-54

AMERICAN LEAGUE WEST

	WON	LOST	PCT.	GB	HOME	ROAD	vs EAST	vs WEST
OAKLAND	103	59	.636	-	51-30	52-29	56-28	47-31
CHICAGO	94	68	.580	9.0	49-31	45-37	47-37	47-31
TEXAS	83	79	.512	20.0	47-35	36-44	45-39	38-40
CALIFORNIA	80	82	.494	23.0	42-39	38-43	42-42	38-40
SEATTLE	77	85	.475	26.0	38-43	39-42	40-44	37-41
KANSAS CITY	75	86	.466	27.5	45-36	30-50	41-42	34-44
MINNESOTA	74	88	.457	29.0	41-40	33-48	42-42	32-46

1990 AMERICAN LEAGUE CLUB MISCELLANEOUS

									DBLHEADERS		
CLUB	VS LHS	VS RHS	GRASS	ARTIF	DAY	NIGHT	1-RUN	X-INN	W	L	S
BALTIMORE	24-32	52-53	65-71	11-14	21-21	55-64	22-28	13-4	0	0	3
BOSTON	30-23	58-51	77-61	11-13	28-22	60-52	31-22	5-8	0	0	2
CALIFORNIA	26-22	54-60	70-68	10-14	18-23	62-59	23-21	10-5	0	0	0
CHICAGO	40-25	54-43	81-54	13-14	22-18	72-50	30-22	5-8	2	0	2
CLEVELAND	34-20	43-65	65-72	12-13	26-20	51-65	16-24	4-5	1	3	3
DETROIT	27-22	52-61	67-71	12-12	23-23	56-60	22-22	5-4	0	0	1
KANSAS CITY	31-21	44-65	22-39	53-47	18-21	57-65	21-26	5-4	1	0	2
MILWAUKEE	21-25	53-63	63-75	11-13	18-34	56-54	18-23	3-9	0	3	1
MINNESOTA	22-26	52-62	26-36	48-52	24-20	50-68	21-19	6-4	1	0	3
NEW YORK	28-27	39-68	56-81	11-14	20-25	47-70	23-29	5-11	2	0	1
OAKLAND	29-15	74-44	87-50	16-9	39-24	64-35	23-18	9-5	1	0	2
SEATTLE	26-22	51-63	30-32	47-53	19-23	58-62	20-28	4-6	0	0	1
TEXAS	29-25	54-54	72-64	11-15	13-16	70-63	37-22	8-5	0	2	1
TORONTO	25-24	61-52	28-35	58-41	26-24	60-52	24-27	4-8	0	0	0

1990 AMERICAN LEAGUE CLUB BATTING

CLUB	AVG	G	AB	R	H	2B	3B	HR	RBI	SH-SF	BB	SO	SB	CS	SLG	OBP
BOSTON	.272	162	5516	699	1502	298	31	106	660	48-44	598	795	53	52	.395	.344
CLEVELAND	.267	162	5485	732	1465	266	41	110	675	54-61	458	836	107	52	.391	.324
KANSAS CITY	.267	161	5488	707	1465	316	44	100	660	31-54	498	879	107	62	.395	.328
MINNESOTA	.265	162	5499	666	1458	281	39	100	625	40-49	445	749	96	53	.385	.324
TORONTO	.265	162	5589	767	1479	263	50	167	729	18-62	526	970	111	52	.419	.328
CALIFORNIA	.260	162	5570	690	1448	237	27	147	646	58-45	566	1000	69	43	.391	.329
SEATTLE	.259	162	5474	640	1419	251	26	107	610	41-54	596	749	105	51	.373	.333
TEXAS	.259	162	5469	676	1416	257	27	110	641	54-44	575	1054	115	48	.376	.331
DETROIT	.259	162	5479	750	1418	241	32	172	714	36-41	634	952	82	57	.409	.337
CHICAGO	.258	162	5402	682	1393	251	44	106	637	75-47	478	903	140	90	.379	.320
MILWAUKEE	.256	162	5503	732	1408	247	36	128	680	59-71	519	821	164	72	.384	.320
OAKLAND	.254	162	5433	733	1379	209	22	164	693	60-48	651	38	992	141	54	.391
BALTIMORE	.245	161	5410	669	1328	234	22	132	623	72-41	660	962	94	52	.370	.330
NEW YORK	.241	162	5483	603	1322	208	19	147	561	37-36	427	1027	119	45	.366	.300
TOTALS	.259	1133	76800	9746	19900	3559	460	1796	9154	683-697	7631	12689	1503	783	.388	.327

1990 AMERICAN LEAGUE CLUB PITCHING

CLUB	W-L	ERA	G	CG	SHO	SV	IP	H	R	ER	HR	HB	BB	SO	WP
OAKLAND	103-59	3.18	162	18	16	64	1456.0	1287	570	514	123	27	494	831	50
CHICAGO	94-68	3.61	162	17	10	68	1449.1	1313	633	581	106	39	548	914	35
SEATTLE	77-85	3.69	162	21	7	41	1443.1	1319	680	592	120	41	606	1064	69
BOSTON	88-74	3.72	162	15	13	44	1442.0	1439	664	596	92	45	519	997	63
CALIFORNIA	80-82	3.79	162	21	13	42	1454.0	1482	706	613	106	38	544	944	50
TEXAS	83-79	3.83	162	25	9	36	1444.2	1343	696	615	113	44	623	997	61
TORONTO	86-76	3.84	162	6	9	48	1454.0	1434	661	620	143	37	445	892	43
KANSAS CITY	75-86	3.93	161	18	8	33	1420.2	1449	709	621	116	46	560	1006	59
BALTIMORE	76-85	4.04	161	10	5	43	1435.1	1445	698	644	161	16	537	776	34
MILWAUKEE	74-88	4.08	162	23	13	42	1445.0	1558	760	655	121	38	469	771	47
MINNESOTA	74-88	4.12	162	13	13	43	1435.2	1509	729	658	134	27	489	872	55
NEW YORK	67-95	4.21	162	15	6	41	1444.2	1430	749	676	144	26	618	909	83
CLEVELAND	77-85	4.26	162	12	10	47	1427.1	1491	737	676	163	40	518	860	50
DETROIT	79-83	4.39	162	15	12	45	1430.1	1401	754	697	154	45	661	856	76
TOTALS	1133-1133	3.91	1133	229	144	637	20182.1	19900	9746	8758	1796	509	7631	12689	775

1990 AMERICAN LEAGUE CLUB FIELDING

CLUB	PCT	G	PO	A	E	TC	DP	TP	PB
TORONTO	.986	162	4362	1720	86	6168	144	0	14
OAKLAND	.986	162	4368	1630	87	6085	152	0	14
BALTIMORE	.985	161	4306	1651	93	6050	151	1	5
MINNESOTA	.983	162	4307	1705	101	6113	161	2	11
CLEVELAND	.981	162	4282	1648	117	6047	146	0	14
BOSTON	.980	162	4326	1743	123	6192	154	0	7
CHICAGO	.980	162	4348	1706	124	6178	169	0	13
NEW YORK	.980	162	4334	1791	126	6251	164	0	27
KANSAS CITY	.980	161	4262	1598	122	5982	161	0	13
SEATTLE	.979	162	4330	1730	130	6190	152	0	18
DETROIT	.979	162	4291	1774	131	6196	178	0	15
TEXAS	.979	162	4334	1721	133	6188	161	0	35
CALIFORNIA	.978	162	4362	1871	142	6375	186	0	15
MILWAUKEE	.976	162	4335	1737	149	6221	152	0	11
TOTALS	.981	1133	60547	24025	1664	86236	2231	3	212

1990 AMERICAN LEAGUE CLUB STARTING PITCHING

CLUB	W-L	ERA	G	CG	SHO	IP	H	R	ER	HR	HB	BB	SO	WP	OPP AVG
BOSTON	69-48	3.32	162	15	4	995.2	947	412	367	56	30	347	677	38	.252
OAKLAND	89-49	3.51	162	18	7	1038.2	972	448	405	99	17	369	552	32	.249
SEATTLE	57-62	3.67	162	21	4	1048.1	939	478	427	88	28	417	775	43	.239
CHICAGO	65-47	3.83	162	17	6	973.2	927	450	414	72	27	339	607	22	.252
CALIFORNIA	62-63	3.92	162	21	5	1048.0	1072	519	456	78	24	381	665	34	.268
KANSAS CITY	51-65	3.93	161	18	5	944.2	983	477	413	75	23	361	622	37	.268
TORONTO	66-52	3.93	162	6	2	968.1	985	448	423	93	27	285	520	25	.266
TEXAS	60-60	3.96	162	25	5	1037.2	960	511	456	87	35	440	751	40	.246
MILWAUKEE	55-57	4.20	162	23	7	958.1	1061	508	447	81	24	278	482	33	.281
BALTIMORE	52-62	4.35	161	10	3	949.1	987	489	459	116	12	358	447	17	.270
MINNESOTA	46-68	4.38	162	13	4	938.1	1014	505	457	90	18	300	546	30	.279
NEW YORK	42-71	4.47	162	15	3	946.1	950	518	470	96	18	385	578	50	.264
CLEVELAND	56-62	4.50	162	12	3	963.1	1057	523	482	118	27	316	530	31	.279
DETROIT .	55-68	5.00	162	15	4	925.1	941	555	514	115	31	438	550	54	.266
TOTALS	825-834	4.06	1133	229	62	13736.0	13795	6841	6190	1264	341	5014	8302	486	.262

1990 AMERICAN LEAGUE CLUB RELIEF PITCHING

CLUB	W-L	ERA	SV	IP	H	R	ER	HR	HB	BB	SO	WP	AVG
OAKLAND	14-10	2.35	64	417.1	315	122	109	24	10	125	279	18	.210
CHICAGO	29-21	3.18	68	475.2	386	183	168	34	12	209	307	13	.227
DETROIT	24-15	3.26	45	505.0	460	199	183	39	14	223	306	22	.246
BALTIMORE	24-23	3.52	43	486.0	458	209	190	45	4	179	329	17	.251
TEXAS	23-19	3.52	36	407.0	383	185	159	26	9	183	246	21	.253
CALIFORNIA	18-19	3.55	42	406.0	410	187	160	28	14	163	279	16	.265
TORONTO	20-24	3.65	48	485.2	449	213	197	50	10	160	372	18	.248
MINNESOTA	28-20	3.67	43	497.1	495	224	203	44	9	189	326	25	.262
NEW YORK	25-24	3.77	41	498.1	480	231	209	48	8	233	331	33	.256
CLEVELAND	21-23	3.78	47	464.0	434	214	195	45	13	202	330	19	.251
SEATTLE	20-23	3.87	41	395.0	380	202	170	32	13	189	289	26	.255
KANSAS CITY	24-21	3.93	33	476.0	466	232	208	41	23	199	384	22	.256
MILWAUKEE	19-31	3.94	42	486.2	497	252	213	40	14	191	289	14	.264
BOSTON	19-26	4.62	44	446.1	492	252	229	36	15	172	320	25	.281
TOTALS	308-299	3.62	637	6446.1	6105	2905	2593	532	168	2617	4387	289	.252

1990 AMERICAN LEAGUE CLUB DESIGNATED HITTING

CLUB	AVG	AB	R	H	2B	3B	HR	RBI	SH-SF	HP	BB	SO	SB	CS	SLG	OBP
CLEVELAND	.293	625	75	183	34	5	14	84	4-3	3	52	92	8	5	.430	.348
CALIFORNIA	.285	617	89	176	35	3	21	87	0-7	6	88	96	2	5	.454	.376
MILWAUKEE	.274	634	79	174	31	3	21	96	1 17	5	49	109	6	11	.432	.323
MINNESOTA.	274	580	65	159	34	2	8	64	3-6	8	62	94	4	7	.381	.349
KANSAS CITY	.268	624	74	167	43	1	14	85	0-8	3	54	99	15	5	.407	.325
SEATTLE	.250	608	68	152	25	0	23	99	0-12	6	72	102	3	4	.405	.330
TEXAS	.245	595	65	146	22	2	17	73	2-3	3	75	134	1	4	.375	.331
OAKLAND	.245	608	76	149	24	2	15	80	1-9	4	79	152	16	8	.365	.331
BOSTON	.244	602	82	147	24	3	17	77	1-7	6	80	113	5	5	.379	.335
CHICAGO	.242	616	79	149	32	3	28	92	4-4	4	65	130	9	4	.440	.316
DETROIT	.235	614	75	144	31	2	15	74	0-9	3	54	103	3	7	.365	.296
NEW YORK	.228	619	66	141	21	1	25	79	0-7	8	49	123	3	1	.386	.290
TORONTO	.220	604	68	133	28	4	14	68	1-11	3	69	132	4	4	.349	.298
BALTIMORE	211	587	68	124	23	1	19	65	2-3	5	88	169	10	3	.351	.318
TOTALS	.251	8533	1029	2144	407	32	251	1123	19-106	67	936	1648	89	73	.395	.326

1990 AMERICAN LEAGUE CLUB PINCH-HITTING

CLUB	AVG	AB	R	H	2B	3B	HR	RBI	SH-SF	HP	BB	SO	GIDP	SLG	OBP
BALTIMORE	.235	115	12	27	2	1	4	27	0-3	0	21	31	1	.374	.345
BOSTON	.215	79	7	17	4	0	1	20	2-5	1	11	18	2	.304	.302
CALIFORNIA	.184	98	4	18	0	1	2	10	0-1	0	10	21	1	.265	.257
CHICAGO	.220	123	14	27	6	1	1	14	6-1	0	10	29	0	.309	.276
CLEVELAND	.260	104	14	27	6	1	3	15	0-1	1	12	22	2	.423	.339
DETROIT	.193	202	21	39	4	0	2	29	3-2	1	38	45	6	.243	.321
KANSAS CITY	.198	96	4	19	2	0	1	13	0-2	0	6	21	2	.250	.240
MILWAUKEE	.190	58	6	11	1	0	0	6	0-0	1	10	13	0	.207	.319
MINNESOTA	.281	139	14	39	5	1	1	21	1-3	1	25	22	5	.353	.387
NEW YORK	.203	182	8	37	5	1	6	21	1-2	4	13	50	5	.341	.269
OAKLAND	.240	154	14	37	7	1	2	26	1-3	0	19	51	3	.338	.318
SEATTLE	.245	147	5	36	3	0	1	19	0-5	0	10	27	3	.286	.284
TEXAS	.220	250	19	55	11	4	3	41	1-1	1	36	68	3	.332	.319
TORONTO	.216	97	4	21	2	1	0	14	0-0	1	11	22	4	.258	.303
TOTALS	.222	1844	146	410	58	12	27	276	15-29	11	232	440	37	.311	.309

1990 AMERICAN LEAGUE TOP 15 QUALIFIERS FOR BATTING CHAMPIONSHIP

(502 OR MORE PLATE APPEARANCES)

BATTER	TEAM	B	AVG	G	AB	R	H	2B	3B	HR	RBI	SH-SF	HB	BB	SO	SB	CS
Brett,G	KC	R	.329	142	544	82	179	45	7	14	87	0-7	0	56	63	9	2
Henderson,R	OAK	L	.325	136	489	119	159	33	3	28	61	2-2	4	97	60	65	10
Palmeiro,R	TEX	L	.319	154	598	72	191	35	6	14	89	2-8	3	40	59	3	3
Trammell,A	DET	R	.304	146	559	71	170	37	1	14	89	3-6	1	68	55	12	10
Boggs,W	BOS	R	.302	155	619	89	187	44	5	6	63	0-6	1	87	68	0	0
Martinez,E	SEA	R	.302	144	487	71	147	27	2	11	49	1-3	5	74	62	1	4
Griffey Jr,K	SEA	L	.300	155	597	91	179	28	7	22	80	0-4	2	63	81	16	11
McGriff,F	TOR	L	.300	153	557	91	167	21	1	35	88	1-4	2	94	108	5	3
James,C	CLE	R	.299	140	528	62	158	32	4	12	70	3-3	4	31	71	4	3
Puckett,K	MIN	R	.298	146	551	82	164	40	3	12	80	1-3	3	57	73	5	4
Greenwell,M	BOS	R	.297	159	610	71	181	30	6	14	73	0-3	4	65	43	8	7
Burks,E	BOS	R	.296	152	588	89	174	33	8	21	89	2-2	1	48	82	9	11
Franco,J	TEX	R	.296	157	582	96	172	27	1	11	69	2-2	2	82	83	31	10
Harper,B	MIN	R	.294	134	479	61	141	42	3	6	54	0-4	7	19	27	3	2
Sheffield,G	MIL	R	.294	125	487	67	143	30	1	10	67	4-9	3	44	41	25	10

1990 AMERICAN LEAGUE TOP 15 QUALIFIERS FOR EARNED-RUN CHAMPIONSHIP

(162 OR MORE INNINGS) # = Mult. Teams

PITCHER	TEAM	T	W-L	ERA	G	GS	CG	SHO	IP	H	R	ER	HR	HB	BB	SO	WP
Clemens,R	BOS	R	21-6	1.93	31	31	7	4	228.1	193	59	49	7	7	54	209	8
Finley,C	CAL	L	18-9	2.40	32	32	7	2	236.0	210	77	63	17	2	81	177	9
Stewart,D	OAK	R	22-11	2.56	36	36	11	4	267.0	226	84	76	16	5	83	166	8
+Appier,K	KC	R	12-8	2.76	32	24	3	3	185.2	179	67	57	13	6	54	127	6
Stieb,D	TOR	R	18-6	2.93	33	33	2	2	208.2	179	73	68	11	10	64	125	5
Welch,B	OAK	R	27-6	2.95	35	35	2	2	238.0	214	90	78	26	5	77	127	2
Wells,D	TOR	L	11-6	3.14	43	25	0	0	189.0	165	72	66	14	2	45	115	7
Hibbard,G	CWS	L	14-9	3.16	33	33	3	1	211.0	202	80	74	11	6	55	92	2
Hanson,E	SEA	R	18-9	3.24	33	33	5	1	236.0	205	88	85	15	2	68	211	10
McCaskill,K	CAL	R	12-11	3.25	29	29	2	1	174.1	161	77	63	9	2	72	78	6
Boddicker,M	BOS	R	17-8	3.36	34	34	4	0	228.0	225	92	85	16	10	69	143	10
Witt,B	TEX	R	17-10	3.37	33	32	7	1	222.0	197	98	83	12	4	110	221	11
Ryan,N	TEX	R	13-9	3.44	30	30	5	2	204.0	137	86	78	18	7	74	232	9
Young,M	SEA	L	8-18	3.52	34	33	7	1	225.1	198	106	88	15	6	107	176	16
Black,B	TOR#	L	13-11	3.57	32	31	5	2	206.2	181	86	82	19	5	61	106	6
Black,B	CLE	L	11-10	3.53	29	29	5	2	191.0	171	79	75	17	4	58	103	6
Black,B	TOR	L	2-1	4.02	3	2	0	0	15.2	10	7	7	2	1	3	3	0

1990 AMERICAN LEAGUE TOP DESIGNATED HITTERS

(BASED ON 100 AB MINIMUM)

BATTER	TEAM	B	AVG	G	AB	R	H	2B	3B	HR	RBI	SH-SF	BB	SO	SB-CS	SLG	OBP
Larkin,G	MIN	S	.336	43	140	14	47	13	1	0	18	2-3	1	24	2-2	.443	.411
Bergman,D	DET	L	.322	51	115	15	37	7	1	1	15	0-2	2	13	1-1	.426	.403
Calderon,I	CWS	R	.304	27	112	20	34	7	0	6	17	0-1	6	7	4-2	.527	.336
James,C	CLE	R	.296	124	477	55	141	27	4	9	57	2-2	4	68	4-3	.426	.340
Brett,G	KC	L	.292	32	120	18	35	14	1	3	16	0-3	2	18	2-0	.500	.333
Baines,H	OAK#	L	.287	125	404	52	116	15	1	16	61	0-6	9	77	0-3	.448	.380
Davis,C	CAL	S	.284	60	225	35	64	13	1	6	30	0-2	3	43	0-2	.431	.375
Parker,D	MIL	L	.281	153	597	68	168	29	3	21	89	0-14	11	102	4-7	.446	.325
Downing,B	CAL	R	.280	87	322	47	90	18	2	14	51	0-4	2	44	0-0	.478	.381
Davis,A	SEA	L	.272	87	301	39	82	16	0	12	52	0-6	8	46	0-2	.445	.387
Tartabull,D	KC	R	.271	32	118	13	32	9	0	4	19	0-2	0	30	0-0	.449	.348
Horn,S	BAL	L	.265	63	204	26	54	11	0	12	34	0-2	1	55	0-0	.495	.345
Perry,G	KC	L	.262	68	263	33	69	12	0	4	35	0-2	2	30	10-2	.354	.322
Olerud,J	TOR	L	.258	90	302	34	78	14	1	10	38	1-4	4	66	0-1	.411	.350
Evans,D	BOS	R	.249	122	445	66	111	18	3	13	63	0-6	5	73	3-4	.391	.347

DESIGNATED HITTING LEADERS (BY DEPARTMENT)

BATTING AVG.	.336	Larkin,G	MIN	**HOME RUNS**	21	Parker,D	MIL
RUNS	68	Parker,D	MIL	**RBI**	89	Parker,D	MIL
HITS	168	Parker,D	MIL	**BASE ON BALLS**	67	Evans,D	BOS
TOTAL BASES	266	Parker,D	MIL	**SLUGGING PCT.**	.527	Calderon,I	CWS
DOUBLES	29	Parker,D	MIL	**ON-BASE PCT.**	.411	Larkin,G	MIN
TRIPLES	4	James,C	CLE				

1990 AMERICAN LEAGUE TOP PINCH HITTERS

(BASED ON 20 AB MINIMUM)

BATTER	TEAM	B	AVG	G	AB	R	H	TB	2B	3B	HR	RBI	HP	BB	SO	SLG	OBP
Mulliniks,R	TOR	L	.364	28	22	2	8	9	1	0	0	7	0	4	4	409	.462
Baerga,C	CLE	S	.355	38	31	8	11	19	5	0	1	9	1	5	8	.613	.447
Reimer,K	TEX	L	.300	45	40	1	12	19	5	1	0	8	0	4	10	.475	.364
Hassey,R	OAK	L	.300	24	20	1	6	8	2	0	0	2	0	2	3	.400	.364
Coles,D	DET#	R	.296	32	27	3	8	8	0	0	0	5	0	2	3	.296	.333
Bradley,S	SEA	L	.286	40	35	1	10	10	0	0	0	5	0	0	5	.286	.270
Moses,J	MIN	S	.280	31	25	2	7	7	0	0	0	1	0	4	1	.280	.367
Cotto,H	SEA	R	.276	35	29	3	8	8	0	0	0	1	0	4	4	.276	.353
Stanley,M	TEX	R	.259	35	27	3	7	12	0	1	1	7	0	6	4	.444	.394
Nokes,M	NYY#	L	.235	35	34	2	8	15	1	0	2	8	0	0	4	.441	.235
Castillo,C	MIN	R	.227	27	22	2	5	5	0	0	0	2	1	1	3	.227	.280
Daugherty,J	TEX	S	.222	52	45	2	10	13	3	0	0	7	1	4	13	.289	.294
Petralli,G	TEX	L	.208	25	24	1	5	8	1	1	0	3	0	1	6	.333	.240
Borders,P	TOR	R	.200	33	25	0	5	6	1	0	0	3	0	5	6	.240	.333
Balboni,S	NYY	R	.200	49	40	2	8	14	0	0	2	5	1	7	20	.350	.327

PINCH HITTING LEADERS (BY DEPARTMENT)

BATTING AVG.	.364	Mulliniks,R . . TOR	**HOME RUNS**	2	Balboni,S . . . . NYY
RUNS	8	Baerga,C . . . CLE			Horn,S . . . . . . BAL
HITS	12	Reimer,K . . . TEX			Nokes,M . . . . . NYY
TOTAL BASES	19	Reimer,K . . . TEX	**RBI**	9	Baerga,C . . . . CLE
		Baerga,C . . . CLE	**BASE ON BALLS**	7	Balboni,S . . . . NYY
DOUBLES	5	Reimer,K . . . TEX	**SLUGGING PCT.**	.613	Baerga,C . . . . CLE
TRIPLES	1	12 PLAYERS TIED	**ON-BASE PCT.**	.462	Mulliniks,R . . . . TOR

AMERICAN LEAGUE TOP ROAD HITTERS, 1990

(502 OR MORE PLATE APPEARANCES)

BATTER	TEAM	AVG	G	AB	R	H	2B	3B	HR	RBI	BB	SO	SB	CS	SLG	OBP
Palmeiro,R	TEX	.350	76	303	34	106	16	1	5	43	10	28	2	2	.459	.367
Henderson,R	OAK	.342	72	269	72	92	21	1	20	39	53	34	31	3	.651	.451
Brett,G	KC	.340	67	256	42	87	27	2	11	41	29	36	5	0	.590	.403
McGriff,F	TOR	.321	76	293	49	94	11	1	21	50	39	71	4	2	.580	.401
Sheffield,G	MIL	.315	62	248	35	78	15	0	7	39	20	19	12	7	.460	.361
James,C	CLE	.310	73	294	35	91	19	3	6	37	16	38	3	3	.456	.347
Griffey Jr.,K	SEA	.308	75	292	46	90	11	3	14	35	29	48	5	7	.510	.369
Harper,B	MIN	.305	68	249	32	76	24	1	5	30	7	12	1	1	.470	.331
Martinez,E	SEA	.305	71	243	38	74	10	1	8	29	32	31	1	0	.453	.393
Parker,D	MIL	.303	80	317	38	96	14	2	12	46	21	44	3	2	.473	.344
Eisenreich,J	KC	.300	72	260	31	78	17	2	3	22	17	32	7	7	.415	.343
Jacoby,B	CLE	.298	77	292	44	87	14	1	4	34	27	37	0	2	.394	.356
Hrbek,K	MIN	.294	71	245	33	72	11	0	14	36	37	29	3	2	.510	.391
Sierra,R	TEX	.293	79	307	32	90	20	1	6	50	26	35	4	0	.423	.343
Davis,A	SEA	.289	68	242	21	70	10	0	5	28	38	30	0	1	.393	381

ROAD HITTING LEADERS (BY DEPARTMENT)

BATTING AVG.	.350	Palmeiro,R . . TEX
RUNS	72	Henderson,R . OAK
HITS	106	Palmeiro,R . . TEX
TOTAL BASES	175	Henderson,R . Oak
		Fielder,C . . . DET
DOUBLES	27	Brett,G . . . . . KC
TRIPLES	5	4 Players Tied for First Place
HOME RUNS	26	Fielder,C . . . DET
RBI	72	Fielder,C . . . DET
BASE ON BALLS	56	McGwire,M . . OAK
SLUGGING PCT.	.651	Henderson,R . OAK
ON-BASE PCT.	.451	Henderson,R . OAK

BLUE JAYS IN FIRST PLACE
(Sole Possession-before games on the 1st)

MAY 1st	JUNE 1st	JULY 1st	AUG. 1st	SEPT.1st	OCT. 1st
1981	1983	1983	1985	1985	1987
1985	1985	1985		1989	1989

1990 MAJOR LEAGUE LEADERS

AMERICAN LEAGUE		BATTING		NATIONAL LEAGUE
GEORGE BRETT, KC	.329	AVERAGE	.335	WILLIE McGEE, STL
ROBERTO KELLY, NY	162	GAMES	162	J0E CARTER, SD
HAROLD REYNOLDS, SEA	642	AT BATS	634	JOE CARTER, SD
RICKEY HENDERSON, OAK	119	RUNS	116	RYNE SANDBERG, CHI
RAPHAEL PALMIERO, TEX	191	HITS	192	LENNY DYKSTRA, PHI
				BRETT BUTLER, SF
CECIL FIELDER, DET	339	TOTAL BASES	344	RYNE SANDBERG, CHI
RAPHAEL PALMIERO, TEX	136	SINGLES	160	BRETT BUTLER, SF
JODY REED, BOS	45	DOUBLES	40	GREGG JEFFERIES, CHI
GEORGE BRETT, KC	45			
TONY FERNANDEZ, TOR	17	TRIPLES		MARIANO DUNCAN, CIN
CECIL FIELDER, DET	51	HOME RUNS	40	RYNE SANDBERG, CHI
CECIL FIELDER, DET	132	RBI	22	MATT WILLIAMS, SF
RICKEY HENDERSON, OAK	65	STOLEN BASES	77	VINCE COLEMAN, STL
BRIAN HARPER, MIN	25	LONGEST HITTING STREAK	23	LENNY DYKSTRA, PHI
CECIL FIELDER, DET	.592	SLUGGING PCTE	.565	BOBBY BONDS, PIT
RICKEY HENDERSON, OAK	.439	ON-BASE PCT	.418	LENNY DYKSTRA, PHI
DAVE PARKER, MIL	14	SACRIFICE FLIES	15	BOBBY BONILLA, PIT
MIKE GALLEGO, OAK	17	SACRIFICE HITS	39	JAY BELL, PIT
BILLY RIPKEN, BAL	17			
MARK McGWIRE, OAK	110	WALKS	104	JACK CLARK, SD
WADE BOGGS, BOS	19	INTENTIONAL WALKS	21	ANDRE DAWSON, CHI
			21	EDDIE MURRAY, LA
PHIL BRADLEY, BAL-CHI	11	HIT BY PITCH	8	GLEN DAVIS, HOU
CECIL FIELDER, DET	182	STRIKEOUTS	169	ANDRES GALARRAGA, MON
IVAN CALDERON, CHI	26	GIDP MOST		DALE MURPHY, ATL-PHI

AMERICAN LEAGUE		PITCHING		NATIONAL LEAGUE
ROGER CLEMENS, BOS	1.92	ERA	2.21	DANNY DARWIN, HOU
BOB WELCH, OAK	27	WINS	22	DOUG DRABEK, PIT
TIM LEARY, NY	19	LOSSES	19	JOSE DeLEON, PIT
BOBBY THIGPEN, CHI	57	SAVES	33	JOHN FRANCO, NY
JACK MORRIS, DET	36	STARTS	35	TOM BROWNING, CIN
DAVE STEWART, OAK	36		35	GREG MADDUX, CHI
			35	FRANK VIOLA, NY
ROGER CLEMENS, BOS	4	SHUTOUTS	4	MIKE MORGAN, LA
DAVE STEWART, OAK	4		4	BRUCE HURST, SD
DAVE STEWART, OAK	267.0	INNINGS	249.2	FRANK VIOLA, NY
JIM ABBOTT, CAL	246	HITS	242	GREG MADDUX, CHI
NOLAN RYAN, TEX	232	STRIKEOUTS	233	DAVID CONE, NY
CHARLIE HOUGH, TEX	119	WALKS	90	JOHN SMOLTZ, ATL
DAVID JOHNSON, BAL	30	HOME RUNS	28	DENNIS RASMUSSEN, SD
TIM LEARY, NY	23	WILD PITCHES	14	JOHN SMOLTZ, ATL
MELIDO PEREZ, CHI	4	BALKS	5	4 PLAYERS TIED

BASEBALL WRITER'S ASSOCIATION OF AMERICA
BBWAA
TORONTO CHAPTER - 1991

EXECUTIVE
CHAIRMAN - NEIL MacCARL, TORONTO STAR
VICE CHAIRMAN - LARRY MILLSON, GLOBE AND MAIL
SECRETARY/TREASURER - STEVE MILTON, HAMILTON SPECTATOR

MEMBERS:
STEVE McALLISTER, CANADIAN PRESS
ROSS HOPKINS, CANADIAN PRESS
DOUG FOLEY, HAMILTON SPECTATOR
JOHN KERNAGHAN, HAMILTON SPECTATOR
STEVE MILTON, HAMILTON SPECTATOR
LARRY SICINSKI, HAMILTON SPECTATOR
PHIL BINGLEY, TORONTO STAR
MILT DUNNELL, TORONTO STAR
NEIL MacCARL, TORONTO STAR
DAVE PERKINS, TORONTO STAR
JIM PROUDFOOT, TORONTO STAR
ALLAN RYAN, TORONTO STAR
TOM SLATER, TORONTO STAR
STEVE BUFFERY, TORONTO SUN
BOB ELLIOT, TORONTO SUN*
KEN FIDLIN, TORONTO SUN
GEORGE GROSS, TORONTO SUN
JIM HUNT, TORONTO SUN
BILL LANKHOF, TORONTO SUN
JIM O'LEARY, TORONTO SUN
WAYNE PARRISH, TORONTO SUN
STEVE SIMMONS, TORONTO SUN
MIKE SIMPSON, TORONTO SUN
HUGH STUART, TORONTO SUN
MIKE ZEISBERGER, TORONTO SUN

HONOURARY MEMBERS:
TRENT FRAYNE
LARRY MILLSON

1990 SEASON IN REVIEW. TORONTO BLUE JAYS

WINS AND LOSSES: The Blue Jays completed the 1990 season with an 86-76 record, second place, two games behind the Boston Red Sox...This season's record was three wins less than last season, when the Blue Jays finished first in the American League East, two games ahead of the Orioles...The club record for wins in a season still remains at 99, which was achieved in 1985 when the Blue Jays won their first A.L. East Divisional crown...The Blue Jays are the only Major League team to have a plus .500 record over the past 8 seasons- the New York Mets have done it the past seven seasons...Toronto finished the season 42-39 on the **ROAD**- the seventh consecutive year that they have been over .500 on the road...At **SkyDome**, they finished with a 44-37 record- the ninth consecutive season that the Blue Jays have had a winning season at Home...Overall vs **AL East**, Toronto was 42-36 (22-17 at SkyDome and 20-19 on the road), while compiling a 44-40 record vs the **AL West** (22-20 at home and 22-20 on the road)...Toronto was the only Eastern Division club to have a plus .500 record vs both divisions...The Blue Jays had plus .500 records against seven of the 13 other clubs in the AL...Their best record vs an AL club this season was vs Minnesota(9-3)...The Red Sox proved to be the club's biggest nemesis this season, as the Blue Jays were just 3-10 vs Boston...Toronto was 8-5 overall vs Boston in 1989...Toronto enjoyed a season sweep of the Twins in Minnesota, going 6-0 at the Metrodome...The Blue Jays did however, have difficulty with the Athletics in Toronto, where the A's won 5 of 6 games...The club did not participate in any doubleheaders this season...Most Games +.500, 14-games(9/20 <82-68>, 9/24 <84-70>...Most Games -.500, 1 game, 4/9 <0-1>, 4/11<1-2>, 5/24 <21-22>.

BY THE MONTH: April 12-9....May 14-14....June 15-13...July 14-12...
At ALL-STAR BREAK 47-38, 2nd, 0.5GBL...August 13-16...Sept/Oct 18-12

BY THE DAY: Sunday 18-7...Monday 12-10...Tuesday 13-12...Wednesday 10-15...
Thursday 7-9...Friday 13-12....Saturday 13-11

THE MANAGER: 1990 was Cito Gaston's first full season as a Major League manager... In 1989 he took over on May 15th after Jimy Williams was dismissed as Blue Jay Manager...Cito guided the Jays to an early first place lead in April...Under Gaston, the Blue Jays have a combined 163-125 won-loss record...Cito is the Blue Jays fifth manager since their inception in 1977.

BLUE JAYS IN THE STANDINGS: Toronto lost their season opener to the Rangers in Texas by a score of 4-2...The Blue Jays then won 6 of their next 9 games, placing them in a tie for 1st place...Toronto then moved into 1st place on the 19th of April- where they remained until the 27th when they lost to the White Sox and fell to 1/2 game back of first place...During the next month, the Blue Jays fell to no farther than 3.5 GBL and were no lower than 4th place...Toronto returned to first place on the 28th of May and remained there for only four days...The club continued to contend for the AL East lead through the month of June...Toronto returned to first place on the 12th of June, defeating the Twins 5-4...The Blue Jays remained in 1st for 13 days until a loss to Boston at Fenway Park on the 25th put them a 1/2 game behind...Toronto was below .500 for only 3 days in 1990; the last being on 5/24...The largest first place lead by Toronto was 2.0 games on 6/18...The most games out of first place in '90 was 6.5 GBL from 8/30-9/4.

BATTING: The Blue Jays hit .265 overall, tied for 4th in the AL...On the Road they led the AL at .265 while at the SkyDome they hit .264...In the AL, they ranked 1st in Runs(767), Total Bases(2343), Triples(50) and Slugging(.419),2nd in Hits(1479), HR(167) and SF(62)-a club record...Of their 167 HR, 93 were hit at SkyDome...Their 18 Sacrifice Hits were a Major League record for the fewest in a season, a record previous held by the 1985 Blue Jays...Their 970 strikeouts equalled the club record set in 1987.

PITCHING: The Blue Jays finished with a team ERA of 3.84, 7th in the AL...They had only six Complete Games, the fewest in franchise history...The 48 saves were a club record and were third in the AL...They yielded only a club record 445 BB which lead the AL for fewest...Opposing batters hit .260.

PITCHING ANALYSIS:	W-L-S	ERA	GM	IP	H	R	ER	HB	HR	BB	Ks
STARTERS	66-52	3.93	162	968.1	985	448	423	27	93	285	520
RELIEVERS	20-24-48	3.64	317	485.2	449	213	197	10	50	160	372

PITCHING POINTS: In 162 games: the BLUE JAYS used 3 or more pitchers in 106 games, and 4 or more in 45-gms;BLUE JAYS' starters went 5 innings or less in 49-games; went 6 innings or more 100 times, 7 inn., or more, 64 times and 8 inn., or more, 24 times.

FIELDING: The Blue Jays set a club mark(.984 in 1986) and were tied with Oakland for highest pct(.986) in the AL...They led the AL in fewest errors(86), their previous low was 100 in 1986...Manny Lee led all second basemen in Fldg Pct(.993), Fred McGriff was 3rd among firstbasemen, Tony Fernandez was 2nd to Cal Ripken at SS and Kelly Gruber was 3rd among thirdbasemen.

SKYDOME DATA: The Blue Jays were 44-37 at home in '90...When the roof was-open, 12-18, when closed 29-17 and closed during the game, 3-2...All time(includes post season)--open, 37-39, closed 41-18, and closed during the game, 5-2...This was the first full season for the Blue Jays at the SkyDome...The SkyDome provided the ideal venue for the setting of the new Major League attendance record- 3,885,284...The club averaged 47,966 fans per game this season (last season avg. 48,562- [54 dates])...The club sold out 66 games, including the last 59, at SkyDome during the season...Over the last two seasons 119 dates have been sold out(including three post season)...Toronto hit a total of 93 HR at home while opponents hit 82...30 of the home games saw the roof open...The Blue Jays hit 26 HR with the roof open and hit 67 when it was closed...SkyDome Home Runs:Bell: 11, Borders: 10, Felix 7, Fernandez 2, Gruber 23, Hill 7, Lee 2, McGriff 14, Mulliniks 1, Myers 3, Olerud 11, Whiten 1.

EJECTIONS: In 1990, a total of 5 Blue Jays were ejected from games...Cito Gaston was ejected six times...Tony Fernandez was thrown out of a game on 6/27 for arguing a foul ball...Newcomer, Kenny Williams was ejected on 9/31 while arguing balls and strikes...John Candelaria also received an ejection from umpire Joe Brinkman for arguing balls and strikes on 9/25 vs Milwaukee...Pitching coach, Galen Cisco was ejected in Boston on 9/29 for arguing balls and strikes.

SWEEPS: Toronto Blue Jays swept seven series this year, all of which were 3- game series...The first series sweep came @ Seattle(5/25-27)...The Twins were swept in the Metrodome(6/12-14) and (8/17-19)...The Yankees went down twice, (6/15-17)(9/17-19)...Toronto swept the Angels at SkyDome, July 3-5...Cleveland was swept, (8/31-9/2)...Chicago went down in Toronto, 9/7-9 for the last sweep...OPPONENTS sweeps; Chicago at Comiskey, 3-g(4/27-29)...Seattle, 3-g(5/15-17) at SkyDome...Oakland, 2-g(5/21-22) at SkyDome...At California, 2-g(5/23-24)...At Boston, 4-g(6/25-28)...At New York, 3-g(8/20-22).

STREAKS: The Blue Jays' longest win streak this season was 6 games- (three times), 12-17, Sept 5-11 and Sept 14-19...In 1989 the Blue Jays' longest win streak was also six games...Toronto also had two five game win streaks in '90(5/25-29) and (7/3-7)...The longest losing streak of the season for the Blue Jays was six games; occuring between 6/25-30(last season: 4 games)...Toronto lost five games in a row between 8/24-28(Boston and Milwaukee).

DOUBLEHEADERS: The Blue Jays did not participate in any doubleheaders in 1990...SkyDome has only seen one doubleheader since it's inaugural season- July 19th, 1989 vs the Angels.

CLOSE GAMES: In 1990, the Blue Jays were 36-46 in close games (one or two runs)...23-27 in one run games (13-13 at home/ 10-14 on the road), and 13-19 in two run games (8-9 at home and 5-10 on the road).

THE ROSTER: Toronto used a total of 41 players including 19 pitchers in 1990---both equalled club marks.

ROOKIES: A total of 11 rookies played for the Blue Jays in 1990, namely, pitchers: Willie Blair, Steve Cummings, Rick Luecken and Bob MacDonald...The position players that played in Toronto were as follows: catchers-Carlos Diaz and Greg Myers, outfielders-Glenallen Hill and Mark Whiten, DH-1B--John Olerud, 3B-Tom Quinlan, IF-Luis Sojo....The only rookies who spent the entire season with the Blue Jays were John Olerud and Glenallen Hill...Olerud hit 14 HR and had 48 RBI while batting .265(95-358). He saw action mostly as the DH but did play 15 games at first base...Hill batted .231(60-260), 12HRS, 32 RBI and appeared in 84 games during the 1990 campaign...Greg Myers split the catching with Borders. He injured his left shoulder and spent some time on the DL.He was assigned to Syracuse for four days on medical rehabilitation on 5/20...Carlos Diaz filled in for the injured Myers in May and hit .333 in 4 games...Willie Blair began the season with Toronto and was sent to Syracuse in early August- (with Toronto was 3-5, 4.06ERA, 27G, 6GS, 68.2IP, 66H, 33R, 31ER, 4HR, 28BB, 43K)...Bob MacDonald was called up from Knoxville on 8/13 and appeared in his first ML game on the 14th of August vs the White Sox...Rick Luecken was picked purchased from Atlanta in late September and appeared in only one game in 1990 as a Blue Jay-(9.00ERA, 1G, 1.0IP, 2H, 1R/ER, 1HR, 1BB)...Tom Quinlan saw action in only one game and went 1-2 vs the Tigers...Luis Sojo was called up to the Blue Jays on 7/14 to replace Felix and played in 33 games (.225 /18-80)...Mark Whiten was seen in a Toronto uniform from 7/12-8/13 and was called up in September...With the Blue Jays he hit (.273/24-88)...Steve Cummings was recalled from Syracuse on 5/8 and while with Toronto was 0-0-0 in 6 appearances with a 5.11ERA in 12.1IP.

PITCHERS HOME RUN BREAKDOWN:

	1R	2R	3R	GS	TOTAL
ACKER	3	3	2	1	9
BLACK	1	1			2
BLAIR	3	1			4
CANDELARIA	2				2
CERUTTI	12	9	2		23
CUMMINGS	4				4
FLANAGAN	3				3
HENKE	4	4			8
KEY	12	5	3		20
KILGUS	1		1		2
LEITER					
LUECKEN	1				1
MACDONALD					
STIEB	9	2			11
STOTTLEMYRE	7	7	4		18
WARD	4	2	2	1	9
WELLS	8	5		1	14
WILLS	7	3	1	2	13
BLUE JAYS	81	42	15	5	143

CATCHERS-RUNNERS THROWN OUT

BORDERS(35-85/41.2%)
MYERS (17-57/29.8%)
DIAZ (1-2/50.0%)

HIT STREAKS:

BELL 11-games(May 29- June 10)
BORDERS 7-games(July 28-August 3)
FELIX 7-games (May 21- May 27)
FERNANDEZ 15-games(April 10-25)
GRUBER 15-games(Sept.10-25)
HILL 6-games(April 25-May 1)
LEE 9-games (May 17-30)
McGRIFF 11-games(August 28-September 9)
MULLINIKS 7-games(August 4- August 11)
MYERS 7-games (April 17- April 26)
OLERUD 9-games (July 24- August 2)
SOJO 4-games (July 14- July 17)
WHITEN 4-games (September 23-26)
WILSON 12-games (September 4-17)

SHUTOUTS:

BLUE JAYS

May 28	at Oakland	W 1-0	Stieb(9.0)
June 20	vs Boston	W 11-0	Cerutti(8.0), Ward(1.0)
July 6	vs Seattle	W 1-0	Wells(8.0), Henke(1.0)
July 12	at California	W 5-0	Wells(8.0), Henke(1.0)
July 27	vs Texas	W 1-0	Stieb(7.0), Ward(1.0), Henke(1.0)
August 18	at Minnesota	W 3-0	Key(7.0), Henke(2.0)
Sept 1	at Cleveland	W 8-0	Stottlemyre(8.1), Candelaria(1.2)
Sept 2	at Cleveland	W 3-0	Stieb(9.0)...No-Hitter
Sept 8	vs Chicago	W 3-0	Stieb(8.0), Henke(1.0)

OPPONENTS

May 2	at Cleveland	L 3-0	Black(8.1), Jones(0.2)
June 26	at Boston	L 3-0	Gardner(6.0), Murphy(2.0), Reardon(1.0)
June 29	vs Oakland	L 5-0	Stewart(9.0)..No-Hitter
July 13	at California	L 2-0	Abbott(9.0)
July 22	at Oakland	L 3-0	Moore(8.2), Honeycutt(0.1)
August 24	vs Boston	L 2-0	Kiecker(8.0), Gray(1.0))
August 25	vs Boston	L 1-0	Clemens(9.0)
Augsut 26	vs Boston	L 1-0	Harris(7.2), Gray(1.1)
Sept 3	at Detroit	L 5-0	Terrell(7.0), Gleaton(2.0)
Sept 26	at Milwaukee	L 6-0	Robinson(9.0)

R. HOWARD WEBSTER AWARD WINNERS: Established in 1982 and named after the club's Honorary Chairman of the Board, Mr. R. Howard Webster, recognizing the Most Valuable Player on each of the Blue Jays' minor league affiliates...The following are the 1990 winners:

Syracuse: Mark Whiten, OF, (.290, 14HR, 48RBI in 104 games)
Knoxville: Tom Quinlan, INF, (.258, 15HR, 51RBI in 141 games)
Dunedin: Jeff Kent, INF, (.277, 16HR, 60RBI in 132 games)
Myrtle Beach: Mike Ogliaruso, RHP, (14-9, 2.52ERA, 26GS, 164.1IP, 160K)
St. Catharines: Carlos Delgado, C, (.283, 6HR, 39RBI in 67 games)
Medicine Hat: Brent Bowers, OF, (.274, 3HR, 27RBI in 60 games)
Santo Domingo: Mariano Dotel,SS(.338).

LABATT'S "BLUE" PLAYER OF THE MONTH AWARDS: The following are the award winners for this season...Voting for the awards is done by the Toronto Chapter of the Baseball Writers Association of America...Memebers of the BBWAA select the Player and Pitcher of the Month based on an overall apppraisal of their performance(s) during the month.

	PLAYER OF THE MONTH	PITCHER OF THE MONTH
APRIL	Kelly Gruber	Duane Ward
MAY	Kelly Gruber	Dave Stieb
JUNE	George Bell	Tom Henke
JULY	Fred McGriff	Dave Stieb
AUGUST	Fred McGriff	Jimmy Key
SEPT/OCT	Kelly Gruber	Jimmy Key

OTHER ACCOLADES: Blue Jays left fielder and DH, George Bell was twice named the American League Player of the Week for the weeks ending 6/11 (.464, 13H, 28AB, 2-2B, 2 HR, 11 RBI) and 6/24 (.500, 14H, 28AB, 5 HR, 11 RBI, 9 R, 1.107 SLG%)...Third baseman, Kelly Gruber received AL Player of the Month honours for the month of September(.352, 32H, 91AB, 8-2B, 3-3B, 8-HR, 30-RBI, 20-R, 3-SB, .769 SLG, .411 OBP)...Gruber also was named the AL Player of the Week for the week ending 9/16 (.464 13-28, 14 RBI, 2 HR).

BLUE JAY RELIEF PITCHING -1990

	IRE	FBE	LONGEST OUTING
ACKER	24-40	34-59	4.0
BLACK	0-0	1-1	2.0
BLAIR	14-20	18-21	5.2
CANDELARIA	8-11	7-12	3.1
CERUTTI	3-5	6-7	2.2
CUMMINGS	3-3	3-4	1.0
GILLES	2-2	1-2	1.0
HENKE	26-32	45-61	2.1
KILGUS	3-5	7-11	3.1
LEITER	2-2	4-4	3.0
LUECKEN	0-0	1-1	1.0
MACDONALD	3-3	3-4	1.0
WARD	9-31	61-73	4.0
WELLS	10-14	16-18	3.0
WILLS	22-28	26-40	4.0

[SAVE-SITUATION]: ACKER[1-3]; BLACK[0-1]; CANDELARIA[1-1]; HENKE[32-38]; WARD[11-20]; WELLS[3-3]

	Batting with Bases Loaded:	Batting with Runners in Scoring Position
BELL	....(1-8/.125, 1HR <Brown> 6RBI)	.....(41-149/.275, 6HR, 67RBI
BORDERS	......(2-7/.286, 5RBI)	.....(20-89/.225, 2Hr, 28RBI)
DUCEY	.....(1-2/.500, 2RBI)	.....(6-12/.500, 7RBI)
EPPARD	....	....(0-2/.000)
FELIX	.....(2-9/.222, 7RBI)	.....(31-105/.295, 3HR, 48RBI)
FERNANDEZ	.....(6-10/.500, 1HR, 12RBI)	.....(47-152/.309, 3HR, 60RBI)
GRUBER	.....(4-14/.286, 1HR, 13RBI)	.....(47-149/.315, 13HR, 93RBI)
HILL	.....(3-10/.300, 1HR, 9RBI)	.....(14-56/.250, 2HR, 20RBI)
LAWLESS	....(0-1/.000)	.....(1-5/.200, 1RBI)
LEE	.....(2-11/.182, 5RBI)	.....(25-101/.248, 1HR, 35RBI)
LIRIANO	.....(1-3)/.333, 1RBI)	.....(12-53/.226, 14RBI)
McGRIFF	.....(2-10/.200, 8RBI)	.....(34-129/.264, 5HR, 48RBI)
MULLINIKS	.....(2-5/.400, 3RBI)	.....(12-33/.364, 13RBI)
MYERS	.....(0-6/.000, 1RBI)	.....(12-71/.169, 2HR, 19RBI)
OLERUD	.....(1-4/.250, 4RBI)	.....(25-85/.294, 2HR, 27RBI)
SOJO	....	.....(7-26/.269, 1HR, 9RBI)
VIRGIL	....	....(0-1/.000)
WHITEN	....(0-4/.000)	.....(3-19/.158, 4RBI)
WILLIAMS	....(0-1/.000)	.....(3-17/.176, 6RBI)
WILSON	.....(2-9/.222, 5RBI)	.....(35-136/.257, 46RBI)
BLUE JAYS	....(29-116/.250, 4HR, 81RBI)	.....(375-1390/.270, 40HR, 545RBI)

BLUE JAYS' BIGGEST INNING: 10R in the 4th inn., of the BLUE JAYS' 13-5 win over Milw, on 6/10...**OPPONENTS' BIGGEST INNING**: 9R in the 4th, of an 14-6 Sea., win on 5/17.

BLUE JAYS' BACK-TO-BACK HR's: BORDERS/LEE, 4th inn., vs. Tigers' DuBois on 5/6...FELIX/GRUBER, 6th inn., vs. Oak's Young, Nelson, 5/22...LEE/FELIX, 3rd inn., 5/27 vs., M's Johnson...LEE/FELIX, 5th inn., vs. Oak's Young on 5/30...HILL/BORDERS, 7th inn., vs. Det's GIBSON on 8/8...McGRIFF/MYERS, 6th inn., vs CHI's McDowell on 9/9.

OPPONENTS' BACK-TO-BACK HR's:...Snyder and Maldonado, 2nd inning vs STIEB on 4/26 vs. Indians...Downing and Bichette, 7th inning vs Ward on 7/14 @ Angels...D.Henderson/J.Canseco, 3rd inning vs Cerutti @ Oakland, on 7/20...Maldonado and James, 6th inning vs Stottlemyre on 9/22 at SkyDome vs Indians.

BLUE JAYS IN THE STANDINGS:

	1st	2nd	3rd	4th	5th	6th	7th	POS., IN STANDINGS	
April: 21-gms/22-days	8	5	7	0	2	0	0	12- 9,	3rd, 1.5 GBL
May: 27-gms/31 days	5	10	14	2	0	0	0	26-23,	1st, +0.5GBL
June: 28-gms/30-days	13	11	6	0	0	0	0	41-36,	2nd, 3.5 GBL
July: 26-gms/31-days	12	19	0	0	0	0	0	55-48,	T1st, 0.0 GBL
August: 29-gms/31-days	2	29	0	0	0	0	0	68-64,	2nd, 6.5 GBL
Sept/Oct: 30-gms/33-days	10	23	0	0	0	0	0	86-76,	2nd, 2.0 GBL

ON THE SHELF: The Blue Jays used the DL only FOUR times in 1990-...the following Blue Jays were on the DL...C-GREG MYERS, 15-day,-left shoulder-May 5-25th...LHP-JIMMY KEY,15-day, pulled right hamstring, May 23- June 22nd...OF-GLENALLEN HILL, 15-day, July 6th-21st-cuts and scrapes, feet & knees...JUNIOR FELIX, 21-day, July 13th-Aug 8th-torn muscle in right calf-had emergency surgery July 13th...As well GLENALLEN HILL had an appendectomy on Oct 1st but was not placed on the DL.

ATTENDANCE: The Blue Jays led all 26 Major League teams in attendance with **3,885,284** for an average of 47,966 (81 dates)...Blue Jays sold-out 66 games at SkyDome this season including the last 59 consecutive...The largest crowd was 49,918 on August 23 vs. the Red Sox...The 3 MILLION barrier was broken August 25 in date # 64 which is a new MAJOR LEAGUE RECORD for fewest dates to reach that figure...The LA DODGERS had the previous mark of 67 dates in 1982...The American League record of 3,375,883 set by the Blue Jays in 1989 was broken Sunday, 9/9 vs CHI(date #71)...The Major League record of 3,608,881 set by the 1982 LA DODGERS was broken Monday, September 17th with a crowd of 49,902...Overall HOME and ROAD the BLUE JAYS drew **5,925,056**, a new Major League record for Total Attendance -Home and Road- previous record was 5,859,072 set by the 1982 LA DODGERS.

MULTIPLE RUN INNINGS:

	1R	2R	3R	4R	5R	6R	7R	8R	9R	10R
JAYS	216	128	42	22	5	4	2	1		1
OPP	191	98	38	22	4	6	1		1	

STARTS IN THE BATTING ORDER:

	GS	GS BREAKDOWN	1st	2nd	3rd	4th	5th	6th	7th	8th	9th
BELL	142	106-LF/36-DH			1	124	17				
BORDERS	83	83-C					9	34	34	6	
DUCEY	18	18-LF		1				11	5		1
FELIX	125	97-RF/27-CF/1-DH	47		8			1	2		67
FERNANDEZ	161	161-SS	50	111							
GRUBER	148	143-3B/5-RF			148						
HILL	68	22-LF/32-RF/14-DH	1		1		2	15	25	8	16
LAWLESS	3	1-3B/1-DH/1-LF									3
LEE	112	112-2B	1						10	88	13
LIRIANO	45	45-2B	3						1	36	5
MCGRIFF	153	148--1B/5-DH			6	36	111				
MULLINIKS	20	14-3B/6-DH			6		5	4	3	2	
MYERS	79	79-C						18	59	2	
OLERUD	101	86-DH/15-1B				2	17	76	6		
QUINLAN	1	1-3B									
SOJO	15	5-2B/4LF/3-3B/2DH/1SS5	1							6	3
VIRGIL	1	1-DH							1		
WH!TEN	20	20-RF					1	2	11	6	
WILLIAMS	16	6-RF/2CF/5LF/3DH	2						4	8	2
WILSON	146	132-CF/8-LF/6-DH	53		42						51

INNING SCORES:

	1	2	3	4	5	6	7	8	9	10	11	12	13	14	15
JAYS (767)	75	85	79	83	117	76	97	82	63	6	3	0	1	0	0
OPP (661)	83	74	78	68	64	100	77	63	44	1	3	0	6	0	0

LAST HOME RUN:

BELL . . . . 09/16 . vs . . . BAL
BORDERS . . . . 09/11 . @ . . . KC
FELIX . . . . 09/30 . @ . . . BOS
FERNANDEZ . . . . 09/11 . @ . . . KC
GRUBER . . . . 09/29 . @ . . . BOS
HILL . . . . 08/14 . @ . . . CHI
LEE . . . . 06/17 . @ . . . NYY
LIRIANO . . . . 04/20 . vs . . . KC
MCGRIFF . . . . 10/02 . @ . . . BAL
MULLINIKS . . . . 09/05 . @ . . . DET
MYERS . . . . 09/09 . vs . . . CHI
OLERUD . . . . 10/03 . @ . . . BAL
SOJO . . . . 08/31 . @ . . . CLE
WHITEN . . . . 09/24 . @ . . . MIL
WILSON . . . . 09/04 . @ . . . DET

MULTIPLE RBI GAMES:

	2RBI	3RBI	4RBI	5RBI	6RBI	TOT
BELL	15	6	1		1	23
BORDERS	7	4				'11
DUCEY	2					2
FELIX	11	3				14
FERNANDEZ	10	3	1			14
GRUBER	20	8	5			33
HILL	5	1	2			8
LEE	3	2				5
LIRIANO	4					4
McGRIFF	14	7	1			22
MULLINIKS	1					1
MYERS	2	2				4
OLERUD	8	4				12
SOJO				1		1
WHITEN	2					2
WILLIAMS	1					1
WILSON	8	1	1			10

GLANCING @ THE BLUE JAYS

AT ALL-STAR BREAK. . . . 47-38, 2nd, 0.5 GBL
AFTER ALL-STAR BREAK . 39-38
Apr. '90/'89/'88 . . . . 12-9/9-16/9-13
May '90/'89/'88 . . . . 14-14/11-15/13-16
June '90/'89/'88 . . . . 15-13/17-10/17-11
July '90/'89/'88 . . . . 14-12/15-12/12-14
August '90/'89/'88 . . . . . . 13-16/20-9/14-14
Sept/Oct.'90/'89/'88 . . . . . 18-12/17-11/22-7
Under CITO GASTON . . . 163-125
vs starting RHP/LHP 61-52/25-24
BJ's/OPP scoring first 59-23/27-53
GMS decided final AB 12-16
Franchise record 1069-1140-2
Home/Road 44-37/42-39
vs EAST/WEST 42-36/44-40
On Grass/Artificial 28-35/58-41
Day/Night 26-24/60-52
Extra Innings 4-8
90 Dome-Open/cld/other . . 12-18/29-17/3-2
All-time*/open/clsd/other . . 37-39/41-18/5-2 *includes post-season

WHEN	AHEAD	TIED	TRAILING
After 6 innings	69-5	8-10	9-61
After 7 innings	75-2	5-12	6-62
After 8 innings	75-2	7-8	4-66
After 9 innings	N/A	4-8	N/A

GAMES HIT IN:

	1H	2H	3H	4H	5H	TOT
BELL	49	30	10		1	90
BORDERS	46	17	5	1		69
DIAZ	1					1
DUCEY	5	4	1			10
FELIX	61	20	4	2		87
FERNANDEZ	55	35	14	1		105
GRUBER	54	27	14	2		97
HILL	32	9	3			44
LAWLESS	1					1
LEE	47	15	6			68
LIRIANO	18	5	2			25
MCGRIFF	64	29	8	4	1	106
MULLINIKS	14	6				20
MYERS	35	9	1	1		46
OLERUD	39	23	2			64
QUINLAN	1					1
SOJO	8	5				13
WHITEN	7	7	1			15
WILLIAMS	10		1			11
WILSON	5	35	11			98

BLUE JAYS 1990 STATISTICS

GAMES PLAYED - 162 + = ROOKIE

PLAYER	AVG	G	AB	R	H	2B	3B	HR	RBI	SH-SF	HP	BB	SO	SB	CS	GIDP
Bell,G	.265	142	562	67	149	25	0	21	86	0-11	3	32	80	3	2	14
Borders,P	.286	125	346	36	99	24	2	15	49	1-3	0	18	57	0	1	17
+Diaz,C	.333	9	3	1	1	0	0	0	0	1-0	0	0	2	0	0	0
Ducey,R	.302	19	53	7	16	5	0	0	7	0-1	1	7	15	1	1	0
Eppard,J	.200	6	5	0	1	0	0	0	0	0-0	1	0	2	0	0	0
Felix,J	.263	127	463	73	122	23	7	15	65	2-5	2	45	99	13	8	4
Right	.211		152		32	8	1	9	22	2-2	1	15	41			1
Left	.289		311		90	15	6	6	43	0-3	1	30	58			3
Fernandez,T	.276	161	635	84	175	27	17	4	66	2-6	7	71	70	26	13	17
Right	.234		205		48	6	2	1	13	0-3	2	31	19			6
Left	.295		430		127	21	15	3	53	2-3	5	40	51			11
Gruber,K	.274	150	592	92	162	36	6	31	118	1-13	8	48	94	14	2	14
+Hill,G	.231	84	260	47	60	11	3	12	32	0-0	0	18	62	8	3	5
Lawless,T	.083	15	12	1	1	0	0	0	1	0-0	0	0	1	0	2	0
Lee,M	.243	117	391	45	95	12	4	6	41	1-3	0	26	90	3	1	9
Right	.242		178		43	8	2	6	20	0-1	0	6	41			5
Left	.244		213		52	4	2	0	21	1-2	0	20	49			4
Liriano,N	.212	50	170	16	36	7	2	1	15	1-1	1	16	20	3	5	5
Right	.214		28		6	0	1	0	4	0-0	0	5	4			1
Left	.211		142		30	7	1	1	11	1-1	1	11	16			4
McGriff,F	.300	153	557	91	167	21	1	35	88	1-4	2	94	108	5	3	7
Mulliniks,R	.289	57	97	11	28	4	0	2	16	0-1	0	22	19	2	1	2
+Myers,G	.236	87	250	33	59	7	1	5	22	1-4	0	22	33	0	1	12
+Olerud,J	.265	111	358	43	95	15	1	14	48	1-4	1	57	75	0	2	5
+Quinlan,T	.500	1	2	0	1	0	0	0	0	0-1	0	0	1	0	0	0
+Sojo,L	.225	33	80	14	18	3	0	1	9	0-0	0	5	5	1	1	1
Virgil,O	.000	3	5	0	0	0	0	0	0	0-0	0	0	3	0	0	0
+Whiten,M	.273	33	88	12	24	1	1	2	7	0-1	0	7	14	2	0	2
Right	.316		38		12	1	1	1	4	0-1	0	3	9			0
Left	.240		50		12	0	0	1	3	0-0	0	4	5			2
Williams,K	.194	49	72	13	14	6	1	0	8	0-1	1	7	18	7	2	1
Wilson,M	.265	147	588	81	156	36	4	3	51	6-4	0	31	102	23	4	10
Right	.245		188		46	10	2	2	21	0-2	0	14	36			4
Left	.275		400		110	26	2	1	30	6-2	0	17	66			6
DH	.220	162	604	68	133	28	4	14	68	1-11	3	69	132	4	4	14
PH	.216	71	97	4	21	2	1	0	14	0-0	1	11	22	0	0	4
Toronto	.265	162	5589	767	1479	263	50	167	729	18-62	28	526	970	111	52	125
Opponents	.260	162	5524	661	1434	259	38	143	632	48-38	37	445	892	95	67	115

PITCHER—R/L	W-L	ERA	G	GS	CG	SHO	SV	IP	H	R	ER	HR	HB	BB	SO	WP
Acker,J—R	4-4	3.83	59	0	0	0	1	91.2	103	49	39	9	3	30	54	4
Black,B—L	2-1	4.02	3	2	0	0	0	15.2	10	7	7	2	1	3	3	0
+Blair,W—R	3-5	4.06	27	6	0	0	0	68.2	66	33	31	4	1	28	43	3
Candelaria,J—L	0-3	5.48	13	2	0	5	0	21.1	32	13	13	2	2	11	19	2
Cerutti,J—L	9-9	4.76	30	23	0	0	0	140.0	162	77	74	23	4	49	49	4
+Cummings,S—R	0-0	5.11	6	2	0	0	0	12.1	22	7	7	4	1	5	4	0
Flanagan,M—L	2-2	5.31	5	5	0	0	0	20.1	28	14	12	3	0	8	5	0
+Gilles,T—R	1-0	6.75	2	0	0	0	0	1.1	2	1	1	0	0	0	1	0
Henke,T—R	2-4	2.17	61	0	0	0	32	74.2	58	18	18	8	1	19	75	6
Key,J—L	13-7	4.25	27	27	0	0	0	154.2	169	79	73	20	1	22	88	0
Kilgus,P—L	0-0	6.06	11	0	0	0	0	16.1	19	11	11	2	1	7	7	0
Leiter,A—L	0-0	0.00	4	0	0	0	0	6.1	1	0	0	0	2	0	5	0
+Luecken,R—R	0-0	9.00	1	0	0	0	0	1.0	2	1	1	1	0	1	0	0
+MacDonald,B—L	0-0	0.00	4	0	0	0	0	2.1	0	0	0	0	0	2	0	0
Stieb,D—R	8-6	2.93	33	33	2	2	0	208.2	179	73	68	11	10	64	125	5
Stottlemyr,T—R	13-17	4.34	33	33	4	0	0	203.0	214	101	98	18	8	69	115	6
Ward,D—R	2-8	3.45	73	0	0	0	11	127.2	101	51	49	9	1	42	112	5
Wells,D—L	11-6	3.14	43	25	0	0	3	189.0	165	72	66	14	2	45	115	7
Wills,F—R	6-4	4.73	44	4	0	0	0	99.0	101	54	52	13	1	38	72	1
TORONTO	86-76	3.84	162	162	6	9	48	1454.0	1434	661	620	143	37	445	892	43
OPPONENTS	76-86	4.42	162	162	18	10	46	1447.2	1479	767	711	167	28	526	970	73

1990 BLUE JAYS STARTING PITCHERS

PITCHER	T	W-L	ERA	GS	CG	IP	H	R	ER	HR	HB	BB	SO	AVG.
BLACK	L	1-1	3.95	2	0	13.2	9	6	6	1	0	2	3	.191
BLAIR	R	0-3	6.00	6	0	30.0	37	20	20	2	1	14	21	.296
CANDELARIA	L	0-2	7.04	2	0	7.2	11	6	6	2	2	5	4	.344
CERUTTI	L	8-9	4.74	23	0	133.0	152	73	70	22	3	44	48	.293
CUMMINGS	R	0-0	3.72	2	0	9.2	17	4	4	2	0	5	3	.415
FLANAGAN	L	2-2	5.31	5	0	20.1	28	14	12	3	0	8	5	.329
KEY	L	13-7	4.25	27	0	154.2	169	79	73	20	1	22	88	.281
STIEB	R	18-6	2.93	33	2	208.2	179	73	68	11	10	64	125	.230
STOTTLEMYRE	R	13-17	4.34	33	4	203.0	214	101	98	18	8	69	115	.274
WELLS	L	10-5	3.11	25	0	167.2	152	63	58	11	1	42	97	.242
WILLS	R	1-0	3.60	4	0	20.0	17	9	8	1	1	10	11	.230
BLUE JAYS		66-52	3.93	162	6	968.1	985	448	423	93	27	285	520	.266

1990 BLUE JAYS RELIEF PITCHERS

PITCHER	T	W-L	ERA	APP	GF	SV	IP	H	R	ER	HR	HB	BB	SO	AVG
Acker,J	R	4-4	3.83	59	19	1	91.2	103	49	39	9	3	30	54	.281
Black,B	L	1-0	4.50	1	1	0	2.0	1	1	1	1	1	1	0	.167
Blair,W	R	3-2	2.56	21	8	0	38.2	29	13	11	2	0	14	22	.209
Candelaria,J	L	0-1	4.61	11	5	1	13.2	21	7	7	0	0	6	15	.362
Cerutti,J	L	1-0	5.14	7	1	0	7.0	10	4	4	1	1	5	1	.357
Cummings,S	R	0-0	10.13	4	2	0	2.2	5	3	3	2	1	0	1	.500
Gilles,T	R	1-0	6.75	2	1	0	1.1	2	1	1	0	0	0	1	.333
Henke,T	R	2-4	2.17	61	58	32	74.2	58	18	18	8	1	19	75	.213
Kilgus,P	L	0-0	6.06	11	4	0	16.1	19	11	11	2	1	7	7	.306
Leiter,A	L	0-0	0.00	4	2	0	6.1	1	0	0	0	0	2	5	.050
Mac Donald,B	L	0-0	0.00	4	1	0	2.1	2	0	0	1	0	3	0	.200
Ward,D	R	2-8	3.45	73	39	11	127.2	101	51	49	9	1	42	112	.221
Wells,D	L	1-1	3.38	18	8	3	21.1	13	9	8	3	1	3	18	.176
Wills,F	R	5-4	5.01	40	6	0	79.0	84	45	44	12	0	28	61	.275
TOTALS (156GAMES)		20-24	3.64	316	155	48	484.2	449	212	196	50	10	160	372	.248

	HOME W	HOME L	ROAD W	ROAD L	TOTALS W	TOTALS L
vs.BALTIMORE	5	2	3	3	8	5
vs.BOSTON	2	4	1	6	3	10
vs.CLEVELAND	4	3	5	1	9	4
vs.DETROIT	4	2	4	3	8	5
vs.MILWAUKEE	2	4	4	3	6	7
vs.NEW YORK	5	2	3	3	8	5
TOTALS vs EAST	22	17	20	19	42	36
vs.CALIFORNIA	4	2	1	5	5	7
vs.CHICAGO	5	1	2	4	7	5
vs.KANSAS CITY	3	3	4	2	7	5
vs.MINNESOTA	3	3	6	0	9	3
vs.OAKLAND	1	5	4	2	5	7
vs.SEATTLE	2	4	4	2	6	6
vs.TEXAS	4	2	1	5	5	7
TOTALS vs. WEST	22	20	22	20	44	40
OVERALL TOTALS	44	37	42	39	86	76
SHUTOUTS	4	4	5	6	9	10
SHO-INDIVIDUALS	0	2	2	2	2	4
EXTRA INNINGS	1	5	3	3	4	8
HOME-RUN DECISIONS	13	13	11	14	24	27
TWO-RUN DECISIONS	8	9	5	10	13	19
vs. LH STARTERS	12	11	13	13	25	24
vs. RH STARTERS	32	26	29	26	61	52
GRASS FIELDS	0	0	28	35	28	35
ARTIFICIAL FIELDS	44	37	14	4	58	41
DAY GAMES	17	16	8	8	25	24
NIGHT GAMES	27	21	34	31	61	52

	TOR	OPP.
DOUBLE PLAYS	144	156
TRIPLE PLAYS	0	0
LEFT ON BASE	1113	1069
GRAND SLAM HR	4	5
HOME RUNS —HOME	93	82
HOME RUNS—ROAD	74	61

DBLHEADERS (HOME)
WON 0 LOST 0 SPLIT O

DOUBLEHEADERS (ROAD)
WON 0 LOST 0 SPLIT O

ATTENDANCE
HOME 3,885,284 (81 DATES) 47,966 AVG
ROAD 2,039,772 (81 DATES) 25,182 AVG

	W	L
STARTERS	66	52
RELIEVERS	20	24
STREAKS	6	6

1990 BLUE JAYS INDIVIDUAL FIELDING

PITCHER	T	PCT	RANK	G	GS	PO	A	E	TC	DP
Acker,J	R	1.000	0	0	59	5	19	0	24	0
Black,B#	L	1.000	12	3	2	0	6	0	6	0
+Blair,W	R	1.000	0	6	27	3	6	0	9	0
Candelaria,J#	L	1.000	0	13	2	1	6	0	7	0
Cerutti,J	L	1.000	0	30	23	11	18	0	29	2
+Cummings,S	R	1.000	0	6	2	1	1	0	2	0
Flanagan,M	L	.857	0	5	5	0	6	1	7	0
+Gilles,T	R	1.000	0	2	0	0	1	0	1	0
Henke,T	R	1.000	0	61	0	6	5	0	11	0
Key,J	L	.968	0	27	27	8	22	1	31	3
Kilgus,P	L	1.000	0	11	0	1	3	0	4	0
Leiter,A	L	1.000	0	4	0	1	1	0	2	0
+Luecken,R	R	.000	0	1	0	0	0	0	0	0
+Mac, Donald,B	L	.000	0	4	0	0	0	0	0	0
Stieb,D	R	.941	24	33	33	24	40	4	68	3
Stottlemyr,T	R	.979	9	33	33	17	30	1	48	5
Ward,D	R	.964	0	73	0	9	18	1	28	0
Wells,D	L	1.000	1	43	25	7	32	0	39	1
Wills,F	R	1.000	0	44	4	9	10	0	19	2

CATCHER	T	PCT	RANK	G	GS	PO	A	E	TC	DP	PB
Borders,P	R	.993	6	115	83	515	46	4	565	6	6
+Diaz,C	R	1.000	0	0	9	13	3	0	16	0	0
+Myers,G	R	.993	4	87	79	411	30	3	444	4	8
Virgil,O	R	1.000	0	0	2	1	0	0	1	0	0

FIRST BASE	T	PCT	RANK	G	GS	PO	A	E	TC	DP
McGriff,F	L	.996	3	147	147	1246	126	6	1378	119
Mulliniks,R	R	1.000	0	3	0	11	0	0	11	1
+Olerud,J	L	.986	0	18	15	133	10	2	145	100

SECOND BASE	T	PCT	RANK	G	GS	PO	A	E	TC	DP
Lawless,T	R	1.000	0	1	0	4	1	0	5	1
Lee,M	R	.993	1	112	112	259	286	4	549	65
Liriano,N	R	.983	0	49	45	93	132	4	229	26
+Sojo,L	R	.969	0	15	5		16	15	1	323

THIRD BASE	T	PCT	RANK	G	GS	PO	A	E	TC	DP
Gruber,K	R	.955	3	145	123	280	19	422	21	0
Lawless,T	R	.800	0	4	1	3	1	5	0	0
Mulliniks,R	R	.949	0	22	12	25	2	39	4	0
+Quinlan,T	R	1.000	0	1	0	1	0	1	0	0
+Sojo,L	R	.875	0	4	2	5	1	8	1	0

SHORTSTOP	T	PCT	RANK	G	GS	PO	A	E	TC	DP
Fernandez,T	R	.989	2	161	297	480	9	786	93	0
Lee,M	R	1.000	0	9	6	15	0	21	1	0
+Sojo,L	R	.842	0	5	6	10	3	19	3	0

OUTFIELDERS	T	PCT	RANK	G	GS	PO	A	E	TC	DP
Bell,G	R	.979	0	106	226	4	5	235	1	0
Ducey,R	R	1.000	0	19	37	0	0	37	0	0
Felix,J	R	.966	32	125	244	11	9	264	3	0
Gruber,K	R	1.000	0	6	6	0	0	6	0	0
+Hill,G	R	.983	0	60	115	4	2	121	0	0
Lawless,T	R	1.000	0	2	6	0	0	6	0	0
+Sojo,L	R	1.000	0	5	10	1	0	11	0	0
+Whiten,M	R	1.000	0	30	60	3	0	63	0	0
Williams,K	R	1.000	0	30	36	0	0	36	0	0
Wilson,M	R	.992	5	141	370	5	3	378	2	0

1990 BLUE JAYS ROAD HITTERS

BATTER	AVG	G	AB	R	H	2B	3B	HR	RBI	SH-SF	HP	BB	SO	SLG	OBP
Bell,G	.274	72	288	31	79	13	0	10	45	0-9	1	16	39	.424	.306
Borders,P	.297	62	182	12	54	11	1	5	21	1-0	0	6	34	.451	.319
Diaz,C	.000	3	1	0	0	0	0	0	0	0-0	0	0	1	.000	.000
Ducey,R	.375	7	24	2	9	3	0	0	5	0-1	0	1	7	.500	.385
Eppard,J	.000	3	2	0	0	0	0	0	0	0-0	1	0	1	.000	.333
Felix,J	.282	60	227	38	64	10	1	8	36	1-1	0	21	49	.441	.341
Fernandez,T	.242	80	314	38	76	10	5	2	28	2-4	2	40	34	.325	.328
Gruber,K	.254	73	287	44	73	23	2	8	56	0-7	4	31	47	.432	.328
Hill,G	.225	36	120	22	27	3	3	5	15	0-0	0	7	33	.425	.268
Lawless,T	.000	5	3	1	0	0	0	0	0	0-0	0	0	1	.000	.000
Lee,M	.224	59	201	24	45	8	2	4	22	1-2	0	15	45	.343	.275
Liriano,N	.195	23	82	3	16	3	1	0	3	0-0	1	5	10	.256	.250
McGriff,F	.321	76	293	49	94	11	1	21	50	0-1	1	39	71	.580	.401
Mulliniks,R	.264	29	53	7	14	0	0	1	5	0-1	0	12	10	.321	.394
Myers,G	.234	44	128	18	30	5	1	2	9	1-2	0	9	14	.336	.281
Olerud,J	.257	53	171	18	44	8	0	3	22	0-3	0	28	32	.357	.356
Quinlan,T	.500	1	2	0	1	0	0	0	0	0-0	1	0	1	.500	.667
Sojo,L	.231	22	65	12	15	2	0	1	7	0-0	0	4	5	.308	.275
Virgil,O	.000	1	1	0	0	0	0	0	0	0-0	0	0	1	.000	.000
Whiten,M	.288	22	59	8	17	0	1	1	4	0-1	0	5	8	.373	.338
Williams,K	.276	23	29	5	8	3	1	0	3	0-1	1	2	6	.448	.333
Wilson,M	.281	78	317	50	89	20	2	3	31	2-4	0	19	52	.385	.318
TOTALS	.265	81	2849	382	755	133	21	74	362	8-37	12	260	501	.404	.325

1990 BLUE JAYS DESIGNATED HITTERS

BATTER	AVG	G	AB	R	H	2B	3B	HR	RBI	SH-SF	HP	BB	SO	SLG	OBP
Bell,G	.232	36	138	16	32	9	0	3	17	0-5	1	12	19	.362	.288
Borders,P	.000	1	1	0	0	0	0	0	0	0-0	0	0	0	.000	.000
Felix,J	.250	1	4	1	1	0	0	0	0	0-0	0	0	2	.250	.250
Gruber,K	1.000	1	1	1	1	0	1	0	3	0-0	0	0	0	3.000	1.000
Hill,G	.196	20	56	8	11	1	2	0	3	0-0	0	4	17	.286	.250
Lawless,T	.000	5	3	0	0	0	0	0	0	0-0	0	0	1	.000	.000
McGriff,F	.136	6	22	1	3	0	0	1	3	0-1	0	3	9	.273	.231
Mulliniks,R	.038	10	26	0	1	1	0	0	1	0-0	0	2	8	.077	.107
Olerud,J	.258	90	302	34	78	14	1	10	38	1-4	1	44	66	.411	.350
Sojo,L	.125	3	8	2	1	0	0	0	0	0-0	0	1	0	.125	.222
Virgil,O	.000	1	4	0	0	0	0	0	0	0-0	0	0	2	.000	.000
Whiten,M	.000	2	2	0	0	0	0	0	0	0-0	0	0	0	.000	.000
Williams,K	.083	9	12	2	1	0	0	0	2	0-1	1	1	5	.083	.200
Wilson,M	.160	6	25	3	4	3	0	0	1	0-0	0	2	3	.280	.222
TOTALS	.220		604	68	133	28	4	14	68	1-11	3	69	132	.349	.298

1990 BLUE JAYS PINCH HITTERS

BATTER	AVG	APP	AB	R	H	2B	3B	HR	RBI	SH-SF	HP	BB	SO	SLG	OBP
Borders,P	.200	33	25	0	5	1	0	0	3	0-0	0	5	6	.240	.333
Eppard,J	.200	6	5	0	1	0	0	0	0	0-0	1	0	2	.200	.333
Felix,J	.000	2	2	0	0	0	0	0	0	0-0	0	0	2	.000	.000
Gruber,K	.500	2	2	1	1	0	1	0	3	0-0	0	1	0	1.500	.500
Hill,G	.286	9	7	0	2	0	0	0	0	0-0	0	2	0	.286	.286
Lee,M	.000	3	3	0	0	0	0	0	0	0-0	0	0	0	.000	.000
Liriano,N	.000	2	2	0	0	0	0	0	0	0-0	0	0	0	.000	.000
Mulliniks,R	.364	28	22	2	8	1	0	0	7	0-0	0	4	4	.409	.462
Myers,G	.286	7	7	0	2	0	0	0	0	0-0	0	0	1	.286	.286
Olerud,J	.143	8	7	0	1	0	0	0	1	0-0	0	1	2	.143	.250
Sojo,L	.000	4	4	0	0	0	0	0	0	0-0	0	0	0	.000	.000
Whiten,M	.000	3	3	0	0	0	0	0	0	0-0	0	0	0	.000	.000
Williams,K	.125	10	8	1	1	0	0	0	0	0-0	0	1	2	.125	.222
TOTALS	.216	97	4	21	25	2	1	0	14	0-0	1	11	22	.258	.303

HITTING FOR THE CYCLE

Third baseman Kelly Gruber is the only Blue Jays' player to hit for the cycle...Gruber collected four hits and a career high six RBI, April 16th, 1989 at Exhibition Stadium vs the Kansas City Royals...Gruber homered in the first inning vs Floyd Bannister; a two-run double—the second inning, also against Bannister; a two-run triple vs Tom Gordon—the 7th inning; and, an RBI single—the 9th inning vs Jerry Don Gleaton...Only three opponents have hit for the cycle vs the Blue Jays...They are: Mike Cubbage, Minnesota Twins, July 27, 1978 (Metropolitan Stadium); Rich Gedman, Boston Red Sox, September 18, 1985 (Fenway Park) and George Brett, Kansas City Royals, July 25, 1990 (SkyDome).

1990 BLUE JAYS DETAILED HITTING

	AVG.	G	AB	R	H	HR	RBI
SEASON	.265	162	5589	767	1479	167	729
HOME	.264	81	2740	385	724	93	367
ROAD	.265	81	2849	382	755	74	362
VS RIGHT	.271	-	3745	513	1014	109	490
VS LEFT	.252	-	1844	254	465	58	239
PINCH HITTING	.216	-	97	4	21	0	14
DES. HITTING	.220	162	604	68	133	14	68
APRIL	.284	21	707	107	201	31	105
MAY	.243	28	942	121	229	34	118
JUNE	.276	28	1000	167	276	37	155
JULY	.239	26	896	104	214	21	95
AUGUST	.270	29	991	132	268	18	125
SEPT./OCT.	.263	30	1053	136	291	26	131
AT ALL-STAR	.263	85	2903	427	764	108	409
AFTER ALL-STAR	.266	77	2686	340	715	59	320
BALTIMORE	.292	13	448	65	131	15	63
BOSTON	.246	13	447	54	110	9	51
CLEVELAND	.297	13	474	69	141	22	68
DETROIT	.261	13	440	71	115	20	69
MILWAUKEE	.286	13	454	70	130	10	67
NEW YORK	.257	13	470	69	121	13	63
VS EAST DIV.	.274	78	2733	398	748	89	381
VS WEST DIV.	.256	84	1856	369	731	78	348
CALIFORNIA	.270	12	415	55	112	8	52
CHICAGO	.243	12	382	50	93	9	49
KANSAS CITY	.279	12	434	62	121	14	59
MINNESOTA	.305	45	423	75	129	13	32
OAKLAND	.197	12	385	33	76	13	32
SEATTLE	.230	12	413	49	93	9	41
TEXAS	.259	12	413	45	107	9	41

ON-BASE PCT. .328 **SLUGGING PCT. - .419** **TOTAL BASES - 2343**

1990 BLUE JAYS DETAILED PITCHING

	ERA	G	W	L	IP	H	ER
SEASON	3.84	162	86	76	1454.0	1434	620
HOME	3.86	81	44	37	749.0	761	321
ROAD	3.82	81	42	39	705.0	673	299
APRIL	4.26	21	12	9	184.0	186	87
MAY	3.93	28	14	14	254.0	247	111
JUNE	4.27	28	15	13	255.0	272	121
JULY	3.36	26	14	12	236.0	233	88
AUGUST	3.59	29	13	16	258.0	249	103
SEPT./OCT.	3.71	30	18	12	267.0	247	110
AT ALL-STAR	3.99	85	47	38	765.0	777	339
AFTER ALL-STAR	3.67	77	39	38	689.0	657	281
BALTIMORE	4.00	13	8	5	114.2	106	51
BOSTON	4.20	13	3	10	111.1	119	52
CLEVELAND	3.20	13	9	4	121.0	101	43
DETROIT	4.07	13	8	5	115.0	117	52
MILWAUKEE	4.74	13	6	7	114.0	123	60
NEW YORK	3.47	13	8	5	124.1	127	48
VS EAST DIV.	3.93	78	42	36	700.1	693	306
VS WEST DIV.	3.75	84	44	40	754.2	741	314
CALIFORNIA	3.62	12	5	7	107.0	110	43
CHICAGO	3.46	12	7	5	104.0	97	40
KANSAS CITY	3.85	12	7	5	111.0	118	47
MINNESOTA	3.25	12	9	3	108.0	102	39
OAKLAND	4.08	12	5	7	106.0	93	48
SEATTLE	3.88	12	6	6	109.0	110	47
TEXAS	4.10	12	5	7	109.2	111	50

OPPONENTS BATTING AVERAGE: .260 **SO PER 9.0 IP: 5.52** **BB PER 9.0 IP: 2.75**

TORONTO BLUE JAYS
1990 PLAYER TRANSACTIONS

DATE	PLAYER	TRANSACTION
March 29	Bob MacDonald-LHP,	
	Pedro Munoz-OF	Optioned to Syracuse
	Tom Quinlan-3B	Optioned to Knoxville
April 1	Alex Sanchez-RHP	
	Randy Knorr-C	Optioned to Syracuse
April 3	Derek Bell-OF	
	Mark Whiten-OF	Optioned to Syracuse
	Rick Trlicek-RHP	Optioned to Dunedin
	Jimmy Rogers-RHP	
	Pat Hentgen-RHP	
	Nate Cromwell-LHP	Optioned to Knoxville
April 6	Luis Sojo-IF	Optioned to Syracuse
April 8	Steve Cummings-RHP	Optioned to Syracuse
	Ozzie Virgil-C	Contract purchased from Syracuse

OPENING DAY ROSTER

PITCHERS(12) Jim Acker, Willie Blair, John Cerutti, Mike Flanagan, Tom Henke, Jimmy Key, Paul Kilgus, Dave Stieb, Todd Stottlemyre, Duane Ward, David Wells, Frank Wills
CATCHERS(3) Pat Borders, Greg Myers, Ozzie Virgil
INFIELDERS(8) Tony Fernandez, Kelly Gruber, Tom Lawless, Manny Lee, Nelson Liriano, Fred McGriff, Rance Mulliniks, John Olerud,
OUTFIELDERS(4) George Bell, Junior Felix, Glenallen Hill, Mookie Wilson

April 30	Paul Kilgus-LHP	Optioned to Syracuse
	Ozzie Virgil-C	Outrighted to Syracuse
May 4	Bob MacDonald-LHP	Optioned transferred from Syracuse to Knoxville
May 5	Greg Myers-C	Placed on 15-day disabled list
	Carlos Diaz-C	Contract purchased from Syracuse
May 8	Mike Flanagan-LHP	Released
	Steve Cummings-RHP	Recalled from Syracuse
May 21	Greg Myers-C	Sent to Syracuse on Rehabilitation Assignment
May 23	Jimmy Key-LHP	Placed on disabled list
May 25	Greg Myers-C	Recalled form injury Rehabilitation Assignment at Syracuse and reinstated from disabled list
	Carlos Diaz-C	Outrighted to Syracuse
June 2	Paul Kilgus-LHP	Recalled from Syracuse
June 6	Steve Cummings-RHP	Optioned to Syracuse
June 7	Jimmy Key-LHP	Assigned to Dunedin on Rehabilitation Assignment
	Tom Gilles-RHP	Contracted purchased from Syracuse
June 18	Kenny Williams-OF	Claimed on waivers from Detroit
	Jimmy Key-LHP	Reinstated to disabled list from injury Rehabilation Assignment at Dunedin
June 19	Tom Gilles-RHP	Optioned to Syracuse
June 21	Paul Kilgus--LHP	Optioned to Syracuse
June 22	Jimmy Key -LHP	Reinstated from disabled list
July 6	Glenallen Hill-OF	Placed on 15-day disabled list
July 12	Mark Whiten-OF	Recalled from Syracuse
	Tom Gilles-RHP	Recalled from Syracuse, not to report. Outrighted to Syracuse
July 13	Junior Felix-OF	Placed on disabled list
July 14	Luis Sojo-IF	Recalled from Syracuse
July 21	Tom Lawless-IF	Released
	Glenallen Hill-Of	Reinstated from disabled list
July 27	John Candelaria-LHP	Acquired from Minnesota in exchange for IF-Nelson Liriano and OF-Pedro Munoz
August 9	Junior Felix-OF	Reinstated from disabled list
	Willie Blair-RHP	Optioned to Syracuse
August 13	Mark Whiten-OF	Optioned to Syracuse
	Bob MacDonald-LHP	Recalled from Knoxville
August 29	Bob MacDoanld-LHP	Optioned to Syracuse
August 31	Mark Whiten-OF	Recalled from Syracuse
	Paul Kilgus-LHP	Recalled from Syracuse not to report and outrighted to Syracuse
Sept 1	Willie Blair-RHP	Recalled from Syracuse
	Carlos Diaz-C	Contract purchased from Syracuse
Sept 3	Tom Quinlan-3B	Recalled from Knoxville
Sept 4	Al Leiter-LHP	
	Rob Ducey-OF	
	Jim Eppard-IF	Contracts purchased from Syracuse
	Bob MacDoanld-LHP	Recalled from Syracuse
Sept 17	Bud Black-LHP	Acquired from Cleveland in exchange for RHPs Mauro Gozzo, Alex Sanchez and Steve Cummings

Sept 24	Rick Leucken-RHP	Contract purchased from Atlanta(NL)
	Nate Cromwell-LHP	Contract assigned to Atlanta(NL) on a waiver claim
Oct 24	Rick Hacker	Appointed third base coach
	Bud Black-LHP	Declares for free agency
Oct 26	Jim Eppard-IF	
	Rick Leucken-RHP	
	John Candelaria-LHP	Released
	Rance Mulliniks-IF	Declared Free Agency
Oct 31	George Bell-OF	Declared Free Agency
Nov 6	Nate Cromwell-LHP	Acquired from Atlanta in exchange for Earl Sanders-RHP
	Alex Sanchez-RHP	Acquired form Cleveland Indians in exchange for RHP-Willie Blair
Nov 26	Ken Dayley-LHP	Signed as a free agnet
Dec 2	Devon White-OF	
	Willie Fraser-RHP	
	Marcus Moore-RHP	Acquired from the California Angels in exchange for OF-Junior Felix, IF-Luis Sojo and C-Ken Rivers
Dec 3	Ricky Rhodes-RHP	Drafted in the Rule 5 draft from New York Yankees.
Dec 5	Rance Mulliniks-IF	Re-signed as a free agent
	Pat Tabler-IF	Signed as a free agent
	Joe Carter-OF	
	Roberto Alomar-IF	Acquired from San Diego Padres in exchange for SS-Tony Fernandez and IF-Fred McGriff
Dec 20	John Cerutti-LHP	Declared a Free Agent as not tendered a contract.
Jan 15/91	Rene Gonzales-IF	Acquired from the Baltimore Orioles for LHP-Rob Blumberg

1990 TORONTO BLUE JAYS HIGHS AND LOWS

*New Club Record
#Ties Club Record

TEAM BATTING

Most Runs, Game, Blue Jays	17	April 20, Kansas City(H)
Most Runs, Game, Opponents	11	April 11, Texas(H)
Most Runs, Game, Both Clubs	23	April 20, Tor-17, KC-6(H)
Most Runs, Inning, Blue Jays	10	June 10, 4th inn, Milwaukee(A)
Most Runs, Inning, Opponents	9	May 17, 3rd inn, Seattle(H)
Most Hits, Game, Blue Jays	19	April 20, Kansas City(H) April 30, Cleveland(A) Sept 30, Boston(A)
Most Hits, Game, Opponents	19	June 6, Minneosta(A)
Most Hits, Game, Both Clubs	30	April 23, Tor-17, Clev-13(H)
Most Hits, Inning, Blue Jays	9	June 20, Boston(H), 8th inning
Most Hits, Inning, Opponents	6	three times
Most Extra-base Hits, Game, Blue Jays	11	June 7, Minnesota(H)
Most Extra-base Hits, Game, Opponents	7	July 14, California(A)
Most Home Runs, Game, Blue Jays	5	April 20, Kansas City(H) May 6, Detroit(H)
Most Home Runs, Game, Opponents	6	July 14, California(A)
Most Home Runs, Inning, Blue Jays	3	May 6, Detroit(H), 4th inning May 22, Oakland(H), 6th inning
Most Home Runs, Inning, Opponents	3	July 14, California(A), 7th inning August 7, Detroit(H), 9th inning
Most Stolen Bases, Game, Blue Jays	4	May 13, Detroit(A) August 5, Texas(A)
Most Stolen Bases, Game, Opponents	4	April 9, Texas(A)
Most Stolen Bases, Inning, Blue Jays	2	five times
Most Singles, Game, Blue Jays	#17	Sept 30, Boston(A)
Most Singles, Game, Opponents	14	April 15, Kansas City(A)
Most Doubles, Game, Blue Jays	*8	June 7, Minnesota(H)
Most Doubles, Game, Opponents	4	April 13, Kansas City(A)
Most Triples, Game, Blue Jays	3	September 25, Milwaukee(A)
Most Triples, Game, Opponents	2	May 30, Oakland(A)
Most Total Bases, Game, Blue Jays	38	April 20, Kansas City(H)
Most Total Bases, Game, Opponents	21	April 11, Texas(H)
Most Left On Base, Blue Jays	14	July 14, California(A)
Most Left On Base, Opponents	12	April 15, Kansas City(A)

TEAM FIELDING

Most Double Plays, Game, Blue Jays	3	six times
Most Double Plays, Game, Opponents	4	May 18, California(H)
Most Errors, Game, Blue Jays	3	six times
Most Errors, Game, Opponents	4	July 4, California(H)

TEAM PITCHING

Pitchers, Most Strikeouts, Game, Blue Jays	11	July 29, Texas(H)
Pitchers, Most Strikeouts, Game, Opponents	15	July 28, Texas(H)
Pitchers, Most Walks, Game, Blue Jays	10	September 5, Detroit(A)
Pitchers, Most Walks, Game, Opponents	9	April 10, Texas(H) September 23, Cleveland(A)

INDIVIDUAL BATTING

Most Runs, Game	4	Gruber,June 8, Milwaukee(A)
Most Hits, Game	5	McGriff, Sept 1, Cleveland(A) Bell, Sept 24, Milwaukee(A)
Most Doubles, Game	2	Many Times
Most Triples, Game	2	Fernandez, June 5, Minnesota(H)
Most Home Runs, Game	2	Bell(3), Gruber(4), Hill(1), McGriff(3), Olerud(1)
Most Runs Batted In, Game	6	Bell, June 8, Milwukee(A)
Most Extra-Base Hits, Game	3	Gruber, September 22, Cleveland(A) Wilson, May 13, Detroit(A)
Most Total Bases, Game	9	Bell(2), Gruber(2), Hill(1), McGriff(2), Olerud(1)
Most Stolen Bases, Game	2	Felix, April 21, Kansas City(H) Wilson, May 13, Detroit(A)
Longest Hitting Streak	15	Tony Fernandez Kelly Gruber
Grand Slams 1		Bell, April 11, Texas(H) Hill, August 14, Chicago(A) Fernandez, Sept 11, Kansas City(A) Gruber, Sept 29, Boston(A)
Inside the Park Home Run	None	

INDIVIDUAL PITCHING

Most Strikeouts, Game	9	Wells, June, Minnesota(H) Stieb, Sept 2, Cleveland(A)
Most Strikeouts, Game, Reliever	7	Ward, August 2, Texas(A)
Most Walks, Game	6	Wills, Sept 4, Detroit(A)
Low Hit, Complete Game	0	Stieb, Sept 2, Cleveland(A)
Most Home Runs Allowed	3	Key, May 6, Detroit(H)
Most Innings, Game, Starter	9	Stieb(2), Stottlemyre(2)
Most Innings, Game, Reliever	5.2	Blair, June 25, Bost(A)
Longest Winning Streak	5	Stieb
Longest Losing Streak	6	Ward, May 19- July 24
Most Consecutive Scoreless innings, Starter	21	0—Wells, July 1-17
Most Consecutive Scoreless innings, Reliever	16	1—Ward, April 10-29

TEAM MISCELLANEOUS

Longest Winning Streak	3	three times
Longest Home Winning Streak	6	September 14-19
Longest Road Winning Streak	6	June 12-17
Longest Losing Streak	6	June 25-30
Longest Home Losing Streak	6	August 23-28
Longest Road Losing Streak	4	June 25-28
Longest Game, Innings	15	June 22, New York(H)
Longest Game, Time, Nine Innings	3:44	August 31, Cleveland (A)
Longest Game, Time, Extra Innings	4:53	June 22, New York(H)
Fastest Game, Time	2:05	July 13, California(A)
Largest Margin, Victory	11	April 20, Kansas City(H), 17-6, June 20, Boston(H), 11-0
Largest Margin, Loss	8	May 17, Seattle(H), 14-6 August 3, Texas(A), 9-1
Largest Crowd, SkyDome	49,918	August 23, Boston
Smallest Crowd, SkyDome	34,129	April 23, Cleveland
Largest Crowd, Road	46,612	June 9, Milwaukee
Smallest Crowd, Road	5,111	May 1, Cleveland
Furthest from First Place	6.5 GB	

JIM ACKER

4 GMS TO 400
23 K TO 450

ROBERTO ALOMAR

52 GMS TO 500
3 HITS TO 500
10 SB TO 100

PAT BORDERS

25 GMS TO 300
9 DOUBLES TO 50
1 RBI TO 100

JOE CARTER

59 AB TO 4000
8 DOUBLES TO 200
2 RBI TO 650
1 SB TO 150

KEN DAYLEY

25 GMS TO 400
9 SAVES TO 50

ROB DUCEY

11 RUNS TO 50
29 GMS TO 150

JIM EPPARD

18 GMS TO 100
11 HITS TO 50

WILLIE FRASER

40 GMS TO 200
55.2 INNINGS TO 600
28 K TO 300

KELLY GRUBER

281 AB TO 2500
79 RUNS TO 400
17 HR TO 100
10 HITS TO 600

TOM HENKE

19 GMS TO 400
4 K TO 600
83 IP TO 600

GLENALLEN HILL

25 HITS TO 100
11 RBI TO 50
13 WINS TO 100

JIMMY KEY

16 GS TO 200
98 K TO 800

MANNY LEE

13 GMS TO 500
9 RUNS TO 150
11 DOUBLES TO 50
19 RBI TO 150

AL LEITER

2 GS TO 25
30.1 IP TO 150
31 K TO 150

RANCE MULLINIKS

225 GMS TO 1500
33 RUNS TO 450
4 HR TO 75
89 HITS TO 1000

GREG MYERS

35 HITS TO 100
16 RUNS TO 50
197 AB TO 500

JOHN OLERUD

33 GMS TO 150
5 RUNS TO 50
2 RBI TO 50
2 HITS TO 100

DAVE STIEB

10 GAMES TO 400
333.1 IP TO 3000
43 K TO 1600
18 GS TO 400

TODD STOTTLEMYRE

12 GMS TO 100
33 GS TO 100
71.1 IP TO 500
5 K TO 250
25 RBI TO 500

PAT TABLER

6 GMS TO 1000(AL)
27 RUNS TO 450
20 DOUBLES TO 200
4 HR TO 50

DUANE WARD

23 GMS TO 250
9 SAVES TO 50
16.1 IP TO 400
6 K TO 350

DAVID WELLS

23 GS TO 50
31 IP TO 400
19 K TO 300
44 GMS TO 200

DEVON WHITE

269 AB TO 2500
49 HITS TO 600
9 DOUBLES TO 100
27 SB TO 150
9 RBI TO 250

MARK WHITEN

12 AB TO 100
17 GMS TO 50
26 HITS TO 50

KENNY WILLIAMS

23 HITS TO 250
4 SB TO 50
30 RUNS TO 150

FRANK WILLS

28.2 IP TO 450
21 K TO 300
3 WINS TO 25

MOOKIE WILSON

161 HITS TO 1500
147 AB TO 5000
26 BB TO 300
40 RBI TO 450
8 TRIPLES TO 75

Pitcher in Caps - Complete Game
r - Relief Pitcher

	W-L	POS	GB	OPP'NT	D/N	SCORE	WINNER	LOSER
APRIL								
9	0-1	T5	1	@TEX	N	L2-4	Ryan(1-0)	Stottlemyre(0-1)
10	1-1	3	1	TEX	N	W2-1	Stieb(1-0)	Hough(0-1)
11	1-2	5	2	TEX	N	L5-11	Brown(1-0)	Cerutti(0-1)
12	2-2	T3	.5	TEX	N	W7-1	Flanagan(1-0)	Moyer(0-1)
13	3-2	T2	.5	@KC	N	W3-1	Key(1-0)	S.Davis(0-1)
14	3-3	T2	1	@KC	D	L1-3	Saberhagen(1-0)	Stottlemyre(0-2)
15	4-3	3	.5	@KC	D	W5-4	Stieb(2-0)	rCrawford(0-1)
16	5-3	2	---	BALT	D	W4-2	Cerutti(1-1)	Tibbs(0-1)
17	6-3	2	---	BALT	N	W8-2	Flanagan(2-0)	Ballard(0-2)
18	6-4	2	---	BALT	N	L5-8	Harnisch(1-0)	rWills(0-1)
19	6-4	1	+.5	**OFF**				
20	7-4	1	+1	KC	N	W17-6	Stottlemyre(1-2)	Saberhagen(1-1)
21	8-4	1	+1	KC	D	W5-1	Stieb(3-0)	Gubicza(1-2)
22	8-5	1	+1	KC	D	L1-7	Gordon(1-0)	Cerutti(1-2)
23	9-5	1	+1.5	CLEV	N	W12-9	rWills(1-1)	rWickander(0-1)
24	10-5	1	+1.5	CLEV	N	W4-3	Key(2-0)	Swindell(1-2)
25	11-5	1	+1.5	CLEV	N	W5-3	Stottlemyre(2-2)	rNichols(0-1)
26	11-6	1	+.5	CLEV	D	L3-4	Candiotti(3-0)	Stieb(3-1)
27	11-7	2	.5	@CHGO	N	L1-6	Hibbard(2-1)	Cerutti(1-3)
28	11-8	3	.5	@CHGO	N	L4-5	Kutzler(1-0)	Flanagan(2-1)
29	11-9	3	1.5	@CHGO	D	L3-10	King(1-0)	Key(2-1)
30	12-9	3	1.5	@CLEV	N	W10-4	Stottlemyre(3-2)	Bearse(0-2)
MAY								
1	13-9	3	1.5	@CLEV	N	W4-3	Stieb(4-1)	Candiotti(3-1)
2	13-10	3	2	@CLEV	N	L0-3	Black(3-0)	Cerutti(1-4)
3	13-10	3	2.5	**OFF**				
4	13-11	3	2.5	DET	N	L1-3	Petry(2-1)	Flanagan(2-2)
5	14-11	3	2	DET	D	W5-1	STOTTLEMYRE(4-2)	Robinson(1-3)
6	15-11	2	1	DET	D	W11-7	Key(3-1)	Dubois(0-1)
7	16-11	2	1	CHGO	N	W6-1	Stieb(5-1)	McDowell(1-2)
8	16-12	2	2	CHGO	N	L1-4	Hibbard(3-2)	Cerutti(1-5)
9	17-12	2	1	CHGO	N	W4-3	rWills(2-1)	rEdwards(0-1)
10	17-13	2	1.5	@DET	N	L5-10	Robinson(2-3)	Stottlemyre(4-3)
11	18-13	2	1.5	@DET	N	W4-2	Key(4-1)	Dubois(0-2)
12	18-13	3	1	@DET	**PPD: RAIN-RESCHEDULED MONDAY, MAY 14th**			
13	19-13	2	---	@DET	D	W6-3	rWells(1-0)	Morris(2-5)
14	20-13	1	---	@DET	D	W8-3(10)	rWard(1-0)	rHennemann(0-3)
15	20-14	1	+.5	SEA	N	L3-4(10)	rComstock(1-1)	rAcker(0-1)
16	20-15	2	.5	SEA	N	L2-4	Holman(6-2)	Stottlemyre(4-4)
17	20-16	3	1.5	SEA	D	L6-14	R.Johnson(3-2)	Key(4-2)
18	20-17	3	2.5	CALF	N	L2-4	Abbott(2-3)	Stieb(5-2)
19	20-18	4	2.5	CALF	D	L9-11	rFraser(1-2)	rWard(1-1)
20	21-18	3	2.5	CALF	D	W5-1	rWills(3-1)	Langston(3-4)
21	21-19	3	2.5	OAK	D	L1-4	Welch(5-2)	Stottlemyre(4-5)
22	21-20	3	3.5	OAK	N	L4-5	Young(2-1)	rWills(3-2)
23	21-21	3	3.5	@CALF	N	L4-5	rBailes(1-0)	rWard(1-2)
24	21-22	4	3.5	@CALF	N	L3-4(11)	rHarvey(2-1)	rHenke(0-1)
25	22-22	3	3	@SEA	N	W3-1(11)	rAcker(1-1)	rSwift(2-2)
26	23-22	3	1.5	@SEA	N	W11-4	rWills(4-2)	Holman(6-3)
27	24-22	2	2	@SEA	N	W5-1	Cerutti(2-5)	R.Johnson(3-3)
28	25-22	1	+.5	@OAK	N	W1-0	STIEB(6-2)	MOORE(4-4)
29	26-22	1	+.5	@OAK	N	W2-1	Wells(2-0)	STEWART(8-2)
30	26-23	2	---	@OAK	D	L5-8	rBurns(1-0)	Blair(0-1)
31	26-23	1	+.5	**OFF**				
JUNE								
1	26-24	3	.5		N	L1-7	Higuera(5-1)	Stott'myre(4-6)
2	26-25	3	1.5	MILW	D	L6-7	rFossas(2-3)	rWells(2-1)
3	27-25	3	.5	MILW	D	W7-4	Stieb(7-2)	Knudson(3-3)
4	27-25	3	.5	**OFF**				
5	28-25	3	.5	MINN	N	W7-3	Wells(3-1)	Smith(4-5)
6	28-26	3	1.5	MINN	D	L5-12	rCandelaria(7-1)	Blair(0-2)
7	29-26	2	1.5	MINN	N	W10-3	Stottlemyre(5-6)	Tapani(6-4)
8	30-26	2	1.5	@MIL	N	W11-5	rGilles(1-0)	rCrim(2-2)
9	31-26	2	1.5	@MIL	N	W7-3	Stieb(8-2)	Bosio(4-4)
10	32-26	2	.5	@MIL	N	W13-5	Wells(4-1)	Navarro(2-2)
11	32-27	2	.5	@MIL	N	L1-4	Krueger(3-3)	Blair(0-3)
12	33-27	1	+.5	MINN	N	W5-4	Stottlemyre(6-6)	rCandelaria(7-2)
13	34-27	1	+.5	MINN	N	W10-1	Cerutti(3-5)	West(2-4)
14	35-27	1	+1.5	MINN	N	W7-1	Stieb(9-2)	Anderson(2-9)
15	36-27	1	+1.5	@NY	N	W5-4	Wells(5-1)	rRobinson(0-5)
16	37-27	1	+1.5	@NY	N	W2-1(11)	rWills(5-2)	rMills(0-2)
17	38-27	1	+1.5	@NY	D	W8-1	STOTTLEMYRE(7-6)	LaPoint(4-6)
18	38-27	1	+2	**OFF**				
19	38-28	1	+1	BOS	N	L2-4	Kiecker(2-3)	rWard(1-3)
20	39-28	1	+2	BOS	N	W11-0	Stieb(10-2)	Gardner(1-4)
21	39-29	1	+1.5	NY	N	L6-7	rMills(1-2)	rAcker(1-2)
22	39-30	1	+.5	NY	N	L7-8(15)	rCadaret(2-4)	rBlair(0-4)
23	40-30	1	+.5	NY	D	W8-4	Stottlemyre(8-6)	Leary(3-10)
24	41-30	1	+.5	NY	D	W8-3	Cerutti(4-5)	Cary(4-3)
25	41-31	2	.5	@BOS	N	L8-10	rLamp(1-2)	rBlair(0-5)
26	41-32	2	1.5	@BOS	N	L0-3	Gardner(2-4)	Wells(5-2)
27	41-33	2	2.5	@BOS	N	L5-9	Boddicker(10-3)	Key(4-3)
28	41-34	2	3.5	@BOS	N	L3-4	Clemens(12-3)	STOTTLEMYRE(8-7)
29	41-35	2	3.5	OAK	N	L0-5	STEWART(10-6)	Cerutti(4-6)
30	41-36	2	3.5	OAK	D	L4-9	Welch(13-2)	Stieb(10-3)

	W-L	POS	GB	OPP'NT	D/N	SCORE	WINNER	LOSER
JULY								
1	42-36	2	3.5	OAK	D	W4-3	Blair(1-5)	rBurns(2-2)
2	42-37	2	4.5	OAK	D	L2-3	Moore(6-7)	Key(4-4)
3	43-37	2	3.5	CAL	N	W5-2	Stottlemyre(9-7)	Blyleven(7-5)
4	44-37	2	3.5	CAL	N	W4-2	Cerutti(5-6)	Abbott(5-7)
5	45-37	2	2.5	CAL	N	W9-2	Stieb(11-3)	McCaskill(6-5)
6	46-37	2	1.5	SEA	N	W1-0	Wells(6-2)	Holman(8-7)
7	47-37	2	.5	SEA	D	W4-2	Key(5-4)	Swan(1-2)
8	47-38	2	.5	SEA	D	L3-6	YOUNG(3-9)	Stottlemyre(9-8)
9	OFF							
10	ALL STAR BREAK							
11	OFF							
12	48-38	2	---	@CAL	N	W5-0	Wells(7-2)	McCaskill(6-6)
13	48-39	2	---	@CAL	N	L0-2	ABBOTT(6-7)	STOTTLEMYRE(9-9)
14	48-40	2	.5	@CAL	N	L7-8	rEichhorn(1-4)	rWard(1-4)
15	48-41	2	.5	@CAL	D	L2-3	FINLEY(12-4)	rHenke(0-2)
16	49-41	1	+ .5	@SEA	N	W4-3	Key(6-4)	Hanson(10-7)
17	49-42	2	.5	@SEA	N	L5-7	rJackson(4-3)	rWard(1-5)
18	49-43	2	1.5	@SEA	D	L2-5	YOUNG(4-10)	Stottlemyre(9-10)
19	49-43	2	1	OFF				
20	50-43	2	.5	@OAK	N	W8-6	Cerutti(6-6)	Young(5-4)
21	51-43	1	+ .5	@OAK	D	W2-1	Stieb(12-3)	Sanderson(11-6)
22	51-44	1	+ .5	@OAK	D	L0-3	Moore(9-8)	Key(6-5)
23	51-44	1	+1	OFF				
24	51-45	1	+1	KC	N	L3-5(13)	rFarr(8-4)	rWard(1-6)
25	51-46	T1	---	KC	N	L1-6	McGaffigan(1-0)	Stottlemyre(9-11)
26	52-46	1	+1	KC	N	W7-5	Cerutti(7-6)	Appier(5-4)
27	53-46	1	+1	TEX	N	W1-0	Stieb(13-3)	Hough(7-7)
28	53-47	1	+1	TEX	D	L2-3(13)	rArnsberg(4-1)	rWills(5-3)
29	54-47	1	+1	TEX	D	W10-8	rAcker(2-2)	rMcMurty(0-1)
30	55-47	1	+1	@BAL	N	W9-2	Stottlemyre(10-11)	Milacki(4-8)
31	55-48	T1	---	@BAL	N	L4-6	McDonald(3-0)	Cerutti(7-7)
AUGUST								
1	56-48	T1	---	@BAL	N	W7-4	Stieb(14-3)	rBallard(1-10)
2	56-49	2	.5	@TEX	N	L4-5(11)	rArnsberg(5-1)	rCandelaria(7-4)
3	56-50	2	1.5	@TEX	N	L1-9	MOYER(1-3)	Wells(7-3)
4	56-51	2	2.5	@TEX	N	L2-3	WITT(10-8)	Stottlemyre(10-12)
5	57-51	2	1.5	@TEX	N	W6-4	Cerutti(8-7)	RYAN(11-5)
6	57-52	2	2	@TEX	N	L3-4	Hough(9-7)	Stieb(14-4)
7	58-52	2	2	DET	N	W11-5	Key(7-5)	Morris(9-14)
8	59-52	2	1	DET	N	W8-3	Wells(8-3)	Terell(0-1)
9	59-53	2	2	DET	N	L4-5	Robinson(9-9)	Stottlemyre(10-13)
10	59-54	2	2	MINN	N	L3-7	WEST(6-7)	Cerutti(8-8)
11	60-54	2	2	MINN	D	W7-4	Stieb(15-4)	rLeach(2-4)
12	60-55	2	3	MINN	D	L4-5	Anderson(5-15)	Key(7-6)
13	61-55	2	2	@CHI	N	W4-3	rWard(2-6)	rThigpen(4-5)
14	62-55	2	2	@CHI	N	W12-4	Stottlemyre(11-13)	Hibbard(9-7)
15	62-56	2	2	@CHI	N	L3-4	McDowell(9-6)	Candelaria(7-5)
16	62-56	2	2	OFF				
17	63-56	2	2	@MINN	N	W5-1	Stieb(16-4)	Erickson(3-3)
18	64-56	2	1	@MINN	N	W3-0	Key(8-6)	ANDERSON(5-16)
19	65-56	2	---	@MINN	D	W9-1	Wells(9-3)	Guthrie(4-6)
20	65-57	2	1	@NY	N	L5-6(11)	rCadaret(5-4)	rAcker(2-3)
21	65-58	2	1	@NY	N	L2-3	Cary(5-8)	Candelaria(7-6)
22	65-59	2	2	@NY	N	L2-4	Hawkins(4-10)	Cerutti(8-9)
23	66-59	2	1	BOS	N	W4-3	rHenke(1-2)	rHesketh(0-1)
24	66-60	2	2	BOS	N	L0-2	Kiecker(5-6)	rWard(2-7)
25	66-61	2	3	BOS	D	L0-1	CLEMENS(19-5)	Wells(9-4)
26	66-62	2	4	BOS	D	L0-1	Harris(11-5)	Stottlemyre(11-14)
27	66-63	2	5	MIL	N	L2-6	Navarro(5-5)	Stieb(16-5)
28	66-64	2	6	MIL	N	L2-6	NAVARRO(5-5)	Stieb(16-5)
29	67-64	2	6	MIL	N	W7-3	Key(9-6)	Knudson(10-7)
30	67-64	2	6.5	OFF				
31	68-64	2	6.5	@CLEV	N	W12-8	rAcker(3-4)	Swindell(10-8)
SEPTEMBER								
1	69-64	2	6.5	@CLEV	N	W8-0	Stottlemyre(12-14)	Candiotti(13-10)
2	70-64	2	6.5	@CLEV	D	W3-0	STIEB(17-5)	Black(10-9)
3	70-65	2	6.5	@DET	D	L0-5	Terrell(4-2)	Key(9-7)
4	70-66	2	6.5	@DET	N	L1-3	rGibson(4-4)	rWard(2-8)
5	71-66	2	5.5	@DET	N	W7-3	Wells(10-4)	Parker(3-2)
6	71-66	2	5.5	OFF				
7	72-66	2	5.5	CHI	N	W3-1	Stottlemyre(13-14)	Perez(12-13)
8	73-66	2	5.5	CHI	D	W3-0	Stieb(18-5)	FERNANDEZ(2-3)
9	74-66	2	4.5	CHI	D	W6-1	Key(10-7)	McDowell(12-7)
10	75-66	2	4	@KAN	N	W6-1	Wells(11-4)	Wagner(0-1)
11	76-66	2	3.0	@KAN	N	W8-4	Wills(6-3)	M.Stottlemyre(0-1)
12	76-67	2	4	@KAN	N	L5-7	Gordon(11-10)	Stottlemyre(13-15)
13	76-68	2	4	BAL	N	L3-5	Mesa(1-2)	Stieb(18-6)
14	77-68	2	3	BAL	N	W8-7	rBlair(2-5)	rOlson(5-5)
15	78-68	2	2	BAL	D	W4-3	rBlair(3-5)	rSchilling(1-2)
16	79-68	2	1	BAL	D	W6-5	RHenke(2-2)	rPrice(3-4)
17	80-68	2	1	NYY	N	W6-4	rCerutti(9-9)	rPlunk(5-3)
18	81-68	T1	---	NYY	N	W3-2	rBlack(12-10)	rGuetterman(10-7)
I9	82-68	1	+1	NYY	N	W7-6	Key(11-7)	Leary(9-19)
20	82-68	1	+1	OFF				
21	82-69	T1	---	CLEV	N	L1-2(13)	Valdez(1-1)	rWills(6-4)
22	82-70	T1	---	CLEV	D	L2-5	Shaw(3-4)	Stottlemyre(13-16)
23	83-70	1	+1	CLEV	D	W5-4(10)	rAcker(4-4)	rC.Ward(1-3)
24	84-70	1	+1.5	@MIL	N	W9-5	Key(12-7)	Navarro(7-7)
25	84-71	1	+1.5	@MIL	N	L4-8	Krueger(6-8)	Black(12-11)
26	84-72	1	+ .5	@MIL	N	L0-6	ROBINSON(12-4)	Wells(11-5)
27	84-72	T1	---	OFF				
28	84-73	2	1	@BOS	N	L6-7	rReardon(4-3)	rHenke(2-3)
29	84-74	2	2	@BOS	D	L5-7	Clemens(21-6)	Stottlemyre(13-17)
30	85-74	2	1	@BOS	D	W10-5	Key(13-7)	rHesketh(0-4)
OCTOBER								
1	85-75	2	2	@BALT	N	L3-6	Mesa(3-2)	Wells(11-6)
2	86-75	2	1	@BALT	N	W2-1	Black(13-11)	Johnson(13-9)
3	86-76	2	2	@BALT	N	L2-3	rOlson(6-5)	rHenke(2-4)

TORONTO BLUE JAYS

American League

MANAGER: Cito Gaston
RECORD: 86-76 (2nd)
ALL-STARS: George Bell, Kelly Gruber, Dave Stieb
LEAGUE LEADERS: Tony Fernandez (17 triples, 161 games-SS, 786 total chances-SS, 297 putouts-SS, 480 assists-SS); Kelly Gruber (123 putouts-3B), Manny Lee (.993 fielding percentage-2B); Dave Stieb (68 total chances-P); Todd Stottlemyre (5 double plays-P).

MOST USED LINEUP

C	Pat Borders (115)
1B	Fred McGriff (147)
2B	Manny Lee (112)
3B	Kelly Gruber (145)
SS	Tony Fernandez (161)
OF	Mookie Wilson (141)
OF	Junior Felix (125)
OF	George Bell (106)
St	Dave Stieb (36) Todd Stottlemyre
Rel	Duane Ward (73)

DUNEDIN BLUE JAYS

Florida State League

MANAGER: Dennis Holmberg
RECORD: 84-52 (3rd)
ALL-STARS: Jeff Kent, Juan De La Rosa, Greg O'Halloran, Anthony Ward
LEAGUE LEADERS: Domingo Cedeno (124 games-SS, 633 total chances-SS, 215 putouts-SS, 382 assists-SS, 74 double plays-SS); Jesse Cross (12.9 strikeouts per 9 IP-relief pitchers); Juan De La Rosa (529 at-bats); Ray Giannelli (18 home runs, 1/23.11 home runs per at-bats ratio); Jeff Kent (680 total chances-2B, 261 putouts-2B, 404 assists-2B, 83 double plays-2B); Anthony Ward (181.1 innings pitched, 137 strikeouts); Dave Weathers (27 games started).

MOST USED LINEUP

C	Jason Townley (90)
1B	Ray Giannelli (79)
2B	Jeff Kent (128)
3B	Mark Young (51)
SS	Domingo Cedeno (124)
OF	Juan De La Rosa (129)
OF	Ryan Thompson (116)
OF	Tim Hodge (89)
St	Dave Weathers (27)
Rel	Al Silverstein (45)

SYRACUSE CHIEFS

International League

MANAGER: Bob Bailor
RECORD: 62-83 (6th)
ALL-STARS: Luis Sojo, Mark Whiten.
LEAGUE LEADERS: Rob Ducey (4 double plays-OF); Jim Eppard (.310 batting average, 143 hits, 131 games-1B, .991 fielding percentage-1B, 1,113 total chances-1B, 1,010 putouts-1B, 93 assists-1B, 100 double plays-1B); Doug Linton (3 shutouts, 177.1 innings pitched); Luis Sojo (9 sacrifice flies); Ed Sprague (519 at-bats, 132 games-3B, 364 total chances-3B, 240 assists-3B).

MOST USED LINEUP

C	Carlos Diaz (77)
1B	Jim Eppard (131)
2B	Luis Sojo (67)
3B	Ed Sprague (132)
SS	Paul Runge (96)
OF	Rob Ducey (119)
OF	Derek Bell (104)
OF	Mark Whiten (92)
St	Doug Linton (26)
Rel	Tom Gilles 43)

MYRTLE BEACH BLUE JAYS

South Atlantic League

MANAGER: Mike Fischlin
RECORD: 77-63 (4th)
ALL-STARS: Shawn Holtzclaw
LEAGUE LEADERS: Gregg Martin (.135 batting average against-relief pitchers).

MOST USED LINEUP

C	Eric Brooks (60)
1B	William Abare (113)
2B	Billy Parese (118)
3B	Brad Mengel (103)
SS	Hector Mercedes (97)
OF	Shawn Holtzclaw (117)
OF	Nigel Wilson (97)
OF	Rick Holifield (89)
St	Aaron Small (27)
Rel	Eric Bradley (46)

1990 BLUE JAYS MINOR LEAGUE MONTHLY AWARDS

	PLAYER	PITCHER
April	Greg O'Halloran-Dunedin	Mike Timlin-Dunedin
May	William Suero-Knoxville	Denis Boucher-Dunedin
June	Ray Giannelli-Dunedin	Bob MacDonald-Knoxville
July	Nigel Wilson-Myrtle Beach	Greg Martin-Myrtle
August	Jim Eppard-Syracuse	Paul Menhart-Myrtle Beach

KNOXVILLE BLUE JAYS
Southern League

MANAGER: John Stearns
RECORD: 67-77 (6th)
ALL-STARS: William Suero, Eddie Zosky

LEAGUE LEADERS: Pete Blohm (3 shutouts); Tom Quinlan (139 games-3B, 103 putouts-3B); Paul Rodgers (142 games, 41 stolen bases, 14 sacrifice hits, 139 games-OF, 350 total chances-OF, 330 putouts-OF); Jimmy Rogers (30 games started); Greg Williams (9.05 baserunners per 9 IP ratio-relief pitchers); Eddie Zosky (.941 fielding percentage-SS, 196 putouts-SS, 80 double plays-SS).

MOST USED LINEUP

C	Randy Knorr (96)
1B	Domingo Martinez (83)
2B	William Suero (130)
3B	Tom Quinlan (139)
SS	Eddie Zosky (115)
OF	Paul Rodgers (129)
OF	Shawn Jeter (129)
OF	Bernie Nunez (101)
St	Jimmy Rogers (30)
Rel	Earl Sanders (37)

ST. CATHARINES BLUE JAYS
New York-Penn League

MANAGER: Doug Ault
RECORD: 29-47 (14th)
ALL-STARS: Carlos Delgado

LEAGUE LEADERS: Carlos Delgado (540 total chances-C, 471 putouts-C, 62 assists-C, 6 double plays-C); Wally Heckel (10 sacrifice hits, .973 fielding percentage-2B, 157 putouts-2B, 47 double plays-2B); Sam Mandia (13.50 strikeouts per 9 IP ratio-relief pitchers); Wilberto Rojas (50 doubleplays-1B); Shawn Scott (12 assists-OF).

MOST USED LINEUP

C	Carlos Delgado	(60)
1B	Wilberto Rojas	(60)
2B	Wally Heckel	(71)
3B	David Tollison	(41)
SS	Ciro Ambrosio	(40)
OF	Shawn Scott	(75)
OF	Anton Mobley	(63)
OF	Robert Perez	(51)
St	Rick Steed	(14)
	Mike L. Taylor	(14)
Rel	Russell Filter	(19)

MEDICINE HAT BLUE JAYS
Pioneer League

MANAGER: Garth Iorg
RECORD: 20-46 (7th)
ALL-STARS: None.

LEAGUE LEADERS: Brent Bowers (.992 fielding percentage-OF); Mark Choate (6 hit-by-pitch); Tim Hyers (61 games-1B, 565 total chances-1B, 516 putouts-1B).

MOST USED LINEUP

C	Kris Harmes (36)
1B	Tim Hyers (61)
2B	Mark Choate (51)
3B	Howard Battle (52)
SS	Hector Tavarez (37)
OF	Brent Bowers (60)
OF	Felix Septimo (37)
OF	Ron Reams (32)
St	Paul Spoljaric (13)
Rel	Thomas Hotchkiss (20)

ALL-TIME WON-LOST BREAKDOWN

	X-INN	DH	SHUTOUTS	1-RUNS	HRS
TORONTO vs	W-L	W-L-S	W-L	W-L	F-A
Baltimore	5-8	2-7-2	10-15	24-22	158-178
Boston	7-9	1-2-4	5-14	26-33	142-189
California	9-10	1-0-1	8-11	22-27	132-158
Chicago	7-1	3-0-4	13-9	26-24	141-136
Cleveland	13-5	4-3-8	2-11	31-27	163-136
Detroit	13-10	2-1-2	11-7	26-31	187-192
Kansas City	7-5	0-3-0	12-9	23-22	116-112
Milwaukee	6-9	1-8-2	4-15	22-27	124-137
Minnesota	6-9	1-3-1	10-8	19-27	150-121
New York	12-13	1-5-4	5-10	27-22	157-179
Oakland	3-12	1-2-2	9-9	26-24	143-147
Seattle	8-8	1-1-1	12-8	24-17	164-132
Texas	9-11	1-0-3	6-9	26-29	140-142
Total	105-111	18-35-34	107-135	322-333	1917-1959

BATTER	POS	'90 CLUB	AVG.	G	AB	R	H	2B	3B	HR	RBI	BB	SO	SB
ABARE, Bill	IF	Myrtle Beach	.251	118	391	49	98	19	0	10	44	59	121	1
AMBROSIO, Ciro	IF	St. Catharines	.245	68	216	24	53	12	2	0	22	43	51	7
BATTLE, Howard	IF	Medicine Hat	.266	61	233	25	62	17	1	5	32	15	38	5
BEACOM, Chris	IF	Dunedin	.227	84	238	26	54	14	4	2	24	17	52	0
BELL, Derek	OF	Syracuse	.261	109	402	54	105	13	5	7	56	23	75	21
BOWERS, Brent	OF	Medicine Hat	.274	60	212	30	58	7	3	3	27	31	35	19
BROOKS, Eric	C	Mrytle Beach	.263	68	213	26	56	8	0	3	22	44	34	1
CARLTON, Drew	IF	St. Catharines	.248	71	254	26	63	11	1	6	24	25	73	4
CEDENO, Domingo	IF	Dunedin	.221	124	493	64	109	12	10	7	61	48	127	10
CHOATE, Mark	IF	Medicine Hat	.234	62	214	30	50	7	1	2	22	33	51	11
COOLBAUGH, Mike	IF	Medicine Hat	.190	58	211	21	40	9	0	2	16	13	47	3
CRUMP, Gerry	IF	Medicine Hat	.000	1	5	0	0	0	0	0	0	0	2	0
DANIELS, Lee	OF	Medicine Hat	.168	31	95	3	16	3	0	0	9	7	39	4
de la Cruz, Hector	IF/OF	Syracuse	.234	83	235	27	55	9	0	4	19	17	54	4
DELGADO, Carlos	C	St. Catharines	.283	67	226	29	64	13	0	6	39	35	65	2
de la Rosa, Juan	OF	Dunedin	.257	131	529	57	136	19	8	10	76	19	98	9
DIAZ, Carlos	C	Syracuse	.203	77	251	18	51	10	0	1	19	17	51	2
DUCEY, Rob	OF	Syracuse	.267	127	438	53	117	32	7	7	47	60	87	13
DZIADKOWIEC, Andy	C	Knoxville	.221	38	122	7	27	3	0	0	12	11	20	2
	C	Syracuse	.000	1	3	0	0	0	0	0	0	0	1	0
EPPARD, Jim	IF	Syracuse	.310	133	461	72	143	18	3	4	48	47	49	5
ESCOBAR, Jose	IF	Syracuse	.270	79	252	16	68	6	2	0	17	18	35	3
GARCIA, Anastacio	C	Medicine Hat	.188	18	48	3	9	12	3	0	0	3	4	12
GARRISON, Webster	IF	Syracuse	.198	37	101	12	20	5	1	0	10	14	20	0
GIANNELLI, Ray	IF	Dunedin	.288	118	416	64	120	18	1	18	57	66	56	4
HARMES, Kris	C	St. Catharines	.500	3	10	1	5	0	0	0	1	0	2	0
	C/IF	Medicine Hat	.261	50	165	18	43	8	1	1	18	24	21	2
HECKEL, Wally	IF	St. Catharines	.203	73	197	30	40	2	0	0	10	33	64	6
HINES, Keith	OF	Medicine Hat	.262	38	126	15	33	2	4	3	14	14	41	4
HODGE, Tim	OF	Dunedin	.244	91	291	30	71		2	3	30	37	90	5
HOLIFIELD, Rick	OF	Myrtle Beach	.201	99	279	37	56	9	2	3	18	28	88	13
HOLTZCLAW, Shawn	OF	Myrtle Beach	.252	133	476	63	120	28	1	14	72	52	123	1
HUDIK, Matthew	IF	St. Catharines	.148	18	27	4	4	2	0	0	1	2	2	2
HYERS, Tim	IF	Medicine Hat	.219	61	224	29	49	7	2	2	19	29	22	4
IRISH, Jeff	C	St. Catharines	.135	16	37	2	5	0	0	0	0	8	11	1
		Dunedin	.200	10	15	2	3	0	0	0	1	4	5	0
JAIME, Juan	C	Myrtle Beach	.197	66	203	14	40	4	1	4	21	14	34	1
JETER, Shawn	OF	Knoxville	.273	131	461	67	126	25	2	4	43	39	95	25
KENT, Jeff	IF	Dunedin	.277	132	447	72	124	32	2	16	60	53	98	17
LOEB, Marc	C	Medicine Hat	.302	29	96	15	29	5	0	2	12	14	28	2
MAKSUDIAN, Mike	IF/OF/C	Knoxville	.287	121	422	51	121	22	5	8	55	50	66	6
MARTINEZ, Domingo	IF	Knoxville	.257	128	463	52	119	20	3	17	67	51	81	2
MARQUEZ, Edgar	OF/C	St. Catharines	.176	36	102	6	18	3	0	2	7	10	39	4
MENGEL, Brad	IF/OF	Myrtle Beach	.273	115	403	50	110	17	1	5	47	36	80	4
MERCEDES, Hector	IF	Myrtle Beach	.196	98	326	37	64	11	0	4	24	14	77	7
MILLER, Scott	IF/OF	Myrtle Beach	.249	96	313	41	78	18	0	4	32	44	44	5
	IF	Dunedin	.214	17	42	2	9	0	0	0	5	2	7	0
MOBLEY, Anton	OF	St. Catharines	.185	66	211	26	39	4	2	7	25	27	90	4
	OF	Myrtle Beach	.181	52	177	20	32	1	0	6	13	11	78	1
MONTALVO, Robert	IF	St. Catharines	.183	38	115	11	21	2	0	0	5	21	19	1
	IF	Myrtle Beach	.200	45	125	15	25	1	0	0	11	9	14	2
MONZAN, Jose	C	Dunedin	.303	30	76	11	23	5	1	0	7	10	18	1
	C	Knoxville	.333	1	3	1	1	0	0	0	0	0	0	0
MORRISON, Brian		Knoxville	.000	1	1	0	0	0	0	0	0	0	1	0
MUNZO, Pedro	OF	Syracuse	.319	86	317	41	101	22	3	7	56	24	64	16
MYERS, Greg	C	Syracuse	.182	3	11	0	2	1	0	0	2	1	1	0
NUNEZ, Bernie	OF	Knoxville	.233	104	313	30	73	11	5	2	39	16	67	10
O'HALLORAN, Greg	C	Dunedin	.284	121	465	70	132	26	4	11	75	37	70	2
PARESE, Bill	IF	Myrtle Beach	.237	121	439	67	104	16	5	5	46	60	73	16
PEDERSON, Stu	OF	Syracuse	.296	96	301	34	89	12	1	2	34	42	40	5
PEREZ, Robert	OF	St. Catharines	.261	52	207	20	54	10	2	5	25	8	34	7
	OF	Myrtle Beach	.292	21	72	8	21	2	0	1	10	3	9	2
PROVENCE, Todd	IF/OF	Myrtle Beach	.236	98	330	55	78	15	2	10	38	43	117	12
	IF/OF	Dunedin	.197	19	61	10	12	3	1	1	6	3	22	2
QUERCUTO, Juan	IF	St. Catharines	.200	9	20	0	4	1	0	0	2	2	4	0
QUINLAN, Tom	IF	Knoxville	.258	141	481	70	124	24	6	15	51	49	157	8
REAMS, Ron	IF/OF	Medicine Hat	.243	48	206	28	50	10	2	3	15	5	30	12
RIVERS, Ken	OF/C	Myrtle Beach	.299	100	358	51	107	18	2	12	67	31	61	0
	C	Syracuse	.000	1	1	0	0	0	0	0	0	0	0	0
ROBERTS, Lonell	IF/OF	Medicine Hat	.212	38	118	14	25	2	0	0	8	5	29	8
RODGERS, Paul	OF	Knoxville	.228	142	482	64	110	15	4	4	35	49	84	41
ROJAS, Wilberto	IF	St. Catharines	.231	63	212	21	49	2	1	4	19	20	56	1
RUNGE, Paul	IF/OF	Syracuse	.232	119	392	45	91	10	3	6	31	59	67	3
SCHUNK, Jerry	IF	Knoxville	.288	85	274	32	79	13	1	3	31	9	25	8
	IF	Syracuse	.240	26	100	8	24	4	0	0	7	3	10	1
SCOTT, Shawn	OF	St. Catharines	.284	75	278	30	79	10	2	1	14	30	54	31
SEPTIMO, Felix	OF	Medicine Hat	.219	43	155	15	34	5	5	2	17	10	62	4
SOJO, Luis	IF	Syracuse	.296	75	297	39	88	12	3	6	25	14	23	10
SPRAGUE, Ed	IF	Syracuse	.239	142	519	60	124	23	5	20	75	31	100	4
SUERO., William	IF	Knoxville	.263	133	483	80	127	29	7	16	60	78	78	40
SZEKELY, Joe	C	Syracuse	.174	50	155	17	27	3	2	5	16	10	20	1
TAVAREZ, Hector	IF	Medicine Hat	.279	39	136	18	38	7	2	0	12	9	28	4

BATTER	POS	'90 CLUB	AVG.	G	AB	R	H	2B	3B	HR	RBI	BB	SO	SB
TAVERAS, Marcos	OF	Dunedin	.258	41	62	16	16	2	1	2	6	7	15	2
TAYLOR, Mike	IF	Dunedin	.237	69	169	29	40	7	0	0	14	32	37	8
	IF/OF	Knoxville	.133	12	15	2	2	0	0	0	2	2	6	1
THOMPSON, Ryan	OF	Dunedin	.231	117	438	56	101	15	5	6	37	20	100	18
TOLLISON, David	IF	St. Catharines	.214	42	154	14	33	6	0	2	14	13	25	2
TOWNLEY, Jason	C	Dunedin	.292	119	397	58	116	22	1	11	63	41	82	1
VIRGIL, Ozzie	IF	Syracuse	.143	28	84	5	12	2	0	0	7	9	16	0
WHITEN, Mark	OF	Syracuse	.290	104	390	65	113	19	4	14	48	37	72	14
WILSON, Nigel	OF	Mrytle Beach	.273	110	440	77	120	23	9	16	62	30	71	22
YAN, Julian	IF	Knoxville	.244	113	389	55	95	18	3	15	48	25	108	2
YORRO, Jacinto	OF	St. Catharines	.231	28	91	10	21	2	0	1	12	8	14	1
YOUNG, Mark	IF/OF	Dunedin	.237	117	409	72	97	14	6	5	38	58	88	31
ZOSKY, Eddie	IF	Knoxville	.271	115	450	53	122	20	7	3	45	26	73	3

PITCHER	R/L	'90 CLUB	W-L	ERA	G	GS	CG	SV	IP	HR	R	ER	BB	SO
ADAMS, Morgan	R	Medicine Hat	0-1	8.49	13	2	0	0	23.1	37	26	22	20	17
AYLMER, Robert	L	St. Catharines	1-2	3.68	12	0	0	2	14.2	18	9	6	4	11
		Dunedin	2-3	2.64	20	0	0	2	30.2	32	15	9	8	19
BICKNELL, Greg	R	Myrtle Beach	5-4	3.65	34	15	0	0	120.2	118	63	49	45	89
BLAIR, Willie	R	Syracuse	0-2	4.74	3	3	1	0	19.0	20	13	10	8	6
BLOHM, Pete	R	Syracuse	0-1	7.20	4	0	0	0	5.0	5	7	4	3	4
		Knoxville	5-5	4.50	30	12	3	2	108.0	101	58	54	37	53
		Dunedin	1-0	1.29	2	0	0	1	7.0	5	1	1	0	6
BLUMBERG, Rob	L	Myrtle Beach	13-4	2.16	25	23	1	0	129.1	101	43	31	68	128
BOUCHER, Denis	L	Dunedin	17-0	.75	9	9	2	0	60.0	45	8	5	8	62
		Syracuse	8-5	3.85	17	17	2	0	107.2	100	51	46	37	80
BRADLEY, Eric	R	Myrtle Beach	2-4	3.31	46	0	0	8	73.1	80	34	27	19	77
BROW, Scott	R	St. Catharines	3-1	2.27	9	7	0	0	39.2	34	18	10	11	39
BROWN, Daren	R	Myrtle Beach	11-7	4.11	25	25	0	0	142.1	153	81	65	51	120
BROWN, Tim	R	Dunedin	2-3	4.43	36	0	0	1	67.0	76	41	33	18	55
BUCHANAN, Bob	L	Syracuse	5-3	3.52	24	6	1	5	64.0	63	32	25	25	21
BURLEY, Travis	R	Medicine Hat	3-4	6.69	12	7	0	0	36.1	34	32	27	37	23
BURRELL, Scott	R	St. Catharines	1-4	5.86	7	7	0	0	27.2	29	20	18	15	24
CROMWELL, Nate	L	Knoxville	5-14	5.56	27	23	2	0	121.1	119	85	75	91	79
CROSS, Jesse	R	Dunedin	13-7	3.29	28	18	0	0	139.1	100	54	51	70	126
CUMMINGS, Steve	R	Syracuse	5-3	3.11	16	13	4	0	81.0	76	31	28	37	34
DARLEY, Ned	R	Medicine Hat	0-4	4.71	9	8	0	0	28.2	29	24	15	26	13
DELACRUZ, Hector	R	Syracuse	0-0	9.00	1	0	0	0	1.0	3	7	1	3	1
DEPASTINO, Rich	R	Dunedin	6-3	5.02	22	14	0	0	84.1	85	54	47	57	72
DUEY, Kyle	R	Medicine Hat	4-6	3.86	15	11	0	0	72.1	72	38	31	34	54
FILTER, Russell	R	St.Catharines	0-2	4.50	19	0	0	2	22.0	28	13	11	7	21
FLENER, Huck	L	St. Catharines	4-3	3.36	14	7	0	1	61.2	45	29	23	33	46
FLETCHER,David	R	Medicine Hat	0-0	14.73	3	0	0	0	3.2	8	6	6	4	1
GANOTE, John	R	St. Catharines	3-0	2.73	18	0	0	4	29.2	26	9	9	7	33
GARCIA, Rafael	R	MedicineHat	3-5	5.05	13	8	0	1	57.0	68	44	32	32	37
GILLES, Tom	R	Syracuse	3-3	2.14	43	0	0	5	71.1	58	22	17	20	44
GILLIGAN, John	R	Medicine Hat	1-6	2.75	18	2	1	1	55.2	58	28	17	10	43
GOZZO, Mauro	R	Syracuse	3-8	3.58	34	10	0	7	98.0	87	46	39	44	62
GUZMAN, Juan	R	Knoxville	11-9	4.24	37	21	2	1	157.0	145	84	74	80	138
HALL, Daren	R	Knoxville	3-5	4.86	28	0	0	1	33.1	29	23	18	33	28
HENTGEN, Pat	R	Knoxville	9-5	3.05	28	26	0	0	153.1	121	57	52	68	142
HORSMAN, Vince	L	Knoxville	2-1	4.63	8	0	0	0	11.2	11	7	6	5	10
		Dunedin	4-7	3.24	28	0	0	1	50.0	53	21	18	15	41
HOTCHKISS, Tom	R	Medicine Hat	1-2	4.91	20	0	0	0	36.2	42	24	20	23	29
HUTSON, Scott	R	Myrtle Beach	0-2	4.85	13	1	0	2	26.0	21	15	14	13	25
JONES, Chris	R	Knoxville	4-4	5.05	37	0	0	1	76.2	79	49	43	39	58
		Syracuse	0-0	3.98	10	0	0	1	20.1	22	10	9	4	19
JONES, Dennis	L	Knoxville	0-1	7.97	9	4	0	0	20.1	13	22	18	34	25
JORDAN, Ricardo	L	Dunedin	0-2	2.38	13	2	0	0	22.2	15	9	6	19	16
KARSAY, Steve	R	St. Catharines	1-1	.79	5	5	0	0	22.2	11	4	2	12	25
KEY, Jimmy	L	Dunedin	2-0	2.50	3	3	0	0	18.0	21	7	5	3	14
KILGUS, Paul	L	Syracuse	6-8	2.94	20	17	7	0	125.2	116	47	41	39	75
KISTAITIS, Dale	L	Medicine Hat	1-4	4.50	12	10	0	0	52.0	44	37	26	29	54
KIZZIAH, Daren	R	Myrtle Beach	6-6	3.47	35	6	1	4	98.2	103	56	38	35	48
KOWER, Frank	R	St. Catharines	0-1	2.84	15	0	0	2	31.2	38	14	10	11	17
KULINA, Kenny	L	Myrtle Beach	3-3	4.60	28	0	0	3	47.0	50	30	24	20	40
LEITER, Al	L	Dunedin	0-0	2.63	6	6	0	0	24.0	18	8	7	12	14
		Syracuse	3-8	4.62	15	14	1	0	78.0	59	43	40	68	69
LINTON, Doug	R	Syracuse	10-10	3.40	26	26	8	0	177.1	174	77	67	67	113
LLOYD, Graeme	L	Myrtle Beach	5-2	2.72	19	6	0	6	49.2	51	20	15	16	42
LOYND Mike	R	Syracuse	4-8	3.68	24	8	0	1	85.2	68	39	35	34	65
LYSANDER, Rick	R	Syracuse	0-1	6.92	10	0	0	0	13.0	18	10	10	7	8
MACDONALD, Bob	L	Knoxville	1-2	1.89	36	0	0	15	57.0	37	17	12	29	54
		Syracuse	0-2	5.40	9	0	0	2	8.1	4	5	5	9	6
MANDIA, Sam	R	St. Catharines	1-1	2.70	8	0	0	2	16.2	12	6	5	8	25
		Myrtle Beach	0-1	.64	9	0	0	4	14.0	6	1	1	4	16
MARCON, Dave	L	St. Catharines	3-5	3.61	16	4	0	2	52.1	53	27	21	12	44
MARTIN, Gregg	R	Myrtle Beach	2-4	2.39	37	0	0	16	49.0	22	16	13	34	71
		Dunedin	2-1	3.77	12	0	0	6	14.1	10	7	6	11	16
MARTINEZ, Domingo	R	Knoxville	0-0	3.00	3	0	0	0	3.0	5	1	1	0	3
MENHART, Paul	R	Myrtle Beach	3-0	.59	5	4	1	0	30.2	18	5	2	5	18
		St. Catharines	0-5	4.05	8	8	0	0	40.0	34	27	18	19	38

PITCHER	R/L	'90 CLUB	W-L	ERA	G	GS	CG	SV	IP	HR	R	ER	BB	SO
MILLER, Scott	R	Medicine Hat	0-0	1.19	19	0	0	5	22.2	18	12	3	13	19
NELLENBACK, Rodney	R	St. Catharines	0-0	3.52	5	0	0	1	7.2	8	4	3	0	10
NOWAK, Rich	R	Myrtle Beach	1-2	2.33	5	5	0	0	27.0	17	8	7	12	29
OGLIARUSO, Mike	R	Myrtle Beach	14-9	2.52	26	26	2	0	164.1	132	57	46	61	160
OLVARES, Jose	L	Myrtle Beach	0-1	3.86	8	0	0	0	11.2	13	6	5	7	5
ORMAN, Rick	L	Medicine Hat	1-2	8.42	19	0	0	1	25.2	39	28	24	16	24
PEDERSON, Stu	L	Syracuse	0-0	9.00	1	0	0	0	1.0	2	1	1	1	0
PEREZ, Jose	R	Medicine Hat	0-3	10.74	11	4	0	0	31.0	47	44	37	15	21
RAUTH, Chris	R	Knoxville	0-1	6.75	8	0	0	0	17.1	23	16	13	13	16
REESE, Jason	R	Medicine Hat	1-0	6.48	17	0	0	0	25.0	31	19	18	27	19
RHEA, Allen	R	St. Catharines	2-4	3.22	16	4	0	0	44.2	49	18	16	13	42
ROGERS, Jimmy	R	Knoxville	9-12	4.47	31	30	2	0	173.1	179	98	86	104	113
RUDOLPH, Blaine	R	Dunedin	3-0	3.11	35	5	0	4	81.0	71	37	28	45	62
SANCHEZ, Alex	R	Syracuse	5-9	5.71	22	22	1	0	112.0	111	77	71	79	65
SANDERS, Earl	R	Knoxville	4-4	4.75	37	0	0	2	60.2	63	41	32	57	39
SCHUNK, Jerry	R	Knoxville	0-0	.00	2	0	0	0	2.1	3	0	0	0	1
SHEA, John	L	Syracuse	8-5	3.64	40	0	0	3	81.2	83	45	33	40	58
SILVERSTEIN, Al	R	Dunedin	7-5	2.26	45	0	0	6	75.2	52	28	19	34	70
SINGER, Thomas	L	St. Catharines	2-3	4.66	13	4	0	1	38.2	38	24	20	23	44
SMALL, Aaron	R	Myrtle Beach	9-9	2.80	27	27	1	0	147.2	150	72	46	56	96
SPOLJARIC, Paul	L	Medicine Hat	3-7	4.34	15	13	0	1	66.1	57	43	32	35	62
STEED, Ricky	R	St. Catharines	3-6	3.07	14	14	0	0	73.1	58	32	25	39	72
TAYLOR, Michael	L	St. Catharines	4-6	3.88	14	14	1	0	72.0	66	35	31	49	54
TIMLIN, Mike	R	Dunedin	1-2	1.73	17	0	0	8	26.0	20	6	5	7	21
		Knoxville	7-2	1.43	42	0	0	22	50.1	36	11	8	16	46
TRLICEK, Rick	R	Dunedin	5-8	3.73	26	26	0	0	154.1	128	74	64	72	125
WANISH, John	R	Myrtle Beach	3-5	4.24	35	2	0	5	74.1	78	41	35	37	69
WAPNICK, Steve	R	Syracuse	0-1	5.06	11	1	0	2	16.0	16	9	9	6	19
WARD, Anthony	L	Dunedin	14-6	2.83	27	26	1	0	181.1	150	63	57	39	137
WATSON, Mathew	R	St. Catharines	1-3	4.70	16	2	0	0	38.1	30	28	20	29	39
WEATHERS, Dave	R	Dunedin	10-7	3.70	27	27	2	0	158.0	158	82	65	59	96
WILCOX, Greg	R	Medicine	Hat	2-2	4.21	13	1	0	36.1	39	22	17	27	49
WILLIAMS, Woody	R	Knoxville	7-9	3.14	42	12	0	5	126.0	111	55	44	39	74
		Syracuse	0-1	10.00	3	0	0	0	9.0	15	10	10	4	8
WISHNEVSKI, Rob	R	Syracuse	2-5	6.66	9	8	0	0	48.2	65	40	36	23	28
		Knoxville	6-3	3.83	20	17	1	1	105.2	84	54	45	39	74

1990 BLUE JAYS MINOR LEAGUE OFFENSIVE LEADERS

RBI	RUNS	HITS
DE LA ROSA-76	SUERO-80	EPPARD-143
O'HALLORAN-75	WILSON-77	DE LA ROSA-136
SPRAGUE-75	EPPARD-72	O'HALLORAN-132
HOLTZCLAW-72	KENT-72	SUERO-127
MARTINEZ-67	YOUNG-72	JETER-67
RIVERS-67	O'HALLORAN-70	KENT-124
KNORR-64	QUINLAN-70	QUINLAN-124
TOWNLEY-63	JETER-67	ZOSKY-122
WILSON-62	PARESE-67	MAKSUDIAN-121
CEDENO-61	WHITEN-65	GIANNELLI-120
		HOLTZCLAW-120
		WILSON-120

BATTING AVERAGE	AT BATS	ON BASE PCT.
EPPARD-.310	DE LA ROSA-529	GIANNELLI-.385
RIVERS-.298	SPRAGUE-519	PEDERSON-.385
PEDERSON-.296	CEDENO-493	EPPARD-.374
TOWNLEY-.292	SUERO-483	RIVERS-.373
WHITEN-.290	RODGERS-482	SUERO-.372
GIANNELLI-.288	QUINLAN-481	MAKSUDIAN-.364
MAKSUDIAN-.284	HOLTZCLAW-476	DUCEY-.360
O'HALLORAN-.284	O'HALLORAN-465	KENT-.360
KENT-.277	MARTINEZ-463	TOWNLEY-.360
KNORR-.276	EPPARD-461	WHITEN-.353
		JETER-461

TOTAL BASES	SLUGGING PCT.	HOME RUNS
SUERO-218	WILSON-.475	SPRAGUE-20
SPRAGUE-217	WHITEN-.467	GIANNELLI-18
WILSON-209	GIANNELLI-.466	MARTINEZ-17
KENT-208	KENT-.465	KENT-16
QUINLAN-205	RIVERS-.461	SUERO-16
DE LA ROSA-201	SUERO-.461	WILSON-16
O'HALLORAN-199	TOWNLEY-.436	QUINLAN-15
MARTINEZ-196	O'HALLORAN-.428	YAN-15
GIANNELLI-194	QUINLAN-.426	HOLTZCLAW-14
HOLTZCLAW-192	MARTINEZ-.423	WHITEN-14

LAST TIME—BLUE JAYS

NO-HITTER: Dave Stieb, Sept. 2, 1990 at Cleveland (won 3-0)
ONE-HITTER: Dave Stieb, Aug 26, 1989 vs Kansas City (won 8-0)
TWO-HITTER: John Cerutti, Aug 2, 1989 vs Kansas City (won 8--0)
10- OR MORE STRIKEOUTS, ONE GAME: Dave Stieb (11), Aug 4, 1989 vs New York (won 2-1)
SHUTOUT: Dave Stieb (8.0), Tom Henke (1.0), Sept 8, 1990 vs Chicago (won 3-0)
BACK-TO-BACK SHUTOUTS, SAME PITCHER: Dave Stieb, Sept 18, 24, 30, 1988
PITCHER TO BAT: Dave Stieb, Aug 29, 1980 vs Minnesota
PITCHER TO APPEAR OFFENSIVELY: Dave Stieb, May 17, 1988, pinch runner vs Texas
CONSECUTIVE SHUTOUTS: Todd Stottlemyre (7.1), John Candelaria (1.2) (8-0 at Cleveland),, Sept 1; Dave Stieb (3-0 at Cleveland), Sept 2, 1990
CONSECUTIVE SHUTOUTS—COMPLETE GAMES: Jimmy Key (1-0) at Boston), Sept 28: Dave Stieb (4-0 vs Baltimore), Sept 30, 1988
INSIDE-THE-PARK HOME RUN: Junior Felix, June 2, 1989 at Boston
TWO HOME RUNS, ONE GAME: Kelly Gruber, Sept 8, 1990 vs Chicago
BACK-TO-BACK HOME RUNS: Fred McGriff, Greg Myers, Sept 9, 1990 vs Chicago
BACK-TO-BACK-TO-BACK HOME RUNS: Ernie Whitt, Jesse Barfield, Kelly Gruber, Sept 12, 1987 vs New York (8th inning)
FIVE HITS, ONE GAME: George Bell, Sept 24, 1990 at Milwaukee
THREE OR MORE STEALS, ONE GAME: Lloyd Moseby, Sept 10, 1989 at Cleveland
STEALING HOME: Lloyd Moseby, July 27, 1987 vs Boston (1st inning)
BATTING FOR THE CYCLE: Kelly Gruber, April 16, 1989 vs Kansas City
THREE HOME RUNS, ONE GAME: George Bell, April 4, 1988 at Kansas City
GRAND SLAM HOME RUN: Kelly Gruber, Sept 29, 1990 at Boston
FOUR HITS, ONE GAME: Fred McGriff, Sept 30, 1990 at Boston
PINCH HIT HOME RUN: Lee Mazzilli, Sept 9, 1989 at Cleveland
TWO HITS, SAME INNING: Junior Felix, June 23, 1989 at Oakland (first inning)
1-0 GAME: Lost vs Boston, Aug 26, 1990
BACK-TO-BACK COMPLETE GAMES: Jimmy Key (beat Boston 1-0), Dave Stieb (beat Baltimore 4-0), Sept 28; 30, 1988
BACK-TO-BACK COMPLETE GAME VICTORIES: Jimmy Key (beat Boston 1-0), Dave Stieb (beat Baltimore 4-0), Sept 28;30, 1988

LAST TIME—OPPONENTS

PERFECT GAME: Len Barker at Cleveland (won 3-0) May 15, 1981
NO-HITTER: Dave Stewart (Oakland won 5-0, June 29, 1990
ONE-HITTER: Kirk McCaskill (Angels won 9-0), at California, April 28, 1989
TWO-HITTER: Greg Harris (7.2IP, 2H), Jeff Gray (1.1IP), vs Boston (Boston won 1-0)
TEN OR MORE STRIKEOUTS: Mark Gubicza (10), Aug 12, 1989 at Kansas City (Toronto won 2-0)
SHUTOUT: Ron Robinson (9.0) at Milwaukee, Sept 26, 1990 (Brewers won 6-0)
BACK-TO-BACK SHUTOUTS: 2-0 and 1-0, 15 inn at Oakland July 26-27, 1986 (9 pitchers combined)
INSIDE-THE-PART HOME RUN: Jim Sundberg, Texas, Sept 4, 1988 (Frank Wills)
TWO HOME RUNS, ONE GAME: Joe Carter, at Cleveland, Sept 9, 1989
THREE HOME RUNS ONE GAME: Tom Brunansky, at Boston, Sept 29, 1990
GRAND SLAM HOME RUN: Sam Horn (Baltimore), at Toronto, Sept 14, 1990
BACK-TO-BACK HOME RUNS: Candy Maldonado, Chris James (Cleveland), at Toronto, Sept 14, 1990 (6th inning)
BACK-TO-BACK-TO-BACK HOME RUNS: Rudy Law, Bryan Little, Harold Baines, at Chicago, Aug 24, 1985 (9th inning)
FIVE HITS, ONE GAME: Kirby Puckett (Minnesota), at Toronto, June 6, 1990
FOUR HITS, ONE GAME: George Brett (Kansas City), at Kansas City, Sept 12, 1990
TWO OR MORE STEALS, ONE GAME: Rickey Henderson (2), at Oakland, Oct 4, 1989 (GM 2-ALCS)
PINCH HIT HOME RUN: Sam Horn (Slam), vs Baltimore, Sept 14, 1990

BASE THEFTS ABOUND: On August 5, 1984 at Baltimore the Blue Jays set a club record with seven stolen bases. Dave Collins and Willie Upshaw each set personal highs with four and two respectively while Lloyd Moseby picked up one. Ironically, not one of the seven bases figured in the scoring of a Blue Jays 4-3 win.

NUM	YTD M/D	OPP	H/R	D/N	TIME OF GAME	ATTENDANCE	HOME	ROAD	H/R DATE
1	4/09	TEX	R	N	3:07	40,907		40,907	1
2	4/10	TEX	H	N	2:59	49,673	49,673		1
3	4/11	TEX	H	N	2:46	35,031	84,704		2
4	4/12	TEX	H	N	2:38	35,354	120,058		3
5	4/13	KC	R	N	2:23	20,522		61,429	2
6	4/14	KC	R	D	2:22	25,930		87,359	3
7	4/15	KC	R	D	3:09	21,925		109,284	4
8	4/16	BAL	H	D	2:35	40,301	160,359		4
9	4/17	BAL	H	N	2:36	38,212	198,571		5
10	4/18	BAL	H	N	3:06	41,181	239,752		6
11	4/20	KC	H	N	3:04	49,151	288,903		7
12	4/21	KC	H	D	3:02	49,121	338,024		8
13	4/22	KC	H	D	2:54	49,056	387,080		9
14	4/23	CLE	H	N	3:04	34,139	421,219		10
15	4/24	CLE	H	N	2:32	35,203	456,422		11
16	4/25	CLE	H	N	2:29	38,168	494,590		12
17	4/26	CLE	H	D	2:41	44,174	538,764		13
18	4/27	CWS	R	N	2:29	10,965		120,249	5
19	4/28	CWS	R	N	2:48	15,395		135,644	6
20	4/29	CWS	R	D	2:40	12,936		148,580	7
21	4/30	CLE	R	N	2:36	6,253		154,833	8
YTD TOTAL						**693,764**	**538,764**	**154,833**	
22	5/01	CLE	R	N	2:46	5,111		159,944	9
23	5/02	CLE	R	N	2:17	5,985		165,929	10
24	5/04	DET	H	N	2:42	49,146	587,910		14
25	5/05	DET	H	D	2:45	49,219	637,129		15
26	5/06	DET	H	D	2:53	49,206	686,335		16
27	5/07	CWS	H	N	3:08	41,384	727,719		17
28	5/08	CWS	H	N	3:05	41,101	768,820		18
29	5/09	CWS	H	N	2:54	43,128	811,948		19
30	5/10	DET	R	N	3:03	11,296		177,225	11
31	5/11	DET	R	N	2:55	17,376		194,601	12
32	5/13	DET	R	D	2:53	17,068		211,669	13
33	5/14	DET	R	D	3:38	10,833		222,502	14
34	5/15	SEA	H	N	3:25	41,108	853,056		20
35	5/16	SEA	H	N	2:42	45,640	898,696		21
36	5/17	SEA	H	D	2:55	47,283	945,979		22
37	5/18	CAL	H	N	2:57	49,339	995,318		23
38	5/19	CAL	H	D	3:18	49,335	1,044,653		24
39	5/20	CAL	H	D	2:45	49,421	1,094,074		25
40	5/21	OAK	H	D	2:49	49,471	1,143,545		26
41	5/22	OAK	H	D	3:0	149,559	1,193,104		27
42	5/23	CAL	R	N	2:53	25,179		247,681	15
43	5/24	CAL	R	N	3:54	24,460		272,141	16
44	5/25	SEA	R	N	3:32	15,341		287,482	17
45	5/26	SEA	R	N	3:14	25,018		312,500	18
46	5/27	SEA	R	N	3:02	25,889		338,389	19
47	5/28	OAK	R	N	2:43	45,005		383,394	20
48	5/29	OAK	R	N	2:41	25,255		408,649	21
49	5/30	OAK	R	D	2:53	24,257		432,906	22
YTD TOTAL						**1,625,959**	**1,193,104**	**432,906**	
50	6/01	MIL	H	N	2:48	49,698	1,242,802		28
51	6/02	MIL	H	D	3:27	49,553	1,292,355		29
52	6/03	MIL	H	D	3:17	49,702	1,342,057		30
53	6/05	MIN	H	N	2:48	49,741	1,391,798		31
54	6/06	MIN	H	D	3:05	49,652	1,441,450		32
55	6/07	MIN	H	N	2:28	49,845	1,491,295		33
56	6/08	MIL	R	N	3:28	27,021		459,927	23
57	6/09	MIL	R	N	3:03	46,612		506,539	24
58	6/10	MIL	R	N	3:16	18,091		524,630	25
59	6/11	MIL	R	N	2:37	17,701		542,331	26
60	6/12	MIN	R	N	2:44	18,298		560,629	27
61	6/13	MIN	R	N	2:59	17,086		577,715	28
62	6/14	MIN	R	N	2:28	18,679		596,394	29
63	6/15	NYY	R	N	3:13	31,827		628,221	30
64	6/16	NYY	R	N	3:53	26,061		654,282	31
65	6/17	NYY	R	D	2:26	38,173		692,455	32
66	6/19	BOS	H	N	2:34	49,907	1,541,202		34
67	6/20	BOS	H	N	2:49	49,857	1,591,059		35
68	6/21	NYY	H	N	3:28	49,883	1,640,942		36
69	6/22	NYY	H	N	4:53	49,808	1,690,750		37
70	6/23	NYY	H	D	3:13	49,858	1,740,608		38
71	6/24	NYY	H	D	3:09	49,806	1,790,414		39
72	6/25	BOS	R	N	3:14	32,591		725,046	33
73	6/26	BOS	R	N	2:39	33,244		758,290	34
74	6/27	BOS	R	N	2:59	32,961		791,251	35
75	6/28	BOS	R	N	2:46	34,547		825,798	36
76	6/29	OAK	H	N	2:27	49,817	1,840,231		40
77	6/30	OAK	H	D	3:04	49,865	1,890,096		41
YTD TOTAL						**2,715,843**	**1,890,096**	**825,74798**	

NUM	YTD M/D	OPP	H/R	D/N	TIME OF GAME	ATTENDANCE	HOME	ROAD	H/R DATE
78	7/01	OAK	H	D	3:15	49,857	1,939,953		42
79	7/02	OAK	H	D	2:35	49,855	1,989,808		43
80	7/03	CAL	H	N	2:53	49,836	2,039,644		44
81	7/04	CAL	H	N	2:53	49,831	2,089,475		45
82	7/05	CAL	H	N	2:55	49,838	2,139,313		46
83	7/06	SEA	H	N	2:28	49,872	2,189,185		47
84	7/07	SEA	H	D	2:22	49,899	2,239,084		48
85	7/08	SEA	H	D	2:35	49,816	2,288,900		49
86	7/12	CAL	R	N	2:59	27,365		853,163	37
87	7/13	CAL	R	N	2:05	35,001		888,164	38
88	7/14	CAL	R	N	3:40	34,466		922,630	39
89	7/15	CAL	R	D	2:48	31,609		954,239	40
90	7/16	SEA	R	N	2:45	24,838		979,077	41
91	7/17	SEA	R	N	3:00	14,274		993,351	42
92	7/18	SEA	R	D	2:32	15,867		1,009,218	43
93	7/20	OAK	R	N	3:15	40,171		1,049,389	44
94	7/21	OAK	R	D	2:40	43,097		1,092,486	45
95	7/22	OAK	R	D	2:10	43,821		1,136,307	46
96	7/24	KC	H	N	4:07	49,884	2,338,784		50
97	7/25	KC	H	N	2:30	49,855	2,388,639		51
98	7/26	KC	H	N	2:40	49,862	2,438,501		52
99	7/27	TEX	H	N	2:37	49,882	2,488,383		53
100	7/28	TEX	H	D	4:15	49,850	2,538,233		54
101	7/29	TEX	H	D	3:20	49,853	2,588,086		55
102	7/30	BAL	R	N	2:57	43,638		1,179,945	47
103	7/31	BAL	R	N	3:24	37,771		1,217,716	48
YTD TOTAL						**3,805,802**	**2,588,086**	**1,217,716**	
104	8/01	BAL	R	N	3:17	40,625		1,258,341	49
105	8/02	TEX	R	N	3:34	30,809		1,289,150	50
106	8/03	TEX	R	N	2:33	23,728		1,312,878	51
107	8/04	TEX	R	N	2:36	35,211		1,348,089	52
108	8/05	TEX	R	N	3:02	41,523		1,389,612	53
109	8/06	TEX	R	N	3:01	28,645		1,418,257	54
110	8/07	DET	H	N	2:44	49,894	2,637,980		56
111	8/08	DET	H	N	3:11	49,897	2,687,877		57
112	8/09	DET	H	N	3:00	49,911	2,737,788		58
113	8/10	MIN	H	N	2:22	49,888	2,787,676		59
114	8/11	MIN	H	D	2:45	49,873	2,837,549		60
115	8/12	MIN	H	D	2:18	49,892	2,887,441		61
116	8/13	CWS	R	N	3:15	28,961		1,447,218	55
117	8/14	CWS	R	N	2:46	24,314		1,471,532	56
118	8/15	CWS	R	N	2:46	27,947		1,499,479	57
119	8/17	MIN	R	N	2:42	28,173		1,527,652	58
120	8/18	MIN	R	N	2:12	32,601		1,560,253	59
121	8/19	MIN	R	D	2:31	29,004		1,589,257	60
122	8/20	NYY	R	N	3:38	21,661		1,610,257	61
123	8/21	NYY	R	N	2:46	22,315		1,633,273	62
124	8/22	NYY	R	N	2:45	25,088		1,658,321	63
125	8/23	BOS	H	N	3:12	49,918	2,937,359		62
126	8/24	BOS	H	N	2:45	49,914	2,987,273		63
127	8/25	BOS	H	D	2:47	49,890	3,037,163		64
128	8/26	BOS	H	D	2:49	49,897	3,087,060		65
129	8/27	MIL	H	N	2:28	49,892	3,136,952		66
130	8/28	MIL	H	N	2:27	49,871	3,186,823		67
131	8/29	MIL	H	D	2:42	49,909	3,236,732		68
132	8/31	CLE	R	N	3:44	12,508		1,670,829	64
YTD TOTAL						**4,907,561**	**3,236,732**	**1,670,869**	
133	9/01	CLE	R	N	2:46	16,547		1,687,376	65
134	9/02	CLE	R	D	2:27	23,640		1,711,016	66
135	9/03	DET	R	D	2:32	33,658		1,744,674	67
136	9/04	DET	R	N	3:07	14,760		1,759,434	68
137	9/05	DET	R	N	3:14	16,677		1,776,111	69
138	9/07	CWS	H	N	2:38	49,885	3,286,617		69
139	9/08	CWS	H	D	2:26	49,898	3,336,515		70
140	9/09	CWS	H	D	2:37	49,870	3,386,385		71
141	9/10	KC	R	N	2:42	22,158		1,798,269	70
142	9/11	KC	R	N	2:47	18,493		1,816,762	71
143	9/12	KC	R	N	2:51	20,135		1,836,897	72
144	9/13	BAL	H	N	3:16	49,875	3,436,260		72
145	9/14	BAL	H	N	3:34	49,893	3,486,153		73
146	9/15	BAL	H	D	2:55	49,888	3,536,041		74
147	9/16	BAL	H	N	3:05	49,886	3,585,927		75
148	9/17	NYY	H	N	2:55	49,902	3,635,829		76
149	9/18	NYY	H	N	2:52	49,887	3,685,716		77
150	9/19	NYY	H	N	2:50	49,890	3,735,606		78
151	9/21	CLE	H	N	3:41	49,894	3,785,500		79
152	9/22	CLE	H	D	2:46	49,883	3,835,383		80
153	9/23	CLE	H	D	3:22	49,901	3,885,284		81
154	9/24	MIL	R	N	3:10	8,769		1,845,606	73
155	9/25	MIL	R	N	3:06	8,576		1,854,242	74
156	9/26	MIL	R	N	2:41	8,804		1,863,046	75
157	9/28	BOS	R	N	3:13	35,735		1,898,781	76
158	9/29	BOS	R	D	3:27	35,444		1,934,225	77
159	9/30	BOS	R	D	3:37	34,403		1,968,628	78
YTD TOTAL						**5,853,952**	**3,885,284**	**1,968,628**	
160	10/01	BAL	R	N	3:01	24,442		1,993,070	79
161	10/02	BAL	R	N	2:22	19,789		2,012,859	80
162	10/03	BAL	R	N	3:04	26,913		2,039,772	81
YTD TOTAL						**5,925,056**	**3,885,284**	**2,039,772**	

1990 BLUE JAYS ATTENDANCE

	AT SKYDOME			ON THE ROAD		
CLUB	DATES	AVERAGE	TOTAL	DATES	AVERAGE	TOTAL
BALTIMORE	7	45,605	319,236	6	32,196	193,178
BOSTON	6	48,897	299,383	7	34,132	238,925
CLEVELAND	7	43,052	301,362	6	11,674	70,044
DETROIT	6	49,546	297,273	7	17,381	121,668
MILWAUKEE	6	49,771	298,625	7	19,368	135,574
NEW YORK	7	49,862	349,034	6	27,521	165,125
EAST	39	48,804	1,1864,913	39	23,705	924,514
CALIFORNIA	6	49,600	297,600	6	29,680	178,080
CHICAGO	6	45,878	275,266	6	20,086	120,518
KANSAS CITY	6	49,488	296,929	6	21,527	129,163
MINNESOTA	6	49,815	298,891	6	23,974	143,841
OAKLAND	6	49,737	298,424	6	36,934	221,606
SEATTLE	6	47,270	283,618	6	20,205	121,227
TEXAS	6	44,941	269,643	6	33,471	200,823
WEST	42	48,104	2,020,371	42	26,554	1,115,258
TOTAL	81	47,966	3,885,284	81	25,182	2,039,772

ATTENDANCE RECORDS

Largest Home	50,286	Fri.,Oct. 6/89	Oakland
Smallest Home	10,074	Tues., Apr. 17/79	Chicago
Largest Opening Day	49,673	Tues., Apr. 10/90	Texas
Largest Day	50,076	Sat., Oct. 7/89	Oakland
Smallest Day	10,074	Thurs., Apr. 17/79	Chicago
Largest Night	50,286	Fri., Oct. 6/89	Oakland
Smallest Night	10,125	Tues., May 3/83	Texas
Doubleheader(Day)	48,641	Mon., July 17/89	California
Doubleheader(TN)	45,102	Tues., Aug. 2/83	New York
Series, Four Dates (Home)	199,619	Aug 22-26/90 (4 Games)	Boston
Series, Four Dates (Road	133,343	June 25-28/90 (4 Games)	Boston
Series, Three Dates (Home)	149,702	Aug. 7-9/90 (3 Games)	Detroit
Series, Three Dates (Road)	127,089	July 20-22/90 (3 Games)	California
Series, Two Dates (Home)	99,774	June(19-20/90 (2 Games)	Boston
Series, Two Dates (Road	49,639	May 23-24/90 (2 Games)	California
Largest Road	61,340	Fri., May 23/86	Cleveland
Smallest Road	1,205	Thurs., Apr. 12/79	Chicago
Season, Home	3,885,284	1990	
Season, Road	2,039,772	1990	
Season, Home & Road	5,925,056	1990	

OPPONENTS' RECORDS IN TORONTO

	LARGEST		SMALLEST	
Baltimore	49,893	Sept. 14/90	11,080	Sept. l3/79
Boston	49,918	Aug. 23/90	10,428	Apr. 23/82
California	49,838	July 5/90	11,295	May l5/78
Chicago	49,898	Sept. 8/90	10,074	Apr. l7/79
Cleveland	49,894	Sept. 21/90	10,173	Apr. 20/83
Detroit	49,911	Aug. 9/90	10,087	Apr. l3/82
Kansas City	49,884	July 24/90	10,169	Apr. l7/78
Milwaukee	49,909	Aug. 29/90	10,127	Apr. l4/83
Minnesota	49,892	Aug. 12/90	10,155	May l/79
New York	49,902	Sept. 17/90	13,306	Apr l9/78
Oakland	49,865	June 30/90	11,339	May 9/78
Seattle	49,899	July 7/90	10,213	June ll/79
Texas	49,882	July 27/90	10,101	Apr. 27/82

BLUE JAYS ON THE ROAD

AT	LARGEST		SMALLEST	
BALTIMORE	47,387	Aug. 23/83	7,053	Sept. 6/79
BOSTON	35,735	Sept 28/90	7,542	April l6/82
CALIFORNIA	49,906	April 29/89	10,239	June 7/77
CHICAGO	41,043	April l0/79	1,205	April l2/79
CLEVELAND	61,340	May 23/86	2,724	April 28/77
DETROIT	52,528	April 7/78	6,210	Sept. 22/80
KANSAS CITY	41,086	April 8/85	14,740	April l0/85
MILWAUKEE	53,852	May 6/79	5,298	April 2l/82
MINNESOTA	53,067	April 8/88	2,830	Sept. 20/82
NEW YORK	55,367	May 27/78	9,685	April l8/77
OAKLAND	46,770	July 4/85	1,289	August l4/79
SEATTLE	43,200	April 4/84	4,113	June l/79
TEXAS	43,705	July 23/83	6,819	May l3/82

TWENTY LARGEST HOME CROWDS

ATTENDANCE	DATE	OPPONENT	EVENT
50,286	Friday, October 6, 1989	Oakland	Game #3 - LCS
50,076	Saturday, October 7, 1989	Oakland	Game #4 - LCS
50,024	Sunday, October 8, 1989	Oakland	Game #5 - LCS
49,918	Thursday, August 23, 1990	Boston	Night Game
49,914	Friday, August 24, 1990	Boston	Night Game
49,911	Thursday, August 9, 1990	Detroit	Night Game
49,909	Wednesday, August 29, 1990	Milwaukee	Back-To-School Day
49,907	Tuesday, June 19, 1990	Boston	Night Game
49,902	Monday, September 17, 1990	New York	Night Game
49,901	Sunday, September 23, 1990	Cleveland	Day Game
49,899	Saturday, July 7, 1990	Seattle	Bowlerama Day
49,898	Saturday, September 8, 1990	Chicago	Day Game
49,897	Wednesday, August 8, 1990	Detroit	Coffee Mug Day
	Sunday, August 26, 1990	Boston	Day Game
49,894	Tuesday, August 7, 1990	Detroit	Pennant Day
	Friday, September 21, 1990	Cleveland	Night Game
49,893	Friday, September 14, 1990	Baltimore	Night Game
49,892	Sunday, August 12, 1990	Minnesota	Old-Timers/Day Game
	Monday, August 27, 1990	Milwaukee	Night Game
49,890	Wednesday, September 19, 1990	New York	Night Game
	Saturday, August 25, 1990	Boston	Camera Day
49,888	Friday, August 10, 1990	Minnesota	Night Game
	Saturday, September 15, 1990	Baltimore	Night Game
49,887	Tuesday, September 18, 1990	New York	Night Game
49,885	Friday, September 7, 1990	Chicago	Night Game

HOW THEY HAVE DRAWN

Attendance Re-Cap l977 - 1990

RANK	CLUB	DATES	ATTENDANCE	AVERAGE
1	NEW YORK	83	2,881,215	34,713
2	DETROIT	88	2,761,616	31,382
3	BOSTON	86	2,593,736	30,160
4	MILWAUKEE	88	2,418,599	27,484
5	BALTIMORE	85	2,363,156	27,802
6	CHICAGO	79	2,188,051	27,697
7	OAKLAND	81	2,185,905	26,986
8	KANSAS CITY	80	2,185,319	27,316
9	CALIFORNIA	79	2,159,879	27,340
10	CLEVELAND	81	2,074,761	25,614
11	MINNESOTA	77	2,073,949	26,934
12	TEXAS	76	1,945,680	25,601
13	SEATTLE	77	1,668,616	21,670
TOTAL		1060	29,500,482	27,830

1990 AMERICAN LEAGUE ATTENDANCE

CLUB	HOME TOTAL	AVERAGE	DATES	ROAD TOTAL	AVERAGE	DATES
TORONTO	3,885,284	47,966	81	2,039,772	25,182	81
OAKLAND	2,900,217	36,253	80	2,597,920	32,886	79
CALIFORNIA	2,555,688	31,552	81	2,079,229	25,356	82
BOSTON	2,528,986	31,612	80	2,398,442	29,980	80
BALTIMORE	2,415,189	30,572	79	1,998,020	25,616	78
KANSAS CITY	2,244,956	28,781	78	2,073,923	25,924	80
TEXAS	2,057,911	25,406	81	1,980,565	25,392	78
NEW YORK	2,006,436	25,080	80	2,399,178	29,619	79
CHICAGO	2,002,357	25,346	79	2,205,062	27,912	79
MILWAUKEE	1,752,900	22,189	79	2,181,099	27,609	79
MINNESOTA	1,751,584	21,894	80	2,003,575	25,687	78
SEATTLE	1,509,727	18,639	81	2,193,421	27,418	80
DETROIT	1,495,785	18,697	80	2,134,797	26,356	81
CLEVELAND	1,225,240	16,337	75	2,047,257	25,591	80
TOTALS	30,332,260	27,228	1114	30,332,260	27,228	1114

1976 . . . March 26 **. . .** American League votes to expand to Toronto, awarding franchise to group consisting of Imperial Trust, Ltd., Labatt's Breweries, and the Canadian Imperial Bank of Commerce. June 18 . . . Metro Baseball, Ltd., appoints Peter Bavasi, Executive Vice-President and General Manager of new franchise. August 12 . . . Directors select "Blue Jays" from over 4,000 names and 30,000 entries in a Name the Team contest. August 25 . . . Blue Jays announce Dunedin, Florida as spring training site. September 22 . . . Roy Hartsfield appointed field manager. October 8 . . . Club reveals distinctive "Blue Jays logo" as season ticket sales begin. October 22 . . . Blue Jays acquire first player in purchase of catcher Phil Roof from the Chicago White Sox. November 5 . . . Blue Jays announce first trade at conclusion of expansion draft, sending Al Fitzmorris to Cleveland for catcher Alan Ashby and infielder outfielder Doug Howard.

1977 . . . March 11 **. . .** Blue Jays defeat New York Mets 3-1 at Dunedin, Florida, in first spring training game. April 7 . . . 44,649 brave snow and freezing temperatures as Major League baseball makes a successful debut in Toronto. Doug Ault becomes an instant hero hitting two home runs in the Blue Jays 9-5 win over the Chicago White Sox. August 9 . . . Blue Jays defeat Minnesota 6-2 in front of 23,450 which pushes the home attendance to 1,219,551 and establishes a new attendance record for a first-year expansion club after only 50 home dates. September 10 . . . Roy Howell drives in nine runs with five hits, including two home runs and two doubles as the Blue Jays inflict a 19-3 loss on the New York Yankees. Jays' total is most runs scored against the Yankees in New York in over a half century. September 15 . . . Blue Jays awarded 9-0 forefit win over Baltimore Orioles as Orioles' manager Earl Weaver removes team from field in fifth inning. October 2 . . . Blue Jays complete their first year with a 54-107 record with 1,701,052 having made their way to Exhibition Stadium to see the team in their inaugural season. November 24 . . . Board of Directors names Peter Bavasi, President and Chief Operating Officer of Toronto Blue Jays Baseball Club.

1978 . . . April 22 . . . Jim Clancy gets the credit for a 4-2 Jacket Day win over the Chicago White Sox in front of 44,327 including Prime Minister Pierre Trudeau and in doing so helps his own cause by starting the Blue Jays first ever triple play. June 26 . . . Blue Jays explode for 24 runs on 24 hits en route to a 24-10 shellacking of the Baltimore Orioles.

1979 . . . September 23 **. . .** Blue Jays complete home season as an expansion record total of 4,695,288 have come to see Blue Jays baseball in the first 3 seasons. October 18 . . . Bobby Mattick named Field Manager for the 1980 season. November 26 . . . Alfredo Griffin named co-winner of the American League's Rookie of the Year Award. December 2-7 . . . The Blue Jays play host to the first Winter Meetings held outside the United States since 1936.

1980 . . . September 12 **. . .** Blue Jays defeat Baltimore 7-5 to win their 60th game of the season and in doing so set a then new club record for victories in a single season. September 26 . . . Continuing to break all attendance records for expansion teams the Blue Jays play host to their 6 millionth fan. October 5 . . . Toronto defeats Boston 4-1 to chalk up their 67th win of the season, 8 more victories than ever before.

1981 . . . October 7 **. . .** Bobby Mattick resigns as Field Manager to become Executive Co-Ordinator, Baseball Operations. October 15 . . . Bobby Cox, former Atlanta Braves Manager (1978-81) named Blue Jays Manager for the 1982 season. November 24 . . . Peter Bavasi, President & Chief Operating Officer resigns.

1982 . . . July 22 **. . .** N.E. Hardy appointed Chief Executive Officer. September 11 . . . Blue Jays set then club mark for road attendance surpassing the previous mark of 1,285,409. October 3 . . . Blue Jays set then club marks for best home (44-37) and road (34-47) records...Club establishes an American League record for the fewest games behind an American league leader for a last place club (17) since divisional play started in 1969....Toronto wins 78th game to tie Cleveland for sixth place, the first season that the club did not finish in 7th place.

1983 . . . May 23 **. . .** Lloyd Moseby becomes third consecutive Blue Jays player to capture AL player of the week honours (others being Luis Leal and Dave Stieb) marking only the second time, league history that one club had captured the honour for three consecutive weeks. June 6 . . . Blue Jays become the last club to make a roster move when Dave Collins is placed on the disabled list. July 4 . . . Blue Jays lead the AL East at the All-Star break, a club first. July 25 . . . Blue Jays are tied for first place, then the latest date that the club was ever in first place. August 2 . . . 45,102 (a then record crowd) see Blue Jays sweep TN-DH from the Yankees. September 19 . . . Lloyd Moseby becomes first Blue Jays player to score 100 runs. September 20 . . . Willie Upshaw becomes first Blue Jay to drive in 100 runs. October 2 . . . Blue Jays finish season at 89-73, 4th place, 9 GB, then the first time the franchise had finished above .500.

1984 . . . April 17 . . . Blue Jays set record with 9,104 season tickets sold. April 28 . . Blue Jays gain sole possession of second place, a position they would never relinquish. May 27 . . . Alfredo Griffin has his major league leading consecutive game streak snapped at 392-games. June 2 . . . Blue Jays win their 19th one-run game in a row. August 5 . . . Blue Jays steal seven bases in a 5-3 win at Baltimore. August 5 . . . Cliff Johnson sets a new major league record with his 19th career pinch hit home run. September 2 . . Blue Jays reach 22-games over .500 (79-57) for a then new club mark. September 19 . . . Blue Jays become the 18th major league franchise to surpass the two million mark in home attendance. September 23 . . . Blue Jays draw 2,110,009 at home-then a new franchise mark. September 29 . . . Blue Jays clinch second place-then their highest standing ever.

1985 . . . April 16 . . .Blue Jays placing 11,500 ceiling on season tickets. May 1...Jimmy Key becomes the club's first starting LHP to win a game since Oct. 4/80 (614-games). May 20...Blue Jays gain solo possession of 1st place which they would not relinquish. June 8-9...Blue Jays draw back-to-back 40,000 home crowds for first time. June 27...Blue Jays surpass one million mark in home attendance, earliest ever. July 21...Blue Jays win their 10th straight home win and push first place lead to a club record 9.5-games. July 27...Blue Jays average home attendance, surpasses the 30,000 mark for the first time ever. September 11...Blue Jays surpass the two million mark for first time. September 12-15...Blue Jays and Yankees set an AL record for a 4-game series (214,510). September 29...Blue Jays move to a club record 41-games over .500 (98-57). October 4...47,686 see the Blue Jays play New York - a new club mark. October 5...Blue Jays captured first division title (American League East). October 6...Blue Jays draw 2,468,925 at home - then a new club mark. October 25...Jimy Williams succeeds Bobby Cox as manager.

1986. . . Blue Jays place a sealing of 14,000 season tickets...Blue Jays celebrate 10th anniversary season. April 15...Club's first home rainout since July 4, 1983...Game vs the Orioles was made up the next day. May 6...Jesse Barfield cracks 2HR's vs Oakland to become the club's all-time franchise leader at 93. June 20...Cliff Johnson HR's vs Detroit for his major league leading 20th career pinch hit HR. June 27...Damaso Garcia ties a major league record with four doubles vs NY. July 10...Damaso Garcia becomes the first player to register 1000 hits in a Blue Jays uniform. July 28...Jim Clancy becomes the first pitcher to record 100 wins in a Blue Jay uniform. September 22...Tony Fernandez becomes the first Blue Jays player to reach the 200 hit mark in one season while he and Jesse Barfield become the first Blue Jays to win a Rawlings Gold Glove for defensive excellence.

1987 . . . June 2...Blue Jays embark on a club record 11-game win streak. July 1...Blue Jays set a club record when a Canada Day crowd of 47,828 saw the Yankees. July 14... George Bell participates in All-Star Game and first Blue Jay ever selected by the fans. September 14...Ernie Whitt becomes the second Blue Jays player to have a 3HR game (vs Orioles) as Blue Jays set a Major League Record with a 10HR game vs the Orioles. September 30...Blue Jays final home attendance reached 2,778,429, the Most Ever for an AL East team and to lead AL in attendance for first time ever. November 17th...George Bell named AL MVP. December 8th...George Bell is named the ML Player of the Year by The Sporting News.

1988 . . . April 3...George Bell becomes the first major leaguer to hit 3HR's on Opening Day...April 11...Blue Jays defeat the Yankees in their home opener before their largest Opening Day crowd (45,185)...May 31...Dave Stieb tosses his first career 1 Hitter, defeating Milwaukee 9-0...June 4...Blue Jays complete a 4-game sweep at Fenway Park, their first sweep ever at Fenway...July 12...Dave Stieb makes his sixth All-Star game appearance, placing him tied/7th on the All-time pitchers list...September 5...George Bell is named AL Player of the Week for the period ending September 4...Was the only league player to be twice honoured in 1988...September 30...Dave Stieb became the sixth modern ML pitcher to toss consecutive 1H'ers when he blanked the Orioles 4-0...October 2...Blue Jays finish the season with a 22-7 September/October, a club record...

1989 . . . January 10...Paul Beeston named President of the Blue Jays...April 16...Kelly Gruber becomes the first franchise player to hit for the cycle, that at Exhibition Stadium against Kansas City...May 15...Jimy Williams is dismissed as manager, replaced on an interim basis by Cito Gaston...It was the club's first managerial change in franchise history to take place during a season...May 28...Blue Jays play their final game at Exhibition Stadium, defeating Chicago 9-5...May 31...Cito Gaston is named as the fifth manager in franchise history through the end of the 1989 season...June 3...Blue Jays overcome a 10-0 seventh inning deficit to defeat Boston 13-11 in 12 innings...June 5...Blue Jays lose 5-3 to Milwaukee in the club's first game at SkyDome...July 9...Blue Jays win 2-0 at Detroit for the club's first-ever sweep at Tiger Stadium...August 4...Dave Stieb loses a perfect game after 8.2 innings when New York's Roberto Kelly doubles...August 31...Blue Jays defeat Chicago 5-1 to move into a first place tie with Baltimore...They would remain in first place for the remainder of the season...September 4...George Bell is named American League Player of the Month for August...September 16...49,501 watch the Blue Jays defeat the Indians as the Blue Jays set an American League record for home attendance...September 30...Blue Jays defeat Baltimore 4-3 to capture their second divison title in five seasons...October 8...Blue Jays draw 50,024 for Game; 5 of the ALCS marking the 41st consecutive sellout at SkyDome...December 17...An era ends as Ernie Whitt is traded to the Atlanta Braves...He was the club's final link with the 1976 Expansion Draft.

1990 . . . APRIL 10, the BLUE JAYS begin their first full season at SkyDome . . .June 29, Dave Stewart of Oakland pitches the first No-Hitter in Toronto and at the SkyDome . . . August 14, George Bell ties a Major League record with 3 Sacrifice Flies in a game vs the White Sox . . . August 18, Mr. R. Howard Webster, the Blue Jays' Honourary Chairman passes away at age 80 . . . September 2, Dave Steib pitches the club's first NO-HITTER vs the Cleveland Indians at Cleveland—final score: Toronto 3, Cleveland 0...September 19, with a crowd of 49,902, the BLUE JAYS set a Major League season attendance record, breaking the old record set by the L.A. Dodgers in 1982 . . . The new record stands at 3,885,284 . . .October 3, Blue Jays set a team record along with the Oakland Athletics for club fielding with a .986 average . . . December 5, the BLUE JAYS make a blockbuster trade with San Diego, trading Tony Fernandez and Fred McGriff for Roberto Alomar and Joe Carter . . . December 14, Mr. N.E. Hardy steps down as the Blue Jays' Chairman of the Board and CEO and is appointed Honourary Chairman as Mr. William R. Ferguson is named Chairman of the Board and Mr. P.N.T. Widdrington is appointed Vice-Chairman and Chief Executive Officer.

THE ORIGINAL BLUE JAYS
American League Expansion Draft Selections

November 5, 1976

1. Bob Bailor, if-of, Baltimore
2. Jerry Garvin, lhp, Minnesota
3. Jim Clancy, rhp, Texas
4. Gary Woods, of, Oakland
5. Rico Carty, if-dh, Cleveland
6. Butch Edge, rhp, Milwaukee
7. Al Fitzmorris, rhp, Kansas City
8. Al Woods, of, Minnesota
9. Mike Darr, rhp, Baltimore
10. Pete Vuckovich, rhp, Chicago
11. Jeff Byrd, rhp, Texas
12. Steve Bowling, of, Milwaukee
13. Dennis DeBarr, lhp, Detroit
14. Bill Singer, rhp, Minnesota
15. Jim Mason, if, New York
16. Doug Ault, if, Texas
17. Ernie Whitt, c, Boston
18. Mike Weathers, if, Oakland
19. Steve Staggs, if, Kansas City
20. Steve Hargan, rhp, Texas
21. Garth Iorg, if, New York
22. Dave Lemanczyk, rhp, Detroit
23. Larry Anderson, rhp, Milwaukee
24. Jesse Jefferson, rhp, Chicago
25. Dave McKay, if, Minnesota
26. Tom Bruno, rhp, Kansas City
27. Otto Velez, of, New York
28. Mike Willis, lhp, Baltimore
29. Sam Ewing, of, Chicago
30. Leon Hooten, rhp, Oakland

ALL TIME BLUE JAYS ROSTER
MANAGERS, COACHES AND PLAYERS

1977 thru 1990

Total number of players — 211
(Includes all players who have participated in one or more official American League games.)

MANAGERS

Cox, Bobby ('82—'85)
Gaston, Cito ('89—)
Hartsfield, Roy ('77—'79)
Mattick, Bobby ('80—'81)
Williams, Jimy ('86—'89)

COACHES

Cisco, Galen ('88; '90—)
Doerr, Bobby ('77—'81)
Felske, John ('80—'81)
Gaston, Cito ('82—'89)
Guerrero, Epy ('81)
Leppert, Don ('77—'79)
Llenas, Winston ('88)
McLaren, John ('86—'90)
Menke, Denis ('80—'81)
Miller, Bob ('77—'79)
Moore, Jackie ('77—'79)
Smith, Billy ('84—'88)
Squires, Mike ('89—)
Sullivan, John ('82—)
Tenace, Gene ('90—)
Torres, Hector ('90—)
Warner, Harry ('77—'80)
Widmar, Al ('80—'89)
Williams, Jimy ('80—'85)

PLAYERS

A
Acker, Jim (rhp) ('83—'86; '89—)
Adams, Glenn (dh) ('82)
Ainge, Dan (if-of) ('79—'81)
Aikens, Willie (dh-lb) ('84—'85)
Alberts, Butch (dh) ('78)
Alexander, Doyle (rhp) ('83—'86)
Allenson, Gary (c) ('85)
Aquino, Luis (rhp) ('86)
Ashby, Alan (c) ('77—'78)
Ault, Doug (lb-of) ('77—'78; '80)

B
Bailor, Bob (if-of-p) ('77—'80)
Bair, Doug (rhp) ('88)
Baker, Dave (if) ('82)
Barfield, Jesse (of) ('81—'89)
Barlow, Mike (rhp) ('80—'81)
Batiste, Kevin (OF) ('89)
Beamon, Charlie (lb-dh) ('81)
Bell, George (of) ('81; '83—'90)
Beniquez, Juan (of-dh) ('87—'88)
Berenguer, Juan (rhp) ('81)
Black, Bud (lhp) ('90)
Blair, Willie (rhp) ('90)
Bomback, Mark (rhp) ('81—'82)
Bonnell, Barry (of) ('80—'83)
Borders, Pat (c-if) ('88—)
Bosetti, Rick (of) ('78—'81)
Bowling, Steve (of) ('77)
Braun, Steve (if-dh) ('80)
Brenley, Bob (c) ('89)
Brown, Bobby (of) ('79)
Bruno, Tom (rhp) ('77)
Buice, DeWayne (rhp) ('89)
Burroughs, Jeff (dh) ('85)
Buskey, Tom (rhp) ('78—'80)
Butera, Sal (c) ('88)
Byrd, Jeff (rhp) ('77)

C
Cabrera, Francisco (c) ('89)
Campusano, Sil (of) ('88)
Candelaria, John (lhp) ('90)
Cannon, J.J. (of) ('79)
Carty, Rico (dh) ('78—'79)
Castillo, Tony (lhp) ('88—'89)
Caudill, Bill (rhp) ('85—'86)
Cerone, Rick (c) ('77—'79)
Cerutti, John (lhp) ('85—'90)
Clancy, Jim (rhp) ('77—'88)
Clark, Bryan (lhp) ('84)
Clarke, Stan (lhp) ('83; '85—'86)
Coleman, Joe (rhp) ('78)
Collins, Dave (of) ('83—'84)
Cooper, Don (rhp) ('83)
Cox, Ted (if) ('81)
Cruz, Victor (rhp) ('78)
Cummings, Steve (rhp) ('89—'90)

D
Darr, Mike (rhp) ('77)
Davis, Bob (c) ('80)
Davis, Dick (of) ('82)
Davis, Steve (lhp) ('85—'86)
DeBarr, Dennis (lhp) ('77)
DeWillis, Jeff (c) ('87)
Diaz, Carolos (c) ('90—)
Ducey, Rob (of) ('87—)

E
Edge, Butch (rhp) ('79)
Eichhorn, Mark (rhp) ('82; '86—'88)
Eppard, Jim (ph) ('90—)
Espinosa, Nino (rhp) ('81)
Ewing, Sam (if-of-dh) ('77—'78)

F
Fairly, Ron (if-of) ('77)
Felix, Junior (of) ('89—'90)
Fernandez, Tony (if) ('83—'90)
Fielder, Cecil (dh-1b) ('85—'88)
Filer, Tom (rhp) ('85)
Flannigan, Mike (lhp) ('87—'90)
Freisleben, Dave (rhp) ('79)

G
Garcia, Damaso (if) ('80—'86)
Garcia, Pedro (if) ('77)
Garvin, Jerry (lhp) ('77—'82)
Geisel, Dave (lhp) ('82—'83)
Gilles, Tom (rhp) ('90—)
Gomez, Luis (if) ('78—'79)
Gordon, Don (rhp) ('86—'87)
Gott, Jim (rhp) ('82—'84)
Gozzo, Mauro (rhp) ('89)
Griffin, Alfredo (if) ('79—'84)
Grilli, Steve (rhp) ('79)
Gruber, Kelly (if-of) ('84—)

H
Hargan, Steve (rhp) ('77)
Hartenstein, Chuck (rhp) ('77)
Hearron, Jeff (c) ('85—'86)
Henke, Tom (rhp) ('85—)
Hernandez, Pedro (if,-of) ('79; '82)
Hernandez, Toby (c) ('84)
Hernandez, Xavier (rhp) ('89)
Hill, Glenallen (of) ('89—)
Hodgson, Paul (of) ('80)
Horton, Willie (dh) ('78)
Howell, Roy (if) ('77—'80)
Huffman, Phil (rhp) ('79)
Hutton, Tommy (if-of) ('78)

I
Infante, Alex (if) ('87—'89)
Iorg, Garth (if-of) ('78; '80—'87)

J
Jackson, Roy Lee (rhp) ('81—'84)
Jefferson, Jesse (rhp) ('77—'80)
Johnson, Anthony (of) ('82)
Johnson, Cliff (dh) ('83—'86)
Johnson, Jerry (rhp) ('77)
Johnson, Joe (rhp) ('86—'87)
Johnson, Tim (if) ('78—'79)

K
Kelly, Pat (c) ('80)
Key, Jimmy (lhp) ('84—)
Kilgus, Paul (lhp) ('90—)
Kirkwood, Don (rhp) ('78)
Klutts, Mickey (if) ('83)
Kucek, Jack (rhp) ('80)
Kusick, Craig (if-p) ('79)

L
Lamp, Dennis (rhp) ('84—'86)
Lavelle, Gary (lhp) ('85—'87)
Lawless, Tom (if) ('89—'90)
Leach, Rick (lb-of-p) ('84—'88)
Leal, Luis (rhp) ('80—'85)
Lee, Manny (if) ('85—)
Leiter, Al (lhp) ('89—)
Lemanczyk, Dave (rhp) ('77—'80)
Lemongello, Mark (rhp) ('79)
Liriano, Nelson (if) ('87—'90)
Luebber, Steve (rhp) ('79)
Luecken, Rick (rhp) ('90)

M
MacDonald, Bob (lhp) ('90—)
Macha, Ken (if) ('81)
Macha, Mike (if) ('80)
Mahler, Mickey (lhp) ('86)
Manrique, Fred (if) ('81; '84)
Martinez, Buck (c) ('81—86)
Mason, Jim (if) ('77)
Matuszek, Len (dh) ('85)
Mayberry, John (lb) ('78—'82)
Mazzilli, Lee (of-dh) ('89)
McGriff, Fred (lb) ('86—'90)
McKay, Dave (if) ('77—'79)
McLaughlin, Joey (rhp) ('80—'84)
Miller, Dyar (rhp) ('79)
Milner, Brian (c) ('78)
Mirabella, Paul (lhp) ('80—'81)
Moffitt, Randy (rhp) ('83)
Moore, Balor (lhp) ('78—'80)
Moore, Charlie (c) ('87)
Morgan, Mike (rhp) ('83)
Moseby, Lloyd (of) ('80—'89)
Mulliniks, Rance (if) ('82—)
Murphy, Tom (rhp) ('77—'79)
Murray, Dale (rhp) ('81—'82)
Musselman, Jeff (lhp) ('86—'89)
Musselman, Ron (rhp) ('84—'85)
Myers, Greg (c) ('87; '89—)

N
Nicosia, Steve (c) ('85)
Niekro, Phil (rhp) ('87)
Nordbrook, Tim (if) ('77)
Nordhagen, Wayne (of-dh) ('82)
Nunez, Jose (rhp) ('87—'89)

O
Olerud, John (lb-dh) ('89—)
Oliver, Al (dh) ('85)
Orta, Jorge (of-dh) ('83)

P
Petralli, Geno (c) ('82—'84)
Powell, Hosken (of-dh) ('82—'83)

Q
Quinlan, Tom (lf) ('90—)

R
Rader, Doug (if) ('77)
Ramos, Domingo (if) ('80)
Revering, Dave (lb-dh) ('82)
Roberts, Leon (of-dh) ('82)
Robertson, Bob (lb-dh) ('79)
Roof, Phil (c) ('77)
Ross, Mark (rhp) ('88)

S
Sanchez, Alex (rhp) ('89)
Schrom, Ken (rhp) ('80; '82)
Scott, John (of) ('77)
Senteney, Steve (rhp) ('82)
Sharperson, Mike (if) ('87)
Shepherd, Ron (of) ('84—'86)
Singer, Bill (rhp) ('77)
Sojo, Luis (if) ('90)
Solaita, Tony (lb-dh) ('79)
Staggs, Steve (if) ('77)
Stark, Matt (c) ('87)
Stieb, Dave (rhp-of) ('79—)
Stottlemyre, Todd (rhp) ('88—)

T
Thornton, Lou (of) ('85; '87—'88)
Todd, Jackson (rhp) ('79—'81)
Torres, Hector (if) ('77)

U
Underwood, Tom (lhp) ('78—'79)
Upshaw, Willie (if-of) ('78; '80—'87)

V
Velez, Otto (if-of-dh) ('77—'82)
Virgil, Ozzie (c) ('89—'90)
Vuckovich, Pete (rhp) ('77)

W
Wallace, Dave (rhp) ('78)
Ward, Duane (rhp) ('86—)
Webster, Mitch (of) ('83—'85)
Wells, David (lhp) ('87—)
Wells, Greg (lb-dh) ('81)
Whiten, Mark (of) ('90—)
Whitmer, Dan (c) ('81)
Whitt, Ernie (c) ('77—'78; '80—'89)
Wilborn, Ted (of-pr) ('79)
Wiley, Mark (rhp) ('78)
Williams, Kenny (of) ('90—)
Williams, Matt (rhp) ('83)
Willis, Mike (lhp) ('77—'81)
Wills, Frank (rhp) ('88—)
Wilson, Mookie (of) ('89—)
Woods, Al (of) ('77—'82)
Woods, Gary (of) ('77—'78)

AMERICAN LEAGUE CHAMPIONSHIP SERIES 1985

As the Blue Jays entered post season play for the first time, they would face the Kansas City Royals in the first ever best-of-seven American League Championship Series. . . The Blue Jays, who finished nine games ahead of the Royals in the loss column, were the favourites and would enjoy the extra home game.

In Game 1 Dave Stieb lived up to superstar billing, shutting out the Royals on three hits through eight innings with no base runner advancing past second base. The Blue Jays struck quickly with two runs in the second, three in the third and one in the fourth. The Blue Jays offense was sparked by 2 RBI performances by Ernie Whitt and Tony Fernandez.

Game 2 was a much more even affair with the Blue Jays eeking out a 6-5, 10-inning win. The Royals jumped into a quick 3-0 lead after $3\frac{1}{2}$ innings primarily on the strength of a 2 run HR by Willie Wilson in the 3rd inning. The Blue Jays rallied and took the lead on a George Bell sacrifice fly in the 8th. The Royals rallied, however in the 9th a on pinch hit HR by Pat Sheridan with the go ahead run being delivered in the 10th on a Frank White single. The Blue Jays won it in the bottom of the 10th on a two-out 2 run single by Al Oliver. On to Kansas City, the Blue Jays were up 2-games to none.

In Game 3, George Brett put on a baseball clinic going 4-4, 2 HR's, 3 RBI with 4 runs scored enroute to a 6-5 Royals win. Leading 5-2 after $4\frac{1}{2}$ innings the Blue Jays squandered the lead for good in the 8th when Brett led off the inning with a single and eventually scored.

Game 4, the Blue Jays came within one win of a World Series berth with a 3-1 come-from-behind victory. The Blue Jays won the game dramatically with 3 runs in the top of the ninth inning, the big blow being a 2 run pinch hit double by Al Oliver.

In Game 5, LHP Danny Jackson went the distance checking Toronto on 8 hits and scoring a run in each of the first two innings. Blue Jays still led the series 3-games to 2.

The Blue Jays and Royals returned to Exhibition Stadium for Game 6. Entering the 5th inning tied at 2-2 George Brett once again delivered the decisive blow with a solo HR. And, with 3.2 shutout innings of relief from Buddy Black and Dan Quisenberry, the Royals pulled even in the series for the first time at three-games apiece.

October 16th – Game 7 – Dave Stieb, the ace of the Toronto staff vs eventual Cy Young Award winner Bret Saberhagen. The Royals came out on top 6-2 shellacking Dave Stieb for six runs in 5.2 innings. The big blow being a wind-assisted bases clearing triple by Jim Sundberg to cap a four run 6th inning.

The Kansas City Royals became only the 5th club in major league history to trail a series 3-games to one and comeback to win the series. The Blue Jays? They slumped immediately after scoring five runs in the 5th inning of Game 3 scoring only eight runs in the last 40 innings.

BATTER	AVG	G	AB	R	H	2B	3B	HR	RBI-GW	SH-SF	HP	BB	SO	SB-CS	E
BARFIELD	.280	7	25	3	7	1	0	1	4-0	0-0	0	3	7	1-1	1
BELL	.321	7	28	4	9	3	0	0	1-0	0-1	1	0	4	0-1	0
BURROUGHS	.000	1	1	0	0	0	0	0	0-0	0-0	0	0	0	0-0	0
FERNANDEZ L	.333		9	2	3	1	0	0	1-0	0-1	0	0	0	0-0	2
FERNANDEZ R	.333		15	0	5	1	0	0	1-0	0-0	0	1	2	0-0	0
FERNANDEZ T	.333	7	24	2	8	2	0	0	2-0	0-1	0	1	2	0-0	2
FIELDER	.333	3	3	0	1	1	0	0	0-0	0-0	0	0	1	0-0	0
GARCIA	.233	7	30	4	7	4	0	0	1-0	0-0	0	3	3	0-0	0
HEARRON	.000	2	0	0	0	0	0	0	0-0	0-0	0	0	0	0-0	0
IORG	.133	6	15	1	2	0	0	0	0-0	0-0	0	1	3	0-0	0
JOHNSON	.368	7	19	1	7	2	0	0	2-0	0-0	0	1	4	0-0	0
LEE L	.000		0	0	0	0	0	0	0-0	0-0	0	0	0	0-0	0
LEE R	.000		0	0	0	0	0	0	0-0	0-0	0	0	0	0-0	0
LEE T	.000	1	0	0	0	0	0	0	0-0	0-0	0	0	0	0-0	0
MOSEBY	.226	7	31	5	7	1	0	0	4-0	0-0	0	2	3	1-0	0
MULLINIKS	.364	5	11	1	4	1	0	1	3-0	0-0	0	2	2	0-0	0
OLIVER	.375	5	8	0	3	1	0	0	3-2	0-0	1	0	0	0-0	0
THORNTON	.000	2	0	1	0	0	0	0	0-0	0-0	0	0	0	0-0	0
UPSHAW	.231	7	26	2	6	2	0	0	1-0	0-0	1	1	4	0-0	1
WHITT	.190	7	21	1	4	1	0	0	2-1	0-0	0	2	4	0-0	0
DH HITTERS	.370		27	2	10	3	0	0	5-2	0-0	1	1	4	0-0	0
PH HITTERS	.462		13	0	6	2	0	0	4-1	0-0	0	0	2	0-0	0
TOTALS	.269		242	25	65	19	0	2	23-3	0-2	3	16	37	2-2	4
OPPONENTS	.225		227	26	51	9	1	7	26-4	4-2	1	22	51	2-4	6

PITCHER		W-L	ERA	G	GS	CG	SHO	SV	IP	H	R	ER	HR	HB	BB	SO	WP
ACKER	R	0-0	0.00	2	0	0	0	0	6.0	2	0	0	0	0	0	5	0
ALEXANDER	R	0-1	8.71	2	2	0	0	0	10.1	14	10	10	4	0	3	9	1
CLANCY	R	0-1	9.00	1	0	0	0	0	1.0	2	1	1	0	0	1	0	0
HENKE	R	2-0	4.26	3	0	0	0	0	6.1	5	3	3	1	0	4	4	0
KEY	L	0-1	5.19	2	2	0	0	0	8.2	15	5	5	1	0	2	5	0
LAMP	R	0-0	0.00	3	0	0	0	0	9.1	2	0	0	0	0	1	10	0
LAVELLE	L	0-0	0.00	1	0	0	0	0	0.0	0	0	0	0	0	1	0	0
STIEB	R	1-1	3.10	3	3	0	0	0	20.1	11	7	7	1	1	10	18	0
TOTALS		3-4	3.77	17	7	0	0	0	62.0	51	26	26	7	1	22	51	1
OPPONENTS		4-3	3.16	18	7	1	1	1	62.2	65	25	22	2	3	16	37	3

Championship Series '85 (continued)

GAME 1
at TORONTO
Tuesday, October 8

				R	H	E
Kansas City	0 0 0	0 0 0	0 0 1	1	5	1
Toronto	0 2 3	1 0 0	0 0 X	6	11	0

LEIBRANDT, Farr (3), Gubicza (5), Jackson (8), and Sundberg
STIEB, Henke (9), and Whitt
HR: None
T-2:24; A-39,115

GAME 2
at TORONTO
Wednesday, October 9

				R	H	E
Kansas City	0 0 2	1 0 0	0 0 1 1	5	10	3
Toronto	0 0 0	1 0 2	0 1 0 2	6	10	0

Black, QUISENBERRY (8), and Sundberg
Key, Lamp (4), Lavelle (8), HENKE (8), and Whitt
HR: Kansas City (2) – Wilson, Sheridan
T-3:39; A-34,029

GAME 3
at KANSAS CITY
Friday, October 11

				R	H	E
Toronto	0 0 0	0 5 0	0 0 0	5	13	1
Kansas City	1 0 0	1 1 2	0 1 X	6	10	1

Alexander, Lamp (6), CLANCY (8), and Whitt
Saberhagen, Black (5) FARR (5), and Sundberg
HR: Toronto (2) – Barfield, Mulliniks Kansas City (3) – Brett (2), Sundberg
T-2:51; A-40,224

GAME 4
at KANSAS CITY
Saturday, October 12

				R	H	E
Toronto	0 0 0	0 0 0	0 0 3	3	7	0
Kansas City	0 0 0	0 0 1	0 0 0	1	2	0

Stieb, HENKE (7), and Whitt, Hearron (9)
LEIBRANDT, Quisenberry (9), and Sundberg
HR: None
T-3:02; A-41,112

GAME 5
at KANSAS CITY
Sunday, October 13

				R	H	E
Toronto	0 0 0	0 0 0	0 0 0	0	8	0
Kansas City	1 1 0	0 0 0	0 0 X	2	8	0

KEY, Acker (6), and Whitt
JACKSON, and Sundberg
HR: None
T-2:21; A-40,046

GAME 6
at TORONTO
Tuesday, October 15

				R	H	E
Kansas City	1 0 1	0 1 2	0 0 0	5	8	1
Toronto	1 0 1	0 0 1	0 0 0	3	8	2

GUBICZA, Black (6), Quisenberry (9) (S), and Sundberg
ALEXANDER, Lamp (6), and Whitt, Hearron (8)
HR: Kansas City (1) – Brett
T-3:12; A-37,557

GAME 7
at TORONTO
Wednesday, October 16

				R	H	E
Kansas City	0 1 0	1 0 4	0 0 0	6	8	0
Toronto	0 0 0	0 1 0	0 0 1	2	8	1

Saberhagen, LEIBRANDT (4), Quisenberry (9), and Sundberg
STIEB, Acker (6), and Whitt
HR: Kansas City (1) – Sheridan
T-2:49; A-32,084

SCORE BY INNINGS

				R	H	E
Kansas City	3 2 3	3 2 9	0 1 2 1	26	51	6
Toronto	1 2 4	2 6 3	0 1 4 2	25	65	4

E—Balboni (2), Brett (2), Fernandez (2), Sundberg, Upshaw, Smith, Barfield
DP—Kansas City (7), Toronto (4)
LOB—Kansas City (44), Toronto (49)
SB—Barfield, Moseby, Wilson, Smith
S—Biancalana, McRae, Wilson, White
SF—Fernandez, Bell, White, Motley
WP—Black (2), Alexander, Gubicza
HBP—Bell (by Black), Oliver (by Saberhagen), McRae (by Stieb)
ATT—264,167

AMERICAN LEAGUE CHAMPIONSHIP SERIES 1989

For the second time in five seasons, the Blue Jays were American League East Division Champions. The Blue Jays would face the Oakland Athletics who had the best record in the Major Leagues in 1989.

Game #1: The Blue Jays surrendered 2-0 and 3-1 leads as the Athletics scored three times in the sixth and twice in the eighth to win 7-3. In the sixth inning Mark McGwire cracked a lead off HR to tie the game and two runs scored when Carney Lansford's double play ball was botched. Dave Stewart allowed five hits over eight innings for the win.

Game #2: The Athletics tallied twice in the fourth inning and three in the sixth en route to a 6-3 win. A's outfielder Rickey Henderson was a one-man wrecking crew going 2-for-2 with two runs scored and four stolen bases. Athletics' righthander Mike Moore allowed just three hits and an unearned run in seven innings.

Game #3: The Blue Jays snapped a five game post season losing streak dating back to 1985 with a convincing 7-3 win. The Blue Jays jumped on Athletics' starter Storm Davis for four runs on four hits in the fourth inning and salted the game away with another three runs in the seventh inning. The win ran the Blue Jays' record to 11-0 at SkyDome with the roof closed. Overcoming a 3-0 Athletics' lead Mookie Wilson and Tony Fernandez paced the Blue Jays with two hits apiece, the latter with two doubles.

Game #4: The Athletics took a commanding 3-1 lead in games with a 6-5 win over the Blue Jays. Rickey Henderson was again a major catalyst with two HR's which accounted for four RBI. The Blue Jays collected 13 hits, 11 of which were singles and attempted to overcome a 5-2 deficit with one run in the sixth and seventh innings and two in the eighth.

Game #5: The Blue Jays spotted the Athletics a 4-0 lead into the seventh inning before eventually losing the game 4-3 and the best-of-seven series in five-games. Trailing 4-1 after eight innings the Blue Jays scored twice in the ninth inning on a leadoff HR by George Bell and a sacrifice fly by Kelly Gruber.

Epilogue: In essence it was Rickey Henderson defeating the Blue Jays four-games to one. Henderson batted .400, slugged 1.000, had a .609 on-base percentage and swiped a LCS record eight stolen bases. The Blue Jays hit .242 as a team (compared to Oakland's .272) with only eight of their hits being for extra bases. They were outscored 8-3 in the first three innings and 12-7 in the middle three before outscoring the Athletics 11-6 in the final three innnings. Unfortunately it is virtually impossible to consistently battle back from an early inning deficit. Although anything can happen in a "short series" the best team of the regular season continued that charted course into post-season, winning eight of nine contests.

BATTER		AVG	G	AB	R	H	2B	3B	HR	RBI	SH-SF	HP	BB	SO	SB-CS	E
BELL		.200	5	20	2	4	0	0	1	2	0-1	0	0	3	0-0	0
BORDERS		1.000	1	1	0	1	0	0	0	1	0-0	0	0	0	0-0	0
FELIX	T	.273	3	11	0	3	1	0	0	3	0-0	0	0	2	0-0	0
FELIX	R	.500	—	2	—	1	0	0	0	1	0-0	0	0	0	--	—
FELIX	L	.222	—	9	—	2	1	0	0	2	0-0	0	0	2	--	—
FERNANDEZ	T	.350	5	20	6	7	3	0	0	1	0-0	0	1	2	5-0	0
FERNANDEZ	R	1.000	—	1	—	1	1	0	0	0	0-0	0	0	0	--	—
FERNANDEZ	L	.316	—	19	—	6	2	0	0	1	0-0	0	1	2	--	—
GRUBER		.294	5	17	2	5	1	0	0	1	0-1	0	3	2	1-0	0
LEE	T	.250	2	8	2	2	0	0	0	0	0-0	0	0	1	0-0	0
LEE	R	.667	—	3	—	2	0	0	0	0	0-0	0	0	0	--	—
LEE	L	.000	—	5	—	0	0	0	0	0	0-0	0	0	1	--	—
LIRIANO	T	.429	3	7	1	3	0	0	0	1	0 0	0	2	0	3-0	1
LIRIANO	R	1.000	—	1	—	1	0	0	0	0	0-0	0	0	0	--	—
LIRIANO	L	.333	—	6	—	2	0	0	0	1	0-0	0	2	0	--	—
MAZZILLI	T	.000	3	8	0	0	0	0	0	0	0-0	0	0	2	0-0	0
MAZZILLI	R	.000	—	0	—	0	0	0	0	0	0-0	0	0	0	--	—
MAZZILLI	L	.000	—	8	—	0	0	0	0	0	0-0	0	0	2	--	—
McGRIFF		.143	5	21	1	3	0	0	0	3	0-0	0	0	4	0-0	1
MOSEBY		.313	5	16	4	5	0	0	1	2	0-0	0	5	2	1-0	0
MULLINIKS		.000	1	1	0	0	0	0	0	0	0-0	0	0	1	0-0	0
WHITT		.125	5	16	1	2	0	0	1	3	0-1	0	2	3	0-0	0
WILSON	T	.263	5	19	2	5	0	0	0	2	0-0	0	2	2	1-0	0
WILSON	R	.000	—	1	—	0	0	0	0	0	0-0	0	1	0	--	—
WILSON	L	.278	—	18	—	5	0	0	0	2	0-0	0	1	2	--	—
PITCHERS		.000	18	0	0	0	0	0	0	0	0-0	0	0	0	0-0	0
BLUE JAYS		.242	5	165	21	40	5	0	3	19	0-3	0	15	24	11-0	2
ATHLETICS		.272	5	158	26	43	9	1	7	23	3-2	1	20	32	13-2	3

PITCHER		W-L	ERA	G	GS	CG	SHO	SV	IP	H	R	ER	HR	HB	BB	SO	WP
ACKER	R	0-0	1.42	5	0	0	0	0	6.1	4	2	1	0	1	1	4	0
CERUTTI	L	0-0	0.00	2	0	0	0	0	2.2	0	0	0	0	0	3	1	0
FLANAGAN	L	0-1	10.38	1	1	0	0	0	4.1	7	5	5	3	0	1	3	0
HENKE	R	0-0	0.00	3	0	0	0	0	2.2	0	0	0	0	0	0	3	0
KEY	L	1-0	4.50	1	1	0	0	0	6.0	7	3	3	1	0	2	2	0
STIEB	R	0-2	6.35	2	2	0	0	0	11.1	12	8	8	2	0	6	10	0
STOTTLEMYRE	R	0-1	7.20	1	1	0	0	0	5.0	7	4	4	1	0	2	3	0
WARD	R	0-0	7.36	2	0	0	0	0	3.2	6	3	3	0	0	3	5	1
WELLS	L	0-0	0.00	1	0	0	0	0	1.0	0	1	0	0	0	2	1	0
BLUE JAYS		1-4	5.02	5	5	0	0	0	43.0	43	26	24	7	1	20	32	1
ATHLETICS		4-1	3.89	5	5	0	0	3	44.0	40	21	19	3	0	15	24	1

GAME 1
at OAKLAND
Tuesday, October 3 (night)

Toronto . . . . . 0 2 0 1 0 0 0 0 0 — 3 5 1
Oakland . . . . . 0 1 0 0 1 3 0 2 X — 7 11 0

STIEB, Acker (6), Ward (8), and Whitt
STEWART, Eckersley (9), and Steinbach
HR: Toronto (1)-Whitt; Oakland (2)-D. Henderson, McGwire
T-2:52; A-49,435

GAME 2
at OAKLAND
Wednesday, October 4 (day)

Toronto . . . . . 0 0 1 0 0 0 0 2 0 — 3 5 1
Oakland . . . . . 0 0 0 2 0 3 1 0 X — 6 9 1

STOTTLEMYRE, Acker (6), Wells (6), Henke (7), Cerutti (8), and Whitt
MOORE, Honeycutt (8), Eckersley (8) (S), and Hassey
HR: Oakland (1)-Parker
T-3:20; A-49,444

GAME 3
at TORONTO
Friday, October 6 (night)

Oakland . . . . . 1 0 1 1 0 0 0 0 0 — 3 8 1
Toronto . . . . . 0 0 0 4 0 0 3 0 X — 7 8 0

DAVIS, Honeycutt (7), Nelson (7), M. Young (8), and Steinbach
KEY, Acker (7), Henke (9), and Whitt
HR: Oakland (1)-Parker
T-2:54; A-50,268

GAME 4
at TORONTO
Saturday, October 7 (day)

Oakland . . . . . 0 0 3 0 2 0 1 0 0 — 6 11 1
Toronto . . . . . 0 0 0 1 0 1 1 2 0 — 5 13 0

WELCH, Honeycutt (6), Eckersley (8) (S), and Hassey
FLANAGAN, Ward (5), Cerutti (8), Acker (9), and Whitt, Borders (7)
HR: Oakland (3)-R. Henderson 2, Canseco
T-3:29; A-50,076

GAME 5
at TORONTO
Sunday, October 8 (day)

Oakland . . . . . 1 0 1 0 0 0 2 0 0 — 4 4 0
Toronto . . . . . 0 0 0 0 0 0 0 1 2 — 3 9 0

STEWART, Eckersley (9) (S), and Steinbach
STIEB, Acker (7), Henke (9), and Whitt
HR: Toronto (2)-Moseby, Bell
T-2:52; A-50,024

SCORE BY INNINGS

Oakland . . . . . 2 1 5 3 3 6 4 2 0 — 26 43 3
Toronto . . . . . 0 2 1 6 0 1 4 5 2 — 21 40 2

AWARDS

LABATT'S 'BLUE' PLAYER OF THE MONTH

Voting is conducted after each Blue Jays game, home and away, by a panel of accredited media personalities to select the outstanding Blue Jays player. The player with the greatest point total at the end of the season receives the Labatt's 'Blue' Most Valuable Player Award, along with $1000 and a cheque in a matching amount donated to the player's favourite charity. Monthly winners receive $500 and a matching amount to their favourite charity along with the Labatt's 'Blue' Player of the Month Trophy. In 1983 the award was split into separate 'Player' & 'Pitcher' awards.

PLAYER OF THE MONTH

Year	April	May	June	July	August	Sept.	Most Valuable Player
1977	Velez	Fairly	Fairly	Rader	Bailor	Bowling	Bailor
1978	Howell	Bosetti	Howell	Mayberry	Bailor	Bailor & Bosetti	Howell
1979	Mayberry	Griffin	Underwood	Velez	Griffin	Griffin	Griffin
1980	Stieb	Woods	Mayberry	Woods	Garcia	Mayberry	Mayberry
1981	Todd	Bonnell	---	---	Moseby	Stieb	Stieb
1982	Barfield	Bonnell	Upshaw	Garcia	Garcia	Clancy	Garcia
1983	Barfield	Upshaw	Johnson	Moseby	Moseby	Upshaw	Moseby & Upshaw
1984	Upshaw	Collins	Upshaw	Mulliniks	Bell	Collins	Bell
1985	Upshaw	Garcia	Bell	Mulliniks	Barfield	Moseby	Barfield
1986	Bell	Barfield	Fernandez	Bell	Moseby	Barfield	Bell
1987	Bell	Bell	Moseby	Fernandez	Bell	Moseby	Bell
1988	Gruber	McGriff	Gruber	McGriff	Whitt	Fernandez	McGriff
1989	McGriff	Liriano	Gruber	McGriff	Bell	Bell	Bell
1990	Gruber	Gruber	Bell	McGriff	McGriff	Gruber	Gruber

PITCHER OF THE MONTH

Year	April	May	June	July	August	Sept.	Most Valuable Pitcher
1983	Stieb	Stieb	Gott	Clancy	Stieb	Alexander	Stieb
1984	Stieb	Alexander	Stieb	Stieb	Stieb & Clancy	Alexander	Stieb
1985	Caudill	Stieb	Stieb	Stieb	Henke	Alexander	Stieb
1986	Alexander	Eichhorn	Key	Clancy	Eichhorn	Stieb	Key
1987	Key	Key	Clancy	Key	Cerutti	Flanagan	Key
1988	Cerutti	Stieb	Ward	Key	Clancy	Stieb	Stieb
1989	Key	Key	Cerutti	Henke	Stieb	Stieb	Stieb
1990	Ward	Stieb	Henke	Stieb	Key	Key	Stieb

Most Valuable Pitcher: 1978 - Clancy & Underwood 1979 - Underwood
1980 - Clancy 1981 - Stieb 1982 - Stieb

TORONTO CHAPTER BBWAA AWARD WINNERS

YEAR	PLAYER OF THE YEAR	PITCHER OF THE YEAR	ROOKIE OF THE YEAR	GOOD GUY	MOST IMPROVED
1977	Bob Bailor	Dave Lemanczyk	Bob Bailor	Roy Hartsfield	---
1978	Bob Bailor ---	Jim Clancy Victor Cruz	Victor Cruz ---	Mike Cannon ---	Alan Ashby ---
1979	Alfredo Griffin	Tom Underwood	Alfredo Griffin	John Silverman	Rick Cerone
1980	John Mayberry	Jim Clancy	Damaso Garcia	Howard Starkman	Al Woods
1981	Dave Stieb	Dave Stieb	---	Bob Mattick	Joey McLaughlin
1982	Damaso Garcia	Dave Stieb	Jesse Barfield	Buck Martinez	Jim Clancy
1983	Lloyd Moseby	Dave Stieb	Jim Acker	Ernie Whitt	Lloyd Moseby
1984	Dave Collins	Doyle Alexander	Tony Fernandez	Dave Collins	Dave Collins
1985	Jesse Barfield	Dennis Lamp	---	Rance Mulliniks	Dennis Lamp
1986	Jesse Barfield	Mark Eichhorn	Mark Eichhorn	Garth Iorg	Rick Leach
1987	George Bell	Jimmy Key	Jeff Musselman	Garth Iorg	Lloyd Moseby
1988	Fred McGriff	Dave Stieb	Pat Borders	John Cerutti	Kelly Gruber
1989	George Bell	Tom Henke	Junior Felix	Kelly Gruber	Todd Stottlemyre
1990	Kelly Gruber	Dave Steib	John Olerud	Jeff Ross Tommy Craig	Pat Borders

THE SPORTING NEWS AWARDS

Pitcher of the Year (AL)
1982 — Dave Stieb
1987 — Jimmy Key

Rookie Pitcher of the Year (AL)
1986 — Mark Eichhorn

Silver Slugger (AL)
1982 — Damaso Garcia, 2B
1983 — Lloyd Moseby, OF
1985 — George Bell, OF
1986 — George Bell, OF
1986 — Jesse Barfield, OF
1987 — George Bell, OF
1989 — Fred McGriff, 1B
1990 — Kelly Gruber, 3B

All-Star Team (AL)
1982 — Damaso Garcia, 2B
1982 — Dave Stieb, P
1983 — Lloyd Moseby, OF
1985 — Damaso Garcia, 2B
1986 — Tony Fernandez, OF
1986 — George Bell, OF
1987 — George Bell, OF
1987 — Jimmy Key, LHP
1988 — Ernie Whitt, C
1989 — Fred McGriff, 1B
1990 — Kelly Gruber, 3B

Manager of the Year (ML)
1985 — Bobby Cox

Rawlings Gold Glove (AL)
1986 — Tony Fernandez, SS
1986 — Jesse Barfield, OF
1987 — Tony Fernandez, SS
1987 — Jesse Barfield, OF
1988 — Tony Fernandez, SS
1989 — Tony Fernandez, SS
1990 — Kelly Gruber, 3B

Major League Player of the Year
1987 — George Bell

American League Player of the Year
1987 — George Bell

R. HOWARD WEBSTER AWARDS

In 1982 the Blue Jays established a set of awards to be bestowed annually upon the 'Most Valuable Player' on each Blue Jay farm club.

The awards are named in honor of R. HOWARD WEBSTER, who was the first Chairman of the Board for the Toronto Blue Jays.

AAA—Syracuse Chiefs: 1982-Tony Fernandez; 1983-Tony Fernandez; 1984-Fred Manrique; 1985-Rick Leach; 1986-Mike Sharperson; 1987-Todd Stottlemyre; 1988-Alexis Infante; 1989-Glenallen Hill; 1990-Mark Whiten
AA—Knoxville Blue Jays: 1982-Tim Thompson; 1983-Dave Shipanoff; 1984-Mike Sharperson; 1985-Steve Davis; 1986-Glenallen Hill; 1987-Geronimo Berroa; 1988-Alex Sanchez; 1989-Derek Bell; 1990-Tom Quinlan
A—Kinston Blue Jays: 1982-Dave Shipanoff; 1983-Jose Escobar; 1984-Luis Aquino; 1985-Eric Yelding;
A—Ventura Blue Jays: 1986-Greg Myers
A—Dunedin Blue Jays: 1987-Steve Cummings; 1988-Pedro Munoz; 1989-Nate Cromwell; 1990-Jeff Kent
A—Florence Blue Jays: 1982-Ken Kinnard; 1983-Cecil Fielder; 1984-Pat Borders; 1985-Sil Campusano; 1986-Pedro Munoz
A—Myrtle Beach Blue Jays: 1987-Doug Linton; 1988-Luis Sojo; 1989-Ray Giannelli; 1990-Mike Ogliaruso
A—St. Catharines Blue Jays: 1986-Willie Blair; 1987-Derek Bell; 1988-Woody Williams; 1989-Greg O'Halloran; 1990-Carlos Delgado
Rookie—Medicine Hat Blue Jays: 1982-Chris Johnston; 1983-Ronnie Robbins; 1984-Rob Ducey; 1985-Geronimo Berroa; 1986-Mark Whiten; 1987-Andy Dziadkoweic; 1988-Eddy Mendez; 1989-Shawn Holtzclaw; 1990-Brent Bowers
Rookie—Bradenton Blue Jays: 1982-Esteban Bolivar; 1983-Santiago Escobar; 1984-Santiago Garcia; 1985-Domingo Martinez; 1988-Wilberto Rojas
Dominican League—Santo Domingo: 1987-Marcos Taveras; 1988-Wilberto Rojas; 1989-Richard Orman; 1900-Mariano Dotel

BASEBALL WRITERS ASSOCIATION OF AMERICA AWARDS

Rookie of the Year (AL)	Most Valuable Player (AL)	Manager of the Year (AL)
1979 — Alfredo Griffin	1987 — George Bell	1985 — Bobby Cox

AMERICAN LEAGUE ALL-STAR TEAM (UPI)

1982 — Damaso Garcia, 2B	1986 — Tony Fernandez, SS	1987 — Jimmy Key, LHP
1983 — Lloyd Moseby, OF	1987 — George Bell, OF	1989 — Fred McGriff, 1B
1986 — Jesse Barfield, OF	1987 — Tom Henke, RP	1990 — Kelly Gruber, 3B

MAJOR LEAGUE ALL-STAR TEAM (AP)

1982 — Damaso Garcia, 2B	1986 — Jesse Barfield, RF	1987 — Jimmy Key, LHP
1986 — Tony Fernandez, SS	1987 — George Bell, OF	

AMERICAN LEAGUE EXECUTIVE OF THE YEAR (UPI)

1985 — Pat Gillick

AMERICAN LEAGUE MANAGER OF THE YEAR (UPI)

1985 — Bobby Cox

AMERICAN LEAGUE MANAGER OF THE YEAR (AP)

1985 — Bobby Cox

BASEBALL AMERICA

All-Star Team (AL)		Player of the Year (AL)
1983 — Dave Stieb-P	1987 — Jimmy Key-SP	1987 — George Bell
1983 — Lloyd Moseby-OF	1987 — Tom Henke-RP	
1984 — Dave Stieb-P	1989 — George Bell-OF(E)	
1986 — Tony Fernandez-SS	1989 — Dave Stieb-P(E)	
1986 — Jesse Barfield-OF	1990 — Kelly Gruber	
1987 — George Bell-OF		

Baseball Man of the Year in Canada (Toronto—Montreal BBWAA)
Peter Bavasi — 1977; Pat Gillick — 1983
Jesse Barfield — 1986; Cito Gaston — 1989

American League Player of the Month
Otto Velez, April, 1977
Alfredo Griffin, September, 1979
Lloyd Moseby, August 1983
Fred McGriff, April, 1989
George Bell, August, 1989
Kelly Gruber, September, 1990

American League Pitcher of the Month
Dave Stieb, April, 1980
Dave Stieb, May, 1983
Doyle Alexander, Sept. 1984
Dave Stieb, May, 1985
Jim Clancy, May, 1987

All-Star Game Selections (* voted)
Ron Fairly, of — 1977
Roy Howell, 3B — 1978
Dave Lemanczyk, p, Roy Hartsfield, coach — 1979
Dave Stieb, p, Ken Carson, trainer — 1980
Dave Stieb, p, — 1981
Jim Clancy, p, — 1982
Dave Stieb, p, — 1983
Dave Stieb, p; Damaso Garcia, 2B,
Alfredo Griffin, ss — 1984
Dave Stieb, p; Damaso Garcia, 2b; Jimmy Key, p; Ernie Whitt, c; Bob Cox, Coach — 1985
Jesse Barfield, of; Lloyd Moseby, of; Tony Fernandez, ss — 1986
*George Bell, of; Tony Fernandez, ss; Tom Henke, p — 1987
Dave Stieb, p — 1988
Tony Fernandez, ss; Kelly Gruber, 3B, 1989
George Bell, OF; Kelly Gruber, 3B; Dave Stieb, RHP, 1990

Latin American All-Star Team-TSN
Damaso Garcia, 2b — 1985
George Bell, of — 1985

American League Player of the Week
Otto Velez, July 23-29, 1979
Dave Stieb, April 21-27, 1981
Jim Clancy, June 14-20, 1982
Jim Clancy, Sept. 27-Oct. 3, 1982
Luis Leal, May 9-15, 1983
Dave Stieb, May 16-22, 1983
Lloyd Moseby, May 23-29, 1983
Cliff Johnson, June 20-26, 1983
Jesse Barfield, August 29-Sept. 4, 1983
Willie Upshaw, April 21-28, 1985
Lloyd Moseby, Sept. 2-Sept. 8, 1985
Lloyd Moseby, Aug. 18-24, 1986
George Bell, Sept. 1-7, 1986
Jim Clancy, May 19-24, 1987
George Bell, June 8-14, 1987
George Bell, July 27-Aug. 2, 1987
George Bell, April 4-10, 1988
George Bell, August 29-September 4, 1988
Nelson Liriano, May 15-21, 1989
Junior Felix, May 29-June 4, 1989
George Bell, August 14-20, 1989
Lloyd Moseby, Sept. 4-10, 1989
Kelly Gruber, April 23-29, 1990
George Bell, June 5-11, 1990
George Bell, June 18-24, 1990
Kelly Gruber, Sept 9-16, 1990

All-Rookie Team — Topps
1977 — Bob Bailor, ss; Doug Ault, 1B; Jerry Garvin, LHP
1978 — Rick Bosetti, of
1979 — Alfredo Griffin, ss; Dan Ainge, 2B
1980 — Damaso Garcia, 2B
1987 — Jeff Musselman

All-Rookie Team — Baseball Digest
1977 — Bob Bailor, cf; Jerry Garvin, LHP
1978 — Rick Bosetti, cf
1979 — Alfredo Griffin, ss; Dan Ainge, 2B
1980 — Damaso Garcia, 2B

Rolaids Relief Awards
Bill Caudill, April 1985
Toronto Blue Jays, 1985
Tom Henke, July, 1989

CANADIAN BASEBALL HALL OF FAME

THE CANADIAN BASEBALL HALL OF FAME was inaugurated in 1983 to honour those who have made a major contribution to Canadian baseball.

The Blue Jays organization have great pride in three of their own who have been inducted into Canada's Baseball Hall of Fame.

DR. RON TAYLOR, inducted in 1985 was a right-handed relief pitcher with five major league teams from 1962 to 1972.

Taylor, who helps in the game today as team physician for the Blue Jays, appeared in two World Series working seven innings without allowing a run.

In 1964, Taylor led the World Champion St. Louis Cardinals in appearances with 63 and saved game four of the World Series vs the Yankees with four innings of shutout ball.

In 1969, as a member of the New York Mets, Taylor led the club in saves (13) and appearances (59) and picked up a World Series save against the Baltimore Orioles.

Taylor started his career in 1962 with Cleveland and also pitched for Houston and San Diego.

He pitched 799 innings in 491 games for a record of 45 wins, 43 losses, 72 saves and a 3.93 ERA.

BOBBY PRENTICE, inducted in 1986, is one of Canada's most successful amateur scouts.

Prentice, who joined the Blue Jays as Director of Canadian Scouting on Nov. 1, 1976 had been associated for 17 years as a scout with the Detroit Tigers.

During his 10 full-time and seven part-time seasons as a Tiger scout, Prentice was responsible for signing of such Canadians as John Hiller, George Korince and Mike Kilkenny—three Canadians who pitched in the Tiger organization through the 1960s.

Prentice was also instrumental in the Tigers drafting of Dave Lemanczyk, who was playing for Guelph of the Inter-County League in Ontario. Lemanczyk went on to a major league career which included a stop with the Blue Jays.

He played in the Cleveland Indian organization for nine years between 1949 and 1957. As a power hitting infielder, Prentice led his club in home runs four times and led the Three I (Class B) League in RBI in 1950.

As a member of the American Association pennant-winning Indianapolis team in 1955, he was a teammate of such Indian greats as Herb Score and Rocky Colavito.

His greatest involvement in Canadian baseball comes as an inspiration to seek continued improvement for amateur baseball. He is directly involved in projects such as the National Baseball Institute, Pearson Cup Game and co-ordination of clinics for coaches and players across Canada.

REGGIE CLEVELAND, 43 from Swift Current, Saskatchewan, played twelve seasons in the Major Leagues. He was inducted into the Canadian Baseball Hall of Fame in 1986. During his career he played with St. Louis, Boston, Texas and Milwaukee. CLEVELAND holds the distinction of being the only Canadian pitcher ever to start a World Series game. His lifetime record is 103 wins and 103 losses, with an ERA of 3.97 in 1,744 innings pitched. He was hired as the pitching coach of the Medicine Hat Blue Jays in November, 1990.

BATTING STATISTICS AS BLUE JAYS ('77 thru '90)

BATTER	AVG	G	AB	R	H	2B	3B	HR	RBI	SH-SF	HP	BB	SO	SB-CS
ADAMS	.258	30	66	2	17	4	0	1	11	0-3	0	4	5	0-0
AINGE	.220	211	665	57	146	19	4	2	37	12-3	4	37	128	12-5
AIKENS	.205	105	254	23	52	8	0	12	31	0-1	2	32	62	0-0
ALBERTS	.278	6	18	1	5	1	0	0	0	0-0	0	0	2	0-0
ALLENSON	.118	14	34	2	4	1	0	0	3	0-0	0	0	10	0-0
ASHBY	.230	205	660	52	152	31	3	11	58	14-2	3	78	82	1-3
AULT	.234	247	693	66	162	28	5	17	86	5-4	7	70	105	4-5
BAILOR	.264	523	1878	230	495	75	19	8	138	21-11	15	127	107	46-28
BAKER	.250	9	20	3	5	1	0	0	2	1-0	2	3	3	0-0
BARFIELD	.265	1032	3463	530	919	162	27	179	527	13-24	27	342	855	55-40
BATISTE	.250	6	8	1	2	0	0	0	0	0-0	0	0	5	0-0
BEAMON	.200	8	15	1	3	1	0	0	0	0-0	0	2	2	0-0
BELL	.286	1181	4528	641	1294	237	32	202	740	0-59	35	255	563	59-27
BENIQUEZ	.288	66	139	15	40	7	1	6	29	1-2	1	13	19	0-0
BONNELL	.281	457	1504	184	422	76	14	33	187	10-13	6	114	187	28-12
BORDERS	.274	275	741	73	203	41	6	23	99	4-6	1	32	126	2-2
BOSETTI	.252	376	1422	149	359	69	8	17	119	13-10	8	69	170	23-30
BOWLING	.206	89	194	19	40	8	1	1	13	3-2	0	37	41	2-3
BRAUN	.273	37	55	4	15	2	0	1	9	0-0	0	8	5	0-0
BRENLY	.170	48	88	9	15	3	1	1	6	1-0	0	10	17	1-0
BROWN	.000	4	10	1	0	0	0	0	0	0-0	0	2	1	0-0
BURROUGHS	.257	86	191	19	49	9	3	6	28	0-2	0	34	36	0-1
BUTERA	.233	23	60	3	14	2	1	1	6	1-0	0	1	9	0-0
CABRERA	.167	3	12	1	2	1	0	0	0	0-0	0	1	3	0-0
CAMPUSANO	.218	73	142	14	31	10	2	2	12	2-1	4	9	33	0-0
CANNON	.177	131	192	30	34	1	1	1	9	3-0	1	1	48	14-4
CARTY	.269	236	848	99	228	42	0	32	123	1-0	1	82	86	4-2
CERONE	.229	255	851	79	195	39	6	11	91	8-4	2	66	84	1-7
COLLINS	.291	246	843	114	245	36	19	3	78	8-5	11	76	108	91-21
COX	.300	16	50	6	15	4	0	2	9	0-0	0	5	10	0-1
DAVIS, B	.189	123	307	24	58	13	0	5	27	14-0	2	17	40	0-0
DAVIS, D	.286	3	7	0	2	0	0	0	2	0-1	0	0	1	0-0
DeWILLIS	.120	13	25	2	3	1	0	1	2	1-0	0	2	12	0-0
DIAZ	.333	9	3	1	1	0	0	0	0	1-0	0	0	2	0-0
DUCEY	.251	121	231	39	58	14	1	1	26	3-4	1	29	57	6-2
EPPARD	.200	6	5	0	1	0	0	0	0	0-0	1	0	2	0-0
EWING	.267	137	300	27	80	8	2	6	43	3-1	0	24	51	1-1
FAIRLY	.279	132	458	60	128	24	2	19	64	8-2	2	58	58	0-4
FELIX	.261	237	878	135	229	37	15	24	111	2-8	5	78	200	31-20
FERNANDEZ	.289	1028	3952	510	1142	192	61	40	404	26-32	26	285	344	138-62
FIELDER	.243	218	506	67	123	19	2	31	84	0-3	3	46	144	0-2
GARCIA, D.	.288	902	3572	453	1028	172	26	32	296	27-20	18	110	284	194-86
GARCIA, P.	.208	41	130	10	27	10	1	0	9	3-0	3	5	21	0-0
GOMEZ	.227	212	576	50	131	14	3	0	42	21-3	0	40	58	3-10
GRIFFIN	.250	873	3151	346	789	117	50	13	84	67-22	14	134	280	76-72
GRUBER	.266	688	2219	321	590	111	19	83	326	9-26	25	138	351	61-19
HEARRON	.200	16	30	2	6	1	0	0	4	0-0	0	3	9	0-0
HERNANDEZ, P.	.000	11	9	2	0	0	0	0	0	0-0	0	0	3	0-0
HERNANDEZ, T.	.500	3	2	1	1	0	0	0	0	0-0	0	0	0	0-0
HILL	.240	103	312	51	75	11	3	13	39	0-0	0	21	74	10-4
HODGSON	.220	20	41	5	9	0	1	1	5	2-0	0	3	12	0-1
HORTON	.205	33	122	12	25	6	0	3	19	0-1	0	3	29	0-0
HOWELL	.272	516	1954	219	532	101	17	43	234	12-11	13	178	337	5-6
HUTTON	.254	64	173	19	44	9	0	2	9	5-0	0	19	12	1-2
INFANTE	.185	40	27	8	5	0	0	0	0	1-0	0	2	5	1-0
IORG	.258	931	2450	251	633	125	16	20	238	21-19	11	114	288	22-17
JOHNSON, A.	.235	70	98	17	23	2	1	3	14	1-1	0	11	26	3-13
JOHNSON, C.	.273	400	1175	162	321	58	3	54	202	1-10	12	178	203	0-3
JOHNSON, T.	.212	110	165	15	35	4	1	0	9	5-1	1	16	31	0-2
KELLY	.286	3	7	0	2	0	0	0	0	0-0	0	0	4	0-0
KLUTTS	.256	22	43	3	11	0	0	3	5	0-0	1	1	11	0-1
KUSICK	.204	24	54	3	11	1	0	2	7	0-1	1	7	7	0-0
LAWLESS	.207	74	82	21	17	1	0	0	4	1-1	0	7	13	12-3
LEACH	.283	376	763	95	216	46	6	8	95	0-9	3	67	99	0-2
LEE	.259	487	1311	141	339	39	13	13	131	10-10	0	86	246	13-11
LIRIANO	.251	318	1022	132	257	45	9	11	101	18-7	5	96	133	44-19
MACHA, K.	.200	37	85	4	17	2	0	0	6	0-1	0	8	15	1-1
MACHA, M.	.000	5	8	0	0	0	0	0	0	0-0	0	0	1	0-0
MANRIQUE	.189	24	37	1	7	0	0	0	2	0-0	1	0	13	0-1
MARTINEZ	.221	454	1100	114	243	63	2	35	154	11-23	4	123	175	2-5
MASON	.165	22	79	10	13	3	0	0	2	2-0	0	7	10	1-1
MATUSZEK	.212	62	151	23	32	6	2	2	15	0-4	0	11	24	2-1
MAYBERRY	.256	549	1803	215	461	62	6	92	272	5-16	21	257	247	3-4
MAZZILLI	.227	28	66	12	15	3	0	4	11	0-1	2	17	16	2-0
McGRIFF	.278	578	1944	348	540	99	8	125	305	2-13	11	352	495	21-10
McKAY	.223	287	934	96	208	33	11	10	79	24-3	4	34	160	7-6
MILNER	.444	2	9	3	4	0	1	0	2	0-0	0	0	1	0-0
MOORE	.215	51	107	15	23	10	1	1	7	4-0	1	13	12	0-0
MOSEBY	.257	1392	5124	768	1319	242	60	149	651	38-40	50	547	1015	255-86
MULLINIKS	.282	1015	2771	354	782	192	13	66	364	13-23	5	370	421	12-10
MYERS	.215	111	303	34	65	9	1	5	23	1-4	0	24	45	0-2
NICOSIA	.267	6	15	0	4	0	0	0	1	0-0	0	0	0	0-0
NORDBROOK	.175	31	63	10	11	0	1	0	1	1-0	1	4	11	1-0
NORDHAGEN	.270	72	185	12	50	6	0	1	20	0-2	0	10	22	0-2
OLERUD	.268	117	366	45	98	15	1	14	48	1-4	1	57	76	0-2
OLIVER	.251	61	187	20	47	6	1	5	23	0-0	1	7	13	0-0
ORTA	.237	103	245	30	58	6	3	10	38	0-4	0	19	29	1-2
PETRALLI	.314	25	51	3	16	2	0	0	1	1-0	0	5	7	0-0
POWELL	.250	152	348	49	87	13	4	4	33	0-4	0	17	31	6-4
QUINLAN	.500	1	2	0	1	0	0	0	0	0-0	1	0	1	0-0
RADER	.240	96	313	47	75	18	2	13	40	4-5	3	38	67	2-1
RAMOS	.125	5	16	0	2	0	0	0	0	0-0	0	2	5	0-0
REVERING	.215	55	135	15	29	6	0	5	18	0-2	0	22	30	0-3
ROBERTS	.229	40	105	6	24	4	0	1	5	0-1	0	7	16	1-1
ROBERTSON	.103	15	29	1	3	0	0	1	1	0-0	0	3	9	0-0
ROOF	.000	3	5	0	0	0	0	0	0	0-0	0	0	1	0-0
SCOTT	.240	79	233	26	56	9	0	2	15	6-0	0	8	39	10-8
SHARPERSON	.208	32	96	4	20	4	1	0	9	1-0	1	7	15	2-1
SHEPHERD	.167	115	108	23	18	6	0	2	5	1-0	0	5	37	3-1
SOJO	.225	33	80	14	18	3	0	1	9	0-0	0	5	5	1-1

BATTER	AVG	G	AB	R	H	2B	3B	HR	RBI	SH-SF	HP	BB	SO	SB-CS
SOLAITA	.265	36	102	14	27	8	1	2	13	0-2	0	17	16	0-0
STAGGS	.258	72	291	37	75	11	6	2	28	3-1	0	36	38	5-9
STARK	.083	5	12	1	0	0	0	0	0	0-0	0	0	0	0-0
STIEB	.000	1	1	1	0	0	0	0	0	0-0	0	0	0	0-0
THORNTON	.237	79	76	24	18	1	1	1	8	0-0	1	3	24	1-1
TORRES	.241	91	266	33	64	7	3	5	26	5-4	1	16	33	1-1
UPSHAW	.265	1115	3710	538	982	177	42	112	478	33-26	21	390	565	76-50
VELEZ	.257	522	1531	204	394	76	10	72	243	9-14	11	278	333	6-9
VIRGIL	.125	12	16	2	2	1	0	1	2	0-0	0	4	6	0-0
WEBSTER	.206	41	34	11	7	2	1	0	4	0-0	0	2	8	0-1
WELLS	.247	32	73	7	18	5	0	0	5	0-0	0	5	12	0-2
WHITEN	.273	33	88	12	24	1	1	2	7	0-1	0	7	14	2-0
WHITMER	.111	7	9	0	1	1	0	0	0	0-0	0	1	2	0-0
WHITT	.253	1218	3514	424	888	164	15	131	518	20-36	4	403	451	22-24
WILBORN	.000	22	12	3	0	0	0	0	0	1-0	0	2	7	0-1
WILLIAMS	.194	49	72	13	14	6	1	0	8	0-1	1	7	18	7-2
WILSON	.275	201	826	113	227	45	5	5	68	9-5	2	34	139	35-5
WOODS, A.	.270	595	1958	228	529	97	14	33	188	31-15	3	164	176	23-24
WOODS, G.	.211	68	246	22	52	10	1	0	17	3-0	2	8	39	6-4

PITCHING STATISTICS AS BLUE JAYS ('77 thru '90)

* Left Handed

PITCHER	W-L	ERA	G	GS	CG	SV	SHO	IP	H	R	ER	HR	HB	BB	SO	WP
ACKER	23-17	3.84	227	13	0	13	0	436.0	458	216	186	33	23	170	229	16
ALEXANDER	46-26	3.56	106	103	25	0	3	750.0	752	315	297	81	14	172	392	16
AQUINO	1-1	6.35	7	0	0	0	0	11.1	14	8	8	2	0	3	5	1
BAILOR	0-0	7.71	3	0	0	0	0	2.1	4	2	2	2	0	1	0	0
BAIR	0-0	4.05	10	0	0	0	0	13.1	14	6	6	2	0	3	8	1
BARLOW	3-1	4.11	52	1	0	5	0	70.0	79	40	32	5	6	27	24	5
BERENGUER	2-9	4.31	12	11	1	0	0	71.0	62	41	34	7	3	35	29	1
BLACK*	2-1	4.02	3	2	0	0	0	15.2	10	7	7	2	1	3	3	0
BLAIR	3-5	4.06	27	6	0	0	0	68.2	66	33	31	4	1	28	43	3
BOMBACK	6-10	4.74	36	19	0	0	0	150.0	171	86	79	16	4	60	55	9
BRUNO	0-1	7.85	12	0	0	0	0	18.1	30	181	16	4	1	13	9	3
BUICE	1-0	5.82	7	0	0	0	0	17.0	13	12	11	2	0	13	10	1
BUSKEY	9-12	3.86	85	0	0	7	0	158.2	156	73	68	22	1	55	85	3
BYRD	2-13	6.18	17	17	1	0	0	87.1	98	68	60	5	0	68	40	3
CANDELARIA*	0-3	5.48	13	2	0	1	0	21.1	32	13	13	2	2	11	19	2
CAUDILL	6-10	4.09	107	0	0	16	0	105.2	89	51	48	15	4	52	78	0
CASTILLO*	2-1	4.68	31	0	0	1	0	32.2	33	19	17	2	1	12	24	3
CERUTTI*	46-37	3.87	191	108	7	2	2	772.1	800	378	332	110	16	254	369	30
CLANCY	128-140	4.10	352	345	73	1	11	2204.2	2185	1104	1005	219	28	814	1237	82
CLARK*	1-2	5.91	20	3	0	0	0	45.2	66	33	30	6	1	22	21	7
CLARKE*	1-2	6.18	24	0	0	0	0	27.2	31	19	19	7	0	17	18	0
COLEMAN	2-0	4.60	31	0	0	0	0	60.2	67	34	31	6	1	30	28	5
COOPER	0-0	6.75	4	0	0	0	0	5.0	8	4	4	3	0	0	5	0
CRUZ	7-3	1.71	32	0	0	9	0	47.1	28	10	9	0	1	36	51	3
CUMMINGS	2-0	3.78	11	4	0	0	0	33.1	40	16	14	5	2	16	12	1
DAVIS*	2-1	5.12	13	5	0	0	0	31.2	31	21	18	7	0	18	27	1
DARR	0-1	33.75	1	1	0	0	0	1.1	3	5	5	1	1	4	1	0
DEBARR*	0-1	5.91	14	0	0	0	0	21.1	29	14	14	1	0	8	10	2
EDGE	3-4	5.23	9	9	1	0	0	51.2	60	32	30	6	1	24	19	4
EICHHORN	24-18	2.98	202	7	0	15	0	389.1	334	139	129	29	19	138	306	11
ESPINOSA	0-0	9.00	1	0	0	0	0	1.0	4	1	1	0	0	0	0	0
FILER	7-0	3.88	11	9	0	0	0	48.2	38	21	21	6	0	18	24	0
FLANAGAN*	26-27	3.96	76	76	3	0	1	452.1	480	217	198	39	11	150	194	9
FREISLEBEN	2-3	4.95	42	2	0	3	0	91.0	101	57	50	5	2	54	35	6
GARVIN*	20-41	4.46	196	65	15	8	1	606.0	648	318	300	74	13	219	320	17
GEISEL*	1-4	4.39	63	2	0	5	0	84.0	79	43	41	10	4	48	72	2
GILLES	1-0	6.75	2	0	0	0	0	1.1	2	1	1	0	0	0	1	0
GORDON	0-1	6.06	19	0	0	1	0	32.2	36	25	22	3	1	11	16	0
GOTT	21-30	4.25	99	65	8	2	3	442.1	422	233	209	37	11	183	276	11
GOZZO	4-1	4.83	9	3	0	0	0	31.2	35	19	17	1	1	9	10	0
GRILLI	0-0	0.00	1	0	0	0	0	2.1	1	0	0	0	0	0	1	0
HARGAN	1-3	5.22	6	5	1	0	0	29.1	36	17	17	2	0	14	11	2
HARTENSTEIN	0-2	6.59	13	0	0	0	0	27.1	40	22	20	8	1	6	15	0
HENKE	26-25	2.52	340	0	0	151	0	457.0	338	139	128	39	6	133	545	16
HERNANDEZ	1-0	4.76	7	0	0	0	0	22.2	25	15	12	2	1	8	7	1
HUFFMAN	6-18	5.77	31	31	2	0	1	173.0	220	130	111	25	0	68	56	5
JACKSON	24-21	3.50	190	2	0	30	0	337.0	307	148	131	30	7	128	204	10
JEFFERSON	22-56	4.75	127	37	21	1	4	666.1	718	385	352	82	8	266	307	9
JOHNSON, Je.	2-4	4.60	43	0	0	5	0	86.0	91	50	44	9	0	54	54	2
JOHNSON, Jo.	10-7	4.42	30	29	0	0	0	154.2	171	83	76	13	5	40	66	5
KEY*	87-56	3.47	251	184	20	10	4	1269.2	1212	538	489	129	17	301	702	25
KILGUS*	0-0	6.06	11	0	0	0	0	16.1	19	11	11	2	1	7	7	0
KIRKWOOD	4-5	4.24	16	9	3	0	0	68.0	76	36	32	6	0	25	29	3
KUCEK	3-8	6.75	23	12	0	1	0	68.0	83	56	51	9	1	41	35	3
KUSICK	0-0	4.91	1	0	0	0	0	3.2	32	2	2	1	0	0	0	0
LAMP	21-14	4.20	149	7	0	13	0	263.2	286	145	123	21	1	88	143	9
LAVELLE*	7-10	3.77	92	0	0	9	0	100.1	90	50	42	7	0	55	67	1
LEACH*	0-0	27.00	1	0	0	0	0	1.0	2	3	3	1	0	2	0	0
LEAL	51-58	4.14	165	151	27	1	3	946.0	958	476	435	101	22	320	491	23
LEITER*	0-0	2.08	5	1	0	0	0	13.0	10	3	3	1	0	4	9	1
LEMANCZYK	27-45	4.68	95	82	25	0	3	575.0	632	334	299	52	13	212	240	36
LEMONGELLO	1-9	6.29	18	10	2	0	0	83.0	97	64	58	14	3	34	40	2
LUEBBER	0-0	INF	1	0	0	0	0	0	2	1	1	0	0	1	0	0
LUECKEN	0-0	9.00	1	0	0	0	0	1.0	2	1	1	1	0	1	0	0
MacDONALD*	0-0	0.00	4	0	0	0	0	2.1	0	0	0	0	0	2	0	0
MAHLER*	0-0	0.00	2	0	0	0	0	1.0	1	0	0	0	1	0	0	0
McLAUGHLIN	22-24	3.88	195	10	0	31	0	341.0	343	169	147	36	5	148	207	10
MILLER	0-0	10.57	10	0	0	0	0	15.1	27	18	18	3	0	5	7	2
MIRABELLA*	5-12	4.64	41	23	3	0	1	145.1	171	89	75	13	4	73	62	4
MOFFITT	6-2	3.77	45	0	0	10	0	57.1	52	27	24	5	1	24	38	0
MOORE*	12-17	4.96	102	37	7	1	0	348.1	376	213	192	39	19	164	148	11
MORGAN	0-3	5.16	16	4	0	0	0	45.1	48	26	26	6	0	21	22	3
MURPHY	9-12	4.00	79	1	0	9	0	164.1	173	76	73	18	1	63	67	9
MURRAY	9-7	2.92	67	0	0	11	0	126.1	127	50	41	3	3	37	72	5

PITCHER	W-L	ERA	G	GS	CG	SV	SHO	IP	H	R	ER	HR	HB	BB	SO	WP
MUSSELMAN,J	20-11	4.26	94	19	0	3	0	190.1	182	99	90	14	6	98	100	9
MUSSELMAN,R	5-2	3.79	36	4	0	1	0	73.2	77	35	31	4	0	34	38	3
NIEKRO	0-2	8.25	3	3	0	0	0	12.0	15	11	11	4	0	7	7	1
NUNEZ	5-3	4.40	56	12	0	0	0	137.0	127	71	67	15	1	77	131	7
ROSS	0-0	4.91	3	0	0	0	0	7.1	5	6	4	0	0	4	4	0
SANCHEZ	0-1	10.03	4	3	0	0	0	11.2	16	13	13	1	0	14	4	1
SCHROM	2-0	5.44	23	0	0	1	0	46.1	45	29	28	5	0	34	21	1
SENTENEY	0-0	4.91	11	0	0	0	0	22.0	23	16	12	5	0	6	20	1
SINGER	2-8	6.79	13	12	0	0	0	59.2	71	54	45	5	2	39	33	3
STIEB	166-123	3.37	390	382	101	1	30	2666.2	2337	1097	989	205	118	937	1557	47
STOTTLEMYRE	24-32	4.51	88	67	4	0	0	428.2	460	227	215	44	17	159	245	12
TODD	7-10	4.27	45	26	7	0	0	215.0	224	117	102	31	7	68	99	9
UNDERWOOD*	15-30	3.88	64	62	19	0	2	424.2	414	218	183	46	11	182	267	18
VUCKOVICH	9-7	3.47	53	8	3	8	1	148.0	143	64	57	13	5	59	123	12
WALLACE	0-0	3.86	6	0	0	0	0	148.0	12	6	6	1	0	11	7	1
WARD	16-22	3.67	217	2	0	41	0	367.2	313	165	150	18	11	176	336	29
WELLS*	25-18	3.29	156	27	0	10	0	369.0	333	147	135	31	4	116	281	23
WILEY	0-0	6.75	2	0	0	0	0	2.2	3	2	2	0	0	1	2	0
WILLIAMS	1-1	14.63	4	3	0	0	0	8.0	13	13	13	5	1	7	5	0
WILLIS*	7-21	4.59	144	6	1	15	0	296.0	312	161	151	36	3	123	149	9
WILLS	9-5	4.38	78	8	0	0	0	191.0	188	97	93	19	2	74	132	6

BLUE JAY CAREER GAMES BY POSITION

FIRST BASEMEN

Willie Upshaw	950
John Mayberry	494
Fred McGriff	474
Doug Ault	179
Cecil Fielder	65

SECOND BASEMEN

Damasco Garcia	869
Manny Lee	344
Garth Iorg	338
Nelson Liriano	288
Dave McKay	226

THIRD BASEMEN

Rance Mulliniks	720
Kelly Gruber	598
Garth Iorg	556
Roy Howell	490

SHORTSTOP

Tony Fernandez	1010
Alfredo Griffin	839
Luis Gomez	168
Manny Lee	99
Bob Bailor	69
Hector Torres	68

OUTFIELDERS

Lloyd Moseby	1349
George Bell	1066
Jesse Barfield	996
Al Woods	531
Barry Bonnell	530
Bob Bailor	404

CATCHERS

Ernie Whitt	1139
Buck Martinez	441
Rick Cerone	251
Pat Borders	226
Alan Ashby	205

PITCHERS

Dave Stieb	390
Jim Clancy	352
Tom Henke	340
Jimmy Key	251
Jim Acker	227
Duane Ward	217
Mark Eichhorn	202
Jerry Garvin	196
Joey McLaughlin	195
John Cerutti	191
Roy Lee Jackson	190
Luis Leal	165

In the Blue Jays first fourteen seasons, the following number of players have been utilized at each position

Catcher	26
First Basemen	33
Second Basemen	24
Third Basemen	32
Shortstop	18
Outfielders	53
Pitchers	83

BLUE JAYS HOME RUNS, FIRST MAJOR LEAGUE APPEARANCE

When Al Woods batted for Steve Bowling in the 5th inning on April 7, 1977 he became the 11th player in major league history to hit a home run as a pinch hitter in his first at bat.
Junior Felix on May 4, 1989 became the 11th major leaguer to homer on his first major league pitch vs California's Kirk McCaskill (solo).

BLUE JAYS' TRADES

DATE	CLUB	OBTAINED	FOR
11-5-76	Cleveland	Alan Ashby, c Doug Howard, 1b-of	Al Fitzmorris, rhp
12-6-76	Cleveland	Rick Cerone, c John Lowenstein, of	Rico Carty, 1b-of
2-17-77	San Diego	Jerry Johnson, rhp	Dave Roberts, c-if
2-24-77	Oakland	Ron Fairly, 1b-of	Mike Weathers, if
3-29-77	Cleveland	Hector Torres, if	John Lowenstein, of
5-9-77	Texas	Roy Howell, if	Steve Hargan, rhp Jim Mason, if
12-6-77	St. Louis	Tom Underwood, lhp Victor Cruz, rhp	Peter Vuckovich, rhp John Scott, of
12-8-77	California	Pat Kelly, c Butch Alberts, 1b-of	Ron Fairly, 1b-of
3-3-78	St. Louis	Rick Bosetti, of	Tom Bruno, rhp
3-3-78	Cleveland	Rico Carty, dh	Dennis DeBarr, lhp
4-28-78	Milwaukee	Tim Johnson, inf	Tim Nordbrook, inf
8-15-78	Oakland	Willie Horton, dh Phil Huffman, rhp	Rico Carty, dh
9-12-78	San Diego	Mark Wiley, rhp	Andrew Dyes, of
11-27-78	Houston	Mark Lemongello, rhp Joe Cannon, of Pedro Hernandez, inf	Alan Ashby, c
12-5-78	Houston	Don Pisker, of	Gary Woods, of
12-6-78	Cleveland	Alfredo Griffin, inf Phil Lansford, 3b	Victor Cruz, rhp
11-1-79	New York (AL)	Chris Chambliss, 1b Paul Mirabella, lhp Damaso Garcia, inf	Tom Underwood, lhp Rick Cerone, c Ted Wilborn, of
12-5-79	Atlanta	Barry Bonnell, of Joey McLaughlin, rhp Pat Rockett, inf	Chris Chambliss, 1b Luis Gomez, ss
12-12-80	New York (NL)	Roy Lee Jackson, rhp	Bob Bailor, if-of
4-6-81	New York (NL)	Mark Bomback, rhp	Charlie Puleo, rhp
5-11-81	Milwaukee	Buck Martinez, c	Gil Kubski, of
6-10-81	Oakland	Future considerations	Rick Bosetti, of
11-18-81	New York (AL)	Aurelio Rodriguez, if	Mike Lebo, c
12-28-81	Minnesota	Hosken Powell, of	Greg Wells, 1b
12-28-81	Chicago (NL)	Dave Geisel, lhp	Paul Mirabella, lhp
3-25-82	Kansas City	Rance Mulliniks, if	Phil Huffman, rhp
4-2-82	Chicago (AL)	Wayne Nordhagen, of-dh	Aurelio Rodriguez, 3b
5-5-82	New York (AL)	Dave Revering, 1b-dh Jeff Reynolds, 3b	John Mayberry, 1b
6-15-82	Philadelphia	Dick Davis, of	Wayne Nordhagen, of (to Pittsburgh)
10-27-82	New York (AL)	Tucker Ashford, 3b	'conditional'
11-5-82	Oakland	Cliff Johnson, dh	Al Woods, of
12-9-82	New York (AL)	Dave Collins, of Mike Morgan, rhp Fred McGriff, 1b	Dale Murray, rhp Tom Dodd, of-c
2-4-83	Kansas City	Cecil Fielder, 1b	Leon Roberts, of
2-4-83	New York (NL)	Jorge Orta, dh-of	Steve Senteney, rhp
12-9-83	Seattle	Bryan Clark, lhp	Barry Bonnell, of
12-19-83	Kansas City	Willie Aikens, if-dh	Jorge Orta, dh-of
12-8-84	Oakland	Bill Caudill, rhp	Dave Collins, of Alfredo Griffin, ss
1-26-85	San Francisco	Gary Lavelle, lhp	Jim Gott, rhp Jack McKnight, rhp Augie Schmidt, if
4-1-85	Philadelphia	Len Matuszek, 1b-dh	Dave Shipanoff, rhp Jose Escobar, if Ken Kinnard, of
7-9-85	Los Angeles	Al Oliver, dh	Len Matuszek, 1b-dh
8-29-85	Texas	Cliff Johnson, dh	Matt Williams, rhp Greg Ferlenda, rhp Jeff Mays, rhp
7-5-86	Atlanta	Duane Ward, rhp	Doyle Alexander, rhp
7-6-86	Atlanta	Joe Johnson, rhp	Jim Acker, rhp
2-2-87	Atlanta	Craig McMurtry, rhp	Damaso Garcia, if Luis Leal, rhp
7-14-87	Kansas City	Juan Beniquez, of-dh	Luis Aquino, rhp
8-31-87	Baltimore	Mike Flanagan, lhp	Oswald Peraza, rhp Jose Mesa, rhp
4-30-89	New York (AL)	Al Leiter, lhp	Jesse Barfield, of
7-31-89	New York (NL)	Mookie Wilson, of	Jeff Musselman, lhp Mike Brady, rhp
8-24-89	Atlanta	Jim Acker, rhp	Tony Castillo, lhp Francisco Cabrera, c
9-17-89	Atlanta	Ricky Trlicek, rhp	Ernie Whitt, c Kevin Batiste, of
7-27-90	Minnesota	John Candelaria, lhp	Nelson Liriano, if Pedro Munoz, of
9-17-90	Cleveland	Bud Black, lhp	Mauro Gozzo, rhp Alex Sanchez, rhp Steve Cummings, rhp
11-6-90	Atlanta	Nate Cromwell, lhp	Earl Sanders, rhp
11-6-90	California	Devon White, of Willie Fraser, rhp Marcus Moore, rhp	Junior Felix, of Luis Sojo, if Ken Rivers, c
12-5-90	San Diego	Joe Carter, of Roberto Alomar, if	Tony Fernandez, ss Fred McGriff, 1b
1-15-91	Baltimore	Rene Gonzales, if	Rob Blumberg, lhp

BLUE JAYS FREE AGENT PICKS (Still in Blue Jays Organization)

1977-90 DRAFT

Player	Pos.	Year Drafted	Round Phase	#	Player	Pos.	Year Drafted	Round Phase	#
Dave Stieb	RHP	1978-June	REG.	5	David Weathers	RHP	1988-June	REG.	3
David Wells	LHP	1982-June	SEC.	2	Eric Brooks	C	1988-June	REG.	4
Jimmy Key	LHP	1982-June	REG.	3	Bill Parese	SS	1988-June	REG.	5
Pat Borders	3B	1982-June	REG.	6	Mike Ogliaruso	RHP	1988-June	REG.	6
Glenallen Hill	OF	1983-June	REG.	9	Robert Montalvo	SS	1988-June	REG.	7
Greg Myers	C	1984-June	REG.	3	Marshall Holifield	OF	1988-June	REG.	21
Shawn Jeter	OF	1985-June	REG.	7	Tim Brown	RHP	1988-June	REG.	25
Paul Rodgers	OF	1985-June	REG.	11	Rick Nowak	RHP	1988-June	REG.	26
Todd Stottlemyre	RHP	1985-June	SEC.	1	Woody Williams	RHP	1988-June	REG.	28
Mark Whiten	OF	1986-Jan	REG.	18	Jason Hutson	RHP	1988-June	REG.	30
Andy Dziadkowiec	C	1986-June	REG.	3	Ray Giannelli	3B	1988-June	REG.	38
Pat Hentgen	RHP	1986-June	REG.	5	Eddie Zosky	SS	1989-June	REG.	1
Jerry Schunk	SS	1986-June	REG.	6	Brent Bowers	OF	1989-June	REG.	2.A
Randy Knorr	1B-C	1986-June	REG.	10	John Olerud	1B	1989-June	REG.	3
Carlos Diaz	C	1986-June	REG.	14	Ricky Steed	RHP	1989-June	REG.	5
John Shea	LHP	1986-June	REG.	17	Marc Loeb	C	1989-June	REG.	6
Tom Quinlan	SS	1986-June	REG.	27	Jeff Irish	C	1989-June	REG.	7
Darren Hall	RHP	1986-June	REG.	28	Lonell Roberts	OF	1989-June	REG.	8
Doug Linton	RHP	1986-June	SEC.	43	Shawn Holtzclaw	OF	1989-June	REG.	10
Alex Sanchez	RHP	1987-June	REG.	1	Walt Heckel	2B	1989-June	REG.	12
Derek Bell	OF	1987-June	REG.	2	Mike Taylor	LHP	1989-June	REG.	13
Rob Wishnevski	RHP	1987-June	REG.	3	Jeff Kent	2B	1989-June	REG.	20
Mike Timlin	OF	1987-June	REG.	5	Gregg Martin	RHP	1989-June	REG.	21
Jason Townley	C	1987-June	REG.	7	Aaron Small	OF	1989-June	REG.	22
Nate Cromwell	LHP	1987-June	REG.	11	Sean Hearn	OF	1989-June	REG.	24
Ryan Thompson	OF	1987-June	REG.	13	Daren Brown	RHP	1989-June	REG.	29
Mark Young	OF	1987-June	REG.	16	Kris Harmes	C	1989-June	REG.	36
Bob MacDonald	LHP	1987-June	REG.	19	Daren Kizziah	RHP	1989-June	REG.	37
Ed Sprague	3B	1988-June	REG.	1	Greg Bicknell	RHP	1989-June	REG.	39
Tim Hodge	C	1988-June	REG.	2	Don Mengel	3B	1989-June	REG.	43

BLUE JAYS FREE AGENT DRAFT PICKS

(Signed from June, 1990)

Player	Pos.	Year Drafted	Round Phase	#	Player	Pos.	Year Drafted	Round Phase	#
Steve Karsay	RHP	1990-June	REG.	1	Carlos Santiago	OF	1990-June	REG.	19
Chris Weinke	3B	1990-June	REG.	2	Matthew Wilke	SS	1990-June	REG.	20
Tim Hyers	1B	1990-June	REG.	2	Raphael Garcia	RHP	1990-June	REG.	21
Felipe Crespo	3B	1990-June	REG.	3	Sam Mandia	RHP	1990-June	REG.	22
Howard Battle	SS	1990-June	REG.	4	Dave Marcon	LHP	1990-June	REG.	26
Scott Burrell	RHP	1990-June	REG.	5	Thomas Hotchkiss	RHP	1990-June	REG.	27
David Tollison	2B	1990-June	REG.	6	Robert Adkins	RHP	1990-June	REG.	28
Scott Brow	RHP	1990-June	REG.	7	Dale Kistaitis	LHP	1990-June	REG.	29
Paul Menhart	RHP	1990-June	REG.	8	Ciro Ambrosio	SS	1990-June	REG.	30
Greg Flener	LHP	1990-June	REG.	9	Gregory Wilcox	RHP	1990-June	REG.	31
Tom Singer	LHP	1990-June	REG.	10	Kyle Duey	RHP	1990-June	REG.	32
Daniel Viitala	OF	1990-June	REG.	11	Scott Miller	SS	1990-June	REG.	34
Mark Choate	SS	1990-June	REG.	12	Ricardo Jordan	LHP	1990-June	REG.	37
Matthew Watson	RHP	1990-June	REG.	14	Donald Boston	1B	1990-June	REG.	39
Travis Burley	RHP	1990-June	REG.	15	Joe Ganote	RHP	1990-June	REG.	41
Mike Coolbaugh	SS	1990-June	REG.	16	Roberto Duran	OF	1990-June	REG.	42
Allen Rhea	LHP	1990-June	REG.	17	Travis Baptist	LHP	1990-June	REG.	45
Ronald Reams	OF	1990-June	REG.	18					

1990 BLUE JAYS FIRST CHOICE IN JUNE DRAFT

1977	Tom Goffena-SS, #25	1984	Dane Johnson-RHP, #46
1978	Lloyd Moseby-OF, #2	1985	Greg David-OF, #25
1979	Jay Schroeder-C, #3	1986	Earl Sanders-RHP, #26
1980	Garry Harris-SS, #2	1987	Alex Sanchez-RHP, #17
1981	Matt Williams-RHP, #5	1988	Ed Sprague-3B, #25
1982	Augie Schmidt-SS, #2	1989	Eddie Zosky-SS, #19
1983	Matt Stark-C, #9	1990	Steve Karsay-RHP, #22

BLUE JAYS OPENING DAY LINEUPS

1977

Opening Game – Home
April 7, 1977 – 44,649

John Scott	– LF
Hector Torres	– SS
Doug Ault	– 1B
Otto Velez	–DH
Gary Woods	– CF
Steve Bowling	– RF
Pedro Garcia	– 2B
Dave McKay	– 3B
Rick Cerone	– C
Bill Singer	– P

Chi 220 001 000 -5-15-0
Tor 112 120 02x -9-16-3

Brett, Barrios (4), Hamilton (7), LaGrow (8) & Downing.
Singer, Johnson (5), Vuckovich (8) & Cerone.
W–Johnson; L–Brett, S–Vuckovich; HRS-Zisk, Ault (2), A. Woods.

1978

Opening Game – Away
April 7, 1978 at Detroit 52,528

Rick Bosetti	– CF
Al Woods	– LF
Roy Howell	– 3B
Rico Carty	–DH
John Mayberry	– 1B
Tommy Hutton	– RF
Dave McKay	– 2B
Luis Gomez	– SS
Alan Ashby	– C
Dave Lemanczyk	– P

Tor 020 000 000 -2-5-0
Det 011 300 10x -6-10-1

Lemanczyk, Jefferson (4) & Ashby; Fidrych & May.
W–Fidrych;
L–Lemanczyk: HRS–May, Mankowski, Thompson.

1979

Opening Game – Away
April 5, 1979 at Kansas City 37,754

Alfredo Griffin	– SS
Bob Bailor	– RF
Roy Howell	– 3B
Rico Carty	–DH
John Mayberry	– 1B
Rick Bosetti	– CF
Bobby Brown	– LF
Dave McKay	– 2B
Rick Cerone	– C
Tom Underwood	– P

Tor 000 020 000 -2-7-3
K.C. 091 001 00x -11-11-2

Underwood, Moore (2), Murphy (5), Freisleben (8) & Cerone.
Leonard, Mingori (7) & Porter, Wathan (7).
W–Leonard; L–Underwood, S–Mingori.

1980

Opening Game – Away
April 9, 1980 at Seattle 22,588

Alfredo Griffin	– SS
Bob Bailor	– RF
John Mayberry	– 1B
Otto Velez	–DH
Roy Howell	– 3B
Barry Bonnell	– LF
Rick Bosetti	– CF
Damaso Garcia	– 2B
Ernie Whitt	– C
Dave Lemanczyk	– P

Tor 200 001 030 -6-9-1
Sea 410 100 20x -8-12-2

Lemanczyk, Buskey (1), Moore (3), Jefferson (6), J. McLaughlin (8) & Whitt, Davis (7).
Parrott, B. McLaughlin (7), Heaverlo (8) & Stinson.
W–Parrott; L–Lemanczyk; S–Heaverlo; HRS–Mayberry (2), Simpson (1).

1981

Opening Game – Away
April 9, 1981 at Detroit 51,452

Alfredo Griffin	– SS
Lloyd Moseby	– CF
Otto Velez	–DH
John Mayberry	– 1B
Willie Upshaw	– LF
Damaso Garcia	– 2B
Barry Bonnell	– RF
Danny Ainge	– 3B
Ernie Whitt	– C
Jim Clancy	– P

Tor 001 010 000 -2-5-1
Det 001 010 310 -6-8-1

Clancy, McLaughlin (7), Willis (7), Jackson (8) & Whitt.
Morris & Parrish
W–Morris;
L–McLaughlin;
HR–Hebner

1982

Opening Game – Home
April 9, 1982 – 30,216

Alfredo Griffin	– SS
Al Woods	– LF
Lloyd Moseby	– CF
Willie Upshaw	– 1B
John Mayberry	–DH
Jesse Barfield	– RF
Ernie Whitt	– C
Damaso Garcia	– 2B
Rance Mulliniks	– 3B
Mark Bomback	– P

Milw 600 107 010 -15-16-2
Tor 000 020 000 -4-8-2

Vuckovich, Easterly (7), Bernard (8), Jones (9) & Moore.
Bomback, Murray (1), Garvin (4), Gott (5), McLaughlin (9) & Whitt
W–Vuckovich; L–Bomback; HRS–Oglivie, Whitt

1983

Opening Game – Away
April 5, 1983 – at Boston 33,842

Damaso Garcia	– 2B
Dave Collins	– LF
Willie Upshaw	– 1b
Cliff Johnson	–DH
Jesse Barfield	– RF
Ernie Whitt	– C
Lloyd Moseby	– CF
Rance Mulliniks	– 3B
Alfredo Griffin	– SS
Dave Stieb	– P

Tor 041 020 000 -7-9-0
Bos 000 001 000 -1-3-0

Stieb, Jackson (7) & Whitt
Eckersley, Hurst (5), Johnson (9) & Gedman
W–Stieb; L–Eckersley; S–Jackson; HRS–Mulliniks, Upshaw, Stapleton

1984

Opening Game – Away
April 4, 1984 – at Seattle 43,200

Damaso Garcia	– 2B
Rance Mulliniks	– 3B
Lloyd Moseby	– CF
Willie Upshaw	– 1B
Cliff Johnson	–DH
George Bell	– LF
Jesse Barfield	– RF
Ernie Whitt	– C
Alfredo Griffin	– SS
Jim Clancy	– P

Tor 001 000 100 0 -2-7-0
Sea 000 000 101 1 -3-9-1

Clancy, Lamp (8) & Whitt.
Moore, Stanton (9) & Kearney, Mercado (9)
W–Stanton; L–Lamp
HRS–Whitt, Phelps

1985

Opening Game – Away
April 8, 1985 at Kansas City – 41,086

Damaso Garcia	– 2B
Lloyd Moseby	– CF
George Bell	– LF
Jesse Barfield	– RF
Jeff Burroughs	–DH
Willie Upshaw	– 1B
Buck Martinez	– C
Garth Iorg	– 3B
Tony Fernandez	– SS
Dave Stieb	– P

Tor 010 000 000 -1-5-1
KC 000 000 20x -2-6-2

Stieb, Lavelle (7), & Whitt.
Black, Quisenberry (8) & Sundberg, Wathan (8)
W–Black; L–Stieb, SV–Quisenberry

1986

Opening Game – Away
April 8, 1986 at Texas – 40,602

Lloyd Moseby	– CF
Tony Fernandez	– SS
Rance Mulliniks	– 3B
Willie Upshaw	– 1B
George Bell	– LF
Jesse Barfield	– RF
Ernie Whitt	– C
Cecil Fielder	–DH
Damaso Garcia	– 2B
Dave Stieb	– P

Tor 000 003 000 -3-10-1
Tex 000 330 00x -6-8-0

Stieb, Eichhorn (5), & Whitt.
Guzman, Harris (9) & Slaught, Porter (6)
W–Guzman; L–Stieb; S–Harris
HRS–Slaught, Parrish

1987

Opening Game – Home
April 6, 1987 – 40,404

Tony Fernandez	– SS
Rance Mulliniks	– 3B
Lloyd Moseby	– CF
George Bell	– LF
Jesse Barfield	– RF
Willie Upshaw	– 1B
Ernie Whitt	– C
Fred McGriff	–DH
Mike Sharperson	– 2B
Jimmy Key	– P

Clev 000 200 100 -3-6-1
Tor 120 013 00x -7-11-0

Key, Eichhorn (8), Henke (9) & Whitt.
Candiotti, Jones (6), Bailes (7), Waddell (8) & Bando
W–Key L–Candiotti
HRS–Moseby, Upshaw

1988

Opening Game – Away
April 4, 1988 at Kansas City – 40,648

Nelson Liriano	– 2B
Lloyd Moseby	– LF
Tony Fernandez	– SS
George Bell	–DH
Rance Mulliniks	– 3B
Ernie Whitt	– C
Jesse Barfield	– RF
Fred McGriff	– 1B
Sil Campusano	– CF
Jimmy Key	– P

Tor 010 300 010 -5-9-0
KC 200 000 100 -3-11-1

Key, Wells (7), Eichhorn (7), Henke (8) & Whitt.
Saberhagen, Quisenberry (9) & MacFarlane.
W–Key L–Saberhagen
SV–Henke
HRS–Bell (3), Brett

1989

Opening Game – Away
April 3, 1989 at Kansas City – 38,595

Lloyd Moseby	– CF
Rance Mulliniks	– 3B
Tony Fernandez	– SS
George Bell	– LF
Fred McGriff	– 1B
Jesse Barfield	– RF
Ernie Whitt	– C
Nelson Liriano	– DH
Manny Lee	– 2B
Jimmy Key	– P

Tor 010 200 100 -4-10-0
KC 000 000 300 -3-9-0

Key, Ward (6), Henke (9) & Whitt.
Gubicza, Gordon (8) & Boone
W–Key; L–Gubicza, SV–Henke

1990

Opening Game — Away
April 9, 1990 at Texas
40,907

Tony Fernandez	— SS
Mookie Wilson	— CF
Kelly Gruber	— 3B
George Bell	— LF
Fred McGriff	— 1B
John Olderud	— DH
Greg Myers	— C
Nelson Liriano	—2B
Junior Felix	— RF
Todd Stottlemyre	— P

Tor 000 000 020 -2-3-0
Tex 201 000 10X -4-7-0

Stottlemyre, Wells (4), Wills (6), Acker (8) & Myers.
Ryan, Jeffcoat (6), Russell (8) & Petralli.
W-Ryan; SV-Russell; L-Stottlemyre
HRS-Baines, Palmeiro

HOME OPENERS

April 14, 1978–35,761

Det 311 100 002 -8-13-3
Tor 201 006 00x -10-12-0

Slaton, Wilcox (3), Hiller (6), Taylor (8) & May.
Garvin, Moore (3), Kirkwood (3), Murphy (9) & Ashby.
W–Kirkwood; L–Wilcox; S– Murphy; HRS–LeFlore, Thompson.

April 13, 1979–40,035

KC 000 010 -1-2-0
Tor 001 21x -4-7-0

STOPPED BY RAIN AFTER $5^1/_2$ INNINGS.
Splittorff (L) & Porter; Clancy (W) & Cerone.
HR–Howell.

April 16, 1980–12,688

Milw 002 000 000 -2-6-2
Tor 220 400 21x -11-12-0

Slaton, Cleveland (4) Augustine (4), Boitano (7), McClure (8) & Moore.
Stieb & Whitt.
W–Stieb; L–Slaton; HR– Howell.

April 13, 1981–25,112

NY 100 000 000 -1-5-0
Tor 000 300 20x -5-7-0

John, Underwood (7), Bird (8) & Cerone.
Clancy, Jackson (8) & Whitt.
W–Clancy; SV–Jackson; L–John.

April 9, 1983–36,459

NY 000 000 220 -4-9-2
Tor 020 000 05x -7-10-3

Gott, McLaughlin (7), Geisel (7), Jackson (7) & Whitt. Alexander, Gossage (8) & Cerone.
W–Jackson; L–Gossage; HR–Barfield.

April 17, 1984–35,602

Balt 000 020 000 -2-6-0
Tor 000 002 01x -3-9-0

Boddicker, T. Martinez (6), Stewart (8) & Dempsey
Alexander, Key (8), Lamp (9) & Whitt, Martinez (7)
W–Key; L–T. Martinez; SV–Lamp; HR–Lowenstein.

April 16, 1985–41,284

Tex 000 040 212 -9-12-1
Tor 000 030 001 -4-10-3

Mason, Noles (7) & Slaught.
Leal, Musselman (5), Lamp (7) & Martinez
HR–Iorg.
W–Mason; L–Leal; SV–Noles.

April 14, 1986–43,587

Balt 001 010 000 -2-9-1
Tor 100 000 000 -1-4-0

Boddicker & Dempsey
Alexander & Whitt
W–Boddicker; L–Alexander.

April 11, 1988–45,185

NY 300 211 020 -9-12-2
Tor 603 003 14x -17-20-1

Rhoden, John (3), Gutterman (4), Stoddard (5), Guante (6), Hudson (8) & Slaught.
Flanagan, Ward (5), Wells (6) & Whitt.
W–Wells; L–Rhoden; HRS–Gruber (2).

April 14, 1989–46,028

KC 000 000 000 -0-2-0
Tor 000 000 21 × -3-11-1

Key & Borders
Leibrandt, Montgomery (8), Gleaton (8), Aquino (8) & MacFarlane
W–Key; L–Leibrandt

April 10, 1990—49,673

Tex 000 000 001 -1-5-0
Tor 000 020 00x -2-6-0

Hough, Bohanon (6), Mielke (7), Rogers (7) & Petralli
Stieb, Henke (7), Ward (8), Wells (8) &Myers, Borders (8)
W-Stieb; SV-Wells
L-Hough
HR-Sierra

OPENING DAY RECORDS

OVERALL RECORD: 5-9
HOME OPENERS: 11-3
MOST RUNS: 9, Tor-9 vs Chicago, April 7/77
MOST HITS: 16, Tor-9 vs Chicago, April 7/77
FEWEST HITS: 3, 1990
MOST RUNS, OPPONENT: 15-Milwaukee at Toronto-4, April 9/82
MOST HITS, OPPONENT: 16-Milwaukee at Toronto, April 9/82
FEWEST HITS, OPPONENT: 3-Boston vs Toronto, April 5/83
EARLIEST OPENING DAY: April 4/84, Toronto-2 at Seattle-3; April 4/88, Toronto at Kansas City
LATEST OPENING DAY: April 9, 1981, 1982 & 1990
RECORD VS OPPONENTS: Boston, 1-0; Chicago, 1-0; Cleveland, 1-0; Detroit, 0-2; Kansas City, 2-2; Milwaukee, 0-1; Seattle, 0-2; Texas, 0-2
MOST STARTS: Dave Stieb, Jimmy Key (3)
MOST WINS: Jimmy Key, 2
MOST LOSSES: Dave Lemanczyk, -2; Dave Stieb, -2

BLUE JAYS YEAR-BY-YEAR

WON-LOST

Year	W-L	H	R	PCT	Home POS	GB	Attendance	Manager
1977	**54-107**	**25-55**	**29-52**	**.335**	**7th**	**45.5**	**1,701,052**	**Roy Hartsfield**
1978	59-102	37-44	22-58	.366	7th	50	1,562,585	Roy Hartsfield
1979	53-109	32-49	21-60	.327	7th	50.5	1,431,651	Roy Hartsfield
1980	67-95	35046	32-49	.414	7th	36	1,400,327	Bob Mattick
1981	16-42 (1st half)	17-36	20-33	276	7th	19	—	Bob Mattick
	21-27 (2nd half)			.438	7th	7.5	755,083	Bob Mattick
1982	78-84	44-37	34-47	.481	T6th	17	1,275,978	Bobby Cox
1983	89-73	48-33	41-40	.549	4th	9	1.930,415	Bobby Cox
1984	89-73	49-32	40-41	549	2nd	15	2,110,009	Bobby Cox
1985	99-62	54-26	45-36	.615	1st	+2	2,468,925	Bobby Cox
1986	86-76	42-39	44-37	.531	4th	9.5	2,455,477	Jimy Williams
1987	96-66	52-29	44-37	.593	2nd	2	2,778,429	Jimy Williams
1988	87-75	45-36	42-39	.537	T3rd	2	2,595,175	Jimy Williams
1989	89-73	46-35	43-38	.549	1st	+2	3,375,883	Jimy Williams/
1990	86-76	44-37	42-39	.531	2nd	2.0	3,885,284	Cito Gaston

CLINCHING/ELIMINATION DATES

Year	Date	GP	EliminatedBy	H/A	Score Tor-Opp	Division Winner	GBL
*1977	Aug. 30	129	Did not play	-	-	New York	33
#1978	Aug. 29	133	Texas	A	4-1	New York	30.5
1979	Aug. 19	123	California	A	2-4	Baltimore	41
†1980	Sept. 7	137	Chicago	H	7-6	New York	27
‡1981	May 17	34	sCleveland	A	0-1	New York	10
	Sept. 22	39	Oakland	H	2-4	Milwaukee	5.5
1982	Sept. 14	143	aDid not play	-	-	Milwaukee	19
1983	Sept. 21	153	Seattle	H	4-3	Baltimore	11
1984	Sept. 18	151	Boston	H	10-3	Detroit	13
1985	Oct. 5	160	New York	H	5-1	Toronto	+2
1986	Sept. 28	156	Boston	A	3-12	Boston	9
1987	Oct. 4	162	Detroit	A	0-1	Detroit	2
1988	Sept. 25	156	Cleveland	A	3-4	Boston	7.5
1989	Sept. 30	161	Baltimore	H	4-3	Toronto	+2
1990	Oct. 3	162	Baltimore	A	2-3	Boston	2

*New York defeated Seattle, 6-6, to eliminate Blue Jays
#Boston (leader on Aug. 29) defeated Seattle, 10-5, to eliminate Blue Jays
†New York defeated Claifornia, 4-1, to eliminate Blue Jays
2nd game of DH
s1st game of DH
‡Split-Season
aMilwaukee defeated Detroit, 6-3, to eliminate Blue Jays

STANDING BY MONTH

	May 1st (GB)	June 1st (GB)	July 1st (GB)	Aug. 1st (GB)	Sept. 1st (GB)
1977	5(03)	7(-9)	7(-13.5)	7(-23)	7(-32.5)
1978	7(-6.5)	7(-16)	7(-25.5)	7(27)	7(30.5)
1979	6(-7)	7(-19)	7(-30.51)	7(-39.5)	7(-45)
1980	1(+1)	3(-5.5)	7(-14)	7(-18.57)	7(-24)
*1981	7(-5)	7(-14)	—	—	6(-3)
1982	5(-5)	7(-9/0	7(-11)	7(-10)	7(17.5)
1983	6(-2)	1(+0.5)	1(+2)	4(-2.5)	5(7.5)
1984	2(-6)	2(5.51)	2(-10)	2(-12)	2(-9.5)
1985	1(+0.5)	1(+4)	1(+3.5)	1(7.5)	1(+5)
1986	7(-5)	7(-10)	5(-10.5)	4(-5.5)	2(-3.5)
1987	3(5.5)	2(-2)	2(-2)	2(2.5)	2(-1)
1988	6(-7)	6(-12)	T5(-9)	6(-11.5)	5(-10.5)
1989	7(-3.5)	7(-7.5)	4(-7)	2(-3)	T1
1990	3(-1.5)	1(+0.5)	2(-3.5)	T1	2(-5.5)

*SPLIT-SEASON

PITCHING

YEAR	W-L	ERA	G	RE	CG	SHO	SV	IP	H	R	ER	HR	BB	SO	HB	WP
1977	54-107	4.57	348	187	40	3	20	1428	1568	822	725	152	623	771	20	62
1978	59-102	4.55	374	213	35	5	23	1429	1529	775	723	149	614	758	22	47
1979	53-109	4.82	357	195	44	7	11	1417	1537	862	759	165	594	613	40	64
1980	67-95	4.19	448	286	39	9	23	1466	1523	762	683	135	635	705	28	41
1981	37-69	3.81	295	189	20	4	18	953	908	466	404	72	377	451	36	41
1982	78-84	3.95	382	220	41	13	25	1444	1428	701	633	147	493	776	25	38
1983	89-73	4.12	419	257	43	8	32	1445	1434	726	662	145	517	835	42	25
1984	89-73	3.86	420	257	34	10	33	1464	1433	696	628	140	528	875	34	42
1985	99-62	3.29	477	316	18	9	47	1448	1312	588	529	147	484	823	26	36
1986	86-76	4.08	453	290	16	12	44	1476	1467	733	669	164	487	1002	45	38
1987	96-66	3.74	—	—	18	8	43	1454	1323	655	605	158	567	1064	22	56
1988	87-75	3.80	455	293	16	17	47	1449	1404	680	611	143	528	904	59	48
1989	89-73	3.58	439	293	12	12	38	1467	1408	651	584	99	478	849	45	58
1990	86-76	3.84	479	317	6	9	48	1454	1434	661	620	143	445	892	37	43

BATTING

YEAR	AVG.	G	AB	R	H	TB	2B	3B	HOMERS T-H-A
1977	.252	161	5419	605	1367	2099	230	41	100-45-55
1978	.250	161	5430	590	1358	1947	217	39	98-50-48
1979	.251	162	5423	613	1362	1968	253	34	95-50-45
1980	.251	162	5571	624	1398	2131	249	53	126-56-70
1981	.226	106	3521	329	797	1163	137	23	61-34-27
1982	.262	162	5526	651	1447	2117	262	45	106-62-44
1983	.277	162	5581	795	1546	2431	268	58	167-101-66
1984	.273	163	5687	750	1555	2395	275	58	1143-59-84
1985	.269	161	5508	759	1482	2343	281	53	158-75-83
1986	.269	163	5716	809	1540	2438	285	35	181-87-94
1987	.269	162	5635	845	1514	2512	277	38	215-101-114
1988	.268	162	5557	763	1491	2330	271	47	158-78-80
1989	.260	162	5581	731	1449	2220	265	40	142-64-78
1990	.265	162	5589	767	1479	2343	263	50	167-93-74

YEAR	RBI	BB	SO	SH-SF	HP	SB-CS	LOB	SLUG PCT	GIDP
1977	552	499	819	81-34	23	65-55	1094	.365	156
1978	550	448	645	77-37	23	28-52	1075	.359	124
1979	562	448	663	65-38	36	75-56	1064	.363	131
1980	580	448	813	63-34	33	67-72	1083	.383	119
1981	314	284	556	44-18	20	66-57	658	.330	72
1982	605	415	749	48-50	28	118-81	1071	.383	107
1983	748	510	810	36-54	32	131-71	1106	.436	117
1984	702	460	816	35-49	52	193-67	1177	.421	90
1985	714	503	807	21-44	30	143-77	1067	.425	121
1986	767	496	848	24-49	33	110-59	1099	.427	122
1987	790	555	970	30-35	38	126-50	1126	.446	136
1988	706	521	935	34-50	31	107-36	1105	.419	145
1989	685	521	923	30-53	31	144-58	1102	.398	124
1990	729	526	970	18-62	28	111-52	1113	.419	125

FIELDING

YEAR	PCT	PO	A	E	TC	DP	TP	PB	RANK
1977	.974	4285	1798	164	6247	133	0	7	13
1978	.979	4288	1763	128	6179	163	1	16	5
1979	.975	4251	1878	158	6287	186	2	8	12
1980	.979	4398	1939	133	6470	206	0	8	3
1981	.975	2860	1164	105	4129	102	0	4	14
1982	.978	4331	1768	136	6235	146	0	7	11
1983	.981	4336	1637	115	6088	148	0	7	3
1984	.980	4392	1669	123	6184	166	0	9	4
1985	.980	4344	1729	125	6198	164	0	3	7
1986	.984	4428	1682	100	6210	150	0	9	1
1987	.982	4362	1700	111	6173	148	0	13	4
1988	.982	4347	1737	110	6194	170	0	12	4
1989	.980	4401	1864	127	6392	164	0	16	6
1990	.986	4362	1720	86	6168	144	0	14	1

DESIGNATED HITTING

YEAR	AVG	AB	R	H	2B	3B	HR	RBI	SH-SF	BB	SO	HP	SB-CS	SLUG %	RANK
1977	.269	583	75	157	27	2	22	87	9-8	76	108	4	4-4	.436	5
1978	.250	621	75	155	25	0	25	96	1-8	52	83	1	2-3	.411	10
1979	.260	599	71	156	37	1	18	82	1-6	66	74	1	3-2	.416	8
1980	.229	599	73	137	21	4	22	84	1-5	75	129	1	1-0	.387	14
1981	.212	363	45	77	14	2	13	36	3-2	64	75	4	3-6	.369	13
1982	.238	596	52	142	18	3	8	56	1-8	60	91	0	7-16	.319	14
1983	.250	604	86	151	29	3	34	113	1-6	81	101	5	0-2	.477	12
1984	.270	612	91	165	32	1	27	93	0-4	79	121	5	4-4	.458	4
1985	.247	600	77	148	22	5	13	78	0-8	61	85	1	5-5	.365	6
1986	.242	616	86	149	26	3	20	83	0-2	67	119	5	2-4	.391	10
1987	.258	592	101	153	32	3	38	97	0-3	83	160	5	3-3	.515	7
1988	.288	612	90	176	33	3	25	95	3-5	81	126	1	3-1	.474	1
1989	.216	589	67	127	23	4	8	55	0-4	69	105	6	10-0	.309	14
1990	.220	604	65	133	28	4	14	68	1-11	69	132	3	4-4	.349	13

PINCH HITTING

YEAR	AVG	AB	R	H	2B	3B	HR	RBI	SH-SF	BB	SO	HP	OBP	SLUG %
1977	.280	93	10	26	2	1	5	23	1-2	11	17	0	.349	.484
1978	.236	123	11	29	4	0	2	18	0-1	15	22	2	.326	.317
1979	.231	52	5	12	3	0	4	14	0-0	11	12	0	.365	.519
1980	.280	100	10	28	4	0	3	15	0-0	14	15	1	.374	.410
1981	.234	77	4	18	3	0	1	15	0-0	11	19	0	.330	.312
1982	.271	262	24	71	14	0	4	53	1-3	39	48	1	.364	.370
1983	.290	200	26	58	8	0	5	42	0-5	28	36	1	.372	.405
1984	.284	215	29	61	10	2	6	39	1-4	30	51	1	.368	.433
1985	.222	167	18	37	4	1	4	29	3-4	19	31	1	.319	.329
1986	.277	155	19	43	8	1	4	32	0-4	21	26	0	.356	.419
1987	.234	167	—	39	6	1	3	28	1-3	33	37	1	.358	.335
1988	.202	129	14	26	3	1	2	18	0-0	22	31	1	.322	.287
1989	.264	121	14	32	10	0	3	13	4-0	17	24	0	.355	.421
1990	.216	97	4	21	2	1	0	14	0-0	11	22	1	.303	.258

* League Leader #Based on 250 AB's

BATTING

YEAR	AVG. (350 AB's)	AB	R	H
1977	B. Bailor, .310	B. Bailor, 496	B. Bailor, 62	B. Bailor, 154
	R. Howell, .316			
1978	R. Howell, .270	B. Bailor, 621	B. Bailor, 74	B. Bailor, 164
1979	A. Griffin, .287	A. Griffin, 624	A. Griffin, 81	A. Griffin, 179
1980	Al Woods, .300	A. Griffin, 653	A. Griffin, 63	A. Griffin, 166
1981	D. Garcia, .252#	A. Griffin, 388	L. Moseby, 36	L. Moseby, 88
1982	D. Garcia, .310	W. Upshaw, 580	D. Garcia, 89	D. Garcia, 185
1983	L. Moseby, .315	W. Upshaw, 579	L. Moseby, 104	W. Upshaw, 177
1984	D. Collins, .308	D. Garcia, 633	L. Moseby, 97	D. Garcia, 180
1985	R. Mulliniks, .295	G. Bell, 607	J. Barfield, 94	G. Bell, 167
1986	T. Fernandez, .310	T. Fernandez, 687	J. Barfield, 107	T. Fernandez, 213
1987	T. Fernandez, .322	G. Bell, 610	G. Bell, 111	G. Bell, 188
1988	M. Lee, .291	T. Fernandez, 648	F. McGriff, 100	T. Fernandez, 186
1989	G. Bell, .297	G. Bell, 613	F. McGriff, 98	G. Bell, 182
1990	F. McGriff, .297	T. Fernandez, 635	K. Gruber, 92	T. Fernandez, 175

YEAR	2B	3B	HR	RBI
1977	R. Fairly, 24	S. Staggs, 6	R. Fairly, 19	R. Fairly, 64
				D. Ault, 64
1978	B. Bailor, 29	D. McKay, 8	J. Mayberry, 22	J. Mayberry, 70
1979	R. Bosetti, 35	A. Griffin, 10	J. Mayberry, 21	J. Mayberry, 74
1980	D. Garcia, 30	A. Griffin, 15*	J. Mayberry, 30	J. Mayberry 82
1981	A. Griffin, 19	A. Griffin, 6	J. Mayberry, 17	J. Mayberry, 43
				L. Moseby, 43
1982	D. Garcia, 32	L. Moseby, 9	W. Upshaw, 21	W. Upshaw, 75
1983	R. Mulliniks, 34	A. Griffin, 9	J. Barfield, 27	W. Upshaw, 104
			W. Upshaw, 27	
1984	G. Bell, 39	D. Collins, 15*	G. Bell, 26	L. Moseby, 92
		L. Moseby, 15*		
1985	J. Barfield, 34	T. Fernandez, 10	G. Bell, 28	G. Bell, 95
1986	G. Bell, 38	T. Feranadez, 9	J. Barfield, 40*	J. Barfield, 108
				G. Bell, 108
1987	G. Bell, 32	T. Fernandez, 8	G. Bell, 47	G. Bell, 134*
1988	T. Fernandez, 41	L. Moseby, 7	F. McGriff, 34	G. Bell, 97
1989	G. Bell, 41	T. Fernandez, 9	F. McGriff, 36	G. Bell, 104
1990	K. Gruber,36	T. Fernandez, 17*	F. McGriff, 35	K. Gruber, 118
	M. Wilson, 36			

YEAR	BB	SO	SLUGGING %	ON BASE %
1977	O. Velez, 65	O. Velez, 87	R. Fairly, 465	R. Howell, .370
1978	J. Mayberry, 61	D. McKay, 90	J. Mayberry, .416	J. Mayberry, .330
1979	J. Mayberry, 69	R. Howell, 91	J. Mayberry, .461	J. Mayberry, .374
1980	J. Mayberry, 77	R. Howell, 92	O. Velez, .487	O. Velez, .368
1981	O. Velez, 55	L. Moseby, 86	J. Mayberry, .452#	O. Velez, .366#
1982	W. Upshaw, 52	L. Moseby, 106	W. Upshaw, .443	B. Bonnell, .345
1983	C. Johnson, 67	J. Barfield, 110	W. Upshaw, .515	L. Moseby, .380
1984	L. Moseby, 78	L. Moseby, 122	C. Johnson, .507	C. Johnson, .393
1985	L. Moseby, 76	J. Barfield, 143	J. Barfield, .536	R. Mulliniks, .387
1986	W. Upshaw, 78	J. Barfield, 146	J. Barfield, .559	J. Barfield, .368
1987	L. Moseby, 70	J. Barfield, 141	G. Bell, .605	T. Fernandez, .379
1988	F. McGriff, 79	F. McGriff, 1459	F. McGriff, .552	F. McGriff, .376
1989	F. McGriff, 119	F. McGriff, 132	F. McGriff, .525	F. McGriff, .399
1990	F. McGriff, 94	F. McGriff, 108	F. McGriff, .530	F. McGriff, .400

Year	SB	SH	SF
1977	B. Bailor, 15	A. Ashby, 10	O. Velez, 6
1978	R. Bosetti, 6	L. Gomez, 19	J. Mayberry, 7
1979	A. Griffin, 21	A. Griffin, 16	R. Bosetti, 7
1980	A. Griffin, 18	A. Griffin, 10	A. Griffin, 5
		L. Moseby, 10	R. Howell, 5
1981	D. Garcia, 13	A. Woods, 8	L. Moseby, 4
1982	D. Garcia, 54	A. Griffin, 11	G. Iorg, 7
1983	D. Collins, 31	A. Griffin, 11	W. Upshaw, 7
	D. Garcia		
1984	D. Collins, 60	A. Griffin, 13	B. Martinez, 9
1985	L. Moseby, 37	T. Fernandez, 7	G. Bell, 8
1986	L. Moseby, 32	T. Fernandez, 5	R. Leach, 7
			L. Moseby, 7
1987	L. Moseby, 39	G. Iorg, 6	G. Bell, 9
1988	L. Moseby, 31	K. Gruber, 5	G. Bell, 8
		N. Liriano, 5	
1989	L.Moseby, 24	N. Liriano, 10	G. Bell, 14
1990	T. Fernandez,. 26	M. Wilson, 6	K. Gruber, 13

Year	Pinch-Hits		Hitting Streaks	
1977	Sam Ewing	—9	Roy Howell (May 10-25)	—15
1978	Otto Velez	—8	Dave McKay (May 19-June 2)	—16
1979	Otto Velez	—5	Alfredo Griffin (Aug 28-Sep.t 12)	—14
1980	Steve Braun	—9	Alfredo Griffin (Aug 13-Sept 1)	—19
			John Mayberry (May 31-June 18)	—11
1981	Willie Upshaw	—4	Damaso Garcia (May29-June 9)	—11
1982	Wayne Mulliniks	—11	Damaso Garcia (Aug 4-21)	—20
1983	Rance Mulliniks	—10	Damaso Garcia (June 21-July 16)	*—21
			Lloyd Moseby (July 27-Aug 16)	*—21
1984	Cliff Johnson	—11	Damaso Garcia (April 15-May 1)	—14
1985	Rance Mulliniks	—9	Jesse Barfield (May 8-26)	—16
			Damaso Garcia (July 23-Aug 10)	—16
1986	Garth Iorg	—10	Damaso Garcia (June 15-July 8)	—8
	Rick Leach	—10		
1987	Rance Mulliniks	—8	Tony Fernandez (Aug 23-Sept 18	—18
1988	Rance Mulliniks	—6	Kelly Gruber (June 22-July 4)	—12
1989	Bob Brenly	—6	George Bell (Aug 8-31)	—22
1990	Rance Mulliniks	—8	Tony Fernandez (Apr 10-25)	—15
			Kelly Gruber (Sept 10-25)	—15

PITCHING

YEAR	W	L	ERA (MIN 140 INN)	G
1977	D. Lemanczyk, 13	J. Garvin, 18	P. Vuckovich, 3.47	P. Vuckovich, 53
1978	J. Clancy, 10	J. Jefferson, 16	J. Clancy, 4.09	T. Murphy, 50
1979	T. Underwood, 9	P. Huffman, 18	T. Underwood, 3.69	T. Buskey, 44
1980	J. Clancy, 13	J. Clancy, 16	J. Clancy, 3.30	J. Garvin, 61
1981	D. Stieb, 11	L. Leal, 13	D. Stieb, 3.19	J. McLaughlin, 40
1982	D. Stieb, 17	L. Leal, 15	D. Stieb, 3.25	D. Murray, 56
1983	D. Stieb, 17	J. Gott, 14	D. Stieb, 3.04	J. McLaughlin, 50
1984	D. Alexander, 17	J. Clancy, 15	D. Stieb, 2.83	J. Key, 63
1985	D. Alexander, 17	D. Stieb, 13	D. Stieb, 2.48*	G. Lavelle, 69
1986	Jim Clancy, 14	Jimmy Key, 14	Mark Eichhorn, 14	Jim Clancy, 14
1987	Jimmy Key, 17	Jim Clancy, 11	J. Key, 2.76*	Mark Eichhorn, 89
1988	D. Stieb, 16	J. Clancy, 13	M. Flanagan, 13	D. Stieb, 3.04
	D. Ward, 64			
1989	D. Stieb, 17	J. Key, 14	J. Cerutti, 3.07	D. Ward, 66
1990	D. Stieb, 18	T. Stottlemyre, 17	D. Stieb, 2.93	D. Ward, 73

YEAR	GS	CG	SV	
1977	J. Garvin, 34	D. Lemanczyk, 34	J. Garvin, 12	P. Vuckovich, 8
1978	J. Clancy, 30	J. Jefferson, 30	T. Underwood, 30	J. Jefferson, 9 V. Cruz, 9
1979	T. Underwood, 32	T. Underwood, 12	T. Buskey, 7	
1980	J. Clancy, 34	J. Clancy, 15	J. Garvin, 8	
1981	D. Stieb, 25	D. Stieb, 11	J. McLaughlin, 10	
1982	J. Clancy, 40*	D. Stieb, 19	D. Murray, 11	
1983	D. Stieb, 36	D. Stieb, 14	R. Moffitt, 10	
1984	J. Clancy, 36*	D. Alexander, 11	D. Stieb, 11	R.L. Jackson, 10
	J. Key, 10			
1985	D. Alexander, 36	D. Stieb, 8	B. Caudill, 14	
	D. Stieb, 36			
1986	Jimmy Key, 35	Jim Clancy, 6	Tom Henke, 27	
1987	Jimmy Key, 36	Jimmy Key, 8	Tom Henke, 34*	
1988	M. Flanagan, 34	D. Stieb, 8	Tom Henke, 25	
1989	D. Stieb, 33	J. Key, 33	J. Key, 5	T. Henke, 20
1990	D. Stieb, 33	T. Stottlemyre, 4	T. Henke, 32	
	T. Stottlemyre, 33			

YEAR	SHO	IP	SO	BB
1977	J. Garvin, 1	J. Clancy, 1	P. Vuckovich, 1	D. Lemanczyk, 252.0
	J. Garvin, 127	D. Lemanczyk, 87		
1978	J. Jefferson, 2	J. Jefferson, 211.2	T. Underwood, 140	J. Clancy, 91
1979	D. Lemanczyk, 3	T. Underwood, 227.0	T. Underwood, 127	T. Underwood, 95
1980	D. Stieb, 4	J. Clancy, 250.2	J. Clancy, 152	J. Clancy, 128
1981	D. Stieb, 2	D. Stieb, 183.2	D. Stieb, 89	J. Clancy, 64
1982	D. Stieb, 5	D. Stieb, 288.1	D. Stieb, 149	L. Leal, 79
1983	D. Stieb, 4	D. Stieb, 278.0	D. Stieb, 187	D. Stieb, 83
1984	D. Alexander, 2	L. Leal, 2	D. Stieb, 2	D. Stieb, 267.0
	D. Stieb, 198	J. Clancy, 88	D. Stieb, 88	
1985	D. Stieb, 2	D. Stieb, 265.0	D. Stieb, 167	D. Stieb, 96
1986	J. Clancy, 3	J. Key, 232.0	M. Eichhorn, 166	D. Stieb, 87
1987	J. Clancy,1	J. Key, 1	D. Stieb, 1	J. Key, 261.0
	J. Clancy, 180	D. Stieb, 87		
1988	D. Stieb, 4	M. Flanagan, 211.0	D. Stieb, 147	M. Flanagan, 80
1989	D. Stieb, 2	J. Key, 216.0	D. Ward, 122	D. Stieb, 76
1990	D. Stieb, 2	D. Stieb, 208.2	D. Stieb, 125	T. Stottlemyre, 69

BLUE JAYS' MAJOR LEAGUE DRAFT SELECTIONS

The Major League Draft is held annually during the winter meetings. Players on a minor league roster with three years of pro ball may be drafted for $50,000. Prior to 1985 the draft price was $25,000. The drafted player must remain with his new club for the full season or be offered back to his original club for $25,000. The drafting is in reverse order of previous seasons records and alternating between leagues.

Following this majcr league draft a separate selection is held by National Association clubs from class AAA to A levels. A "AAA" selection price is $12,000. A "AA" selection is $4,000.

Following are the Blue Jays' Major League Draft Selections:

1977—Willie Upshaw-1B, OF, Syracuse (NYY)
Andy Dyes-OF, Denver (MTL)
1978—Ted Wilborn-OF, Tacoma (NYY)
Bob Davis-C, Hawaii (S.D.)
1979—Mike Macha-IF, Richmond (ATL)
1980—George Bell-OF, Oklahoma City (PHIL)
Dan Whitmer-C, Salt Lake City (CALF)
1981—Jim Gott-RHP, Springfield (ST.L)
Anthony Johnson-OF, Denver, (MTL)
1982—Jim Acker-RHP, Richmond (ATL)
Mercedes Esquer-LHP, Portland (PITT)
1983—Kelly Gruber-IF, Charleston (CLEV)
Terry Cormack-C, Richmond (ATL)
1984—Manny Lee-IF, Tucson, (HOUS)
Louis Thornton-OF, Tidewater (NYM)
1985—Jose DeJesus-RHP, Omaha)KC)
1986—Jose Nunez-RHP, Omaha (KC)
1990—Ricky Rhodes, RHP, Columbus (NYY)

Following are players drafted from the Blue Jays:

1981—Ramon Lora-C, by Los Angeles
Domingo Ramos-IF, by Seattle
1983—Dave Geisel-LHP, by Seattle
1984—Mike Morgan-RHP, by Seattle
1986—Cliff Young-LHP, by Oakland
Stan Clarke-LHP, by Seattle
1987—Joe Johnson-RHP, by California
Santiago Garcia-IF, by Chicago W.S.
1988—Colin McLaughlin-RHP, by Seattle
Chris Jones-RHP, by Los Angeles
Geronimo Berroa-OF, by Atlanta
Matt Start-C, by Atlanta
Eric Yelding-IF, by Chicago Cubs
1989—Steve Wapnick-RHP, by Detroit
Sil Campusano-OF, by Philadelphia
Xavier Hernandez-RHP, by Houston

AVERAGE (350 AB)

1.	Fernandez	.322	1987
2.	Bonnell	.318	1983
3.	Howell	.316	1977
4.	Moseby	.315	1983
5.	Bailor	.310	1977
	Garcia	.310	1982
	Fernandez	.310	1986
8.	Bell	.309	1986
9.	Collins	.308	1984
	Bell	.308	1987

GAMES

1.	Fernandez	163	1986
2.	Bosetti	162	1979
	Griffin	162	1982
	Griffin	162	1983
5.	Fernandez	161	1985
	Fernandez	161	1990
	McGriff	161	1989
8.	Upshaw	160	1982
	Upshaw	160	1983
10.	Bell	159	1984
	Bell	159	1986
	Barfield	159	1987

HITS

1.	Fernandez	213	1986
2.	Bell	198	1986
3.	Bell	188	1987
4.	Fernandez	186	1987
	Fernandez	186	1988
6.	D. Garcia	185	1982
7.	G. Bell	182	1989
8.	D. Garcia	180	1984
9.	Griffin	179	1979
10.	Upshaw	177	1983
	Bell	177	1984

AT BATS

1.	Fernandez	687	1986
2.	Griffin	653	1980
3.	Fernandez	648	1988
4.	Bell	641	1986
5.	Fernandez	635	1990
	D. Garcia	633	1984
7.	Griffin	624	1979
8.	Bailor	621	1978
9.	Bosetti	619	1979
10.	Bell	614	1988

RUNS

1.	Bell	111	1987
2.	Barfield	107	1986
3.	Moseby	106	1987
4.	Moseby	104	1983
5.	Bell	101	1986
6.	McGriff	100	1988
7.	Upshaw	99	1983
8.	McGriff	98	1989
9.	Moseby	97	1984
10.	Barfield	94	1985

SINGLES

1.	Fernandez	161	1986
2.	Griffin	145	1979
	D. Garcia	145	1982
4.	Fernandez	144	1987
5.	D. Garcia	138	1984
6.	Fernandez	136	1988
7.	D. Garcia	132	1985
8.	D. Garcia	129	1983
9.	Bailor	127	1978
10.	Fernandez	127	1990

DOUBLES

1.	Fernandez	41	1988
	Bell	41	1989
3.	Bell	39	1984
4.	Bell	38	1986
5.	Gruber	36	1990
	Wilson	36	1990
7.	Bosetti	35	1979
	Barfield	35	1986
	McGriff	35	1988
10.	Mulliniks	34	1983
	Barfield	34	1985

TRIPLES

1.	Fernandez	17	1990
	Griffin	15	1980
	Collins	15	1984
	Moseby	15	1984
5.	Griffin	10	1979
	Fernandez	10	1985
7.	Howell	9	1980
	Moseby	9	1982
	Griffin	9	1983
	Upshaw	9	1984
	Barfield	9	1985
	Fernandez	9	1986
	Fernandez	9	1989

HOME RUNS

1.	Bell	47	1987
2.	Barfield	40	1986
3.	McGriff	36	1989
4,	McGriff	35	1990
5.	McGriff	34	1988
6.	Bell	31	1986
7.	Gruber	31	1990
8.	Mayberry	30	1980
9.	Bell	28	1985
	Barfield	28	1987
11.	Barfield	27	1983
	Upshaw	27	1983
	Barfield	27	1985

EXTRA BASE HITS

1.	Bell	83	1987
2.	Barfield	77	1986
3.	Bell	75	1986
4.	McGriff	73	1988
5.	Gruber	73	1990
6.	Barfield	70	1985
7.	Bell	69	1984
8.	McGriff	66	1989
9.	Bell	62	1985
10.	Moseby	61	1984
	Bell	61	1989

TOTAL BASES

1.	Bell	369	1987
2.	Bell	341	1986
3.	Barfield	329	1986
4.	Gruber	303	1990
5.	Bell	302	1984
6.	Upshaw	298	1983
7.	McGriff	296	1988
8.	McGriff	295	1990
9.	Fernandez	294	1986
10.	Bell	291	1985

RUNS BATTED IN

1.	Bell	134	1987
2.	Gruber	118	1990
3.	Barfield	108	1986
	Bell	108	1986
5.	Upshaw	104	1983
	Bell	104	1989
7.	Bell	97	1988
8.	Moseby	96	1987
9.	Bell	95	1985
10.	McGriff	92	1989

SLUGGING (350 AB)

1.	Bell	.605	1987
2.	Barfield	.559	1986
3.	McGriff	.552	1988
4.	Barfield	.536	1985
5.	Bell	.532	1986
6.	McGriff	.530	1990
7.	McGriff	.525	1989
8.	Upshaw	.515	1983
9.	Gruber	512	1990
10.	Barfield	.510	1983

ON-BASE

1.	McGriff	.400	1990
2.	McGriff	.399	1989
3.	Johnson	.393	1984
4.	Mulliniks	.387	1985
5.	Moseby	.380	1983
6.	Fernandez	.379	1987
7.	Upshaw	.377	1983
8.	Johnson	.376	1983
	McGriff	.376	1988
10	Mayberry	.374	1979
	Mulliniks	.374	1983

STOLEN BASES

1.	Collins	60	1984
2.	D. Garcia	54	1982
3.	Moseby	39	1987
4.	Moseby	37	1985
5.	Moseby	32	1986
	Fernandez	32	1987
7.	Collins	31	1983
	D. Garcia	31	1984
	Moseby	31	1988
10.	D. Garcia	28	1985

STRIKEOUTS (BATTER)

1.	McGriff	149	1988
2.	Barfield	146	1986
3.	Barfield	143	1985
4.	Barfield	141	1987
5.	McGriff	132	1989
6.	Moseby	124	1987
7.	Moseby	122	1984
	Moseby	122	1986
9.	Barfield	110	1983
10.	Barfield	108	1988
	McGriff	108	1990

BASE ON BALLS

1.	McGriff	119	1989
2.	McGriff	94	1990
3.	McGriff	79	1988
4.	Moseby	78	1984
	Upshaw	78	1986
6.	Mayberry	77	1980
7.	Moseby	76	1985
8.	Fernandez	71	1990
9.	Moseby	70	1987
	Moseby	70	1988

HITTING STREAKS

1.	Bell	22	1989
2.	D. Garcia	21	1983
	Moseby	21	1983
4.	D. Garcia	20	1982
5.	Griffin	19	1980
6.	D. Garcia	18	1986
	Fernandez	18	1987
8.	Mayberry	17	1980
	Bell	17	1987
	D. Garcia	17	1982

PINCH-HITS

1.	Nordhagen	11	1982
	Johnson	11	1984
3.	Powell	10	1982
	Mulliniks	10	1983
	Iorg	10	1986
	Leach	10	1986
7.	Ewing	9	1977
	Braun	9	1980
	Iorg	9	1982
	Mulliniks	9	1985

PINCH AT BATS

1.	Johnson	39	1983
2.	Johnson	34	1984
3.	Leach	31	1986
4.	Powell	30	1982
5.	Ewing	29	1978
	Orta	29	1983
	Burroughs	29	1985
8.	Iorg	28	1986
	Leach	28	1987
10.	Ewing	27	1977
	Mulliniks	27	1983
	Iorg	27	1985

ERA (162 INNINGS)

1.	Stieb	2.48	1985
2.	Key	2.76	1987
3.	Stieb	2.83	1984
4.	Stieb	2.93	1990
5.	Key	3.00	1985
6.	Stieb	3.04	1983
	Stieb	3.04	1987
8.	Cerutti	3.07	1989
9.	Alexander	3.13	194
10.	Wells	3.14	1990

WINS

1.	Stieb	18	1990
2	Stieb	17	1982
	Stieb	17	1983
	Stieb	17	1989
	Alexander	17	1984
	Alexander	17	1985
	Key	17	1987
8.	Clancy	16	1982
	Stieb	16	1984
	Stieb	16	1988

LOSSES

1.	Garvin	18	1977
	Huffman	18	1979
3.	Jefferson	17	1977
4.	Stottlemyre	17	1990
5.	Clancy	16	1980
	Underwood	16	1979
	Jefferson	16	1978
	Lemanczyk	16	1977
9.	Clancy	15	1984
	Leal	15	1982
	Stieb	15	1980

SAVES

1.	Henke	34	1987
2.	Henke	32	1990
3.	Henke	27	1986
4.	Henke	25	1988
5.	Henke	20	1989
6.	Ward	15	1988
	Ward	15	1989
8.	Caudill	14	1985
9.	Henke	13	1985
10.	Murray	11	1982
	Ward	11	1990

GAMES PITCHED

1.	Eichhorn	89	1987
2.	Ward	73	1990
3.	Henke	72	1987
4.	Lavelle	69	1985
	Eichhorn	69	1986
6.	Musselman	68	1987
7.	Caudill	67	1985
8.	Ward	66	1989
9.	Ward	64	1988
	Henke	64	1989

GAMES STARTED

1.	Clancy	40	1982
2.	Leal	38	1982
	Stieb	38	1982
4.	Clancy	37	1987
5.	Stieb	36	1983
	Clancy	36	1984
	Alexander	36	1985
	Stieb	36	1986
	Key	36	1987
10.	Leal	35	1983
	Alexander	35	1984
	Leal	35	1984
	Stieb	35	1984

COMPLETE GAMES

1.	Stieb	19	1982
2.	Clancy	15	1980
3.	Stieb	14	1980
	Stieb	14	1983
5.	Garvin	12	1977
	Underwood	12	1979
7.	Lemanczyk	11	1977
	Lemanczyk	11	1979
	Stieb	11	1981
	Clancy	11	1982
	Clancy	11	1983
	Alexander	11	1984
	Stieb	11	1984

INNINGS PITCHED

1.	Stieb	288.1	1982
2.	Stieb	178.0	1983
3.	Stieb	267.0	1984
4.	Clancy	266.2	1982
5.	Stieb	265.0	1985
6.	Alexander	261.2	1984
7.	Key	261.0	1987
8.	Alexander	260.2	1985
9.	Lemanczyk	252.0	1977
10.	Clancy	250.2	1980

STRIKEOUTS (PITCHER)

1.	Stieb	198	1984
2.	Stieb	187	1983
3.	Clancy	180	1987
4.	Stieb	167	1985
5.	Eichhorn	166	1986
6.	Key	161	1980
7.	Clancy	152	1987
8.	Stieb	147	1988
9.	Alexander	142	1985
10.	Stieb	141	1982
	Key	141	1986

SHUTOUTS

1.	Stieb	5	1982
2.	Stieb	4	1980
	Stieb	4	1983
	Stieb	4	1988
5.	Lemanczyk	3	1979
	Clancy	3	1982
	Clancy	3	1986
8.	Jefferson	2	1978
	Clancy	2	1980
	Jefferson	2	1980
	Stieb	2	1981
	Stieb	2	1985
	Key	2	1986
	Stieb	2	1989
	Stieb	2	1990

BLUE JAYS ALL TIME 'TOP TEN' BATTING DEPARTMENTS

GAMES

Moseby	1392
Whitt	1218
Bell	1181
Upshaw	1115
Barfield	1032
Fernandez	1028
Mulliniks	1015
Iorg	931
Garcia, D.	902
Griffin	873

AT BATS

Moseby	5124
Bell	4528
Fernandez	3952
Upshaw	3710
Garcia, D.	3572
Whitt	3514
Barfield	3463
Griffin	3151
Mulliniks	2771
Iorg	2450

RUNS

Moseby	768
Bell	641
Upshaw	538
Barfield	530
Fernandez	510
Garcia, D.	453
Whitt	424
McGriff	348
Griffin	346
Mulliniks	354

HITS

Moseby	1319
Bell	1294
Fernandez	1142
Garcia, D.	1028
Upshaw	982
Barfield	919
Whitt	888
Griffin	789
Mulliniks	782
Iorg	633

DOUBLES

Moseby	242
Bell	237
Fernandez	192
Mulliniks	192
Upshaw	177
Garcia, D.	172
Whitt	164
Barfield	162
Iorg	125
Griffin	117

TRIPLES

Fernandez	61
Moseby	60
Griffin	50
Upshaw	42
Bell	32
Barfield	27
Garcia, D.	26
Collins	19
Bailor	19
Gruber	19

HOME RUNS

Bell	202
Barfield	179
Moseby	149
Whitt	131
McGriff	125
Upshaw	112
Mayberry	92
Gruber	83
Velez	72
Mulliniks	66

TOTAL BASES

Moseby	2128
Bell	2201
Barfield	1672
Upshaw	1579
Fernandez	1576
Whitt	1475
Garcia, D.	1348
Mulliniks	1198
Griffin	1045
McGriff	1030

RUNS BATTED IN

Bell	740
Moseby	651
Barfield	527
Whitt	518
Upshaw	478
Fernandez	404
Mulliniks	364
Garcia, D.	296
Gruber	326
McGriff	305

EXTRA BASE HITS

Bell	471
Moseby	451
Barfield	368
Upshaw	331
Whitt	310
Fernandez	293
Mulliniks	271
McGriff	232
Garcia, D.	230
Gruber	213

BATTING AVG. (300 GP)

Fernandez	.289
Bell	.286
Garcia, D.	.287
Leach	.283
Mulliniks	.282
Bonnell	.281
McGriff	.278
Johnson, C.	.273
Howell	.272
Woods, A.	.270
Gruber	.266
Upshaw	.265
Barfield	.265

SLUGGING PCT (300 GP)

McGriff	.530
Bell	.486
Barfield	.483
Velez	.461
Mayberry	.450
Gruber	.445
Mulliniks	.432
Whitt	.420
Bonnell	.416
Moseby	.415

STOLEN BASES

Moseby	255
Garcia, D.	194
Fernandez	138
Collins	91
Griffin	76
Upshaw	76
Gruber	61
Bell	59
Barfield	55
Bailor	46

BB

Moseby	547
Whitt	403
Upshaw	390
Mulliniks	370
McGriff	352
Barfield	342
Fernandez	285
Velez	278
Mayberry	257
Bell	255

SO

Moseby	1015
Barfield	855
Upshaw	565
Bell	563
McGriff	495
Whitt	451
Mulliniks	421
Gruber	351
Fernandez	344
Howell	337

HP

Moseby	50
Bell	35
Barfield	27
Fernandez	26
Gruber	25
Mayberry	21
Upshaw	21
Garcia, D.	18
Bailor	15
Griffin	14

SH

Griffin	67
Moseby	38
Upshaw	33
Woods, A.	31
Garcia, D.	27
Fernandez	26
McKay	24
Bailor	21
Gomez	21
Iorg	21

SF

Bell	59
Moseby	40
Whitt	36
Fernandez	32
Gruber	26
Upshaw	26
Barfield	24
Martinez	23
Mulliniks	23
Griffin	22

BLUE JAYS ALL TIME 'TOP TEN' — PITCHING DEPARTMENTS

ERA (400 IP)		WINS		LOSSES		INNINGS PITCHED	
Henke	2.52	Stieb	166			Gott	30
Stieb	3.37	Clancy	128	Clancy	140	Stieb	2666.2
Key	3.47	Key	87	Stieb	123	Clancy	2204.2
Alexander	3.56	Leal	51	Leal	58	Key	1269.2
Acker	3.84	Alexander	46	Jefferson	56	Leal	946.0
Cerutti	3.87	Cerutti	46	Key	56	Cerutti	772.1
Underwood	3.88	Lemanczyk	27	Lemanczyk	45	Alexander	750.0
Flanagan	3.96	Flanagan	26	Garvin	41	Jefferson	666.1
Clancy	4.10	Wells	25	Cerutti	37	Garvin	606.0
Leal	4.14	Henke	24	Stottlemyre	32	Lemanczyk	575.0
				Underwood	30	Henke	457.0

STRIKEOUTS		BASES ON BALLS		W-L PCT (300 IP)		GAMES	
Stieb	1557	Stieb	937	Alexander	.639	Stieb	390
Clancy	1237	Clancy	814	Key	.608	Clancy	352
Key	702	Leal	320	Wells	.581	Henke	340
Henke	545	Key	301	Acker	.575	Key	251
Leal	491	Jefferson	266	Stieb	.574	Acker	227
Alexander	392	Cerutti	254	Eichhorn	.571	Ward	217
Cerutti	369	Garvin	219	Cerutti	.554	Eichhorn	202
Ward	336	Lemanczyk	212	Henke	.510	Garvin	196
Garvin	320	Gott	183	Jackson	.533	McLaughlin	195
Jefferson	307	Underwood	182	Flanagan	.491	Cerutti	191
						Jackson	190

SHUTOUTS		SAVES		GAMES STARTED		COMPLETE GAMES	
Stieb	30	Henke	151	Stieb	382	Stieb	101
Clancy	11	Ward	41	Clancy	345	Clancy	73
Key	4	McLaughlin	31	Key	184	Leal	27
Jefferson	4	Jackson	30	Leal	151	Alexander	25
Alexander	3	Caudill	16	Cerutti	108	Lemanczyk	25
Gott	3	Willis	15	Alexander	103	Jefferson	21
Leal	3	Eichhorn	15	Lemanczyk	82	Key	20
Lemanczyk	3	Lamp	13	Flanagan	76	Underwood	19
Underwood	2	Acker	13	Stottlemyre	67	Garvin	15
Cerutti	2	Murray	11	Garvin	65	Gott	8
				Gott	65		

HOME RUNS ALLOWED		HIT BATSMEN		WILD PITCHES	
Clancy	219	Stieb	118	Clancy	82
Stieb	205	Clancy	28	Stieb	47
Key	129	Acker	23	Lemanczyk	36
Cerutti	110	Leal	22	Cerutti	30
Leal	101	Moore	19	Ward	29
Jefferson	82	Eichhorn	19	Key	25
Alexander	81	Key	17	Leal	23
Garvin	74	Stottlemyre	17	Wells	23
Lemanczyk	52	Cerutti	16	Underwood	18
Underwood	46	Alexander	14	Garvin	17
				Alexander	16
				Acker	16

YOUNGEST BLUE JAYS

Three teenagers have performed for the Blue Jays.

	Birthdate	Date of 1st Game	Age at 1st Game
Brian Milner	Nov. 17/59	June 23, 1978	18 yrs, 7months, 6 days
Fred Manrique	Nov. 5/61	Aug. 23, 1981	19 yrs, 9months, 18 days
Manny Lee	June 17/65	April 10, 1985	19 yrs, 9months, 24 days

BLUE JAYS .300 HITTERS

(350 or more At-Bats)

YEAR	PLAYER	AVG	YEAR	PLAYER	AVG	YEAR	PLAYER	AVG
1977	Bob Bailor	.310	1983	Damaso Garcia	.307	1984	Cliff Johnson	.304
1977	Roy Howell	.316	1983	Lloyd Moseby	.315	1986	Tony Fernandez	.317
1980	Al Woods	.300	1983	Willie Upshaw	.306	1986	George Bell	.309
1982	Damaso Garcia	.310	1984	Rance Mulliniks	.324	1987	Tony Fernandez	.322
1983	Barry Bonnell	.318	1984	Dave Collins	.308	1987	George Bell	.308
						1990	Fred McGriff	.300

BLUE JAYS WITH 80 RBI

YEAR	PLAYER	RBI	YEAR	PLAYER	RBI	YEAR	PLAYER	RBI
1980	John Mayberry	82	1985	Jesse Barfield	84	1988	George Bell	97
1983	Willie Upshaw	104	1986	Jesse Barfield	108	1988	Fred McGriff	82
1983	Lloyd Moseby	81	1986	George Bell	108	1988	Kelly Gruber	81
1984	Lloyd Moseby	92	1986	Lloyd Moseby	86	1989	George Bell	104
1984	George Bell	87	1987	George Bell	134	1989	Fred McGriff	92
1984	Willie Upshaw	84	1987	Lloyd Moseby	96	1990	George Bell	86
1985	George Bell	95	1987	Jesse Barfield	89	1990	Kelly Gruber	118
						1990	Fred McGriff	88

BLUE JAYS WITH 20 HOME RUNS

YEAR	PLAYER	HR's	YEAR	PLAYER	HR's	YEAR	PLAYER	HR's
1978	Rico Carty	20	1984	George Bell	26	1987	Lloyd Moseby	26
1978	John Mayberry	22	1985	George Bell	28	1987	Fred McGriff	20
1979	John Mayberry	21	1985	Jesse Barfield	27	1988	Fred McGriff	34
1980	John Mayberry	30	1986	Jesse Barfield	40	1988	George Bell	24
1980	Otto Velez	20	1986	George Bell	31	1989	Fred McGriff	36
1982	Willie Upshaw	21	1986	Lloyd Moseby	21	1990	Kelly Gruber	31
1983	Jesse Barfield	27	1987	George Bell	47	1990	Fred McGriff	35
1983	Willie Upshaw	27	1987	Jesse Barfield	28	1990	George Bell	21
1983	Cliff Johnson	22						

BLUE JAYS 15-GAME WINNERS

YEAR	PITCHER	W	L	YEAR	PITCHER	W	L
1982	Dave Stieb	17	14	1984	Doyle Alexander	17	10
1982	Jim Clancy	16	14	1987	Jimmy Key	17	8
1983	Dave Stieb	17	12	1987	Jim Clancy	15	11
1983	Jim Clancy	15	11	1988	Dave Stieb	16	8
1984	Doyle Alexander	17	6	1989	Dave Stieb	17	8
1984	Dave Stieb	16	8	1990	Dave Stieb	18	6

THE YEARLY BLUE JAY PINCH-HITTING LEADER:

YEAR	PLAYER	HITS	YEAR	PLAYER	HITS	YEAR	PLAYER	HITS
1977	Sam Ewing	9	1982	Wayne Nordhagen	11	1986	Garth Iorg	10
1978	Otto Velez	8	1983	Rance Mulliniks	10	1987	Rance Mulliniks	8
1979	Otto Velez	5	1984	Cliff Johnson	11	1988	Rance Mulliniks	6
1980	Steve Braun	9	1985	Rance Mulliniks	9	1989	Bob Brenly	6
1981	Willie Upshaw	4	1986	Rick Leach	10	1990	Rance Mulliniks	8

BLUE JAYS WITH 20 STOLEN BASES

YEAR	PLAYER	SB	YEAR	PLAYER	SB	YEAR	PLAYER	SB
1979	Alfredo Griffin	21	1985	Lloyd Moseby	37	1987	Tony Fernandez	32
1982	Damaso Garcia	54	1985	Damaso Garcia	28	1988	Lloyd Moseby	31
1983	Dave Collins	31	1985	George Bell	21	1988	Kelly Gruber	23
1983	Damaso Garcia	31	1985	Jesse Barfield	22	1989	Lloyd Moseby	24
1983	Lloyd Moseby	27	1986	Lloyd Moseby	32	1989	Tony Fernandez	22
1984	Dave Collins	60	1986	Tony Fernandez	25	1990	Tony Fernandez	26
1984	Damaso Garcia	46	1986	Willie Upshaw	23	1990	Mookie Wilson	23
1984	Lloyd Moseby	39	1987	Lloyd Moseby	39			

BLUE JAYS' YEARLY HOME RUN LEADERS —AT HOME

Kelly Gruber holds the Blue Jay record for home runs in a season at home as he hit 23 in 1990 at SkyDome.

YEAR	PLAYER	HR	YEAR	PLAYER	HR	YEAR	PLAYER	HR
1977	Ron Fairly	10	1982	Willie Upshaw	11	1988	Fred McGriff	18
1978	John Mayberry	12	1983	Jesse Barfield	22	1989	Fred McGriff	18
1979	John Mayberry	13	1984	George Bell	12	1990	Kelly Gruber	23
1980	Otto Velez	12	1985	Jesse Barfield	15			
1981	John Mayberry	10	1986	Jesse Barfield	16			
1982	Jesse Barfield	11	1987	George Bell	19			

BLUE JAYS' YEARLY HOME RUN LEADERS —ON THE ROAD

YEAR	PLAYER	HR	YEAR	PLAYER	HR	YEAR	PLAYER	HR
1977	Ron Fairly	9	1979	Otto Velez	8	1985	George Bell	18
1977	Doug Rader	9	1980	John Mayberry	20	1986	Jesse Barfield	24
1977	Otto Velez	9	1981	John Mayberry	7	1987	George Bell	28
1978	Rico Carty	10	1982	Willie Upshaw	10	1988	Fred McGriff	16
1978	John Mayberry	10	1983	Cliff Johnson	12	1990	Fred McGriff	21
1979	John Mayberry	8	1984	George Bell	14			

LONGEST WINNING & LOSING STREAKS

YEAR	WON	LOST	YEAR	WON	LOST
1977	3	11	1984	7	6
1978	5	9	1985	9	6
1979	4	7	1986	9	5
1980	6	8	1987	11	7
1981	4	12	1988	6	6
1982	6	6	1989	6	4
1983	5	6	1990	6	3

MILESTONE VICTORIES

VICTORY #	DATE	OPPONENT	SCORE	WINNER	LOSER
1	Apr. 7/77	vs Chicago	9–5	Jerry Johnson	Ken Brett
100	Aug. 13/78	vs Kansas City	3–2(10)	Mike Willis	Al Hrabosky
200	July 11/80	vs Cleveland	6–3	Dave Stieb	Wayne Garland
300	June 19/82	at Oakland	3–1(12)	Joey McLaughlin	Bob Owchinko
400	July 18/83	vs Kansas City	8–2	Jim Clancy	Larry Gura
500	Aug. 5/84	at Baltimore	4–3	Jimmy Key	Tippy Martinez
600	Aug. 20/85	at Cleveland	3–2	Jimmy Key	Roy Smith
625	Oct. 5/85	vs New York	5–1	Doyle Alexander	Joe Cowley
700	Sept. 3/86	vs Cleveland	3–1	Dave Stieb	Tom Candiotti
800	Sept. 18/87	at New York	6–3	Jim Clancy	Neil Allen
900	Apr. 16/89	vs Kansas City	2–1	David Wells	Bret Saberhagen
983	Sept. 30/89	vs Baltimore	4–3	Frank Wills	Mark Williamson
1000	May 9/90	vs Chicago	4-3	Frank Wills	Wayne Edwards

*1985 AL East Pennant Clincher
#1989 AL East Pennant Clincher

PITCHERS WITH OVER NINE INNINGS IN ONE GAME

PITCHER	DATE	OPPONENT	INNINGS	W-L-S	SCORE
Jerry Garvin	May 25/77	Oak.	9.2	L	L5-6(10)
Dave Lemanczyk	July 14/77	at Chi	11.0	W	W5-3(11)
Dave Lemanczyk	July 17/77	at Det (2nd)	11.0	L	L6-7 (11)
Dave Lemanczyk	Oct. 2/77	Clev (1st)	11.0	W	W2-1(11)
Jesse Jefferson	May 23/78	Bost	12.0	W	W2-1(12)
Tom Underwood	Sept.3/79	at Balt (1st)	10.0	ND	L11-2 (11)
Jesse Jefferson	May 16/80	Oak	11.0	W	W1-0(11)
Dave Stieb	May 17/80	Oak	12.0	ND	L2-4(14)
Dave Stieb	Aug. 9/80	KC	10.0	ND	W4-3(14)
Dave Stieb	Sept. 16/82	Calf	11.0	ND	W2-1(12)
Dave Stieb	May 11/83	at Chi	10.0	W	W3-1(10)
Dave Stieb	May 16/83	at Milw	10.0	W	W2-1(10)
Jim Clancy	Sept. 24/83	at Oak	9.1	L	L1-2(10)
Jimmy Key	June 6/85	Det	10.0	ND	W2-0(12)
Jimmy Key	June 17/86	at Milw	10.0	ND	W2-1(12)
Jimmy Key	July 27/86	at Oak	10.0	ND	L0-1(15)
Mike Flanagan	Oct. 3/87	at Det	11.0	ND	L2-3(12)
John Cerutti	Apr. 30/89	at Calf'	10.0	ND	L0-1(11)

Player	Date	OPP	Pitchers
DOUG AULT (1)	April 7, 1977	Chicago	Ken Brett
OTTO VELEZ	April 25, 1977	Boston	Luis Tiant, Bill Campbell
OTTO VELEZ	June 5, 1977	at Oakland	Vida Blue, Joe Coleman
ROY HOWELL (1)	Sept. 10, 1977	at New York	Catfish Hunter, Ken Clay
RICO CARTY (1)	April 27, 1978	at Kansas City	Larry Gura
JOHN MAYBERRY	May 22, 1978	Boston	Allen Ripley
JOHN MAYBERRY	May 26, 1978	at New York	Jim Beattie, Sparky Lyle
JOHN MAYBERRY	June 26, 1978	Baltimore	Joe Kerrigan, Larry Harlow
OTTO VELEZ	July 26, 1979	Texas	Doc Medich, Doyle Alexander
JOHN MAYBERRY	August 26, 1979	California	Nolan Ryan
JOHN MAYBERRY	April 9, 1980	at Seattle	Mike Parrott
JOHN MAYBERRY	June 1, 1980	at New York	Tom Underwood, Rich Gossage
JOHN MAYBERRY	August 14, 1980	at Milwaukee	Moose Haas
JOHN MAYBERRY	July 16, 1980	at Seattle	Glenn Abbott
JOHN MAYBERRY	May 30, 1981	Oakland	Mike Norris
OTTO VELEZ (4)	June 3, 1981	California	Geoff Zahn
JOHN MAYBERRY (10)	April 25, 1982	Boston	Bob Ojeda, Mark Clear
WILLIE UPSHAW	June 7, 1982	Cleveland	John Denny
WILLIE UPSHAW	August 17, 1982	Cleveland	Ed Whitson
LLOYD MOSEBY	April 19, 1983	Cleveland	Rick Sutcliffe, Dan Spillner
ERNIE WHITT	May 23, 1983	Detroit	Milt Wilcox
LLOYD MOSEBY	May 29, 1983	Boston	Dennis Eckersley
JESSE BARFIELD	June 14, 1983	Oakland	Tom Underwood
CLIFF JOHNSON	June 21, 1983	Minnesota	Bryan Oelkers, Jim Lewis
MICKEY KLUTTS (1)	June 26, 1983	at Seattle	Manny Castillo
LLOYD MOSEBY	August 2, 1983	New York (1st g)	Matt Keough
JESSE BARFIELD	August 29, 1983	Boston (1st g)	John Tudor
JESSE BARFIELD	Sept. 1, 1983	Baltimore	Jim Palmer
JESSE BARFIELD	Sept. 2, 1983	Detroit (1st g)	Juan Berenguer, Doug Bair
ERNIE WHITT	Sept. 4, 1983	Detroit	Glenn Abbot, Aurelio Lopez
CLIFF JOHNSON	April 6, 1984	at California	Jim Slaton
WILLIE UPSHAW	April 26, 1984	Oakland	Mike Warren
BUCK MARTINEZ (1)	June 23, 1984	at Boston	Rich Gale, Mike Brown
JESSE BARFIELD	July 1, 1984	Oakland	Curt Young, Keith Atherton
DAMASO GARCIA	July 3, 1984	California	Tommy John
JESSE BARFIELD	July 6, 1984	Seattle	Edwin Nunez
CLIFF JOHNSON (3)	July 15, 1984	at Oakland	Keith Atherton, Chris Codiroli
WILLIE AIKENS (11)	Sept. 14, 1984	at Detroit	Jack Morris
WILLIE UPSHAW (4)	April 28, 1985	at Texas	Mike Mason, Greg Harris
JESSE BARFIELD	June 5, 1985	Minnesota	Mike Smithson
JESSE BARFIELD	July 31, 1985	at Baltimore	Dennis Martinez
JESSE BARFIELD	May 6, 1986	Oakland	Moose Haas, Steve Ontiveros
LLOYD MOSEBY	June 28, 1986	at New York	Joe Niekro, Alfonso Pulido
JESSE BARFIELD	July 3, 1986	at Boston	Oil Can Boyd, Mike Brown
RANCE MULLINIKS	July 3, 1986	at Boston	Oil Can Boyd, Mike Brown
GEORGE BELL	July 19, 1986	at California	John Candelaria, Donnie Moore
GEORGE BELL	July 21, 1986	at Seattle	Mark Huismann
JESSE BARFIELD	July 21, 1986	at Seattle	Mark Huismann, Karl Best
LLOYD MOSEBY	August 5, 1986	Kansas City	Scott Bankhead, Buddy Black
JESSE BARFIELD	Sept. 17, 1986	Detroit	Jack Morris
JESSE BARFIELD	October 1, 1986	at New York	Ron Guidry
GEORGE BELL	April 26, 1987	at Chicago	Jose DeLeon, Bobby Thigpen
JESSE BARFIELD	May 1, 1987	vs Texas	Jose Guzman, Mitch Williams
JESSE BARFIELD (15)	May 8, 1987	at Texas	Jose Guzman
GEORGE BELL	May 9, 1987	at Texas	Ed Correa, Dale Mohorcic
LLOYD MOSEBY	May 10, 1987	at Texas	Bobby Witt, Dale Mohorcic
GEORGE BELL	May 22, 1987	at Seattle	Scott Bankhead
KELLY GRUBER	May 22, 1987	at Seattle	Scott Bankhead, Jerry Reed
GEORGE BELL	May 25, 1987	at Seattle	Mike Morgan, Steve Shields
GEORGE BELL	June 8, 1987	at New York	Rick Rhoden, Rich Bordi
GEORGE BELL	June 11, 1987	at Baltimore	John Habyan
RANCE MULLINIKS	June 24, 1987	at Detroit	Jack Morris
GARTH IORG (1)	July 20, 1987	at Texas	Charlie Hough
GEORGE BELL	July 29, 1987	vs Boston	Bruce Hurst
FRED McGRIFF	August 4, 1987	at Chicago	Neil Allen
GEORGE BELL	August 30, 1987	vs Oakland	Jose Rijo, Dennis Lamp
ERNIE WHITT (3)	Sept. 12, 1987	vs New York	Rick Rhoden, Bill Fulton
GEORGE BELL	Sept. 14, 1987	vs Baltimore	Eric Bell, Mike Kinnunen
RANCE MULLINIKS (3)	Sept. 14, 1987	vs Baltimore	Ken Dixon, Eric Bell
LLOYD MOSEBY (7)	Sept. 29, 1987	vs Milwaukee	Chris Bosio
KELLY GRUBER	April 11, 1988	vs New York	Cecilio Guante, Charles Hudson
FRED McGRIFF	May 3, 1988	at Seattle	Mike Campbell
FRED McGRIFF	June 15, 1988	vs Cleveland	Greg Swindell, Dan Schatzeder
CECIL FIELDER	June 15, 1988	vs Cleveland	Greg Swindell, Dan Schatzeder
FRED McGRIFF	July 17, 1988	at Oakland	Curt Young, Gene Nelson
CECIL FIELDER (2)	July 24, 1988	at Seattle	Mark Langston, Rod Scurry
FRED McGRIFF	August 2, 1988	vs Minnesota	Charlie Lea, Jim Winn
FRED McGRIFF	April 11, 1989	at New York	Dave LaPoint
FRED McGRIFF	July 21, 1989	at Seattle	Gene Harris
FRED McGRIFF	August 23, 1989	vs Detroit	Jeff Robinson

Player	Date	OPP	Pitchers
Kelly Gruber	April 24, 1990	vs Clevland	Greg Swindell
Kelly Gruber	May 6, 1990	vs Detroit	Urbano Lugo
Glenallen Hill (1)	May 17, 1990	vs Seattle	Randy Johnson, Gene Harris
Kelly Gruber	May 22, 1990	vs Oakland	Curt Young, Gene Nelson
George Bell	June 8, 1990	at Milwaukee	Mark Knudson
George Bell	June 21, 1990	vs New York	Andy Hawkins, Dave Righetti
John Olerud (1)	June 21, 1990	vs New York	Andy Hawkins, Alan Mills
George Bell	June 24, 1990	vs New York	Chuck Cary
Fred McGriff	June 28, 1990	at Boston	Roger Clemens
Fred McGriff	July 12, 1990	at California	Kirk McCaskill, Mike Fetters
Fred McGriff (11)	Sept. 2, 1990	at Cleveland	Bud Black, Jesse Orosco
Kelly Gruber (6)	Sept. 8, 1990	vs Chicago	Alex Fernandez

BLUE JAYS PINCH HIT HOME RUNS

Date	Player	H/A	Opponent
April 7, 1977	Al Woods	H	Off Francisco Barrios, Chicago, (5th inning, one on) (tied major league record as 11th player to homer as pinch-hitter In first major league at bat)
April 14, 1977	Otto Velez	H	Off John Hiller, Detroit (8th inning, two on)
April 21, 1977	Al Woods	A	Off Dick Tidrow, at New York (9th inning, none on)
August 9, 1977	Doug Ault	H	Off Tom Burgmeier, Minnesota (4th inning, none on)
August 24, 1977	Doug Rader	A	Off Mike Kekich, at Seattle (4th inning, none on)
June 26, 1978	John Mayberry	H	Off Joe Kerrigan, Baltimore (2nd inning, one on)
July 1, 1978	Sam Ewing	H	Off Sid Monge, Cleveland (8th inning, one on)
June 17, 1979	Otto Velez	H	Off Bob Lacey, Oakland (7th inning, two on)
July 4, 1979	Otto Velez	A	Off Dave Tobik at Detroit (11th inning, two on)
August 6, 1979	Rico Carty	H	Off Steve Mingori, Kansas City (8th inning, none on)
Sept. 22, 1979	Rico Carty	H	Off Jim Kaat, New York (4th inning, one on)
May 6, 1980	Roy Howell	A	Off Don Aase, California (7th inning, one on)
June 14, 1980	Bob Davis	H	Off Dave Rajsich, Texas (6th inning, none on)
August 7, 1980	Doug Ault	A	Off Rick Waits, Cleveland (7th inning, one on)
April 24, 1981	Willie Upshaw	A	Off Rich Gossage, New York (8th inning, none on)
April 24, 1982	Jesse Barfield	H	Off Tom Burgmeier, Boston (8th inning, three on)
June 23, 1982	Ernie Whitt	A	Off Mike Stanton, Seattle (9th inning, none on)
July 21, 1982	Ernie Whitt	H	Off Dan Quisenberry, Kansas City (9th inn., none on)
July 24, 1982	Jesse Barfield	A	Off Kevin Hickey, Chicago (8th inning, two on)
April 29, 1983	Mickey Klutts	H	Off Dick Tidrow, Chicago (7th inning, none on)
May 22, 1983	Cliff Johnson	H	Off Tippy Martinez, Baltimore (8th inning, none on)
June 25, 1983	Buck Martinez	A	Off Ed Vande Berg, Seattle (9th inning, none on)
July 14, 1983	Rance Mulliniks	A	Off Dennis Lamp, Chicago (7th inning, two on)
July 20, 1983	Ernie Whitt	H	Off Mike Armstrong, Kansas City (7th inning, two on)
August 1, 1984	Ernie Whitt	H	Off Bret Saberhagen, Kansas City (8th inning, one on)
August 3, 1984	Willie Aikens	A	Off Bill Swaggerty, Baltimore (6th inning, two on)
August 5, 1984	Cliff Johnson	A	Off Tippy Martinez, Baltimore (8th inning, none on)
August 14, 1984	George Bell	A	Off Tom Waddell, Cleveland (8th inning, none on)
August 28, 1984	Jesse Barfield	H	Off Bert Roberge, Chicago (7th inning, one on)
Sept. 25, 1984	Kelly Gruber	A	Off Al Nipper, Boston (9th inning, one on)
April 24, 1985	Jeff Burroughs	H	Off Larry Gura, Kansas City (3rd inning, two on)
April 27, 1985	Willie Aikens	A	Off Tommy Boggs, Texas (9th inning, one on)
June 12, 1985	Rance Mulliniks	A	Off Rich Bordi, New York (10th inning, none on)
Sept. 25, 1985	Jeff Burroughs	H	Off Bruce Hurst, Boston (9th inning, none on)
June 13, 1986	Cliff Johnson	H	Off Willie Hernandez, Detroit (8th inning, none on)
June 14, 1986	Rick Leach	H	Off Jack Morris, Detroit (7th inning, none on)
June 14, 1986	Buck Martinez	H	Off Willie Hernandez, Detroit (9th inning, one on)
June 15, 1986	Garth Iorg	H	Off Chuck Cary, Detroit (6th inning, two on)
June 28, 1987	Fred McGriff	A	Off Jay Aldrich, Milwaukee (8th inning, none on)
July 24, 1987	Juan Beniquez	H	Off Dan Schatzeder, Minnesota (7th inning, two on)
September 4, 1987	Cecil Fielder	H	Off Dennis Powell, Seattle (10th inning, none on)
May 23, 1988	Fred McGriff	A	Off Odell Jones, Milwaukee (8th inning, none on)
July 3, 1988	Jesse Barfield	H	Off Rick Honeycutt, Oakland (7th inning, none on)
May 5, 1989	Nelson Liriano	H	Off Brian Harvey, California, (9th inning, none on)
June 13, 1989	Kelly Gruber	A	Off Dan Plesac, Milwaukee, (9th inning, none on)
September 9, 1989	Lee Mazzilli	A	Off Rich Yett, Cleveland, (6th inning, none on)

NON-PITCHERS WHO PITCHED FOR THE BLUE JAYS

Player	Position	Pitched	W-L	ERA	G	GS	IP	H	BB	SO
Bailor, Bob	IF/OF	1980	0-0	7.71	3	0	2.1	4	1	0
Kusick, Craig	1B	1979	0-0	4.91	1	0	3.2	3	0	0
Leach, Rick	1B/OF	1984	0-0	27.00	1	0	1.0	2	2	0

BLUE JAYS INSIDE THE PARK HOMERS

Date	Player	H/A	Opponent
August 21, 1977	DOUG RADER	A	California
July 9, 1979	AL WOODS	H	Milwaukee
August 28, 1979	ALFREDO GRIFFIN	H	Oakland
September 17, 1980	ROY HOWELL	A	New York
April 25, 1981	LLOYD MOSEBY	A	New York
June 7, 1982	WILLIE UPSHAW	H	Cleveland
April 14, 1983	WILLIE UPSHAW	H	Milwaukee
May 25, 1983	JORGE ORTA	H	Detroit
May 30, 1983	LLOYD MOSEBY	A	Detroit
September 14, 1983	BARRY BONNELL	A	Seattle
June 6, 1984	GEORGE BELL	A	Detroit
August 10, 1984	TONY FERNANDEZ	H	Baltimore
June 12, 1986	KELLY GRUBER	H	Detroit
May 16, 1988	KELLY GRUBER	A	Chicago
June 2, 1989	JUNIOR FELIX (SLAM)	A	Boston

BLUE JAYS WHO HAVE HIT THREE HOME RUNS IN A GAME

Player	Date	OPP	Pitchers
OTTO VELEZ	May 4, 1980	vs Cleveland (1ts g)	Dan Spillner Wayne Garland,, Sid Monge
ERNIE WHITT	Sept. 14, 1987	vs Baltimore	Ken Dixon (2), Tony Arnold
GEORGE BELL	April 4, 1988	at Kansas City	Bret Saberhagen

BLUE JAYS GRAND SLAM HOME RUNS

Date	Player	H/A	Opponent
June 27, 1977	Hector Torres	H	Off Ron Guidry, New York (5th inning)
May 7, 1978	Rick Bosetti	A	Off Enrique Romo, Seattle (8th inning)
July 31, 1978	Rico Carty	H	Off Jack Billingham, Detroit (1st inning)
July 3, 1979	Roy Howell	A	Off Jack Billingham, Detroit (1st inning)
August 27, 1979	Roy Howell	H	Off Craig Minetto, Oakland (6th inning)
Sept. 7, 1979	Rico Carty	A	Off Rick Waits, Cleveland (5th inning)
April 26, 1980	Barry Bonnell	A	Off Mike Caldwell, Milwaukee (9th inning)
May 4, 1980 (1st g.)	Otto Velez	H	Off Dan Spillner, Cleveland (1st inning)
April 24, 1982	Jesse Barfield)	H	Off Tom Burgmeier, Boston (8th inning)
May 1, 1983	Barry Bonnell	H	Off Dick Tidrow, Chicago (7th inning)
June 5, 1983	Buck Martinez	A	Off Tim Stoddard, Baltimore (6th inning)
Sept. 11, 1983	Willie Upshaw	H	Off Chris Codiroli, Oakland (1st inning)
April 20, 1984	Lloyd Moseby	H	Off Mike Witt, California (6th inning)
June 23, 1985	Ernie Whitt	H	Off Bruce Kison, Boston (6th inning)
July 9, 1985	George Bell	A	Off Ed Vande Berg, Seattle (13th inning)
August 2, 1985	George Bell	H	Off Glen Cook, Texas (4th inning)
May 22, 1986	Ernie Whitt	A	Off Richard Dotson, Chicago (4th inning)
June 20, 1986	George Bell	H	Off Dave Righetti, New York (9th inning)
August 31, 1986	Lloyd Moseby	H	Off Mark Portugal, Minnesota (3rd inning)
June 11, 1987	George Bell	A	Off John Habyan, Baltimore (5th inning)
June 23, 1987	Willie Upshaw	A	Off Jeff Robinson, Detroit (4th inning)
August 27, 1987	George Bell	H	Off Greg Cadaret, Oakland (5th inning)
April 19, 1988	Jesse Barfield	H	Off Bret Saberhagen, Kansas City (3rd inning)
Sept. 4, 1988	George Bell	H	Off Mitch Williams, Texas, (9th inning)
Sept. 13, 1988	Jesse Barfield	H	Off Paul Gibson, Detroit, (7th inning)
April 7, 1989	Tony Fernandez	A	Off Bobby Witt, Texas, (2nd inning)
May 2, 1989	Rance Mulliniks	H	Off Bob Welch, Oakland, (1st inning)
June 2, 1989	Junior Felix	A	Off Bob Stanley, Boston, (9th inning)
June 4, 1989	Ernie Whitt	A	Off Lee Smith, Boston (9th inning)
July 7, 1989	Pat Borders	A	Off Guillermo Hernandez, Detroit, (8th inning)
July 21, 1989	Fred McGriff	A	Off Gene Harris, Seattle, (3rd inning)
July 22, 1989	Lloyd Moseby	A	Off Dennis Powell, Seattle, (9th inning)
Sept. 1, 1989	Glenallen Hill	H	Off Mark Guthrie, Minnesota, (4th inning)
April 11, 1990	George Bell	H	Off Kevin Brown, Texas (3rd inning)
August 14, 1990	Glenallen Hill	A	Off Adam Peterson, Chicago, (7th inning)
Sept. 11, 1990	Tony Fernandez	A	Off Mel Stottlemyre, Kansas City, (2nd inning)
Sept. 29, 1990	Kelly Gruber	A	Off Dennis Lamp, Boston, (9th inning)

BACK-TO-BACK-TO-BACK HOME RUNS: The Blue Jays have hit three consecutive home runs, twice in their ten year history. The first time it happened was April 26, 1984 vs Oakland at Exhibition Stadium. In the bottom of the 6th inning with one out Willie Upshaw had a solo home run to left on the first pitch. George Bell followed with another home run to left on a 3-2 count. Jesse Barfield completed the trio of home runs with one to right field on 0-1 pitch. All three home runs came off RHP, Mike Warren. Final score of game was Oakland 7, Toronto 4. The last time was September 12, 1987 vs. the Yankees at Exhibition Stadium. With two out in the 8th inning Ernie Whitt hit a three-run HR against Tom Fulton. That was followed by solo shots by Jesse Barfield and Kelly Gruber also against Fulton. The final score was Toronto 13, New York 1.

HOME RUNS IN CONSECUTIVE GAMES

George Bell hit four home runs in four consecutive games (August 23, 24, 25, 26) in 1985 to set the club record.

The following players have hit home runs in three consecutive games.

RON FAIRLY	— June 27 & 28th (1st & 2nd g), 1977
DOUG RADER	— July 9, 10 & 11, 1977
JOHN MAYBERRY	— September 14, 16 & 17, 1980
LLOYD MOSEBY	— July 2, 3, & 4, 1982
GEORGE BELL	— April 11, 12 & 13, 1985
JESSE BARFIELD	— May 19, 20 & 21, 1985
ERNIE WHITT	— May 24, 25, & 26, 1985
JESSE BARFIELD	— April 30, May 1 & 2, 1986
CLIFF JOHNSON	— June 12, 13 & 14, 1986
GEORGE BELL	— July 19, 20 & 21, 1985
JESSE BARFIELD	— July 21, 22 & 23, 1986
JESSE BARFIELD	— September 30, October 1 & 3, 1986
GEORGE BELL	— June 23, 24 & 26, 1987
LLOYD MOSEBY	— July 29, 31, August 2, 1987
GEORGE BELL	— July 21, 23, 24, 1988
JESSE BARFIELD	— August 21, 22, 23, 1988
FRED McGRIFF	— August 22, 23, 24, 1988
KELLY GRUBER	— July 13, 14, 15, 1989
KELLY GRUBER	— April 23, 24, 25, 1990
KELLY GRUBER	— June 6, 7, 8,1990

HOW LONG DID IT TAKE

LONGEST OFFICIAL GAME	
HOME	5.20-May 17/88 vs Texas-14 innings
ROAD	5.23-Sept. 9.89 vs Cleveland-16 innings
SHORTEST OFFICIAL GAME	1.04-Sept. 15/77 vs Baltimore (forfeit, 4.5 innings)
LONGEST NINE-INNING GAME	
HOME	4.15-April 11/88 vs New York
ROAD	3.59-June 17/88 vs Detroit
SHORTEST NINE-INNING GAME	
ROAD	1.39-June 16/77 vs Detroit
HOME	1.33-Sept. 28/82 (1st g) vs Minnesota

AVERAGE TIME OF NINE-INNING GAME

	Home	Away	AL
1977	2.27	2.27	2.31
1978	2.24	2.23	2.24
1979	2.23	2.24	2.32
1980	2.24	2.28	2.36
1981	2.31	2.27	2.34
1982	2.29	2.28	2.37
1983	2.34	2.36	2.38
1984	2.35	2.39	2.37
1985	2.39	2.46	2.45
1986	2.46	2.47	2.48
1987	2.50	2.54	2.51
1988	2.47	2.52	2.48
1989	2.43	2.51	2.48
1990	2.51	2.52	2.49

BLUE JAYS SWITCH-HITTERS

Alan Ashby	-C	Tony Fernandez	-IF
Dave McKay	-IF	Mitch Webster	-OF
Bobby Brown	-OF	Manny Lee	-IF
Alfredo Griffin	-IF	Nelson Liriano	-IF
Ted Wilborn	-OF	Junior Felix	-OF
Geno Petralli	-C/IF	Lee Mazzilli	OF/DH
Dave Collins	-OF	Mookie Wilson	-OF
		Mark Whiten	-OF

FIVE HITS

Roy Howell
—Sept. 10/77 vs New York (A) (5 for 6; 4 runs; 1—1B; 2—2B; 2HR; 9 RBI)
Rick Bosetti
—Apr. 27/79 vs Milwaukee (H) (5 for 5; 2 runs; 4—1B; 1—2B; 1RBI)
Barry Bonnell
—Apr. 10/82 vs Milwaukee (H) (5 for 5; 1 run; 4—1B; 1—2B)
Damaso Garcia
—June 19/82 vs Oakland (A) (5 for 5; 1 run; 5—1B)
George Bell (2)
—April 6/88 vs Kansas City (A) (5 for 5; 3 runs; 3-1B, 2-2B)
—Sept. 24/90 vs vs Milwaukee (A) (5 for 5; 1 run; 3-1B, 2-2B)
Kelly Gruber
—June 12/89 vs Detroit (H) (5 for 6; 4-1B; 1-2B; 3-RBI)
Fred McGriff
—Sept. 1/90 vs Cleveland (A) (5 for 5; 1 run, 3 1B, 1 2B, 1 HR)

FOUR HITS

Alan Ashby (1)
Bob Bailor (6)
Jesse Barfield (11)
George Bell (5)
Barry Bonnell (3)
Pat Borders (1)
—April 30/90 vs Cleveland (A) 3-1B, 1-2B
Rick Bosetti (3)
Rico Carty (1)
Dave Collins (4)
Ted Cox (1)
Rob Ducey (1)
—Sept. 26/88 vs Boston (A) 2-2B; 2-1B
Ron Fairly (2)
Junior Felix (5)
Tony Fernandez (8)
Damaso Garcia (9)
Alfredo Griffin (5)
Kelly Gruber (6)
—May 22/87 vs Seattle (A) 2—1B; 2—HR
—Apr. 11/88 vs New York (H) 1-1B; 1-2B; 2-HR
—Apr. 16/89 vs Kansas City (H) 1—1b; 1—2B; 1—3B; 1—HR
—May 28/89 vs Chicago (H) 2—1B; 2—2B
—April 25/90 vs Cleveland (H) 2-1B, 1-2B, 1-HR
—Sept. 14/90 vs Baltimore (H) 2-1B, 2-B
Roy Howell (9)
Garth Iorg (2)
Cliff Johnson (2)
Rick Leach (1)
Manny Lee (1)
—Apr. 11/89 vs New York (A) 3—1B; 1—2B
Nelson Liriano (3)
Buck Martinez (2)
Len Matuszek (1)
John Mayberry (2)
Lloyd Moseby (7)
Fred McGriff (6)
Dave McKay (1)
Rance Mulliniks (1)
—June 13/85 vs Boston (A) 1—1B; 2—2b; 1—HR
Greg Myers (1)
—June 10/90 vs Milwaukee (A) 3-1B, 1-2B
Willie Upshaw (5)
Otto Velez (2)
Ernie Whitt (5)
Mookie Wilson (2)
—Aug. 15/89 vs Boston (A) 3—1B; 1—2B
—Aug. 26/89 vs Milwaukee (H) 4—1B
Al Woods (6)

BLUE JAYS BREAK AL AND MAJOR LEAGUE ATTENDANCE RECORD

In 1990, the TORONTO BLUE JAYS set an American League attendance record as well as a Major League attendance record with a season attendance mark of 3,885,284...TORONTO had set the previous American League record of 3,375,883 in 1989 breaking the Twins' 1988 American League mark of 3,030,672...The Los Angeles Dodgers had previously held the Major League record of 3,608,881 set in 1982...The BLUE JAYS broke the record on Monday, September 17th, 1990 (date #75) when they hosted the New York Yankees...The average attendance per game for 1990 was 47,966 ((81 dates)...66 of the games at SkyDome were sell-outs, including the last 59 consecutive...The three million barrier was broken on date #64 (August 25) - a new Major League record...The BLUE JAYS also set a Major League record for total attendance in a season (Home and Road) with 5,925,056 breaking the 1982 L.A. Dodgers record of 5,859,072.

The Three Million Club. The 1989 home attendance mark of 3,375,883 was the fourth highest in major league history. Here's a listing of the three million club:

1.	Toronto Blue Jays	3,885,284	1990
2.	Los Angeles Dodgers	3,608,881	1982
3.	Los Angeles Dodgers	3,510,313	1983
4.	Toronto Blue Jays	3,375,883	1989
5.	Los Angeles Dodgers	3,347,845	1978
6.	Los Angeles Dodgers	3,264,593	1985
7.	Los Angeles Dodgers	3,249,287	1980
8.	Los Angeles Dodgers	3,134,824	1984
9.	St. Louis Cardinals	3,082,000	1989
10.	St. Louis Cardinals	3,072,122	1987
11.	New York Mets	3,055,445	1988
12.	New York Mets	3,034,124	1987
13.	Minnesota Twins	3.030.672	1988
14.	Los Angeles Dodgers	3,023,208	1986
15.	Los Angeles Dodgers	3,002,396	1990

BLUE JAYS BIGGEST INNINGS

Inning	Runs	H/A	Date	OPP	Score	Winner	Loser
1st	7	A	June 23, 1989	Oak	10-8	Buice	Young
2nd	9	H	June 26, 1978	Balt	24-10	Underwood	Flanagan
3rd	7	H	April 19, 1988	KC	12-3	Clancy	Saberhagen
3rd	7	H	August 21, 1988	Milw	8-4	Key	August
4th	10	A	June 10, 1990	Milw	13-5	Wells	Navarro
5th	8	H	May 26, 1989	Chi	11-0	Key	Hillegas
6th	10	A	August 3, 1987	Chi	14-5	Musselman	Bannister
7th	9	H	May 15, 1978	Calf	10-6	Moore	Hartzell
7th	9	H	June 19, 1987	Milw	15-6	Musselman	Clear
8th	8	A	May 28, 1986	Minn	14-8	Clancy	Blyleven
9th	11	A	July 20, 1984	Sea	12-7	Acker	Mirabella
10th	5	A	April 11, 1989	NY	11-6	Henke	Righetti
10th	5	A	May 14, 1990	Det	8-3	Ward	Henneman
11th	5	A	July 22, 1983	Tex	10-5	Moffitt	Schmidt
12th	3	A	April 22, 1988	NY	6-4	Wells	Stoddard
13th	5	A	July 9, 1985	Sea	9-4	Musselman	Vande Berg
14th	5	A	April 29, 1981	Milw	5-0	Leal	Easterly
14th	5	A	June 21, 1989	Calf	6-1	Henke	Minton
15th	3	A	June 12, 1983	Calf	6-5	Clarke	Brown
16th	2	A	September 9, 1989	Clev	7-5	Wills	Kaiser
17th	1	A	October 4, 1980	Bost	7-6	Leal	Stanley

OPPONENTS BIGGEST INNINGS

Inning	Runs	H/A	Date	OPP	Score	Winner	Loser
1st	8	H	August 25, 1979	Calf	2-24	Frost	Moore
2nd	9	H	April 5, 1979	KC	2-11	Leonard	Underwood
3rd	9	H	May 17, 1990	Sea	6-14	Johnson	Key
4th	8	A	August 17,1989	Balt	6-11	Ballard	Cerutti
5th	8	H	September 17, 1988	Clev	3-12	Swindell	Key
6th	7	H	July 25,1987	Minn	9-13	Schatzeder	Musselman
7th	11	H	August 6, 1979	KC	12-16	Mingori	Stieb
8th	8	H	June 30, 1977	NY	5-11	Hunter	Garvin
9th	6	A	September 7, 1979	Clev	8-9	Reuschel	Buskey
9th	6	H	May 15, 1985	Calf	6-9	Moore	Caudill
10th	4	A	September 17, 1980	NY	7-8	T. Underwood	Kucek
10th	4	H	May 10, 1981	Bost	5-9	Burgmeier	Jackson
10th	4	A	August 24, 1982	Balt	3-7	D.Martinez	McLaughlin
10th	4	A	August 24, 1983	Balt	4-7	T.Martinez	McLaughlin
11th	4	H	June 28, 1977	NY	1-5	(2nd)	Tidrow
12th	5	H	July 1, 1987	NY	1-6	Clements	Musselman
13th	6	H	June 2, 1982	NY	6-12	Rawley	McLaughlin
14th	2	H	May 17, 1980	Oak	2-4	Keough	McLaughlin
14th	2	H	May 17, 1988	Tex	6-7	Mohorcic	Eichhorn
15th	2	H	August 28, 1980	Minn	5-7	Verhoeven	Jefferson
15th	2	A	June 12, 1983	Calf	6-5	Clarke	Brown
15th	2	H	June 22, 1990	NY	7-8	Cadaret	Blair

BLUE JAYS ALL-TIME WON-LOST BREAKDOWN

	Home	Road	Day	Night	vs East	vs West	1-Run	Extra Inn's.	DH's W-L-S
1977	25-55	29-52	27-39	27-68	31-58	23-49	17-27	4-11	1-7-8
1978	37-44	22-58	20-42	39-60	28-61	31-41	23-30	7-8	3-8-6
1979	32-49	21-60	21-44	32-65	22-56	31-53	19-28	2-10	0-3-7
1980	35-46	32-49	29-27	38-68	28-50	39-45	23-21	10-8	5-1-4
1981	17-36	20-33	16-27	21-42	15-27	22-42	10-17	1-8	0-5-0
1982	44-37	34-47	30-28	48-56	33-45	45-39	28-30	10-5	3-3-2
1983	48-33	41-40	35-23	54-50	39-39	50-34	24-20	11-6	1-1-4
1984	49-32	40-41	32-27	57-46	37-41	52-32	34-25	6-12	2-4-1
1985	54-26	45-36	34-24	65-38	44-33	55-29	26-21	12-5	2-0-1
1986	42-39	44-37	30-30	56-46	42-36	44-40	22-25	10-13	1-2-1
1987	52-29	44-37	29-28	67-38	44-34	52-32	27-24	10-7	0-1-0
1988	45-36	42-39	24-30	63-45	47-31	40-44	21-17	6-6	0-0-0
1989	46-35	43-38	22-29	67-44	46-32	43-41	25-22	13-4	1-0-0
1990	44-37	42-39	26-24	60-52	42-36	44-40	24-27	4-8	0-0-0

	APR. W-L	MAY W-L	JUNE W-L	JULY W-L	AUG. W-L	SEPT./ OCT. W-L	AT ALL-STAR W-L	AFTER ALL-STAR W-L	TOTALS W-L
H	6-4	5-10	3-9	5-10	3-8	3-14	18-27	7-28	25-55
1977A	4-7	3-7	7-8	2-11	7-10	6-9	16-31	13-21	29-52
T	10-11	8-17	10-17	7-21	10-18	9-23	34-58	20-49	54-107
H	4-7	7-7	6-8	7-7	10-3	3-12	19-23	18-21	37-44
1978A	4-6	2-11	3-9	6-11	6-11	1-10	13-30	9-28	22-58
T	8-13	9-18	9-17	13-18	16-14	4-22	32-53	27-49	59-102
H	3-8	3-15	6-5	5-6	6-8	9-7	14-32	18-17	32-49
1979A	4-7	2-8	6-14	3-11	5-9	1-11	15-32	6-28	21-60
T	7-15	5-23	12-19	8-17	11-17	10-18	29-64	24-45	53-109
H	3-1	8-9	7-7	5-10	6-8	6-11	18-19	17-27	35-46
1980A	6-6	5-5	3-10	6-7	5-12	7-9	15-24	17-25	32-49
T	9-7	13-14	10-17	11-17	11-20	13-20	33-43	34-52	67-95
H	2-7	5-10	0-5	—	4-8	6-6	7-22	10-14	17-36
1981A	5-5	4-10	0-5	—	5-2	6-11	9-20	11-13	20-33
T	7-12	9-20	0-10	—	9-10	12-17	16-42	21-27	37-69
H	5-6	6-5	7-10	9-4	7-8	10-4	19-24	25-13	44-37
1982A	3-6	7-9	5-4	6-8	6-12	7-8	18-23	16-24	34-47
T	8-12	13-14	12-14	15-12	13-20	17-12	37-47	41-37	78-84
H	4-4	12-6	6-3	8-8	7-6	11-6	23-15	25-18	48-33
1983A	4-6	6-3	10-9	7-4	8-13	6-5	20-18	21-22	41-40
T	8-10	18-9	16-12	15-12	15-19	17-11	43-33	46-40	89-73
H	5-5	15-2	9-5	7-6	6-5	7-9	34-15	15-17	49-32
1984A	8-4	4-4	4-11	7-8	12-7	5-7	16-19	24-22	40-41
T	13-9	19-6	13-16	14-14	18-12	12-16	50-34	39-39	89-73
H	5-4	9-2	11-5	10-4	5-3	12-8	26-13	28-13	54-26
1985A	8-3	8-6	5-8	8-6	12-7	6-6	27-22	18-24	45-36
T	13-7	17-8	16-13	18-10	17-10	18-14	53-35	46-37	99-62
H	4-7	7-5	10-8	5-5	11-5	5-9	26-25	16-14	42-39
1986A	5-4	7-10	7-3	10-6	7-5	8-9	21-18	23-19	44-37
T	9-11	14-15	17-11	15-11	18-10	13-18	47-43	39-33	86-76
H	7-4	7-3	8-7	12-4	5-6	13-5	28-16	24-13	52-29
1987A	5-4	9-8	9-4	3-8	12-6	6-7	23-20	21-17	44-37
T	12-8	16-11	17-11	15-12	17-12	19-12	51-36	45-30	96-66
H	4-9	6-5	10-4	4-8	7-7	14-3	23-24	22-12	45-36
1988A	5-4	7-11	7-7	8-6	7-7	8-4	19-22	23-17	42-39
T	9-13	13-16	17-11	12-14	14-14	22-7	42-46	45-29	87-75
H	4-5	8-9	6-5	6-8	14-4	8-5	20-23	26-12	46-35
1989A	5-11	3-6	11-5	9-4	6-5	9-6	22-22	21-16	43-38
T	9-16	11-15	17-10	15-12	20-9	17-11	42-45	47-28	89-73
H	9-4	5-9	6-8	9-5	5-8	10-3	26-23	18-14	44-37
1990A	3-5	9-5	9-5	5-7	8-8	8-9	21-15	21-24	42-39
T	12-9	14-14	15-13	14-12	13-16	18-12	47-38	39-38	86-76

BLUE JAYS WORLD SERIES/LCS SHARES:

The Blue Jays have qualified for a share of the World Series/league championship pool six times in their fourteen year history.

Here are the individual share/total of all shares that Blue Jays players have received.

1984	$3,557.49/$129,965.54	(2nd place-East)
1985	$26,697.41/$975.671.41	(1st place-East)
1987	$5,663.88/$202,767.15	(2nd place-East)
1988	$885.98/$37,405.87	(T 3rd place-East)
1989	$37,927.84/$1,513,851.10	(1st place-East)
1990	$8,308.18/$343,153.88	(2nd place-East)

HIGHEST SCORING GAMES

(13 or More Runs Scored)

BY BLUE JAYS

DATE		OPPONENT	SCORE	BLUE JAYS PITCHER OF RECORD
June 26, 1978	vs	Baltimore	24-10	Tom Underwood
Sept. 10, 1977	at	New York	19-3	Jim Clancy
June 26, 1983	at	Seattle	19-7	Jim Acker
Sept. 14, 1987	vs	Baltimore	18-3	Jim Clancy
April 11, 1988	vs	New York	17-9	David Wells
April 20, 1990	vs	Kansas City	17-6	Todd Stottlemyre
May 14, 1987	at	Minnesota	16-4	Dave Stieb
June 22, 1986	vs	New York	15-1	Jimmy Key
May 9, 1987	at	Texas	15-4	Dave Stieb
June 19, 1987	vs	Milwaukee	15-6	Jeff Musselman
June 15, 1988	vs	Cleveland	15-3	Dave Stieb
Sept. 27, 1988	at	Boston	15-9	Mike Flanagan
April 16, 1989	vs	Kansas City	15-8	David Wells
May 28, 1986	at	Minnesota	14-8	Jim Clancy
June 27, 1986	at	New York	14-7	Jim Acker
June 29, 1987	vs	New York	14-15	Tom Henke
Aug. 3, 1987	at	Chicago	14-5	Jeff Musselman
July 18, 1978	at	Seattle	13-12 (10)	Tom Murphy
June 14, 1983	vs	Oakland	13-7	Roy Lee Jackson
Aug. 2, 1983 (2nd gm)	vs	New York	13-6	Matt Williams
Sept. 17, 1983	at	Minnestoa	13-3	Luis Leal
April 5, 1984	at	Seattle	13-5	Luis Leal
Sept. 29, 1985	at	Milwaukee	13-5	Jim Acker
Aug. 16, 1986	vs	Texas	13-1	Jimmy Key
Aug. 30, 1987	vs	Oakland	13-3	Jim Clancy
Sept. 12, 1987	vs	New York	13-1	Jimmy Key
June 16, 1988	at	Detroit	13-5	Mike Flanagan
June 4, 1989	at	Boston	13-11	Duane Ward
June 10, 1990	at	Milwaukee	13-5	David Wells

BY OPPONENTS

DATE		OPPONENT	SCORE	BLUE JAYS PITCHER OF RECORD
Aug. 25, 1979	vs	California	2-24	Balor Moore
June 3, 1981	vs	California	6-17	Jim Clancy
May 8, 1979	at	Minnesota	6-16	Mike Willis
Aug. 6, 1979	vs	Kansas City	12-16	Dave Stieb
Aug. 31, 1983	vs	Cleveland	11-16	Jim Acker
Aug. 15, 1984 (1st gm)	at	Cleveland	1-16	Luis Leal
Sept. 25, 1977 (1st gm)	vs	New York	0-15	Jerry Garvin
April 9, 1982	vs	Milwaukee	4-15	Mark Bomback
June 3, 1984	vs	New York	2-15	Jim Clancy
June 29, 1987	vs	New York	14-15	Tom Henke
July 26, 1977	vs	Texas	0-14	Jim Clancy
Sept. 9, 1979	at	Cleveland	10-14	Tom Buskey
July 20, 1983	vs	Kansas City	8-14	Dave Stieb
Sept. 25, 1984	at	Boston	6-14	Dave Stieb
April 9, 1987	vs	Cleveland	3-14	Joe Johnson
Aug. 6, 1987	at	Cleveland	5-14	Jim Clancy
May 17, 1990	vs	Seattle	6-14	Jimmy Key
June 17, 1978	at	Texas	2-13	Jim Clancy
July 22, 1979	at	Minnesota	1-13	Dave Lemanczyk
Aug. 23, 1981	vs	Chicago	2-13	Luis Leal
Aug. 22, 1984	vs	Cleveland	3-13	Jim Clancy
Sept. 18, 1985	at	Boston	1-13	Jim Clancy
May 9, 1986	at	Seattle	3-13	Dave Stieb
July 25, 1987	vs	Minnesota	9-13	Jeff Musselman
September 20, 1988	vs	Boston	2-13	Jeff Musselman
May 14, 1989	at	Minnesota	1-13	Mike Flanagan

TORONTO'S BEST WON/LOST RECORDS

G	W-L	YR	G	W-L	YR	G	W-L	YR	G	W-L	YR
1	1-0	(77/83/87/88/89)	41	27-14	(84/85)	81	49-32	(84/85)	121	75-46	(85)
2	2-0	(87/88)	42	28-14	(84/85)	82	50-32	(84/85)	122	76-46	(85)
3	2-1	(77/83-87/88)	43	29-14	(84/85)	83	51-32	(85)	123	77-46	(85)
4	3-1	(77/84/86)	44	30-14	(84/85)	84	52-32	(85)	124	77-47	(85)
5	3-2	(77/84/86/88)	45	31-14	(84/85)	85	53-32	(85)	125	78-47	(85)
6	4-2	(77)	46	31-15	(84/85)	86	53-33	(85)	126	79-47	(85)
7	5-2	(77)	47	32-15	(84)	87	53-34	(85)	127	79-48	(85)
8	5-3	(77/84)	48	33-15	(84)	88	53-35	(84/85)	128	80-48	(85)
9	5-4	(77/80/84/85-87)	49	34-15	(84)	89	54-35	(84)	129	81-48	(85)
10	6-4	(84/85/87)	50	34-16	(84/85)	90	54-36	(85)	130	81-49	(85)
11	7-4	(84/85)	51	35-16	(85)	91	54-37	(84/85)	131	82-49	(85)
12	8-4	(84)	52	36-16	(85)	92	55-37	(84/85)	132	82-50	(85)
13	9-4	(84)	53	36-17	(84/85)	93	56-37	(84/85)	133	83-50	(85)
14	9-5	(84/90)	54	36-18	(84/85)	94	57-37	(85)	134	84-50	(85)
15	10-5	(90)	55	36-19	(84/85)	95	58-37	(85)	135	84-51	(85)
16	9-7	(90)	56	37-19	(85)	96	59-37	(85)	136	85-51	(85)
17	11-6	(90)	57	38-19	(85)	97	60-37	(85)	137	86-51	(85)
18	11-7	(85/90)	58	38-20	(85/87)	98	61-37	(85)	138	87-51	(85)
19	12-7	(85)	59	39-20	(87)	99	62-37	(85)	139	88-51	(85)
20	13-7	(85)	60	39-21	(87)	100	63-37	(85)	140	88-52	(85)
21	14-7	(85)	61	39-22	(84/85/87)	101	63-38	(85)	141	89-52	(85)
22	14-8	(85/87)	62	40-22	(84/87)	102	64-38	(85)	142	90-52	(85)
23	15-8	(85/86/87)	63	41-22	(84/87)	103	65-38	(85)	143	91-52	(85)
24	15-9	(80/84/85/87)	64	41-23	(84)	104	66-38	(85)	144	91-53	(85)
25	15-10	(80/84/85/87)	65	41-24	(84/87)	105	67-38	(85)	145	91-54	(85)
26	16-10	(84/85/87)	66	42-24	(84)	106	67-39	(85)	146	92-54	(85)
27	17-10	(84/87)	67	42-25	(84/87)	107	68-39	(85)	147	93-54	(85)
28	18-10	(84)	68	43-25	(84)	108	69-39	(85)	148	93-55	(85)
29	18-11	(84/85/87)	69	43-26	(84/85/87)	109	69-40	(85)	149	94-55	(85)
30	19-11	(85/87)	70	44-26	(87)	110	69-41	(85)	150	95-55	(85)
31	20-11	(85/87)	71	44-27	(85/87)	111	70-41	(85)	151	95-56	(85)
32	21-11	(87)	72	45-27	(85/87)	112	70-42	(85)	152	95-57	(85)
33	21-12	(87)	73	45-28	(85/87)	113	71-42	(85)	153	96-57	(85)
34	21-13	(84/85/87)	74	46-28	(85)	114	72-42	(85)	154	97-57	(85)
35	22-13	(84)	75	46-29	(85)	115	72-43	(85)	155	98-57	(85)
36	23-13	(84)	76	46-30	(85)	116	72-44	(85)	156	98-58	(85)
37	24-13	(84)	77	47-30	(85)	117	73-44	(85)	157	98-59	(85)
38	24-14	(84/85)	78	47-31	(85)	118	73-45	(85)	158	98-60	(85)
39	25-14	(84/85)	79	48-31	(85)	119	74-45	(85)	159	98-61	(85)
40	26-14	(84/85)	80	48-32	(84/85)	120	74-46	(85)	160	99-61	(85)
									161	99-61	(85)
									162	96-66	(85)

MARATHONS IN BLUE JAYS' HISTORY

Date	Opponent	H/A	Innings	Score	Winner	Loser
Oct. 4/80	Boston	A	17 (1st)	7-6	Leal	Stanley
July 3/88	Oakland	H	16	8-9	Burns	Cerutti
Sept. 9/89	Cleveland	A	16	7-5	Wills	Kaiser
*Aug. 28/80	Minnesota	H	15	5-7	Verhoeven	Jefferson
May 23/81	Oakland	A	15	2-3	Jones	Leal
June 12/83	California	A	15	6-5	Clarke	Brown
July 27/86	Oakland	A	15	0-1	Leiper	Clarke
June 22/90	New York	H	15	7-8	Cadaret	Blair
May 17/80	Oakland	H	14	2-4	Keough	McLaughlin
Aug. 9/80	Kansas City	H	14	4-3	Willis	Eastwick
July 31/78	Detroit	H	14	8-7	Coleman	Sykes
Sept. 24/78	Boston	H	14	6-7	Drago	Buskey
Apr. 29/81	Milwaukee	A	14	5-0	Leal	Easterley
Sept. 21/85	Milwaukee	H	14	2-1	Lamp	Darwin
May 17/88	Texas	H	14	6-7	Mohorcic	Eichhorn
June 21/89	California	A	14	6-1	Henke	Minton
Aug. 22/89	Detroit	H	14	3-2	Gozzo	E. Nunez
June 8/77	California	A	13	1-2	Laroche	Bruno
July 15/77	Detroit	H	13	8-6	Vuckovich	Crawford
May 28/78	New York	A	13	5-6	Gossage	Murphy
June 20/78	Detroit	H	13	3-4	Hiller	Willis
June 8/80	Minnesota	A	13 (2nd)	6-4	McLaughlin	Arroyo
Sept. 14/80	Baltimore	H	13	4-3	Barlow	D. Martinez
Sept. 17/80#	New York	A	13	7-8	T. Underwood	Kucek
Sept. 22/81	Oakland	H	13 (1st)	2-3	Beard	Leal
June 6/82	New York	H	13	6-12	Rawley	McLaughlin
June 30/83	Cleveland	H	13	6-5	McLaughlin	Anderson
Apr. 20/84	California	H	13	6-10	Sanchez	Acker
July 25/84	Kansas City	A	13	4-5	Quisenberry	Clark
Aug. 15/84	Cleveland	A	13 (2nd)	3-4	Jeffcoat	Key
July 9/85	Seattle	A	13	9-4	Musselman	Vande Berg
Aug. 13/86	Baltimore	A	13	6-7	Aase	Aquino
April 14/87	Chicago	H	13	4-3	Eichhorn	McKeon
Sept. 27/87	Detroit	H	13	2-3	Henneman	Nunez
June 22/89	Oakland	A	13	4-2	Hernandez	Corsi
Sept. 19/89	Boston	H	13	6-5	Henke	Harris
July 24/90	Kansas City	H	13	3-5	Farr	Ward
July 28/90	Texas	H	13	2-3	Arnsberg	Wills
Sept. 21/90	Cleveland	H	13	1-2	Valdez	Wills

*Suspended game, due to CNE curfew—completed on August 29th
#Suspended game, due to rain—completed on September 18th

LIFETIME HOME RUNS-AL-BY PARKS

	Balt	Bost	Cal	Chi	Clev	Det	KC	Milw	Minn	NY	Oak	Sea	Tex	Tor(#)
BORDERS	1	1	0	1	0	1	1	1	1	0	0	1	0	13(11)
CARTER	7	13	5	4	69	3	1	10	14	6	5	5	5	4 (1)
GRUBER	7	7	1	3	2	2	0	2	0	3	1	5	4	55(29)
HILL	1	0	0	1	2	0	0	0	1	0	0	0	0	8 (8)
LEE	0	1	0	0	0	2	0	0	0	1	1	1	1	6 (3)
MULLINIKS	3	5	7	1	2	5	0	1	4	2	6	3	1	31 (1)
MYERS	0	0	0	0	0	0	0	1	0	1	0	0	0	3 (3)
OLERUD	2	1	0	0	0	0	0	0	0	0	0	0	0	11(11)
TABLER	0	3	2	2	23	1	2	1	1	0	1	1	2	2 (0)
WHITE	2	1	28	4	5	1	0	1	2	3	1	5	3	3 (1)
WHITEN	0	0	0	0	0	0	0	1	0	0	0	0	0	1 (1)
WILLIAMS	1	0	2	8	3	3	0	0	1	0	2	2	2	2 (1)
WILSON	1	0	0	0	0	2	0	0	0	0	0	0	1	1 (1)
TOTAL	100	103	98	81	179	107	49	71	81	89	68	125	84	981(156)

#=AT SKYDOME

TRIPLE PLAYS

By Toronto

APR. 22/78 vs. Chicago at Toronto-With Jim Clancy pitching in the Chicago second, after Bobby Bonds homered Lamar Johnson doubled and stayed at second on an infield hit by Ron Blomberg. Junior Moore followed with an attempted bunt that was lined to Clancy who threw to John Mayberry at first to double Blomberg. Mayberry then fired the ball to Luis Gomez at second and Johnson was tripled up before he could return to the bag. Final Score Toronto 4 Chicago 2

SEPT. 7/79 at Cleveland-With Phil Huffman pitching in Cleveland's eighth and the bases loaded, Ted Cox grounded to third baseman, Roy Howell, who stepped on the bag forcing Mike Hargrove, threw to second baseman, Luis Gomez, who erased Rick Manning and then relayed to first baseman, John Mayberry to nip Cox. Final Score Cleveland 9 Toronto 8

SEPT. 21/79 vs New York at Toronto-With Tom Underwood pitching in New York's seventh, Chris Chambliss and Roy Staiger were at first and second on consecutive singles. Damaso Garcia, the batter, lined sharply to second baseman Dave McKay, who threw to Craig Kusick at first to double Staiger. Kusick relayed to shortstop Alfredo Griffin at second base to catch Chambliss off base for the third out. Final Score-Toronto 3 New York 2

By Opposition

SEPT. 9/78 vs. Baltimore at Toronto-With Scott McGregor pitching in the Blue Jays sixth Doug Ault and Dave McKay hit consecutive singles to put Toronto runners on first and second. Rick Cerone followed with a hard grounder to Doug DeCinces who stepped on third for the first out and then threw to Rick Dauer at second for a forceout. Dauer then fired the ball to first baseman Eddie Murray, beating Cerone to the bag. Final Score-Baltimore 4 Toronto 0

BLUE JAYS HOME POSTPONEMENTS

1. April 22, 1977, vs. Boston (Friday—Day)
2. April 23, 1977, vs. Boston (Saturday—Day)
3. September 24, 1977, vs. New York (Saturday—Day)
4. September 30, 1977, vs. Cleveland (Friday—Night)
5. October 1, 1977, vs. Cleveland (Saturday—Day)
6. April 20, 1978, vs. New York (Thursday—Day)
7. May 8, 1978, vs. Oakland (Monday—Night)
8. May 14, 1978, vs. Seattle (Sunday—Day)
9. June 12, 1978, vs. Minnesota (Monday—Night)
10. May 25, 1979 vs. Boston (Friday—Night)
11. April 14, 1980, vs. Milwaukee (Monday—Opening Day)
12. April 28, 1980, vs. Kansas City (Monday—Night)
13. May 13, 1980, vs. Seattle (Tuesday—Night)
14. June 19, 1980, vs. Chicago (Thursday—Night)
15. May 5, 1981, vs. Cleveland (Tuesday—Night)—Fog
16. August 30, 1981, vs. Kansas City (Sunday—Day)
17. September 21, 1981, vs. Oakland (Monday—Night)
18. June 5, 1982, vs. Cleveland (Satuday—Day)
19. June 25, 1982, vs. Minnesota (Friday—Night)
20. September 14, 1982, vs. Oakland (Tuesday—Night)
21. April 30, 1983, vs. Chicago (Saturday—Day)
22. May 29, 1983, vs. Boston (Sunday—2nd g—DH)
23. July 4, 1983, vs. Seattle (Monday—Night)
24. April 30, 1984, vs. Texas (Monday—Night) (Winds)
25. April 16, 1986, vs. Baltimore (Wednesday—Day)
26. September 10, 1986, vs. New York (Wednesday—Night)
27. October 4, 1986, vs. Milwaukee (Saturday—Day)
28. April 15, 1988, vs. Minnesota (Friday—Night) (Cold)
29. May 17, 1989 vs California (Sunday—Day)

AT THE ALL STAR BREAK

AVERAGE

1977	Bailor	.332
1982	Bonnell	.325
1986	Bell	.316
1984	Bell	.314

HOMERUNS

1987	Bell	29
1986	Barfield	21
1989	McGriff	20
1990	Gruber	20
1987	Barfield	19
1985	Bell	18
1990	McGriff	18

RBI

1987	Bell	76
1990	Gruber	66
1990	Bell	60
1986	Barfield	65
1986	Bell	65
1985	Bell	58
1984	Upshaw	55

WINS

1990	Stieb	11
1987	Clancy	10
1988	Stieb	10
	4 others at	9

LOSSES

1979	Underwood	12
1988	Clancy	11
	4 others at	10

STRIKEOUTS

1987	Key	98
1984	Stieb	95
1985	Stieb	95
1987	Clancy	94
	2 tied at	83

AT THE ALL-STAR BREAK:

YEAR	W-L	POS.	GBL	HOME ATTENDANCE
1977	34-58	7th	-19	1,020,152
1978	32-53	7th	-26	804,890
1979	29-64	7th	-31.5	785,030
1980	33-43	7th	-17	675,556
1981*	16-42	7th	-19	426,795
1982	37-47	7th	-11.5	637,057
1983	43-33	1st	+1	786,503
1984	50-34	2nd	-7	1,247,799
1985	53-35	1st	+2.5	1,123,502
1986	47-43	5th	-10.5	1,442,158
1987	51-36	2nd	-3	1,413,455
1988	42-46	6th	-11.5	1,473,480
1989	42-45	T4th	-7	1,559,163
1990	47-38	2nd	-0.5	2,288,900

TORONTO BLUE JAYS IRON MAN STREAK (active players)

Mookie Wilson currently holds the Blue Jays Iron Man record, by playing in 25 games between September 7th, 1990 and October 3, 1990...The streak is still intact heading into the 1991 season...The All-Time Blue Jays record is 403 set by Tony Fernandez between September 21, 1984 and June 24, 1987.

BASEBALL RECORDS HELD or TIED BY BLUE JAYS

MAJOR LEAGUE RECORDS SET

Most Home Runs, None on Base, Game, Club-7, by Boston vs Toronto, July 4/77
Fewest Sacrifice Hits, Club, Season-18, Toronto, 1990
Most Home Runs, Club, Game-10 Toronto vs Baltimore, Sept. 14/87
Most Home Runs, opening day game-3, George Bell, April 4, 1988
Highest Fielding Average, Shortstop, Season-.992, Tony Fernandez, 1989

MAJOR LEAGUE RECORDS TIED

Home Run, First Time at Bat in Major Leagues, as Pinch Hitter-Al Woods, April 7/77, fifth inning
Most Grounded into Double Play, Extra-Inning Game, Club-6, by Toronto vs Minnesota, August 29/77, first game (10 innings)

Most Home Runs, Opening Game of Season-2, Doug Ault, Toronto April 7/77, John Mayberry, Toronto, April 9/80
Highest Fielding Percentage, Club, Season-.976, Oakland, Toronto
Most Players, 100 or More Hits, Club, Season-9, 1983
Most Doubles, Games-4, Damasco Garcia, June 27/86 at New York
Most Pinch-Hit Home Runs, Club, Game-2, Toronto, June 14/86 vs Detroit
Most Errors, First Baseman, Inning-3, Willie Upshaw, Toronto, July 1/86 at Boston, Fifth Inning.
Most Players with two or more Home Runs, Club, Game-3 Toronto vs Baltimore Sept. 14/87 (Bell, Mulliniks, Whitt)
Most Home Runs, both Club, Game-11, Toronto (10), Baltimore (1) Sept. 14/87
Most Players with 100 hits or more, Club, Season-9, 1988
Most Consecutive One-Hit Games-2, Dave Stieb, September 24,30, 1988
Fewest Complete Games, Club, Season-6
Fewest 1-0 Games Lost-0, 1988
Fewest Doubleheaders, Club, Season-0, 1990
Hitting Home Run, First Major League At-Bat-Junior Felix, May 4, 1989
Most Sacrifice Flies, Both Clubs, Game-5, Toronto (4) vs Chicago (1), August 14, 1990

AMERICAN LEAGUE RECORDS SET

Most Sacrifice Flies Allowed, Season-70, 1977, Toronto
Most Long Hits, Game, Both Clubs-19, Minnesota (12) vs Toronto (7), May 8/79
Most Consecutive Hits Allowed, Pitcher, Start of Game-5, Luis Leal, June 2/80
Most Three-base Hits, Switch-hitter, Season-15, Alfredo Griffin, 1980
Most Runs, Both Clubs-Ninth Inning-15, Toronto (11), Seattle (4), July 20/84
Largest attendance, 4-game series, Blue Jays at New York, September 12-15, 1985 (214,510)
Most Games Played, Shortstop, Season-163, Tony Fernandez, 1986
Longest Nine Inning Night Game by Time-3:59, Detroit vs Blue Jays, June 17, 1988
Highest Home Attendance, Club, Season-3,375,883

AMERICAN LEAGUE RECORDS TIED

Most Players 2 + Two-base Hits, Inning, Club-2, vs Baltimore, June 26/78, 2nd inning
Most Home Runs, Doubleheader, Hitting Homers Each Game-4, Otto Velez, May 4/80 (3, 1st game, 10 innings; 1, 2nd game)
Most Games, Switch-Hitter Season-163, Tony Fernandez, 1986
Most Home Runs on Road, Righthanded Batter, Season-28, George Bell, 1987
Most Games Pitched in Relief, Season-89, Mark Eichhorn, 1987
Most Games allowing Zero Hits or One Hit, Season-3, Dave Stieb, 1988

BLUE JAYS LONGEST HITTING STREAKS

Club Record: 22 games, George Bell, 1989
21 games, Damaso Garcia, 1983
21 games, Lloyd Moseby, 1983
20 games, Damaso Garcia, 1982
19 games, Alfredo Griffin, 1980
18 games, Damaso Garcia, 1986
18 games, Tony Fernandez, 1987
17 games, John Mayberry, 1980
17 games, Damaso Garcia, 1982
17 games, George Bell, 1987
16 games, Dave McKay, 1978
16 games, Jesse Barfield, 1985
16 games, Damaso Garcia, 1985
16 games, Tony Fernandez, 1989
15 games, Roy Howell, 1977
15 games, George Bell, 1986
15 games, Kelly Gruber, 1989
15 games, Tony Fernandez, 1990
15 games, Kelly Gruber, 1990

BLUE JAYS EXTRA-INNING RECORDS

	GP	W-L		GP	W-L
1977	15	4-11	1984	18	6-12
1978	15	7-8	1985	17	12-5
1979	12	2-10	1986	23	10-13
1980	18	10-8	1987	16	10-6
1981	9	1-8	1988	12	6-6
1982	15	10-5	1989	17	13-4
1983	17	11-6	1990	12	4-8

BLUE JAYS WHO LED LEAGUE IN FIELDING

Rance Mulliniks, 3B, 1984	.968	Jimmy Key, P, 1986	1.000
Rance Mulliniks, 3B, 1985	.971	Fred McGriff, 1B, 1988	.997
Rance Mulliniks, 3B, 1986	.975	Tony Fernandez, SS, 1989	. 992
Tony Fernandez, SS, 1986	.983	Manny Lee, 2B, 1990	.993

ATTENDANCE RECORD: The largest crowd ever to see the Blue Jays at Exhibition Stadium was 47,828 to see the Blue Jays lose to the New York Yankees 6-1 on July 1, 1987...The largest crowd at SkyDome was 50,268 on October 6, 1989 vs Oakland Athletics in Game #3 of the ALCS...The largest crowd to see a regular season game at SkyDome was 49,918 on August 23, 1990 vs the Boston Red Sox.

THREE CANADIANS have worn the Blue Jays uniform in the history of the franchise. Infielder Dave McKay was a member of the Blue Jays from 1977-79...A native of Vancouver, McKay played 3B in the club's inaugural game, April 7, 1977...Paul Hodgson, an outfielder from Fredericton, New Brunswick, played with the Blue Jays in 1980...Outfielder Rob Ducey, born in Toronto but a resident of nearby Cambridge, Ontario debuted with the Blue Jays in 1987. In addition to these three players there have been two other Canadians on the club's 40-Man Roster...They are: RHP-Dave Shipanoff (Oct. 1982-April 1984) and LHP-Denis Boucher (Nov. 1990-)

NAME THE TEAM CONTEST

The Blue Jays were named in a contest conducted in June and July of 1976. Over 30,000 individual entries ere received, suggesting over 4,000 names for the new American League club. From the list of names submitted, specially-appointed panels of judges selected ten names to submit to the Board of Directors. The Directors chose the name "Blue Jays" from that list and announced their decision on August 12th, at which time the team officially became the Toronto Blue Jays Baseball Club.

A total of 154 people submitted the name Blue Jays, and a drawing was held to select a grand prize winner from those who submitted the name. Dr. William Mills of Etobicoke, Ontario, won a pair of season tickets for 1977 and an all-expenses paid trip for himself and his family to watch the Blue Jays at spring training in Dunedin, Florida. Nine runners-up also won season tickets.

BLUE JAYS LOGO

The Blue Jays logo was created by the Toronto design firm of Savage Sloan, Ltd. It depicts a stylized Blue Jay on a red baseball outline incorporating a red maple leaf. The logo features two shades of blue, and red. It was selected to represent three facets of the club's identity: the team name, baseball, and the fact that the team is Canadian.

LONGEST RAIN DELAYS

(Exhibition Stadium)

3 hours, 34 minutes - vs Cleveland, August 2, 1987 (3 hours, 34 minutes to start. Game started at 5:09 P.M. and ended at 7:55 P.M. T-2:46)

3 hours, 18 minutes - vs Boston, September 26, 1985 (3 hours, 18 minutes delay to start. Game started at 10:53 P.M. and ended at 1:02 A.M. T-2:09)

3 hours, 16 minutes - vs Boston, June 22, 1985 (3 hours, 16 minutes delay bottom of 5th inning. Game started at 1:39 P.M. and ended at 7:47 P.M. T-2:25)

3 hours, 1 minute - vs Boston, June 17, 1984 (1 hour, 33 minutes delay to start and 1 hour, 28 minutes delay at start of bottom of the 5th inning. Game started at 3:08 P.M. and ended at 7:47 P.M. T-2:48)

2 hours, 47 minutes - vs Boston, June 11, 1986 (2 hours, 47 minutes delay to start. Game started at 10:22 P.M. and ended at 12:51 A.M. T-2:29)

2 hours, 13 minutes - vs Chicago, August 23, 1988 (2 hours, 13 minutes delay to start. Game started at 9:48 P.M. and ended at 12:28 A.M. T-2:40)

LATEST ENDING GAMES

1:02 A.M. - at Baltimore (Memorial Stadium), August 3, 1984. T-2:45, rain delay 2 hours, 7 minutes in top of 4th. Blue Jays - 5, Orioles - 2.

1:02 A.M. - Boston (Exhibition Stadium), September 26, 1985. T-2:09. 3 hours, 18 minutes delay to start. Red Sox - 4, Blue Jays - 1.

SUSPENDED GAMES: The Blue Jays have played two suspended games in their history...The first game was August 28, 1990 in a 7-5, 15-inning loss to Minnesota...The game was suspended after 14 innings due to a 5pm Canadian National Exhibition curfew...The last suspended game was an 8-7, 13 inning loss at New York on September 17, 1980 which was completed the next day...Play was halted with the Blue Jays batting in the 10th inning.

CANADIAN PLAYERS IN BLUE JAYS ORGANIZATION

Name	Position	Birthdate	Hometown	1990 Club
Boucher, Denis	LHP	March 7/68	Lachine, PQ	Dunedin/Syracuse
Butler, Richard	OF	May 7/73	Toronto, ON	
Butler, Robert	OF	April 10/70	Toronto, ON	
Ducey, Rob	OF	May 24/65	Cambridge, ON	Toronto
Horsman, Vince	LHP	March 9/67	Dartmouth, NS	Dunedin/Knoxville
Jeffrey, Scott	LHP	May 6/74	Yarmouth, NS	
Leystra, Jeff	RHP	May 30/73	Corunna, ON	
O'Halloran, Greg	C	May 21/68	Mississauga, ON	Dunedin
Spoljaric, Paul	LHP	Sept. 24/70	Kelowna, BC	Medicine Hat
Wilson, Nigel	OF	Jan. 12/70	Ajax, ON	Myrtle Beach

BLUE JAY - "BIG" RBI GAMES

9-Roy Howell, Sept. 10/77 vs New York (A)
7-John Mayberry, June 26/78 vs Baltimore (H)
7-Otto Velez, May 4/80 vs Cleveland (H) (1st g)
7-George Bell, May 9/87 vs Texas (A)
6-Roy Howell, July 3/79 vs Detroit (A)
6-Barry Bonnell, May 3/80 vs Cleveland (H)
6-Lloyd Moseby, Aug. 19/81 vs Kansas City
6-Damaso Garcia, May 10/85 vs Seattle (H)
6-Jesse Barfield, May 18/86 vs Cleveland (H)
6-George Bell, June 11/87 vs Baltimore (A)
6-Ernie Whitt, September 12/87 vs New York (H)
6-Ernie Whitt, September 27/8 vs Baltimore (A)
6-Kelly Gruber, April 16/89 vs Kansas City (H)
6-George Bell, June 8/90 vs Milwaukee (A)

THREE HOME RUNS IN A GAME: Did you know that Otto Velez, Ernie Whitt and George Bell are the only Blue Jays players to hit three HR's in one Game?...Velez hit his in the first game of a DH on May 4, 1980 vs Cleveland at the expense of Dan Spillner, Wayne Garland and Sid Monge...Whitt hit his against Baltimore on September 14, 1987 vs Ken Dixon (2) and Tony Arnold...Bell hit his on Opening Day, 1988, April 4 at Kansas City vs Bret Saberhagen (3)...Bell became the first major leaguer to hit three home runs on Opening Day...Six opponents have hit three home runs in a game off Blue Jay pitching...Four did it at Exhibition Stadium...John Mayberry (Kansas City) on June 1, 1977; Cliff Johnson (New York) on June 30, 1977; Eddie Murray (Baltimore) on September 14, 1980; Jim Rice (Boston) on August 29, 1983 (2nd game)...Cecil Fielder (Detroit) hit three at the SkyDome on May 6, 1990...The sixth player is Tom Brunansky (Boston) who hit three vs the Blue Jays on September 29, 1990 at Fenway Park.

RAWLINGS GOLD GLOVE AWARD

JESSE BARFIELD (OF) and TONY FERNANDEZ (SS) in 1986 became the first Blue Jays in the club's history to win Gold Gloves. Both BARFIELD (OF) and FERNANDEZ (SS) were repeat winners in 1987. Fernandez went on to capture honours in 1988, and 1989. Kelly Gruber (3B) captured his first Gold Glove in 1990.

The famous Rawlings Gold Glove Award, symbolic of fielding excellence, was first introduced by Rawlings in 1957. One major league team was selected the first year and included players like Gil Hodges, Nelson Fox, Roy McMillan and Frank Malzone in the infield, Willie Mays, Al Kaline and Minnie Minoso in the outfield, Bobby Shantz on the mound and Sherm Lollar behind the plate.

Since 1958, the Rawlings Gold Glove Award* has been presented annually to the eighteen players, nine in each league, by position. These outstanding players are judged and selected as the best fielding players at their respective position by the major league coaches and managers prior to the conclusion of the regular baseball season. Managers and coaches may not select players from their own club and only vote for players in their own league. Votes are tabulated for Rawlings by The Sporting News.

1-0 GAMES: The Blue Jays are 15-13 in 1-0 games...By year they are: 1979 (0-3); 1980 (5-0); 1981 (0-2); 1982 (0-1); 1984 (2-0); 1985 (1-0); 1986 (1-2); 1987 (0-2); 1988 (3-0); 1989 (0-1); 1990 (3-2). The club's last 1-0 win was July 27, 1990 vs Texas with Dave Stieb getting the victory...The last 1-0 loss was August 26, 1990 vs Boston with Todd Stottlemyre taking the loss after allowing one run through 8 innings.

PITCHERS-10 or more strikeouts in a game

April 14/77 —Jerry Garvin vs Detroit (H)-10
June 26/77 —Pete Vuckovich vs Baltimore (A)-12
Sept. 28/78 —Jim Clancy vs Boston (H)-10
May 16/80 —Jesse Jefferson vs Oakland (H)-10
Sept. 5/80 —Jim Clancy vs Chicago (H)-11
June 19/82 —Jim Clancy vs Oakland (A)-10 (10 inn)
May 6/83 —Dave Stieb vs Kansas City (H)-10
Sept. 4/83 —Dave Stieb vs Detroit (H)-11 (10 inn)
May 4/84 —Dave Stieb vs Kansas City (A)-10 (10 inn)
Aug.24/84 —Luis Leal vs Minnesota (A)-10
Aug. 26/84 —Dave Stieb vs Minnesota (A)-10
Aug. 31/84 —Dave Stieb vs Minnesota (H)-10
July 23/85 —Doyle Alexander vs Seattle (H)-11
July 7/86 —Jimmy Key vs Seattle (H)-10
July 9/87 —Jose Nunez vs Kansas City (H)-11
July 12/87 —Jim Clancy vs Kansas City (H)-11
Sept. 9/87 —Jim Clancy vs Milwaukee (A)-10
April 19/88 —Jim Clancy vs Kansas City (H)-12
Aug. 22/88 —Dave Stieb vs Chicago (H)-12
April 24/89 —Jimmy Key vs Oakland (A)-10
Aug. 4/89 —Dave Stieb vs New York (H)-11

LOW HIT GAMES BY BLUE JAYS

NO-HITTER

Sept. 2/90 —Dave Stieb, Toronto-3 at Cleveland-0

ONE HIT GAMES

April 24/79 —Dave Lemanczyk, Toronto-2 at Texas-0, Putnam single in third
August 27/79 —Phil Huffman, Oakland-0 at Toronto-7, Essian single in sixth
May 30/82 —Jim Gott (6 innings), Roy Lee Jackson (3 innings) Toronto-6 at Baltimore-0, Dempsey single in the fifth
Sept. 28/82 —Jim Clancy, Minnesota-0 at Toronto-3, Bush bloop single in ninth to break up perfect game
May 14/83 —Luis Leal (5 innings), Roy Lee Jackson (4 innings) Toronto-8 at Cleveland-1, Bando single in eighth
May 22/86 —Jimmy Key, Toronto-5 at Chicago-0, Guillen single in 5th
May 31/88 —Dave Stieb, Milwaukee-0 at Toronto-9, Surhoff single in 4th
Sept. 24/88 —Dave Stieb, Toronto-1 at Cleveland-0, Franco single in 9th with two out
Sept. 30/88 —Dave Stieb, Baltimore-0 at Toronto-4, Traber single in 9th with two out
April 10/89 —Dave Stieb, Toronto-8 at New York-0, Quirk single in 5th
August 26/89 —Dave Stieb, Milwaukee-0 at Toronto-7, Yount single in 6th

TWO HIT GAMES

Sept. 15/77 —Jim Clancy, Baltimore-0 at Toronto-4, five innings forfeit, Bumbry double and Skaggs single in third
May 2/78 —Tom Underwood, Toronto-1 at Oakland-2, North double and Alexander homer in fourth
April 13/79 —Jim Clancy, Kansas City-1 at Toronto-4, 5;s1/;i2 innings - rain stopped - Otis single in first, Patek single in fifth
August 7/79 —Tom Underwood, Kansas City-2 at Toronto-3, Brett single in second, McRae homer in third
July 27/80 —Jesse Jefferson, Seattle-0 at Toronto-5, Simpson single in fourth and Roberts single in eighth
Sept. 18/80 —Luis Leal, Toronto-2 at New York-1, Jackson and Spencer, singles in fourth
October 3/81 —Dave Stieb (8.1 inn), Jerry Garvin (.1 inn), Joey McLaughlin (.1 inn), Toronto-4 at Seattle-1, Anderson homered in third, Zisk homered in ninth (both off Stieb)
August 10/82 —Dave Stieb, Boston-0 at Toronto-4, Lansford single in second, Allenson single in third
Sept. 6/82 —Dave Stieb, Toronto-3 at Oakland-1, Armas homered in seventh, Burroughs single in eighth
July 14/83 —Luis Leal, Toronto-8 at Chicago-0, Luzinski and Baines singles in fourth
June 16/84 —Luis Leal, Boston at Toronto-7, Miller single in second, Rice double in seventh
July 3/84 —Jim Gott, California-0 at Toronto-4, Carew single in fourth, Reggie Jackson single in fifth
Sept. 2/84 —Doyle Alexander, Minnesota-0 at Toronto-6, Brunansky single in second, Putnam double in seventh
Sept. 5/85 —Doyle Alexander, Minnesota-0 at Toronto-7, Hrbek double in fourth, Gagne single in sixth
May 25/86 —John Cerutti (8IP), Bill Caudill (1IP), Toronto-8 at Cleveland-1, Carter single in the 1st, Tabler single in 2nd
July 5/86 —Jim Clancy (8IP), Tom Henke (1IP), California-3 at Toronto-7, Burleson single in 4th, Pettis single in 8th
May 3/87 —Jim Clancy (8.1IP), Tom Henke (.2IP), Texas-1 at Toronto-3, O'Brien single in 5th, Petralli double in 9th
May 18/87 —Jim Clancy, Toronto-12 at California-0, McLemore single in 6th, White single in 7th
August 27/87 —Jimmy Key (6IP), Mark Eichhorn (.2IP), Jeff Musselman (1.1IP), Tom Henke (1IP), Oakland-4 at Toronto-9, Canseco single in 1st, Lansford home run in 1st
July 15/88 —Jimmy Key, Toronto-1 at Oakland-0, Baylor double and Gallego single in 2nd
August 13/88 —Jeff Musselman (7IP), Duane Ward (2IP), Seitzer triple in 1st, White single in 2nd
April 14/89 —Jimmy Key, Kansas City-0 at Toronto-3, Seitzer and Tartabull singles in 7th
August 2/89 —John Cerutti, Kansas City-0 at Toronto-8, Brett double in 7th, Wilson double in 9th
August 4/89 —Dave Stieb, New York-1 at Toronto-2, Kelly double with two out in 9th, followed by a single by Sax

GENERAL

CATEGORY	RECORD	YEAR
Doubleheaders, Most Played	17	1978
Doubleheaders, Fewest Played	0	1990
oubleheaders, Best Record	5-1-4	1980
Doubleheaders, Most Wins	5	1980
Doubleheaders, Most Losses	8	1978
Doubleheaders, Most Split	8	1977
Extra Innings, Most Wins	13	1989
Extra Innings, Most Losses	13	1986
Extra Innings, Most Played	23	1986
Extra Innings, Fewest Played	9	1981
Games	163	1984, 1986
Games Won	99	1985
Games Lost	109	1979
Games Won, Consecutively	11	June 2-13, 1987
Games Lost, Consecutively	12	May 31-June 11 & August 10, 1981
Home Wins, Consecutive	10	July 21-28, August 2-3, 1985
Home Losses, Consecutive	9	Aug. 26-28, Sept. 2-5 (dh)-6 1977
Road Wins, Consecutive	7	Apr. 14, 26-May 1, 1985; May 25; June 8-13, 1987
Road Losses, Consecutive	10	Aug. 19-22, Sept. 3(dh), 6-9, 1979
(over two seasons)	10	1977 (9), 1978 (1)
Games Won, Highest Percentage	.615	(99-62) 1985
Home Record, Best	54-26	(.675) 1985
Road Record, Best	45-36	(.556) 1985
Homestand, Best	10-1	May 17-27, 1984
Homestand, Worst	0-6	Sept. 26-Oct. 1, 1980
Home Wins, Fewest	25	1977
Road Wins, Fewest	21	1979
Home Losses, Most	55	1977
Road Losses, Most	60	1979
Road Trip, Best	6-1	June 8-14, 1987
Road Trip, Worst	0-6	Sept. 26-Oct. 1, 1978
Road Trip, Worst	0-6	July 19-23, 1979
Road Trip, Worst	0-6	Sept. 3-9, 1979
One Club, Most Wins vs	12	vs Baltimore, 1987
One Club, Most Losses vs	12	Boston (77) & Milwaukee, (78)
One Club, Most Home Wins	6	Balt., 1978, 1987; Tex., 1982 1987; Minn., 1984; Sea., 1985, Det., 1989
One Club Home Losses	6	Bost. (77); Clev. (78); Det. (79); Balt. (82)
One Club, Most Road Wins	7	Boston, 1988
One Club, Most Road Losses	8	Milwaukee, 1978
One Run Games, Most	59	1984
One Run Games, Most Wins	34	1984
One Run Games, Most Losses	30	1978, 1982
One Run Games, Fewest Wins	17	1977
One Run Games, Fewest Losses	20	1983
Two Run Games, Most	38	1980
Two Run Games, Most Wins	20	1980
Two Run Games, Most Losses	23	1979
Two Run Games, Fewest Wins	7	1984
Two Run Games, Fewest Losses	12	1984
Day Games, Played	65	1979
Day Games, Most Won	35	1983
Day Games, Most Lost	44	1979
Night Games, Played	111	1989
Night Games, Most Won	67	1987, 1989
Night Games, Most Lost	68	1977, 1980
Players Used, Most	43	1989, 1990
Players Used, Fewest	33	1983, 1984
Pitchers Used, Most	19	1979, 1989, 1990
Players Used, Fewest	13	1982, 1984
Righthanders, Most Wins vs	75	1985
Lefthanders, Most Wins vs	37	1990
Righthanders, Most Losses vs	75	1979
Lefthanders, Most Losses vs	44	1982
Shutouts, Both Teams, Most	24	1978, 1981
Shutouts, Most Wins	13	1982
Shutouts, Most Losses	20	1981
Shutouts, Fewest Won	3	1977
Shutouts, Fewest Lost	4	1984
Shutouts, Most vs One Team	4	vs Detroit, 1989
Shutouts, Most By Opponents	4	vs Milwaukee, 1978, vs Bost., 1990
Winning Margin, Highest	16	vs New York, Sept. 10, 1977
Winning Margin, Highest by Foe	22	vs California, Aug. 25, 1979
Artificial Turf, Most Won	64	1985
Artificial Turf, Most Lost	60	1977 & 1978
Natural Turf, Most Won	38	1989
Natural Turf, Most Lost	52	1978

BATTING

CATEGORY	RECORD	YEAR
At Bats, Most	5716	1986
Batting Average, Highest	.277	1983
Batting Average, Lowest	.250	1978
Batting Average, Lowest	.226	(106 games) 1981
Grounded Into Double Plays, Most	156	1977
Grounded Into Double Plays, Most	91	1984
Hit By Pitcher, Most	52	1984
Hit By Pitcher, Fewest	23	1977 & 1978
Hits, Most	1555	1984
Hits, Fewest	1358	1978
Hits vs One Club, Most	152	vs Detroit, 1978
Hits vs One Club, Fewest	73	vs California, 1978
Home Runs, Most	215	1987
Home Runs, Fewest	95	1979
Home Runs, Home Most	101	1983 & 1987
Home Runs, Home Fewest	45	1977
Home Road, Most	114	1987
Home Runs, Fewest	44	1982
Home Runs vs One Club, Most	31	vs Baltimore, 1987
Home Runs vs One Club, Fewest	2	vs KC & Minn, 1977
	2	vs Minn & Oak, 1978
Grand Slams, Most	8	1989
Inside The Park, Most	4	1983
Left On Base, Most	1177	1984
Left On Base, Fewest	1064	1979
Singles, Most	1069	1984
Singles, Fewest	970	1980
Doubles, Most	285	1986
Doubles, Fewest	217	1978
Triples, Most	68	1984
Triples, Fewest	34	1979
Most Extra-Base Hits	530	1987
Pinch Hits, Most	71	1982
Pinch Hits, Fewest	12	1979
Pinch Hits Home Runs, Most	6	1984
Pinch Hit Average, Highest	.290	1983
Runs Batted In, Most	790	1987
Runs Batted In, Fewest	550	1978
Runs Scored, Most	845	1987
Runs Scored, Fewest	590	1978
Sacrifices, Most	81	1977
Sacrifices, Fewest	18	1990
Sacrifice Flies, Most	62	1990
Slugging Percentage, Highest	.446	1987
Slugging Percentage, Lowest	.358	1978
Slugging Percentage, Lowest	.330	(106 games) 1981
Stolen Bases, Most Stolen	193	1984
Stolen Bases, Times Caught	81	1982
Stolen Bases, Fewest Stolen	28	1978
Strikeouts, Most	970	1987, 1990
Strikeouts, Fewest	645	1978
Total Bases, Most	2512	1987
Total Bases, Fewest	1947	1978
Walks, Most	555	1987
Walks, Fewest	415	1982
On-Base Percentage, Highest	.372	1983
On-Base Percentage, Lowest	.293	1977
On-Base Percentage, Lowest	.288	(106 games) 1981

FIELDING

CATEGORY	RECORD	YEAR
Assists, Most	1939	1980
Assists, Fewest	1637	1983
Chances Total, Most	6468	1980
Chances Total, Fewest	6088	1983
Double Plays, Most	206	1980
Double Plays, Fewest	133	1977
Errors, Most	164	1977
Errors, Fewest	86	1990
Fielding Average, Highest	.986	1906
Fielding Average, Lowest	.974	1977
Passed Balls, Most	16	1978, 1989
Passed Balls, Fewest	3	1985
Putouts, Most	4428	1986
Putouts, Fewest	4251	1979
Triple Plays	2	1979
Most Errorless Games	103	1990
Most Consecutive Errorless Games	11	1986

PITCHING

CATEGORY	RECORD	YEAR
Complete Games, Most	44	1979
Complete Games, Fewest	6	1990
Earned Run Average, Lowest	3.29	1985
Earned Run Average, Highest	4.81	1979
Hit Batsmen, Most	45	1986, 1989
Hit Batsmen, Fewest	20	1977
Hits, Most	1568	1977
Hits, Fewest	1312	1985
Home Runs, Most	165	1979
Home Runs, Fewest	99	1989
Home Runs, Home Most	94	1977
Home Runs, Home Fewest	50	1989
Home Runs, Road Most	91	1979
Home Runs, Road Fewest	49	1989
One Hit Games	3	1988
Runs, Most	862	1979
Runs, Fewest	588	1985
Earned Runs, Most	758	1979
Earned Runs, Fewest	529	1985
Relief Appearances, Most	336	1987
Relief Appearances, Fewest	187	1977
Saves, Most	48	1905
Saves, Fewest	11	1979
Strikeouts, Most	1064	1987
Strikeouts, Fewest	611	1979
Walks, Most	635	1980
Walks, Fewest	445	1990
Wild Pitches, Most	63	1979
Wild Pitches, Fewest	25	1983
Shutouts, Most	13	1982
Shutouts, Fewest	3	1977
1-0 Games, Won, Most	5	1980
1-0 Games, Lost, Most	3	1979

SEASON INDIVIDUAL RECORDS

R - Right hand batter
B - Switch hitter
L - Left hand batter
* - League Leader

BATTING

Highest Average (502 Plate App.)	(R)	.310	Bob Bailor-'77
		.310	Damaso Garcia-'82
	(L)	.315	Lloyd Moseby-'83
	(B)	.322	Tony Fernandez-'87
Highest Average (100 games)	(R)	.318	Barry Bonnell-'83
	(L)	.324	Rance Mulliniks-'84
	(B)	.322	Tony Fernandez-'87
Highest Average as Blue Jay	(R)	.318	Barry Bonnell-'83
	(L)	.324	Rance Mulliniks-'84
	(B)	.322	Tony Fernandez-'87
Most Games	(R)	162	Rick Bosetti-'79
	(L)	160	Willie Upshaw-'82/'83
	(B)	*163	Tony Fernandez-'86
Most at Bats	(R)	641	George Bell-'86
	(L)	592	Lloyd Moseby-'84; '87
	(B)	687	Tony Fernandez-'86
Most Runs	(R)	111	George Bell-'87
	(L)	106	Lloyd Moseby-'87
	(B)	91	Tony Fernandez-'86
Most Hits	(R)	198	George Bell-'86
	(L)	177	Willie Upshaw-'83
	(B)	213	Tony Fernandez-'86
Most Total Bases	(R)	369	George Bell-'87
	(L)	296	Willie Upshaw-'83
		296	Fred McGriff-'88
	(B)	294	Tony Fernandez-'86
Highest Slugging Percentage	(R)	.605	George Bell-'87
	(L)	.552	Fred McGriff-'88
	(B)	441	Junior Felix-'90
Most Singles	(R)	145	Damaso Garcia-'82
	(L)	117	Willie Upshaw-'83
	(B)	*161	Tony Fernandez-'86
Most Extra Base Hits	(R)	83	George Bell-'87
	(L)	71	Fred McGriff-'88
	(B)	52	Tony Fernandez-'86
Most Doubles	(R)	41	George Bell-'89
	(L)	35	Fred McGriff-'88
	(B)	41	Tony Fernandez-'88

Most Triples	(R)	9	Jesse Barfield-'85
	(L)	*15	Lloyd Moseby-'84
			Tony Fernandez-'90
	(B)	17	Tony Fernandez-'90
Most Home Runs	(R	47	George Bell-'87
	(L)	36	Fred McGriff-'89
	(B)	15	Junior Felix-'90
Most Home Runs-Home	(R)	23	Kelly Gruber-'90
	(L)	18	Fred McGriff-'88, '89
Most Home Runs-Road	(R)	28	George Bell-'87
	(L)	21	Fred McGriff-'90
Most Grand Slam Homers	(R)	2	George Bell-'85; '87
		2	Jesse Barfield-'88
	(L)	2	Roy Howell-'79
Most Runs Batted In	(R)	*134	George Bell-'87
	(L)	104	Willie Upshaw-'83
	(B)	70	Tony Fernandez-'88
Most Base On Balls	(R)	69	Jesse Barfield-'86
	(L)	119	Fred McGriff-'89
	(B)	71	Tony Fernandez-'90
Most Times Striking Out	(R)	146	Jesse Barfield-'86
	(L)	149	Fred McGriff-'88
	(B)	99	Junior Felix-'90
Most Sacrifice Bunts	(R)	19	Luis Gomez-'78
	(L)	12	Alfredo Griffin-'84
	(B)	16	Alfredo Griffin-'79
Most Sacrifice Flies	(R)	14	George Bell-'89
	(L)	7	John Mayberry-'78
		7	Willie Upshaw-'83
		7	Lloyd Moseby-'84
		7	Rick Leach-'86
		7	Lloyd Moseby-'86
	(B)	10	Tony Fernandez-'89
Most Sacrifices Total	(R)	22	Luis Gomez-'78
	(L)	16	Alfredo Griffin-'84
	(B)	20	Alfredo Griffin-'79
Most Times Hit by Pitch	(R)	9	Damaso Garcia-'84
	(L)	8	John Mayberry-'81
		8	Lloyd Moseby-'82 & '84
	(B)	9	Dave Collins-'84
Most Times GIDP	(R)	21	Rico Carty-'79
		21	George Bell-'88
	(L)	16	Roy Howell-'77
Fewest Times GIDP (100 games)	(R)	2	Buck Martinez-'84
	(L)	3	Fred McGriff-'87
	(B)	0	Dave Collins-'84
Fewest Times Striking Out	(R)	21	Bob Bailor-'78
(502) Plate App.)	(L)	38	Al Woods-'77
Most Pinch-Hits	(R)	11	Wayne Nordhagen-'82
		11	Cliff Johnson-'84
	(L)	10	Hosken Powell-'82
		10	Rance Mulliniks-'83
		10	Rick Leach-'86
Most Stolen Bases		60	Dave Collins-'84
Most Caught Stealing		23	Alfredo Griffin-'80

PITCHING

Most Wins	(R)	18	Dave Stieb-'90
	(L)	17	Jimmy Key-'87
Most Home Wins	(R)	12	Doyle Alexander-'84
		12	Dave Stieb-'88
	(L)	10	Jimmy Key-'85/'87
		10	Jeff Musselman-'87
Most Road Wins	(R)	10	Dave Stieb-'89
	(L)	8	John Cerutti-'87
		8	Jimmy Key-'88
Most Losses	(R)	18	Phil Huffman-'79
	(L)	18	Jerry Garvin-'77
Most Home Losses	(R)	10	Jesse Jefferson-'77
		10	Dave Stieb-'80
	(L)	9	Jerry Garvin-'80
Most Road Losses	(R)	12	Luis Leal-'82
	(L)	9	Jerry Garvin-'77
Most Decisions	(R)	31	Dave Stieb-'82
	(L)	28	Jerry Garvin-'77
Highest Winning Pct (10 decisions)	(R)	.750	Dave Stieb-'90
	(L)	.733	John Cerutti-'87
Lowest ERA (162 IP)	(R)	*2.48	Dave Stieb-'85
	(L)	*2.76	Jimmy Key-'87
Lowest ERA (100 IP)	(R)	1.72	Mark Eichhorn-'86
	(L)	*2.76	Jimmy Key-'87

SEASON INDIVIDUAL RECORDS, PITCHING (Continued)

Most Appearances	(R)	89	Mark Eichhorn-'87
	(L)	69	Gary Lavelle-'85
Most Games Started	(R)	40	Jim Clancy-'82
	(L)	36	Jimmy Key-'87
Most Complete Games	(R)	19	Dave Stieb-'82
	(L)	12	Jerry Garvin-'77
		12	Tom Underwood-'79
Most Shutouts	(R)	5	Dave Stieb-'82
	(L)	2	Jimmy Key-'86
Most Innings Pitched	(R)	288.1	Dave Stieb-'82
	(L)	261.0	Jimmy Key-'87
Most Hits Allowed	(R)	278	Dave Lemanczyk-'77
	(L)	247	Jerry Garvin-'77
Most Runs Allowed	(R)	143	Dave Lemanczyk-'77
	(L)	127	Jerry Garvin-'77
Most Earned Runs Allowed	(R)	125	Jim Clancy-'84
	(L)	114	Jerry Garvin-'77
Most Home Runs Allowed	(R)	29	Dave Stieb-'86
	(L)	33	Jerry Garvin-'77
Most Bases on Balls	(R)	128	Jim Clancy-'80
	(L)	95	Tom Underwood-'79
Most Strikeouts	(R)	198	Dave Stieb-'84
	(L)	161	Jimmy Key-'87
Most Hit Batsmen	(R)	*15	Dave Stieb-'86
	(L)	9	Tom Underwood-'79
Most Balks	(R)	6	Mark Eichhorn-'88
	(L)	5	Jimmy Key-'87
Most Wild Pitches	(R)	20	Dave Lemanczyk-'77
	(L)	11	Tom Underwood-'79
Most Relief Appearances	(R)	89	Mark Eichhorn-'87
	(L)	69	Gary Lavelle-'85
Most Relief Wins	(R)	14	Mark Eichhorn-'86
	(L)	12	Jeff Musselman-'87
Most Relief Losses	(R)	10	Tom Buskey-'79; Duane Ward-'89
	(L)	7	Mike Willis-'78
		7	Jerry Garvin-'80
		7	Gary Lavelle-'85
Most Saves	(R)	34	Tom Henke-'87
	(L)	10	Jimmy Key-'84
Most Decisions in Relief	(R)	20	Mark Eichhorn-'86
	(L)	17	Jeff Musselman-'87
Highest Total of Wins & Saves	(R)	36	Tom Henke-'86
(Relief Only)	(L)	15	Jeff Musselman-'87
Innings Pitched In Relief	(R)	157.0	Mark Eichhorn-'86
	(L)	92.1	Mike Willis-'77
Most Games Finished	(R)	62	Tom Henke-'87
Most Consecutive Won, Season	(R)	11	Dennis Lamp-'85
	(L)	6	Jimmy Key-'85
Most Consecutive Lost, Season	(R)	9	Jeff Byrd-'77
	(L)	10	Jerry Garvin-'77
		10	Paul Mirabella-'80
Best Start	(R)	11-0	Relief/Dennis Lamp-'85
	(R)	7-0	Starter/Tom Filer-'85
	(L)	5-0	Jerry Garvin-'77

MISCELLANEOUS

Most Consecutive Wins	11	Dennis Lamp	Apr. 6-Oct. 6/85
Most Consecutive Losses (Season)	10	Jerry Garvin	June 16-Aug. 7/77
	10	Jerry Garvin	May 21-July 23/78
	10	Paul Mirabella	May 23-Sept. 29/80
	9	Jeff Byrd	Aug. 11-Sept. 27/77
	9	Tom Underwood	Apr. 5-June 10/79
	9	Juan Berenguer	Aug. 24-Oct. 2/81
Most Consecutive Losses	13	Tom Underwood	Aug. 28-Sept. 26/78 (4) & Apr. 5-June 10/79 (9)
Most Consecutive Shutouts	3	Dave Stieb	Sept. 18-24-30/88
Most Consecutive Complete Games	7	Dave Stieb	June 18-July 21/80
Most Consecutive Scoreless Innings	31	Dave Stieb	Sept. 13-18-24-30/88
Most Consecutive Games, one or more RBI's	8	Willie Upshaw	Sept. 11-20/83
Most Consecutive Hits	8	Rance Mulliniks	Aug. 24-27/84
Most Consecutive Times Reached Base	10	Rance Mulliniks	Aug. 24-27/84
Most Consecutive Games Reached Base Safely	26	Lloyd Moseby	1983
Most Consecutive Hits, Team	8	vs Minnesota (A) (1st inning)	Aug. 23/86

Most Home Runs, One Inning	3	vs Seattle (A) (9th inning)	June 23/82
		vs Detroit (H) (4th inning)	May 23/83
		vs Oakland (H) (6th inning) (Cons.)	Apr. 26/84
		vs Detroit (A) (4th inning)	June 5/84
		vs Oakland (H) (7th inning)	Aug. 30/87
		vs New York (H) (8th inning) (Cons.)	Sept. 12/87
		vs Baltimore (H) (2nd inning)	Sept. 14/87
Home Runs in Consecutive AB's	3	Cliff Johnson	June 20-21/83
Most Consecutive Stolen Bases	19	Damaso Garcia	1982
Most Runs, One Inning	11	vs Seattle (A) (9th inning)	July 20/84
Most Hits, One Inning	11	vs Seattle (A) (9th inning)	July 20/84
Most Batters, One Inning	16	vs Seattle (A) (9th inning)	July 20/84
Most Consecutive Errorless Games	11	1986	
Most Errorless Games	103	1990	
Most Errors, Game	6	Texas (A)	May 13/82
Most Double Plays, Game	5	California (A)	May 7/80
	5	Boston (H)	Sept. 25/85, 13 innings
Most Innings, Home	15	vs Minnesota	Aug. 28/80
Most Innings, Road	17	vs Boston	Oct. 4/80 (1st game)
Hitting Streak	22	George Bell	1989
Most Consecutive Times Shutout	3	May 13-15/81	
Most Consecutive Complete Games	4	Sept. 20, 21, 23, 24/83	
Most Consecutive Shutout Games	3	May 21, 22, 23/83	
Most Consecutive Shutout Innings	28	June 4, 5, 6, 7/85	
Most Consecutive Games Played	403	Tony Fernandez	Sept. 21/84-June 24/87
Consecutive Games with At Least One Home Run	13	(17 Home Runs)	May 19-June 2/85
Most Years, Pitcher	12	Jim Clancy	1977-1988
	12	Dave Stieb	1979-1990
Most Years, Non-Pitcher	12	Ernie Whitt	1977-1989

FIELDING—SEASON

Based on 100 games

CATEGORY	RECORD	PLAYER	YEAR
First Basemen			
Games, Most	159	Willie Upshaw, 1983/Fred McGriff,	1989
Putouts, Most	1460	Fred McGriff,	1989
Assists, Most	131	Willie Upshaw,	1986
Errors, Most	21	Willie Upshaw,	1983
Errors, Fewest	5	Fred McGriff,	1988
Total Chances, Most	1592	Fred McGriff,	1989
Double Plays, Most	148	Fred McGriff,	1989
Best Percentage	.997	Fred McGriff,	1988
Second Basemen			
Games, Most	149	Damaso Garcia,	1984
Putouts, Most	316	Damaso Garcia,	1980
Assists, Most	471	Damaso Garcia,	1980
Errors, Most	16	Damaso Garcia,	1980
Errors, Fewest	4	Manny Lee,	1990
Total Chances, Most	803	Damaso Garcia,	1980
Double Plays, Most	112	Damaso Garcia,	1980
Best Percentage	.993	Manny Lee,	1990
Third Basemen			
Games, Most	156	Kelly Gruber,	1988
Putouts, Most	123	Kelly Gruber,	1990
Assists, Most	349	Kelly Gruber,	1988
Errors, Most	22	Roy Howell, 1978/Kelly Gruber,	1989
Errors, Fewest	6	Rance Mulliniks,	1986
Total Chances, Most	477	Kelly Gruber,	1988
Double Plays, Most	31	Kelly Gruber,	1988
Best Percentage	.975	Rance Mulliniks,	1986

Shortstop

Games, Most	163	Tony Fernandez, 1986
Putouts, Most	319	Alfredo Griffin, 1982
Assists Most	501	Alfredo Griffin, 1979
Errors, Most	37	Alfredo Griffin, 1979
Errors, Fewest	6	Tony Fernandez, 1989
Total Chances, Most	824	Alfredo Griffin, 1982
Double Plays, Most	126	Alfredo Griffin, 1980
Best Percentage	.992	Tony Fernandez, 1989

Catchers

Games, Most	136	Rick Cerone, 1979
Putouts, Most	803	Ernie Whitt, 1987
Assists, Most	71	Alan Ashby, 1977
Errors, Most	13	Rick Cerone, 1979
Errors, Fewest	4	Ernie Whitt, 1988 / Pat Borders, 1990
Passed Balls, Most	12	Ernie Whitt, 1989
Total Chances, Most	863	Ernie Whitt, 1987
Double Plays, Most	11	Alan Ashby, 1977 & Ernie Whitt, 1980
Best Percentage	.994	Ernie Whitt, 1984/1987/1988

Outfielders

Games, Most	162	Rick Bosetti, 1979
Putouts, Most	473	Lloyd Moseby, 1984
Assists, Most	22	Jesse Barfield, 1985
Errors, Most	15	George Bell, 1988
Errors, Fewest	2	(108g)Dave Collins, 1984
Total Chances, Most	497	Rick Bosetti, 1979
Double Plays, Most	8	Jesse Barfield, 1985, 1986
Best Percentage	.992	Lloyd Moseby, 1982 & Jesse Barfield, 1986/1987/Mookie Wilson, 1990

Pitchers

Games, Most	89	Mark Eichhorn, 1987
Putouts, Most	34	Dave Stieb, 1985 & Jim Clancy, 1986
Assists, Most	66	Jerry Garvin, 1977
Errors, Most	8	Jesse Jefferson, 1977
Total Chances, Most	92	Dave Stieb, 1985
Double Plays, Most	8	Dave Stieb, 1980
Best Percentage	1.000	Phil Huffman, 1979
(35 or more chances)		Jerry Garvin, 1978
		Luis Leal, 1982 & 1984
		Jimmy Key, 1986
		Mark Eichhorn, 1986
		Dave Stieb, 1988 1989
		Mike Flanagan, 1988 1989
		John Cerutti, 1988
		David Wells, 1990

BLUE JAY ALL-TIME FIELDING TEAM

(100 Games)	Year	PCT	G	PO	A	E	TC	DP
Fred McGriff—1B	1988	.997	153	1344	93	5	1442	143
Manny Lee—2B	1990	.993	112	259	286	4	549	65
Rance Mulliniks—3B	1986	.975	110	60	176	6	242	13
Tony Fernandez—SS	1989	.992	163	260	475	6	741	93
Lloyd Moseby—OF	1982	.992	145	361	4	3	368	0
Ernie Whitt—C	1987	.994	113	803	55	5	863	10
Jerry Garvin—P	1978	1.000	26	9	28	0	37	1
Phil Huffman—P	1979	1.000	31	7	30	0	37	0
Luis Leal—P	1982	1.000	38	17	31	0	48	2
Luis Leal—P	1984	1.000	35	12	30	0	42	3
Jimmy Key—P	1986	1.000	36	18	42	0	60	4
Mark Eichhorn—P	1986	1.000	69	16	21	0	37	1
Dave Stieb—P	1988	1.000	32	19	26	0	45	3
Mike Flanagan—P	1988	1.000	34	6	35	0	41	2
John Cerutti—P	1988	1.000	46	13	27	0	40	2
Mike Flanagan—P	1989	1.000	30	8	33	0	41	4
Dave Stieb—P	1989	1.000	33	18	29	0	47	1
David Wells—P	1990	1.000	43	7	32	0	39	1

(35 or more chances for pitchers)

BATTING

Category	Record	Opponent	Date
Runs	24	Baltimore (H)	June 26/78
Hits	24	Baltimore (H)	June 26/78
Singles	17	Milwaukee (A)	Sept. 29/78
	17	Boston (A)	Sept. 30/90
	15	Boston (H) (14 Inn)	Sept. 24/85
	14	Detroit (H)	July 4/78
Doubles	8	Minnesota (H)	June 7/90
Triples	4	Cleveland (H)	July 29/83
	4	Oakland (H)	Sept. 11/83
	4	Seattle (H)	July 5/84
Home Runs	10	Baltimore (H)	Sept. 14/87
Total Bases	53	Baltimore (H)	Sept. 24/87
Runs Batted in	24	Baltimore (H)	June 26/78
Extra Base Hits	12	Baltimore (H)	Sept. 14/87
Left On Base	16	Chicago (H)	April 16/78
	20	Chicago (H)	April 16/78
	20	Cleveland (A) (13 Inn) (2nd g)	August 15/84
Strikeouts	19	California (A) (13 Inn)	June 8/77
	18	California (A) (9 Inn)	June 8/77
	18	Texas (A) (9 Inn)	July 25/89
Base On Balls	13	Chicago (H)	April 16/79
Stolen Bases	7	Baltimore (A)	August 5/84
		Milwaukee (H)	April 14/83
Sacrifice Hits	4	Cleveland (A)	Sept. 17/77
	4	Chicago (A)	August 14/90
GIDP	6	Minnesota (A) (10 Inn)	Aug. 29/77 (1st game)
	5	Texas (A)	April 23/79
Best Shutout Victory	12-0	California (A)	May 18/87
	11-0	Oakland (H)	April 25/84
	11-0	Boston (H)	June 20/90
Worst Shutout Defeat	0-15	New York (H)	Sept. 25/77 (1st game)
Best Winning Margin	16	New York (A) (Tor-19, NY-3)	Sept. 10/77
Worst Losing Margin	22	California (H) (Tor-2, Cal-24)	August 25/79
Most Consecutive Games, one or more HRs	13	(17 homers)	1985

PITCHING

Category	Record	Opponent	Date
Most Runs	24	California (H)	August 25/79
Most Earned Runs	19	California (H)	August 25/79
Most Unearned Runs	6	Kansas City (A)	April 5/79
Most Hits	26	California (H)	August 25/79
Most Hits	26	California (H)	August 25/79
Most Home Runs	8	Boston (A)	July 4/77
Most Strikeouts	17	Oakland (H) (16 inn.)	July 3/88
	14	Seattle (H)	July 7/86
	12	Baltimore (H)	June 26/77
Most Walks	14	Cleveland (A)	Sept. 9/79
Most Wild Pitches	4	Boston (A)	July 3/86
Most Hit Batsmen	3	Chicago (H)	August 23/81
Longest 1-0 game, won	12 innings	Boston (A)	Sept. 26/86
Longest 1-0 game, lost	15 innings	Oakland (A)	July 27/86

GAME INDIVIDUAL RECORDS

BATTING

Category	Record	Player	Opponent	Date
At Bats	9	Alfredo Griffin (17 innings)	Boston (A), 1st g	Oct. 4/80
	8	Barry Bonnell & John Mayberry (17 innings)	Boston (A), 1st g	Oct. 4/80
Runs	4	Al Woods & Roy Howell	New York (A)	Sept. 10/77
		Otto Velez & Bob Bailor	Baltimore (H)	June 26/78
		Lloyd Moseby	Cleveland (H)	April 19/83
		Ernie Whitt	Cleveland (H)	May 25/85
		Kelly Gruber	Kansas City (H)	April 16/89
		Kelly Gruber	Milwaukee (A)	June 8/90
Hits	5	Roy Howell	New York (A)	Sept. 10/77
		Rick Bosetti	Milwaukee (H)	April 27/79
		Barry Bonnell	Milwaukee (H)	April 10/82
		Damaso Garcia	Oakland (A)	June 19/82

BATTING (Cont...)

Category	Record	Player	Opponent	Date
		George Bell	Kansas City (A)	April 6, /8888
		Kelly Gruber	Kansas City (H)	April 16/89
		Fred McGriff	Cleveland (A)	Sept. 1/90
		George Bell	Milwaukee (A)	Sept. 24/90
Doubles	4	Damaso Garcia	New York (A)	June. 27/86
Triples	2	Alfredo Griffin	Minnesota (A)	May 8/79
		Alfredo Griffin	Milwaukee (A)	April 25/80
		Barry Bonnell	Oakland (H)	May 16/83
		Garth Iorg	Boston (H); 2nd g	Aug. 29/83
		Lloyd Moseby	New York (H)	June 1/84
		Dave Collins	Seattle (H)	July 5/84
		Tony Fernandez	Minnesota (H)	June 5/90
Home Runs	3	Otto Velez	Cleveland (H), 1st g	May 4/80
		Ernie Whitt	Baltimore (H)	Sept. 14/87
		George Bell	Kansas City (A)	April 4/88
Total Bases	13	Roy Howell	New York (A)	Sept. 10/77
RBI's	9	Roy Howell	New York (A)	Sept. 10/77
Sacrifice Bunts	2	Many Times		
Sacrifice Flies	3	George Bell	Chicago (A)	August 14/90
Strikeouts	4	Dave McKay	Cleveland (A)	April 28/77
		Otto Velez	California (A)	June 7/77
		Dave McKay	California (A)	July 14/78
		Willie Horton	New York (H), 2nd g	Sept. 20/78
		Lloyd Moseby	Detroit (A)	Sept. 24/80
		Jesse Barfield	New York (A)	May 26/82
		Jesse Barfield	Oakland (A)	June 19/82
		Jesse Barfield	Texas (H)	Aug. 16/86
		Fred McGriff	Minnesota (H)	July 26/87
		Fred McGriff	California (H)	Aug. 31/87
		Lloyd Moseby	Minnesota (H)	April 16/88
		Pat Borders	Texas (A)	May 26/88
		John Olerud	Oakland (H)	May 21/90
Walks	4	Alfredo Griffin & John Mayberry	Chicago (H)	April 16/79
Stolen Bases	4	Damaso Garcia	Oakland (H)	April 25/84
		Dave Collins	Baltimore (A)	August 5/84
Hit By Pitch	2	Jesse Barfield	Seattle (A)	May 11/86

PITCHING

Category	Record	Player	Opponent	Date
Innings	12	Jesse Jefferson	Boston (H)	May 23/78
		Dave Stieb	Oakland (H)	May 17/80
Hits	13	Pete Vuckovich	Boston (A)	July 6/77
		Dave Lemanczyk	Detroit (H)	May 28/79
		Dave Stieb	Minnesota (H)	Aug. 29/80
		Jim Clancy	Seattle (A)	June 23/82
Runs	10	Luis Leal	Cleveland (A)	Aug. 15/84
Earned Runs	10	Luis Leal	Cleveland (A)	Aug. 15/84
		Jesse Jefferson	Chicago (A)	April 11/78
Unearned Runs	6	Tom Underwood	Kansas City (A)	April 5/79
Home Runs	4	Chuck Hartenstein	Boston (A)	July 4/77
		Jerry Garvin	Seattle (H)	Sept. 4/77
		Jesse Jefferson	Chicago (A)	April 11/78
		Dave Lemanczyk	Chicago (A)	April 12/78
		Balor Moore	Texas (H)	Aug. 21/78
		Jackson Todd	Detroit (H)	Sept. 30/80
		Jimmy Key	Oakland (H)	May 6/86
Strikeouts	12	Pete Vuckovich	Baltimore (A)	June 26/77
		Jim Clancy	Kansas City (H)	April 19/88
		Dave Stieb	Chicago (H)	August 22/88
Walks	9	Jesse Jefferson	Baltimore (H)	June 18/77
		Jim Clancy	Chicago (A)	August 30/84
Hit Batsmen	2	Dave Lemanczyk (11 innings)	Chicago (A), 2nd g	July 13/77
		Balor Moore	New York (A)	Sept. 28/78
		Tom Underwood (2 times)	Milwaukee (A)	May 3/79
			California (A)	Aug. 18/79
	2	Dave Stieb (6 times)	Boston (H)	Sept. 27/80
			Detroit (A)	April 11/81
			Texas (H)	Aug. 25/81
			Chicago (A)	Sept. 4/81
			Kansas City (A)	April 8/85
			Kansas City (A)	Aug. 9/85
		Jim Clancy	Chicago (A)	June 8/81
		Luis Leal	Chicago (H)	Aug. 23/81
		Jim Acker	Boston (A)	June 30/86
		Mark Eichhorn	Seattle (A)	May 22/87
		Joe Johnson	Cleveland (H)	April 9/87
Wild Pitches	4	John Cerutti	Boston (A)	July 2/86

PITCHERS Record		Player	Opponent	Date
Most Putouts	4	Dave Lemanczyk	Boston (H)	Sept. 7/77
		Jackson Todd	New York (A)	April 25/81
		Luis Leal	Chicago (A)	May 9/83
		Jim Clancy	California (H)	June 18/83
		Jim Clancy	Kansas City (A)	July 13/83
Most Assists	8	Jim Clancy	Seattle (A)	April 4/84
Most Errors	2	Jesse Jefferson	Minnesota (H)	Aug. 9/77
		Tom Underwood	Oakland (A)	May 2/78
		Tom Underwood	California (A)	June 5/79
		Jack Kucek	Detroit (A)	July 3/80
Most Double Plays	3	Dave Lemanczyk	Boston (H)	Sept. 7/77
Most Total Chances	8	Jim Clancy	Seattle (A)	April 4/84

CATCHERS				
Most Putouts	15	Ernie Whitt	Seattle (H)	July 7/86
	15	Ernie Whitt (13 innings)	Boston (H)	Sept. 19/89
Most Assists	4	Buck Martinez (12 innings)	Oakland (A)	May 24/81
	3	Rick Cerone (5 times)	Last time, Oakland (H)	Aug. 29/79
		Bob Davis	Oakland (A)	June 8/79
			Texas (A)	June 21/80
	3	Ernie Whitt (7 times)	Last time, Milwaukee (A)	May 21/88
		Buck Martinez	Seattle (H)	April 23/84
Most Errors	2	Ernie Whitt	California (A)	Sept. 28/83
Most Passed Balls	2			
	2	Ernie Whitt	Texas (A)	April 14/84
		Charlie Moore	Milwaukee (H)	Sept. 30/87
Most Total Chances	17	Ernie Whitt (15 innings)	Oakland (A)	May 23/81
	15	Ernie Whitt	Oakland (A)	June 18/82
	15	Ernie Whitt	Seattle (H)	July 7/86
	15	Ernie Whitt (13 innings)	Boston (H)	Sept. 19/89

FIRST BASEMEN				
Most Putouts	21	Doug Ault (13 innings)	Detroit (H)	July 15/77
	21	Rick Leach (14 innings)	Milwaukee (H)	Sept. 21/85
	20	John Mayberry	Seattle (H)	Sept. 2/79
Most Assists	4	Doug Ault (3 times)	Detroit (H)	April 13/77
			Seattle (A)	June 11/77
			Boston (H)	Sept. 7/77
		John Mayberry	Chicago (H)	April 18/79
		Willie Upshaw (6 times)	Milwaukee (A)	April 22/82
			New York (H)	Aug. 27/82
			Kansas City (A)	July 13/83
			California (A)	July 20/86
			New York (A)	Sept. 30/86
			Kansas City (A)	July 5/87
Most Errors	3	Willie Upshaw	Boston (A)	July 1/86
Most Double Plays	5	John Mayberry	California (A)	May 7/80
Most Total Chances	21	Doug Ault (13 innings)	Detroit (H)	July 15/77
	21	Rick Leach (14 innings)	Milwaukee (H)	Sept. 21/85
	20	John Mayberry	Seattle (H)	Sept. 2/79

SECOND BASEMEN				
Most Putouts	8	Dave McKay	New York (A), 2nd g	May 28/78
		Damaso Garcia	Kansas City (H)	May 7/82
		Dan Ainge	Texas (A)	July 8/79
		Dan Ainge (11 Innings)	Milwaukee (A)	July 19/79
		Manny Lee	Minnesota (A)	Sept. 14/89
		Nelson Liriano (10 innings)	California (A)	April 29/89
		Manny Lee	Boston (H)	Aug. 25/90
Most Assists	10	Dave McKay	Kansas City (H)	Aug. 12/78
Most Errors	3	Garth Iorg	California (A)	April 28/78
		Alfredo Griffin	Cleveland (H)	Aug. 22/84
Most Double Plays	4	Dan Ainge (10 Innings)	New York (H)	June 28/79
			Texas (A)	July 8/79
		Damaso Garcia	Seattle (A)	July 16/80
			Milwaukee (H)	April 22/81
			Boston (H)	Sept. 25/85
Most Total Chances	15	Dave McKay	New York (A), 2nd g	May 28/78
		Damaso Garcia	Kansas City (H)	May 7/82
		Nelson Liriano (10 innings)	California (A)	April 29/89

THIRD BASEMEN

Most Putouts 6	Dan Ainge (12 Innings)	Texas (A)	June 5/81
5	Roy Howell (2 times)	Milwaukee (H)	April 17/80
		Chicago (A)	June 11/80
Most Assists 9	Roy Howell	Milwaukee (H), 2nd g	June 14/78
Most Errors 3	Dave Baker	Oakland (H), 2nd g	Sept. 15/82
. . . . 3	Kelly Gruber	Baltimore (A)	June 27/89
Most Double Play . . 3	Roy Howell	Texas (A)	July 8/79
		Boston	Sept. 26/79
Most Total Chances 11	Roy Howell	Milwaukee (H), 2nd g	June 14/78
		Milwaukee (H)	April 17/80

SHORTSTOPS

Most Putouts 7	Alfredo Griffin	Texas (A)	Sept. 2/81
Most Assists 9	Alfredo Griffin	Boston (A)	July 27/82
	Alfredo Griffin	Kansas City (H)	May 7/83
	Tony Fernandez (10 innings)	Kansas City (A)	Aug. 10/85
	Tony Fernandez	New York (A)	Sept. 14/85
	Manny Lee	New York (H)	April 18/89
Most Errors 3	Hector Torres	Baltimore (A)	June 24/77
	Alfredo Griffin	Texas (A)	May 13/82
	Luis Sojo	Cleveland (A)	Aug. 31/90
Most Double Play . . 5	Alfredo Griffin	California (A)	May 7/80
Most Total Chances 14	Alfredo Griffin	Oakland (H)	July 29/80

OUTFIELDERS

Most Putouts . . . 10	Lloyd Moseby (10 inn.)	New York (H) 1st g	Aug. 2/83
9	Rick Bosetti	New York (H)	May 19/78
	Bob Bailor	Oakland (A)	June 9/79
	Lloyd Moseby	Seattle (A)	June 23/82
	Lloyd Moseby	California (H)	May 31/87
Most Assists 3	Steve Bowling	Oakland (H)	Aug. 27/77
	Rick Bosetti	Detroit (H)	May 28/79
Most Errors 2	Al Woods	Seattle (A)	June 1/79
		New York (A)	June 21/79
	Otto Velez	Kansas City (H)	Aug. 9/79
	Bob Bailor	Baltimore (A)	Sept. 20/80
	George Bell (4 times)	California (A)	July 20/88
		Minnesota (A)	July 25/88
		Minnesota (H)	August 3/88
		Detroit (A)	July 8/89
Most Double Play . . 2	Rick Bosetti	Detroit (H)	May 28/79
	Bob Bailor	Boston (H)	May 20/80
	Jesse Barfield	Seattle (A)	July 9/85
Most Total Chances 10	Lloyd Moseby (10 inn.)	New York (H) 1st g	Aug. 2/83
9	Rick Bosetti	New York (H)	May 19/78
	Bob Bailor	Detroit (H)	June 21/78
		Oakland (A)	June 9/79
	Lloyd Moseby	Seattle (A)	June 23/82

TEAM RECORDS—MONTH

CATEGORY	RECORD	YEAR
Wins	20	August—89
	22	Sept/Oct.—88
Losses	23	Sept./Oct.—77/May—79
Batting Average	.293	July—83
Runs	167	June -90
Hits	324	August—83
2B	57	July & August—83
3B	16	June & July—84
HRs	46	June—86
RBIs	155	June-90
SB	47	August—84
Complete Games	11	June—79
Shutouts	6	Sept—88
Home Runs—Opponents	42	August—82
ERA (Low)	2.71	July—85
ERA (High)	5.96	July—77
Slugging Avg	.465	Sept./Oct.—83
Best Record	19-6	Sept/Oct.—88
	22-7	May—84
Worst Record	4—22	Sept./Oct.—78

INDIVIDUAL PITCHING—MONTH

Games	18	Mark Eichhorn	June '87
Wins	6	Roy Lee Jackson (Relief)	May '84
	6	Dave Stieb	May '88
	5	Dave Lemanczyk	June '77
		Doyle Alexander	September '83 & '84
		Dave Stieb	May '83
		Tom Filer	August '85
		Jim Clancy	July '86
		Jim Clancy	May '87
Losses	7	Jesse Jefferson	August '80
IP	60.2	Doyle Alexander	September '84
Saves	10	Tom Henke	July '87
ERA	1.09	Dave Stieb	April '80 (33 IP)
	0.94	Dave Stieb	July '90 (28.2IP)
	0.48	Tom Buskey	August '79 (8 app.)
	0.48	Mark Eichhorn	April '86
	0.00	Tom Henke	April '87 (12 app.)
	0.00	John Cerutti	August '88 (8 app.)
Complete Games	5	Tom Underwood	June '79
Starts	8	Luis Leal	August '82
	8	Jimmy Key	Sept./Oct. '87
SHO	3	Dave Stieb	September '88

INDIVIDUAL BATTING—MONTH

At Bats	134	Lloyd Moseby	August '83
Hits	47	Lloyd Moseby	August '83
Runs	26	Lloyd Moseby	August '83
2B	12	Jesse Barfield	August '85
3B	5	Alfredo Griffin	May '79
	5	Lloyd Moseby	June '84
HRs	11	George Bell	May '87/June '87
RBIs	31	George Bell	May '87
Total Bases	78	Lloyd Moseby	August '83
		George Bell	May '87
Extra Base Hits	19	George Bell	August '84
		George Bell	August '87
		Kelly Gruber	September '90
	20	Kelly Gruber	Sept/Oct '90
Bases on Balls	30	Fred McGriff	Aug./Sept. '89
SH	5	Dave McKay	September '77
SF	5	Lloyd Moseby	July '84
	5	George Bell	September '89
	5	George Bell	August '90
SB	18	Dave Collins	August '84
Avg	.442	Otto Velez	April '77 (52 AB)
Slugging	.865	Otto Velez	April '77 (52 AB)
	.769	Kelly Gruber	September '90

OPPONENTS BATTING AVERAGE VS BLUE JAYS- CAREER LEADERS (75AB)

AVG	HITS	HRS	RBI
WOCKENFUSS, .376	YOUNT, 222	RICE, 34	BRETT, 107
KELLY, .364	BRETT, 182	EVANS (DW), 27	YOUNT, 107
POLONIA, .361	TRAMMELL, 169	MURRAY, 25	RICE, 100
RAY, .361	WHITAKER, 165	GRICH, 23	MURRAY, 89
EASLER, .356	RICE, 164	DeCINCES, 22	EVANS (DW), 87
HISLE, .349	MOLITOR, 157	PARRISH L., 22	FISK, 77
OLIVER, .349	COOPER, 153	ARMAS, 21	COOPER, 73
RIPKEN C., .349	MURRAY, 153	BRETT, 21	WINFIELD, 69
BOGGS, .345	HENDERSON, 146	THOMAS, 21	RIPKEN C., 67
ALMON, .342	LEMON, 140	YOUNT, 21	TRAMMELL, 66
CANSECO, .342	BOGGS, 136	LYNN, 20	WHITAKER, 65
BRETT, .341	MATTINGLY, 135	JACKSON (Re), 19	BAINES, 64
MATTINGLY, .341	LANSFORD, 132	LEMON, 19	JACKSON (Re), 64
JOYNER, .340	EVANS (DW), 128	GRICH, 63	

CATEGORY	RECORD	YEAR
Rookies on 25-man roster, opening day	9	1977
Rookies on opening day starting lineup	4	1977
Rookies to appear during season	16	1977
Major league debuts	9	1987, 1989
Greatest number of rookies on 25-man roster at one time	12	July 1-13, 23-27, 1977
Youngest rookie	Brian Milner-18 yrs, 7 mos, 6 days, 1978	
Oldest rookie	Dave Wallace-30 yrs, 8 mos, 26 days, 1978	
Total number of at bats by rookies	2,477	1977
Total number of hits by rookies	649	1977
Combined rookies' batting average	.262	1977
Total number of innings pitched by rookies	557	1977
Games started by rookies	68	1977
Games won by rookies	31	1986
Greatest number of rookies in starting lineup, game	7	(many times) 1977
Highest average (500 plate appearances)	310	Bob Bailor, 1977
Most games	153	Alfredo Griffin, 1979
Most at bats	624	Alfredo Griffin, 1979
Most hits	179	Alfredo Griffin, 1979
Most runs	81	Alfredo Griffin, 1979
Most total bases	227	Alfredo Griffin, 1979
Most extra-base hits	41	Damaso Garcia, 1980
Most doubles	30	Damaso Garcia, 1980
Most triples	10	Alfredo Griffin, 1979
Most home runs	20	Fred McGriff, 1987
Most runs batted in	64	Doug Ault, 1977
Most bases on balls	60	Fred McGriff, 1987
Most times striking out	104	Fred McGriff, 1987
Fewest times striking out (502 plate appearances)	26	Bob Bailor, 1977
Most sacrifice bunts	16	Alfredo Griffin, 1979
Most sacrifice flies	4	Alfredo Griffin, 1979 John Olerud, 1990
Highest slugging percentage	.505	Fred McGriff, 1987
Most stolen bases	21	Alfredo Griffin, 1979
Most stolen base attempts	37	Alfredo Griffin, 1979
Most times caught stealing	16	Alfredo Griffin, 1979
Most times ground into double plays	20	Doug Ault, 1977
Fewest times grounded into double plays (502 plate appearances)	5	Rick Bosetti, 1978
Longest hitting streak	14	Alfredo Griffin, 1979
Longest hitting streak, start of career	8	Jesse Barfield, 1981

PITCHING

Most wins	14	Mark Eichhorn, 1986
Most losses	18	Jerry Garvin, 1977; Phil Huffman, 1979
Most decisions	28	Jerry Garvin, 1977
Most games	69	Mark Eichhorn, 1986
Most games started	34	Jerry Garvin, 1977
Most relief appearances	69	Mark Eichhorn, 1986
Most games finished	34	Mark Eichhorn, 1986
Most saves	10	Jimmy Key, 1984; Mark Eichhorn, 1986
Lowest era (162 IP)	4.19	Jerry Garvin, 1977
Lowest era (100 IP)	1.72	Mark Eichhorn,, 1986
Most innings pitched	244.2	Jerry Garvin, 1977
Most runs allowed	130	Phil Huffman, 1979
Most ER allowed	114	Jerry Garvin, 1977
Most home runs allowed	33	Jerry Garvin, 1977
Most bases on balls	85	Jerry Garvin, 1977
Most strikeouts	166	Mark Eichhorn, 1986
Most hit batsmen	7	Mark Eichhorn, 1986
Most wild pitches	8	Jim Gott, 1982; John Cerutti, 1986
Most walks	3	
	3	Jeff Musselman, 1987 Todd Stottlemyre, 1988
Most pickoffs	22	Jerry Garvin, 1977

BLUE JAYS ROOKIES

1977 (16): Doug Ault, Bob Bailor, Steve Bowling, Tom Bruno, *Jeff Byrd, Rick Cerone, *Jim Clancy, *Mike Darr, *Dennis DeBarr, Sam Ewing, *Jerry Garvin, *Steve Staggs, Ernie Whitt, *Mike Willis, *Al Woods, Gary Woods, *Major League debut (8)
1978 (7): *Butch Alberts, Rick Bosetti, *Victor Cruz, *Garth Iorg, *Brian Milner, *Willie Upshaw, Dave Wallace, *Major Leage debut (5)

1979 (9): *Dan Ainge, *Bobby Brown, J.J. Cannon, *Butch Edge, Alfredo Griffin, *Pedro Hernandez, *Phil Huffman, *Dave Stieb, *Ted Wilborn, *Major League debut (7)

1980 (8): Damaso Garcia, *Paul Hodgson, *Pat Kelly, *Luis Leal, Mike Macha, *Lloyd Moseby, Domingo Ramos, *Ken Schrom, *Major League debut (5)

1981 (5): *Jesse Barfield, *George Bell, *Fred Manrique, *Greg Wells, Dan Whitmer, *Major League debut (4)

1982 (9): *Dave Baker, Jesse Barfield, *Mark Eichhorn, *Jim Gott, Pedro Hernandez, Anthony Johnson, *Geno Petralli, Ken Schrom, *Steve Senteney, *Major League debut (5)

1983 (6): *Jim Acker, *Stan Clarke, *Tony Fernandez, Geno Petralli, *Mitch Webster, *Matt Williams, *Major League debut (5)

1984 (7): Tony Fernandez, *Kelly Gruber, *Toby Hernandez, *Jimmy Key, Fred Manrique, *Ron Shepherd, Mitch Webster, *Major League debut (4)

1985 (10): *John Cerutti, Stan Clarke, *Steve Davis, *Cecil Fielder, Kelly Gruber, *Jeff Hearron, *Manny Lee, Ron Shepherd, *Lou Thorton, Mitch Webster, *Major League debut (6)

1986 (13): *Luis Aquino, John Cerutti, Stan Clarke, Steve Davis, Mark Eichhorn, Cecil Fielder, *Don Gordon, Kelly Gruber, Jeff Hearron, Joe Johnson, *Fred McGriff, *Jeff Musselman, Duane Ward, *Major League debut (4)

1987 (12): *Jeff DeWillis, *Rob Ducey, *Alexis Infante, *Nelson Liriano, Fred McGriff, Jeff Musselman, *Greg Myers, *Jose Nunez, *Mike Sharperson, *Matt Stark, Duane Ward, *David Wells, *Major League debut (9)

1988 (7): *Tony Castillo, David Wells, *Todd Stottlemyre, *Pat Borders, Alexis Infante, *Silvestre Campusano, Rob Ducey, *Major League debut (4)

1989 (12): *Kevin Batiste, *Francisco Cabrera, Tony Castillo, *Steve Cummings, *Junior Felix, *Mauro Gozzo, *Xavier Hernandez, *Glenallen Hill, Alexis Infante, Greg Myers, *John Olerud, *Alex Sanchez, *Major League debut (9)

1990 (11): *Willie Blair, Seve Cummings, *Carlos Diaz, Glenallen Hill, *Rick Luecken, *Bob MacDonald, Greg Myers, John Olerud, *Tom Quinlan, *Luis Sojo, *Mark Whiten

* = Major League Debut (7)

BLUE JAYS ROOKIES IN 1991

Pitchers (9): Denis Boucher, Nate Cromwell, Pat Hentgen, Bob MacDonald, Ricky Rhodes, Alex Sanchez, Mike Timlin, Ricky Trlicek, David Weathers

Catchers (2): Carlos Diaz, Randy Knorr

Infielders (3): Tom Quinlan, Jerry Schunk, William Suero,

Outfielders (2): Derek Bell, Mark Whiten

FORFEIT GAME: The Blue Jays have played one forfeit game, a 9-0 decision vs Baltimore on September 15, 1977...In that game Clancy had held the Orioles to two-hits over five innings before Earl Weaver pulled his club off the field...His reason was that the tarps on the Blue Jays bullpen created a hazard for his players.

BATTING DATA: The 215 HR's hit by the BLUE JAYS in 1987 was a club record and enabled the BLUE JAYS to have the sixth most HR's in the American League history behind the 1961 Yankees (240), 1987 Tigers and 1963 Twins (225), the 1964 Twins (221) and the 1982 Brewers (216)...It also placed eighth overall on the major league list...National League clubs which have eclipsed the 200 HR mark include the 1953 and 1955 Brooklyn Dodgers (208, 201), the 1956 Cincinnati Reds (221), the 1987 Chicago Cubs (209) and San Francisco Giants (205).

	HOME	AWAY	TOTAL
	W-L	W-L	W-L
1977	2-5	3-5	5-10
1978	6-2	1-6	7-8
1979	2-4	0-7	2-11
1980	2-5	0-6	2-11
1981	1-2	1-3	2-5
1982	1-6	2-4	3-10
1983	4-2	2-5	6-7
1984	5-2	4-2	9-4
1985	4-1	4-3	8-4
1986	2-5	3-3	5-8
1987	6-0	6-1	12-1
1988	6-1	2-4	8-5
1989	3-3	3-4	6-7
1990	5-2	3-3	8-5
TOTAL	49-40	34-56	83-96

SYNOPSIS: Lifetime vs the Orioles, the BLUE JAYS are 83-96, 49-40 at Toronto (8-5, at SkyDome) and 34-56 at Memorial Stadium...BLUE JAYS won their first series in the last five at Baltimore in 1990 (July 30-Aug 1)...TORONTO has won five of the last seven season series since 1984...Season series record is (5-9-0).

LAST SWEEP: BY TORONTO: At Toronto: September 30-October 2, 1988 (3-games); At Baltimore: September 21-23, 1987 (3-games).

LAST SWEEP: BY BALTIMORE:: Toronto: August 30-September 1, 1982 (3-games); At Baltimore: August 24-26, 1982 (3-games).

SERIES SWEPT: BY TORONTO: 2-game (2), 3-game (6), 4-game (1)
BY BALTIMORE: 3-game (8), 4-game (1)

LONGEST WIN STREAK: BY TORONTO: 6-games, May 10-August 11, 1984.
BY BALTIMORE: 15-games, September 8, 1978-September 6, 1979.

MOST RUNS, GAME: BY TORONTO: 24 runs, 24-10, June 26, 1978 at Toronto
BY BALTIMORE: 12 runs, 12-5, August 26, 1982 at Baltimore

WIDEST MARGIN VICTORY: BY TORONTO: 15 runs, 18-3, September 14, 1987 at Toronto
BY BALTIMORE: 0 runs, 4 times, last time: 16-6, June 27, 1989 at Baltimore.

BOSTON RED SOX

	HOME	AWAY	TOTAL
	W-L	W-L	W-L
1977	2-6	1-6	3-12
1978	2-5	2-6	4-11
1979	3-4	1-5	4-9
1980	2-5	0-6	2-11
1981	0-4	0-0	0-4
1982	3-3	3-4	6-7
1983	3-4	3-3	6-7
1984	4-2	4-3	8-5
1985	4-3	0-6	4-9
1986	3-3	3-4	6-7
1987	4-3	3-3	7-6
1988	4-2	7-0	11-2
1989	2-5	6-0	8-5
1990	2-4	1-6	3-10
TOTAL	37-53	39-48	76-101

SYNOPSIS: The BLUE JAYS are 76-101 lifetime vs the Red Sox, 37-53 at Toronto (4-9 at SkyDome) and 39-48 at Fenway Park...BLUE JAYS were 6-0 at Fenway Park in 1989, only to go 1-6 at Fenway in 1990...Last season, TORONTO lost five games by one run to Boston...Prior to 1990, the BLUE JAYS had won 15 games consecutively at Fenway Park, dating back to 1987...Season series record is (4-10-0).

LAST SWEEP: BY TORONTO: At Toronto: June 15-17, 1984 (3-games); at Boston: August 14-16, 1989 (3-games).

LAST SWEEP: BY BOSTON: AT TORONTO: April 23-25, 1982 (3-games); at Boston: June 5-28, 1990 (4-games)

SERIES SWEPT: BY TORONTO: 2-game (1), 3-game (2), 4-game (1)
BY BOSTON: 2-game (1), 3-game (5), 4-game (3)

LONGEST WIN STREAK: BY TORONTO: 6-games; June 2-11, 1988
BY BOSTON: 7-games; September 26, 1980-May 11, 1981

MOST RUNS, GAME: BY TORONTO: 24 runs, twice, last time 15-9 at Boston September 27, 1988.
BY BOSTON: 20 runs, 14-6, at Boston, September 25, 1984.

WIDEST MARGIN VICTORY: BY TORONTO: 11 runs, 11-0, June 20, 1990 at Toronto
BY BOSTON: 12 runs, 13-1, September 18, 1985 at Boston.

	HOME W-L	AWAY W-L	TOTAL W-L
1977	1-4	3-2	4-6
1978	2-3	1-4	3-7
1979	3-3	2-4	5-7
1980	4-2	5-1	9-3
1981	3-3	3-3	6-6
1982	3-3	1-5	4-8
1983	4-2	4-2	8-4
1984	2-4	3-3	5-7
1985	5-1	2-4	7-5
1986	2-4	4-2	6-6
1987	5-1	2-4	7-5
1988	2-4	4-2	6-6
1989	2-4	3-3	5-7
1990	4-1	1-5	5-7
TOTAL	42-39	38-44	80-84

SYNOPSIS: The BLUE JAYS are 80-84 lifetime vs the Angels, 42-39 at Toronto (6-2 at SkyDome) and 38-44 at Anaheim Stadium...The BLUE JAYS have had identical records vs the Angels for the past two seasons (5-7)...The last time the BLUE JAYS posted a season series record above .500 was in 1987 (7-5)...Each team swept one series during 1990 - (California- (2 game), at California [May 23-24], TORONTO- (3 game), at SkyDome [July 3,4,5])...Season series record is (4-7-3).

LAST SWEEP: BY TORONTO: At Toronto: July 3-5, 1990 (3-games); At California: June 19-21, 1989.

LAST SWEEP: BY CALIFORNIA: At Toronto: April 20-22, 1984 (3-games); At California: May 23-24, 1990 (2-games).

SERIES SWEPT: BY TORONTO: 2-game (1); 3-game (5); 4-game (1)
BY CALIFORNIA: 2-game (3); 3-game (5)

LONGEST WIN STREAK: BY TORONTO: 5-games, June 19-August 17, 1989.
BY CALIFORNIA: 5-games, 2 times, last time: April 8-July 2, 1984.

MOST RUNS, GAME: BY TORONTO: 12 runs, 2 times, last time: 12-2, July 18, 1988 at California
BY CALIFORNIA: 24 runs, 24-2, August 25, 1979 at Toronto

WIDEST MARGIN VICTORY: BY TORONTO: 12 runs, 12-0, May 18, 1987 at California
BY CALIFORNIA: 22 runs, 24-2, August 25, 1979 at Toronto

CHICAGO WHITE SOX

	HOME W-L	AWAY W-L	TOTAL W-L
1977	2-3	1-5	3-8
1978	4-1	2-3	6-4
1979	1-5	4-2	5-7
1980	5-1	2-4	7-5
1981	2-4	3-3	5-7
1982	2-4	2-4	4-8
1983	2-4	5-1	7-5
1984	4-2	4-2	8-4
1985	5-1	4-2	9-3
1986	4-2	2-4	6-6
1987	3-3	5-1	8-4
1988	4-2	1-5	5-7
1989	5-1	6-0	11-1
1990	5-1	2-4	7-5
TOTAL	48-34	43-40	91-74

SYNOPSIS: Lifetime vs the White Sox, the BLUE JAYS are 91-74, 48-34 at Toronto (8-1 at SkyDome) and 43-40 at Comiskey Park...
TORONTO has had a winning record at home vs the White Sox for the last seven seasons (1983, 2-4)...The BLUE JAYS are 14-4 at home vs the White Sox over the last three seasons...It was the seventh time in the last eight seasons that the BLUE JAYS have played at least .500 vs Chicago...Season series record (8-5-1).

LAST SWEEP: BY TORONTO: At Toronto: September 7-9, 1990 (3-games); At Chicago: September 4-6, 1989.

LAST SWEEP: BY CHICAGO: At Toronto: April 16-18, 1979 (3-games); At Chicago: April 27-29, 1990.

SERIES SWEPT: BY TORONTO: 2-game (2), 3-game (6)
BY CHICAGO: 2-game (5), 3-game (3)

LONGEST WIN STREAK: BY TORONTO: 7 games, May 28-April 27, 1990
BY CHICAGO: 6-games, July 14, 1977-April 21, 1978

MOST RUNS, GAME: BY TORONTO: 11 runs, 11-1, May 20, 1989 at Chicago
BY CHICAGO: 16 runs, 16-7, July 11, 1982 at Toronto

WIDEST MARGIN VICTORY: BY TORONTO: 10 runs, 11-1, May 20, 1989 at Chicago
BY CHICAGO: 11 runs, 13-2, August 23, 1981 at Toronto

	HOME W-L	AWAY W-L	TOTAL W-L
1977	1-5	4-4	5-9
1978	2-6	2-4	4-10
1979	4-2	1-6	5-8
1980	4-3	1-5	5-8
1981	1-1	1-3	2-4
1982	3-4	3-3	6-7
1983	4-2	5-2	9-4
1984	5-2	2-4	7-6
1985	4-2	5-2	9-4
1986	5-2	5-1	10-3
1987	4-2	4-3	8-5
1988	5-2	2-4	7-6
1989	5-1	3-4	8-5
1990	4-3	5-1	9-4
TOTALS	51-37	43-46	94-83

SYNOPSIS: The BLUE JAYS are 94-83 lifetime vs the Tribe, 51-37 at Toronto (7-3 at SkyDome) and 43-46 at Cleveland...The BLUE JAYS won the season series from the Tribe in 1990 (9-4) for the eighth consecutive season and are 37-16 at home during that stretch...The 51 wins at home are second only to Texas (52)...The three home losses by the BLUE JAYS was the first since 1982...Both of the BLUE JAYS' tie games have come at Cleveland...The only No-hitter in BLUE JAYS history came vs Cleveland on September 2, 1990...Season series record is (8-6-0).

LAST SWEEP:	BY TORONTO: At Toronto: September 15-17, 1989 (3-games); At Cleveland: August 31-September 2, 1990 (3-games).
LAST SWEEP:	BY CLEVELAND: At Toronto: September 4-5, 1978 (2-games); At Cleveland: May 29-31, 1989 (3-games).
SERIES SWEPT:	BY TORONTO: 2-game (1), 3-game (5), 4-game (2)
SERIES SWEPT:	BY CLEVELAND: 2-game (2), 3-game (3), 4-game (2)
LONGEST WIN STREAK:	BY TORONTO: 7-games, August 23, 1984-June 1, 1985
	BY CLEVELAND: 7-games, April 26-July 9, 1977
MOST RUNS, GAME:	BY TORONTO: 15 runs, 15-3, June 15, 1988 at Toronto
	BY CLEVELAND: 16 runs, 16-11, April 31, 1983 at Toronto
WIDEST MARGIN VICTORY:	BY TORONTO: 12 runs, 15-3, June 15, 1988 at Toronto
	BY CLEVELAND: 15 runs, 16-1, August 15, 1984 (1) at Cleveland

DETROIT TIGERS

	HOME W-L	AWAY W-L	TOTAL W-L
1977	5-3	0-7	5-10
1978	2-5	4-4	6-9
1979	1-6	3-3	4-9
1980	1-5	3-4	4-9
1981	1-3	3-3	4-6
1982	4-2	3-4	7-6
1983	4-3	3-3	7-6
1984	2-4	3-4	5-8
1985	5-2	2-4	7-6
1986	4-2	5-2	9-4
1987	4-3	2-4	6-7
1988	4-2	4-3	8-5
1989	6-1	5-1	11-2
1990	4-2	4-3	8-5
TOTAL	47-43	44-49	91-92

SYNOPSIS: The BLUE JAYS are 91-92 lifetime vs the Tigers, 47-43 at Toronto (10-3 at SkyDome) and 44-49 at Tiger Stadium...The BLUE JAYS have now won the season series from the Tigers in four of the last five seasons and each of the last three years at Detroit (1st time in franchise history)...BLUE JAYS 14-5 at home over the last three seasons...Last series loss to the Tigers was the final series of the 1987 season at Tiger Stadium...Season series record is (7-7-0).

LAST SWEEP:	BY TORONTO: At Toronto August 22-24, 1989 (3-games); At Detroit: July 7-9, 1989 (3-games)
LAST SWEEP:	BY DETROIT: At Toronto: September 7-9, 1984 (3-games); At Detroit: October 1-3, 1987 (3-games)
SERIES SWEPT:	BY TORONTO: 3-game (3)
	BY DETROIT: 2-game (3), 3-game (6), 4-game (1)
LONGEST WIN STREAK:	BY TORONTO: 8-games, June 11, 1989-May 4, 1990
	BY DETROIT: 5-games, 3 times, last time- April 21-May 31, 1979
MOST RUNS, GAME:	BY TORONTO: 13 runs, 13-5, June 16, 1988 at Detroit
	BY DETROIT: 12 runs, 12-3, June 17, 1988 at Detroit
WIDEST MARGIN VICTORY:	BY TORONTO: 9 runs, 12-3, June 12, 1984 at Toronto
	BY DETROIT: 9 runs, 9-0, June 15, 1977 at Detroit

	HOME W-L	AWAY W-L	TOTAL W-L
1977	1-4	1-4	2-8
1978	2-3	3-2	5-5
1979	3-3	0-6	3-9
1980	2-4	1-5	3-9
1981	2-5	2-1	4-6
1982	2-4	2-5	4-6
1983	4-3	1-5	5-8
1984	5-1	2-4	7-5
1985	2-4	3-3	5-7
1986	3-3	4-2	7-5
1987	4-2	0-6	4-8
1988	4-2	4-2	8-4
1989	3-3	2-4	5-7
1990	2-4	4-3	6-7
TOTAL	41-40	32-47	73-87

SYNOPSIS: The BLUE JAYS are 73-87 lifetime vs the Royals, 41-40 at Toronto (4-5 at SkyDome) and 32-47 at Royals Stadium...The 73 wins vs Kansas City are the fewest vs any opponent...The BLUE JAYS have not lost a home series to the Royals since 1985 when they went 2-4...Since 1985 the club is 31-29 vs the Royals and 17-13 at home...Season series record is (5-7-2).

LAST SWEEP:	BY TORONTO: At Toronto April 19-20, 1988 (2-games); At Kansas City: July 28-30, 1986 (3-games)
LAST SWEEP:	BY KANSAS CITY: At Toronto: June 10-11, 1981 (2-games); At Kansas City: July 3-5, 1987 (4-games)
SERIES SWEPT:	BY TORONTO: 2-game (3), 3-game (3)
	BY KANSAS CITY: 2-game (5), 3-game (3), 4-game (2)
LONGEST WIN STREAK:	BY TORONTO: 5-games, April 27-May 6, 1984
	BY KANSAS CITY: 7-games, August 10, 1980-August 17, 1981
MOST RUNS, GAME:	BY TORONTO: 17 runs, 17-6, April 20, 1990 at Toronto
	BY KANSAS CITY: 16 runs, 16-12, August 12, 1979 at Toronto
WIDEST MARGIN VICTORY:	BY TORONTO: 11-runs, 17-6, April 20, 1990
	BY KANSAS CITY: 10 runs, 11-1, August 6, 1988 at Toronto

MILWAUKEE BREWERS

	HOME W-L	AWAY W-L	TOTAL W-L
1977	4-4	3-4	7-8
1978	3-4	0-8	3-12
1979	2-5	1-5	3-10
1980	3-3	5-2	8-5
1981	2-5	2-1	4-6
1982	2-4	2-5	4-9
1983	4-3	1-5	5-8
1984	2-4	1-6	3-10
1985	5-2	4-2	9-4
1986	2-5	4-2	6-7
1987	2-5	2-4	4-9
1988	3-3	3-4	6-7
1989	4-3	3-3	7-6
1990	2-4	4-3	6-7
TOTAL	40-54	35-54	75-108

SYNOPSIS: The BLUE JAYS are 75-108 lifetime vs the Brewers, 40-54 at Toronto (6-7 at SkyDome) and 35-54 at County Stadium...Against Milwaukee, the BLUE JAYS hold the worst overall record vs any team and their second worst road record (1st Baltimore- 34-56)...Toronto was 6-7 vs Milwaukee in 1990, one of two Eastern clubs that the BLUE JAYS had losing records against (Boston 3-10)...Toronto has finished at .500 or below for 11 of the past 14 seasons...Season series record (3-11-0).

LAST SWEEP:	BY TORONTO: At Toronto April 16-17, 1980 (2-games); At Milwaukee: September 27-29, 1985 (3-games)
LAST SWEEP:	BY MILWAUKEE: At Toronto: September 28-30, 1987 (3-games); At Milwaukee: June 25-27, 1984, (4-games)
SERIES SWEPT:	BY TORONTO: 2-game (2), 3-game (1)
	BY MILWAUKEE: 2-game (4), 3-game (4), 4-game (3)
LONGEST WIN STREAK:	BY TORONTO: 5-games, April 14-27, 1980
	BY MILWAUKEE: 8-games, August 6, 1977-June, 14, 1978
MOST RUNS, GAME:	BY TORONTO: 15 runs, 15-6, June 19, 1987 at Toronto
	BY MILWAUKEE: 15 runs, 15-4, April 9, 1982 at Toronto
WIDEST MARGIN VICTORY:	BY TORONTO: 9 runs, 15-6, June 19, 1987 at Toronto
	BY MILWAUKEE: 11 runs, 15-4, April 9, 1982 at Toronto

	HOME W-L	AWAY W-L	TOTAL W-L
1977	1-4	0-5	1-9
1978	2-3	2-3	4-6
1979	1-5	0-6	1-11
1980	2-4	3-3	5-7
1981	1-2	0-3	1-5
1982	4-2	3-3	7-5
1983	4-2	3-3	7-5
1984	6-0	5-1	11-1
1985	5-1	3-3	8-4
1986	5-1	3-3	8-4
1987	5-1	4-2	9-3
1988	3-3	2-4	5-7
1989	3-3	0-6	3-9
1990	3-3	6-0	9-3
TOTALS	45-34	34-45	79-79

SYNOPSIS: The BLUE JAYS are 79-79 lifetime vs the Twins, 45-34 at Toronto (6-4 at SkyDome) and 34-45 at Minnesota (5-20 at Metropolitan Stadium/29-25 at the Metrodome)...Toronto reversed its 1989 record of 0-6 at the Metrodome by posting a perfect 6-0 record (two three game sweeps) at Minnesota in 1990...The BLUE JAYS have won 38 of the last 54 games played at the Metrodome including 31 of the last 39 dating back to 1984...Toronto has had a .500 or better record at home vs the Twins for the last nine seasons...Season series record (7-7-0).

LAST SWEEP: BY TORONTO: At Toronto: April 28-29, 1987 (2-games); At Minnesota: August 17-19, 1990 (3-games)

LAST SWEEP: BY MINNESOTA: At Toronto: June 16-17, 1980 (2-games); At Minnesota: September 12-14, 1989 (3-games)

SERIES SWEPT: BY TORONTO: 2-game (4); 3-game (5)
BY MINNESOTA: 2-game (5); 3-game (6); 4-game (1)

LONGEST WIN STREAK: BY TORONTO: 10-games, August 24, 1986-July 16, 1987
BY MINNESOTA: 8-games, July 15, 1979-June 8, 1980

MOST RUNS, GAME: BY TORONTO: 16 runs, 16-4, June 14, 1987 at Minnesota
BY MINNESOTA: 16 runs, 16-8, May 8, 1979 at Minnesota

WIDEST MARGIN VICTORY: BY TORONTO: 12 runs, 16-4, June 14, 1987 at Minnesota
BY MINNESOTA: 12 runs twice, last time- 13-1, May 14, 1989 at Minnesota

NEW YORK YANKEES

	WON W-L	LOST W-L	TOTAL W-L
1977	2-7	4-4	6-9
1978	3-5	1-6	4-11
1979	1-5	0-6	1-11
1980	2-5	1-5	3-10
1981	1-1	2-1	3-2
1982	5-2	2-4	7-6
1983	4-2	2-5	6-7
1984	4-3	1-5	5-8
1985	2-4	5-2	7-6
1986	2-5	4-2	6-7
1987	2-4	5-2	7-6
1988	2-5	5-1	7-6
1989	2-4	4-3	6-7
1990	5-2	3-3	8-5
TOTAL	38-51	41-48	79-99

SYNOPSIS: The BLUE JAYS are 79-99 lifetime vs the Yankees, 38-51 at Toronto (7-3 at SkyDome) and 41-48 at Yankee Stadium...The 38 wins are the fewest wins at home vs any club, while 99 losses are the second highest total vs any opponent (Milwaukee- 108)...The BLUE JAYS have not lost a season series at Yankee Stadium since 1984 when they went 1-5...Toronto swept the Yankees at home for the first time ever during 1990 (3 game series- September 17-19)...1990 marked just the fourth time that the BLUE JAYS have won the season series at home vs New York...Season series record (5-9-0).

LAST SWEEP: BY TORONTO: At Toronto: September 17-19, 1990 (3-games); At New York: June 15-17, 1990 (3-games)

LAST SWEEP: BY NEW YORK: At Toronto: April 17-19, 1989 (3-games); At New York: August 20-22, 1990 (3-games)

SERIES SWEPT: BY TORONTO: 3-game (5)
BY NEW YORK: 3-game (9)

LONGEST WIN STREAK: BY TORONTO: 4-games, 2 times, last time- October 1, 1986-June 10, 1987
BY NEW YORK: 8-games, September 22, 1979-May 24, 1980

MOST RUNS, GAME: BY TORONTO: 19 runs, 19-3, September 10, 1977 at New York
BY NEW YORK: 15 runs, 15-4, June 29, 1987 at Toronto

WIDEST MARGIN VICTORY: BY TORONTO: 14 runs, 15-1, June 22, 1986 at Toronto
BY NEW YORK: 13 runs, 15-2, June 3, 1984 at Toronto

	HOME W-L	AWAY W-L	TOTAL W-L
1977	0-5	3-2	3-7
1978	4-2	0-5	4-7
1979	4-2	4-2	8-4
1980	2-4	2-4	4-8
1981	2-4	0-6	2-10
1982	3-3	6-0	9-3
1983	4-2	2-4	6-6
1984	4-2	4-2	8-4
1985	3-3	4-2	7-5
1986	3-3	1-5	4-8
1987	2-4	3-3	5-7
1988	0-6	3-3	3-9
1989	3-3	2-4	5-7
1990	1-5	4-2	5-7
TOTAL	35-48	38-44	73-92

SYNOPSIS: The BLUE JAYS are 73-92 lifetime vs the Athletics, 35-48 at Toronto (3-7 at SkyDome) and 38-44 at the Coliseum...The 92 losses are the most vs any western division club and the 73 wins being tied with K.C. for the fewest vs any opponent...The BLUE JAYS were 5-7 in 1990, the third time in four seasons that they have posted that mark...Toronto has only one six of the past 24 games played at Toronto...Dave Stewart of Oakland pitched a no-hitter on June 29 at Toronto, for only the second no-hitter vs the BLUE JAYS...Season series record (4-9-1).

LAST SWEEP: BY TORONTO: At Toronto September 15, 1982 (2-games); At Oakland: April 29-30, 1985 (2-games)

LAST SWEEP: BY OAKLAND: At Toronto : May 21-22, 1990 (2-games); At Oakland: May 4-5, 1988 (2-games)

SERIES SWEPT: BY TORONTO: 2-game (3), 3-game (3)
BY OAKLAND: 2-game (6), 3-game (6), 4-game (1)

LONGEST WIN STREAK: BY TORONTO: 8-games, June 18-September 15, 1982
BY OAKLAND: 9-games, July 22, 1980-May 11, 1980

MOST RUNS, GAME: BY TORONTO: 16 runs, 16-6, September 11, 1983, at Toronto
BY OAKLAND: 12 runs, twice, last time- 12-1, May 11, 1980 at Oakland

WIDEST MARGIN VICTORY: BY TORONTO: 11 runs, 12-1, May 18, 1980 at Toronto
BY OAKLAND: 11 runs, 2 times, last time- 12-1, May 11, 1980 at Oakland

SEATTLE MARINERS

	HOME W-L	AWAY W-L	TOTAL W-L
1977	2-3	4-1	6-4
1978	1-4	1-4	2-8
1979	3-3	1-5	4-8
1980	4-2	2-4	6-6
1981	2-1	1-2	3-3
1982	3-3	2-4	5-7
1983	3-3	5-1	8-4
1984	3-3	4-2	7-5
1985	6-0	4-2	10-2
1986	3-3	3-3	6-6
1987	5-1	5-1	10-2
1988	4-2	3-3	7-5
1989	4-2	3-3	7-5
1990	2-4	4-2	6-6
TOTAL	45-34	42-37	87-71

SYNOPSIS: The BLUE JAYS are 87-71 lifetime vs the Mariners, 45-34 at Toronto (4-5 at SkyDome) and 42-37 at the Kingdome...The Mariners are one of only two clubs that the BLUE JAYS have a lifetime winning road record against (Chicago- 43-40)...With a 6-6 record in 1990, the BLUE JAYS have now won or split the season series in each of the past eight seasons...In 1990, Toronto lost their first home series to the Mariners since 1978 (1-4)...Season series record (7-3-4).

LAST SWEEP: BY TORONTO: At Toronto: September 4-6, 1987 (3-games); At Seattle: May 25-27, 1990 (3-games)

LAST SWEEP: BY SEATTLE: At Toronto: May 15-17, 1990 (3-games); At Seattle: August 20-22, 1979 (3-games)

SERIES SWEPT: BY TORONTO: 2-game (4), 3-game (6)
BY SEATTLE: 3-game (6)

MOST RUNS, GAME: BY TORONTO: 19 runs, 19-7, June 26, 1983 at Seattle
BY SEATTLE: 14 runs, 14-6, May 17, 1990 at Toronto

WIDEST MARGIN VICTORY: BY TORONTO: 12 runs, 19-7, June 26, 1983 at Seattle
BY SEATTLE: 10-runs, 13-3, May 9, 1986 at Seattle

	HOME W-L	AWAY W-L	TOTAL W-L
1977	2-4	2-3	4-7
1978	4-1	3-3	7-4
1979	3-3	2-4	5-7
1980	3-3	2-4	5-7
1981	0-2	2-4	2-6
1982	6-0	2-4	8-4
1983	5-1	3-3	8-4
1984	3-3	3-3	6-6
1985	4-2	5-1	9-3
1986	4-2	3-3	7-5
1987	6-0	3-3	9-3
1988	4-2	2-4	6-6
1989	4-2	3-3	7-5
1990	4-2	1-5	5-7
TOTAL	52-27	36-47	88-74

SYNOPSIS: The BLUE JAYS are 88-74 lifetime vs the Rangers, 52-27 at Toronto (6-3 at SkyDome) and 36-47 at Arlington Stadium...88 wins is the third highest total vs any opponent with 52 home wins being the most vs any opponent...Lost the seasons series in 1990 for the first time since 1981...BLUE JAYS have gone 4-2 at home for five out of the last six seasons...Since 1985, Toronto has gone 25-10 at home vs the Rangers and is undefeated in their last 16 home series...Season series record (7-5-2).

LAST SWEEP:	BY TORONTO: At Toronto: September 1-4, 1988 (4-games); At Texas: April 26-28, 1985 (3-games)
LAST SWEEP:	BY TEXAS: At Toronto: May 17-18, 1988 (2-games); At Texas: June 5-7, 1981, (3-games)
SERIES SWEPT:	BY TORONTO: 2-game (2), 3-game (5), 4-game (2)
	BY TEXAS: 2-game (4), 3-game (1)
LONGEST WIN STREAK:	BY TORONTO: 6-games, August 10, 1986-May 9, 1987
	BY TEXAS: 4-games, 2 times, last time- April 22-August 9, 1986
MOST RUNS, GAME:	BY TORONTO: 15 runs, 15-4, May 9, 1987 at Texas
	BY TEXAS: 14 runs, 14-0, July 26, 1977 at Toronto
WIDEST MARGIN VICTORY:	BY TORONTO: 12 runs, 13-1, August 16, 1986 at Toronto
	BY TEXAS: 14 runs, 14-0, July 26, 1977 at Toronto

OPPOSING BATTERS VS BLUE JAYS

	1990					LIFETIME				
	AVG.	AB	HITS	HR	RBI	AVG.	AB	HITS	HR	RBI
Afenir, Troy	.333	3	1	0	0	.333	3	1	0	0
Aguayo, Luis	-	-	-	-	-	.261	23	6	0	1
Allanson, Andy	-	-	-	-	-	.247	85	21	0	0
Allred, Beau	-	-	-	-	-	.333	8	3	0	0
Alomar, Sandy	.125	40	5	1	4	.125	40	5	1	4
Anderson, Brady	.185	27	5	0	3	.179	56	10	0	3
Anderson, Kent	.429	7	3	0	1	.276	29	8	0	2
Armas, Tony	-	-	-	-	-	.254	418	106	21	61
Azocar, Oscar	.267	15	4	0	2	.267	15	4	0	2
Backman, Wally	-	-	-	-	-	.154	13	2	0	0
Baerga, Carlos	.143	28	4	0	1	.143	28	4	0	1
Baines, Harold	.250	28	7	2	6	.267	416	111	20	64
Baker, Doug	-	-	-	-	-	.286	7	2	0	1
Balboni, Steve	.226	31	7	3	3	.222	248	55	15	42
Barfield, Jesse	.170	47	8	1	2	.200	70	14	2	3
Barrett, Marty	.250	4	1	0	1	.250	252	63	2	28
Beane, Bill	-	-	-	-	-	.176	17	3	0	1
Bell, Juan	-	-	-	-	-	.000	4	0	0	0
Belle, Joey	.000	3	0	0	1	.333	18	6	1	4
Bergman, Dave	.200	10	2	0	0	.254	114	29	3	15
Bichette, Dante	.231	26	6	3	7	.180	50	9	3	11
Blankenship, Lance	.200	5	1	0	0	.227	22	5	0	0
Blowers, Mike	.067	15	1	0	2	.067	15	1	0	2
Boggs, Wade	.300	50	15	2	7	.345	394	136	4	39
Boone, Bob	.444	18	8	0	2	.229	293	67	1	28
Bosley, Thad	.000	1	0	0	0	.136	22	3	0	2
Boston, Daryl	-	-	-	-	-	.237	93	22	1	3
Bradley, Phil	.308	13	4	0	0	.327	223	73	5	14
Bradley, Scott	.222	18	4	0	2	.244	123	30	0	8
Braggs, Glenn	.000	8	0	0	0	.248	125	31	3	15
Brantley, Mickey	-	-	-	-	-	.214	84	18	1	4
Brett, George	.373	51	19	2	8	.341	533	182	21	107
Briley, Greg	.160	25	4	0	3	.277	47	13	3	9
Brock, Greg	.261	23	6	0	3	.265	132	35	3	15
Brookens, Tom	.400	5	2	0	0	.219	302	66	5	30
Brower, Bob	-	-	-	-	-	.267	45	12	1	1
Browne, Jerry	.154	52	8	0	2	.272	136	37	0	14
Brumley, Mike	.222	18	4	0	1	.235	34	8	0	1
Brunansky, Tom	.222	18	4	0	1	.259	247	64	10	27
Buckner, Bill	-	-	-	-	-	.289	204	59	2	26

	1990 AVG.	1990 AB	1990 HITS	1990 HR	1990 RBI	LIFETIME AVG.	LIFETIME AB	LIFETIME HITS	LIFETIME HR	LIFETIME RBI
Buechele, Steve	.200	35	7	3	12	.207	184	38	10	32
Buhner, Jay	-	-	-	-	-	.179	28	5	0	3
Burks, Ellis	.200	45	9	0	2	.230	148	34	3	14
Bush, Randy	.143	7	1	0	1	.209	230	48	4	25
Calderon, Ivan	.267	45	12	3	7	.236	195	46	8	18
Canale, George	-	-	-	-	-	.000	1	0	0	0
Canseco, Ozzie	.000	7	0	0	0	.000	7	0	0	0
Canseco, Jose	.419	31	13	4	13	.342	187	64	17	54
Carter, Joe	-	-	-	-	-	.251	251	63	9	37
Castillo, Carmelo	.250	24	6	0	0	.226	124	28	1	18
Cerone, Rick	.250	8	2	0	0	.289	190	55	3	18
Clark, Dave	-	-	-	-	-	.262	42	11	1	5
Clark,Jack	-	-	-	-	-	.133	30	4	1	5
Cochrane, Dave	.500	2	1	0	0	.400	5	2	0	0
Cole, Alex	.333	15	5	0	0	.333	15	5	0	0
Coles, Darnell	-	-	-	-	-	.185	54	10	1	2
Cotto, Henry	.220	50	11	2	5	.177	130	23	4	17
Daugherty, Jacy	.231	13	3	0	0	.333	15	5	0	0
Davis, Alvin	.414	29	12	2	8	.298	252	75	7	42
Davis, Bo	-	-	-	-	-	.250	4	1	0	0
Davis, Chili	.222	27	6	0	3	.250	112	28	4	17
Deer, Rob	.222	36	8	0	5	.203	182	37	10	30
Devereaux, Mike	.167	48	8	1	2	.176	85	15	2	6
Diaz, Mario	.333	15	5	0	2	.320	25	8	0	2
Disarcina, Gary	.143	7	1	0	0	.235	17	4	0	0
Downing, Brian	.316	19	6	2	2	.251	411	103	14	49
Dwyer, Jim	.077	13	1	0	0	.305	190	58	10	32
Eisenreich, Jim	.213	47	10	1	7	.213	89	19	1	8
Engle, Dave	-	-	-	-	-	.000	3	0	0	0
Esasky, Nick	-	-	-	-	-	.333	54	18	2	5
Espinoza, Alvino	.256	43	11	0	2	.275	91	25	0	7
Espy, Cecil	.000	3	0	0	0	.141	64	9	0	2
Evans, Dwight	.237	38	9	1	6	.257	499	128	27	87
Felder, Mike	.286	21	6	0	2	.263	114	30	1	13
Fermin, Felix	.286	35	10	0	6	.275	69	19	0	6
Fielder, Cecil	.383	47	18	7	14	.383	47	18	7	14
Finley, Steve	.242	33	8	1	7	.217	46	10	1	7
Fisk, Carlton	.344	32	11	0	4	.264	462	122	18	77
Fletcher, Scott	.171	41	7	0	1	.255	298	76	2	33
Franco, Julio	.333	42	14	0	5	.300	363	109	3	51
Francona, Tito	-	-	-	-	-	.471	17	8	1	5
Gaetti, Gary	.310	42	13	2	9	.229	350	80	13	46
Gagne, Greg	.167	24	4	1	4	.258	182	47	4	31
Gallagher, Dave	.333	6	2	0	1	.250	84	21	1	8
Gallego, Mike	.231	26	6	0	3	.260	100	26	0	9
Gantner, Jim	.208	24	5	0	1	.267	409	109	3	37
Gedman, Rich	-	-	-	-	-	.244	221	54	7	32
Geren, Bob	.286	21	6	1	3	.333	30	10	1	3
Giles, Brian	.455	11	5	3	8	.455	11	5	3	8
Gladden, Don	.256	39	10	0	0	.245	159	39	3	13
Gonzales, Mariano	-	-	-	-	-	.286	14	4	0	1
Gonzales, Rene	.000	6	0	0	0	.108	37	4	0	3
Grebeck, Craig	.125	16	2	0	1	.125	16	2	0	1
Green, Gary	.200	5	1	0	0	.200	5	1	0	0
Greenwell, Mike	.356	45	16	1	8	.302	172	52	7	34
Griffey, Ken, Jr.	.260	50	13	0	2	.314	86	27	1	6
Griffey, Ken, Sr.	-	-	-	-	-	.289	152	44	5	21
Guillen, Ozzie	.242	33	8	0	3	.246	236	58	1	17
Hale, Chip	-	-	-	-	-	.167	6	1	0	0
Hall, Mel	.344	32	11	2	4	.244	164	40	4	19
Hamilton, Jeff	.267	15	4	0	1	.267	15	4	0	1
Harper, Brian	.300	30	9	0	4	.319	72	23	2	11
Hassey, Ron	.118	17	2	0	1	.243	259	63	5	29
Heath, Mike	.294	34	10	0	1	.235	289	68	3	21
Heep, Danny	.200	5	1	0	1	.241	29	7	1	5
Hemond, Scott	.000	4	0	0	0	.000	4	0	0	0
Henderson, Dave	.217	46	10	3	9	.296	314	93	18	54
Henderson, Rickey	.294	34	10	2	7	.293	498	146	15	55
Hernandez, Keith	.231	26	6	1	4	.231	26	6	1	4
Higgins, Mark	-	-	-	-	-	.143	7	1	0	0
Hill, Donnie	.222	27	6	1	2	.251	167	42	5	19
Hinzo, Tommy	-	-	-	-	-	.273	33	9	1	2
Hoffman, Glenn	-	-	-	-	-	.545	11	6	0	0
Hoiles, Chris	-	-	-	-	-	.250	4	1	0	1
Horn, Sam	.273	22	6	2	5	.289	45	13	4	13
Howell, Jack	.276	29	8	0	1	.292	171	50	5	17
Howard, Steve	.286	7	2	0	0	.286	7	2	0	0
Hrbek, Kent	.206	34	7	1	3	.249	366	91	15	55
Hubbard, Glenn	-	-	-	-	-	.115	26	3	0	1
Hulett, Tim	.000	2	0	0	0	.231	13	3	0	2
Huson, Jeff	.120	25	3	0	1	.120	25	3	0	1
Incaviglia, Pete	.256	43	11	1	8	.237	194	46	8	27
Jackson, Bo	.355	31	11	2	6	.221	140	31	6	21

	1990					LIFETIME				
	AVG.	AB	HITS	HR	RBI	AVG.	AB	HITS	HR	RBI
Jacoby, Brook	.326	46	15	1	4	.291	309	90	9	36
James, Chris	.171	41	7	1	3	.171	41	7	1	3
James, Dion	.381	21	8	0	1	.429	35	15	1	6
Javier, Stan	-	-	-	-	-	.228	57	13	1	5
Jefferson, Stan	-	-	-	-	-	.333	18	6	1	6
Jeltz, Steve	.158	19	3	0	1	.158	19	3	0	1
Jennings, Doug	.400	10	4	0	0	.400	10	4	0	0
Johnson, Lance	.265	34	9	0	1	.222	54	12	0	1
Jones, Tracy	-	-	-	-	-	.125	8	1	0	2
Jorgensen, Terry	-	-	-	-	-	.000	5	0	0	0
Jose, Felix	.174	23	4	0	1	.174	23	4	0	1
Joyner, Wally	.514	35	18	2	7	.340	206	70	8	41
Karkovice, Ron	.333	6	2	0	1	.167	60	10	0	5
Kelly, Roberto	.400	55	22	1	6	.364	121	44	1	17
Kittle, Ron	.100	10	1	0	0	.228	171	39	17	30
Komminsk, Brad	-	-	-	-	-	.048	21	1	0	1
Kreuter, Chad	.000	6	0	0	0	.182	11	2	0	0
Kunkel, Jeff	.167	24	4	0	0	.193	83	16	1	5
Kutcher, Randy	.250	4	1	0	0	.125	24	3	0	1
Lansford, Carney	.242	33	8	0	2	.283	466	132	11	57
Larkin, Gene	.267	30	8	1	2	.288	104	30	2	11
Laudner, Tim	-	-	-	-	-	.190	126	24	1	9
Leach, Rick	-	-	-	-	-	.556	9	5	0	0
Lemon, Chet	.343	35	12	2	5	.266	526	140	19	62
Leonard, Jeff	.238	42	10	2	8	.231	108	25	2	13
Lusader, Scott	-	-	-	-	-	.286	14	4	1	2
Lynn, Fred	-	-	-	-	-	.261	468	122	20	56
Lyons, Steve	.250	8	2	1	1	.246	130	32	2	7
Maas, Kevin	.250	20	5	2	3	.250	20	5	2	3
Macfarlane, Mike	.231	26	6	2	3	.267	45	12	2	3
Mack, Shane	.292	24	7	2	8	.292	24	7	2	8
Magrann, Tom	-	-	-	-	-	.000	4	0	0	0
Maldonado, Candy	.200	45	9	4	7	.200	45	9	4	7
Manrique, Fred	.333	24	8	0	4	.290	107	31	2	21
Manto, Jeff	.200	5	1	0	0	.200	5	1	0	0
Marshall, Mike	.364	11	4	0	2	.364	11	4	0	2
Martinez, Carlos	.250	24	6	1	4	.242	66	16	2	8
Martinez, Edgar	.364	44	16	0	5	.321	81	26	1	10
Marzano, John	.000	1	0	0	0	.308	13	4	0	1
Mattingly, Don	.233	43	10	0	3	.341	396	135	14	62
McDowell, Oddibe	-	-	-	-	-	.243	148	36	6	16
McCray, Rodney	.000	2	0	0	0	.000	2	0	0	0
McGuire, Mike	-	-	-	-	-	.250	4	1	0	0
McGwire, Mark	.093	43	4	0	1	.225	160	36	9	31
McKnight, Jeff	.385	13	5	0	1	.385	13	5	0	1
McLemore, Mark	-	-	-	-	-	.300	50	15	0	7
McCrae, Brian	.250	8	2	0	0	.250	8	2	0	0
Medina, Luis	-	-	-	-	-	.182	33	6	2	3
Melendez, Francisco	-	-	-	-	-	.5	2	1	0	3
Melvin, Bob	.258	31	8	0	2	.241	58	14	0	4
Mercado, Orlando	-	-	-	-	-	.000	2	0	0	0
Merullo, Matt	-	-	-	-	-	.200	5	1	0	1
Meulens, Hensley	.200	10	2	1	2	.200	10	2	1	2
Meyer, Joey	-	-	-	-	-	.364	33	12	2	10
Milligan, Randy	.318	22	7	1	3	.346	52	18	2	9
Molitor, Paul	.273	55	15	3	10	.284	552	157	12	59
Moreland, Keith	-	-	-	-	-	.222	36	8	0	2
Morman, Russ	-	-	-	-	-	.278	18	5	0	0
Morris, Hal	-	-	-	-	-	.250	4	1	0	0
Moseby, Lloyd	.171	35	6	2	4	.171	35	6	2	4
Moses, John	.125	8	1	0	0	.231	91	21	0	9
Murray, Eddie	-	-	-	-	-	.295	518	153	25	89
Newman, Al	.190	21	4	0	0	.247	89	22	0	3
Nokes, Matt	.154	13	2	0	2	.236	89	21	4	12
O'Brien, Charlie	.083	12	1	0	0	.237	38	9	2	2
O'Brien, Pete	.300	20	6	1	2	.246	338	83	17	49
Orsulak, Joe	.250	12	3	0	3	.355	62	22	1	13
Ortiz, Jr.	.167	12	2	0	1	.167	12	2	0	1
Orton, John	.143	7	1	0	0	.143	7	1	0	0
Pagliarulo, Mike	-	-	-	-	-	.184	174	32	3	15
Palacios, Rey	-	-	-	-	-	0	0	0	0	0
Palmeiro, Rafael	.390	41	16	1	6	.287	87	25	3	11
Parker, Dave	.302	53	16	4	7	.267	105	28	6	17
Parrish, Lance	.206	34	7	2	5	.247	425	105	22	61
Pasqua, Dan	.200	20	4	0	0	.178	107	19	0	9
Pecota, Bill	.235	17	4	0	1	.286	42	12	1	3
Pena, Tony	.279	43	12	0	4	.279	43	12	0	4
Perry, Gerald	.314	35	11	1	2	.314	35	11	1	2
Pedrique, Al	-	-	-	-	-	.200	5	1	0	0
Petralli, Geno	.056	18	1	0	0	.286	91	26	1	14
Pettis, Gary	.326	46	15	0	2	.247	247	61	3	19
Phelps, Ken	-	-	-	-	-	.254	114	29	11	31
Phillips, Tony	.259	54	14	1	4	.235	247	58	3	25

	1990					LIFETIME				
	AVG.	AB	HITS	HR	RBI	AVG.	AB	HITS	HR	RBI
Plantier, Phil	.250	4	1	0	0	.250	4	1	0	0
Polidor, Gus	-	-	-	-	-	.143	21	3	0	1
Polonia, Luis	.333	30	10	0	2	.361	97	35	3	10
Presley, Jim	-	-	-	-	-	.246	236	58	8	30
Puckett, Kirky	.319	47	15	0	4	.274	339	93	5	33
Quintana, Luis	.244	41	10	1	4	.292	65	19	1	8
Quirk, Jamie	.429	7	3	0	4	.234	167	39	5	25
Randolph, Willie	.214	28	6	1	1	.223	188	42	6	22
Ray, Johnny	.355	31	11	0	3	.361	144	52	0	20
Reed, Jody	.327	55	18	1	3	.276	116	32	1	8
Reimer, Kevin	.200	5	1	0	0	.200	5	1	0	0
Reynolds, Harold	.213	47	10	0	5	.242	211	51	0	15
Richie, Rob	-	-	-	-	-	.100	10	1	0	0
Ripken, Billy	.316	38	12	1	2	.268	97	26	1	3
Ripken, Cal	.288	52	15	3	9	.349	338	118	18	67
Rivera, Luis	.175	40	7	0	2	.174	69	12	0	4
Romero, Ed	.000	5	0	0	0	.217	175	38	0	9
Romine, Kevin	.125	8	1	0	1	.340	50	17	0	2
Russell, John	.333	18	6	0	1	.333	18	6	0	1
Ryal, Mark	-	-	-	-	-	.333	3	1	0	0
Salas, Mark	.429	14	6	0	1	.293	82	24	2	6
Sanders, Deion	.091	11	1	0	0	.091	11	1	0	0
Santana, Rafael	.000	1	0	0	0	.000	1	0	0	0
Sax, Steve	.264	53	14	0	4	.282	110	31	1	11
Schaefer, Danny	.000	1	0	0	0	.000	1	0	0	0
Schofield, Dick	.130	23	3	0	0	.200	215	43	2	5
Schroeder, Bill	.286	7	2	0	0	.239	109	26	2	5
Schu, Rick	.385	13	5	0	0	.241	83	20	2	3
Schulz, Jeff	.583	12	7	0	3	.583	12	7	0	3
Seitzer, Kevin	.302	53	16	0	0	.282	174	49	1	12
Sequi, David	.455	11	5	1	4	.455	11	5	1	4
Sheets, Larry	.240	25	6	2	6	.286	168	48	7	22
Sheffield, Gary	.214	28	6	0	1	.236	55	13	0	5
Shelby, John	.231	13	3	0	0	.231	13	3	0	0
Shumpert, Terry	.000	2	0	0	0	.000	2	0	0	0
Sierra, Ruben	.373	51	19	1	8	.309	217	67	9	33
Sinatro, Matt	.375	8	3	0	0	.294	17	5	0	0
Skinner, Joel	.143	7	1	0	0	.25	56	14	1	4
Slaught, Don	-	-	-	-	-	.241	199	48	4	22
Snyder, Cory	.184	38	7	1	5	.193	207	40	12	31
Sorrento, Paul	-	-	-	-	-	.500	4	2	0	0
Sosa, Sammy	.394	33	13	3	10	.348	46	16	3	11
Spiers, Billy	.294	34	10	0	3	.224	67	15	0	3
Stanley, Mike	.214	14	3	0	1	.237	59	14	0	2
Steinbach, Terry	.280	25	7	0	1	.263	95	25	4	16
Stillwell, Kurt	.161	31	5	0	5	.196	92	18	2	15
Stone, Jeff	.500	2	1	0	1	.286	7	2	0	1
Strange, Doug	-	-	-	-	-	.187	16	3	0	0
Sundberg, Jim	-	-	-	-	-	.257	343	88	8	38
Surhoff, B.J.	.422	45	19	0	11	.326	141	46	2	27
Sveum, Dale	.333	9	3	1	4	.221	136	30	3	22
Tabler, Pat	.187	16	3	0	1	.275	284	78	4	35
Tartabull, Danny	-	-	-	-	-	.260	169	44	6	24
Tettleton, Mickey	.233	30	7	1	4	.263	133	35	5	23
Thomas, Frank	.500	18	9	0	2	.500	18	9	0	2
Thurman, Gary	.250	8	2	0	1	.261	23	6	0	2
Tolleson, Wayne	.000	5	0	0	0	.241	166	40	1	10
Traber, Jim	-	-	-	-	-	.233	90	21	4	8
Trammell, Allan	.380	50	19	3	10	.304	556	169	14	66
Valle, Dave	.267	15	4	0	2	.220	91	20	3	16
Vaughn, Greg	.381	21	8	0	4	.333	33	11	1	6
Velarde, Randy	.125	8	1	0	0	.256	39	10	0	9
Venable, Max	.231	13	3	0	3	.333	21	7	0	3
Ventura, Robin	.174	23	4	0	0	.174	23	4	0	0
Vizquel, Omar	.333	12	4	0	0	.277	47	13	1	3
Walewander, Jim	-	-	-	-	-	.385	26	10	0	1
Walker, Greg	-	-	-	-	-	.197	213	42	3	14
Ward, Gary	.250	28	7	1	1	.255	357	91	12	37
Ward, Turner	.500	8	4	0	1	.500	8	4	0	1
Washington, Claudell	-	-	-	-	-	.282	170	48	3	18
Webster, Mitch	.241	29	7	2	5	.241	29	7	2	5
Weiss, Walt	.333	36	12	0	5	.256	82	21	0	10
Wellman, Brad	-	-	-	-	-	.364	22	8	0	2
Whitaker, Lou	.133	30	4	0	2	.282	586	165	9	65
White, Devon	.100	30	3	1	2	.208	168	35	5	19
White, Frank	.080	25	2	0	3	.187	482	90	5	36
Wilkerson, Curtis	-	-	-	-	-	.248	117	29	1	8
Willard, Jerry	.000	1	0	0	0	.000	1	0	0	0
Williams, Dana	-	-	-	-	-	0	0	0	0	0
Williams, Eddie	-	-	-	-	-	.150	20	3	0	1
Williams, Kenny	.167	6	1	0	0	.238	63	15	2	4
Wilson, Willie	.280	25	7	0	4	.249	466	116	2	31
Winfield, Dave	.256	43	11	3	5	.307	387	119	18	69

	1990 AVG.	AB	HITS	HR	RBI	LIFETIME AVG.	AB	HITS	HR	RBI
Winters, Matt	-	-	-	-	-	.250	4	1	0	0
Worthington, Craig	.256	43	11	1	7	.266	94	25	2	16
Young, Mike	-	-	-	-	-	.194	124	24	4	10
Yount, Robin	.234	47	11	1	7	.340	652	222	21	107
Zuvella, Paul	-	-	-	-	-	.235	17	4	1	1

OPPOSING PITCHERS

1990 SEASON	ERA	W-L-S	G	IP	ER	LIFETIME ERA	W-L-S	G	IP	ER
Abbott, Jim	2.48	2-1-0	4	29.0	8	2.63	3-2-0	7	51.1	15
Abbott, Paul	-	---	-	-	-	-	-	-	-	-
Adkins, Steve	6.75	0-0-0	1	4.0	3	6.75	0-0-0	1	4.0	3
Aguilera, Rick	0.00	0-0-0	1	1.0	0	0.00	1-0-0	2	8.0	0
Akerfelds, Darrel	-	-	-	-	-	19.06	0-2-0	2	5.2	12
Aldrich, Jay	13.50	0-0-0	1	1.1	2	4.15	1-0-0	2	4.1	2
Alexander, Doyle	-	-	-	-	-	3.91	5-4-0	16	103.2	45
Allen, Neil	-	-	-	-	-	4.66	0-2-0	10	36.2	19
Alvarez, Wilson	-	-	-	-	-	INF	0-1-0	1	0.0	3
Andersen, Larry	0	0-0-0	1	0.2	0	0.00	0-0-0	1	0.2	0
Anderson, Allan	4.38	1-2-0	3	24.2	12	3.72	3-3-0	9	58.0	24
Appier, Kevin	6.00	0-1-0	1	6.0	4	6.00	0-1-0	1	6.0	4
Aquino, Luis	11.57	0-0-0	2	4.2	6	2.66	2-0-0	5	20.1	6
Arnsberg, Brad	1.59	2-0-0	3	5.2	1	2.25	2-0-0	4	8.0	2
Atherton, Keith	-	-	-	-	-	7.60	1-4-1	25	34.1	29
August, Don	-	-	-	-	-	4.26	3-1-0	4	19.0	9
Bailes, Scott	12.27	1-0-0	5	3.2	5	2.70	5-1-1	22	53.1	16
Ballard, Jeff	6.52	0-2-0	5	9.2	7	4.21	3-6-0	13	66.1	31
Bankhead, Scott	0.00	0-0-0	1	5.0	0	3.08	6-2-0	10	64.1	22
Barfield, John	0.00	0-0-1	2	1.0	0	0.00	0-0-1	2	1.0	0
Bannister, Floyd	-	-	-	-		3.70	9-10-0	26	170.1	70
Bautista, Jose	0.00	0-0-0	1	0.1	0	6.87	0-1-0	5	18.1	14
Bearse, Kevin	27.00	0-1-0	2	2.1	7	27.00	0-1-0	2	2.1	7
Berenguer, Juan	7.94	0-0-0	4	5.2	5	3.79	3-1-0	17	57.0	24
Black, Bud	1.17	1-1-0	2	15.1	2	3.21	11-5-0	27	137.1	49
Blyleven, Bert	5.59	0-1-0	2	9.2	6	3.58	8-10-0	20	148.1	59
Boddicker, Mike	4.73	1-0-0	2	13.1	7	4.33	8-11-0	24	162.0	78
Booker, Greg	-	-	-	-	-	4.50	0-0-0	1	2.0	1
Bohanon, Brian	0.00	0-0-0	1	1.0	0	0.00	0-0-0	1	1.0	0
Bolton, Tom	9.39	0-0-0	2	7.2	8	10.6	4-0-0	0	6	11.0
Boone, Dan	0.00	0-0-0	1	2.1	0	0.00	0-0-0	1	2.1	0
Bosio, Chris	5.87	0-1-0	1	7.2	5	4.88	2-5-0	12	55.1	30
Boyd, Dennis	-	-	-	-	-	4.43	1-1-0	3	22.1	11
Brown, Kevin	3.43	1-0-0	3	21.0	8	3.32	2-1-0	6	40.2	15
Burns, Todd	5.79	1-1-0	3	4.2	3	2.00	3-1-1	8	18.0	4
Cadaret, Greg	1.69	2-0-0	5	16.0	-	3.82	2-2-0	14	30.2	13
Campbell, Mike	-	-	-	-	-	7.80	0-2-0	3	15.0	13
Candelaria, John	0.00	1-1-0	2	5.2	0	3.2	6-4-0	11	64.1	23
Candiotti, Tom	5.75	1-2-0	3	20.1	13	4.7	24-7-0	12	80.0	42
Capel, Mike	INF	0-0-0	1	0.0	0	INF	0-0-0	1	0.0	3
Cary, Chuck	8.00	1-1-0	2	9.0	8	5.00	2-1-0	3	18.0	10
Clark, Bryan	11.57	0-0-0	4	2.1	3	4.10	3-2-0	16	37.1	17
Clemens, Roger	1.17	3-0-0	3	23.0	3	2.25	9-4-0	18	132.0	33
Clutterbuck, Bryan	-	-	-	-	-	7.20	0-0-0	1	5.0	4
Comstock, Keith	1.23	1-0-0	7	7.1	1	0.90	1-0-0	8	10.0	1
Cook, Mike	-	-	-	-	-	4.26	0-1-0	5	12.2	6
Corsi, Jim	-	-	-	-	-	8.10	0-1-0	4	6.2	6
Crawford, Steve	10.80	0-1-0	4	3.1	4	4.30	3-1-1	26	58.2	28
Crim, Chuck	7.94	0-1-1	4	5.2	5	4.94	0-2-5	19	27.1	15
Davis, Steve	-	---	-	-	-	20.25	0-0-0	1	1.1	3
Davis, Mark	1.86	0-0-2	6	9.2	2	1.86	0-0-2	6	9.2	2
Davis, Storm	4.82	0-1-0	2	9.1	5	3.66	6-4-0	18	103.1	42
Dawley, Bill	-	---	-	-	-	0.00	0-0-0	1	4.1	0
Dopson, John	-	---	-	-	-	17.18	0-1-0	1	3.2	7
Dotson, Richard	-	---	-	-	-	2.99	9-10-0	24	159.2	53
Drummond, Tim	7.36	0-0-0	1	3.2	3	7.36	0-0-0	1	3.2	3
Dubois, Brian	11.37	0-2-0	2	6.1	8	4.43	0-3-0	4	20.1	10
Dunne, Mike	-	---	-	-	-	7.41	0-3-0	3	17.0	14
Eave, Gary	1.50	0-0-0	1	6.0	1	1.50	0-0-0	1	6.0	1
Eckersley, Dennis	0.00	0-0-4	4	5.0	0	2.99	9-5-11	33	150.1	50
Edens, Tom	7.71	0-0-0	3	4.2	-	7.71	0-0-0	3	4.2	4
Edwards, Wayne	3.00	0-1-1	3	6.0	2	3.00	0-1-1	3	6.0	2
Eichhorn, Mark	1.29	1-0-2	5	7.0	1	1.29	1-0-2	5	7.0	1
Elvira, Narcisco	INF	0-0-0	1	0.0	1	INF	0-0-0	1	0.0	1
Erickson, Scott	2.70	0-1-0	1	6.2	2	2.70	0-1-0	1	6.2	2
Farr, Steve	0.90	1-0-0	4	10.0	1	3.02	2-2-3	23	44.2	15

	1990 SEASON					LIFETIME				
	ERA	W-L-S	G	IP	ER	ERA	W-L-S	G	IP	ER
Farrell, John	6.52	0-0-0	2	9.2	7	3.83	2-1-0	4	44.2	19
Filer, Tom	-	---	-	-	-	5.73	2-1-0	4	22.0	14
Fernandez, Alex	1.69	0-1-0	2	16.0	3	1.69	0-1-0	2	16.0	3
Fetters, Mike	5.11	0-0-0	4	12.1	7	5.11	0-0-0	4	12.1	7
Finley, Chuck	2.00	1-0-0	1	9.0	2	6.16	2-2-0	8	30.2	21
Fossas, Tony	0.00	1-0-0	2	3.0	0	1.50	2-0-0	9	12.0	2
Fraser, Willie	3.24	1-0-0	5	8.1	3	4.28	2-1-0	11	33.2	16
Gardner, Wes	3.38	1-1-0	4	13.1	5	3.70	1-3-1	13	41.1	17
Gibson, Paul	2.13	1-0-0	6	12.2	3	4.64	1-1-0	18	42.2	22
Gleaton, Jerry Don	2.45	0-0-1	6	7.1	2	4.50	0-0-4	17	18.0	9
Gonzales, German	-	---	-	-	-	13.50	0-0-0	2	3.1	5
Gordon, Tom	2.36	2-0-0	4	26.2	7	2.44	5-1-0	13	51.2	14
Gray, Jeff	5.63	0-0-3	8	8.0	5	5.63	0-0-3	8	8.0	5
Guante, Cecilio	6.00	0-0-0	2	3.0	2	6.63	0-1-0	16	19.0	14
Gubicza, Mark	6.75	0-1-0	1	4.0	3	4.74	4-7-0	14	79.2	42
Guetterman, Lee	3.86	0-1-1	4	9.1	4	2.56	1-1-3	21	45.2	13
Gullickson, Bill	-	---	-	-	-	1.29	1-0-0	1	7.0	1
Guthrie, Mark	8.10	0-1-0	2	10.0	9	6.33	1-2-0	4	21.1	15
Guzman, Jose	-	---	-	-	-	5.24	1-0-0	6	34.1	20
Hall, Drew	-	---	-	-	-	0.90	0-0-0	4	10.0	1
Hanson, Erik	5.14	0-1-0	1	7.0	4	3.21	1-1-0	2	14.0	5
Hardy, John	-	---	-	-	-	0.00	0-0-0	1	2.0	0
Harnisch, Pete	3.86	1-0-0	2	14.0	6	3.54	2-0-0	3	20.1	8
Harris, Greg	3.86	1-0-0	2	9.1	4	4.14	3-4-2	10	45.2	21
Harris, Gene	18.00	0-0-0	1	1.0	2	9.35	0-1-0	3	8.2	9
Harris, Reggie	0.00	0-0-0	1	3.0	0	0.00	0-0-0	1	3.0	0
Harvey, Bryan	5.14	1-0-0	4	7.0	4	3.13	4-1-1	12	23.0	8
Hawkins, Andy	2.53	1-0-0	3	21.1	6	4.50	3-2-0	7	46.0	23
Henneman, Mike	5.14	0-1-2	5	7.0	4	4.46	4-3-3	22	36.1	18
Hernandez, Guillermo	-	---	-	-	-	3.57	2-5-6	29	35.1	14
Hesketh, Joe	7.36	0-2-0	2	3.2	3	7.36	0-2-0	2	3.2	3
Hibbard, Greg	3.00	2-1-0	3	18.0	6	3.00	2-1-0	3	18.0	6
Hetzel, Eric	-	---	-	-	-	0.00	1-0-0	1	5.2	0
Hickey, Kevin	0.00	0-0-0	2	0.2	0	6.75	1-0-0	5	2.2	2
Higuera, Teddy	1.80	2-0-0	2	15.0	3	3.81	9-4-0	16	101.2	43
Hillegas, Shawn	-	---	-	-	-	9.58	0-2-0	2	10.1	11
Holman, Brian	4.44	1-2-0	4	26.1	13	3.93	1-2-0	5	34.1	15
Holton, Brian	12.71	0-0-0	2	5.2	8	6.59	0-0-0	4	13.2	10
Honeycutt, Rick	0.00	0-0-1	6	5.0	0	2.60	9-4-4	33	117.2	34
Hough, Charlie	1.83	1-2-0	3	19.2	4	4.52	7-11-0	25	153.1	77
Irvine, Daryl	0.00	0-0-0	2	3.1	0	0.00	0-0-0	2	3.1	0
Jackson, Mike	3.38	1-0-0	4	5.1	-	3.07	1-1-1	10	14.2	5
Jeffcoat, Mike	4.76	0-0-1	2	5.2	3	2.08	0-1-1	3	13.0	3
Johnson, Dave	4.73	0-1-0	2	13.1	-	5.40	0-2-0	4	23.1	14
Johnson, Randy	5.68	1-1-0	2	12.2	8	3.74	2-1-0	3	21.2	9
Jones, Barry	0.00	0-0-0	2	1.2	0	3.38	0-0-0	6	5.1	2
Jones, Doug	1.42	0-0-4	5	6.1	1	1.13	1-1-10	14	24.0	3
Jones, Jimmy	1.59	0-0-0	1	5.2	1	1.59	0-0-0	1	5.2	1
Kaiser, Jeff	-	---	-	-	-	8.10	0-1-0	5	6.2	6
Kiecker, Dana	2.60	2-0-0	3	17.1	5	2.60	2-0-0	3	17.1	5
Kilgus, Paul	-	---	-	-	-	3.47	1-0-0	4	23.1	9
King, Eric	5.40	1-0-0	1	5.0	3	4.93	2-2-1	11	34.2	19
Knackert, Brent	4.91	0-0-0	4	3.2	2	4.91	0-0-0	4	3.2	2
Knudson, Mark	8.80	0-2-0	3	15.1	15	6.18	0-2-0	7	27.2	19
Krueger, Bill	2.70	2-0-0	3	16.2	5	2.51	2-1-1	7	28.2	8
Kutzler, Jerry	5.79	1-0-0	2	9.1	6	5.79	1-0-0	2	9.1	6
Lamp, Dennis	7.88	1-0-0	2	8.0	7	4.66	3-5-4	30	75.1	39
Langston, Mark	5.14	0-1-0	1	7.0	4	5.69	3-9-0	14	91.2	58
La Point, Dave	5.59	0-1-0	4	19.1	12	5.74	2-4-0	11	58.0	37
Leibrandt, Charlie	-	---	-	-	-	4.04	5-6-0	17	111.1	50
Long, Bill	-	---	-	-	-	4.43	1-0-1	8	20.1	10
Leach, Terry	6.23	0-1-0	3	4.1	3	6.23	0-1-0	3	4.1	3
Leary, Tim	11.32	0-2-0	2	10.1	13	11.32	0-2-0	2	10.1	13
Lee, Mark	4.50	0-0-0	1	2.0	1	4.50	0-0-0	1	2.0	1
Luecken, Rick	-	---	-	-	-	9.00	0-0-0	1	1.0	1
Lugo, Urbano	9.00	0-0-0	3	7.0	7	6.20	0-1-0	6	20.1	14
McCarthy, Tom	-	---	-	-	-	2.70	0-0-0	4	6.2	2
Machado, Julio	0.00	0-0-0	1	0.2	0	0.00	0-0-0	1	0.2	0
McCaskill, Kirk	6.00	0-2-0	3	12.0	8	4.27	5-6-0	15	90.2	43
McClure, Bob	-	---	-	-	-	5.40	2-1-0	5	6.2	4
McCullers, Lance	-	---	-	-	-	4.50	0-0-0	3	2.0	1
McDonald, Ben	2.30	1-0-0	2	15.2		2.16	2-0-0	3	16.2	4
McDowell, Jack	5.50	1-2-0	3	18.0	11	5.25	2-2-0	4	24.0	14
McGaffigan, Andy	0.00	1-0-0	1	5.0	0	0.00	1-0-0	1	5.0	0
McMurtry, Craig	INF	0-1-0	1	0.0	3	4.50	0-2-0	5	6.0	3
McWilliams, Larry	16.88	0-0-0	3	2.2	5	16.88	0-0-0	3	2.2	5
Mesa, Jose	3.14	2-0-0	2	14.1	-	4.42	2-1-0	3	18.1	9
Mielke, Gary	3.00	0-0-0	3	6.0	2	4.26	0-0-0	4	6.1	3
Milacki, Bob	12.27	0-1-0	2	3.2	5	6.33	1-2-0	5	21.1	15
Mills, Alan	3.18	1-1-0	3	5.2	2	3.18	1-1-0	3	5.2	2
Minton, Greg	-	---	-	-	-	2.81	2-1-2	11	16.0	5
Mirabella, Paul	3.72	0-0-0	4	9.2	4	3.74	1-1-0	17	33.2	14

	1990					LIFETIME				
	ERA	W-L-S	G	IP	ER	ERA	W-L-S	G	IP	E
Mitchell, John	0.00	0-0-0	2	3.1	0	0.00	0-0-0	2	3.1	0
Mohorcic, Dale	-	---	-	-	-	4.87	2-0-3	19	20.1	11
Monteleone, Rick	-	---	-	-	-	0.00	0-0-0	3	6.1	0
Montgomery, Jeff	5.40	0-0-0	5	5.0	3	2.40	1-0-0	12	15.0	4
Moore, Mike	1.09	2-1-0	3	24.2	3	3.68	6-13-0	24	164.0	67
Morris, Jack	9.26	0-2-0	2	11.2	12	4.31	12-12-0	31	217.0	104
Moyer, Jamie	5.00	1-1-0	3	18.0	10	4.85	2-1-0	4	26.0	14
Murphy, Rob	0.00	0-0-1	4	3.1	0	2.70	1-1-3	12	13.1	4
Nagy, Chuck	4.50	0-0-0	2	8.0	4	4.50	0-0-0	2	8.0	4
Navarro, Jaime	6.35	1-2-0	3	17.0	12	6.00	1-2-0	4	18.0	12
Nelson, Gene	6.75	0-0-0	2	1.1	1	4.53	3-2-2	12	51.2	26
Nichols, Rod	5.40	0-1-0	1	3.1	2	3.42	0-3-0	4	26.1	10
Nieves, Juan	-	---	-	-	-	2.53	4-1-0	6	32.0	9
Nunez, Edwin	2.45	0-0-0	2	3.2	1	2.27	0-2-0	19	39.2	10
Olin, Steve	0.00	0-0-0	5	6.2	0	0.90	0-1-0	9	10.0	1
Olson, Gregg	3.68	1-1-4	7	7.1	3	2.20	1-1-6	13	16.1	4
Orosco, Jesse	2.79	0-0-0	7	9.2	3	2.20	0-0-0	15	16.1	4
Pall, Donn	1.42	0-0-0	4	6.1	1	2.08	0-1-0	9	13.0	3
Parker, Clay	8.10	0-1-0	2	3.1	3	6.75	0-2-0	4	14.2	11
Patterson, Ken	0.00	0-0-0	2	2.1	0	3.38	0-0-0	6	8.0	3
Peraza, Oswald	-	---	-	-	-	2.45	1-0-0	1	7.1	2
Perez, Melido	4.05	0-1-0	1	6.2	3	3.52	3-3-0	7	46.0	18
Peterek, Jeff	-	---	-	-	-	4.00	0-1-0	2	9.0	4
Peterson, Adam	18.00	0-0-0	1	4.0	8	18.00	0-0-0	1	4.0	8
Petry, Dan	1.29	1-0-0	1	7.0	1	4.15	5-4-0	20	110.2	51
Plesac, Dan	4.15	0-0-2	5	4.1	2	2.48	1-3-12	25	29.0	8
Plunk, Eric	2.35	0-1-0	4	7.2	2	2.51	3-3-0	14	43.0	12
Powell, Dennis	-	---	-	-	-	9.53	0-1-1	7	5.2	6
Price, Joe	3.86	0-1-0	4	2.1	1	3.68	0-1-0	8	7.1	3
Radinsky, Scott	3.38	0-0-0	6	2.2	1	3.38	0-0-0	6	2.2	1
Rawley, Shane	-	---	-	-	-	2.51	1-0-0	2	14.1	4
Reardon, Jeff	2.08	1-0-4	5	4.1	1	2.42	1-1-15	21	22.1	6
Reed, Jerry	-	---	-	-	-	1.67	1-1-0	19	27.0	5
Reuss, Jerry	-	---	-	-	-	5.75	2-2-0	11	36.0	23
Righetti, Dave	5.40	0-0-3	5	5.0	3	4.09	7-5-18	45	83.2	38
Robinson, Jeff	-	---	-	-	-	10.80	0-4-0	5	21.2	26
Robinson, Ron	0.00	1-0-0	1	9.0	0	0.00	1-0-0	1	9.0	0
Rogers, Kenny	4.70	0-0-1	6	7.2	4	2.50	1-0-1	13	18.0	5
Rosenberg, Steve	0.00	0-0-1		1.0	0	6.04	0-2-1	7	22.1	15
Russell, Jeff	0.00	0-0-1	1	1.1	0	6.57	2-3-3	15	24.2	18
Ryan, Nolan	3.21	1-1-0	2	14.0	5	.40	6-4-0	12	97.2	26
Saberhagen, Brett	4.76	1-1-0	2	11.1	6	4.56	4-8-1	19	100.2	51
Sanderson, Scott	3.00	0-1-0	2	15.0	5	3.00	0-1-0	2	15.0	5
Savage, Jack	16.88	0-0-0	2	2.2	5	16.88	0-0-0	2	2.2	5
Schilling, Curt	6.75	0-1-0	3	1.1	1	12.46	0-2-0	5	4.1	6
Schmidt, Dave	-	---	-	-	-	3.47	5-4-2	24	57.0	22
Schooler, Mike	0.00	0-0-3	4	4.0	0	2.53	1-1-5	11	10.2	3
Schwabe, Mike	-	---	-	-	-	4.26	0-1-0	1	6.1	3
Seanez, Rudy	-	---	-	-	-	0.00	0-0-0	1	2.0	0
Searcy, Steve	0.00	0-0-0	1	2.2	0	0.00	0-0-0	1	2.2	0
Shaw, Jeff	6.00	1-0-0	2	12.0	8	6.00	1-0-0	2	12.0	8
Segura, Jose	-	---	-	-	-	43.20	0-0-0	2	1.2	8
Shields, Steve	-	---	-	-	-	4.15	0-0-0	9	8.2	4
Smith, Lee	-	---	-	-	-	10.13	0-0-2	8	8.0	9
Smith, Mike	-	---	-	-	-	0.00	0-0-0	1	1.2	0
Smith, Roy	6.30	0-1-0	2	10.0	7	5.82	0-2-0	3	17.0	11
Smithson, Mike	-	---	-	-	-	6.39	2-11-0	19	94.1	67
Snyder, Brian	-	---	-	-	-	13.50	0-0-0	1	0.2	1
Solano, Julio	-	---	-	-	-	0.00	0-0-1	3	3.2	0
Stanley, Bob	-	---	-	-	-	2.77	14-8-7	56	175.1	54
Stewart, Dave	0.50	1-1-0	2	18.0	1	2.32	9-5-0	17	108.2	28
Stoddard, Tim	-	---	-	-	-	6.00	0-2-3	24	24.0	16
Stottlemyre, Mel	9.00	0-1-0	2	5.0	5	9.00	0-1-0	2	5.0	5
Swan, Russ	13.50	0-1-0	1	2.0	3	13.50	0-1-0	1	2.0	3
Swift, Bill	3.24	0-1-0	3	8.1	3	5.23	0-4-0	9	32.2	19
Swindell, Greg	9.26	0-2-0	2	11.2	12	6.52	1-6-0	10	58.0	42
Tanana, Frank	3.38	0-0-0	3	18.2	7	2.61	10-8-0	30	213.2	62
Tapani, Kevin	8.44	0-1-0	2	10.2	10	5.40	1-1-0	3	18.1	11
Telford, Anthony	5.79	0-0-0	1	4.2	3	5.79	0-0-0	1	4.2	3
Terrell, Walt	4.09	1-1-0	2	11.0	5	4.26	5-8-0	15	93.0	44
Thigpen, Bobby	4.50	0-1-3	5	6.0	3	3.76	1-3-8	20	26.1	11
Thurmond, Mark	-	---	-	-	-	0.50	0-0-3	12	18.0	1
Tibbs, Jay	7.20	0-1-0	1	5.0	4	5.93	2-3-0	5	30.1	20
Trout, Steve	-	---	-	-	-	4.50	2-1-0	4	14.0	7
Trujillo, Mike	-	---	-	-	-	3.29	1-0-0	7	13.2	5
Valdez, Sergio	2.08	1-0-0	3	4.1	1	2.08	1-0-0	3	4.1	1
Veres, Randy	2.25	0-0-0	2	4.0	1	3.60	0-0-0	3	5.0	2
Viola, Frank	-	---	-	-	-	5.02	5-12-0	22	141.2	79
Wagner, Hector	7.11	0-1-0	1	6.1	5	7.11	0-1-0	1	6.1	5
Ward, Colby	13.50	0-1-0	3	2.0	3	13.50	0-1-0	3	2.0	3
Wayne, Gary	13.50	0-0-0	3	3.1	5	6.75	0-0-0	7	6.2	5
Wegman, Bill	108.00	0-0-1	0	0.1	4	5.40	3-3-1	8	45.0	27

1990 SEASON	ERA	W-L-S	G	IP	ER	LIFETIME ERA	W-L-S	G	IP	E
Welch, Bob	3.14	2-0-0	2	14.1	5	4.32	3-2-0	6	41.2	20
West, Dave	3.24	1-1-0	2	16.2	6	2.66	2-1-0	3	23.2	7
Weston, Mickey	9.00	0-0-0	1	4.0	4	9.00	0-0-0	1	4.0	4
Wickander, Kevin	4.91	0-1-0	2	3.2	2	4.91	0-1-0	2	3.2	2
Williams, Frank	-	---	-	-	-	1.93	1-0-0	4	4.2	1
Williamson, Mark	6.23	0-0-0	2	4.1	3	4.23	0-2-2	16	27.2	13
Wilmet, Paul	-	---	-	-	-	54.00	0-0-0	1	0.2	4
Witt, Bobby	2.00	1-0-0	1	9.0	2	4.70	3-2-0	10	53.2	28
Witt, Mike	2.25	0-0-0	1	8.0	2	3.67	4-9-0	22	154.2	63
Wojna, Ed	-	---	-	-	-	2.45	0-0-0	3	3.2	1
Yett, Rich	-	---	-	-	-	5.35	1-0-0	14	33.2	20
Young, Curt	-	---	-	-	-	6.84	4-3-0	15	48.2	37
Young, Matt	2.00	2-0-0	2	18.0	4	2.00	2-0-0	5	27.0	6

OPPONENTS CAREER HOMERS AT SKYDOME

ALOMAR 1
BAINES 2
BALBONI 2
BARFIELD . . . 2
BELLE 1
BICHETTE . . . 1
BRADLEY (P) . . 2
BRAGGS 1
BRETT 2
BRILEY 1
BROCK 1
BUECHELE . . . 2
CALDERON . . . 1
CANSECO . . . 4
CARTER 1
CASTILLO 1
CLARK 1
COTTO 2
DEER 1
EISENREICH . . 1
ESASKY 2
EVANS (DW) . . 2
FIELDER 4
FINLEY 1
GAETTI 2
GAGNE 1
GEREN 1
GILES 2
GLADDEN 1
GREENWELL . . 2
HALL 1
HEEP 1
HENDERSON (D) 2
HENDERSON (R) 2
HERNANDEZ . . 1
HILL 1
HORN 1
HRBEK 1
INCAVIGLIA . . . 1
JACKSON (B) . . 1
JAMES (C) . . . 1
JOYNER 2
KITTLE 2
LEMON 3
LEONARD . . . 1
LEYRITZ 1
LYONS 1
MAAS 1
MACK 2
MacFARLANE . 2
MalDONADO . . 2
MARTINEZ . . . 1
MATTINGLY . . 1
McGWIRE 2
MEVLENS 1
MILLIGAN 1
MOLITOR 1
MOSEBY 1
NOKES 2
PARKER 5
PARRISH 1
PHELPS 1
RIPKEN (C) . . . 3
RIPKEN (B) . . . 1
SEGUI 1
SHEETS 1
SIERRA 1
STIENBACH . . 1
TRAMMELL . . . 2
VAUGHN 1
WARD 2
WEBSTER . . . 2
WHITAKER . . . 1
WHITE (D) . . . 1
WILLIAMS (K) . . 1
WINFIELD 1
WORTHINGTON 2
YOUNT 1

OPPONENTS BATTING YEAR-BY-YEAR

	AVG.	AB	R	H	TB	1B	2B	3B	HR H-A-T
1977	.278	5524	822	1568	2361	1074	241	55	94-58-152
1978	.279	5488	775	1529	2371	1037	291	52	75-74-149
1979	.281	5469	862	1537	2408	1042	284	46	91-74-165
1980	.274	5567	762	1523	2240	1105	254	29	75-60-135
1981	.252	3602	466	908	1348	640	168	28	41-3-1-72
1982	.257	5546	701	1428	2275	1011	234	36	75-72-147
1983	.259	5531	726	1434	2254	947	299	43	84-61-145
984	.257	5574	696	1433	2185	1009	236	48	78-62-140
1985	.243	5406	588	1312	2029	917	220	28	78-69-147
1986	.261	5621	733	1467	2283	1008	266	29	89-75-164
1987	.244	5426	655	1323	2145	857	268	40	83-75-158
1988	.251	5484	680	1404	2151	977	250	34	73-70-143
1989	.255	5513	651	1408	2056	997	273	39	50-49-99
1990	.260	5524	661	1434	2198	1756	259	38	82-61-143

OPPONENTS BATTING YEAR-BY-YEAR

(Cont...)

	RBI	BB	SO	SH-SF	HP	SB-CS	LOB	SLUG
1977	762	623	771	64-70	20	84-75	1184	.427
1978	730	614	758	79-51	22	101-66	1192	.432
1979	809	594	613	67-50	40	85-56	1107	.440
1980	720	635	705	92-47	28	115-53	1209	.402
1981	435	377	451	38-36	36	55-35	763	.374
1982	657	493	776	46-31	25	78-46	1109	.410
1983	689	517	835	34-50	42	83-46	1112	.408
1984	662	528	875	54-45	34	75-40	1147	.392
1985	558	484	823	47-41	26	83-44	1072	.375
1986	691	487	1002	59-51	45	95-46	1103	.406
1987	620	567	1064	56-32	22	123-59	1086	.395
1988	632	528	904	61-37	59	120-55	142	.392
1989	610	478	849	61-62	45	115-54	1107	.373
1990	.610	478	849	61-62	45	115-54	1107	.373

OPPONENTS PITCHING YEAR-BY-YEAR

	W-L	ERA	AP	RA	CG	SV	SHO	IP
1977	107-54	3.25	345	184	52	43	15	1452
1978	102-59	3.31	340	179	59	33	19	1450
1979	109-53	3.32	347	185	53	41	15	1444
1980	95-67	3.39	343	181	54	34	12	1481
1981	69-37	2.76	239	133	30	21	20	967
1982	84-78	3.61	397	235	39	37	9	1448
1983	73-89	4.48	413	251	26	33	8	1437.1
1984	73-89	4.08	426	263	26	28	4	1453.0
1985	62-99	4.28	427	266	24	23	4	1427.0
1986	76-86	4.40	480	317	19	38	6	1470.0
1987	66-96	4.72	—	—	26	33	10	1441.1
1988	75-87	4.19	—	—	23	39	3	1442.0
1989	73-89	4.02	—	—	17	38	7	1461.0
1990	76-86	4.42	—	—	18	46	10	1447.2

	H	R	ER	HR	BB	SO	HB	WP
1977	1367	822	525	100	499	819	23	35
1978	1358	590	534	98	448	645	23	32
1979	1362	613	533	95	448	663	36	37
1980	1398	624	558	126	448	813	33	37
1981	797	329	297	61	284	556	20	25
1982	1447	651	581	106	415	749	28	43
1983	1546	795	716	167	510	810	32	45
1984	1555	750	659	143	460	816	52	47
1985	1482	759	679	158	503	807	30	8
1986	1540	809	718	181	496	848	33	46
1987	1514	845	756	215	555	970	38	64
1988	1491	763	671	158	521	935	31	61
1989	1449	731	653	142	521	923	31	52
1990	1479	767	711	167	526	970	28	73

LOW HIT GAMES VS BLUE JAYS

NO HIT GAMES

May 15/81 -Len Barker, Toronto-0 at Cleveland-3, Perfect Game
June 29/90 -Dave Stewart, Oakland -5 at Toronto -0

ONE HIT GAMES

Sept. 3/78 -Chris Knapp, California-3 at Toronto-1, Horton homer in second
July 7/79 -Doc Medich (6.2 inn), Jim Kern (2.1 inn), Toronto-0 at Texas-2, Mayberry single in second
April 30/80 -Larry Gura, Kansas City-3 at Toronto-0, Garcia single in sixth
June 6/80 -Geoff Zahn, Toronto-0 at Minnesota-5, Mayberry single in seventh
Sept. 26/80 -Dennis Eckersley, Boston-3 at Toronto-1, Mayberry home run in fifth
May 27/83 -John Tudor, Boston-2 at Toronto-0, Collins single in fourth
August 13/84 -Mike Boddicker, Baltimore-2 at Toronto-1, Mulliniks double in third
April 23/89 -Nolan Ryan, Texas-4 at Toronto-1, Liriano triple in ninth
April 28/89 -Kirk McCaskill, Toronto-0 at California-9, Liriano double in ninth

TWO HIT GAMES

July 24/77 -Bob Sykes, Toronto-2 at Detroit-6, Ashby single in sixth, Bailor homer in ninth
Oct. 2/77 -(1st game) Jim Bibby (6 inn), Don Hood (4 inn), Larry Andersen (2/3 inn), Cleveland-1 at Toronto-2 (11 innings), G. Woods, singles in sixth and eleventh
April 29/78 -Nolan Ryan, Toronto-0 at California-5, Upshaw triple in third, Cerone single in seventh
August 19/78 -Gary Serum, Toronto-0 at Minnesota-5, Ashby single in third, A. Woods single in fifth
Oct. 1/78 -Luis Tiant, Toronto-0 at Boston-5, Howell single in fourth, Mayberry single in seventh
May 14/79 -Rick Waits, Toronto-0 at Cleveland-1, McKay single in fourth and double in seventh
August 12/79 -(1st game) Ross Baumgarten, Toronto-2 at Chicago-7, Bailor single in first, A. Woods triple in seventh
May 2/80 -Len Barker (7 inn), Mike Stanton (2 inn), Cleveland-6 at Toronto-1, Garcia doubles in third and seventh
July 30/80 -Rich Langford, Oakland-11 at Toronto-1, Griffin home run in seventh and Ault single in eighth
Sept. 5/80 -LaMarr Hoyt, Chicago-3 at Toronto-0, Woods single in second and Iorg single in sixth
May 6/81 -Bert Blyleven, Cleveland-4 at Toronto-1, Moseby double in ninth, Bell single in ninth
April 18/83 -Ron Guidry, Toronto-0 at New York-3, Collins single in first, Martinez single in sixth
June 29/85 -Walt Terrell, Toronto-0 at Detroit-8, Moseby double in first, Upshaw single in seventh
May 23/86 -Don Schulze, Toronto-1 at Cleveland-3, Bell HR and Whitt single in the 2nd
July 26/86 -Eric Plunk (6IP), Dave Leiper (0.1IP), Dave Stewart (1.2IP), Joaquin Andujar (1IP), Toronto-0 at Oakland-2, Moseby single in the 3rd, Leach double in the 4th
August 11/86 -Mike Flanagan (8.1IP), Don Aase (0.2IP), Toronto-1 at Baltimore-3, Shepherd double in the 3rd, Fernandez double in the 9th
April 10/87 -Bruce Hurst, Toronto-0 at Boston-3, Iorg single in 3rd, Fernandez single in 6th.
May 23/89 -Shane Rawley (8IP), Juan Berenguer (0.2IP), Minnesota-1 at Toronto-2, Liriano single in 6th, McGriff single in 7th
April 27/90 -Greg Hibbard (S.0IP), Scott Radinsky (0.0IP) -Bobby Thigpen (0.1IP), Toronto -1 at Chicago -6 Hill and Felix singles in 5th
July 18/90 -Matt Young (9.0), Toronto -2 at Seattle -5 Borders double in 4th, single in 6th
August 26/90 -Greg Harris (7.2IP), Jeff Gray (1.1IP), Boston -1 at Toronto -0, McGriff single in 2nd, Myers single in 8th.

OPPONENTS GRAND SLAM HOME RUNS

DATE	PLAYER/CLUB	H/A	PITCHER
Sept. 6/77	Carlton Fisk, Boston	H	Mike Darr (1st inning)
April 18/78	Amos Otis, Kansas City	H	Dave Lemanczyk (1st inning)
April 25/78	Paul Dade, Cleveland	H	Jerry Garvin (4th inning)
May 26/78	Jim Spencer, New York	A	Tom Murphy (7th inning)
June 24/78	Gary Alexander, Cleveland	A	Mike Willis (4th inning)
August 6/78	Al Cowens, Kansas City	A	Balor Moore (1st inning)
May 22/79	Andre Thornton, Cleveland	H	Mark Lemongello (3rd inning)
June 3/79	Dan Meyer, Seattle	A	Mark Lemongello (3rd inning)
June 10/79	Jim Essian, Oakland	A	Mike Willis (5th inning)
June 13/79 (1st)	Willie Aikens, California	H	Dyar Miller (3rd inning)
June 14/79	Willie Aikens, California	H	Phil Huffman (1st inning)
July 15/79	Dave Edwards, Minnesota	H	Jim Clancy (3rd inning)
August 25/79	Don Baylor, California	H	Balor Moore (1st inning)
Sept. 9/79	Bobby Bonds, Cleveland	A	Tom Buskey (9th inning)
April 22/81	Paul Molitor, Milwaukee	H	Joey McLaughlin (5th inning)
June 7/81	Buddy Bell, Texas	A	Roy Lee Jackson (8th inning)
May 29/82 (2nd)	Benny Ayala, Baltimore	A	Jerry Garvin (7th inning)
June 2/82	Bobby Murcer, New York	H	Mark Bomback (13th inning)
July 11/82	Harold Baines, Chicago	H	Jerry Garvin (2nd inning)
July 30/82	Alan Trammell, Detroit	H	Jim Clancy (4th inning)
August 24/82	Joe Nolan, Baltimore	A	Joey McLaughlin (10th inning)
August 26/82	Eddie Murray, Baltimore	A	Ken Schrom (3rd inning)
June 15/83	Dave Lopes, Oakland	H	Dave Geisel (5th inning)
August 8/83 (2nd)	Ken Griffey, New York	A	Matt Williams (1st inning)
August 20/83	Jim Rice, Boston	A	Dave Stieb (3rd inning)
July 20/84	Alvin Davis, Seattle	A	Roy Lee Jackson (7th inning)
April 19/85	Fritz Connally, Baltimore	H	Doyle Alexander (5th inning)
May 15/85	Jerry Narron, California	H	Bill Caudill (9th inning)

DATE	PLAYER/CLUB	H/A	PITCHER
May 8/86	Wally Joyner, California	A	Jim Acker (3rd inning)
May 9/86	Alvin Davis, Seattle	A	Don Gordon (7th inning)
April 9/87	Cory Snyder, Cleveland	H	Joe Johnson (1st inning)
June 29/87	Don Mattingly, New York	H	John Cerutti (2nd inning)
June 29/87	Dave Winfield, New York	H	Tom Henke (8th inning)
August 6/87	Casey Parsons, Cleveland	H	Mark Eichhorn (6th inning)
August 10/87	Sam Horn, Boston	A	Jose Nunez (8th inning)
July 2/88	Terry Steinbach, Oakland	H	Mike Flanagan (3rd inning)
May 2/89	Mark McGwire, Oakland	H	Tom Henke (9th inning)
July 16/89	Terry Steinbach, Oakland	H	Duane Ward (7th inning)
Sept. 12/89	Kent Hrbek, Minnesota	A	Duane Ward (7th inning)
May 17/90	Brian Giles, Seattle	H	Frank Will (5th inning)
May 22/90	Jose Canseco , Oakland	H	Frank Wills (6th inning)
July 17/90	Alvin Davis, Seattle	A	David Wells (6th inning)
August 3/90	Steve Buechele, Texas	A	Jim Acker (7th inning)
Sept. 14/90	Sam Horn, Baltimore (PH)	H	Duane Ward (6th inning)

1991 IMPORTANT DATES TO REMEMBER

January 5-15	Period in which player may make submission to arbitration.
January 8	Last day until May 1 for former clubs to resign players who refused binding arbitration.
February 1-21	Salary arbitration hearings held.
February 22	First date pitchers, catchers, and injured players can voluntarily work out at spring training.
February 27	First date all others can voluntarily work out at spring training.
March 6	Earliest mandatory date for first spring training workout.
March 14	Earliest date to request major league waivers on selected players or draft-excluded players acquired after August 15, 1989
March 11	Last date to renew contracts.
March 19	First date draft-excluded players acquired after 8-15-88 or players chosen in 1988 Rule 5 selection meeting may be assigned to a National Association club. Also, last date to furnish notice of release and incur only 30 days' salary liability.
March 23	Last date to request unconditional release waivers if you will MAIL notice to player, without incurring full season salary liability.
March 27	Last date to request unconditional release waivers if you will HAND notice to player, without incurring full season salary liability.
April 8	Official opening of the 1991 Championship Season. Beginning this date, Active list to 25 players.
May 7	First day former clubs may resign free agent players who refused binding arbitration and were unsigned after January 8.
May 8	Waivers secured on or after November 11th expire at 5:00 P.M. EDT.
May 2	New waiver period. Waivers secured on/after this date are good through 5:00 P.M. EDT July 31st. Beginning today, outright assignments to National Association may be made with ordinary major league waivers in effect.
May 27	Start of free agent closed period re summer draft.
June 3-5	Summer free agent draft.
July 9	All-Star Game at SkyDome, Toronto
July 31	Waivers secured on or after May 7, 1991 expire 5:00 P.M. EDT.
July 31	New waiver period begins. No assignments of player contracts to other Major League clubs until day after end of championship season except on waiver claim or with waivers in effect.
July 22	Hall of Fame game at Cooperstown
August 15	Last date to bring player up for "full trial" (to avoid "draft-excluded" status.)
September 1	Active player limit increased from 25 to 40. Beginning today, until 30 days of the 1991 season have expired outright assignments to National Association may be made only with special waivers in effect.
October 6	1991 Championship Season Closes.
October 9	Last date for requesting waivers until November 11th.
Close of World Series	Commencement of 15-day period during which eligible players may elect trade or free agency.
November 10	Waivers secured on or after August 1, 1991 expire 5:00 P.M. EST.
November 11	New waiver period begins. Major League waiver requests may be withdrawn by a club on any player only once in each waiver period; subsequent Major League waiver requests in that period are irrevocable.
November (TBA)	Last date to file AAA and AA reserve lists with National Association and Commissioner.
November 20	Last date to file Major League reserve lists with League and Commissioner.
December 20	Last date to tender contracts.

Batting Average (30 AB's)	.514,	Wally Joyner, Calf.	519,	Don Mattingly, NY-1986
Most at Bats	55,	Roberto Kelly, NY		
		Paul Molitor, Milw.		
		Jody Reed, Bos.		
Most Runs	13,	Ricky Henderson, Oak	17,	Ron LeFlore, Det-1977
				Ron LeFlore, Det-1978
Most Hits	22,	Roberto Kelly, NY	27,	Don Mattingly, NY-1986
Most Total Bases	43,	Cecil Fielder, Det	50,	George Brett, KC-1983
Most Doubles	6,	Roberto Kelly, NY	9,	George Brett, KC-1979
		Jody Reed, Bos		
Most Triples	3,	George Brett, KC	3,	Ron LeFlore, Det-1977
		Gary Pettis, Tex		Rick Peters, Det-1981
				Julio Franco, Clev-1983
				Robin Yount, Milw-1987
				Devon White, Cal-1989
				George Brett, KC-1990
				Gary Pettis, Tex-1990
Most Home Runs	7,	Cecil Fielder, Det	7,	Bobby Grich, Cal-1979
				Jim Rice, Bost-1983
				Cecil Fielder, Det-1990
Most Runs Batted In	14,	Cecil Fielder, Det	22,	Carlton Fisk, Bost-1977
Most Sacrifice Bunts	4,	Mike Gallego, Oak	4,	Jim Sundberg, Tex-1977
				Roy Smalley, Minn-1978
				Jim Morrison, Chi-1980
				Mike Gallego, Oak-1990
Most Sacrifice Flies	2,	Brady Anderson, Balt	4,	Gary Gaetti, Minn-1989
		Dwight Evans, Bost		
		Steve Finley, Balt		
		Paul Molitor, Milw		
		Robin Yount, Milw		
Most Times Striking Out	16,	Gary Pettis, Tex	22,	Bo Jackson, KC-1987
Most Walks	10,	Julio Franco, Tex	13,	Jason Thompson, Det-1977
				Butch Wynegar, Minn-1979
				Wade Boggs, Bost-1983
				George Brett, KC-1986
				Willie Randolph, NY-1987
Most Times Hit By Pinch	2,	Cancy Maldonado, Clev	4,	Chet Lemon, Chi-1981
		Jesse Barfield, NY		Don Baylor, Bost-1986
Most Stolen Bases	4,	Greg Briley, Sea	13,	Rickey Henderson, NY-1988
		Julio Franco, Tex		
		Ricky Henderson, Oak		
		Paul Molitor, Milw		
		Gary Pettis, Tex		
Most Times Caught Stealing	4,	Gary Pettis, Tex	4,	Gil Flores, Cal-1977
				Dwayne Murphy, Oak-1980
				Rickey Henderson, Oak-1981
				Brett Butler, Clev-1985
				Rickey Henderson, NY-1988
				Harold Reynolds, Sea-1988
				Gary Pettis, Det-1989
				Gary Pettis, Tex-1990
Most Times GIDP	5,	Ivan Calderson, Chi	6,	Buddy Bell, Clev-1978
		Henry Cotto, Sea		Dave Engle, Minn-1984
Most Wins	3,	Roger Clemens, Bos	4,	Dennis Eckersley, Bost-1978
				Rick Waits, Clev-1978
				Dave Goltz, Minn-1979
				Chuck Rainey, Bost-1979
				Luis Tiant, NY-1979
				Steve Stone, Balt-1980
				Britt Burns, Chi-1982
				Dave Stewart, Oak-1987
Most Losses	2,	13 Pitchers	4,	Danny Darwin, Tex-1983
				Mike Norris, Oak-1980
Most Appearances	8,	Jeff Gray, Bost	10,	Keith Atherton, Oak-Minn-1986
Most Complete Games	2,	Dave Stewart, Oak	4,	Mike Flanagan, Balt-1978
		Matt Young, Sea		Mike Norris, Oak-1990
Most Saves	4,	Dennis Eckersley, Oak	5,	Dan Quisenberry, KC-1983
		Doug Jones, Clev		Jeff Reardon, Minn-1988
		Greg Olson, Balt		
		Jeff Reardon, Bost		
Most Innings Pitched	29.0,	Jeff Robinson, Det	40.0,	Mike Flanagan, Balt-1978
Most Hits Allowed	30,	Brian Holman, Sea	43,	Mike Flanagan, Balt-1978
Most Runs Allowed	16,	Dave LaPoint, NY	23,	Frank Viola, Minn-1985
Most Earned Runs	15,	Mark Knudson, Milw	19,	Mike Caldwell, Milw-1983
Most Homeruns Allowed	6,	Curt Young, Oak	7,	Floyd Bannister, Chi-1987
Most Strikeouts	27,	Tom Gordon, KC	44,	Nolan Ryan, Calf-1977
Most Base on Balls	12,	Andy Hawkins, NY	20,	Nolan Ryan, Calf-1977
Most Hit Batsmen	3,	Brian Holman, Sea	5,	Jose DeLeon, Chi-1987
		Jeff Robinson, Det		
Most Wild Pitches	3,	Greg Cadaret, NY	5,	Charlie Hough, Tex-1986
		Greg Harris, Bost		
		Brian Harvey, Calf		

PLAYER LIMITS: 40 until opening day, when the number must be reduced to 25 until September 1, when it again becomes 40. The minimum number of active players maintained by each club throughout the championship season shall be 25.

TRADING REGULATIONS: The trading deadline is July 31.

Trades may be made with any other major league club in the period from the end of the championship season through July 31 (5.00 pm EDT) without waivers. Waivers are required, however:

1. If the assignment is to another major league club: From August 1 and ending at 5 pm EDT the day after the end of the season.
2. If assignment is to a minor league club, with right of recall, at any time after 3 years from the date the player first reported to a major league club during a championship season.
3. If assigned to a minor league club without right of recall, after acquiring 3 years service: At any time during the year.
4. If assigned to a minor league club, without right of recall, at any time prior to acquiring three years of service, special waivers are required between September 1 and the opening of the following season. If player is claimed, request may be withdrawn. If no claims are made, club has 7-day period in which to make assignment to minor leagues.

WAIVERS: The 1985 collective bargaining agreement brought about changes in the waivers process. Following is information on the new waiver agreements.

SUBSTANTIVE

- The "trading deadline" is now July 31. Waivers are required for any inter- or intra-Major League assignment during the period beginning August 1 and ending at 5 pm ET the day after the end of the season. During the other ten months of the year no waivers are needed.
- It will be easier to compute which players need waivers before they may be optioned: if three years (less one for each previously spent on option) have elapsed since the player actually reported to the Major Leagues for the first time, waivers are required. The date of actual physical reporting will be used as the benchmark instead of the date the player was first placed on a club's 40-man roster.
- The procedure for outright assignments to the National Association remains unchanged from the 31st day of each season until August 31; during this period, ordinary waivers are required. However, from September 1 until the 30th day of the following season, special waivers are required:
- The club must tender a special waiver request specifying that waivers are requested for the purpose of outright assignment to the National Association. The claiming period, as with other waivers, is three business days, and an assignment pursuant to special waivers must be completed by 2 pm ET the seventh day after the waivers were secured.
- Seventy-two-hour waivers, secured on players recalled not to report, continue unaffected except insofar as they no longer suffice for an outright assignment to the National Association during those times in the year when special waivers are required.

PROCEDURAL

- Waiver requests deadline is now 2:00 pm Eastern Time.
- Claiming period is now three business days for all waiver requests, including "special waivers" and waivers for the purpose of unconditional release.
- AL Only and NL Only waivers have been abolished.
- In the event of claims, withdrawals period is two business days.
- A club may withdraw once per waiver period on any one player.
- New waiver periods:
  November 11-30th day of season
  31st day of season-July 31
  August 1-November 10
- "Special waivers" and waivers for the purpose of unconditional release may both be requested during the closed period, October 10-November 10.
- Waiver price for selected and draft-excluded players is now $25,000, and may be set by agreement ($20,000 minimum) in all other waiver assignments. Rules on priority of claim are unchanged.
- Closed period on selected and draft-excluded players now runs from October 10 through the 25th day before Opening Day, and no assignments may be made pursuant to such waivers until 15 days before Opening Day. "Dates to Remember", from the league offices, will specify the correct dates each year.

FREE AGENCY (RE-ENTRY): The 1985 collective bargaining agreement brought about changes in the free agency process. Following is the appropriate information:

Six years of Major League Service continues to be required to be eligible for free agency.

The Re-Entry Draft has been abolished.

A player has 15 days from the first day following the World Series to file for free agency

By December 7, former club must offer to arbitrate or becomes ineligible to sign player. By December 19, player must accept offer or on January 9 former club becomes ineligible to sign the player. (Ineligible club regains eligibility the following May 1.)

If club and player proceed to arbitration, maximum salary cut rules do not apply.

Player who accepts former club's offer to arbitrate is not subject to repeater rights limitations.

SALARY ARBITRATION:

Beginning in 1987, three years Major League Service required for eligibility.

Beginning in 1987, maximum cut rules do not apply if in immediately preceding year player won arbitration increase of over 50%.

Beginning in 1987, arbitrator is officially instructed to give particular attention for purposes of comparison to salaries of players with Major League Service no more than one annual service group higher than player who is arbitrating.

FREE AGENT DRAFT RULE (AMATEUR DRAFT) - REVISED FOR 1987: One selection meeting shall be conducted each year in June to be known at the "Summer Meeting".

Major League Clubs shall select in reverse order of their league standing at the close of the preceeding season (determined by the percentage of games it won). No club may transfer to another club its right to select.

A selected player shall be placed on a club's Negotiation List and shall remain, thereon until the start of the Closed Period (The seven days preceding the Summer Meeting) of the next selection meeting, unless at an earlier date he (1) signs a contract (2) is removed because he was not eligible for selection (3) becomes a College Player by entering or returning to college.

A club may not transfer its Negotiation Right to any other club.

REGULATION GAME: A regulation game consists of nine innings unless extended because of a tie score or shortened because (1) the home team needs none of its half of the ninth or only part of it; or (2) because the umpire-in-chief calls the game after five completed innings. A regulation game may be less than five innings if the home team is ahead after the first of the fifth, or takes the lead or ties the score while at bat in the fifth.

TIE GAME: A regulation game that is called by the umpire-in-chief when both teams have the same number of runs is a tie game. Individual player performances are official and are entered in the records, but the game does not count in the League standings and may be re-scheduled at a later date.

SUSPENDED GAME RULE:

Rule 4.12 SUSPENDED GAMES

(a) A league shall adopt the following rules providing for completion at a future date of games terminated for any of the following reasons:

(1) A curfew imposed by law;

(2) A time limit permissible under league rules;

(3) Light failure or malfunction of a mechanical field device under control of the home club. (Mechanical field device shall include automatic tarpaulin or water removal equipment.);

(4) Darkness because of any law, the lights may not be turned on.

(a) (5) Weather, if the game is called while an inning is in progress and before it is completed, and one of the following situations prevails:

(5) (i) The visiting team has scored one or more runs to tie the score, and the home team has not scored.

(ii) The visiting team has scored one or more runs to take the lead, and the home team has not tied the score or retaken the lead.

(b) Such games shall be known as suspended games. No game called because of a curfew, weather, or a time limit shall be a suspended game unless it has progressed far enough to have been a regulation game under the provisions of Rule 4.10. A game called under the provisions of 4.12(a)(3) or (4) shall be a suspended game at any time after it starts.

(c) By amending NOTE to read as follows:

NOTE: Weather and similar conditions—4.12(a) (1 through 5)—shall take precedence in determining whether a called game shall be a suspended game. A game can only be considered a suspended game if stopped for any of the five (5) reasons specified in Section (a). Any legal game called due to weather with the score tied (unless situation outlined in 4.12(a)(5)(i) prevails) is a tie game and must be replayed in its entirety.

(d) A suspended game shall be resumed and completed as follows:

(1) Immediately preceding the next scheduled single game between the two clubs on the same grounds;

or

(2) Immediately preceding the next scheduled double-header between the two clubs on the same grounds, if no single game remains on the schedule, or

(3) If suspended on the last scheduled date between the two clubs in the city, transferred and played on the grounds of the opposing club, if possible;

(i) Immediately preceding the next scheduled single game, or

(ii) Immediately preceding the next scheduled double-header, if no single game remains on the schedule.

(4) If a suspended game has not been resumed and completed on the last date scheduled for the two clubs, it shall be a called game.

(e) A suspended game shall be resumed at the exact point of suspension of the original game. The completion of a suspended game is a continuation of the original game. The lineup and batting order of both teams shall be exactly the same as the lineup and batting order at the moment of suspension, subject to the rules governing substitution. Any player may be replaced by a player who had not been in the game prior to the suspension. No player removed before the suspension may be returned to the lineup. A player who was not with the club when the game was suspended may be used as a substitute, even if he has taken the place of a player no longer with the club who would not have been eligible because he had been removed from the lineup before the game was suspended.

4.11(d)

A called game ends at the moment the umpire terminates play. **EXCEPTION:** If the game is called while an inning is in progress and before it is completed, the game becomes a SUSPENDED game in each of the following situations:

(1) The visiting team has scored one or more runs to tie the score and the home team has not scored.

(2) The visiting team has scored one or more runs to take the lead and the home team has not tied the score or retaken the lead.

DISABLED LISTS: REGULAR DISABLED LIST: The 21 and 30 day disabled lists were eliminated in August 1990. The 15 day list may be used for as many players as needed

EMERGENCY DISABLED LIST: Maximum number of players on list at one time-no limit. Minimum period of inactivty-sixty (6)) calendar days. Players placed on this list after August 1st shall remain there for the balance of the season. This list may only be used when a club is at the maximum limit of 40 players.

AMERICAN LEAGUE CURFEWS: No inning of an American league night game can start after 1:00 a.m., local time. Any inning started prior to 1:00 a.m. can be completed. Curfews shall be waived for the final series of the season between two teams in each of the cities.

Any game, regardless of length, called because of the time curfew, becomes a suspended game and must be completed from the exact point of interruption before the teams play their next scheduled game against each other.

DEFINITION OF NIGHT GAME: Any game scheduled to start after 6:00 p.m. (i.e. 6:01 p.m., or later), will be considered a night game. If a game is scheduled to start at 6:00 p.m., and is delayed by rain or for any other reason, it will be considered a day game.

However, both games of a twi-night doubleheader shall be considered night games. When afternoon and night games are played on the same date and separate admissions are charged, they will be counted as one day and one night game, and will not be included in doubleheader statistics.

BATTING CHAMPIONSHIP QUALIFICATIONS: A batting champion must have 502 or more actual plate appearances. (The equivalent of 3.1 appearances for each of the 162 scheduled games.). If, however, there is any player with fewer than the required number of plate appearances whose average would be the highest if he were charged with the required number of official at bats, then the player shall be awarded the batting championship.
EARNED-RUN AVERAGE CHAMPION QUALIFICATIONS: To win the earned-run average championship a pitcher must pitch at least as many innings as the number of games scheduled for each club in his league that season and have the lowest earned-run average.
FIELDING CHAMPIONSHIP QUALIFICATIONS: The individual fielding champions shall be the fielders with the highest fielding average at each position, provided:
(1) A catcher must have participated as a catcher in at least one-half the number of games scheduled for each club in his league that season;
(2) An infielder or outfielder must have participated at his position in at least two-thirds of the number of games scheduled for each club in his league that season;
(3) A pitcher must have pitched at least as many innings as the number of games scheduled for each club in his league that season. **EXCEPTION:** If another pitcher has a fielding average as high or higher, and has handled more total chances in a lesser number of innings, he shall be the fielding champion.
DETERMINING THE MAGIC NUMBERS: Determine the number of games yet to be played, add one, then subtract the number of games ahead in the loss column of the standings from the closest opponent.
DETERMINING BATTING AVERAGE: Divide the number of at bats into the number of hits.
DETERMINING AN EARNED-RUN AVERAGE: Multiply the number of earned runs by nine; take the number and divide it by the number of innings pitched.
DETERMINING SLUGGING PERCENTAGE: Divide the total bases of all safe hits by the total times at bat. (At bats do not include walks, sacrifices, hit by pitcher, or times awarded first base because of interference or obstruction.)
DETERMINING ON BASE PERCENTAGE: Add the total of hits, walks and hit by pitches and divide by the total of at-bats, walks, hit by pitches and sacrifice flies.
DETERMINING FIELDING AVERAGE: Divide the total putouts and assists by the total of putouts, assists and errors.
DETERMINING PERCENTAGE OF GAMES WON AND LOST: Divide the number of games won by the total games won and lost.
CONSECUTIVE HITTING STREAKS: A consecutive hitting streak shall not be terminated if the plate appearance results in a base on balls, hit batsman, defensive interference or a sacrifice bunt. A sacrifice fly shall terminate the streak.
CONSECUTIVE-GAME HITTING STREAKS: A consecutive-game hitting streak shall not be terminated if all the player's plate appearances (one or more) result in a base on balls, hit batsman, defensive interference or a sacrifice bunt. The streak shall terminate if the player has a sacrifice fly and no hit. The player's individual consecutive-game hitting streak shall be determined by the consecutive games in which the player appears and is not determined by his club's games.
CONSECUTIVE-GAME PLAYING STREAK: A consecutive-game playing streak shall be extended if the player plays one-half inning on defense, or if he completes a time at bat by reaching base or being put out. A pinch-running appearance only shall not extend the streak. If a player is ejected from a game by an umpire before he can comply with the requirements of this rule, his streak shall continue.
SUSPENDED GAMES: For the purpose of this rule, all performances in the completion of a suspended game shall be considered as occurring on the original date of the game.
"SAVE" RULE: A pitcher shall be credited with a save when he meets all three of the following conditions:
(1) He is the finishing pitcher in a game won by his club, and
(2) He is not the winning pitcher, and
(3) He qualifies under one of the following conditions:
(3) (a) He enters the game with a lead of no more than three runs and pitches for at least one inning, or
(b) He enters the game regardless of the count, with the potential tying run either on base, at bat, or on deck (that is, the potential tying run is either already on base or is one of the first two batsmen he faces), or
(c) He pitches effectively for at least three innings.

DESIGNATED HITTER RULE: A hitter may be designated to bat for the pitcher in any spot in the batting order in any game without affecting the status of the pitcher. The designated hitter must be selected and be included on the lineup cards presented to the umpire-in-chief prior to the game. Failure to do so precludes the use of a designated hitter for that game.
The designated hitter is "locked" into the batting order but may be removed for a pinch-hitter or pinch-runner, who in turn becomes the designated hitter. The designated hitter, while still in the game, may be used defensively but the pitcher then assumes the batting order of the replaced defensive player, thus terminating the designated hitter role.
The designated hitter is eligible for all American League batting titles.
The designated hitter named in the starting lineup must come to bat at least one time, unless the opposition changes pitchers.
SCORING RULE ON PINCH-HITTERS: A player shall be considered a pinch-hitter only if he enters the game as a substitute batter and then only on his first time at bat which must be before he becomes a fielder. If the team bats around and a pinch hitter comes up a second time in the inning in which he first appeared he will not be considered a pinch hitter during that second time up.
A substitute hitter for a Designated Hitter is both a pinch hitter and a designated hitter on his first time at bat. On subsequent trips to the plate he is a Designated Hitter only.
EARNED-RUNS RULE: The determination of earned-run is as follows:
'An earned-run is a run for which the pitcher is held accountable. In determining earned-runs, the inning should be reconstructed without the errors and passed balls; and the benefit of the doubt should always be given to the pitcher in determining which bases would have been reached with errorless play.'
Until 1969, the reliever could not be charged with an earned-run if he entered the game after the side could have been retired but for an error, no matter how many runs he subsequently gave up in that inning. Now, runs, scored by batters who reach base off the reliefer are charged as earned

on that pitcher's record. They are not, however, charged as earned against the team as a whole. Therefore, a discrepancy may occur between the total earned-runs charged against a team and the sum total of the earned-runs charged against the individual pitchers of that team.

DOCTORED BAT: A batter is out for illegal action when he uses or attempts to use a bat that, in the umpire's judgment, has been altered or tampered with in such a way to improve the distance factor or cause an unusual reaction on the baseball. This includes bats that are filled, flat-surfaced, nailed, hollowed, grooved or covered with a substance such as paraffin, wax, etc. No advancement on the bases will be allowed and any out or outs made during a play shall stand. In addition to being called out, the player shall be ejected from the game and may be subject to additional penalties as determined by his League President. (Rule 6.06d).

DETERMINING A "MAJOR LEAGUE YEAR": 172 days constitute a full year in the major leagues.

MAJOR LEAGUE SERVICE:

is credited for each day the player appears on an active roster or major league disabled list or suspended list.

in the case of a player called up from the minor leagues, is credited beginning with the date he physically reports.

in the case of a major league player who is traded and reports in the normal course, service is not interrupted.

in the case of a player sent down to the minor leagues, is credited through the date of the assignment.

in the case of a player who is unconditionally released, is credited through the date waivers were requested.

in the case of a player designated for release or assignment (MLR 2), is credited after the designation, through the date of the actual assignment or the request for unconditional release waivers.

for a player who appears on his club's opening day roster, is credited as of the earliest scheduled opener, without regard to the actual opening date of his own club.

is credited at the rate of 172 days per "year', though the season is actually 182 days long.

is not credited during any period or periods of optional assignment totalling 20 days or more during a single season.

ROOKIE QUALIFICATION: A player shall be considered a rookie unless, during a previous season or seasons, he has (a) exceeded 130 at bats or 50 innings pitched in the major leagues; or (b) accumulated more than 45 days on the active roster of a major league club or clubs during the period of a 25-man limit (excluding time in military service) and time on the disabled list.

GAME WINNING RBI: The RBI that gives the club the lead it never relinquishes. (Note: There does not have to be a game-winning RBI in every game and all game-winning RBIs must conform to RULE 10.04).

PLAYING RULES:

Spectator Interference—batter, runner and other runner(s) will be placed at the base(s) which the umpires feel they would have reached with no interference.

Time—ball is dead, play suspended. This sign used when ball is foul, umpire then pointing to foul territory.

Batted Balls Fair or Foul—if fair, umpire points to fair territory—if foul he raises arms overhead (as in "Time" above) and then turns and points to foul territory, and vocally calls "foul".

SCHEDULE: The AL schedule uses a balanced format in which each club plays twelve games against all 13 opponents, for a total of 156 games. This includes six home contests and six away against each opponent.

However, in order to reach the seasonal total of 162 games, it is necessary to add six games to the above 156 total. This is accomplished by having each club play six additional games within its division—three home and three away, one with each club in its division.

MINIMUM SALARY: The minimum rate of payment to a player for each day of service on a Major League Club for the 1991 season is $100.000 U.S. Funds.

TERMINATION PAY: One full season's pay if player released opening day or later. Thirty days pay for player who is released on the 16th day before opening day or earlier. If players is released after that 16th day prior to opening day he receives one additional day's pay (over the 30 days) for each additional day.

OPPONENTS PITCHING VS BLUE JAYS-CAREER LEADERS (50 IP)

IP	AP	W	L	SV	ERA
Morris, 217.0	Stanley, 56	Flanagan, 17	Moore, 13	Quisenberry, 22	Norris, 2.09
Tanana, 213.2	Righetti, 45	Stanley, 14	Morris, 12	Righetti, 18	Gossage, 2.23
Flanagan, 208.0	Martinez, 42	McGregor, 13	Viola, 12	Reardon, 15	Clemens, 2.25
Stanley, 175.1	Quisenberry, 42	Moore, 12	Boddicker, 11	Plesac, 12	Matlack, 2.29
Bannister, 170.1	Clear, 42	Morris, 12	Hough, 11	Clear, 11	Stewart, 2.32
Guidry, 170.0	Vande Berg, 32	Black, 11	Smithson, 11	Eckersley, 11	Hoyt, 2.36
Moore, 164.0	Moore, 31	Guidry, 11	Bannister, 10	Jones, 10	Quisenberry, 2.36
Boddicker, 162.0	Morris, 31	Gura, 11	Blyleven, 10	Lopez, 10	Martinez (D), 2.36
Dotson, 159.2	Lamp, 30	Haas, 11	Dotson, 10	Lyle, 8A	ase, 2.39
Witt (M), 154.2	Hernandez, 29	Slaton, 11	Darwin, 9	Martinez (T), 8	Ryan, 2.40
John, 154.1	Slaton, 28	Tanana, 10	Langston, 9	Fingers, 7	Niekro (P), 2.42
Hough, 153.1		Zahn, 10	Witt, 9	Stanley, 7	Gordon, 2.44
Eckersley, 150.1					

Television "over the air" broadcast rights are owned by the Labatt Brewing Company and are produced by TV Labatt commercially on the CTV Network (flagship station- CFTO-TV, Toronto and affiliated stations throughout Canada)...Commentators on the CTV Telecasts include play-by-play announcer Don Chevrier, colour commentator Tommy Hutton and host Fergie Olver...The cable/Pay-TV broadcast rights are owned by The Sports Network (TSN)...Jim Hughson will handle the play-by-play for TSN along with colour commentator Buck Martinez...CTV will carry 60 games in 1991 and TSN will also carry 60 games.

JOHN HUDSON
Director of Media Properties
TV Labatt
2 First Canadian Place
Suite # 3200
Toronto, Ontario, M5X 1E7
(416) 361-5050

PETER SISAM
Vice-President, Sports and Business Development
CTV Network
42 Charles Street
9th Floor
Toronto, Ontario, M4Y 1T5
(416) 928-6000

GORDON CRAIG
President and General Manager
The Sports Network
1155 Leslie Street
Don Mills, Ontario
M3C 2J6
(416) 449-2244

DON CHEVRIER,
Play-by-play Announcer

The voice of the Blue Jays on all telecasts throughout the club's 14 year history..."Chevvy" returns for his 15th season...Has been in broadcasting for 34 years...Is one of North American's most highly respected announcers because of his knowledge of the various sports he broadcasts...Has worked for every major network in North America...Personal highlight was broadcasting the 1980 Winter Olympics and the United States gold medal win in hockey...Other major sporting events include the Rome, Montreal and Los Angeles Summer Olympics, the Sapparo, Lake Placid, and Sarajevo Winter Olympics, Commonwealth and Pan-Am Games, Canada/Russia hockey series, CFL football, curling championships, golf, boxing and the USSR-NHL hockey series...Has worked ABC's Monday Night Baseball, sports anchor for ABC Direction Network and boxing for ESPN...Resides in Palm Harbor, FL.

TOMMY HUTTON,
Colour Commentator

Begins his second season as the Colour Commentator on the CTV Network for the Blue Jays games...Hutton was a member of the Yankees broadcast team from 1987-1989 after having spent the previous five seasons as a broadcaster for the Montreal Expos...His major league playing career spanned twelve seasons while playing first base for the Dodgers, Phillies, Blue Jays and Expos...Career .995 fielding percentage as a First Baseman...In addition to his Blue Jay broadcasts in 1990, he was also a member of the ESPN broadcast team...He will return to ESPN in '91 as well.

FERGIE OLVER,
Host

Starting 11th season on Blue Jay telecasts...Former centerfielder in pro baseball...Played two seasons in Chicago White Sox chain, 1962-63...Team-mate in first season at Harlan, Kentucky was former Cy Young Award winner Denny McLain...Returned to Western Canada to play for Saskatoon/Medicine Hat in Western Baseball League (semi-pro)...Started working in radio and TV in Moose Jaw/Regina area and in 1969 came east to CFCF-TV in Montreal...Moved to CFTO-TV in Toronto four months later...Stayed for 15 years before resigning in the fall of 1984...Worked as play-by-play announcer of Blue Jays games televised on The Sports Network...Owns and races standard-bred horses...Resides in Toronto

JIM HUGHSON,
TSN Play-by-play Announcer

Joined The Sports Network in 1986, and is the network's "man for both seasons", covering the Blue Jays in the summer and NHL Hockey in the winter...Began his career in radio broadcasting in 1974...Had a four year stint with CKNW Radio in Vancouver...Moved to Toronto in 1982 where he was the play-by-play man of the Toronto Maple Leafs on CHCH-TV in Hamilton...He also covered the NHL Playoffs for ESPN in 1985...Since 1986 he has been the play-by-play man for "The NHL Tonight" on TSN...In 1990, he joined former Blue Jay catcher, Buck Martinez in the broadcast booth as the play-by-play announcer for the Blue Jays after having spent three seasons as the play-by-play man for Expos telecasts...His other on-air duties include hosting TSN's Sportsdesk and Extra Innings, TSN's live post-game phone-in show...He has also covered Canada Cup Hockey for TSN...The native of Fort St. John, B.C., now resides in Peterborough, Ontario.

BUCK MARTINEZ,
TSN Colour Commentator

Began with The Sports Network in 1987 as the colour commentator for the Blue Jays games...Is a former major league catcher who played with the Kansas City Royals from 1969-1977, the Milwaukee Brewers from 1978-1980 and the Toronto Blue Jays (1981-1986)...During his career he hit .225 with 58 home runs while playing in 1,049 games...He wrote two books while he was with the Blue Jays; "From Worst to First", which chronicles the Blue Jays' 1985 season, and "The Last Out", which notes his final season as a player...Is a native of Redding, California and now resides in Mission Viejo, California.

CTV TELEVISION NETWORK

NTV	St. John's, NF
ATV	Sydney, Halifax, Moncton
CFCF	Montreal, PQ
CJOH	Ottawa, ON
CKCO	Kitchnener
CJBN	Kenora, ON
MCTV	Sudbury, North Bay, Timmins
CHBX	Sault Ste. Marie, ON
CHFD	Thunder Bay, ON
CFTO	Toronto, ON
CKY	Winnipeg, MB
CKCK	Regina, Saskatchewan
CFQC	Saskatoon, Saskatchewan
CITL	Lloydminister, Alberta
CIPA	Prince Albert, Saskatchewan
CICC	Yorkton, Alberta
CFCN	Calgary, Alberta
CFRN	Edmonton, Alberta
BCTV	Vancouver, British Columbia
CHEK	Victoria, British Columbia

BLUE JAYS RADIO BROADCAST

TELEMEDIA RADIO NETWORK
40 HOLLY STREET
TORONTO, ONTARIO
M4S 3C3
(416) 482-9383

VICE-PRESIDENT: PAUL J. WILLIAMS
MANAGER, NETWORK SPORTS: ALLAN DAVIS
MARKETING/PROMOTIONS MANAGER: VICKI McKEE

TOM CHEEK
PLAY-BY-PLAY ANNOUNCER

Returns for his 15th season as the BLUE JAYS' play-by-play man...Off-season functions include appearances and speaking engagements for the BLUE JAYS...51 years old...Only person to see every BLUE JAYS game as a broadcaster...Born in Pensacola, Florida...Attended the Cambridge School of Broadcasting in Boston...Began radio career in Plattsburg, New York and then moved to Burlington, Vermont where for nine years was corporate sales manager and sports director for a group of three radio stations in Burlington and Rutland...Play-by-play experience includes baseball, basketball, football and hockey for the University of Vermont...From 1974 to 1976 was the swing man on Montreal Expos radio broadcasts on television nights...Member of the broadcast team for ABC Sports at the 1980 Winter Olympics at Lake Placid and 1984 Olympics at Sarajevo...Has broadcast college basketball for Mutual Radio Network...Was instrumental in organizing the Burlington International Games (while living in Vermont in 1967)...Married, three children...Wife Shirley, hails from Hemmingford, Quebec...Children Tom Jr. (24), Lisa (22) and Jeffrey (20)...Resides in Burlington, Ontario.

JERRY HOWARTH
PLAY-BY-PLAY ANNOUNCER

Back for his 10th full-season as a member of the BLUE JAYS radio team...Worked a partial schedule of games in 1981 while still sports director and sports talk show host at KWMS radio in Salt Lake City prior to joining the sports department of CJCL radio in Toronto...Born in York, Pennsylvania and grew up in San Francisco...45 years old...Graduated from University of Santa Clara in 1968...Served two years in the armed forces in West Germany...On return, attended Hastings Law School in San Francisco where he met his wife Mary...Started broadcasting career in 1974 with play-by-play of Tacoma Twins Triple A baseball and also for the University of Puget Sound's varsity baseball, basketball and football teams...Moved to Salt Lake City in 1976 and did play-by-play of Salt Lake City Gulls Triple A baseball for three years...Switched to basketball and was the Assistant General Manager of the Utah Pros of the Western Basketball Association and Group Sales Manager for Utah Jazz of the NBA prior to joining KWMS radio in 1980...Resides in Etobicoke with his wife Mary and two children Benjamin (14) and Joseph (12).

RADIO NETWORK
Flagship Station: CJCL 1430, Toronto

Affiliates: CKBB 950 (Barrie, Ont.), CJNR 730 (Blind River, Ont.), CFBG-FM 100.9 (Bracebridge/Gravenhurst, Ont.), CHUC 1450 (Cobourg, Ont.), CKCB 1400 (Collingwood, Ont.), CKNR 1340 (Elliot Lake), CKNS 930 (Espanola, Ont.), CHML 900 (Hamilton, Ont.), CFMK-FM 96.3 (Kingston, Ont.), CKGL-FM 96.7 (Kitchener, Ont.), CHYR 730 (Leamington/Windsor, Ont.), CKLY 910 (Lindsay, Peterborough, Ont.), CJBK 1290 (London, Ont.), CKMP 1230 (Midland, Ont.), CJMR 1320 (Mississauga, Ont.), CJTT 1230 (New Liskard, Ont.), CKAN 1480 (Newmarket, Ont.), CJRN 710 (Niagara Falls, Ont.), CKAT-FM 101.9 (North Bay, Ont.), CFOR 1570 (Orillia, Ont.), CKAR 1350 (Oshawa, Ont.), CFOS 560 (Owen Sound, Ont.), CFPS 1490 (Port Elgin, Ont.), CHOK 1070 (Sarnia, Ont.), CFYN 1050 (Sault Ste. Marie, Ont.), CHNR 1600 (Simcoe, Ont.), CHEQ-FM 101.9 (Smiths Falls/Ottawa, Ont.), CJCS 1240 (Stratford, Ont.), CIGM 790 (Sudbury, Ont.), CKGB 750 (Timmins, Ont.), CJCL 1430 (Toronto, Ont.), CJTN 1270 (Trenton, Ont.), CJSL 1280 (Estevan, Sask.), CFSL 1190 (Weyburn, Sask.), CKLQ 880 (Brandon, Manitoba), CKMW 1570 (Winkler, Man.), CJOB 680 (Winnipeg, Man.), CKDY 1420 (Digby, N.S.), CKEN 1490 (Kentville, N.S.), CKAD 1350 (Middleton, N.S.), CKPE-FM 94.9 (Sydney, N.S.), CKDY-FM 103.3 (Weymouth, N.S.), CFAB 1450 (Windsor, N.S.).

SITE:

MINOR LEAGUE COMPLEX
Cecil P. Englebert Recreational Complex
1700 Solon Avenue
Dunedin, Florida 34698

DUNEDIN STADIUM
at GRANT FIELD
311 Douglas Avenue
Dunedin, Florida 34698

FIRST WORKOUT DATES:
Major League-Pitchers & Catchers—Monday, February 25th.
Balance of Squad—Friday, March 1st.

NOTE: Major League Club opens Spring Training at the Cecil P. Englebert Recreational Complex and will continue to work out at the complex through to March 7st. Commencing March 8th, the Major League Club will move to Grant Field.

All games will be played at Dunedin Stadium

Minor League-Entire Squad—Friday, March 8th.

MAILING ADDRESS:
TORONTO BLUE JAYS
P.O. Box 957
Dunedin, Florida 34697

HOTEL HEADQUARTERS:
RAMADA INN COUNTRYSIDE
2560 U.S. 19 North
Clearwater, Florida 34623

TELEPHONES:

RAMADA INN COUNTRYSIDE	(813) 796-1234
MINOR LEAGUE COMPLEX	(813) 733-9302
DUNEDIN STADIUM OFFICE	(813) 733-9302
PUBLIC RELATIONS OFFICE (Effective March 8nd)	(813) 734-4214
FAX-DUNEDIN STADIUM	(813) 734-7661
FAX-ENGLEBERT COMPLEX	(813) 733-9389

TICKET DATA:

Ticket Office at DUNEDIN STADIUM, 373 Douglas Avenue, Dunedin.	(813) 733-0429
Monday to Saturday: 10:00 a.m. to 3:00 p.m. for Phone Orders	(813) 733-0429

TICKET PRICES: Reserved $7.00 & $6.00 U.S. Funds

DUNEDIN STADIUM
Located at the corner of Douglas Avenue and Beltrees Street in Dunedin, Dunedin Stadium is the spring training home of the Toronto Blue Jays.

DIMENSIONS:

Left-field line	335 ft/102.1 m
Left-centre	380 ft/115.8 m
Centre field	400 ft/121.9 m
Right-centre	365 ft/111.3 m
Right field line	315 ft/ 96.0 m

Fence-Twelve feet high, chain link with screen cover (3.66 m high).
Warning track-12 feet/3.66 m.
Distance from baselines to out-of-play-60 feet at all points (18.29 m).
Batter's eye screen-40 feet by 60 feet/12.2 m by 18.3 m.
Capacity-6218.

SPRING EXHIBITION RESULTS:

					ATTENDANCE		*DUNEDIN-ONLY	
	Home	ROAD	W-L	PCT	*HOME	AVG	ROAD	AVG
1977	5-8	3-8	8-16	.333	21,728	1,671	22,093	2,008
1978	3-8	5-9	8-17	.320	20,009	1,819	36,334	2,595
1979	6-6	6-6	12-12	.500	21,420	1,785	26,496	2,205
1980	5-4	5-3	10-7	.588	15,377	1,709	18,499	2,312
1981	7-6	6-7-1	13-13-1	.500	24,180	1,860	33,391	2,385
1982	7-7	8-5-1	15-12-1	.556	26,442	1,889	37,237	2,660
1983	9-4	7-6	16-10	.615	27,662	2,305	60,461	4,319
1984	8-6	5-10	13-16	.448	32,869	2,739	164,890	9,699
1985	11-4	8-5-1	19-9-1	.679	42,314	3,022	114,226	7,615
1986	10-3	5-9	15-12	.555	43,263	3,328	60,862	4,347
1987	5-5-1	4-6-1	9-11-2	.450	35,101	3,181	55,003	5,000
1988	8-5	10-5-2	18-10-2	.643	42,633	3,279	112,844	6,638
1989	12-4	9-6	21-10	.677	54,270	3,392	77,284	5,152
1990	1-5	3-5	4-10	.286	21,410	3,568	27,695	3,956

The largest spring exhibition crowd at Dunedin Stadium was 6,218 on Tuesday, March 27, 1990 for the game between the Blue Jays and Kansas City Royals and Wednesday, March 13, 1985 for a game with the New York Mets.

The first Blue Jays game ever played was on March 11, 1977 at Grant Field. The Blue Jays defeated the New York Mets 3-1.

The Blue Jays will play their spring exhibition games at the newly expanded and modernized DUNEDIN STADIUM at GRANT FIELD.

Since 1977 the Blue Jays played at Grant Field with a seating capacity of 3,417.

The City of Dunedin, at a cost of approximately $2.4 million have provided a new stadium called Dunedin Stadium at the same location as Grant Field, at the corner of Douglas Avenue and Beltrees Street.

The new stadium was designed by the architect firm of JOHNSTON DANA ASSOCIATES and was built by CASE CONTRACTING Company of Plant City, Florida.

The old structure came down in the first weeks of September 1989.

Some of the features of Dunedin Stadium:

—a symmetrical 'U'-shaped structure with four entrance ramps
—total capacity will be 6218
—seats will be arm chairs (4480 with top eight rows under cover
—bleacher seats (1698) will be located along first base/left field lines
—grade level area for wheelchairs (20 plus 20 for attendants)
—upgrade in lighting standards adequate for AA and AAA
—two new concession stands
—new public restroom facilities
—first-aid room
—security office
—ticket windows
—TV/photographer pits
—press box will provide two radio booths, one television booth plus seating for 25 members of print and electronic media
—media workroom and lounge for hospitality
—umpires room

The actual playing field will remain the same as will the Blue Jays and visitors clubhouses.

As well as the Toronto Blue Jays, the Dunedin Blue Jays of the Class A Florida State League will play at Dunedin Stadium.

The Toronto Blue Jays have committed to the City of Dunedin to continue to play spring exhibition games at Dunedin Stadium through 1999.

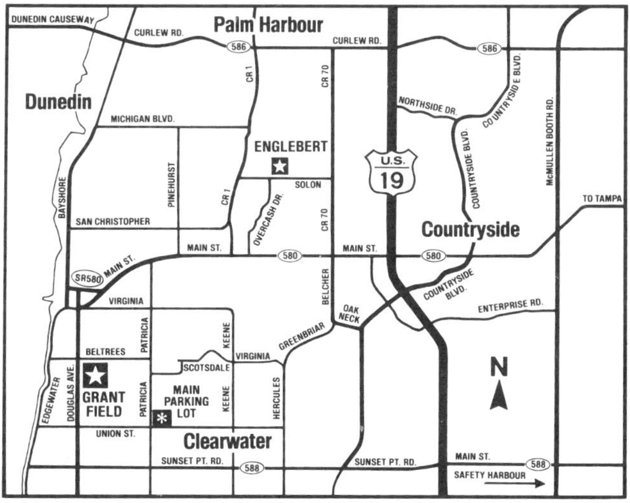

BATTER	AVG	G	AB	R	H	2B	3B	HR	RBI	SH-SF	HB	BB	SO	SB-CS	E
D. Bell	.222	6	9	0	2	2	0	0	3	0-1	0	0	1	0-0	0
G. Bell	.314	9	35	5	11	2	0	0	1	0-0	0	2	6	0-0	0
Borders	.320	8	25	3	8	0	0	0	3	0-0	0	1	5	0-0	1
Delacruz	.000	1	1	0	0	0	0	0	0	0-0	0	0	0	0-0	0
Diaz	.250	3	4	0	1	0	0	0	0	0-0	0	1	0	0-0	0
Ducey	.333	5	12	3	4	2	1	0	0	0-0	0	0	2	0-0	0
Felix	.190	13	42	4	8	1	0	0	2	0-0	0	1	5	2-0	1
Fernandez	.294	10	34	4	10	1	0	0	2	0-0	1	4	4	1-0	1
Gruber	.128	10	39	4	5	1	0	1	3	0-0	0	0	8	0-0	2
Hill	.216	12	37	9	8	2	0	3	8	0-1	0	6	13	0-0	0
Knorr	.667	3	3	0	2	0	0	0	1	0-0	0	0	1	0-0	0
Lawless	.357	6	14	1	5	0	0	0	0	0-0	0	2	0	0-0	0
Lee	.333	6	18	0	6	0	0	1	0	0-0	2	1	0	0-0	0
Liriano	.207	11	29	2	6	0	0	0	4	0-0	0	5	4	1-1	2
McGriff	.250	12	36	6	9	1	0	0	3	0-1	0	2	7	0-1	1
Mulliniks	.286	7	14	3	4	0	0	0	2	0-0	0	3	1	0-0	0
Munoz	.000	1	1	0	0	0	0	0	0	0-0	0	0	0	0-0	0
Myers	.250	6	12	1	3	0	0	1	3	0-0	0	2	2	0-0	0
Olerud	.296	13	27	1	10	2	0	0	6	0-0	0	5	1	0-0	1
Quinlan	.200	3	5	0	1	0	0	0	1	0-0	0	0	1	0-0	0
Runge	.200	6	5	0	1	0	0	0	0	0-0	0	1	1	0-0	0
Sojo	.400	12	20	2	10	0	0	2	0	0-0	0	1	1	0-2	0
Virgil	.444	6	9	3	7	0	0	1	1	0-0	0	0	1	0-0	0
Whiten	.125	7	8	1	1	0	0	0	0	0-0	0	2	4	0-0	0
Wilson	.250	9	36	3	10	1	0	0	3	0-0	0	0	4	0-0	0
Zosky	.000	1	1	0	0	0	0	0	0	0-0	0	0	0	0-0	1
BLUE JAYS	.255	14	486	55	124	18	1	6	49	0-3	1	39	77	5-2	16
OPPONENTS	.270	14	471	72	127	23	1	11	66	2-2	2	45	70	16-4	24

PITCHER	W-L	ERA	G	GS	CG	GF	SHO	SV	IP	H	R	ER	HR	HB	BB	SO-WP
Acker	0-1	0.00	2	0	0	0	0	0	2.1	2	1	0	0	0	1	3-0
Blair	0-1	10.50	7	0	0	4	0	1	6.0	10	7	7	1	0	3	6-0
Cerutti	0-1	2.25	3	3	0	0	0	0	8.0	10	4	2	0	0	1	5-0
Cummings	0-2	12.38	5	0	0	1	0	0	8.0	17	13	11	1	0	4	3-1
Flanagan	0-0	6.00	2	2	0	0	0	0	6.0	8	4	4	1	0	1	3-0
Gozzo	1-1	11.25	2	0	0	0	0	0	4.0	7	5	5	1	1	4	1-1
Henke	0-0	10.50	6	0	0	2	0	0	6.0	8	7	7	2	1	2	4-0
Hentgen	0-0	0.00	1	0	0	0	0	0	2.0	1	0	0	0	0	1	2-0
Key	2-0	3.60	3	2	0	0	0	0	10.0	9	4	4	0	0	2	3-0
Kilgus	1-1	4.26	4	0	0	0	0	0	6.1	8	3	3	1	0	3	6-0
Leiter	0-0	0.00	2	1	0	0	0	0	5.2	2	0	0	0	0	3	0-0
Linton	0-0	9.00	2	0	0	2	0	1	2.0	3	2	2	0	0	0	0-1
MacDonald	0-0	0.00	1	0	0	0	0	0	1.0	0	0	0	0	0	0	1-0
Rogers	0-0	0.00	1	0	0	0	0	0	3.0	0	0	0	0	0	0	1-0
Sanchez	0-1	6.43	3	1	0	0	0	0	7.0	8	6	5	2	0	2	2-1
Stieb	0-1	1.54	3	3	0	0	0	0	11.2	9	2	2	0	0	4	9-0
Stottlemyre	0-0	6.75	3	2	0	0	0	0	8.0	9	6	6	2	0	4	6-0
Trlicek	0-0	4.50	1	0	0	1	0	0	2.0	1	1	1	0	0	1	2-0
Ward	0-0	1.13	5	0	0	1	0	0	8.0	4	1	1	0	0	2	7-0
Wells	0-0	1.50	5	0	0	2	0	0	6.0	1	2	1	0	0	3	0-0
Wishneyski	0-1	13.50	1	0	0	0	0	0	2.0	3	3	3	0	0	3	0-0
BLUE JAYS	4-10	4.83	14	14	0	14	0	2	121.0	127	72	65	11	2	45	70-4
OPPONENTS	10-4	3.17	14	14	0	14	2	6	125.0	124	55	44	6	1	39	77-2

ATTENDANCE		
HOME	21,410 (6 dates)	3,568 AVG.
ROAD	27,695 (8 dates)	3,956 AVG.

DAY	DATE	OPPONENT	SITE		TIME
Fri	March 8	Cardinals	**Dunedin**		1:35 pm
Sat	March 9	Phillies	**Dunedin**	+	1:35 pm
Sun	March 10	Phillies	Clearwater	*	1:05 pm
Mon	March 11	Twins	Fort Myers		1:05 pm
Tue	March 12	Royals	**Dunedin**		1:35 pm
Wed	March 13	Phillies	Clearwater		1:05 pm
Thu	March 14	Red Sox	**Dunedin**	s	1:35 pm
Fri	March 15	Mets	Toronto, ON	*+	7:35 pm
Sat	March 16	Mets	Toronto, ON	*	1:05 pm
Sun	March 17	Orioles	**Dunedin**	*	1:35 pm
Mon	March 18	White Sox	Sarasota		7:05 pm
Tue	March 19	Cardinals	**Dunedin**		1:35 pm
Wed	March 20	Tigers	**Dunedin**		1:35 pm
Thu	March 21	Orioles	**Dunedin**		1:35 pm
Fri	March 22	Cardinals	St. Petersburg		1:05 pm
Sat	March 23	Pirates	**Dunedin**	*	1:35 pm
Sun	March 24	Cardinals	St. Petersburg	*	1:05 pm
Mon	March 25	Twins	**Dunedin**		1:35 pm
Tue	March 26	Rangers	**Dunedin**		1:35 pm
Wed	March 27	Tigers	Lakeland		1:35 pm
Thu	March 28	Rangers	Port Charlotte		1:30 pm
Fri	March 29	White Sox	**Dunedin**		1:35 pm
Sat	March 30	Red Sox	Winter Haven	*	1:05 pm
Sun	March 31	Phillies	**Dunedin**	*	1:35 pm
Mon	April 1	Pirates	Bradenton		1:05 pm
Tue	April 2	Phillies	Clearwater	+	7:35 pm
Wed	April 3	White Sox	**Dunedin**		1:35 pm
Thu	April 4	Royals	Baseball City		1:05 pm
Fri	April 5	Cardinals	St. Petersburg		1:05 pm
Sat	April 6	Mets	Shea Stadium	*+	2:10 pm

bold home game
s split squad
all times local

* TBS Radio
\+ TSN-TV

SPRING TRAINING RECORD

1977-1990

	HOME	ROAD	OVERALL
BALTIMORE	1-2-0	2-0-0	3-2-0
BOSTON	4-4-0	4-7-0	8-11-0
CHICAGO (AL)	9-11-0	12-7-3	21-18-3
CLEVELAND	0-0-0	0-0-1	0-0-1
DETROIT	5-5-0	7-4-0	12-9-0
KANSAS CITY	3-4-0	4-6-0	7-10-0
MILWAUKEE	3-1-0	0-2-0	3-3-0
MINNESOTA	10-4-0	5-9-0	15-13-0
NEW YORK (AL)	2-0-0	0-6-0	2-6-0
SEATT;E	0-0-0	0-1-0	0-1-0
TEXAS	3-4-0	4-3-1	7-7-1
ATLANTA	1-0-0	1-0-0	2-0-0
CINCINNATI	7-4-0	3-5-1	10-9-1
HOUSTON	4-1-0	1-5-0	5-6-1
LOS ANGELES	0-1-0	0-2-0	0-3-0
MONTREAL	8-2-0	3-5-0	11-7-0
NEW YORK (NL)	8-6-0	6-5-0	14-11-0
PHILADELPHIA	11-11-1	15-9-0	26-20-1
PITTSBURGH	9-8-0	6-6-1	15-14-1
ST. LOUIS	10-5-0	9-8-0	19-13-0
at FLORIDA	94-74-1	83-86-6	177-160-7
OTHER	4-1-0	0-4-1	4-5-1
vs NL	58-38-1	45-45-2	103-83-3
vs AL	40-37-0	28-45-5	78-82-5
OVERALL	98-75-1	83-90-7	181-165-8

1991 TORONTO BLUE JAYS SPRING ROSTER

MANAGER: Cito Gaston (43)
COACHES: 1B: Mike Squires (25)
3B Rick Hacker (7)
Pitching: Galen Cisco (42)
Bating: Gene Tenace (18)
Bullpen: John Sullivan (8)

DIRECTOR, PUBLIC RELATIONS: Howard Starkman
MANAGER, TEAM TRAVEL: John Brioux
CLUB PHYSICIAN: Dr. Ron Taylor
TRAINER: Tommy Craig
ASSISTANT TRAINER: Brent Andrews
EQUIPMENT MANAGER: Jeff Ross.

No.	Pitchers (19)	B	T	Ht.	Wt.	Born	Birthplace	Residence	1990 Club	W-L	ERA	G	GS	CG	SV	IP	H	BB	SO	ML SER
34	ACKER, Jim	R	R	6-2	215	09-24-58	Freer, TX	Freer, TX	TORONTO	4-4	3.83	59	0	0	1	91.2	103	30	54	8.000
35	BOUCHER, Denis	R	L	6-1	195	03-07-68	Montreal, PQ	Lachine, PQ	Dunedin	7-0	0.75	9	9	2	0	60.0	45	8	62	
									Syracuse	8-5	3.85	17	17	2	0	107.2	100	37	80	0.000
38	CROMWELL, Nate	L	L	6-1	185	08-23-68	Las Vegas, NV	Las Vegas, NV	Knoxville	5-14	5.56	27	23	2	0	121.1	119	91	79	0.000
46	DAYLEY, Ken	L	L	6-0	180	02-25-59	Jerome, ID	Chesterfield, MO	ST. LOUIS	4-4	3.56	58	0	0	2	73.1	63	30	51	7.094
27	FRASER, Willie	R	R	6-1	208	05-26-64	New York, NY	Irvine, CA	CALIFORNIA	5-4	3.08	45	0	0	2	76.0	69	24	32	4.031
50	HENKE, Tom	R	R	6-5	225	12-21-57	Kansas City, MO	Jefferson City, MO	TORONTO	2-4	2.17	61	0	0	32	74.2	58	19	75	6.059
41	HENTGEN, Pat	R	R	6-2	200	11-13-68	Detroit, MI	Fraser, MI	Knoxville	9-5	3.05	28	26	0	0	153.1	121	68	142	0.000
22	KEY, Jimmy	R	L	6-1	185	04-22-61	Huntsville, AL	Tarpon Springs, FL	Dunedin	2-0	2.50	3	3	0	0	18.0	21	3	14	
									TORONTO	13-7	4.25	27	27	0	0	154.2	169	22	88	7.000
28	LEITER, Al	L	L	6-3	215	10-23-65	Toms River, NJ	Plantation, FL	Dunedin	0-0	2.63	6	6	0	0	24.0	18	12	14	
									Syracuse	3-8	4.62	15	14	1	0	78.0	59	68	69	
									TORONTO	0-0	0.00	4	0	0	0	6.1	1	2	5	2.033
45	MacDONALD, Bob	L	L	6-3	208	04-27-65	East Orange, NJ	Toms River, NJ	Knoxville	1-2	1.89	36	0	0	15	57.0	37	29	54	
									Syracuse	0-2	5.40	9	0	0	2	8.1	4	9	6	
									TORONTO	0-0	0.00	4	0	0	0	2.1	0	2	0	0.046
54	RHODES, Ricky	R	R	6-4	205	05-28-68	Waco, TX	Waco, TX	Greensboro	7-10	3.73	27	27	0	0	154.1	121	95	147	0.000
32	SANCHEZ, Alex	R	R	6-2	195	04-08-66	Concord, CA	San Diego, CA	Syracuse	5-9	5.71	22	22	1	0	112.0	111	79	65	0.025
37	STIEB, Dave	R	R	6-1	195	07-22-57	Santa Ana, CA	Gilroy, CA	TORONTO	18-6	2.93	33	33	2	0	208.2	179	64	125	11.096
30	STOTTLEMYRE, Todd	L	R	6-3	195	05-20-65	Yakima, WA	Yakima, WA	TORONTO	13-17	4.34	33	33	4	0	203.0	214	69	115	2.111
40	TIMLIN, Mike	R	R	6-4	205	03-10-66	Midland, TX	Midland, TX	Dunedin	7-2	1.43	42	0	0	22	50.1	36	16	46	0.000
									Knoxville	1-2	1.73	17	0	0	8	26.0	20	7	21	0.000
52	TRLICEK, Rick	R	R	6-3	200	04-26-69	Houston, TX	Houston, TX	Dunedin	5-8	3.73	26	26	0	0	154.1	128	72	125	0.000
31	WARD, Duane	R	R	6-4	215	05-28-64	Parkview, NM	Las Vegas, NV	TORONTO	2-8	3.45	73	0	0	1	127.2	101	42	112	3.154
36	WELLS, David	L	L	6-4	225	05-20-63	Torrance, CA	Palm Harbor, FL	TORONTO	11-6	3.14	43	25	0	3	189.0	165	45	115	3.019
44	WILLS, Frank	R	R	6-2	210	10-26-58	New Orleans, LA	Destrehan, LA	TORONTO	6-4	4.73	44	4	0	0	99.0	101	38	72	4.035

No.	Catchers (19)	B	T	Ht.	Wt.	Born	Birthplace	Residence	1990 Club	AVG.	G	AB	R	H	2B	3B	HR	RBI	BB	SO	SB	ML SER
10	BORDERS, Pat	R	R	6-2	200	05-14-63	Columbus, OH	Lake Wales, FL	TORONTO	.286	125	346	36	99	24	2	15	49	18	57	0	3.000
39	DIAZ, Carlos	R	R	6-3	190	12-24-64	Elizabeth, NJ	Palm Harbor, FL	Syracuse	.203	77	251	18	51	10	0	1	19	17	51	2	
									TORONTO	.333	9	3	1	1	0	0	0	0	0	2	0	0.053
49	KNORR, Randy	R	R	6-2	205	11-12-68	San Gabriel, CA	Baldwin Park, CA	Knoxville	.276	116	392	51	108	12	1	13	64	31	83	0	0.000
21	MYERS, Greg	L	R	6-2	205	04-14-66	Riverside, CA	Riverside, CA	Syracuse	.182	3	11	0	2	1	0	0	2	1	1	0	
									TORONTO	.236	87	250	33	59	7	1	5	22	22	33	0	1.155

No.	Infielders (19)	B	T	Ht.	Wt.	Born	Birthplace	Residence	1990 Club	AVG.	G	AB	R	H	2B	3B	HR	RBI	BB	SO	SB	ML SER
12	ALOMAR,Roberto	S	R	6-0	185	02-05-68	Ponce, PR	San Diego, CA	SAN DIEGO	.287	147	586	80	168	27	5	6	60	46	72	24	3.000
88	GONZALES, Rene	R	R	6-3	201	09-03-61	Austin, TX	Covina, CA	BALTIMORE	.214	67	103	13	22	3	1	1	12	12	14	1	4.024
17	GRUBER, Kelly	R	R	6-0	185	02-26-62	Houston, TX	Austin, TX	TORONTO	.274	150	592	92	162	36	6	31	118	48	94	14	5.108
4	LEE, Manny	S	R	5-9	166	06-17-65	S.P. de Macoris, DR	SP de Macoris, DR	TORONTO	.243	117	391	45	95	12	4	6	41	26	90	3	4.149
5	MULLINIKS, Rance	L	R	6-0	175	01-15-56	Tulare, CA	El Paso, TX	TORONTO	.289	57	97	11	28	4	0	2	16	22	19	2	12.115
9	OLERUD, John	L	L	6-5	218	08-05-68	Seattle, WA	Bellevue, WA	TORONTO	.265	111	358	43	95	15	1	14	48	57	75	0	1.031
16	QUINLAN, Tom	R	R	6-3	210	03-27-68	St. Paul, MN	Maplewood, MN	Knoxville	.258	141	481	70	124	24	6	15	51	49	157	8	
									TORONTO	.500	1	2	0	1	0	0	0	0	0	1	0	0.031
11	SUERO, William	R	R	5-9	175	11-07-66	Santo Domingo, DR	Santo Domingo, DR	Knoxville	.263	133	483	80	127	29	7	16	60	78	78	40	0.000
15	TABLER, Pat	R	R	6-2	200	02-02-58	Hamilton, OH	Cincinnati, OH	KANSAS CITY	.272	75	195	12	53	14	0	1	19	20	21	0	
									NEW YORK(NL)	.279	17	43	6	12	1	1	1	10	3	8	0	8.078

No.	Outfielders (19)	B	T	Ht.	Wt.	Born	Birthplace	Residence	1990 Club	AVG.	G	AB	R	H	2B	3B	HR	RBI	BB	SO	SB	ML SER
14	BELL, Derek	R	R	6-2	200	12-11-68	Tampa, FL	Tampa, FL	Syracuse	.261	109	402	57	105	13	5	7	56	23	75	21	0.000
29	CARTER, Joe	R	R	6-3	225	03-07-60	Oklahoma City, OK	Leawood, KS	SAN DIEGO	.232	162	634	79	147	27	1	24	115	48	93	22	6.143
20	DUCEY, Rob	L	R	6-2	180	05-24-65	Toronto, ON	Palm Harbor, FL	Syracuse	.267	127	438	53	117	32	7	7	47	60	87	13	
									TORONTO	.302	19	53	7	16	21	5	0	7	7	15	1	1.158
24	HILL, Glenallen	R	R	6-2	210	03-22-65	Santa Cruz, CA	Santa Cruz, CA	TORONTO	.231	84	260	47	60	11	3	12	32	18	62	8	1.034
19	WHITE, Devon	S	R	6-2	182	12-29-62	Kingston, Jamaica	Gilbert, AZ	CALIFORNIA	.217	125	443	57	96	17	3	11	44	44	116	21	
									Edmonton	.364	14	55	9	20	4	4	0	6	7	12	4	4.061
23	WHITEN, Mark	S	R	6-3	215	11-25-66	Pensacola, FL	Pensacola, FL	Syracuse	.290	104	390	65	113	19	4	14	48	37	72	14	
									TORONTO	.273	33	88	12	24	1	1	2	7	7	14	2	0.057
13	WILLIAMS, Kenny	R	R	6-1	195	04-06-64	Berkeley, CA	Puyallup, WA	DETROIT	.133	57	83	10	11	2	0	0	5	3	24	2	
									TORONTO	.194	49	72	13	14	6	1	0	8	7	18	7	3.162
3	WILSON, Mookie	S	R	5-10	175	02-09-56	Bamberg, SC	Bamberg, SC	TORONTO	.265	147	588	81	156	36	4	3	51	31	102	23	10.034

NON-ROSTER PLAYERS

No.	Pitchers (5)	B	T	Ht.	Wt.	Born	Birthplace	Residence	1990 Club	W-L	ERA	G	GS	CG	SV	IP	H	BB	SO	ML SER
66	GUZMAN, Juan	R	R	5-11	190	10-28-66	Santo Domingo, DR	Santo Domingo, DR	Knoxville	11-9	4.24	37	21	2	1	157.0	145	80	138	0.000
47	KARSAY, Steve	R	R	6-3	185	03-24-72	Flushing, NY	College Point, NY	St. Catharines	1-1	0.79	5	5	0	0	22.2	11	12	25	0.000
57	MANZANILLO, Ravelo	L	L	5-10	190	10-17-63	SP de Macoris, DR	SP de Macoris, DR	Vancouver	7-3	3.61	38	6	0	4	92.1	74	60	64	0.010
53	WEATHERS, David	R	R	6-3	205	09-25-69	Lawrenceburg, TN	Leoma, TN	Dunedin	10-7	3.70	27	27	2	0	158.0	158	59	96	0.000
67	WISHNEVSKI, Bob	R	R	6-2	210	1-2-67	Hammond, IN	Valparasio, IN	Knoxville	6-3	3.83	20	17	1	1	105.2	84	39	74	0.000
									Syracuse	2-5	6.66	9	8	0	0	48.2	65	23	28	0.000

No.	Catchers (2)	B	T	Ht.	Wt.	Born	Birthplace	Residence	1990 Club	AVG.	G	AB	R	H	2B	3B	HR	RBI	BB	SO	SB	ML SER
68	DELGADO, Carlos	L	R	6-3	206	06-25-72	Aguadilla, PR	Aguadilla, PR	St. Catharines	.283	67	226	29	64	13	0	6	39	35	65	2	0.000
33	SPRAGUE, Ed	R	R	6-2	215	07-25-67	Castro Valley, CA	Lodi, CA	Syracuse	.239	142	519	60	124	23	5	20	75	31	100	4	0.000

No	Infielders (4)	B	T	Ht.	Wt.	Born	Birthplace	Residence	1990 Club	AVG.	G	AB	T	H	2B	3B	HR	RBI	BB	SO	SB	ML SER
26	EPFARD, Jim	L	L	6-2	181	04-27-60	South Bend, IN	Huntington Beach, CA	Syracuse	.310	133	461	72	143	18	3	4	48	47	49	5	1.079
59	SCHUNK, Jerry	R	R	5-11	180	10-05-65	Hamilton, OH	Cincinnati, OH	Knoxville	.288	85	274	32	79	13	1	3	31	9	25	8	0.000
									Syracuse	.240	26	100	8	24	4	0	0	7	3	10	1	0.000
48	WEINKE, Chris	-	R	6-4	205	07-31-72	St. Paul, MN	St. Paul, MN	DID NOT PLAY PROFESSIONAL													0.000
1	ZOSKY, Eddie	R	R	6-0	175	02-10-68	Whittier, CA	Whittier, CA	Knoxville	.271	115	450	53	122	20	7	3	45	26	73	3	0.000